International Congress on the Study of the Middle Ages

Congrès international d'études sur le Moyen Âge

Internationaler Kongress zum Mittelalter

Congresso internazionale di studi sul Medioevo

Congreso Internacional sobre la Edad Medieval

Internationaal congres voor de studie van de Middeleeuwen

(c. 300-1500)

02-05 July

This programme is available in alternative formats, e.g. Braille, large print, etc., on request.

Large-scale maps and plans are available to print online: www.leeds.ac.uk/ims/imc/maps.html

Table of contents

Welcome

Please find in the following the programme for the International Medieval Congress 2018. Little did I think in 1994 - at the very first IMC - that I would still be here, presenting the Congress programme to you 25 years later.

The IMC 2018 is the 25th Congress since it started in 1994. We feel that this is a significant milestone worth remembering. Not only has medieval studies developed over the last 25 years, but so too has the IMC. Little did we think then that the IMC would grow to have over 2,500 active participants, or that it would continue to have an astonishingly steady number of delegates new to the Congress year on year. This year's Congress has record-breaking numbers: in total, the programme lists 2,545 actively involved participants. We are delighted to welcome some of the original staff members back from 1994 and are planning to hold a celebratory party on Wednesday, 4 July 2018.

It is not just the 25th year of the IMC, but also the 50th anniversary of two closely related Leeds institutions: the Institute for Medieval Studies and the *International Medieval Bibliography*, both initiated in 1967 and instrumental in the setting up and support of the IMC over the years. This milestone provides an opportunity to take stock of what has been achieved and what challenges lie ahead – you will find a number of sessions and round table discussions throughout the programme. See also pp. 9-10 where you will find a brief overview of the last 25 years with some photographs and delegate memories.

We felt that this year's Special Thematic Strand on 'Memory' would make a fine special focus for an anniversary year, while having a broader appeal to many more medievalists. 'Memory' clearly resonated with delegates, with a record 392 sessions dealing with the many aspects of memory - including forgetting. Congratulations to Lucie Doležalová (Institute of Greek & Latin Studies, Univerzita Karlova, Praha) and Jan Čermák (Department of English, Univerzita Karlova, Praha), who so expertly curated this strand and shaped its programme - a monumental task and one fitting for the 25th Congress.

In addition to the many sessions on this special thematic strand, we are delighted to welcome as keynote speakers: Alixe Bovey (Courtauld Institute of Art, University of London) who will present a lecture on 'Historical Present: Fake History, Material Culture, and Collective Misremembering', Mary J. Carruthers (Department of English, New York University) on 'But What Are YOU Remembering For?', Richard Dance (Department of Anglo-Saxon, Norse & Celtic, University of Cambridge) on 'Do Words Remember?: The Etymologist versus the Vikings', Farkas Gabor Kiss (Department for Early Hungarian Literature, Eötvös Loránd University, Budapest) on 'The Metaphors They Lived by: Verbal Imagery of Memory in the Middle Ages', and Jeff Rider (Department of Romance Languages & Literatures, Wesleyan University, Connecticut) on 'I Can't Remember the Middle Ages'.

The remainder of the IMC programme is certainly not to be overlooked. A further 394 sessions, round table discussions, and workshops deal with many other aspects of the Middle Ages. As every year, the Congress is keen to showcase the widest spectrum of research in medieval studies, and we want to ensure that the special thematic strand does not become an exclusive

Congress theme of the year. For 2018, we have created four new strands: Global Medieval Studies, Health & Medicine, Manuscript Studies, and the Mediterranean World, as a reflection of the rise of interest in these areas within the medieval studies communities.

New this year are two more lectures during the Congress. We are delighted to welcome Roland Betancourt (Department of Art History, University of California, Irvine), who will present a lecture on 'Transgender Lives in Byzantium'. This lecture is intended to be the start of a series highlighting new voices in medieval studies. Also new is a lecture sponsored by the Instituto Cervantes and the Centre for the History of Ibero-America at the University of Leeds. Giles Tremlett (*The Guardian / The Economist*) will be talking on 'Black Legends, Bullying Queens, and the Wonders of Moorishland - How Spain Lives Its Medieval Past Today'.

Returning are the annual *Early Medieval Europe* lecture with Paul Fouracre (Department of History, University of Manchester) on 'Lights, Power, and the Moral Economy of Early Medieval Europe', and the annual Medieval Academy of America lecture, with Anne D. Hedeman (Department of Art History, University of Kansas) on 'History and Visual Memory in the Library of King Charles V of France'. Many thanks to the Medieval Academy and *Early Medieval Europe* for their continuing support of medieval studies and the IMC.

IMC 2018 also has a record number of round table discussions, and, following public demand, we have incorporated round table discussions into the daytime session slots to allow for more time for discussion. We do want to encourage debate and dialogue, and we are keen to trial the mixture of formats. We will be following your feedback over the year and during the IMC, so please let us know your thoughts about these and other developments.

On Friday we are delighted to welcome four different Career Development Workshops:

- Organised and sponsored by Medievalist.net - a workshop on '7 Ways a Medievalist Can Earn Income outside Academia'
- Organised and sponsored by The National Archives - a workshop on 'Medieval Records and the National Archives'
- Organised and sponsored by the Royal Armouries - a workshop and excursion on 'Medieval Military Effigies in West Yorkshire'

In addition to the wide-ranging academic programme, we are pleased to have further workshops, concerts, and theatrical performances from Sunday to Thursday. Highlights of the programme include concerts of the music of Oswald von Wolkenstein and of songs from the Ritson Manuscript, as well as workshops on using an astrolabe, goldwork embroidery, Coptic booking, and Jewish scribal arts. We are also proud to host dramatic performances of the Deventer Sister-books and *Spil von Fünfferley betrachtnussen zur Buß* - a 16th-century morality play by Johannes Kolross. For more information, please read more on pp. 459-471.

We also offer a number of specialist excursions to Mount Grace Priory and Jervaulx Abbey, Middleham Castle, Stank Hall, John Rylands Library, Kirkstall Abbey, York Minster, Southwell Minster and Town, and Conisborough Castle.

More details can be found at pp. 449-458. This year, we are particularly proud to present two multi-day excursions, one before the IMC to the early medieval Hadrian's Wall country, led by Richard Morris (Emeritus Professor of Conflict and Culture, University of Huddersfield) and Ian Wood (Emeritus Professor of Early Medieval History, University of Leeds), and the other just after the IMC 2018 to Medieval Castles and Battlefields of the Midlands (with a special focus on the War of the Roses), led by Kelly DeVries (Professor of History, Loyola University Maryland) and Robert C. Woosnam-Savage (Curator of Edged Weapons, Royal Armouries, Leeds). See pp. 55-60 for more on these tours.

On a practical level, the increase in active Congress participants mean that we have added a further building to the mix: the Thackrah Building (adjacent to the Maurice Keyworth Building and within easy walking distance). Back after last year's refurbishment is the Michael Sadler Building, but the basement of the Parkinson Building will be refurbished this year. However, the bookfair will continue to be in its traditional place in the Parkinson Court.

We have been working with University bodies on diversity and inclusiveness, and for 2018 will introduce a quiet room and lactation room facilities. We would ask IMC delegates to respect these facilities. We are keen to further improve the diversity and inclusivity of the IMC, and welcomes feedback and input from delegates past, present and future.

With a record number of delegates in 2018, IMC beds will be in very short supply. We have added additional hotels to our portfolio of accommodation, but would recommend to anyone wishing to stay in IMC accommodation to register as early as possible.

While this programme mainly focusses on this year's Congress, I would like to draw your attention to IMC 2019. We have chosen as the special (not exclusive) focus 'Materialities'. Please see p. 534 for further details.

Before closing, a warm farewell and big thank-you to outgoing Programming and Standing Committee members and IMC staff: Susan Broadbent, Ros Brown-Grant, Keith Busby, Hayley Coulson, Hans-Werner Goetz, Jennifer Palmer, and Nick Westerman. Equally, a warm welcome to Nadia Altschul, Emma Campbell, Pietro Delcorno, Anne E. Lester, Fiona Livermore, Ben Palmer, Dolores López Pérez, Federica Pich, Dominique Stutzmann, and Vanessa Wright. The IMC Committees and its staff make the Congress happen, and all of your dedication and hard work make this (and any of the future) Congress(es) possible.

Keep medievalling!

Axel E. W. Müller

Director, International Medieval Congress

About the IMC

The IMC provides an interdisciplinary forum for sharing ideas relating to all aspects of the Middle Ages.

Organised and administered by the Institute for Medieval Studies at the University of Leeds, since its inception in 1994 the IMC has worked to cultivate the field of medieval studies by bringing researchers from different countries, backgrounds, and disciplines together, providing opportunities for networking and professional development in an open and inclusive environment.

As the largest Congress of its kind in Europe, the IMC regularly attracts more than 2,000 medievalists from all over the world. In addition to the academic programme, the IMC hosts a wide variety of concerts, exhibitions, and excursions, which are open to delegates and the public alike. It also seeks to foster scholarly community by providing spaces for networking and socialising. This year's IMC will be the 25th in its history and will take place 2-5 July 2018 on the northern part of the main campus of the University of Leeds (see map 8, p. 43).

Structure and organisation

Academic support for the IMC is provided by an international Programming Committee, where individual members act as specialists for individual programming strands. They are responsible for assessing proposals, collating individual paper proposals into coherent sessions, and proposing special keynote speakers. For more information see p. 71 and the IMC website: www.leeds.ac.uk/ims/imc/strand_index.html

The IMC is also supported by its Standing Committee, comprising a group of medievalists from the Institute for Medieval Studies. They advise on academic matters such as selection of new Programming Committee members and each year's special thematic strand, as well as advising the IMC administration team on strategic, operational, and developmental issues.

Institute for Medieval Studies

The IMS is home to a thriving community of more than 50 medievalists, as well as an outstanding library. It offers interdisciplinary MA and PhD study, including innovative language teaching and research skills training (see p. 62).

As well as the IMC, the IMS is responsible for producing the *International Medieval Bibliography* (IMB). Since its launch in 1967 this has proved to be an invaluable research tool, which is now also available online and in CD-ROM format to be used by researchers worldwide (see p. 65).

The IMS also acts as series editor for International Medieval Research (IMR), the series which publishes selected papers given at the IMC. So far more than 20 IMR volumes have been produced (see p. 66).

IMC at 25

In July 2018, we at the University of Leeds proudly welcome you to the 25th International Medieval Congress. We are delighted that this year's Congress looks to be the largest yet, with a record number of papers submitted.

In the early 1990s, there was increasing demand for Europe to host its own international conference for medieval studies. Thus, Simon Forde, Director of the International Medieval Institute at the University of Leeds, and Joyce Hill, Director of the Centre for Medieval Studies at the University of Leeds, brought together medievalists from around the world to launch the IMC in 1994.

The very first IMC in 1994 was themed around Gregory of Tours, featured 21 subject strands and had 859 attendees; in 2018, the Congress, celebrating its silver anniversary, will feature 39 regular subject strands and surpass last year's record-breaking attendance of over 2,400 delegates.

We feel it appropriate to honour those attendees who have attended every single Congress so far:

- Kelly DeVries
- Simon Forde
- Sieglinde Hartmann
- Gerhard Jaritz
- Chris Lewis
- Axel Müller
- Caroline Palmer
- Walter Pohl
- Richard Rastall
- Ian Wood

We are very proud of our long-standing members and look forward to welcoming them again in 2018. We are equally proud of every contribution made by the thousands of participants over the years, whether that be organising a session, giving a paper, performing, demonstrating, or working as a member of staff: the IMC would not be what it is without all of you, and for that, we thank you.

What Makes the IMC?

The IMC is the sum of the people who have taken part in various roles over the past 25 years. From its inception to the present day, almost 140 members of staff have worked on the IMC team, helping to plan and co-ordinate the event each year. This does not include the large numbers of temporary staff, many of them students at the University, whom we employ during the Congress week.

From the beginning, the IMC has been advised by a Standing Committee, drawn from medievalists at the University of Leeds. Initially the Standing Committee also assisted with assembling the academic programme, but this task is now undertaken by a Programming Committee of academics from around the world, each one a leader in their field. Over the last 25 years, the IMC has relied on help, input, advice, and many long hours of hard work from over 150 academics worldwide.

Most important to the IMC, however, are the delegates who attend each year. Without their contribution, the event would not be possible. By the end of 2018 we hope that more than 20,000 medievalists from across of the world will have attended at least one IMC!

Bodington & Weetwood

From its inception until 2012, the IMC took place at the two sites of Bodington Hall and Weetwood Hall, located some 6 km (4 miles) north of the main University of Leeds campus; most delegates stayed on-site and many look back on it as a unique bubble in which academics could meet and share ideas.

Fondly remembered by long-standing participants, the final year closed with celebrations featuring a joust, live music, and the last ever Bodington Disco.

'My favourite memory is of the disco dance floor. Medievalists are the best dancers!'

'Glimpsing an anxious young student practising his paper in front of an empty classroom - been there kid!'

Moving to the Main Campus

In 2013 the Congress moved onto the main University of Leeds campus, where there was more space for academic sessions, professional development workshops, and public events, such as the ever-popular Making Leeds Medieval - a one-day event featuring combat displays, a craft fair, re-enactments, and musical entertainment.

The move offered scope for expansion and growth with a wider range of activities for a more immersive experience.

What Next?

By the end of IMC 2018, we will have welcomed over 20,000 medievalists, hosted over 30,000 papers, and enabled countless conversations. Since our beginning in 1994, our aim has been to facilitate discussion in medieval studies and to encourage the exploration of new areas, methods, and disciplines. We hope you will join us in celebrating this milestone and will continue to support us during our next 25 years.

"25 is a great milestone, but it is only the very beginning. Medieval studies and the IMC are growing and developing in fascinating ways. The ambition of the Congress is to help in the shaping of what medieval studies will become."

- Axel E. W. Müller, Congress Director

The IMC Is...

'...an exciting blend of different medievalists from across the globe.'

'...a great opportunity to share current projects and make connections with other scholars.'

'...a fantastic place to learn about new approaches and research.'

-Quotations from anonymous online survey and postcards, IMC 2017

Registration and Payment

We recommend you complete your registration as early as possible, especially if you are booking accommodation. On-campus accommodation is particularly limited, and you may not be able to book a room on campus if you register close to or after the deadline.

The deadline for registrations is **Sunday 13 May 2018**. Any registrations received after this date are subject to a late fee. We do not recommend registering when you arrive at the IMC.

How to Register

You can book and pay for your registration, accommodation, meals, events, and excursion tickets through the University of Leeds Online Store. Payments are processed in GBP (£) and can be made by Switch/Maestro, Visa, or MasterCard.

Once you have completed the registration process, you will receive an automated confirmation email from the Online Store. After we have then processed and completed your registration, you will receive an itemised receipt from us by email. You will receive another copy of your receipt in your registration pack on arrival.

If you want to order some items separately - for example, if you want to book meal tickets after you have paid for your registration - you can do this by returning to the Online Store to purchase additional items.

Concessionary Registration Fees

Reduced fees are available for students, retired, or unwaged scholars. After you complete your registration via the Online Store, you will receive an automated email asking you to send us some proof of your status if you have registered in this category. These can be sent to us as a scanned document attached to an email, as a photocopy by post, or by fax.

Students can provide an image of their student card with expiry date clearly shown, or a letter from their academic department. Unwaged delegates need to provide official state documentation which indicates their status.

If you are retired, you can either send us a copy of your passport indicating your date of birth, a letter from your former employer including your date of retirement, or state documentation indicating that you are retired.

Paper Registration

If you are not able to register through the Online Store or cannot pay online by credit or debit card, you can complete the paper registration form. Please note that this incurs an additional fee to cover administrative costs.

Download the paper form from the IMC website or contact us to receive a copy. We cannot process your booking unless payment is provided in full.

Processing a paper registration form may take up to five weeks in busy periods. You will receive a receipt when it is completed.

Payment by Invoice or Bank Transfer

If you are only able to pay by invoice or bank transfer, please contact the IMC before registering so we can send you instructions about completing your registration. Failure to contact us in advance may lead to a delay in processing your registration.

Friends and Family Members

Non-participating friends and family members can attend the session in which their friend or family member is speaking without having to pay a registration fee. If they wish to attend any other sessions, they will need to register as a delegate and pay the registration fee.

Please provide the name of the friend or family member who will accompany you in the 'Other details' section of your registration form so we can make them a special name badge.

Children at the IMC and Family Registration

Unfortunately, the IMC cannot provide assistance with childcare. However, children are welcome to accompany their parents or guardians. Children under 18 must be supervised by their parents or guardian at all times, including at IMC events.

If you want to bring your children to Leeds, you will need to complete a Family Registration Form instead of using the Online Store. Please contact us to arrange this as soon as possible, as family accommodation is very limited. For more information on family accommodation, see p. 18.

Bursary Recipients

If you have been awarded an IMC Bursary, you can register through the Online Store as normal, and we will then refund you the amount of your bursary. Alternatively, please contact us for an IMC Bursary Recipient Registration Form.

Cancellations

Cancellations received in writing by **Monday 14 May 2018** will secure a refund, minus one half of the Registration and Programming Fee.

Cancellations received by **Saturday 9 June 2018** will secure a refund of 25% of the total amount paid, excluding the Programming and Registration Fee and, if applicable, any hotel accommodation fees.

Refunds will not be made, under any circumstances, for cancellations received after **Saturday 9 June 2018**.

Please inform the IMC administration and, if applicable, your session organiser immediately if you need to withdraw from the programme.

Accommodation on Campus

We offer a variety of accommodation options that can be booked through the Online Store when you register. These include options in a number of halls of residence on campus.

Accommodation on campus is very limited: we recommend that you book as early as possible to reserve a room. We cannot guarantee on-campus accommodation.

University halls of residence offer rooms for single occupancy only. Rooms cannot be shared. If you would like to have a room next to a friend or family member, please make this clear when you register. Although we will do our best to accommodate your request, this cannot be guaranteed.

Staff at halls of residence try to allocate shared bathroom facilities to delegates of the same gender, but this may not always be possible. Please contact us if you have any queries or concerns.

In addition to the facilities listed below, delegates staying in all halls of residence also have access to the University's sports facilities at *the*Edge, including a well-equipped gym, swimming pool, squash courts, and even a climbing wall.

Delegates booking accommodation on campus will receive their registration pack upon checking in at their accommodation.

Alternative Accommodation

If you prefer to book your own accommodation, Visit Leeds can provide information and resources.

Visit Leeds and Art Gallery Shop
The Headrow
Leeds
LS1 3AA
www.visitleeds.co.uk

Charles Morris Hall: Storm Jameson Court

Storm Jameson Court offers award-winning University accommodation and the only fully accessible accommodation on campus. The 23 available accessible rooms are suitable for those with mobility difficulties, visual impairments, or hearing difficulties. Please book as early as possible and explain your access requirements at the time of booking.

There are lifts to every floor of the building, meaning all rooms have step-free access.

- **Breakfast:** Hot and cold buffet provided in the Refectory
- **Availability:** 30 June 2018 (Sat) - 5 July 2018 (Thu)
- **Room Types:** Single occupancy ensuite and limited single occupancy accessible rooms
- **Reception:** 24-hour reception
- **Check-in times:** Check-in possible after 14.00, check-out is at 10.00
- **Provided:** Bedding, towels, shampoo and soap, tea- and coffee-making facilities in kitchen
- **Lift for upper floor access:** Yes
- **Wifi:** Yes
- **Kitchen:** Kitchen and lounge areas are shared between 6-8 rooms. No crockery provided
- **Access to** *the*Edge: Yes

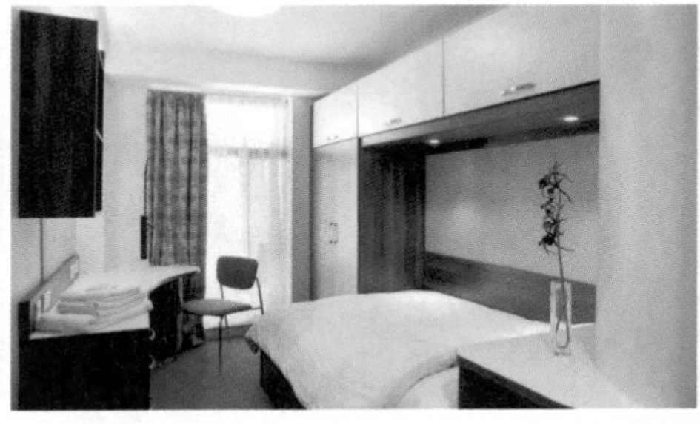

Lyddon Hall

Lyddon Hall consists of a converted 19th-century main hall and an adjacent annexe of converted 19th-century townhouses. Lyddon Hall offers 129 rooms and there are two common rooms available for residents' use in the main hall.

- **Breakfast:** Hot and cold buffet provided in the Refectory
- **Availability:** 30 June 2018 (Sat) - 5 July 2018 (Thu)
- **Room Types:** Single occupancy ensuite and single occupancy shared bathroom in flats of 3-4 rooms
- **Reception:** 24-hour reception located in main hall
- **Check-in times:** Check-in possible after 14.00, check-out is at 10.00
- **Provided:** Bedding, towels, shampoo and soap, tea- and coffee-making facilities in kitchenette
- **Lift for upper floor access:** No. No floor is stair-free.
- **Wifi:** Yes
- **Kitchen:** Kitchenettes are available for guest use and are shared between 5-9 bedrooms. No crockery provided
- **Access to** *the*Edge: Yes

Ellerslie Hall

Ellerslie Hall is situated in a row of converted 19th-century townhouses and comprises 88 rooms. There are two common rooms available for residents' use in the main hall.

- **Breakfast:** Hot and cold buffet provided in the Refectory
- **Availability:** 30 June 2018 (Sat) - 5 July 2018 (Thu)
- **Room Types:** Single occupancy ensuite and single occupancy shared bathroom in flats of 4-5 rooms. Most rooms have their own washbasin
- **Reception:** 24-hour reception located in main hall
- **Check-in times:** Check-in possible after 14.00, check-out is at 10.00
- **Provided:** Bedding, towels, shampoo and soap, tea- and coffee-making facilities in kitchenette
- **Lift for upper floor access:** No. No floor is stair-free
- **Wifi:** Yes
- **Kitchen:** Kitchenettes are available for guest use in the main hall, whilst the annexes each have one large kitchen for 11 people. No crockery provided
- **Access to** *the*Edge: Yes

Map 1: On-Campus Accommodation

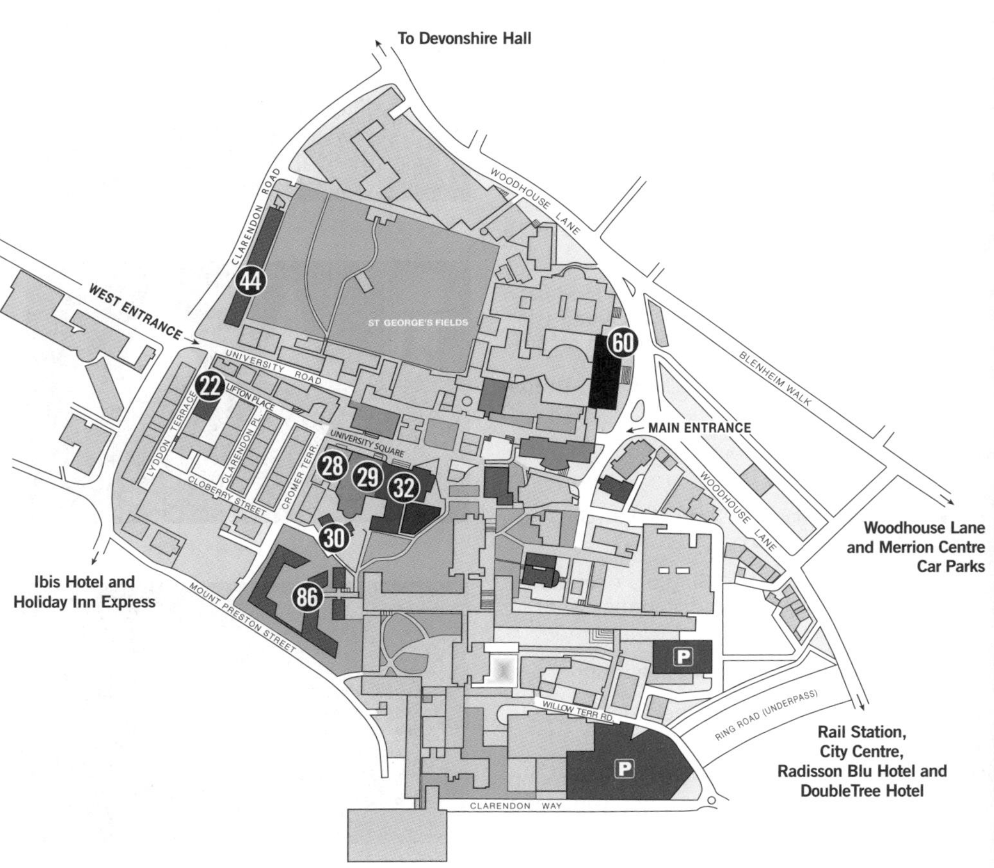

Key

86. Charles Morris Hall - Storm Jameson Court
22. Ellerslie Hall
44. Henry Price Residences
32. Leeds University Union
30. Lyddon Hall
60. Parkinson Building
29. Refectory
28. University House

Accommodation Off-Campus

Devonshire Hall

Devonshire Hall is a University hall of residence in a tranquil neighbourhood 1.4 km (0.9 miles) from campus - approximately a 20-minute walk or a five-minute bus journey.

Public buses 1, 6, 97, and 28 run every few minutes between Cumberland Road and the main campus. Some parking is available on-site and on adjacent streets without the need for a permit. However, a parking space is not guaranteed.

Delegates booking accommodation at Devonshire Hall will receive their registration pack upon checking in on site.

- **Location:** 15 Cumberland Rd, Leeds LS6 2EF
- **Breakfast:** Hot and cold buffet in the on-site dining hall
- **Availability:** 30 June 2018 (Sat) - 5 July 2018 (Thu)
- **Room Types:** Single occupancy ensuite and single occupancy shared bathroom
- **Reception:** 24-hour reception
- **Check-in times:** Check-in possible after 14.00, check-out is at 10.00
- **Provided:** Bedding, towels, shampoo and soap, tea and coffee-making facilities in kitchen
- **Lift for upper floor access:** No. No floor is stair-free
- **Wifi:** Yes
- **Kitchen:** May be located on the top floor. No crockery provided

Hotel Accommodation

IMC delegates can benefit from special inclusive rates at a number of nearby hotels, which are suitable for a variety of budgets and include bed, breakfast, and unlimited internet access.

Delegates booking accommodation through the IMC will receive their registration pack upon checking in at their hotel.

Single, twin, double, and family rooms are available in hotel accommodation. For all shared rooms, please provide the IMC with the names of all guests when registering, as we are required to provide the names of all guests to the hotels.

Parking for hotel accommodation cannot be booked through the IMC and is not included in the prices given below. Where applicable, parking must be arranged directly with the hotel.

If you would like to extend your stay at an IMC hotel accommodation beyond the dates featured on this page, please contact us to arrange this for you.

Additional Hotel Accommodation

We are also working with several other hotels in Leeds that look forward to welcoming IMC delegates in 2018.

For futher information about hotel accommodation options, see the IMC website:
www.leeds.ac.uk/ims/imc/IMC2018/accommodation.html

Family Accommodation

Children are welcome to accompany their parents or guardians to the IMC. Children under 18 must be supervised by their parents or guardian at all times, including at IMC events.

A limited number of family rooms are available at the Radisson Blu; we recommend early booking if you would like to reserve one. Family rooms accommodate up to four people, but larger families can book interconnecting rooms. Children under 16 can eat for free in the Radisson Blu restaurant when accompanied by an adult.

If you would like a family room, do not register through the Online Store - contact us for a Family Registration Form instead.

If you would like to book a family room in any other accommodation, please contact the hotel directly. However, if you need a cot for an infant, most hotels have a limited supply of these; we recommend requesting one as soon as possible.

Holiday Inn Express

The Holiday Inn Express is located just under 2 km (1¼ miles) from the south of the University campus, which is a 25-minute walk.

- **Breakfast:** Buffet breakfast
- **Availability:** 30 June 2018 (Sat) - 5 July 2018 (Thu)
- **Room Types:** Ensuite double bed and twin bed rooms for single or double occupancy. Non-smoking. Family rooms can be booked with the hotel directly
- **Reception:** 24-hour reception
- **Check-in times:** Check-in possible after 14.00, check-out is at 11.00
- **Provided:** Wifi, Freeview TV, fridge, desk, tea- and coffee-making facilities, iron, air conditioning
- **Lift for upper floor access:** Yes
- **Parking:** On-site parking £6.00

Contact:
Cavendish Street/Kirkstall Road
LEEDS
LS3 1LY
Tel: +44 (871) 902-1616 - Option 5
Fax: +44 (113) 242-6300
www.expressleeds.co.uk

Our Holiday Inn Express Hotel in Leeds is as warm and diverse as the city itself.

Based in a great location, it is a 10-15 minute walk from the city centre and just one mile from Leeds Railway Station.

There is a fantastic mix of restaurants in Leeds, so you can try a traditional taste of West Yorkshire or the many intriguing cuisines on offer.

Of course, it would not be Leeds if we didn't mention shopping, with more than 1,000 stores for you to explore.

With our rates, we offer more than just friendly accommodation:

- Start your day with a free continental buffet breakfast including hot choices
- Always be online with free wifi access
- Cheap on-site parking
- Complimentary toiletries from reception

Our Accommodation provides pleasant rooms with modern conveniences including:

- Fully adjustable air conditioning
- Ensuite bathrooms with power showers
- Brand new 32-inch flat screen TVs
- Hairdryer
- Choice of firm or soft pillows
- Tea/coffee making facilities

Ibis Hotel

The Ibis Hotel is located 2 km (1¼ miles) to the south of the University campus, which is a 25-minute walk.

- **Breakfast:** Buffet breakfast
- **Availability:** 30 June 2018 (Sat) - 5 July 2018 (Thu)
- **Room Types:** Ensuite double bed and twin bed rooms for single or double occupancy. Non-smoking
- **Reception:** 24-hour reception
- **Check-in times:** Check-in possible after 14.00, check-out is at 12.00
- **Provided:** Wifi, Freeview TV, hairdryer, desk, tea- and coffee-making facilities
- **Lift for upper floor access:** Yes
- **Parking:** Public outdoor parking, LS1 4PD. Charges apply

Contact:
23 Marlborough Street
LEEDS
LS1 4PB
Tel: +44 (113) 396-9000
www.ibis.com/gb/hotel-3652-ibis-leeds-centre-marlborough-street/index.shtml

Ibis Leeds is situated in the city centre within easy walking distance of the main University campus and Leeds Railway Station. Please feel free to ask at reception for directions or a taxi if preferred.

The hotel features a stylish Restaurant & Bar serving food all day, plus a 24-hour reception service.

The hotel has 168 rooms including comfortable queen-size or twin beds, flat screen TVs, free wifi, tea & coffee making facilities, and an ensuite shower room equipped with power shower.

Driving directions to the hotel are available on request, and a public car park is located opposite the hotel at £10 per 24 hours.

We look forward to welcoming IMC delegates once again to the Ibis Leeds.

Discovery Inn

The Discovery Inn is situated near the train station 1.6 km (1 mile) away from the University campus, which is a 20-minute walk.

- **Breakfast:** Continental buffet
- **Availability:** 1 July 2018 (Sun) - 5 July 2018 (Thu)
- **Room Types:** Ensuite double bed and twin bed rooms for single or double occupancy. Non-smoking. Family rooms can be booked with the hotel directly
- **Reception:** 24-hour reception
- **Check-in times:** Check-in possible after 14.00, check-out is at 11.00
- **Provided:** Wifi, Freeview TV, hairdryer, tea- and coffee-making facilities
- **Lift for upper floor access:** Yes, excluding 6th floor
- **Parking:** Public multi-storey car park Q-Park, Sovereign Square, LS1 4AG

The Discovery Inn is the best value hotel for work, rest, and play in Leeds City Centre! Located just 100 metres from Leeds City Station, the Discovery Inn is an ideal choice for those who want the convenience of a centrally-located hotel without the overinflated price tag.

Each room is well-equipped for a comfortable stay and a good night's sleep regardless of whether you're in Leeds for business or pleasure – ensuite bathroom, tea and coffee-making facilities, complimentary wifi, Freeview TV and hairdryer all come as standard.

We look forward to welcoming IMC delegates to the Discovery Inn Leeds.

Contact:
13-15 Bishopgate Street
LEEDS
LS1 5DY
Tel: +44 (113) 242-2555
http://discovery-inn-leeds.co.uk

The Queens Hotel

The Queens Hotel is located 1.6 km (1 mile) from the University campus, a 20-minute walk. The hotel is situated close to the railway station, shops, bars and restaurants of the city centre.

- **Breakfast:** Buffet breakfast
- **Availability:** 1 July 2018 (Sun) - 5 July 2018 (Thu)
- **Room Types:** Ensuite double bed and twin bed rooms for single or double occupancy. Non-smoking
- **Reception:** 24-hour reception
- **Check-in times:** Check-in possible after 15.00, check-out is at 11.00
- **Provided:** Wifi, TV with Sky, hairdryer, tea- and coffee-making facilities, iron, air conditioning
- **Lift for upper floor access:** Yes
- **Parking:** Valet parking available for £15.95 for 24 hours

Contact:
City Square
LEEDS
LS1 1PJ (use LS1 4DY for sat-nav)
Tel: +44 (113) 243-1323
www.qhotels.co.uk/our-locations/the-queens

QHOTELS

The Queens is the most famous landmark hotel in Leeds. The imposing building with a Portland Stone façade enjoys an enviable location, adjacent to Leeds train station and stands proudly over City Square with restaurants, bars, and shops just a stone's throw away.

The hotel oozes 1930s Art Deco glamour and elegance, but the facilities and service will surpass the expectations of today's business or leisure guest.

Parking...

The main hotel car park, of which there are 80 spaces, is located below the hotel. Guests should park their cars in the drop off point at the front of the hotel and a member of our Concierge team will valet park your car at The Queens Hotel.

Radisson Blu

The Radisson Blu Hotel is approximately 1 km (2/3 mile) south of the University campus, a 15-minute walk. It offers four-star accommodation in single, double, twin, and some family bedrooms.

- **Breakfast:** Continental, North European, and American buffet breakfast
- **Availability:** 30 June 2018 (Sat) - 5 July 2018 (Thu)
- **Room Types:** Ensuite double bed and twin bed rooms for single or double occupancy, as well as family rooms. Non-smoking
- **Reception:** 24-hour reception
- **Check-in times:** Check-in possible after 15.00, check-out is at 12.00
- **Provided:** Wifi, Premium TV channels, tea- and coffee-making facilities, toiletries, hairdryer
- **Lift for upper floor access:** Yes
- **Parking:** Public underground car park, Q-Park The Light, LS2 3AG. Present the chip coin to the reception staff on check-out to receive a discount

Contact:
1 The Light
LEEDS
LS1 8TL
Tel: +44 (113) 236-6000
www.radissonblu.co.uk/hotel-leeds

A warm welcome to the Radisson Blu Hotel Leeds, situated in the heart of the city centre just a short walk from the train station and the University.

Built within the former Leeds Permanent Building Society, this Grade II listed building offers grandeur and opulence whilst providing modern and wow-factor private dining in the flagship FireLake Grill House and Cocktail Bar.

Our 147 fabulously unique bedrooms are refurbished to a modern and luxurious feel. You can also relax in your surroundings with access to our 300MB high speed wifi.

To find out more visit

www.radissonblu.co.uk/hotel-leeds

Located within The Light complex, guests can enjoy use of the leisure facilities of a Nuffield Health Club without even stepping outside (additional charges apply). The complex also offers a large indoor car park.

Parking...

Car parking is available within the Q-Park situated within The Light complex attached to our buildings. Q-Park offers 24-hour security and undercover access into the hotel. 24-hour parking is charged at a reduced rate of £13.00.

Ibis Styles Hotel

The Ibis Styles Hotel is located 1.4 km (0.9 miles) to the south of the University campus, a 20-minute walk.

- **Breakfast:** Continental buffet breakfast
- **Availability:** 1 July 2018 (Sun) - 5 July 2018 (Thu)
- **Room Types:** Ensuite double bed and twin bed rooms for single or double occupancy. Non-smoking
- **Reception:** 24-hour reception
- **Check-in times:** Check-in possible after 14.00, check-out is at 12.00
- **Provided:** Wifi, Freeview TV, hairdryer, desk, tea- and coffee-making facilities, free toiletries
- **Lift for upper floor access:** Yes
- **Parking:** Public multistorey parking, Citipark, Merrion Way, LS2 8BT

Contact:
Wade Lane
LEEDS
LS2 8NJ
Tel: +44 (113) 831-4530
www.ibis.com/gb/hotel-9687-ibis-styles-leeds-city-centre-arena-/index.shtml

A hotel born and bed in Yorkshire, ibis Leeds City Centre Arena is a hotel that's Yorkshire through and through.

Brewed with the very best of Leeds and Yorkshire, this hotel's bustling and modern like the city, and like the county, it's proud to share nods to its past. Iron, wool, and wood combine with northern soul and northern humour to give a hefty slice of glorious Northernism.

ibis Styles Leeds City Centre Arena features a Marco Pierre White New York Italian restaurant and bar. Free wifi is available throughout the property.

Comprising 134 stunning bedrooms, we offer practical and comfortable rooms that will ensure you have one great night's sleep. Every room at this hotel is air-conditioned and is equipped with a flat-screen TV and tea/ coffee making facilities.

The Leeds Marriott Hotel

The Leeds Marriott Hotel is located 1.8 km (1.1 miles) to the south of the University campus, a 25-minute walk.

- **Breakfast:** Cold Continental and hot breakfast
- **Availability:** 1 July 2018 (Sun) - 5 July 2018 (Thu)
- **Room Types:** Ensuite double bed and twin bed rooms for single or double occupancy. Non-smoking
- **Reception:** 24-hour reception
- **Check-in times:** Check-in possible after 15.00, check-out is at 12.00
- **Provided:** Wifi, flat-screen TV, hairdryer, desk, tea- and coffee-making facilities, free toiletries
- **Lift for upper floor access:** Yes
- **Parking:** Valet parking £15 per 24-hour period. Public multi-storey parking is also available nearby at Trinity Leeds

Contact:
4 Trevelyan Square
Boar Lane
LEEDS
LS1 6ET
Tel: +44 (113) 236-6366
www.marriott.co.uk/hotels/travel/lbadt-leeds-marriott-hotel

Located in Leeds city centre, the Marriott is just 5 minutes' walk from Leeds Rail Station opposite Trinity Leeds shopping centre. A sauna, indoor pool, and gym are available in the hotel's leisure centre.

Bathrobes and a hairdryer are included in the modern bathrooms. A flat-screen TV and tea and coffee facilities are provided in each air-conditioned room.

Halal Indian dishes are served in the stylish AM Kitchen & Bar. On-site restaurant Cast Iron Bar & Grill is open for breakfast, lunch, and dinner, offering a wide menu including light bites, burgers and British 28-day aged steaks.

The Principal Met Hotel

The Principal Met Hotel is located 1.4 km (0.9 miles) to the south of the University campus, a 20-minute walk.

- **Breakfast:** Cold Continental and hot breakfast
- **Availability:** 1 July 2018 (Sun) - 5 July 2018 (Thu)
- **Room Types:** Ensuite double bed and twin bed rooms for single or double occupancy. Non-smoking
- **Reception:** 24-hour reception
- **Check-in times:** Check-in possible after 15.00, check-out is at 12.00
- **Provided:** Wifi, flat-screen TV, hairdryer, desk, tea- and coffee-making facilities, free toiletries
- **Lift for upper floor access:** Yes
- **Parking:** None. Public multi-storey parking is available nearby at Leeds Rail Station or Trinity Leeds

Contact:
King Street
LEEDS
LS1 2HQ
Tel: +44 (113) 245-0841
www.phcompany.com/principal/leeds-met-hotel/

Accommodation Contact Details

Charles Morris Hall
Mount Preston Street
University of Leeds
LEEDS
LS2 9JP
Tel: +44 (113) 343-2750

Devonshire Hall
Cumberland Road
LEEDS
LS6 2EQ
Tel: +44 (113) 275-1265

Ellerslie Hall
Lyddon Terrace
LEEDS
LS2 9LQ
Tel: +44 (113) 343-1802

Lyddon Hall
Lyddon Hall
Off Cromer Terrace
LEEDS
LS2 9JW
Tel: +44 (113) 343-7697

Discovery Inn
13-15 Bishopgate St
LEEDS
LS1 5DY
Tel: +44 (113) 242-2555

Holiday Inn Express
Leeds City Centre
Cavendish Street/Kirkstall Road
LEEDS
LS3 1LY
Tel: +44 (871) 902-1616 - Option 5

Ibis Hotel
Ibis Hotel Leeds Centre
23 Marlborough Street
LEEDS
LS1 4PB
Tel: +44 (113) 396-9000

Ibis Styles Hotel
Ibis Styles Leeds City Centre Arena
Wade Lane
LEEDS
LS2 8NJ
Tel: +44 (113) 831-4530

Leeds Marriott Hotel
4 Trevelyan Square
Boar Lane
LEEDS
LS1 6ET
Tel: +44 (113) 236-6366

The Principal Met Hotel
King Street
LEEDS
LS1 2HQ
Tel: +44 (113) 245-0841

The Queens Hotel
City Square
LEEDS
LS1 1PJ
Tel: +44 (113) 243-1323

Radisson Blu Hotel
Radisson Blu Hotel, Leeds
1 The Light
LEEDS
LS1 8TL
Tel: +44 (113) 236-6000

Map 2: Off-Campus Accommodation

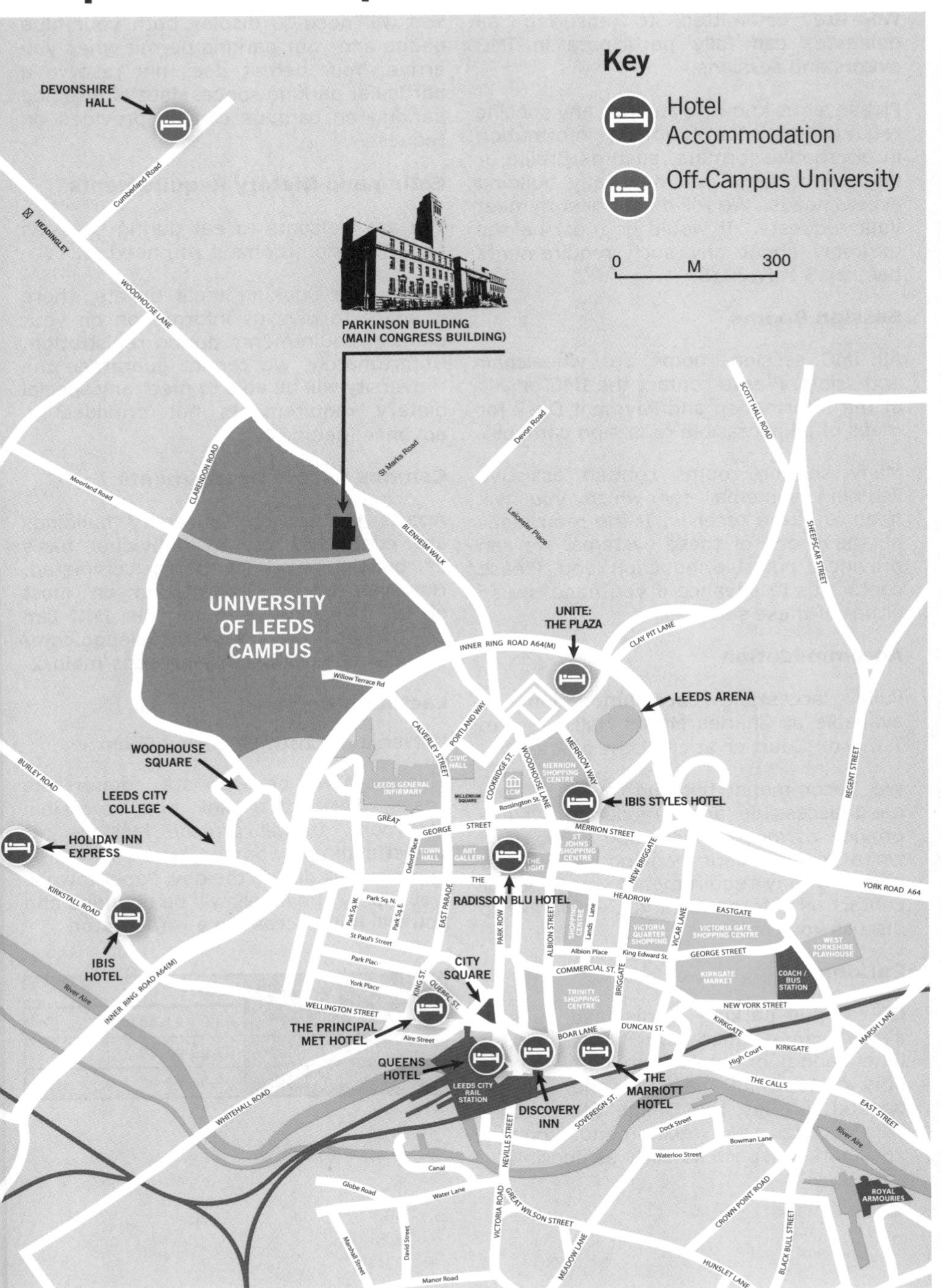
Key
Hotel Accommodation
Off-Campus University
0 M 300
DEVONSHIRE HALL
PARKINSON BUILDING (MAIN CONGRESS BUILDING)
UNIVERSITY OF LEEDS CAMPUS
UNITE: THE PLAZA
LEEDS ARENA
IBIS STYLES HOTEL
WOODHOUSE SQUARE
LEEDS CITY COLLEGE
HOLIDAY INN EXPRESS
IBIS HOTEL
RADISSON BLU HOTEL
CITY SQUARE
THE PRINCIPAL MET HOTEL
QUEENS HOTEL
DISCOVERY INN
THE MARRIOTT HOTEL
LEEDS CITY RAIL STATION
COACH / BUS STATION
ROYAL ARMOURIES
INNER RING ROAD A64(M)
WOODHOUSE LANE
CLARENDON ROAD
BLENHEIM WALK
YORK ROAD A64
HEADROW
GEORGE STREET
MERRION STREET
BOAR LANE
WELLINGTON STREET
WHITEHALL ROAD
KIRKSTALL ROAD
BURLEY ROAD
River Aire

Accessibility

We are committed to ensuring all delegates can fully participate in IMC events and sessions.

Please let us know if you have any specific requirements, for example, information in alternative formats, such as Braille or large print, or if you have any building access needs. We will do our best to meet your requests. It would be most helpful to know about any such requirements before 13 May 2018.

Session Rooms

All IMC session rooms are wheelchair accessible. Please contact the IMC or ask at the Information and Payment Desk for maps of all accessible routes on campus.

Many session rooms contain assistive listening systems, for which you will need to hire a receiver. If the room does not have one of these systems, we can provide a portable induction loop. Please contact us in advance if you need to use either of these services.

Accommodation

Fully accessible accommodation is available at Charles Morris Hall – Storm Jameson Court or at city centre hotels.

We recommend booking early if you need accessible accommodation. Please provide as much information as possible when making your booking so we can help with any requirements you have, or contact us beforehand if you would like to discuss your options.

Parking

On-campus parking in disabled bays is available for delegates who hold a valid EU blue badge, or international equivalent. This costs £7.00 per day and can be booked through the Online Store when you register. We recommend booking your parking space as early as possible.

You will need to display both your blue badge and your parking permit when you arrive. Your permit does not reserve a particular parking space. Maps of disabled parking on campus can be provided on request.

Eating and Dietary Requirements

You are welcome to eat during sessions and in session rooms if you need to.

If you are booking meal tickets, there is space to give us information on your dietary requirements during registration. Unfortunately, we cannot guarantee the University will be able to meet any special dietary requirements not provided in advance (see p. 29).

Campus Access Assessments

Access reports on University buildings are conducted on an individual basis as building work is being completed. However, access information on most of the buildings used for the IMC can be found at www.disabledgo.com/organisations/university-of-leeds/main-2

Lactation Room

University House: Woodsley Room

This room will be a private, comfortable space, close to a sink and accessible bathroom. It will provide facilities for breastfeeding women who want to express milk during the day. Paper towels, wet wipes, and labels will be provided and you will have access to a refrigerator.

Monday 02 July	09.00-21.00
Tuesday 03 July	09.00-21.00
Wednesday 04 July	09.00-21.00
Thursday 05 July	09.00-17.00

Quiet Room

University House: De Grey Room

This room will be open as a quiet place for relaxing away from the lively atmosphere of the IMC. Equipment such as earplugs will be available for you to take a break in your own company.

The quiet room is not intended as a space for socialising or practising your paper: please respect the needs of other delegates. Instructions on using the room will be available inside.

Monday 02 July	09.00-21.00
Tuesday 03 July	09.00-21.00
Wednesday 04 July	09.00-21.00
Thursday 05 July	09.00-17.00

Gender Neutral and Accessible Bathrooms

All single-room accessible toilets on campus are gender neutral. These will be signposted in all buildings used for IMC events.

Additional gender-neutral toilets are also available in Leeds University Union and the Fine Art Building, and will be clearly marked on building plans and signage.

Accessible Entrance to the Parkinson Building

- Facing the main entrance to the Parkinson Building, turn left and pass around the building.
- Go through the arches and turn right.
- Go through a second arch and take the ramp to your right and use the button-operated automatic door.
- Turn left inside the building and follow the corridor. Take the lift on your right and select '0' for Parkinson Court.

The locations of accessible entrances to all University buildings, can be found using the 'Disabled Building Access' filter on the University's campus map: www.leeds.ac.uk/campusmap

Meals and dietary requirements

Breakfast

All accommodation booked through the IMC includes breakfast. For on-campus accommodation, breakfast will be served in the Refectory. If you are staying in any other IMC accommodation, breakfast will be served in the dining hall or restaurant of your accommodation.

Lunch and Dinner

IMC delegates can purchase meal tickets for lunch and dinner through the Online Store during registration, or at the IMC itself from the Refectory Foyer.

We cannot guarantee any meals that are not booked in advance, and it is not possible to sell or exchange unwanted tickets when you arrive.

Tickets can be purchased for hot lunches and dinners that are served in the Refectory, or you can buy a ticket for a packed lunch which will be available to collect from the Marquee.

Special Dietary Requirements

Please provide as much detail as possible about any dietary requirements when you register. We will pass these on to the University's catering team, who will do their best to meet your needs. However, unfortunately we cannot always guarantee that this will be possible - especially if we are not informed in advance.

Kosher Meals

To provide kosher meals, the University orders meals in advance from a specialist supplier. This means you will need to purchase a supplement in addition to each kosher meal, and book well in advance to ensure we can meet your needs.

Supplements can be bought through the Online Store at http://store.leeds.ac.uk/product-catalogue/conference-and-events-office/international-medieval-congress-supplementary-items

Eating on Campus

A number of cafés, bars, and shops are also open on campus.

Old Bar and Terrace Bar in Leeds University Union serve hot food all day, while cold sandwiches, salads, and drinks can be purchased from the Essentials shop. Cafeteria-style meals are also available from the Refectory on a cash basis.

Coffee bars selling hot and cold sandwiches can also be found in Baines Wing, the Maurice Keyworth Building, and the Marjorie and Arnold Ziff Building.

Travelling to the IMC

Air

Leeds is well-situated between Leeds Bradford and Manchester airports. Both airports benefit from regular transport links to Leeds Rail Station.

Leeds Bradford Airport (LBA)

A number of airlines operate at Leeds Bradford Airport, offering links to major hubs such as London Heathrow and Amsterdam Schipol.

The 'Flying Tiger' 757 bus connects the airport to Leeds Rail Station and Leeds City Bus and Coach Station. Taxis directly from the airport can be booked in advance, or reserved at the booking office outside the terminal.

LBA Airport Information

Tel: +44 (871) 288-2288
www.leedsbradfordairport.co.uk

Manchester International Airport (MAN)

Manchester International Airport is approximately 90 km (60 miles) from the University of Leeds main campus. Flights to Manchester can be booked from nearly 200 international airports.

A train station within the airport offers direct, half-hourly services to Leeds Railway Station Monday to Saturday, and hourly services on Sunday.

MAN Airport Information

Tel: +44 (871) 271-0711
www.manchesterairport.co.uk

Coach or Bus

Leeds City Bus and Coach Station is in the centre of Leeds, 2 km (1¼ miles) from the University campus, a 25-minute walk.

Public buses 6, 28, and 97 offer a frequent bus service to the University; tickets are purchased from the driver. Delegates may also take a taxi to the University.

Coach Timetables and Tickets

There is an extensive network of coach services within the UK and, through Eurolines, to cities throughout mainland Europe. This method of travel is usually the least expensive, often a third of the cost of rail travel.

For information concerning timetables and fares, or to book tickets, contact:

National Express
Tel: +44 (871) 781-8178
www.nationalexpress.com

Megabus
Tel: +44 (900) 160-0900
www.megabus.com

Eurolines
www.eurolines.com

Car

Because parking is very limited on campus and public transport links to campus are excellent, we strongly recommend that delegates use alternative methods to travel to Leeds.

Parking on Campus

All cars entering campus are subject to parking charges, including evenings and weekends. Parking permits can be booked through the Online Store when you register at a cost of £7.00 per day – these expire at 24.00 (midnight) on the day for which they were booked. Parking permits do not reserve a particular space.

If you need to use a disabled parking space, please see p.26.

City Centre Parking

Public and private multi-storey car parking facilities are within easy walking distance of campus, including Woodhouse Lane Car Park and Merrion Centre Car Park. You will need to pay for your space at the car park on the day.

By Rail

Leeds Railway Station offers frequent direct services to most major UK cities. Travelling to London King's Cross takes around 2¼ hours. The station is around 1.6 km (1 mile) from campus, a 20-minute walk.

Tickets and Timetables

The following websites will help you find the right trains and book tickets online.

National Rail Enquiries
Tel (UK): 0845 748-4950
Tel (Overseas): +44 (20) 7278-5240
www.nationalrail.co.uk

The Trainline
www.thetrainline.com

Brit Rail (Overseas)
www.britrail.com

Meet and Greet Service

On Sunday 1 and Monday 2 July, the IMC will provide a meet and greet service in the central hall of the station. IMC representatives will help you find the best way to your accommodation, whether by helping you book a taxi, providing walking directions, or providing information on buses.

Sunday 01 July	12.00-23.00
Monday 02 July	07.30-12.30

Map 3: Leeds Rail Station Meet & Greet

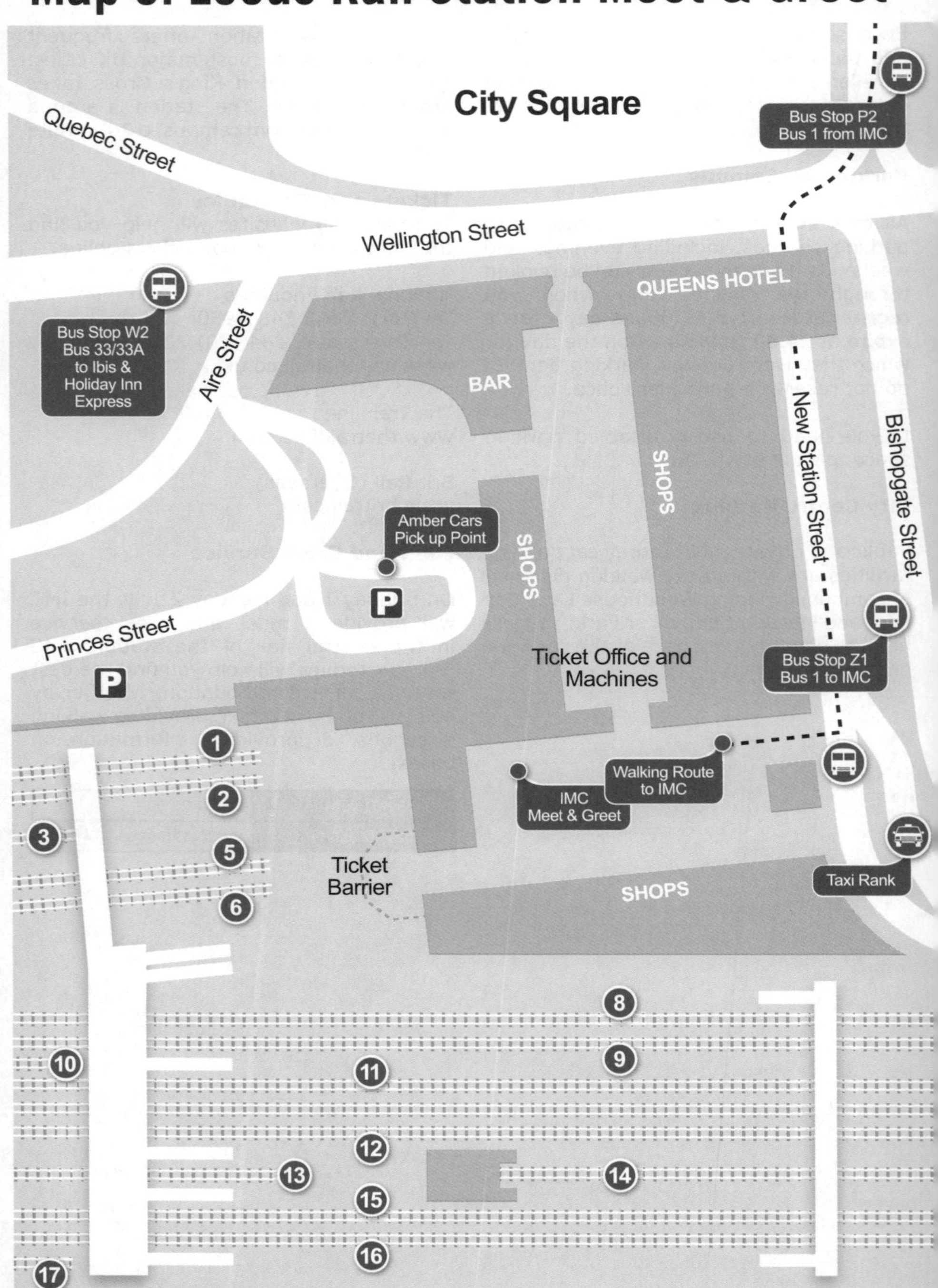
City Square
Quebec Street
Wellington Street
Bus Stop P2
Bus 1 from IMC
Aire Street
Bus Stop W2
Bus 33/33A
to Ibis &
Holiday Inn
Express
QUEENS HOTEL
BAR
SHOPS
New Station Street
Bishopgate Street
Amber Cars
Pick up Point
SHOPS
P
Princes Street
P
Ticket Office and
Machines
Bus Stop Z1
Bus 1 to IMC
Walking Route
to IMC
IMC
Meet & Greet
Ticket
Barrier
SHOPS
Taxi Rank
1
2
3
5
6
8
9
10
11
12
13
14
15
16
17

Map 4: Car Parking

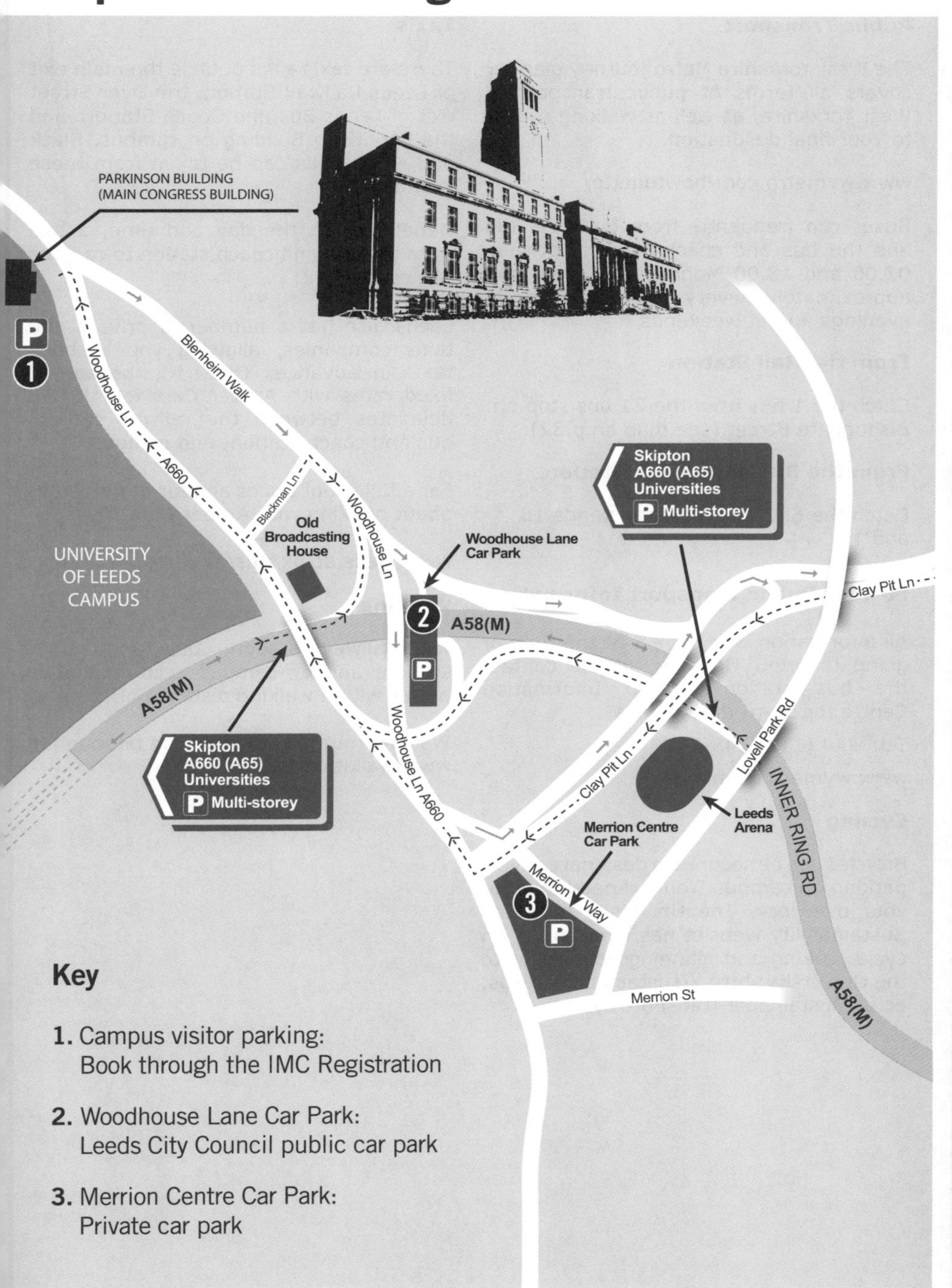

Key

1. Campus visitor parking:
   Book through the IMC Registration
2. Woodhouse Lane Car Park:
   Leeds City Council public car park
3. Merrion Centre Car Park:
   Private car park

Travelling around Leeds

Public Transport

The West Yorkshire Metro journey planner covers all forms of public transport in West Yorkshire, as well as walking routes to your final destination.

www.wymetro.com/howtogetto/

Buses run frequently from both the rail and the bus and coach station between 07.00 and 18.00 Monday to Friday, and approximately every 30 minutes in evenings and at weekends.

From the Rail Station

Catch the 1 bus from the Z1 bus stop on Bishopgate Street (see map on p.32).

From the Bus and Coach Station

Catch the 6, 28, or 97 from stands 18 and 19.

Further Public Transport Information

All information was correct at the time of going to print. However, please contact the bus station's Metro Information Centre for up-to-date details:

Tel: +44 (113) 245-7676
www.wymetro.com

Cycling

Bicycles can be secured in designated cycle parking on campus. You will need to bring your own lock. The University of Leeds Sustainability website has information on cycle parking and planning your route to the University: http://sustainability.leeds.ac.uk/sustainable-transport/cycle/

Taxis

There are taxi ranks outside the main exit of Leeds Railway Station, the Dyer Street exit of Leeds Bus and Coach Station, and the Parkinson Building on campus. Black and white taxis can be taken from these locations.

Depending on the day and time, a taxi from the bus and coach station to campus can cost £6-12.

Leeds also has a number of private hire taxis companies, allowing you to book taxis in advance. The IMC has agreed fixed rates with Amber Cars for all IMC delegates between the railway station, bus and coach station, and campus.

For a full list of prices and for more details about booking with Amber Cars, visit:

www.leeds.ac.uk/ims/imc/travelto.html

Walking

The railway station, bus and coach station, and off-campus accommodation are all within walking distance of campus.

Walking routes and maps can be found at www.walkit.com/cities/leeds/

Arriving at the IMC

When you arrive at the IMC, you will need to collect your registration pack before attending any sessions, events, or excursions.

Registration Packs

Your registration pack will include your receipt, a copy of the *Addenda/ Corrigenda*, and your name badge.

Your IMC name badge is your pass to the IMC. Delegates not displaying their IMC name badge may be refused admission to IMC sessions or activities. The University of Leeds campus is a busy environment; you will therefore be required to wear your name badge at all times for security reasons.

In addition, your name badge will include your IT username and password, and your library access barcode. For more information on computing and library facilities, see pp. 38-39.

Collecting Your Pack

You will need to collect your registration pack before the first IMC session or excursion you plan to attend.

If you have booked your accommodation through the IMC, your pack will be available to collect from your hotel or hall of residence reception. If you arrive before check-in opens at 14.00, you will be able to leave your luggage at your accommodation.

If you have not booked accommodation through the IMC, you will be able to collect your pack from the Registration Pack Collection Desk. On Sunday 1 July this will be in Leeds University Union Foyer; after this date, it will be located at the main entrance to the Parkinson Building.

Sunday 01 July	10.00-19.00
Monday 02 July	08.00-20.00
Tuesday 03 July	08.00-18.00
Wednesday 04 July	08.00-18.00
Thursday 05 July	08.00-13.00

This desk may be very busy at peak times, so we ask you to please leave plenty of time before the start of your session or excursion in order to collect your pack and ask any questions you may have.

Map 5: Main Road Routes to Leeds

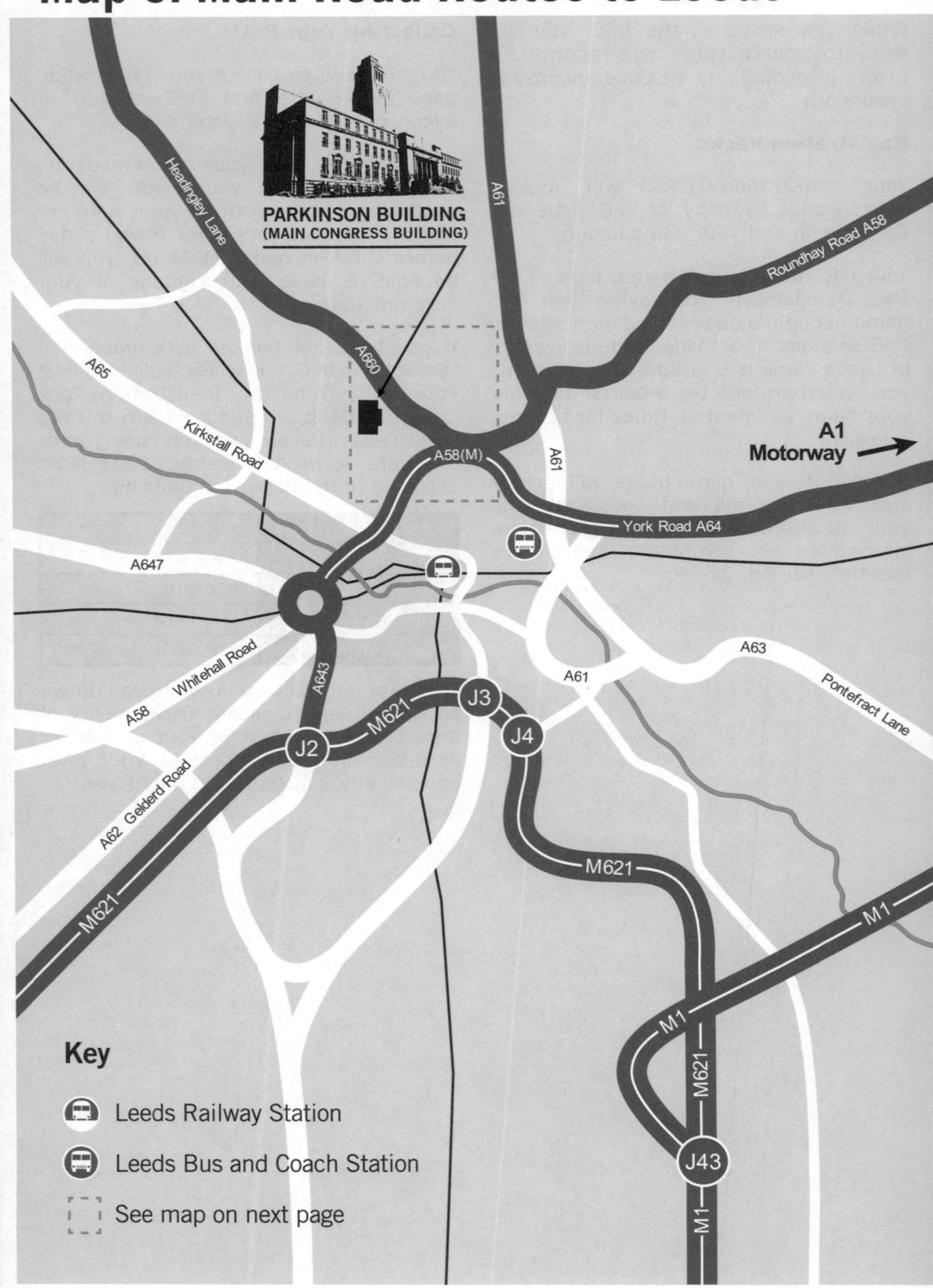

PARKINSON BUILDING
(MAIN CONGRESS BUILDING)
Headingley Lane
A61
Roundhay Road A58
A65
A660
Kirkstall Road
A58(M)
A61
A1
Motorway
York Road A64
A647
Whitehall Road
A643
A58
A63
A61
Pontefract Lane
J3
M621
J4
J2
A62 Gelderd Road
M621
M621
M1
M1
M621
J43
M1
Key
Leeds Railway Station
Leeds Bus and Coach Station
See map on next page

Map 6: Walking Routes to Campus

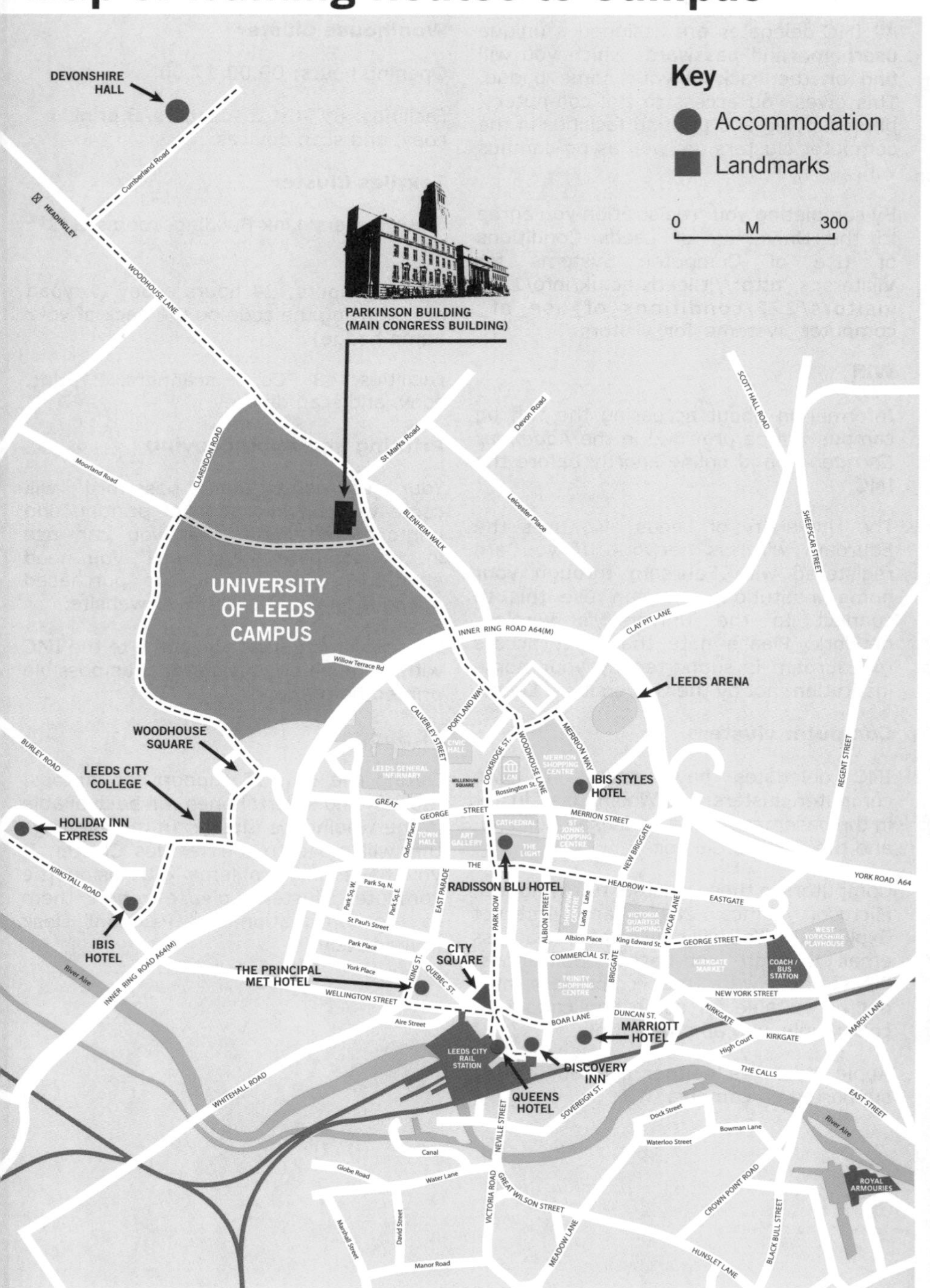

Computing and Printing Facilities

All IMC delegates are assigned a unique username and password, which you will find on the back of your name badge. This gives you access to the computers, photocopying and printing facilities in the computer clusters, as well as on-campus wifi.

By completing your registration you agree to the University of Leeds Conditions of Use of Computer Systems for Visitors: http://it.leeds.ac.uk/info/133/visitors/272/conditions_of_use_of_computer_systems_for_visitors

Wifi

Information about accessing the wifi on campus will be provided in the *Addenda/Corrigenda* and online shortly before the IMC.

The University of Leeds also uses the Eduroam wireless network. If you are registered with Eduroam through your home institution, you can use this to connect to the University's wireless network. Please note that your access to Eduroam is supported by your home institution, not by the University of Leeds.

Computer clusters

IMC delegates have access to two computer clusters: the Woolhouse Cluster in the basement of the Parkinson Building, and the Textiles Cluster.

Computers in these clusters run Windows, Microsoft Office 2013, and Internet Explorer 10. You will only be able to access email through web-based applications. Please be aware that computers may not be suitable for some applications or compatible with all types of file.

Apple Macs are neither catered for nor supported on campus.

Woolhouse Cluster

Opening hours: 09.00-17.00

Facilities: 89 PCs, 2 scanners, 3 print, copy, and scan devices

Textiles Cluster

Clothworkers' Link Building, rooms G33-34

Opening hours: 24 hours a day (keypad access using the code on the back of your name badge)

Facilities: 43 PCs, 2 scanners, 2 print, copy, and scan devices

Printing and Photocopying

Your username and password will come with an allocation of printing and photocopying credit that you can use in the computer clusters. If you need additional credit, it can be purchased online from the University IT website.

We recommend that you come to the IMC with as much of your material as possible printed beforehand.

IT Support

During the day, IT support for laptops, tablets, and smartphones will be available in the Woolhouse Cluster. In the evenings this will move to the Textiles Cluster. If you have any problems with using the computer clusters, please report them to the Information and Payment Desk immediately.

Library Access

The back of your name badge will include a barcode which gives you read-only access to Leeds University Library. One of the largest research libraries in the UK, the University Library holds over 2.7 million books, including extensive holdings relating to medieval studies.

There are several libraries on campus which are available for you to use. If you are looking for a particular book or journal, the online catalogue will give you the name of the right library: https://library.leeds.ac.uk/

Brotherton Library

Arts, social sciences, law, and Special Collections

Opening hours: 08.00-20.00

Computers: Yes

Edward Boyle Library

Science, social sciences and engineering

Opening hours: 08.00-20.00

Computers: Yes

Health Sciences Library

Medicine and health-related subjects

Opening hours: 08.00-20.00

Computers: Yes

Laidlaw Library

High demand collection and core texts

Opening hours: 08.00-20.00

Computers: Yes

Floor plans of individual libraries, including the locations of individual subject collections, can be found at https://library.leeds.ac.uk/about-the-library

Special Collections

The Brotherton Library is also home to Special Collections, which holds more than 200,000 rare books and hundreds of thousands of manuscripts, incunabula, rare books, and archival materials. You are welcome to use Special Collections, but you will need to book an appointment in advance.

For further information, please see https://library.leeds.ac.uk/special-collections-visit

Terms and Conditions

By completing your registration you agree to the 'Institute for Medieval Studies Conditions of Use of the Library', as detailed on our website:

www.leeds.ac.uk/ims/imc/IMC2017/tc_library.html

Presenting and Moderating Sessions

Recommendations for Speakers

- Make sure your paper is presented within the allotted time (20 minutes for sessions with three papers and 15 minutes for sessions with four papers).
- Arrive at least 10 minutes before the session to prepare.
- Speak clearly and slowly so that everyone can follow your paper. The language in which you are speaking may not be the first language of everyone in the audience.
- Support your paper with additional information, using either a slideshow (such as a PowerPoint presentation) or a paper handout. Standard session rooms can hold 28-40 people, but some rooms may hold more.
- Please make sure that all materials you use are clearly legible for delegates with visual impairments. We recommend using the guidelines at www.rnib.org.uk/professionals/accessibleinformation/accessibleformats/Pages/accessible_formats.aspx
- You may wish to produce at least 2 copies in large print for delegates with visual impairments. In addition, remember to describe the images used in your presentation.
- If you are presenting your paper in a language other than English, we recommend producing a short handout summarising the key points of your paper in English.
- If there is a microphone in your session room, please use it so that delegates with hearing impairments can follow your paper.

Using Audio-Visual (AV) Equipment

Every session room at the IMC will include a computer and data projector as standard.

Speakers should include requests to use additional equipment with their paper and session proposals, and we start planning to provide these items soon after the proposal deadline. Some rooms are allocated according to the equipment that can be provided in them.

Although we will do our best, we cannot guarantee that any additional equipment requested after December will be available. Please contact us as early as possible if you will need any other equipment.

Technical Requirements

If you plan to use your own laptop, please make sure you have informed the IMC team. The laptop must have a 'female' VGA monitor output to connect to our projectors.

If you are bringing your presentation to display using the IMC computer in your session room, make sure your presentation is Microsoft-compatible. We recommend bringing your presentation on a USB flash drive / memory stick; you may also consider emailing a copy to yourself as a backup.

Only Microsoft PowerPoint 2013 will be automatically provided on IMC computers. If you need other software and cannot bring your own laptop, contact us as soon as possible.

Some session rooms will be connected to the internet via ethernet cable, while others will use campus wifi. This means that some session rooms may have more reliable internet connections than others. If you plan to access the internet during your paper, we strongly recommend bringing a contingency plan in case of a weak connection.

Apple Macs

Data projectors can be used with Apple Macs, but you will need to bring your own convertor cables, specific to the model of computer. Compatibility cannot be guaranteed for Macs, and the University does not offer technical support for them.

Slide and Overhead Projectors

The University of Leeds has a very limited number of slide and overhead projectors; we cannot guarantee their availability at the time of the Congress.

If you wish to use one of these items, please note that you will need to order it well in advance. We will not be able to provide a slide or overhead projector that you have not requested ahead of time.

We strongly recommend that you come to the IMC with a contingency plan in case this equipment is not available. Wherever possible, please bring your slides or transparencies in an alternative format.

Session Room Support

Each session room is assigned a Session Room Organiser (SRO), who will introduce themselves to the speakers and moderator at the start of the session. They ensure that the room is tidy, that the temperature and lighting are comfortable, that water is available for speakers, and that the correct equipment is provided.

Equipment is available for use 20 minutes before the start of your session, and we recommend that you test the equipment and report any problems. SROs will try to resolve any issues, but they may need to contact a University IT technician for support. Please be patient while waiting for a technician, who may be helping another delegate.

Please make sure you are familiar with the basic functions of the equipment you are using before you arrive. SROs will be assigned to more than one session room, so they will not have time to help every speaker use their equipment during the session.

Moderating a Session

The main duties of a session moderator are:

- To introduce each speaker, being aware there may be non-specialists in the audience
- To make sure each speaker finishes their paper on time, and to be assertive on this issue if necessary
- To make sure the session starts and finishes on time
- To initiate and moderate questions and discussion after the papers, ensuring all of the session's participants adhere to our policy on dignity and mutual respect (see p. 50)
- To be prepared to ask questions if they are not forthcoming from the audience
- To complete our feedback form and return it to the Session Room Organiser at the end of the session.

We strongly recommend that moderators contact all the speakers in their session before the IMC, to get to know each speaker's paper and research.

Map 7: Session Rooms

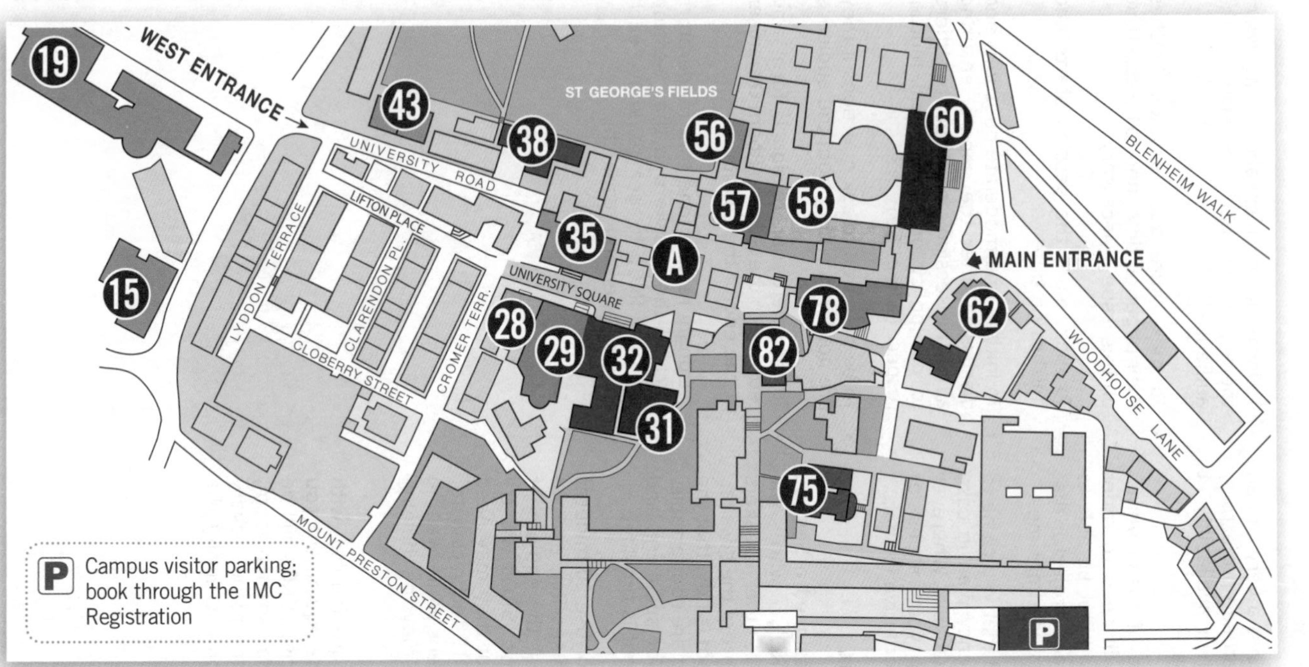

58. Baines Wing
15. Charles Thackrah Building
56. Clothworkers Building North
35. Clothworkers Building South
62. Emmanuel Centre
38. Fine Art Building
57. Great Hall
43. Institute for Transport Studies
32. Leeds University Union
A. The Marquee
19. Maurice Keyworth Building
78. Michael Sadler Buiding
60. Parkinson Building
29. Refectory
75. School of Music: Clothworkers Centenary Concert Hall
82. Social Sciences Building
31. stage@leeds
28. University House

Map 8: IMC Campus Map

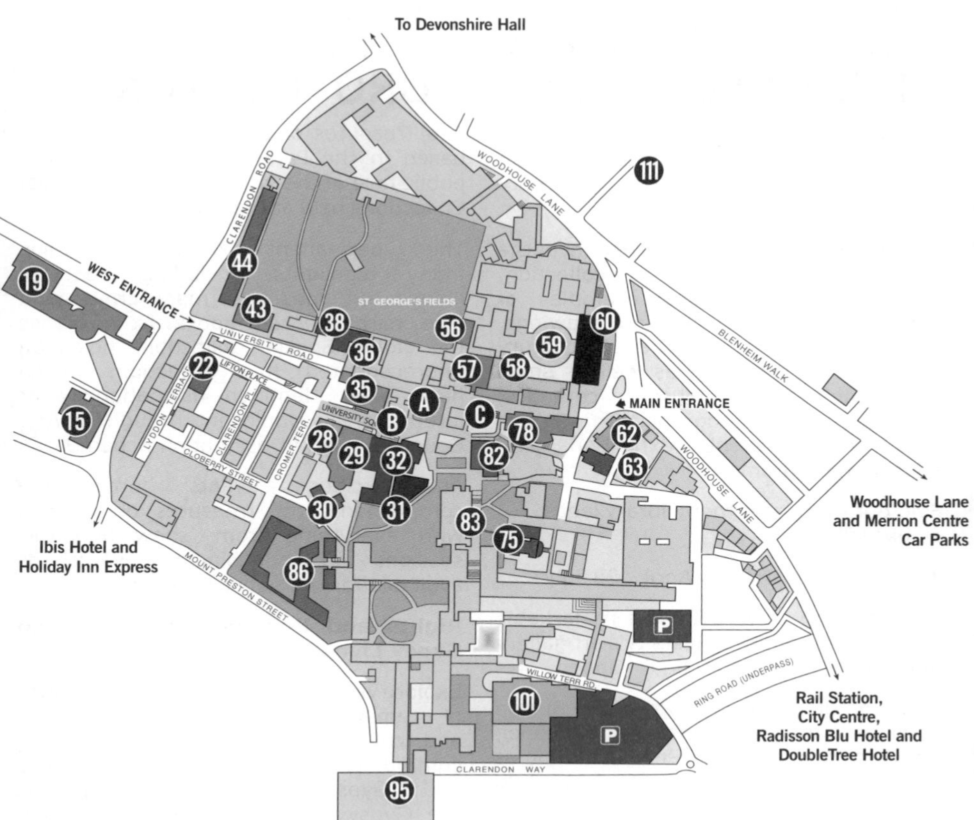

Key

58. Baines Wing
59. Brotherton Library
111. Catholic Chaplaincy (5-7 St Mark's Avenue)
86. Charles Morris Hall
15. Charles Thackrah Building
56. Clothworkers Building North
35. Clothworkers Building South
83. Edward Boyle Library
62. Emmanuel Centre
22. Ellerslie Hall
38. Fine Art Building
57. Great Hall
95. Health Sciences Library
44. Henry Price Residences
43. Institute for Transport Studies
61. Laidlaw Library
32. Leeds University Union
30. Lyddon Hall
A. The Marquee
19. Maurice Keyworth Building
78. Michael Sadler Buiding
60. Parkinson Building
C. Beech Grove Plaza
29. Refectory
75. School of Music: Clothworkers Centenary Concert Hall
82. Social Sciences Building
31. stage@leeds
86. Storm Jameson Court
36. Textiles Computer Cluster (24hr)
101. *the*Edge Sport and Fitness Centre
28. University House
B. University Square

Things to Do on Campus

THE STANLEY & AUDREY BURTON GALLERY

Based in the Parkinson Building, The Stanley & Audrey Burton Gallery is an oasis of calm at the heart of the University of Leeds campus.

Visitors are welcome to experience the University's exceptional art collection, which includes stunning examples of European and British painting, drawings, and prints, dating from the 17th-century up to the present day, as well as small collections of sculpture, ceramics, miniatures, and photographs. The Gallery has a thriving events, exhibitions, and education programme.

Find out more at https://library.leeds.ac.uk/galleries

Transformations (19 April - 28 July)

An exhibition celebrating the remarkable development of the University's art gallery and the people who made it happen.

From the quiet philanthropy of the Burton Family and the incisive vision of its Keeper, Dr Hilary Diaper, the gallery's evolution as the Stanley & Audrey Burton Gallery is told with key highlights from the Collection, including Stanley Spencer, Patrick Heron, Jacob Epstein, Ivon Hitchens, Terry Frost, Atkinson Grimshaw, and many others.

Open: Monday, 13.00-17.00, Tuesday-Saturday, 10.00-17.00. Free admission.

TREASURES OF THE BROTHERTON

The Treasures of the Brotherton Gallery, based in the Parkinson Building, is the public face of the world-renowned Special Collections held at the University of Leeds.

The permanent display contains many highlights, including beautiful illuminated medieval manuscripts and rare early printed books from across the globe. Special Collections holds an unprecedented five collections which have been identified as nationally or internationally significant through the Arts Council England Designation Scheme.

An exciting events programme complements the treasures on display, with everything from 'show and tell' sessions to bookbinding workshops available for the public to enjoy.

Rights and Romance: Representing Gypsy Lives (1 March - 31 July)

Explore visual and fictional representations of Gypsy and Traveller lives, made and collected by non-Travellers. Using community insight from members of Leeds GATE (Gypsy And Traveller Exchange) and the Gypsyville heritage group, this co-curated exhibition challenges stereotypes. Learn about Gypsy and Traveller lives in the past, the struggle for rights, and the community's responses to being represented by those outside it.

Open: Monday, 13.00-17.00, Tuesday-Saturday, 10.00-17.00. Free admission.

ULITA

an Archive of International Textiles

ULITA - an Archive of International Textiles is at St Wilfred's Chapel, Maurice Keyworth Building (next to Leeds University Business School).

The purpose of this accredited museum is to collect, preserve, and document textiles and related items from many of the textile-producing areas of the world for the benefit of scholars, researchers, and the general public.

A research group of the School of Design at Leeds, ULITA is primarily a textiles museum which holds annual exhibitions. The stored collections can be consulted by individuals and small groups by making an appointment.

An online catalogue of its major collections is available: go to http://ulita.leeds.ac.uk/

Open: Tuesday-Thursday, 09.30-16.30, Fridays by appointment. Free admission.

IMC Bookfair

The IMC Bookfair is open in Parkinson Court throughout the IMC. Take advantage of special conference discounts and meet publishers and distributors (see p. 472).

Second-Hand and Antiquarian Bookfair

Meet book dealers and browse a wide variety of titles in Leeds University Union Foyer, Sunday-Tuesday (see p. 473).

Medieval Craft Fair

Discover hand-crafted items inspired by medieval production techniques and aesthetics in Leeds University Union Foyer on Wednesday (see p. 298).

Historical and Archaeological Societies Fair

Find out more about the societies working to preserve and promote the heritage of Leeds, Yorkshire, and the UK, in the Marquee on Thursday (see p. 400).

Events and excursions

The IMC runs a diverse programme of events, workshops, and excursions to historic sites in the region. Tickets can be booked in advance when registering online. All events and excursions are open to the public as well as delegates (see pp. 449-471).

Souvenirs

Take home a memento of your trip to Leeds and pay a visit to our souvenir stall in Leeds University Union Foyer all week.

Making Leeds Medieval

Thursday 05 July, 10.30-18.00

Leeds University Union Foyer, University Square, and the Marquee

As IMC 2018 comes to a close, come and discover all that Making Leeds Medieval has to offer. Performances, demonstrations, and a bustling craft fair and farmers' market will turn University Square into a vibrant scene inspired by the past.

Medieval Craft Fair

Discover hand-crafted items inspired by medieval production techniques and aesthetics, from handmade books to wood and leatherwork. As you browse, meet the exhibitors and learn about the techniques involved in making these exquisite and unique items.

Farmers' Market

A wide range of quality, local produce from the Yorkshire region will be available for purchase, including the not-so-medieval, but undeniably delicious hog roast!

Demonstrations, Displays, and Music

Experience an exciting collection of demonstrations and displays, including the ever-popular live combat displays and, of course, birds of prey.

Meet the demonstrators, view replica weaponry and armour, and see majestic birds of prey including falcons and hawks up close.

Live musical performances throughout the day will accompany the festivities.

Historical & Archaeological Societies Fair

Meet representatives of a number of independent groups involved in preserving local and national history in Leeds, Yorkshire, and the UK as a whole.

These societies will be based in the Marquee during Making Leeds Medieval with a wealth of information and resources.

IMC Timetable

Event	Location	Sunday 01 July	Monday 02 July	Tuesday 03 July	Wednesday 04 July	Thursday 05 July
Meet & Greet	Leeds Railway Station	12.00 23.00	07.30 12.30			
Check-in	University Halls of Residence	Check in from 14.00 on day of arrival				
	Radisson Blu					
	Discovery Inn					
	Queens Hotel					
	Ibis Hotel					
	Ibis Styles					
	Holiday Inn Express					
	Marriott Hotel	Check in from 15.00 on day of arrival				
	The Met Hotel	Check in from 15.00 on day of arrival				
Registration Pack Collection	IMC Accommodation	Collect on arrival at accommodation				
	Refectory Foyer	10.00 22.00				
	Parkinson Court		10.00 19.30	08.00 18.00	08.00 18.00	08.00 13.00
Information and Payment Desk	Refectory Foyer	10.00 22.00	08.00 22.00	08.00 22.00	08.00 22.00	08.00 20.00
IMC Bookfair	Parkinson Court		10.00 19.30	08.30 18.30	08.30 18.30	08.30 13.00
Second-Hand Bookfair	Leeds University Union Foyer	16.00 21.00	08.00 19.00	08.00 17.00		
Medieval Craft Fair	Leeds University Union Foyer				10.30 19.30	10.30 18.00
Historical Societies Fair	The Marquee					10.30 18.00
Making Leeds Medieval	University Square					10.30 18.00
Breakfast	Refectory	07.00-10.00				
	Devonshire Hall	07.00-10.00				
	Marriott Hotel	07.00-11.00	06.30-10.30			
	The Met Hotel	07.00-11.00	06.30-10.00			
	Radisson Blu	06.30-12.00	06.30-10.30			
	Discovery Inn	07.00-10.00				
	Queens Hotel	07.00-10.00				
	Ibis Hotel	06.30-12.30	06.30-10.30			
	Ibis Styles	06.30-12.30	06.30-10.30			
	Holiday Inn Express	07.00-11.00	06.30-09.30			
Lunch	Refectory		12.00-14.00			
Dinner	Refectory	18.00-20.00				

Networking and Socialising

Socialising and networking are important aspects of the IMC, and a number of spaces are available on campus for medievalists to get to know each other informally.

The Marquee

Open exclusively for IMC delegates in University Square

Sunday - Thursday until 23.00

- Complimentary tea and coffee all day for IMC delegates
- Alcoholic and soft drinks available for purchase
- Indoor and outdoor seating

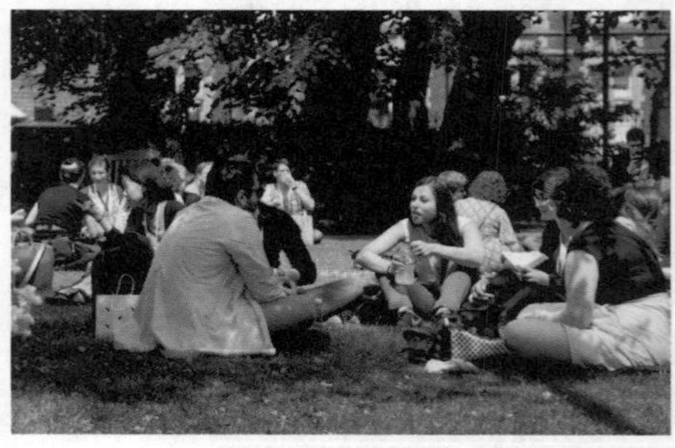

Parkinson Court

Parkinson Building

Monday - Wednesday until 18.00, Thursday to 13.00

- Complimentary tea and coffee all day for IMC delegates
- Centre of the IMC Bookfair

Old Bar

Leeds University Union

Every day until 02.00

- 'Traditional British pub' feel
- Serving traditional Congress Ale
- Alcoholic drinks, pub food, and soft drinks

Terrace Bar

Leeds University Union

Every day until 02.00

- Food served until 22.00 every day
- Indoor and outdoor seating
- Alcoholic and soft drinks served until late

Map 9: Networking and Social Spaces

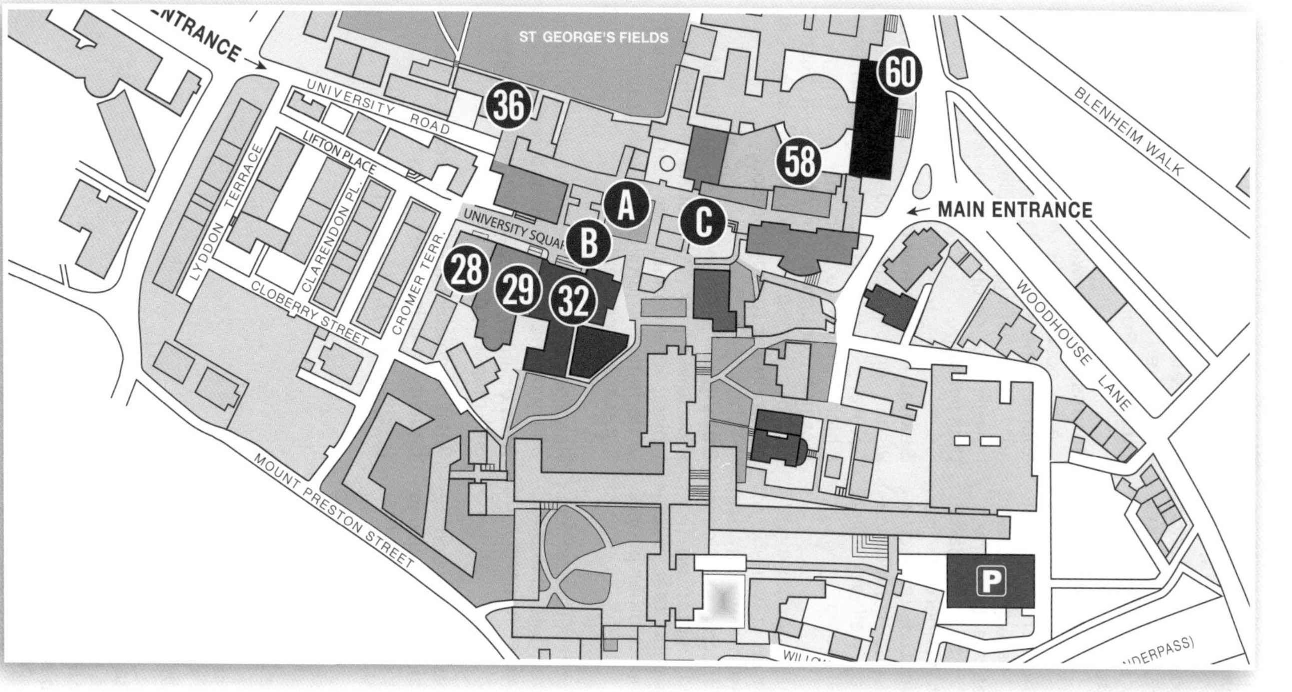

- **58.** Baines Wing Coffee Bar
- **32.** Leeds University Union
- **A.** The Marquee (Complimentary Tea & Coffee)
- **60.** Parkinson Building (Complimentary Tea & Coffee) (Computers available here)
- **C.** Beech Grove Plaza
- **29.** Refectory (Computers available here)
- **36.** Textiles Computer Cluster (24hr) (Computers available here)
- **28.** University House
- **B.** University Square

P Campus visitor parking; book through IMC Registration
Complimentary Tea & Coffee
Computers available here

Policy on Dignity and Mutual Respect

The IMC seeks to create a safe and productive environment for everyone, irrespective of race (including caste, ethnic or national origin, nationality or colour), gender, gender identity and expression, age, sexual orientation, disability, physical appearance, religion, pregnancy or maternity status, marriage or civil partnership status, or any other characteristic.

To ensure that everyone can make the most of the academic, networking, and social opportunities that the IMC offers, the organisers expect all delegates, exhibitors, and staff to adhere to our policy on dignity and mutual respect at all conference venues and conference-related social events, as well as online and in any form of social media.

The IMC is a diverse international event, and attendees come from a variety of different backgrounds with a wide range of opinions and perspectives. Please be mindful of this, and appreciate that behaviours and comments that seem harmless to you may impact other people in different ways.

We do not tolerate any form of harassment or bullying against any delegate, exhibitor, or member of staff, whether in person or online.

If you feel you are being harassed or bullied, notice harassing or bullying behaviour, or have any other concerns, please contact a member of IMC staff immediately. We value your attendance and will help contact security or police, provide escorts, or otherwise help you to feel safe throughout the IMC.

If you are asked to stop a behaviour which is deemed to be inappropriate, we will expect you to comply immediately.

We reserve the right to take action against people who violate these standards, which may include expelling offenders from the IMC with no refund, or banning them from future events.

We use the definitions of harassment, sexual harassment, and bullying used by the University of Leeds in its policy on dignity and mutual respect. **All visitors to the University of Leeds are also expected to comply with this policy and the University's Equality & Inclusion Policy.**

Harassment: Unwanted conduct that has the purpose or effect of either violating another person's dignity or creating an intimidating, hostile, degrading, humiliating, or offensive environment for that person.

Sexual harassment: Unwanted verbal, visual, or physical conduct of a sexual nature, or other conduct based on sex, which affects a person's working or learning conditions or creates a hostile or humiliating working or studying environment for that person.

Bullying: Offensive, intimidating, malicious, or insulting behaviour which intentionally or unintentionally undermines, humiliates, denigrates or injures the recipient.

Read or download the University of Leeds policy on mutual dignity and respect:

www.equality.leeds.ac.uk/DMR/Dignity-and-respect.pdf

Read or download the University of Leeds Equality and Inclusion Policy:

www.equality.leeds.ac.uk/

Social Media Policy

Delegates use social media as a way of sharing research knowledge with the public and allowing people who cannot attend conferences to follow and participate in discussion.

Twitter is the most common social media channel for this purpose. Users of Twitter can search for or click on any hashtag and see all tweets that include it, allowing them to follow the IMC or individual conversations related to it. They can also see every tweet posted by someone that they follow, whether it uses a hashtag or not.

This policy focuses on Twitter, but platforms such as Facebook and Instagram are also used by some researchers. The same principles apply to all social media channels used to talk about IMC 2018.

Many of our delegates tweet regularly, and you should expect other delegates to tweet about your paper unless you have expressly requested otherwise.

Session organisers will be asked to contact the speakers in their session to ask if they would prefer not to be tweeted about. Moderators are asked to make this clear at the start of the session, but they may also wish to remind audiences during questions/comments to make sure latecomers are aware.

Please respect the wishes of individual speakers. If the speaker is happy for you to tweet about their paper:

- Use the year-specific hashtag, e.g. **#IMC2018**, so that Twitter users can see all tweets related to the event.
- Use the specific hashtag for your session, which will be #s followed by the number of the session, e.g. **#s9999**. This allows Twitter users to focus on tweets related to that session.
- Clearly **attribute the content** of the tweet to the speaker and mention them by at least their surname. If they have a Twitter account and you know their Twitter handle, include their Twitter handle instead.
- Always **separate your own comments** about a topic from those of the speaker or any other participants. If you quote anyone directly, use quotation marks.
- **Listen carefully** to the speaker and reflect the content of the paper fairly and accurately.
- **Be respectful and constructive.** Feel free to engage with the speaker's ideas, ask questions and suggest areas of further research, but please do not tweet anything you would not be willing to say in the Q&A session after the paper. Twitter is a public forum where anyone can follow each conversation.

You may also decide to add to the conversation by tweeting links to relevant articles, the speaker's presentation, their online profile or other resources. If you do, links can be shortened to fit into tweets more easily by using sites such as tinyurl.com.

Speakers may be happy for you to take photos of them or their presentations, but **always ask permission first**.

Bursaries and Awards

IMC Bursary Fund

Each year the IMC receives a large number of applications for financial support. The IMC Bursary Fund was established in 1994 as part of our commitment to widening participation at the IMC. The IMC Bursary deadline is mid-October every year and applications are made online via the IMC website.

The Bursary Fund is available to delegates from outside Western Europe, students, independent scholars, retired, and unwaged scholars. The bursaries awarded range in value and may cover all or part of the Registration and Programming Fee, accommodation, and meals.

IMC Bursary Recipients

For the International Medieval Congress 2018 a total amount of almost £15,000 was awarded. 370 applications were received and 97 applicants were awarded bursaries ranging from £100 to £400.

For this year's Congress, bursaries were awarded to participants from Australia, Austria, Belarus, Belgium, Brazil, Canada, Croatia, Czech Republic, Ethiopia, France, Georgia, Germany, Greece, Hungary, Republic of Ireland, Israel, Italy, Japan, Latvia, Libya, Netherlands, New Zealand, Norway, Poland, Romania, Russia, Serbia, Spain, Sweden, Turkey, Ukraine, UK, USA, and Vatican City State.

If you would like to support the IMC Bursary Fund, please use the relevant section when making your booking for the IMC. Even small contributions make a great impact.

Awards and Prizes

We are keen to work with individuals and organisations who are interested in providing further support for individuals who would not otherwise be able to attend the IMC. If you or someone you know would be interested in participating in this way, please get in touch.

Templar Heritage Trust Bursaries

We would like to thank the Templar Heritage Trust (THT) for offering three bursaries of £200 each to IMC delegates.

THT operates as part of the Charities Aid Foundation and makes a number of grants each year in support of academic research and conservation of historic buildings. It takes a particular interest in the literary, architectural, and cultural legacy of the medieval Knights Templar and their period in history.

Sieglinde Hartmann Prize for German Language and Literature

Thanks to the generosity of Sieglinde Hartmann, president of the Oswald von Wolkenstein-Gesellschaft and a long-standing supporter of the IMC, a new prize has been instituted for the 2018 Congress.

The prize of €250 is awarded for the best abstract for any paper proposal in the field of medieval German language and/or medieval German literature.

Leeds Medieval Studies Endowment Fund

The Institute for Medieval Studies received a substantial bequest from a fellow medievalist which enabled us to establish the Leeds Medieval Studies Endowment Fund in 2008.

Part of this fund directly contributes to the IMC Bursary Fund, further assisting medievalists in need of financial support to attend the Congress. In addition, it provides scholarships for MA and PhD students in the Institute for Medieval Studies, internship opportunities, and support for other activities in the medieval studies community.

For further information about leaving a legacy or other ways of making a donation to the International Medieval Congress and Leeds Medieval Studies, please email legacies@leeds.ac.uk.

Pre-Congress Tour

Hadrian's Wall Country in the Early Middle Ages **Price: £595.00**
Friday 29 June - Sunday 01 July 2018

Depart: Parkinson Steps, Friday 08.00
Arrive: Parkinson Steps, Sunday 19.00

Running from sea to sea, part of a frontier that stretched for 150 miles, Hadrian's Wall is one of the world's greatest monuments. This tour explores its continuing political, symbolic, and practical significance in the early Middle Ages. Many medieval sites to be visited were constructed using materials from Roman sources; archaeology increasingly demonstrates the post-Roman use of forts along the Wall.

St Cuthbert's coffin, Durham Cathedral

Some of our earliest written information about the Wall comes from Bede, who said that it had originated as an earthen rampart, built in the time of Emperor Severus, and that it had been reconstructed in stone after the end of the Roman government to counter incursions by the Irish and the Picts. Appropriately, therefore, the tour will include St Paul's Church, Jarrow, which formed part of the monastery where Bede lived and worked 1300 years ago. In Bede's day, Jarrow was one of Europe's most influential centres of learning.

The tour will include a visit to the Open Treasure Gallery at Durham Cathedral - one of Europe's greatest Romanesque structures - where visitors can enter previously hidden spaces.

Hadrian's Wall

This gallery is now the permanent home of the Treasures of St Cuthbert, which include his preserved wooden coffin and pectoral cross as well as other artefacts such as Anglo-Saxon vestments that were gifted to the shrine.

At Hexham we shall examine the sculptural and architectural legacy of the Romanophile St Wilfrid. In c. 674 Queen Æthelthryth of Northumbria made a grant of land to Wilfrid, Bishop of York, to build a Benedictine abbey. The building has seen many changes, but the 7th-century crypt survives. In 2014, the abbey regained ownership of its former monastic buildings and has since developed them into a permanent exhibition and visitor centre.

St Paul's Church, Jarrow

Birdoswald Fort

Lindisfarne Priory

Birdoswald Roman fort stands alongside the longest surviving stretch of the wall. The fort was of the standard 'playing card' plan; a near-complete circuit of the walls survives, along with substantial evidence for how the site was used after Roman rule in Britain ended.

The tour will visit the churches of St Cuthbert, Bewcastle, and Ruthwell to see the Bewcastle and the Ruthwell Crosses, the largest and most elaborately decorated Anglo-Saxon crosses to have survived near-intact.

The third day of the tour is largely devoted to Lindisfarne, also known as Holy Island. Irish monks settled there in 635, founding one of the most important centres of early English Christianity. Now the remains of a modest 12th-century priory can be seen, as well as a select but impressive display of early medieval sculpture. The incoming tide will cover the causeway shortly after our arrival, creating an island for a few hours until the falling tide enables us to re-join the mainland.

Places are limited, so we recommend that you reserve your place on this excursion by completing the Registration Form as early as possible. Sensible footwear is recommended, as there will be a significant amount of walking on uneven surfaces and climbing steep stones steps. It would also be advisable to bring raincoats and sunblock.

This tour will be led by Richard Morris (Emeritus Professor for Conflict and Culture, University of Huddersfield) and Ian Wood (Emeritus Professor of Early Medieval History, University of Leeds).

The price of the tour includes expert guides, entry to sites, individual site guide books, and two nights' accommodation (ensuite), with breakfast and dinner at the hotel, and packed lunches.

Hexham Abbey

Bewscastle Cross, Bewscastle

Post-Congress Tour

The Wars of the Roses: Medieval Castles and Battlefields of the Midlands **Price: £825.00**
International Medieval Congress and the Royal Armouries
Friday 06 July - Monday 09 July 2018

Depart: Parkinson Steps, Friday 08.00
Arrive: Parkinson Steps, Monday 19.00

This year the IMC Post-Congress tour ventures to the 'deep south' of the English Midlands.

In search of medieval castles and battlefields we will discover that many of the sites we visit were associated with some of the great characters involved with the Wars of the Roses, from magnates and lords, such as William, Lord Hastings and Richard Neville, the Earl of Warwick (the 'Kingmaker'), to monarchs like Edward IV and Richard III. We also visit other sites associated with the Wars of the Roses, including two battlefields, that of Tewkesbury (1471), where Edward took control of the throne after defeating the army of Henry VI and Margaret of Anjou, and Bosworth (1485), where Richard III, the last of the Yorkist kings, met his death. We will also see the spot where he was discovered in 2012 and his place of (re)burial at Leicester Cathedral.

These twelve sites range from a magnificent early Bronze Age hill fort to the splendid moated and fortified residences of the later Middle Ages. They include two of England's finest castles, one now a ruin and the other a stately home. In between we will see the place where a saint killed a dragon and discover one of the finest surviving sculptures of medieval England, as well as visiting an abbey that has been described as 'the Westminster Abbey of the feudal baronage'.

A number of castles had their roots in the aftermath of the Norman Conquest as the Normans extended their control over England. Deddington Castle, for example, was the site of the base of William I's half-brother Odo. Many sites in this part of England are noted for their formidable earthworks and their surviving stonework, the latter often of local stone, such as limestone and sandstone. The later use of brick, in the 15th century, will also be found at Kirby Muxlowe.

Kenilworth Castle

And, as ever, the tour provides an opportunity for you to explore and compare these evocative castles in one trip.

Ashby de la Zouch Castle

This castle takes its name from the Zouch family. In 1464 Edward IV granted it to William, Lord Hastings, who was unceremoniously executed in 1483 by Richard, Duke of Gloucester, later Richard III. Although now mostly ruinous, it reveals fascinating domestic details, particularly the layout of its kitchens and the impressive 27.4 m (90 ft) four-storey 'Hastings Tower', one of the best surviving examples of a late-medieval tower house. The castle also has its own underground passage, connecting cellars to the kitchen.

Bosworth Battlefield Heritage Centre

The Centre stands on Ambion Hill, which formed part of the battlefield of Bosworth on 22 August 1485. It was here that Richard III was killed, and Henry Tudor, Earl of Richmond, gained the Crown to become Henry VII, the first of the Tudor monarchs. This date has been regarded by many as the 'end' of the Middle Ages and the beginning of the English Renaissance. On display at the centre are many of the finds, including pieces of shot from the battle. Here the largest

Bosworth Battlefield

concentration of shot from any European medieval battlefield was found, enabling the site of the battle to be identified with certainty in 2010.

Kenilworth Castle

This castle gave its name to Sir Walter Scott's great romantic novel of 1821. This mighty ruin still retains much of its grandeur amidst the remains of artificial water defences and causeway, upon which tournaments were staged. The first castle, built on this site around 1120, was expanded by King John to become one of the largest royal castles in England in the early 13th century. The castle was not just about 'show'; it survived a six-month long siege in 1266.

The Norman tower dominates the site and the later Great Hall, with its huge windows, shows how the residential aspects of the castle overtook any defensive requirements. The reconstructed Elizabethan garden, which opened in 2009, illustrates the magnificence of such settings. Scott's novel about Sir Robert Dudley, Earl of Leicester, and Elizabeth I is set in the latter part of the castle's history, at the time of the famous reception held here in 1575.

Tewkesbury Abbey, Battlefield, and Medieval Townscape

Tewkesbury Abbey, begun in 1121 on the site of an earlier 8th-century Saxon monastery, is the second largest parish church in England. The 45 m (148 ft) Norman tower still dominates the town; it was reputedly from here that Margaret of Anjou watched the total defeat of her Lancastrian army at the battle of Tewkesbury in 1471. In the aftermath Edward IV notoriously entered the abbey and brought out some 13 Lancastrian nobles, including the Duke of Somerset, who had sought sanctuary and had them publicly beheaded in the town marketplace. The Abbey contains much 14th-century stained glass, depicting nobles such as the De Clares, Despensers, and Beauchamps, many of whom are buried here and are marked by their surviving monuments. One of the finest is that of Edward Despenser (c. 1375), which still retains much of its gilding. The alleged remains of Richard III's brother George - 'false, fleeting, perjured Clarence' - are also buried in a vault at Tewkesbury.

Warwick Castl

Minster Lovell Hall and Dovecote

There has been a manor house on this site since the 12th century, but the ruins of Minster Lovell Hall that stand today are the remains of the hall built in 1430s. Later in the 15th century it became the home of Francis, Viscount Lovell, a close friend of Richard III, who reputedly visited the property in 1483. Lovell was one of three supporters of Richard, whose badge was the boar, named in the famous doggerel: 'The Catte, the Ratte and Lovell our dogge rulyth all Englande under a Hogge'. Following the Yorkist defeat at Bosworth, the Hall became property of the Tudor Crown, and Lovell seemingly disappeared after the battle of Stoke in 1487. The hall was eventually abandoned and demolished in the late 18th century, but the remains include traces of its fine hall, tower, and 15th-century dovecote.

Donnington Castle

The residential suites overlook the river to the south, and the undercrofts date to the 14th century. The interiors were much altered through the intervening centuries until it became the stately home it now is, standing within a landscape created by 'Capability' Brown.

Uffington Castle, White Horse, and Dragon Hill

Although not medieval, these three prehistoric sites illustrate the myth and legend at the heart of England. Built in the 7th century BCE, Uffington 'Castle' is actually one of the best preserved Iron Age hillforts in Britain. The large 220 x 160 m (722 x 525 ft) enclosure atop 'Whitehorse Hill' is surrounded by a 12 m (39 ft) wide rampart and would have contained round-houses. This in turn is enclosed by a 3 m (10 ft) deep ditch and an outer rampart. It was entered by a causeway on its western flanks. The famed 'White Horse', which is 111 m (364 ft) long, is probably the oldest chalk-cut hill figure in Britain at over 3000 years old. Its significance is still a mystery, but local legends associate the horse with St George, and 'Dragon Hill' marks the spot where he slew the dragon - its spilt blood so poisonous that flowers never grow on its summit.

Donnington Castle

Once a fashionable 14th-century fortified residence, Deddington Castle had a striking twin-towered gatehouse, now the only substantial remains of the castle left. It was built in the 1380s for Sir Richard Apperbury, Queen's Chamberlain and a knight who served the Black Prince. The gate passage is elaborately vaulted. The

Deddington Castle

This castle is famed for being the alleged site of the abduction of Piers Gaveston by Guy de Beauchamp, Earl of Warwick, before his execution in 1312. The castle began to be used as a quarry in the mid-14th century; now all that survives is the impressive, 15 m (49 ft) high Norman earthwork rampart of the outer bailey and some associated fish ponds to the east. Its other chief point of interest is the sheer scale of its enclosure, some 3.2 hectares (8 acres), which reflects the rank and position of Bishop Odo, half-brother of William the Conqueror, who built the Norman castle on this site not long after 1066 and used Deddington as his Oxfordshire base.

Warwick Castle

For many the exterior of Warwick Castle is the epitome of what a 'real' medieval castle should look like. Although much altered internally, it still exudes magnificence. The present castle encloses its earlier Norman motte-and-bailey of 1068. In 1268 the castle passed to the Beauchamps and, in the 14th century, a major redevelopment of the castle began. Following the death of the Warwick 'the Kingmaker' in 1471, the castle passed to the Duke of Gloucester, who would become Richard III in 1483. His works include the low artillery tower along the north side.

Kirby Muxlowe Castle

castle was bought by Thomas Chaucer, son of the poet Geoffrey Chaucer, and Speaker of the House of Commons, although he probably never lived there. It was heavily damaged in 1646 after a lengthy 20-month siege.

The Beauchamp Chapel, Collegiate Church of St Mary's, Warwick

The world famous Chapel of Our Lady, commonly known as the 'Beauchamp Chapel', contains a number of military effigies, including the stunning life-size gilt-bronze figure of Richard Beauchamp, 13th Earl of Warwick (1382-1439), depicted in full mid 15th-century Italian armour. His son-in-law Richard Neville, 'Warwick the Kingmaker', appears as one of the 'weepers' on his tomb-chest. Described as the finest piece of English 15th-century bronze sculpture, the figure is also encased in a rare original medieval hearse. Also in the chapel lies Sir Robert Dudley, 1st Earl of Leicester (1533-88), favourite and suitor of Elizabeth I, whose seat was Kenilworth Castle.

Kirby Muxlowe Castle

With its fine decorative diaper-pattern brickwork, Kirby Muxlowe, although never completed, still stands as one of the finest example of 15th-century brick castles. Begun by William, Lord Hastings, in 1480, some £1,088 was spent on the construction of this fortified and moated residence. However, after the execution of Hastings in 1483, building work ceased. The Hastings family lived on in the unfinished castle apartments but left in the 16th century. The remains of the castle contain a number of surviving gunports.

Richard III Visitor Centre and Leicester Cathedral, Leicester

In 2012, the skeleton of Richard III was discovered in the grounds of the now demolished Church of the Greyfriars. Despite local folk tales of its desecration, the hurriedly prepared grave was kept intact and now forms part of a centre which tells about the life and death of Richard III as well as the amazing story of the skeleton's discovery. Meticulous scientific studies confirmed he was indeed Richard III, before he was finally laid to rest in a new tomb at the heart of Leicester Cathedral in March 2015, an event that was televised around the world.

This tour will once again be led by Kelly DeVries, Professor of the Department of History, Loyola University, Maryland, and Honorary Historical Consultant to the Royal Armouries, and Robert C. Woosnam-Savage, Curator of Armour and Edged Weapons, Royal Armouries, Leeds and a member of the Greyfriars Research team that discovered and identified the remains of Richard III.

We recommend that you reserve your place on this excursion by registering as early as possible. Sensible footwear is recommended, as there will be a significant amount of walking on uneven surfaces and climbing steep stone steps. It would also be advisable to bring raincoats and sunblock.

The price of the tour includes entry to sites, individual site guidebooks, transport, three nights' accommodation (ensuite), with breakfast and dinner at the hotel, and packed lunches.

The programme may be subject to change.

Leicester Cathedral

Queries and Contact Details

Before the IMC

If you have any queries before the IMC about your paper, registration, meals, events, accommodation, or excursion bookings, please contact us at:

Email: imc@leeds.ac.uk

Tel: +44 (113) 343-3614

Fax: +44 (113) 343-3616

Post:

IMC Administration
Institute for Medieval Studies
Parkinson 1.03
University of Leeds
LEEDS
LS2 9JT

At the IMC

During the IMC, the Information and Payment Desk in the Refectory Foyer will be your first point of contact for queries regarding any aspect of your booking.

Sunday 01 July	10.00-22.00
Monday 02 July	08.00-22.00
Tuesday 03 July	08.00-22.00
Wednesday 04 July	08.00-22.00
Thursday 05 July	08.00-20.00

Please note that payments can only be taken before 19.00 each day.

For general queries, you can also contact the Information Desk in the Parkinson Building.

Emergencies

In emergencies only, please contact the University of Leeds Security Service:

Tel: +44 (113) 343-2222 (or 32222 from any university telephone)

On campus, please use this number instead of contacting emergency services.

Medical Treatment

NHS walk-in centres offer convenient access to treatments for minor illnesses and injuries. The nearest walk-in centre to campus is:

Shakespeare Medical Practice
Cromwell Mount
LEEDS
LS9 7TA
Tel: +44 (113) 295-1132

www.onemedicalgroup.co.uk/shakespeare-medical-practice-leeds

Open: 08.00-20.00, every day.

Pharmacy

Lloyds Pharmacy
166 Woodhouse Lane (opposite the Parkinson Building)
LEEDS
LS2 9HB

Open: 09.00-18.00, Monday-Friday

Emergency Medical Care

If you are experiencing a medical emergency, you can visit the Emergency Department at Leeds General Infirmary, a short walk from campus.

Access to the Emergency Department is via the Jubilee Wing on Calverley Street.

For more information see www.leedsth.nhs.uk/a-z-of-services/emergency-medicine/

Medieval Studies at Leeds

MA in Medieval Studies

PhD in Medieval Studies

A Unique Environment

For 50 years, the University of Leeds has combined exceptional interdisciplinary teaching and research with a close-knit community. Our staff and students have access to some of the best resources for the study of the medieval period.

Internationally renowned for its specialism in Medieval Studies, Leeds is home to the Institute for Medieval Studies (IMS), the *International Medieval Bibliography* (IMB), and the International Medieval Congress (IMC). As a hub of outstanding research, we are committed to developing the next generation of medievalists and pushing the boundaries of academic knowledge and impact.

Believed to be the oldest interdisciplinary centre in the University, the Institute for Medieval Studies has been home to a large community of medievalists since 1967. Professor John Le Patourel, Professor of Medieval History, led a group of pioneers to form a centre of graduate studies; since then, the IMS has flourished, with over 70 staff, students, and associates from around the world.

With resources such as the world-class Brotherton Library and the archives of the Yorkshire Archaeological and Historical Society based at the University, with the British Library's Boston Spa Reading Room nearby, our students have access to some of the best medieval resources in the UK. Many of the medieval manuscripts of the Library can now be viewed online: www.leeds.ac.uk/library/spcoll/.

MS 102, Brotherton Library, University of Leeds. John Sintram, Sermons, c. 1425

The IMS has a long-standing cooperation with the Royal Armouries and Leeds City Museum and Galleries, as well as other regional heritage organisations. In addition, we have also a close association with the Centre d'études supérieures de civilisation médiévale at the University of Poitiers.

Masters of Arts: Medieval Studies or Medieval History

Full-time (12 months) and part-time (24 months)

Our MA programmes focus on building core skills necessary for postgraduate study and interdisciplinary analysis of the Middle Ages. Each student will complete a 10,000 word dissertation on an area of their choice, supervised on an individual basis by one of Leeds's world-leading academic staff. We offer two pathways, based on individual preference, in Medieval Studies or Medieval History.

At Leeds, we are proud to provide the most thorough groundings in medieval languages available in the UK. All Masters students are required to take at least one module of Latin, dependent on their ability; a beginner, within a year, can be fluent in the language through our intensive course. We can also offer vernacular languages such as Old and Middle English, Old French, Old Norse, and Middle High German.

Our teaching and supervision expertise spans 1000 years – our students can choose to tailor their course to a specific theme or spread their interests across our full range of options. IMS students also have the opportunity to attend the IMC free of charge.

This focus on research and analytical skills equips our graduates for success in doctoral study or in the workplace. IMS alumni work across the world in leading academic institutions, heritage organisations, and in areas such as journalism, marketing, and business.

Medieval Studies at Leeds

MA Compulsory Modules

All MA students are required to take:

- Research Methods and Bibliography
- Palaeography
- Medieval Latin

MA Option Modules

- The Margins of Medieval Art
- Vikings, Saxons, and Heroic Culture
- Arthurian Legend: Medieval to Modern
- Preaching History: Understanding Sermons as Literature and Historical Source
- Religious Communities and the Individual Experience of Religion, 1200-1500
- Lifecycles: Birth, Death, and Illness in the Middle Ages
- Warfare in the Age of the Crusades
- The Medieval Tournament: Combat, Chivalry, and Spectacle in Western Europe, 1100-1600
- Gender, Sex, and Love: Byzantium and the West, 900-1200
- Bede's Northumbria
- Making History: Archive Collaborations

Please note optional modules on offer may change from year to year, based on staff availability and other factors.

Doctoral Research in Medieval Studies

The IMS supervises doctoral research on interdisciplinary medieval topics across a wide range of subjects, including: literature, with specialisms in Dante, Anglo-Norman, Latin, Middle English, Old Norse, and French; Christianity, including the Papacy, monastic life and culture, mendicants, the cult of saints, mysticism, and clerical life and culture; medieval medicine; warfare, arms and armour, chivalry and tournaments, and the Crusades; Arabic historiography; the Baltic and East-Central Europe; Scandinavia and Old Norse mythology; the Iberian Peninsula; Jewish-Christian cultural relations, Hebrew illuminated manuscripts, monuments, and art; Anglo-Saxon literature, history and art history; gender studies; music and liturgy; courtly culture; history of the book; music and liturgy; southern Italy; and theology.

or of Ledsham Church, Yorkshire

Our research degrees are designed to prepare doctoral researchers for a career in academia. IMS first-year research students have the opportunity to take taught modules in research methods, Medieval Latin, and a modern foreign language to support their engagement with scholarship.

IMS research students always have two co-supervisors to help to shape the student's project, give bibliographical and methodological guidance, and advise throughout their research. Each student presents an annual paper on their work in progress at a research seminar in the IMS, and is able to attend the IMC free of charge. Research students are also encouraged to give papers at national and international conferences.

Medieval Studies at Leeds

IMS trip to Knaresborough Castle, North Yorkshire

A Community of Scholars

Medieval Studies at Leeds is, first and foremost, a community of scholars, joined together in their pursuit of knowledge. Students can join the Leeds University Union Medieval Society, where film nights, lectures, and trips are organised. The Medieval Group, initially established in 1952, brings together staff, students, and members of the public for seminars and workshops. Reading groups for languages such as Old English, French, and Italian are an informal way for staff and students to discuss medieval sources. At the heart of this community is the Le Patourel Room, a dedicated study space for IMS postgraduate students.

MS 4, fol. 161v. Brotherton Librar University of Leed

Ripon Cathedral, North Yorkshire

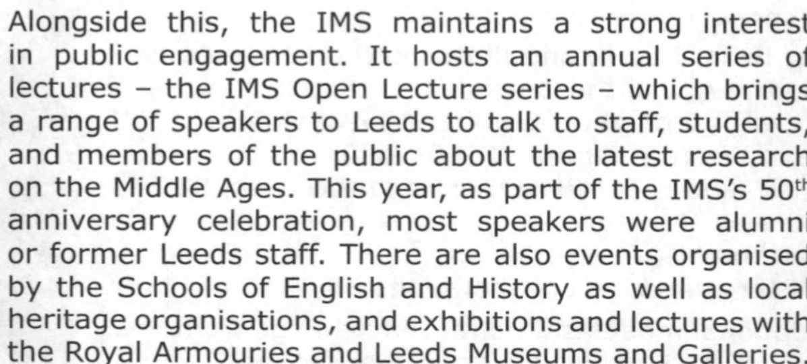

Alongside this, the IMS maintains a strong interest in public engagement. It hosts an annual series of lectures – the IMS Open Lecture series – which brings a range of speakers to Leeds to talk to staff, students, and members of the public about the latest research on the Middle Ages. This year, as part of the IMS's 50th anniversary celebration, most speakers were alumni or former Leeds staff. There are also events organised by the Schools of English and History as well as local heritage organisations, and exhibitions and lectures with the Royal Armouries and Leeds Museums and Galleries.

Students also have a range of paid work and volunteering options open to them. The IMS offers several paid internships to its students in areas such as communications and events management. The Royal Armouries, Leeds City Museum, and other heritage sites in the area offer opportunities to gain experience in the heritage sector.

Medieval sculptu at Lastingham Church, North Yorkshire

IMS trip on New Year's Day to Lud's Chapel in Staffordshire

Located in Yorkshire, Leeds is a thriving modern city with its own medieval sites, such as nearby Kirkstall Abbey, and a strong interest in heritage. Yorkshire, the largest county in the UK, has a variety of medieval sites including abbeys, castles, and settlements. The city of York, with its strong Viking and medieval past, is easily accessible by car, bus, and train from Leeds. As part of the White Rose consortium, we are partnered with the Universities of Sheffield and York to fund the best research in the north of England.

Find out more about the IMS: www.leeds.ac.uk/ims

Medieval church Jarrow, Tyne and Wear

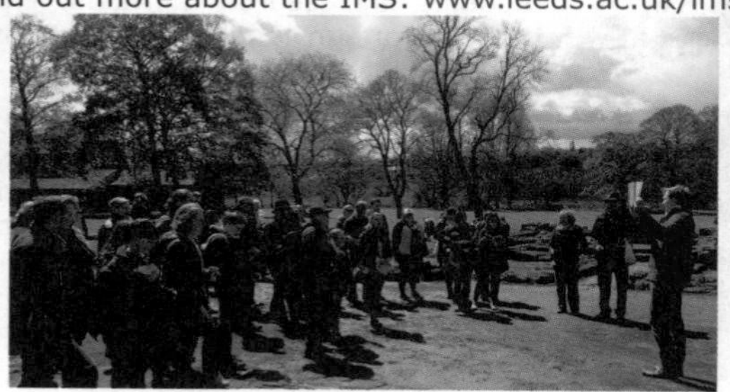

Kirkstall Abbey tour, Leeds

Medieval Studies at Leeds

International Medieval Bibliography

The *International Medieval Bibliography* (IMB), based at Leeds since 1967, is the world's leading multi-disciplinary database of Medieval Studies. The IMB is produced by an editorial team at the University of Leeds, supported by some 40 contributors worldwide. It covers periodical literature and miscellany volumes published in Europe, North America, South America, Australasia, Japan, and South Africa.

The printed IMB appears twice a year, covering most recent publications, totalling over 1100 pages per year. The complete cumulative bibliography is available online via Brepols Publishers. IMB-Online offers 380,000 records of articles, review articles, and scholarly notes on all aspects of Medieval Studies, covering publications in 30 different languages and updated quarterly. The online interface allows sophisticated search possibilities by the use of controlled vocabulary, hierarchical indexes, and authority lists comprising over 120,000 terms. Further information can be found on the IMB website: www.leeds.ac.uk/ims/imb/

IMB - Anniversary Quiz

As part of the 50th anniversary celebrations of the *International Medieval Bibliography*, delegates are invited to take part in the IMB Anniversary Quiz (www.imb2018quiz.com), sponsored by our publisher Brepols.

The quiz is open to all registered delegates of IMC 2018 - you could win a trip to Bruges, Belgium, or one of many book prizes!

This short quiz consists of six questions exploring some of the lesser-known searches and functionalities of the IMB. It is also a chance to discover some of the more unusual articles and subjects covered in the bibliography, whose 120,000+ index terms include such diverse topics as body art, earthquakes, manticores, and planets.

Winners will be announced at the IMC 2018.

IMB artefacts on display at the exhibition celebrating the anniversary of the IMS, *IMB*, and IMC, November 2017

International Medieval Research

The International Medieval Research Series (IMR) is a continuing success, with over 20 previous volumes and several more in various stages of production. Proposals are warmly invited for future volumes of the IMR, which has a strong emphasis on the interdisciplinary study of the European Middle Ages.

Published by Brepols, volumes in the series have consisted primarily of articles based on papers read at sessions of the IMC, complemented by additional contributions that are closely linked with the themes chosen for the original sessions. Themes may be drawn from the thematic strand of a particular year, or other special interests where a coherent volume can be proposed.

Those proposing volumes should either be interested in acting as editor themselves or should nominate an editor, and each volume should have a strong, thematic organisation.

Most of those papers selected will have been, or will be, presented at the IMC. Each paper should be between 5,000 and 8,000 words, with each volume consisting of between ten and twenty articles; articles have been previously published in English, French, German, Italian, and Spanish.

The formal proposal, which should not exceed five pages, follows a proforma and would include, at a minimum, the following information:

- Title of the work
- Author(s)
- Detailed breakdown of contents by article
- The work set within the tradition of scholarship on the topic
- Readership to which it is directed
- Rationale for the volume
- Language(s) of articles
- Special requirements (tables, illustrations, maps)

The formal proposal is then considered by the editorial board, Brepols Publishers, and an external reader, who also comments on the unfinished papers. At this stage the volume can then be conditionally accepted and a conditional contract issued.

Anyone can propose a volume as editor for IMR. If you would like to propose a future volume of the IMR series, for more details on the process of application, or the latest version of the proforma, please email imrseries@leeds.ac.uk.

The most recent volumes in the series include:

- IMR 15: *Languages of Love and Hate: Conflict, Communication, and Identity in the Medieval Mediterranean World*, ed. by Sarah Lambert and Helen J. Nicholson (2012)
- IMR 16: *Representations of Power in Medieval Germany, 800-1500*, ed. by Björn Weiler and Simon MacLean (2006)
- IMR 17: *Behaving like Fools: Voice, Gesture, and Laughter in Texts, Manuscripts, and Early Books*, ed. by Lucy M. Perry and Alexander Schwarz (2010)
- IMR 18: *Medieval Lifecycles: Continuity and Change*, ed. by Isabelle Cochelin and Karen Smyth (2013)
- IMR 19: *Problems and Possibilities of Early Medieval Charters*, ed. by Jonathan Jarrett and Allan Scott McKinley (2013)
- IMR 20: *The Tree: Symbol, Allegory, and Mnemonic Device in Medieval Art and Thought*, ed. by Pippa Salonius and Andrea Worm (2014)
- IMR 21: *Travel and Mobilities in the Middle Ages: From the Atlantic to the Black Sea*, ed. by Marianne O'Doherty and Felicitas Schmieder (2015)
- IMR 22: *Approaches to Poverty in Medieval Europe: Complexities, Contradictions, Transformations, c. 1100–1500*, ed. by Sharon Farmer (2016)
- IMR 23: *Miracles in Canonization Processes: Structures, Functions and Methodologies*, ed. by Christian Krötzl and Sari Katajala-Peltomaa (forthcoming in 2018)
- IMR 24: *Book of Medieval Pleasures*, ed. by Naama Cohen-Hanegbi and Piroska Nagy (forthcoming in 2018)

The editorial board would be pleased to receive informal submissions in the first instance. The informal proposal will then be considered before an invitation for a formal proposal can be extended for submission for consideration by Brepols. The editorial board consists of:

We would like to thank the following organisations for their financial support of the

International Medieval Congress 2018

The University of Leeds

Institute for Medieval Studies
School of English
School of Fine Art, History of Art & Cultural Studies
School of History
School of Languages, Cultures & Societies
School of Philosophy, Religion & History of Science
Conference & Events Office
Leeds University Library
International Office
International Student Office

Daleside Brewery

Early Medieval Europe

Leeds City Council

Leeds Philosophical & Literary Society

Medieval Academy of America

Oswald-von-Wolkenstein Gesellschaft

Royal Armouries

Templar Heritage Trust

Universities' Chaplaincy in Leeds

Yorkshire Archaeological & Historical Society

International Medieval Congress 2018

IMC Staff

Axel E. W. Müller
Congress Director

Marta Cobb
Senior Congress Officer

Nick Westerman
Project Manager

Sarah Parkin
Congress Officer

Natalie Elvin
Congress Officer

Fiona Livermore
Congress Officer

Susan Broadbent
Congress Liaison Assistant

Katy Mathers
Congress Liaison Assistant

Benjamin Palmer
Congress Liaison Assistant

Emma Thornton
Congress Liaison Assistant

IMC Standing Committee

Catherine J. Batt
Pietro Delcorno
Emilia Jamroziak
Catherine E. Karkov
Graham A. Loud
Federica Pich
Vanessa Wright

IMC Programming Committee

Nadia Altschul
University of Glasgow

Bettina Bildhauer
University of St Andrews

Pavel Blažek
Academie Věd České Republiky, Praha

Brenda Bolton
University of London

Emma Campbell
University of Warwick

Jan Čermák
Univerzita Karlova, Praha

Catherine Clarke
University of Southampton

Daniel DiCenso
College of the Holy Cross, Massachussetts

Cora Dietl
Universität Gießen

Lucie Doležalová
Univerzita Karlova, Praha

Simon Forde
Arc Humanities Press, Leeds

Eva Frojmovic
University of Leeds

Helen Fulton
University of Bristol

Andrew Galloway
Cornell University

Julian Gardner
University of Warwick

Sieglinde Hartmann
Universität Würzburg

Anne-Marie Helvétius
Université de Paris VIII - Vincennes-Saint-Denis

Yitzhak Hen
Ben-Gurion University of the Negev, Beer Sheva

Charles Insley
University of Manchester

Gerhard Jaritz
Central European University, Budapest

Kurt Villads Jensen
Stockholms Universitet

Torstein Jørgensen
VID Vitenskapelige Høgskole, Stavanger

Chris Lewis
University of London

Dolores López Pérez
Universitat de Barcelona

Gert Melville
Technische Universität, Dresden

Marco Mostert
Universiteit Utrecht

Cary Nederman
Texas A&M University, College Station

Christian Rohr
Universität Bern

Flocel Sabaté i Curull
Universitat de Lleida

Danuta Shanzer
Universität Wien

Jo Van Steenbergen
Universiteit Gent

Dominique Stutzmann
Centre National de la Recherche Scientifique (CNRS), Paris

Sam Turner
Newcastle University

Shaun Tougher
Cardiff University

Steven A. Walton
Michigan Technological University

Diane Watt
University of Surrey

Jarosław Wenta
Uniwersytet Mikołaja Kopernika, Toruń

Annemarieke Willemsen
Rijksmuseum van Oudheden, Leiden

Strand Index

Today's Excursions

Mount Grace Priory and Jervaulx Abbey	09.00-19.00
Middleham Castle	13.00-19.00
Stank Old Hall, New Hall, and Barn	14.00-18.00

See pp. 449-453 for full details.

* * * * *

'NO GOLD GLITTERS LIKE THAT WHICH IS OUR OWN': MEDIEVAL GOLDWORK EMBROIDERY WORKSHOP

DIRECTED BY
TANYA BENTHAM

UNIVERSITY HOUSE: DE GREY ROOM
11.00-17.00

PRICE: £32.50

From the earliest times, embroidering with gold thread has been a popular way to decorate items and display wealth and prestige across Asia, Europe, and the Middle East. Among the oldest surviving examples of English goldwork are the fragments of the stole and maniple of St Cuthbert, which were found in his coffin and are now on display in Durham Cathedral. Many of the later surviving examples of goldwork are various forms of ecclesiastical embroidery. In the 13th and 14th centuries, English luxury embroidery, sometimes called 'Opus Anglicanum' (English work), enjoyed an international reputation and was imported across Europe. Recently, Opus Anglicanum was the subject of an exhibition at the Victoria and Albert Museum.

This workshop provides a rare opportunity to learn the goldwork embroidery techniques used throughout the medieval period. Participants will learn the basic stitches of goldwork embroidery – surface and underside couching - as well as how to incorporate pearls into their designs. The workshop fee includes all materials. Each participant will produce a compact lozenge-shaped piece that can be converted into a pendant or a key fob.

Tanya Bentham has been a re-enactor for more than 30 years, working for the last 20 as a professional living historian. Her main focus has always been on textiles, especially embroidery, but also making detours into costume, natural dyeing, weaving, millinery, and silversmithing. She has delivered workshops for numerous museums, schools, and community organisations throughout Yorkshire.

The workshop can only accommodate a limited number of participants. Early booking is recommended. Lunch is not included.

SUNDAY 01 JULY 2018

* * * * *

'DRAW THY SWORD IN RIGHT': COMBAT WORKSHOP

DIRECTED BY

DEAN DAVIDSON AND STUART IVINSON, *KUNST DES FECHTENS* (KDF) INTERNATIONAL

LEEDS UNIVERSITY UNION: RILEY SMITH HALL
14.00-16.30

PRICE: £15.00

Have you ever had a desire to learn how to fight like our historical forbears or study the highly effective fighting style that was taught throughout the medieval period? This year *Kunst des Fechtens* (KDF) International brings a workshop on the use of medieval longswords to the Congress participants.

KDF workshops bring a dynamic approach to training, with a martial application of this historical art through practical drills combined with interpretations from historical treatises. Our professional and experienced instructors will be on hand to provide tuition in this noble fighting style.

KDF International is an association of like-minded clubs from across Europe, whose aim is to promote the study, development, and practice of the martial arts tradition of medieval and renaissance Germany, in particular the work of the Master Johannes Liechtenauer. These martial arts have been preserved in numerous treatises and have been unearthed, transcribed, translated, and interpreted into a modern understanding of a subtle, dynamic, and effective martial arts system that looks at the use of a number of weapons and unarmed combat of the time. Founded in 2006, KDF was born from a desire to focus attention on Liechtenauer's works as well as bringing a dynamic approach to training, adding the use of protection as well as free play exercises and bouts to drill and practice as a part of trying to triangulate a truth within their interpretations.

Dean has over 20 years' experience in martial arts and training in historical weapons. He is the KDF International Senior Instructor and European Historical Combat Guild Chapter Master at the Royal Armouries, Leeds. He is an active member of the Society for Combat Archaeology, an international organisation committed to the promulgation of systematic knowledge related to combat and warfare in the past. Dean is passionate about sharing knowledge on this subject and regularly presents at renowned international conferences and seminars, providing a unique insight in to the arms and armour used throughout medieval warfare. He is also a founding member of the Towton Battlefield Frei Compagnie and 3 Swords, a prestigious medieval historical and armed combat interpretation group. Dean holds a Masters in Health Informatics from the Faculty of Medicine at the University of Leeds and is a member of the Leeds University Medieval Society.

Stuart Ivinson has been involved with historical combat for 16 years, joining the European Historical Combat Guild in 2000 and KDF upon its inception in 2006. He is currently an Assistant Instructor at the Leeds Chapter of both organisations. Stuart is also a member of the Society for Combat Archaeology and a founder member of both the Towton Battlefield Society Frei Compagnie and 3 Swords. He has made presentations regarding the display arms and armour for organisations such as the National Archives at Kew, English Heritage, and numerous British museums. Stuart has an MA in Librarianship, an MA in Medieval History, and a P.Dip in Heritage Management. When he is not being Dean's sidekick, he is the Librarian at the Royal Armouries Museum in Leeds.

All weapons are provided by KDF and attendees are asked to arrive wearing indoor training shoes and appropriate and comfortable gym training gear that will allow freedom of movement (i.e. t-shirt and tracksuit bottoms). Please make the instructors aware of any prior medical conditions.

This workshop can only accommodate a limited number of participants. Early booking is recommended.

* * * * *

SECOND-HAND AND ANTIQUARIAN BOOKFAIR

LEEDS UNIVERSITY UNION: FOYER
16.00-21.00

This event is free of charge.

The IMC 2018 Exhibitions and Bookfairs (see pp. 472-474) will open with a three-day specialist Second-Hand and Antiquarian Bookfair. The following booksellers will be among those exhibiting:

Bennett & Kerr Books – Old, rare, and scholarly books on medieval studies.
Chevin Books – Books on most subjects, including archaeology, theology, art, and architecture.
Northern Herald Books – Scholarly books on medieval studies, together with general economic and social history.
Pinwell Books – All aspects of the Middle Ages.
Salsus Books – Medieval and Byzantine Studies, Patristics, and general academic books.
Unsworth's Booksellers – Antiquarian and second-hand books on the Middle Ages.

* * * * *

STRANGE ADVENTURES AND OTHERWORLDLY JOURNEYS

PERFORMED BY
MATTHEW BELLWOOD

LEEDS UNIVERSITY UNION: ROOM 6 - ROUNDHAY
19.30-21.00

The event is free of charge.

Master storyteller Matthew Bellwood brings to life Norse sagas, Celtic legends, and European folk stories in this collection of long-remembered tales from the Middle Ages. Enter into realms where gods battle frost giants, kings hide unexpected secrets, little girls fight wicked witches, and husbands reach out from other worlds to reclaim lost brides.

Matthew Bellwood is a Leeds-based writer and storyteller. His background is in devised theatre, and he has performed at drama festivals in Canada, Germany, and New Zealand, as well as throughout the UK. He currently runs Moveable Feast Productions, a touring Theatre in Education company, for which he has written and produced a wide range of shows and workshops for young people. He also works regularly with A Quiet Word, who create site-specific theatre work in unusual places.

* * * * *

Today's Excursions
John Rylands Library 13.00-19.00
See p. 453 for full details.

* * * * *

SECOND-HAND AND ANTIQUARIAN BOOKFAIR

LEEDS UNIVERSITY UNION: FOYER
08.00-19.00

This event is free of charge.

The IMC 2018 Exhibitions and Bookfairs (see pp. 472-474) will open with a three-day specialist Second-Hand and Antiquarian Bookfair. The following booksellers will be among those exhibiting:

Bennett & Kerr Books – Old, rare, and scholarly books on medieval studies.
Chevin Books – Books on most subjects, including archaeology, theology, art, and architecture.
Northern Herald Books – Scholarly books on medieval studies, together with general economic and social history.
Pinwell Books – All aspects of the Middle Ages.
Salsus Books – Medieval and Byzantine Studies, Patristics, and general academic books.
Unsworth's Booksellers – Antiquarian and second-hand books on the Middle Ages.

* * * * *

Session:	**1**	**Great Hall**
Titles and Speakers:	**KEYNOTE LECTURES 2018:** **BUT WHAT ARE YOU REMEMBERING FOR?** (Language: English) Mary J. Carruthers, Department of English, New York University **DO WORDS REMEMBER?: THE ETYMOLOGIST VERSUS THE VIKINGS** (Language: English) Richard Dance, Department of Anglo-Saxon, Norse & Celtic, University of Cambridge	
Introduction:	Lucie Doležalová, Institute of Greek & Latin Studies, Univerzita Karlova, Praha and Jan Čermák, Department of English, Univerzita Karlova, Praha	
Details:	**But What Are YOU Remembering For?** *This lecture considers the importance of motive in what is now loosely called 'remembering' - as though it were a single, simple phenomenon. Though we now sharply distinguish 'memory' from 'remembering', the Middle Ages knew only one term, for medieval 'vis memorativa' and 'vis reminiscentia' are synonyms.* Memoria *in the scholastic and monastic traditions, though compatible, are quite different in their goals and definitions - I will explore some of these. My lecture touches on the nature of 'rote' and how it is distinct from 'remembering'; the importance of 'forgetting'; and the differences of 'social memory', 'memory of God', and some medieval accounts of Mind.* **Do Words Remember?: The Etymologist versus the Vikings** *English words have some extraordinary stories to tell. The history of English in the medieval period is famously colourful, reflecting centuries of complex interactions between the many languages spoken and written in and around Britain - but it is not always as easy as one might expect to discover the effects of these meetings. In particular, many hundreds of items in the medieval English lexicon have been explained as showing the influence of the early Scandinavian languages. These words are potentially invaluable witnesses to an intense period of Anglo-Scandinavian contact in the Viking Age, but getting them to 'remember' those encounters can be uniquely challenging. By presenting a range of examples from medieval English, including some words for acts of memory and intention, this lecture will explore the pleasures and the perils of trying to recall the Vikings through their linguistic traces, and the multiplicity of voices and approaches that this can involve. Along the way, we will take the opportunity to think about some of the roles of etymology and of etymologists in giving access to the vibrant connections and diversity of the medieval past.* *Please note that admission to this event will be on a first-come, first-served basis as there will be no tickets. Please ensure that you arrive as early as possible to avoid disappointment.*	

COFFEE BREAK: 10.30-11.15

Coffee and Tea will be served at the following locations:

Maurice Keyworth Building: Foyer
Michael Sadler Building: Foyer
Parkinson Building: Bookfair
University Square: The Marquee

See Map 7, p. 44.

Session: **101** **Baines Wing: Room 1.13**
Title: **ANGLO-SAXON RIDDLES, I: MOODS AND MEANINGS**
Sponsor: The Riddle Ages: An Anglo-Saxon Riddle Blog
Organiser: Megan Cavell, Department of English Literature, University of Birmingham and Jennifer Neville, Department of English, Royal Holloway, University of London
Moderator: Megan Cavell
Paper 101-a: **Memories of Fear and the Fear of Memories in the Exeter Book Riddles** (Language: English)
Rafał Borysławski, Institute of English Cultures & Literatures, University of Silesia, Katowice
Paper 101-b: **Humor and the Exeter Book Riddles** (Language: English)
Jonathan Wilcox, Department of English, University of Iowa
Paper 101-c: **Gendered 'Pride' and Noble 'Courage' in the Double Entendre Riddles of the Exeter Book** (Language: English)
Jennifer Neville

Session: **102** **Michael Sadler Building: Banham Theatre**
Title: **PAPERS IN HONOUR OF DEBBY BANHAM, I: ANGLO-SAXON AGRICULTURE - WOMEN, ROYALTY, AND FOOD**
Organiser: Christine Voth, Seminar für Englische Philologie, Georg-August-Universität Göttingen
Moderator: Clare Pilsworth, School of Arts, Languages & Cultures, University of Manchester
Paper 102-a: **Women's Work and Sheep Walks: Economy and Ecology in the Age of Ine** (Language: English)
Alex Woolf, St Andrews Institute of Mediaeval Studies, University of St Andrews
Paper 102-b: **Women, Bread, and the Supernatural** (Language: English)
Martha Bayless, Department of English, University of Oregon
Paper 102-c: **Feeding Lords and Kings: *Feorm* in Anglo-Saxon England** (Language: English)
Rosamond Faith, Wolfson College, University of Oxford

Session: **103** **Baines Wing: Room 2.13**
Title: **SIN, MIRACLES, AND HEAVEN IN BYZANTIUM**
Organiser: IMC Programming Committee
Moderator: Ekaterini Mitsiou, Institut für Byzantinistik & Neogräzistik, Universität Wien
Paper 103-a: **The Analysis of Yohannes of Amidas's Miniature of the Heavenly Jerusalem: Dublin, Chester Beatty Library No. 551** (Language: English)
Anush Sargsyan, Mesrop Mashtots Institute of Ancient Manuscripts (MATENADARAN), Hrazdan, Armenia
Paper 103-b: **Shaping a Christian Society: The Uses of Tariffs and Epitimies in Insular, Continental, and Byzantine Penitentials** (Language: English)
Rebekah Sheldon, Department of History, Saint Louis University, Missouri
Paper 103-c: **Construction of the Past through Miracles in Byzantine Historical Narratives** (Language: English)
Eliso Elizbarashvili, Institute of Oriental Studies, Ilia State University, Georgia

Session: **104** **Baines Wing: Room 2.14**
Title: **EARLY MEDIEVAL BURIAL CULTURE AND THE REUSE OF CEMETERIES**
Organiser: IMC Programming Committee
Moderator: Dóra Mérai, Department of Medieval Studies, Central European University, Budapest
Paper 104-a: **Memory and Cemeteries in 5th-Century Britain** (Language: English)
Janet Kay, Society of Fellows in the Liberal Arts, Princeton University
Paper 104-b: **Lifecycles, Dress, and Gender in a 6th-Century Early Medieval Cemetery: The Example of Cutry, Meurthe-et-Moselle** (Language: English)
Olga Magoula, Department of History & Archaeology, University of Ioannina
Paper 104-c: **From Cemetery to Norman Castle: Control Over the Living and the Dead?** (Language: English)
Therron Welstead, School of Archaeology, History & Anthropology, University of Wales Trinity Saint David

---

Session: **105** **Fine Art Building: SR G.04**
Title: **WARFARE IN EUROPE'S PERIPHERY: IBERIA AND SCANDINAVIA, 12TH-15TH CENTURIES**
Sponsor: De la Lucha de Bandos a la hidalguía universal: transformaciones sociales, políticas e ideológicas en el País Vasco (siglos XIV y XV) Project / Grupo Consolidado de Investigación: Sociedad, poder y cultura (siglos XIV-XVIII) Project
Organiser: Ekaitz Etxeberria, Departamento de Historia Medieval, Moderna y de América, Universidad del País Vasco - Euskal Herriko Unibertsitatea, Vitoria-Gasteiz
Moderator: Fernando Arias Guillén, Facultad de Filosofía y Letras, Universidad de Valladolid
Paper 105-a: **Castles, Cogs, and the *Leiðangr*: Changing Patterns of Warfare in the Scandinavian 'Civil War Period'** (Language: English)
Beñat Elortza, Centre for Scandinavian Studies, Department of History, University of Aberdeen
Paper 105-b: **Military Leadership in 15th-Century Castile** (Language: English)
Ekaitz Etxeberria
Paper 105-c: **Notes on Private Wars in Late Medieval Basque Country** (Language: English)
Jon Andoni Fernández de Larrea Rojas, Departamento de Historia Medieval, Moderna y de América, Universidad del País Vasco - Euskal Herriko Unibertsitatea, Vitoria-Gasteiz

Session: **106** **University House: Beechgrove Room**
Title: **CHRONICLES AND LETTER-BOOKS OF THE 14TH CENTURY**
Sponsor: White Hart Society
Organiser: Chris Given-Wilson, St Andrews Institute of Mediaeval Studies, University of St Andrews
Moderator: David Green, Centre for British Studies, Harlaxton College, University of Evansville
Paper 106-a: **The Calamitous 14th Century: Was It All Bad?** (Language: English)
George B. Stow, Department of History, La Salle University, Pennsylvania
Paper 106-b: ***Cronica bona et compendiosa*: The Composition and Uses of an Unedited Chronicle in England, c. 1377-1410** (Language: English)
Trevor Russell Smith, Institute for Medieval Studies, University of Leeds
Paper 106-c: **The 'Royal Letter Book', Edinburgh University Library MS 183: Potentially a Rich Source of 14th-Century Material** (Language: English)
Louise Gardiner, Centre for Research Collections, University of Edinburgh

Session: **107** **Michael Sadler Building: Room LG.16**
Title: **CITIZENSHIP, IDENTITY, AND CONFLICT IN LATE MEDIEVAL URBAN SOCIETY**
Organiser: Leen Bervoets, Vakgroep Geschiedenis, Universiteit Gent
Moderator: Christian Liddy, Department of History, Durham University
Paper 107-a: **Merchants, Craftsmen, and Taxpayers: Considering the Versatile Background of Burghers in 13th-Century Flanders** (Language: English)
Leen Bervoets
Paper 107-b: **Managing Internal Conflict and Identity in the Cities of the Kingdom of Aragon during the 13th Century** (Language: English)
María Jesús García Arnal, Departamento de Historia Medieval Ciencias y Técnicas Historiográficas y Estudios Árabes e Islámicos, Universidad de Zaragoza
Paper 107-c: **The Fluidity of Status and Identity in Late Medieval France and Flanders** (Language: English)
Bobbi Sutherland, Department of History, University of Dayton, Ohio

Session: **108** **Fine Art Building: Studio Ground Floor**
Title: **BEAUTIFUL ANIMALS**
Sponsor: MAD (Medieval Animal Data Network)
Organiser: Gerhard Jaritz, Department of Medieval Studies, Central European University, Budapest
Moderator: Alice Choyke, Department of Medieval Studies, Central European University, Budapest
Paper 108-a: **Beautiful Creeps: Insects in Byzantine Rhetoric and Poetry** (Language: English)
Floris Bernard, Department of Medieval Studies, Central European University, Budapest
Paper 108-b: **Unicorns: Spiritual and Physical Beauty in Late Medieval Books of Hours** (Language: English)
Mónica Ann Walker Vadillo, Old Operating Theatre Museum, London
Paper 108-c: **Animals and Beauty in Medieval Bestiaries** (Language: English)
Gerhard Jaritz

Session: **109** **Parkinson Building: Room 1.16**
Title: **TRANSCULTURAL APPROACHES TO THE BIBLE: EXEGESIS AND HISTORICAL WRITING IN THE MEDIEVAL WORLDS, I**
Sponsor: Bible & Historiography in Transcultural Iberian Societies, 8th-12th Centuries, Institut für Mittelalterforschung, Österreichische Akademie der Wissenschaften, Wien / FWF Project
Organiser: Matthias Martin Tischler, Institut d'Estudis Medievals, Universitat Autònoma de Barcelona
Moderator: Kristin Skottki, Lehrstuhl für Mittelalterliche Geschichte, Universität Bayreuth
Paper 109-a: **Biblical Allusions as Markers of Social Hierarchy in 12th- and 13th-Century Sources of the Crusades** (Language: English)
Sini Kangas, School of Social Sciences & Humanities, University of Tampere
Paper 109-b: **'To understand the "effeminatos" in all people': Biblical Exegesis and Gendered Pastoral Care** (Language: English)
Lydia Marie Walker, Department of History, University of Tennessee, Knoxville
Paper 109-c: **'Lupi rapaces': Biblical Typology and the Envisioning of Lithuanian Pagans, c. 1200-1400** (Language: English)
Stefan Donecker, Institut für Mittelalterforschung, Österreichische Akademie der Wissenschaften, Wien

Session: **110** **Maurice Keyworth Building: Room 1.04**
Title: **BONAVENTURE OF BAGNOREGIO: IN HIS OWN WORDS**
Sponsor: Franciscaans Studiecentrum, Tilburg University
Organiser: Krijn Pansters, Department of Biblical Sciences & Church History, Tilburg University
Moderator: Neslihan Şenocak, Department of History, Columbia University
Paper 110-a: **Natural and Divine Law: Bonaventure and His Sources** (Language: English)
Lydia Schumacher, Department of Theology & Religious Studies, King's College London
Paper 110-b: **Moral and Spiritual Life: Bonaventure and His Virtues** (Language: English)
Krijn Pansters
Paper 110-c: **Theology and Reality: Bonaventure and His *Lives of Francis*** (Language: English)
Helmut Flachenecker, Institut für Geschichte, Julius-Maximilians-Universität Würzburg

Session: **111** **Baines Wing: Room 2.16**
Title: **WAS THERE AN 11TH CENTURY?, I: INSTITUTIONS**
Sponsor: Department of History, King's College London
Organiser: Rory Naismith, Department of History, King's College London and Danica Summerlin, Department of History, University of Sheffield
Moderator: Alice Taylor, Department of History, King's College London
Paper 111-a: **A Feudal Revolution in Germany?: Comital Office in the Salian Century** (Language: English)
Levi Roach, Department of History, University of Exeter
Paper 111-b: ***Placita, Curiae,* and Making Sense of 11th-Century Legal Institutions: Western France, 980-1120** (Language: English)
Matthew McHaffie, Department of History, King's College London
Paper 111-c: **Canon Law on the Peripheries: Re-Thinking Reform in 11th-Century Church Councils** (Language: English)
Kathleen Cushing, Department of History, Keele University

Session: **112** **Charles Thackrah Building: 1.01**
Title: **NETWORK ANALYSIS FOR MEDIEVAL STUDIES, I: NETWORK ANALYSIS OF MEDIEVAL CHARTERS**
Sponsor: H37 - Histoire & Cultures Graphiques, Université catholique de Louvain, Louvain-la-Neuve / Centre de recherche pratiques médiévales de l'écrit (PraME), Université de Namur
Organiser: Sébastien de Valeriola, Institut de Statistique, Biostatistique et Sciences Actuarielles, Université catholique de Louvain, Louvain-la-Neuve and Nicolas Ruffini-Ronzani, Département d'histoire, Université de Namur
Moderator: Matthew H. Hammond, Department of History, King's College London
Paper 112-a: **'Et se en defaloient de cest paiement...': Personal Pledging and Social Networks, 13th Century** (Language: English)
Sébastien de Valeriola
Paper 112-b: **Recipients and Witnesses of High Medieval Charters: A Social Network Analysis of the German Political System during the Reign of Frederick I Barbarossa, 1152-90** (Language: English)
Clemens Beck, Historisches Institut, Friedrich-Schiller-Universität Jena
Paper 112-c: **A Knowledge Base of Charters from the *Regesta Imperii* for Generating Networks in Medieval Social and Constitutional History** (Language: English)
Christian Knüpfer, Institut für Informatik, Friedrich-Schiller-Universität Jena

Session: **113** **Baines Wing: Room 1.15**
Title: **REMEMBERING WOMEN**
Organiser: IMC Programming Committee
Moderator: Ann R. Christys, Independent Scholar, Leeds
Paper 113-a: **Andalusian Women's Poetry and the Politics of Canonicity** (Language: English)
Mourad El Fahli, Faculté des Lettres et des Sciences Humaines Saïs-Fés, Université Sidi Mohamed Ben Abdellah, Morocco
Paper 113-b: **'Will he remember the elegant doe?': Between Solomon ibn Gabirol and Dunash's Wife** (Language: English)
Nufar Rashkes, Department of Hebrew Literature, Ben-Gurion University of the Negev, Beer-Sheva
Paper 113-c: **Memories of Women and Male 'Barbarism' in the Byzantine Illuminated Book** (Language: English)
Mati Meyer, Department of Literature, Language & Arts, Open University of Israel, Raanana

Session: **114** **Michael Sadler Building: Room LG.17**
Title: **GENDER, NETWORKS, AND COMMUNITY IN LEGAL SOURCES, I: AUTHORITIES AND MINORITIES**
Organiser: Aysu Dinçer, Department of History, University of Warwick and Chiara Ravera, Department of History, University of Nottingham
Moderator: Richard M. Goddard, Department of History, University of Nottingham
Paper 114-a: **A Silent Relationship?: Tracing the Management of Muslims under the Rule of Military Orders in the Iberian Peninsula** (Language: English)
Clara Almagro-Vidal, Centro Interdisciplinar de História, Culturas e Sociedades, Universidade de Évora
Paper 114-b: **Behind Closed Doors?: Medieval Jewish Women in Barcelona and Their Social Network** (Language: English)
Anna Rich-Abad, Department of History, University of Nottingham
Paper 114-c: **'Pour ce que il estoient espars en tant de leus': The Latin Minority in Romania during the 13th and 14th Centuries** (Language: English)
Simon Hasdenteufel, UFR d'Histoire, Université Paris IV - Sorbonne

---

Session: **115** **Michael Sadler Building: Rupert Beckett Theatre**
Title: **DISTAFF, I: DRESS, FAITH, IDENTITY, AND MEMORIALISATION**
Sponsor: Discussion, Interpretation & Study of Textile Arts, Fabrics & Fashions (DISTAFF)
Organiser: Gale R. Owen-Crocker, Department of English & American Studies, University of Manchester
Moderator: Gale R. Owen-Crocker
Paper 115-a: **Stealing the Look: The Augustinian Friars and Their Troublesome Habits** (Language: English)
Alejandra Concha Sahli, Department of History, University College London
Paper 115-b: **From Archbishops to Administrators: Donors of Vestments in the 1295 Inventory of St Paul's Cathedral and Memory Construction** (Language: English)
Lara Howerton, Centre for Medieval Studies, University of Toronto, Downtown
Paper 115-c: **Jewish Garments Intended to Instill and Maintain Religious Memory** (Language: English)
Nahum Ben-Yehuda, Department of Land of Israel Studies & Archaeology, Bar-Ilan University, Ramat Gan

Session:	**116** **University House: Little Woodhouse Room**
Title:	**ESTABLISHING LAW AND ORDER IN LATE MEDIEVAL LIFE AND LITERATURE**
Organiser:	IMC Programming Committee
Moderator:	Arnold Otto, Erzbischöfliches Generalvikariat Erzbistumsarchiv, Paderborn
Paper 116-a:	***Ordnung muss sein*: Measures and Tools Applied against the Routiers in the Middle of the 14th Century in Alsace, Lorraine, and Burgundy** (Language: English) Tamás Ölbei, Histoire et Cultures de l'Antiquité et du Moyen-Âge, Université de Lorraine / Department of History, University of Debrecen
Paper 116-b:	**Bands and Vagabonds: Responses to Group and Individual Crime in the Late Medieval Low Countries** (Language: English) Mireille Juliette Pardon, Department of History, Yale University
Paper 116-c:	**Memory, Law, and the Parable of the Serpent in *Reynard the Fox*** (Language: English) Andreea D. Boboc, Department of English, University of the Pacific, California

Session:	**117** **Baines Wing: Room 1.14**
Title:	**POST-ROMAN GALLAECIA: POWER, RELIGION, AND TERRITORY**
Sponsor:	Antigüedad Tardía y Alta Edad Media en Hispania Research Group (ATAEMHIS), Universidad de Salamanca
Organiser:	Pablo Poveda Arias, Departamento de Prehistoria, Historia Antigua y Arqueología, Universidad de Salamanca
Moderator:	Pablo C. Díaz Martínez, Departamento de Prehistoria, Historia Antigua y Arqueología, Universidad de Salamanca
Paper 117-a:	**Beyond Hydatius: Archaeology of Power in the Interior of Post-Roman Gallaecia** (Language: English) Carlos Tejerizo-García, Instituto de Ciencias del Patrimonio, Consejo Superior de Investigaciones Científicas, Santiago de Compostela
Paper 117-b:	**Bishops and Society: Elite and Non-Elite Contributions to the Development of the Church in Early Medieval Gallaecia** (Language: English) Rebecca A. Devlin, Department of History, University of Louisville, Kentucky
Paper 117-c:	**The Making of a Christian Time in Early Medieval Gallaecia** (Language: English) Marco García Quintela, Departamento de Historia, Universidade de Santiago de Compostela

Session:	**118** **Maurice Keyworth Building: Room 1.09**
Title:	**FRANKS AND MEROVINGIANS: EAST AND WEST**
Sponsor:	Oxford Handbook of the Merovingian World
Organiser:	Isabel Moreira, Department of History, University of Utah
Moderator:	Isabel Moreira
Paper 118-a:	**Frankish Federates and the Creation of the Merovingian Kingdom** (Language: English) Ralph Mathisen, Department of History, University of Illinois, Urbana-Champaign
Paper 118-b:	**A Dark Age in East and West?: Late Merovingian Connections to the Byzantine World** (Language: English) Laury Sarti, Historisches Seminar, Albert-Ludwigs-Universität Freiburg
Paper 118-c:	**The Gundovald Affair in Light of Merovingian 'Domestic Politics'** (Language: English) Till Stüber, Friedrich-Meinecke-Institut, Freie Universität Berlin

Session: **119** **Social Sciences Building: Room 10.05**
Title: **SHARING BOOKS, SHARING MEMORIES: BOOK FRAGMENTS ILLUMINATING INTER-EUROPEAN CONNECTIONS**
Sponsor: National Library of Finland, Helsinki
Organiser: Sara Ellis Nilsson, Historical Studies, Department of Society, Culture & Identity, Malmö University
Moderator: Jaakko Tahkokallio, National Library of Finland, Helsinki
Paper 119-a: **From Paris to Nidaros: French Books in Medieval Norway** (Language: English)
Synnøve Myking, Institutt for lingvistiske, litterære og estetiske studier, Universitetet i Bergen
Paper 119-b: **The Use of English Liturgical Texts in Sweden and Finland** (Language: English)
Olli-Pekka Kasurinen, Department of Philosophy, History, Culture & Art Studies, University of Helsinki
Paper 119-c: **European Book Fragments in Norway: Embracing Chaos in Research Methods** (Language: English)
Åslaug Ommundsen, Institutt for lingvistiske, litterære og estetiske studier, Universitetet i Bergen

Session: **120** **Social Sciences Building: Room 10.06**
Title: **REVENANTS AND CHTHONIC MEMORIES IN MIDDLE ENGLISH LITERATURE**
Organiser: IMC Programming Committee
Moderator: Rose A. Sawyer, Institute for Medieval Studies, University of Leeds
Paper 120-a: **Unforgotten: Revenants and Ghosts in Some Middle English Texts** (Language: English)
Rosanne Gasse, Department of English, Brandon University, Manitoba
Paper 120-b: **History under the 'Grene': Memory, Landscape, and the Post-Conquest Historical Imagination** (Language: English)
Sarah-Nelle Jackson, Department of English, University of British Columbia
Paper 120-c: **The Trope of Memory as a Structuring Motif in *Sir Orfeo*** (Language: English)
Angana Moitra, School of English, University of Kent / Institut für Englische Philologie, Freie Universität Berlin

Session: **121** **Charles Thackrah Building: 1.02**
Title: **LA CULTURA ALFONSÍ COMO LUGAR DE MEMORIA: LITERATURA, SABERES Y PODER MONÁRQUICO**
Organiser: Mechthild Albert, Institut VII: Romanistik, Rheinische Friedrich-Wilhelms-Universität Bonn
Moderator: Mechthild Albert
Paper 121-a: **La cultura alfonsí: Construcción de un lugar de memoria** (Language: Español)
Mechthild Albert
Paper 121-b: **'Calila y Dimna' como instrumento de memoria, legitimación regia y monumento literario** (Language: Español)
Ulrike Becker, Institut VII: Romanistik, Rheinische Friedrich-Wilhelms-Universität Bonn
Paper 121-c: **El tesoro del tío: La cultura alfonsí como lugar de memoria e instrumento de legitimación autorial en la obra de don Juan Manuel** (Language: Español)
Lena Ringen, Institut VII: Romanistik, Rheinische Friedrich-Wilhelms-Universität Bonn

Session: **122** **Maurice Keyworth Building: Room 1.32**
Title: **MNEMONIC DIAGRAMS IN LATE MEDIEVAL PREACHING AND PEDAGOGY**
Sponsor: International Medieval Sermon Studies Society
Organiser: Kimberly Rivers, Department of History, University of Wisconsin-Oshkosh
Moderator: Anne Holloway, Centre for Medieval & Renaissance Studies, Monash University, Victoria
Paper 122-a: **How to Know and Love God: Visual Strategies in Llull's Art and Its Early Reception** (Language: English)
Pamela Beattie, Department of Comparative Humanities, University of Louisville, Kentucky
Paper 122-b: **Schematic Imaging: A Tool for the Late Medieval Preacher** (Language: English)
Holly Johnson, Department of English, Mississippi State University
Paper 122-c: **How to Memorize the Decretals in the Later Middle Ages: Johannes Sintram's Mnemonic Diagram** (Language: English)
Kimberly Rivers

Session: **123** **Maurice Keyworth Building: Room 1.06**
Title: **RECLAIMING THE MIDDLE AGES FOR AFRICA, I: FROM NUBIA TO ETHIOPIA**
Sponsor: Fakultät für Geschichtswissenschaft, Ruhr-Universität Bochum
Organiser: Vincent van Gerven Oei, punctum books, Tirana and Meseret Oldjira, Department of Art & Archaeology, Princeton University
Moderator: Adam Simmons, Department of History, Lancaster University
Paper 123-a: **The Memories of Byzantium as Preserved in Nubia's Political Ideology after the 7th Century** (Language: English)
Effrosyni Zacharopoulou, Independent Scholar, Athens
Paper 123-b: **For Sale: Old Nubian Land Sales and What They Tell Us about Nubian Medieval Economy** (Language: English)
Vincent van Gerven Oei
Paper 123-c: **Early Pan-African Biblical Projects: New Perspectives on Solomon, Sheba, and the Ethiopian 14th-Century Text *Kəbrä Nägäst*** (Language: English)
Wendy Laura Belcher, Department of Comparative Literature, Princeton University
Paper 123-d: **The Influence of Christianity on Nubian Culture** (Language: English)
Abdulrahman Khary, Dongola Association for Nubian Culture & Heritage, International University of Africa, Sudan

Session:	**124** **Maurice Keyworth Building: Room 1.31**
Title:	**REMEMBERING MELODY WITH AND WITHOUT NOTATION**
Organiser:	IMC Programming Committee
Moderator:	Daniel J. DiCenso, College of the Holy Cross, Massachusetts
Paper 124-a:	**Musical Notation as the Trace of Lost Sources: The Fragmentary Exemplars of Trouvère *Chansonnier* V (Paris, Bibliothèque nationale, MS fonds français 24406)** (Language: English) Nicholas Bleisch, King's College, University of Cambridge
Paper 124-b:	**An Apocalyptic Heart: Portraying Sacred Meaning in Baude Cordier's *Belle, bonne, sage*** (Language: English) Rachel McNellis, Department of Music, Case Western Reserve University, Ohio
Paper 124-c:	**Putting Medieval Music into Practice: The Byzantine Musical Performance and Transmission in the Ecumenical Patriarchate of Constantinople** (Language: English) Georgios Karazeris, Centre for Advanced Studies in Music, Istanbul Technical University

Session:	**125** **Michael Sadler Building: Room LG.19**
Title:	**MYTHS AND MYTHOLOGISING IN THE CONSTRUCTION OF HISTORY**
Organiser:	IMC Programming Committee
Moderator:	Daniel Franke, Department of History, Richard Bland College of William & Mary, Virginia
Paper 125-a:	**Lombard Migration Saga: Myth or History?** (Language: English) Peter Bystrický, Institute of History, Slovak Academy of Sciences, Bratislava
Paper 125-b:	**The Forging and Reforging of the Myth: The Construction and Mobilisation of the Norman Myth in the Battle of Hastings of Henry of Huntingdon** (Language: English) Paulo Christian Martins Marques da Cruz, Escola de Filosofia, Letras e Ciências Humanas, Universidade Federal de São Paulo
Paper 125-c:	**Inventing the Hero: The Origins of the Myth of Jaroslav of Sternberg** (Language: English) Jan Malý, Institute of World History, Univerzita Karlova, Praha

Session:	**126** **Social Sciences Building: Room 10.07**
Title:	**WOMEN'S STRATEGIES OF MEMORY, I: TRAUMA AND RECONSTRUCTION**
Organiser:	Lucy Allen, Newnham College, University of Cambridge and Emma Bridget O'Loughlin Bérat, Institut für Anglistik, Amerikanistik und Keltologie, Rheinische Friedrich-Wilhelms-Universität Bonn
Moderator:	Ruen-chuan Ma, Department of English & Literature, Utah Valley University
Paper 126-a:	**A Textile Habitus of Memory in Chaucer's *Legend of Philomela*** (Language: English) Lucy Allen
Paper 126-b:	**Hanna the Maccabi: A Healing and Restorative Memory from a Feminine Sexual Trauma in the Rabbinic Literature** (Language: English) Dvora Lederman Daniely, Department of Education, David Yellin College, Jerusalem
Paper 126-c:	**Re-Membering the Drowned: The Rebellious Recollection of Noah's Wife in the York, Chester, and Towneley Flood Pageants** (Language: English) Daisy Black, School of Humanities, University of Wolverhampton
Paper 126-d:	**Revising 'Remembrance': Custance's Strategies of Memory in Chaucer's *Man of Law's Tale*** (Language: English) Emma Bridget O'Loughlin Bérat

Session:	**127** **Baines Wing: Room 1.16**
Title:	**MEMORY IN TOLKIEN'S MEDIEVALISM, I**
Sponsor:	Cardiff Metropolitan University
Organiser:	Dimitra Fimi, Department of Humanities, Cardiff Metropolitan University
Moderator:	Anna Smol, Department of English, Mount Saint Vincent University, Nova Scotia
Paper 127-a:	**Memory, Lore, and Knowledge in Tolkien's Legendarium** (Language: English) Thomas Honegger, Institut für Anglistik, Friedrich-Schiller-Universität Jena
Paper 127-b:	**World-Building and Memory in the Name-List to the 'Fall of Gondolin'** (Language: English) Andrew Higgins, Independent Scholar, Brighton
Paper 127-c:	**The Smith, the Weaver, and the Librarian: Sub-Creating Memory in Tolkien's Work** (Language: English) Gaëlle Abaléa, Centre d'Etudes Médiévales Anglaises (CEMA), Université Paris IV - Sorbonne
Paper 127-d:	**Tolkien's Typological Imagination** (Language: English) Anna Smol

Session:	**128** **Emmanuel Centre: Wilson Room**
Title:	**Between Memory and Imagination, I: Medieval Religious Encounters from the Silk Road to the Indian Ocean**
Sponsor:	Arc Humanities Press
Organiser:	Shannon Cunningham, Amsterdam University Press / Arc Humanities Press / Medieval Institute Publications, Western Michigan University, Kalamazoo
Moderator:	Alexandra F. C. Cuffel, Centrum für Religionswissenschaftliche Studien, Ruhr-Universität Bochum
Paper 128-a:	**Bordering the World of Islam: Ibn Battuta in the Malay Archipelago** (Language: English) Aglaia Iankovskaia, Peter the Great Museum of Anthropology & Ethnography, St Petersburg / Department of Medieval Studies, Central European University, Budapest
Paper 128-b:	**The Origin of Monotheism in Malabar: From the Perspectives of Muslims, Hindus, Christians, and Jews** (Language: English) Ophira Gamliel, Centrum für Religionswissenschaftliche Studien, Ruhr-Universität Bochum
Paper 128-c:	**Relations between the St Thomas Christians and the Nambuthiri Brahmins in Medieval Kerala in the Context of the Thomas Traditions** (Language: English) Johny Shelly, Department of Political Science, St Aloysius College, Kerala

Session:	**129** **Michael Sadler Building: Room LG.10**
Title:	**Memory in Local Religious Spaces**
Organiser:	IMC Programming Committee
Moderator:	Judit Majorossy, Institut für Geschichte, Universität Wien
Paper 129-a:	**Between Elites and Local Communities: Church Consecrations in Urgell, 10th and 11th Centuries** (Language: English) Rosa Maria Quetglas Munar, Departamento de Historia Medieval, Moderna y Contemporánea, Universidad de Salamanca
Paper 129-b:	**The Manipulation of Memory: Reinventing Local Motifs in Carrión de los Condes** (Language: English) Elizabeth Lastra, Department of the History of Art, University of Pennsylvania
Paper 129-c:	**Indulgences and Memory in the English Parish Context** (Language: English) Ann Brodeur, School of Arts & Sciences, University of Mary, North Dakota

Session: **130** **Charles Thackrah Building: 1.03**
Title: **MYSTICAL MEMORIES, I: MYSTICS REMEMBERED**
Sponsor: Institute for the Study of Spirituality, KU Leuven / Ruusbroecgenootschap, Universiteit Antwerpen
Organiser: Rob Faesen, Institute for the Study of Spirituality, KU Leuven / Ruusbroecgenootschap, Universiteit Antwerpen
Moderator: Rob Faesen
Paper 130-a: **Medieval Mystics in the Popular Press: Remembering the Mystics as Self-Help Experts** (Language: English)
Joanne Maguire Robinson, Department of Religious Studies, University of North Carolina, Charlotte
Paper 130-b: **Jan van Leeuwen: A Remembered Lay Mystic** (Language: English)
John Arblaster, Institute for the Study of Spirituality, KU Leuven / Ruusbroecgenootschap, Universiteit Antwerpen
Paper 130-c: **Middle English Translations of Continental Female Mystics: What Is Remembered and What Is Not?** (Language: English)
Louise Nelstrop, St Benet's Hall, University of Oxford / Department of Theology & Religious Studies, York St John University

---

Session: **131** **Maurice Keyworth Building: Room 1.05**
Title: **MEMORY AND COMMUNITY, I**
Sponsor: Centre d'Études Supérieures de Civilisation Médiévale (CESCM), Université de Poitiers / Centre Nationale de la Recherche Scientifique (CNRS), Institute for Medieval Studies, Leeds
Organiser: Emilia Jamroziak, Institute for Medieval Studies / School of History, University of Leeds
Moderator: Martin Aurell, Centre d'Études Supérieures de Civilisation Médiévale (CESCM), Université de Poitiers
Paper 131-a: **Subscriptions, Community, and Memory in Italian Charters of the 10th-12th Centuries** (Language: English)
Emilie Kurdziel, Centre d'Études Supérieures de Civilisation Médiévale (CESCM), Université de Poitiers
Paper 131-b: **Late Medieval Monastic Memory: Community between Past and Present - The Case Study of Ebrach** (Language: English)
Emilia Jamroziak
Paper 131-c: **Connecting the Dots: How the Community of Plaimpied Developed a Graphical Memory** (Language: English)
Thierry Grégor, Centre d'Études Supérieures de Civilisation Médiévale (CESCM), Université de Poitiers and Estelle Ingrand-Varenne, Centre d'Études Supérieures de Civilisation Médiévale (CESCM), Université de Poitiers / Centre National de la Recherche Scientifique (CNRS), Paris

Session: **132** **Social Sciences Building: Room 10.09**
Title: **BRITISH ARCHAEOLOGICAL ASSOCIATION, I: ARCHITECTURAL MEMORY - REMEMBERING AN EMPIRE, RELIGIOUS COMMUNITIES, AND PATRONS THROUGH BUILDINGS**
Sponsor: British Archaeological Association
Organiser: Harriet Mahood, Graduate Centre for Medieval Studies, University of Reading
Moderator: Harriet Mahood
Paper 132-a: **Visual Memories in Southern Italy: The City of Bari in and out of the Byzantine Empire** (Language: English)
Clare Vernon, Department of History, Archaeology & Classics, Birkbeck, University of London
Paper 132-b: **Church Façades as Sites of Institutional Memory in 12th-Century Spain** (Language: English)
Rose Walker, Courtauld Institute of Art, University of London
Paper 132-c: **Local Memory: Remembering and Being Remembered in the English Parish Church** (Language: English)
Meg Bernstein, Department of Art History, University of California, Los Angeles

Session: **133** **Leeds University Union: Room 2 - Elland Road**
Title: **REMEMBERING THE VIKING AGE AROUND THE IRISH SEA, I: INTERNATIONAL IDENTITIES**
Sponsor: ISMARN: The Irish Sea in the Middle Ages Research Network
Organiser: Lindy Brady, Department of English, University of Mississippi
Moderator: Ben Guy, Department of Anglo-Saxon, Norse & Celtic, University of Cambridge
Paper 133-a: **A Hiberno-Scandinavian Origin Legend: Community and Identity in 11th- and 12th-Century Dublin and the Isles** (Language: English)
Patrick Wadden, Department of History, Belmont Abbey College, North Carolina
Paper 133-b: **Impressions of a 12th-Century Maritime Ruler: Somerled - Viking Warrior, Clan Chieftain, or Traitor to the Scottish King?** (Language: English)
Caitlin Ellis, Department of Anglo-Saxon, Norse & Celtic, University of Cambridge
Paper 133-c: **Viking Age Heroic Biography around the Irish Sea** (Language: English)
Lindy Brady

Session:	**134** **Leeds University Union: Room 4 - Hyde Park**
Title:	**TRANSFORMATION OF COLLECTIVE MEMORY**
Organiser:	IMC Programming Committee
Moderator:	Piotr Oliński, Instytut Historii i Archiwistyki, Uniwersytet Mikołaja Kopernika, Toruń
Paper 134-a:	***Memoria* before *Memoria*** (Language: English) Alexis Fontbonne, Centre D'études en Sciences Sociales du Religieux, École des Hautes Études en Sciences Sociales (EHESS), Université de recherche Paris Sciences et Lettres
Paper 134-b:	**Catholics Missionaries' Cultural-Educational Contribution in Late Medieval Georgia: Historical Memory** (Language: Français) Manana Javakhishvili, School of Arts & Sciences, Ilia State University, Georgia
Paper 134-c:	**Transformation of the Medieval Model of the Georgian Cultural Portrait and Self-Portrait in the Literature of the Last Two Centuries: In the Context of Collective Memory** (Language: English) Nino Pirtskhalava, Institute of Comparative Literature, Ilia State University, Georgia

Session:	**135** **Leeds University Union: Room 5 - Kirkstall Abbey**
Title:	**MEMORY AND THE MATERIALITY OF MEDIEVAL TEXTS, I: CODICES AND COMMUNITIES**
Sponsor:	Centre for Medieval Studies, University of Bristol
Organiser:	Benjamin Pohl, Department of History, University of Bristol
Moderator:	Benjamin Pohl
Paper 135-a:	**'I betake me unto those rockes and monuments': Constructing a Collective Memory of a 'Local' Arthur in William Camden's *Britannia* and John Leland's *Assertio Inclytissimi Arturii*** (Language: English) Mary Bateman, Department of English, University of Bristol
Paper 135-b:	**Codices and Communities: Continuity and Change in Practice from Late Medieval to Early Modern in the Case of Mary Sidney and the Wilton Circle** (Language: English) Rebecca Lyons, Department of English, University of Bristol
Paper 135-c:	**'Scripta volant, verba manent': The Un-Publication of *Floris and Blancheflour* in Medieval and Early Modern England** (Language: English) Leah Tether, Department of English, University of Bristol

Session:	**136** **Charles Thackrah Building: 1.04**
Title:	**MEMORISING TIME: THE *CISIOJANUS* AS A COMPLEX STORAGE OF PRE-MODERN MEMORY**
Organiser:	Silvan Wagner, Lehrstuhl für Ältere Deutsche Philologie, Universität Bayreuth
Moderator:	Silvan Wagner
Paper 136-a:	**Singing the Year All at Once: When *Memoria* Disciplines the Divine Office** (Language: English) Irene Holzer, Institut für Historische Musikwissenschaft, Universität Hamburg
Paper 136-b:	**All Days Are Equal, but Some Days Are More Equal than Others: Late Medieval German *Cisiojani* and Their Structure of Time** (Language: English) Silvan Wagner
Paper 136-c:	**The Memory of Saints and His Stratifications: A Philological Approach to the Study of Italian *Cisiojani*** (Language: English) Nicola De Nisco, Dipartimento di scienze umane e sociali, Università per Stranieri di Perugia

Session:	**137** **Maurice Keyworth Building: Room 1.03**
Title:	**REMEMBERING AND FORGETTING THE ANCIENT CITY, I: URBAN MYTHS**
Sponsor:	ERC Project 'The Impact of the Ancient City'
Organiser:	Javier Martínez-Jiménez, Faculty of Classics, University of Cambridge and Sam Ottewill-Soulsby, Faculty of Classics, University of Cambridge
Moderator:	Andrew Wallace-Hadrill, Faculty of Classics, University of Cambridge
Paper 137-a:	**Remembering the First City: Freculf of Lisieux and the End of Innocence** (Language: English) Sam Ottewill-Soulsby
Paper 137-b:	**Myth and Reality: Mérida - The End of a Great History and the Beginning of a Medieval Legend** (Language: English) Isaac Sastre de Diego, Museo Nacional de Arte Romano, Mérida
Paper 137-c:	**Remembering the Rose Red City: Pilgrimage, Storytelling, and the Shaping of Byzantine Petra** (Language: English) Marlena Whiting, Faculteit der Geesteswetenschappen, Universiteit van Amsterdam

Session:	**138** **Maurice Keyworth Building: Room 1.33**
Title:	**REMEMBERING THE ROYAL HUNT: HUNTING HISTORIES AND ROYAL IDENTITY**
Organiser:	Hagar Barak, Independent Scholar, New York
Moderator:	Eric J. Goldberg, Department of History, Massachusetts Institute of Technology
Paper 138-a:	**'Much of a Hunter - Less of a King': Hunting as Historiographic Allegation and Subject of Anti-Royal Propaganda - The Case of Roman and Bohemian King Wenceslas IV, 1361-1419** (Language: English) Klara Hübner, Department of Auxiliary Historical Sciences & Archive Studies, Masarykova univerzita, Brno
Paper 138-b:	**Pale Reflections?: Cultural Constructions of the Medieval Deer Park in the 16th and Early 17th Centuries** (Language: English) Amanda Richardson, Department of History, University of Chichester
Paper 138-c:	**Desperately Seeking Saint-Denis: Philip Augustus's Boar, Dagobert's Stag, and the Right to Rule in Primat's *Chronicle of Saint-Denis*, c. 1250-1274** (Language: English) Hagar Barak

Session: **139** **University House: Great Woodhouse Room**
Title: **CONSTRUCTING AND RECONSTRUCTING THE PAST**
Organiser: IMC Programming Committee
Moderator: Hugh Kennedy, Department of the Languages & Cultures of the Near & Middle East, School of Oriental & African Studies, University of London
Paper 139-a: **Manipulating Memory and Reconstructing the Past: The 'Abbasid *Dawa* and *Akhbar al-Dawla al-'Abbasiyya*** (Language: English)
Öznur Özdemir, Department of Islamic History, Sakarya University, Turkey
Paper 139-b: **Ibn Battuta's *Rihla*: When Description Becomes Memory** (Language: English)
Rocio Rojas-Marcos, Departamento de Estudios Árabes e Islámicos, Universidad de Sevilla
Paper 139-c: **Recalling the Sacred Past in Avignonese Court Sermons** (Language: English)
Blake R. Beattie, Department of History, University of Louisville, Kentucky

---

Session: **140** **Leeds University Union: Room 6 - Roundhay**
Title: **MONARCHY AND MEMORY, I: KINGSHIP AND MEMORY IN THE BRITISH ISLES**
Sponsor: Royal Studies Network
Organiser: Gabrielle Storey, Department of History, University of Winchester
Moderator: Paul Webster, School of History, Archaeology & Religion, Cardiff University
Paper 140-a: **The Illustration of Kingship in the Manuscripts of Matthew Paris** (Language: English)
Judith Collard, Department of History & Art History, University of Otago, New Zealand
Paper 140-b: **The King's and the Queen's Anniversary: The Commemoration of Eleanor of Castile, 1290-1400** (Language: English)
Anna M. Duch, Division of Humanities & Social Sciences, Columbia State Community College, Tennessee
Paper 140-c: **'The whole stature of a godly man and a large horse': Memory, Masculinity, and the Military Status of Henry VIII** (Language: English)
Emma Levitt, Department of History, University of Huddersfield
Paper 140-d: **'Heroism and Humanity': Depictions and Descriptions of King Robert I, 1800-1950** (Language: English)
Laura Harrison, School of History, Classics & Archaeology, University of Edinburgh

Session: **141** **Parkinson Building: Nathan Bodington Chamber**
Title: **REMEMBERING *ADMONITIO*: EPISCOPAL CRITICISM OF RULERS IN THE MIDDLE AGES, I**
Organiser: Ryan Kemp, Department of History & Welsh History, Aberystwyth University
Moderator: James Palmer, St Andrews Institute of Mediaeval Studies, University of St Andrews
Paper 141-a: **Romancing and Remembering Admonition: Confronting Roman Emperors in Late Antique Early Medieval Italian Hagiography** (Language: English)
Mark Humphries, Centre for Medieval & Early Modern Research (MEMO), Swansea University
Paper 141-b: **Pastor of Muppets: Admonishing 'Sons of the Church' in the Post-Imperial West** (Language: English)
Robin Whelan, Department of History, University of Liverpool
Paper 141-c: **Imperial Confrontation and Episcopal Identity in Late Antique Alexandria** (Language: English)
David Gwynn, Department of History, Royal Holloway, University of London

---

Session: **142** **Baines Wing: Room G.37**
Title: **FAME: PATRONS AND MEMORIES IN BYZANTIUM, I**
Organiser: Francisco Lopez-Santos Kornberger, Centre for Byzantine, Ottoman & Modern Greek Studies, University of Birmingham and Jessica Varsallona, Centre for Byzantine, Ottoman & Modern Greek Studies, University of Birmingham
Moderator: Rebecca Darley, Department of History, Classics & Archaeology, Birkbeck, University of London
Paper 142-a: **'Our pious, just and great Emperors': Echoes of the Imperial Past in Heresiological Texts of the 10th Century** (Language: English)
Carl Dixon, Department of History, University of Nottingham
Paper 142-b: **The Founder's Memory in the Architecture of Late Antique Ravenna: Strategies of Visualisation and Communication Codes** (Language: English)
Maria Cristina Carile, Dipartimento di Beni Culturali, Alma Mater Studiorum, Università di Bologna
Paper 142-c: **Dara in Mesopotamia: Memories of a Byzantine Town from the Emperors to Facebook** (Language: English)
Alessandro Carabia, Centre for Byzantine, Ottoman & Modern Greek Studies, University of Birmingham

Session:	**143**	**Stage@leeds: Stage 3**
Title:	**CRUSADES AND MEMORY, I : ARCHITECTURE AND LANDSCAPE**	
Organiser:	Pagona Papadopoulou, School of History & Archaeology, Aristotle University of Thessaloniki	
Moderator:	Scott Redford, Department of History of Art & Archaeology, School of Oriental & African Studies, University of London	
Paper 143-a:	**The Afterlife of the Lord's Temple and Bayt al-Maqdis: Reinterpreting the Sacred at the *Templum Domini* in Jerusalem in the 12th Century** (Language: English) Heba Mostafa, Department of Art /Graduate Department of Art History, University of Toronto, St. George	
Paper 143-b:	**Royal Authority and Teutonic Power in Sicily after the 3rd Crusade** (Language: English) Dana Katz, Haifa Center for Mediterranean History (HCMH), University of Haifa	
Paper 143-c:	**The Mongol-Crusader Connection: Evolving Architectural Memory after the Battle of *Kösedağ*** (Language: English) Suna Çağaptay, Faculty of Classics, University of Cambridge	

Session:	**144**	**Fine Art Building: SR 1.10**
Title:	**PILGRIM LIBRARIES, I: HISTORY AND MEMORY IN PILGRIMAGE LITERATURE**	
Sponsor:	Leverhulme International Research Network 'Pilgrim Libraries - Books & Reading on the Medieval Routes to Rome & Jerusalem'	
Organiser:	Philip Booth, Department of History, Politics & Philosophy, Manchester Metropolitan University	
Moderator:	Philip Booth	
Paper 144-a:	**Remembering the Fourth Crusade on the Late Medieval Jerusalem Pilgrimage** (Language: English) Nicky Tsougarakis, Department of English, History & Creative Writing, Edge Hill University	
Paper 144-b:	**Wandering in Venice with a Book of Saints: The Pilgrims' Use and Dissemination of Petrus de Natalibus's *Catalogum Sanctorum* during the 15th Century** (Language: English) Laura Grazia Di Stefano, Department of History, University of Nottingham	
Paper 144-c:	**Printing Pilgrimage?: Representations of Jerusalem in the Incunable Editions of the *Book of John Mandeville*** (Language: English) Matthew Coneys, Institute of Modern Languages Research, University of London	

Session:	**145**	**Baines Wing: Room G.36**
Title:	**MARVELS, MEMORY, AND PLACE: INTERDISCIPLINARY PERSPECTIVES ON MEDIEVAL LANDSCAPES**	
Organiser:	Marianne O'Doherty, Department of English / Centre for Medieval & Renaissance Culture, University of Southampton	
Moderator:	Catherine A. M. Clarke, Faculty of Humanities, University of Southampton	
Paper 145-a:	**Eanswythe's Landscape: Inventing 7th-Century Folkestone** (Language: English) Michael Bintley, School of Humanities, Canterbury Christ Church University	
Paper 145-b:	**The Miraculous Landscape in Norman Historical Writing** (Language: English) Leonie V. Hicks, School of Humanities, Canterbury Christ Church University	
Paper 145-c:	**Marvels, Memory, and Place in the 'Marvels of Britain' Tradition** (Language: English) Marianne O'Doherty	

Session:	**146**	**Emmanuel Centre: Room 10**
Title:	**THE MEDIEVAL JEWISH CRAFTSMEN: FACT OR FICTION?**	
Organiser:	Maria Stürzebecher, Kulturdirektion, Landeshauptstadt Erfurt	
Moderator:	Maria Stürzebecher	
Paper 146-a:	**Stones, Masons, Marks: 'Mason's Marks' and Other Signs on Medieval Jewish Gravestones Revisited** (Language: English) Stefanie Fuchs, Institut für Europäische Kunstgeschichte, Universität Heidelberg	
Paper 146-b:	**Blood, Meat, and Politics: How Influence and Interfaith Interactions Were Remembered by Butchers in the Middle Ages** (Language: English) Jörn Roland Christophersen, Seminar für Judaistik, Goethe-Universität, Frankfurt am Main / Arye Maimon-Institut für Geschichte der Juden, Universität Trier	
Paper 146-c:	**What Do We Know about Jewish Goldsmiths and Jewish Seal Engravers in the Middle Ages?** (Language: English) Andreas Lehnertz, Arye Maimon-Institut für Geschichte der Juden, Universität Trier	

Session:	**147**	**Baines Wing: Room 2.15**
Title:	**MEMORY, ETERNITY, AND THE DIVINE IN MEDIEVAL THEOLOGY**	
Organiser:	IMC Programming Committee	
Moderator:	Montague Brown, Department of Philosophy, Saint Anselm College, New Hampshire	
Paper 147-a:	**The Memory of the Ineffable in Augustine and Diadochus of Photike** (Language: English) Georgiana Huian, Faculty of Theology, University of Bern	
Paper 147-b:	**The Place and the Significance of the Presence in John Duns Scotus's Concept of Memory** (Language: English) Barbara Ćuk, Faculty of Philosophy & Religious Studies, University of Zagreb	
Paper 147-c:	**John Wyclif, Albert the Great, and the Alleged Late Aristotle's Afterthoughts about the Eternity of the World** (Language: English) Luigi Campi, Dipartimento di Filosofia, Università degli Studi di Milano	

Session: **148** **University House: St George Room**
Title: **DOMINICAN POVERTY IN THE MIDDLE AGES: COUNSEL, CRITICISM, AND CONFLICT**
Organiser: Cornelia Linde, German Historical Institute London
Moderator: Sita Steckel, Historisches Seminar, Westfälische Wilhelms-Universität Münster
Paper 148-a: **Dominican Influence in the Development of the *Ordo Servorum Mariae*** (Language: English)
Ingrid Würth, Institut für Geschichte, Martin-Luther-Universität Halle-Wittenberg
Paper 148-b: **Franciscans versus Dominicans: An English Debate on Poverty** (Language: English)
Cornelia Linde
Paper 148-c: **'Not friaries, but rather palaces and manor houses': Monastic Criticism against Mendicant Claims of Poverty in Late Medieval Scandinavia** (Language: English)
Johnny Grandjean Jakobsen, Nordisk Forskningsinstitut, Københavns Universitet

Session: **149** **University House: Cloberry Room**
Title: **RE-ENACTMENT AND MEDIEVAL STUDIES, I: MARTIAL ARTS**
Organiser: Melissa Venables, School of English, University of Nottingham
Moderator: Melissa Venables
Paper 149-a: **Understanding the Mechanics of Armour and Weapon Use, Or, How We Know What We Think We Know** (Language: English)
Dean Davidson, Society for Combat Archaeology, Leeds and Stuart Ivinson, Society for Combat Archaeology / Royal Armouries, Leeds
Paper 149-b: **Ice Skating with Skarphéðinn: How Useful, If at All, Are the Icelandic Family Sagas as a Historical Reference for Early Medieval Combat?** (Language: English)
Sam Just, School of English, University of Nottingham
Paper 149-c: **Recreating the Armour of Lionel Lord Welles** (Language: English)
Wayne Reynolds, Towton Battlefield Society

Session: **150** **Michael Sadler Building: Room LG.15**
Title: **SCIENTIFIC, EMPIRICAL, BIBLICAL, AND HAGIOGRAPHICAL KNOWLEDGE IN THE MIDDLE AGES, I: ASTRONOMY, COMPUTUS, AND MEDICINE**
Sponsor: School of Arts, English & Languages, Queen's University Belfast
Organiser: Sarah Baccianti, School of Arts, English & Languages, Queen's University Belfast
Moderator: Ciaran Arthur, School of Arts, English & Languages, Queen's University Belfast
Paper 150-a: **Anglo-Saxons' Visions of Modern Science** (Language: English)
Marilina Cesario, School of Arts, English & Languages, Queen's University Belfast and Pedro Lacerda, School of Mathematics & Physics, Queen's University Belfast
Paper 150-b: **Why Write *Computus* in English?: Vernacularity and Computistical Inquiry** (Language: English)
Rebecca Stephenson, School of English, Drama, Film & Creative Writing, University College Dublin
Paper 150-c: **Pus, Boils, and Amputations: Surgery in Medieval Scandinavia** (Language: English)
Sarah Baccianti

Session:	**151** **Emmanuel Centre: Room 11**
Title:	**INTEGRATING THE SASANIANS, I: IDENTITIES AND POLITICS IN LATE ANTIQUE AND MEDIEVAL IRAN**
Sponsor:	MPS - Middle Persian Studies, Universidade de Brasília / Sonderforschungsbereiche Project 'Visions of Community', Österreichische Akademie der Wissenschaften, Universität Wien
Organiser:	Otávio Luiz Vieira Pinto, Middle Persian Studies Project, Universidade de Brasília
Moderator:	Ricky Broome, Leeds Institute for Clinical Trials Research (LICTR), University of Leeds
Paper 151-a:	**Strangers in a Strange Land: The Ostrogothic Embassy to Khosrow I** (Language: English) Otávio Luiz Vieira Pinto
Paper 151-b:	**Finding Persia: Persian Toponyms and Ethnonyms on the *Tabula Peutingeriana*** (Language: English) Salvatore Liccardo, Institut für Mittelalterforschung, Österreichische Akademie der Wissenschaften, Wien
Paper 151-c:	**(Middle) Persian in the East: The Rise of the Persianate Polities in Late Antique and Early Medieval Central Asia** (Language: English) Khodadad Rezakhani, Department of History, Princeton University

Session:	**152** **Stage@leeds: Stage 2**
Title:	**ENGLAND AND SCOTLAND AT PEACE AND WAR IN THE LATER MIDDLE AGES, I**
Organiser:	Claire Etty, Oxford English Dictionary, Oxford University Press and Andy King, Department of History, University of Southampton
Moderator:	Claire Etty
Paper 152-a:	**A Tale of Two Towns: Roxburgh and Berwick before the Wars of Independence** (Language: English) David Ditchburn, Department of History, Trinity College Dublin
Paper 152-b:	**'Delay is dangerous': Berwick's Experience as an English-Occupied Scottish Town, 1333-1357** (Language: English) Iain A. MacInnes, Centre for History, University of the Highlands & Islands, Dornoch
Paper 152-c:	**Rock and a Hard Place: Roxburgh Castle and Burgh in the Later Middle Ages** (Language: English) Alastair Macdonald, School of Divinity, History & Philosophy, University of Aberdeen

Session:	**153** **Stage@leeds: Stage 1**
Title:	**CREATIVE MEMORIES: SHAPING IDENTITY IN MEDIEVAL CULTURE, I**
Sponsor:	Sächsische Akademie der Wissenschaften zu Leipzig / Forschungsstelle für Vergleichende Ordensgeschichte (FOVOG), Technische Universität, Dresden
Organiser:	Jörg Sonntag, Sächsische Akademie der Wissenschaften zu Leipzig / Technische Universität, Dresden
Moderator:	Mirko Breitenstein, Sächsische Akademie der Wissenschaften zu Leipzig / Forschungsstelle für Vergleichende Ordensgeschichte (FOVOG), Technische Universität Dresden
Paper 153-a:	**Tradition Meets Creativity: The Ambiguous Lifestyle of the Order of St William** (Language: English) Jörg Sonntag
Paper 153-b:	**Memory and Mnemotechnics in Medieval Didactic Games** (Language: English) Sophie Caflisch, Institut für Historische Theologie, Universität Bern
Paper 153-c:	**Between Tradition and Creativity: The Rituals of the Teutonic Order** (Language: English) Nicholas W. Youmans, Forschungsstelle für Vergleichende Ordensgeschichte (FOVOG), Technische Universität Dresden

---

LUNCH

Meal Times

Refectory	12.00-14.00
University Square: The Marquee	12.00-14.00

See Map 9, p. 51.

---

* * * * *

THE CASALE PILGRIM: A JOURNEY INTO JEWISH VISUAL REPRESENTATIONS OF THE HOLY LAND

GALLERY TALK BY
MARCI FREEDMAN

PARKINSON BUILDING: TREASURES OF THE BROTHERTON GALLERY
13.00-14.00

Travel has been a ubiquitous feature within the Jewish world. Whether as merchants, scholars, pilgrims, or refugees, there have always been Jews on the move. The medieval world particularly saw a rise in pilgrimage, making it one of the most studied medieval institutions. Jewish travel has been accompanied by a small, but rich body of Jewish travel writing; nevertheless, these texts remain largely understudied. Amongst these is the Casale Pilgrim, an illustrated pilgrimage through the Holy Land, dated 1597-8. Leeds University Library Special Collections possesses the only known copy (Leeds University Library, Roth MS. 220) making it a true treasure. Part of the manuscript collection of the notable Jewish historian Cecil Roth, this talk will shed light on the Casale Pilgrim and its unique status within the tradition of Jewish travel literature. The manuscript comprises 85 illustrations and offers an artistic interpretation of Jewish holy sites. This talk seeks to address what sites remained important to Jewish travellers (and readers) at the close of the 16th century. It will draw links between the captions and visualisation of Jewish sacred space and how these sites were described and depicted. The talk will also address the roots of this Jewish visual tradition, drawing from parallels in the Christian and Islamic traditions. In offering a frame of reference for this unique manuscript, we will be able to place the Casale pilgrim within the fields of travel literature, 'mental pilgrimage', and illustrated Jewish manuscripts more widely.

Marci Freedman completed an MA in Medieval Studies at the University of Leeds before completing her PhD at the School of Arts, Languages & Cultures at the University of Manchester. Her research areas include textual and intellectual history, with a focus on Jewish travel literature, and knowledge exchange between Jewish and Christian cultures.

Special Collections houses over 200,000 rare books and 7 km of manuscripts and archives, including the celebrated Brotherton Collection. The Special Collections Reading Room is open from 09.00-17.00 during the IMC, and delegates are welcome to pursue their research and explore the collection. More details on how to search and use the collections can be found at https://library.leeds.ac.uk/special-collections.

Please note that admission to this event will be on a first-come, first-served basis as there will be no tickets. Please ensure that you arrive as early as possible to avoid disappointment.

* * * * *

Session:	**199** **Stage@leeds: Stage 1**
Title:	**KEYNOTE LECTURE 2018: THE METAPHORS THEY LIVED BY: VERBAL IMAGERY OF MEMORY IN THE MIDDLE AGES** (Language: English)
Speaker:	Farkas Gabor Kiss, Department for Early Hungarian Literature, Eötvös Loránd University, Budapest
Introduction:	Lucie Doležalová, Institute of Greek & Latin Studies, Univerzita Karlova, Praha and Jan Čermák, Department of English, Univerzita Karlova, Praha
Details:	*Recent research suggests that human cognition relies on metaphor systems in the process of thinking, and metaphors have a fundamental role in human perception and understanding by allowing the mind to construct complex social, cultural, and psychological realities. In this lecture, I will discuss the main medieval trends in metaphoric descriptions of the mental processes of reminiscing and memorisation, focusing on the medieval Western tradition. Everyday mnemonic practices were commonly described using highly sophisticated metaphorical language, as knowledge was supposed to be 'sent to the memory cell', 'impressed on the mind', 'elevated', or 'dilated into the mental space'. The metaphor systems of memory have radically changed from Late Antiquity to the late Middle Ages, and the 12th century marked a turning point in this process, closely reflecting the revival of Greco-Arabic medicine, meditative spirituality, and dialectic thinking. The lack of first-language competence in Latin eased the invention and the acceptance of metaphoric expressions by the speakers, which in turn catalysed the vernacular usage of these phrases. Although I will mainly focus on the evolution of the medieval Latin imagery of memory (using primarily texts from the Victorine school and scholasticism), Arabic, Greek, and other European vernacular traditions will be considered, too.* *Please note that admission to this event will be on a first-come, first-served basis as there will be no tickets. Please ensure that you arrive as early as possible to avoid disappointment.*

Session:	**201** **Baines Wing: Room 1.13**
Title:	**ANGLO-SAXON RIDDLES, II: PATTERNS AND RELATIONSHIPS**
Sponsor:	The Riddle Ages: An Anglo-Saxon Riddle Blog
Organiser:	Megan Cavell, Department of English Literature, University of Birmingham and Jennifer Neville, Department of English, Royal Holloway, University of London
Moderator:	Jennifer Neville
Paper 201-a:	**The Vercelli Book and Enigmatic Reading** (Language: English) Britt Mize, Department of English, Texas A&M University, College Station
Paper 201-b:	**The Awkward Ending of Riddles 21 and 58** (Language: English) Linden Currie, Department of English, Royal Holloway, University of London
Paper 201-c:	**Isidore's *Etymologiae*, Riddles, and the *Physiologus*: Exploring a Triple Connection in Anglo-Saxon England** (Language: English) Mercedes Salvador-Bello, Departamento de Literatura Inglesa y Norteamericana, Universidad de Sevilla

Session:	**202** **Michael Sadler Building: Banham Theatre**
Title:	**PAPERS IN HONOUR OF DEBBY BANHAM, II: ANGLO-SAXON MEDICINE AND AGRICULTURE - TEXT AND PRACTICE**
Organiser:	Christine Voth, Seminar für Englische Philologie, Georg-August-Universität Göttingen
Moderator:	Julia Crick, Department of History, King's College London
Paper 202-a:	**Transmission and Translation in a Late 11th-Century Copy of the *Herbarium*** (Language: English) Bethany Christiansen, Department of English, Ohio State University
Paper 202-b:	**Anglo-Saxon Superfoods** (Language: English) Christina Lee, School of English, University of Nottingham
Paper 202-c:	**Imagining and Re-Creating Anglo-Saxon Agricultural Protection Formulas** (Language: English) Karen L. Jolly, Department of History, University of Hawai'i at Mānoa

Session:	**203** **Baines Wing: Room 2.13**
Title:	**BYZANTINE THEOLOGY IN THE PALAIOLOGAN ERA: PALAMISM BEFORE, DURING, AND AFTER, I**
Organiser:	Tikhon Pino, Department of Theology, Marquette University, Wisconsin
Moderator:	Tikhon Pino
Paper 203-a:	**Palamism before Palamas: The *Filioque* and Byzantine Ecclesiology in the 13th and 14th Centuries** (Language: English) Dmitry Makarov, Department of General Humanities, Urals State Mussorgsky Conservatoire, Russia
Paper 203-b:	**Universals in the Thought of St Gregory Palamas** (Language: English) Dmitry Biriukov, Laboratory of Interdisciplinary Empirical Studies, National Research University Higher School of Economics, Perm
Paper 203-c:	**The Palamite Legacy in Joseph Bryennios** (Language: English) Basil Lourié, Faculty of Social Sciences & Humanities, National Research University Higher School of Economics, St Petersburg

Session: **204** **Baines Wing: Room 2.14**
Title: **AGE OF BEDE, I: SCRIPTURAL INTERACTIONS**
Sponsor: wordpress.bedenet.com
Organiser: Peter Darby, Department of History, University of Nottingham and Máirín MacCarron, Department of History, University of Sheffield
Moderator: Joyce Hill, School of English, University of Leeds
Paper 204-a: **Interactions with Hebrew in Early Anglo-Saxon England** (Language: English)
Damian Fleming, Department of English & Linguistics, Indiana University-Purdue University, Fort Wayne
Paper 204-b: **Bede and the Gospel of John** (Language: English)
Susan Cremin, Independent Scholar, Cork
Paper 204-c: **Bede and the *Vetus Latina*** (Language: English)
John Gallagher, School of English, University of St Andrews

Session: **205** **Fine Art Building: SR G.04**
Title: **SYMBOLISM AND CASTLES, I: DESIGNS OF INNOVATION, IMAGINATION, AND ROMANCE**
Sponsor: Institute of Medieval & Early Modern Studies, Durham University
Organiser: Heidi Richards, Department of Archaeology, Durham University
Moderator: Heidi Richards
Paper 205-a: **Geometry and the Cosmos: Castles as Symbols of Power** (Language: English)
David Rollason, Department of History, Durham University
Paper 205-b: **Gendering Privacy in the Late Medieval Female Residence** (Language: English)
Rachel Delman, Faculty of History, University of Oxford
Paper 205-c: **Castles, Magnificence, and the Display of Power** (Language: English)
Richard Barber, Boydell & Brewer, Woodbridge / Department of History, University of York

Session: **206** **University House: Beechgrove Room**
Title: **PASTORS OF ALL KINDS: ADAPTING PASTORAL CARE FOR LOCAL NEEDS ACROSS ENGLAND, FRANCE, AND GERMANY**
Organiser: Philippa Byrne, St John's College, University of Oxford and Rebecca Springer, Oriel College, University of Oxford
Moderator: Philippa Byrne
Paper 206-a: **Communicating Pastoral Care: What Priests Explained to Their Parishioners in 13th-Century England and France** (Language: English)
Felicity Hill, Corpus Christi College, University of Cambridge
Paper 206-b: **Teaching Pastoral Care in Southern Germany in the 13th Century: Evidence from Abbreviations of Raymond of Penafort's *Summa de Casibus*** (Language: English)
Emily Corran, Department of History, St John's College, University of Oxford
Paper 206-c: **'Preachers, doctors, and any of the elect': Religious Ministry by Lay People in 12th-Century England** (Language: English)
Rebecca Springer

Session:	**207** **Michael Sadler Building: Room LG.16**
Title:	**ALCOHOL AND ADDICTION IN MEDIEVAL LITERATURE**
Sponsor:	Scottish Medieval/Early Modern Studies Postgraduate Network (ScotMEMS)
Organiser:	Martin Laidlaw, Faculty of English, University of Dundee
Moderator:	Sophie Sexon, School of Critical Studies, University of Glasgow
Paper 207-a:	**Mead-iating Masculinity: The Mead-Hall, Drunkenness, and the Renegotiation of Anglo-Saxon Masculinities in the Long 10th Century** (Language: English) Ryan T. Goodman, Department of History, University of Manchester
Paper 207-b:	**'Dred delitable drynke': Alcohol, Memory, and Morality in Medieval Poetry** (Language: English) Martin Laidlaw
Paper 207-c:	**'Now and at the hour of our death': Marian Petitions as Expressions of Behavioural Addiction** (Language: English) Mark Ronan, School of English, Drama & Film, University College Dublin

Session:	**208** **Fine Art Building: Studio Ground Floor**
Title:	**MEDIEVAL BODIES: HUMAN AND ANIMAL**
Sponsor:	Onderzoeksschool Mediëvistiek, Rijksuniversiteit Groningen
Organiser:	Rob Meens, Departement Geschiedenis en Kunstgeschiedenis, Universiteit Utrecht
Moderator:	Rob Meens
Paper 208-a:	**The Valley of the Changing Sheep in the Middle Welsh Tale *Peredur ab Efrawc*** (Language: English) Kiki Calis, Departement Talen, Literatuur en Communicatie, Universiteit Utrecht
Paper 208-b:	**Dehumanising Humans, or Humanising Animals?: The Human-Animal Divide in the Late Middle Ages** (Language: English) Sven Gins, Afdeling Geschiedenis, Rijksuniversiteit Groningen
Paper 208-c:	**Developing a Culture of Sports and Physical Exercise in the Late Middle Ages and the Early Modern Period** (Language: English) Miente Pietersma, Afdeling Geschiedenis, Rijksuniversiteit Groningen

Session: **209** **Parkinson Building: Room 1.16**
Title: **Transcultural Approaches to the Bible: Exegesis and Historical Writing in the Medieval Worlds, II**
Sponsor: Bible & Historiography in Transcultural Iberian Societies, 8th-12th Centuries, Institut für Mittelalterforschung, Österreichische Akademie der Wissenschaften, Wien / FWF Project
Organiser: Matthias Martin Tischler, Institut d'Estudis Medievals, Universitat Autònoma de Barcelona
Moderator: Stefan Donecker, Institut für Mittelalterforschung, Österreichische Akademie der Wissenschaften, Wien
Paper 209-a: **The Chronicle of Sampiro, the Arabs, and the Bible: 11th-Century Christian-Iberian Strategies of Identifying the Cultural and Religious 'Other'** (Language: English)
Patrick Marschner, Institut für Mittelalterforschung, Österreichische Akademie der Wissenschaften, Wien
Paper 209-b: **The Armies of Gog and Magog?: Interpreting Nomadic Invasions as Apocalyptic Events in Western Christian, Eastern Christian, and Islamic Sources** (Language: English)
Nicholas E. Morton, School of Arts & Humanities, Nottingham Trent University
Paper 209-c: **How to Fit the 'Livs' into Sacred History?: Identifying the Cultural 'Other' in the Chronicles of the Livonian Crusade** (Language: English)
Peter Fraundorfer, Institut für Mittelalterforschung, Österreichische Akademie der Wissenschaften, Wien

Session: **210** **Maurice Keyworth Building: Room 1.04**
Title: **The Influence of Jacopo da Varagine's *Legenda aurea* on Homiletics and Hagiography in Later Medieval Europe**
Sponsor: Hagiography Society
Organiser: Carrie Beneš, Division of Social Sciences, New College of Florida
Moderator: M. Michèle Mulchahey, Pontifical Institute of Mediaeval Studies, University of Toronto, Downtown
Paper 210-a: **The *Legenda Aurea* and Dominican Preaching: A System of Communication** (Language: English)
Giovanni Paolo Maggioni, Scienze Umanistiche, Sociali e della Formazione, Universita degli Studi del Molise
Paper 210-b: **Gone but Not Forgotten: Saints Omitted from the *Legenda aurea*** (Language: English)
Samantha Kahn Herrick, Department of History, Syracuse University, New York
Paper 210-c: **Adapting the *Legenda aurea* for a Local Austrian Legendary: The *Pronunciamentum de sanctis* or *Legendarium austriacum minus*** (Language: English)
Manu Radhakrishnan, Institut für Mittelalterforschung, Österreichische Akademie der Wissenschaften, Wien

Session:	**211**	**Baines Wing: Room 2.16**
Title:	**WAS THERE AN 11TH CENTURY?, II: IDEAS**	
Sponsor:	Medieval & Ancient Research Centre (MARCUS), University of Sheffield	
Organiser:	Rory Naismith, Department of History, King's College London and Danica Summerlin, Department of History, University of Sheffield	
Moderator:	Danica Summerlin	
Paper 211-a:	**Male *Adolescentia* in the 11th Century: Some Chronicle Perspectives** (Language: English) Emily J. Ward, Darwin College, University of Cambridge	
Paper 211-b:	**Monastic Formation in the 11th Century: Transformation or Systematisation?** (Language: English) Micol Long, Vakgroep Geschiedenis, Universiteit Gent	
Paper 211-c:	**Subverting the Law?: Scribal Confusion and Legal Doctrine in the 11th Century** (Language: English) Christof Rolker, Institut für Geschichtswissenschaften und Europäische Ethnologie, Otto-Friedrich-Universität Bamberg	

Session:	**212**	**Charles Thackrah Building: 1.01**
Title:	**NETWORK ANALYSIS FOR MEDIEVAL STUDIES, II: THE DYNAMICS OF MEDIEVAL POLITICAL AND PERSONAL NETWORKS**	
Sponsor:	Department for the Study of Religions, Masarykova univerzita, Brno / Reframing the Legal & Historical Past in Late Medieval Scotland, AHRC Project	
Organiser:	David Zbíral, Department for the Study of Religions, Masarykova univerzita, Brno	
Moderator:	Nicolas Ruffini-Ronzani, Département d'histoire, Université de Namur	
Paper 212-a:	**The Dynamic Networks of a Royal Household: Scotland, 1222-1371** (Language: English) Matthew H. Hammond, Department of History, King's College London	
Paper 212-b:	**The Participation of Women (and Some Men) in Languedocian Catharism: A Network Science Perspective, II** (Language: English) David Zbíral	
Paper 212-c:	**Structural Balance: 'Political Factions' and Their Rapid Change in the 13th-Century Holy Roman Empire** (Language: English) Robert Gramsch-Stehfest, Historisches Institut, Friedrich-Schiller-Universität Jena	

Session:	**213**	**Baines Wing: Room 1.15**
Title:	**WOMEN AS LETTER WRITERS AND SCRIBES**	
Organiser:	IMC Programming Committee	
Moderator:	Rachel E. Moss, Corpus Christi College, University of Oxford	
Paper 213-a:	**Margaret Paston's Letters Changing or Not Changing: A Pragmatic Approach in the Analysis of Characters of the Topics in Her Letters** (Language: English) Osamu Ohara, Department of English, Jikei University School of Medicine, Tokyo	
Paper 213-b:	***In memoriam*: The Selwerd Scribe, c. 1470-1490** (Language: English) Merlijn Lotte Krommenhoek, Independent Scholar, Rouveen	
Paper 213-c:	**'How onkynde so euer I haue ben...let me know your mynde': Grievances Remembered, Kindnesses Manipulated, and Charities Sought - Emergence of Female Memory and Identity in Middle English Material Culture** (Language: English) Kenna L. Olsen, Department of English, Mount Royal University, Alberta	

Session:	**214** **Michael Sadler Building: Room LG.17**
Title:	**GENDER, NETWORKS, AND COMMUNITY IN LEGAL SOURCES, II: WORDS AND DEEDS**
Organiser:	Aysu Dinçer, Department of History, University of Warwick and Chiara Ravera, Department of History, University of Nottingham
Moderator:	Denise Bezzina, Centro interuniversitario di ricerca di storia del notariato (NOTARIORUM ITINERA), Università degli Studi di Genova
Paper 214-a:	**Verbal Violence and Gender in Communal Italy: Bologna in the Later Middle Ages** (Language: English) Chloé Tardivel, Laboratoire Identités, Cultures, Territoires (EA337), Université Paris Diderot - Paris 7
Paper 214-b:	**Women in Wills in Genoese Chios between the Late 14th Century and the Early 16th Century** (Language: English) Chiara Ravera
Paper 214-c:	**Women's Voices in Male Script: A Perspective from Medieval Notarial Sources of Porto** (Language: English) Ricardo Seabra, Centro de Investigação Transdisciplinar 'Cultura, Espaço e Memória' (CITCEM) / Faculdade de Letras, Universidade do Porto

Session:	**215** **Michael Sadler Building: Rupert Beckett Theatre**
Title:	**DISTAFF, II: FRENCH DRESSING**
Sponsor:	Discussion, Interpretation & Study of Textile Arts, Fabrics & Fashions (DISTAFF)
Organiser:	Gale R. Owen-Crocker, Department of English & American Studies, University of Manchester
Moderator:	Elizabeth Coatsworth, Institute for Research & Innovation in Art & Design (MIRIAD), Manchester Metropolitan University
Paper 215-a:	**The Mantle Is Not a Cloak: When, Where, and How Nobles Wore Mantles in Old French Literature** (Language: English) Monica L. Wright, Department of Modern Languages, University of Louisiana, Lafayette
Paper 215-b:	**Dressing to Deceive: Cross-Dressing and Identity in Old French Fabliaux** (Language: English) Vanessa Wright, Institute for Medieval Studies, University of Leeds
Paper 215-c:	**The Crusader's Return** (Language: English) Tina Anderlini, Independent Scholar, Russange

Session: **216** **University House: Little Woodhouse Room**
Title: **NEW APPROACHES TO MANUSCRIPTS AND LIBRARIES**
Organiser: IMC Programming Committee
Moderator: Lisa Fagin Davis, Medieval Academy of America, Massachusetts
Paper 216-a: ***Labeculae Vivae*: A Reference Library of Stains Found on Medieval Manuscripts** (Language: English)
Alberto Campagnolo, Preservation Research & Testing Division, Library of Congress, Washington DC and Erin Connelly, Schoenberg Institute for Manuscript Studies, University of Pennsylvania
Paper 216-b: **Get Your Library Card: Medieval Patrons of Medieval Libraries** (Language: English)
Elizabeth Linville, School of Library & Information Studies, University of Alberta
Paper 216-c: **Proteomic Parchment Identification: Cambridge, Trinity College O.3.57** (Language: English)
Natalie Louise James, Independent Scholar, Leeds
Paper 216-d: **The Effect of Digitisation on the Construction of Memory** (Language: English)
Keri Thomas, Independent Scholar, Aberystwyth

Session: **217** **Baines Wing: Room 1.14**
Title: **CHANGE AND CONTINUITY IN 10TH CENTURY WESTERN EUROPE, I: THE RESOURCES OF CENTRAL AUTHORITIES, THE IDENTITIES OF LOCAL LEADERS**
Sponsor: Marie Skłodowska-Curie Action Project 'Central Authority & Local Strength in the Early Middle Ages: Comparing Social Complexity in Northern Iberia & Central Italy (8th-10th Centuries)'
Organiser: Igor Santos Salazar, Departamento de Geografía, Prehistoria y Arqueología, Universidad del País Vasco - Euskal Herriko Unibertsitatea
Moderator: Iñaki Martín Viso, Departamento de Historia Medieval, Moderna y Contemporánea, Universidad de Salamanca
Paper 217-a: **Rulers and Resources in 10th-Century Iberia** (Language: English)
Robert Portass, School of History & Heritage, University of Lincoln
Paper 217-b: **Teofilatto or Teodora?: Women's Roles in the Construction of the Identity and Power of Roman Families** (Language: English)
Maddalena Betti, Dipartimento di Scienze Umane, Sociali e della Salute, Università di Cassino e del Lazio
Paper 217-c: **'Omnia disponebat ut soliti sunt modo Romani facere': Fiscal Lands, Private Wealth, and the Archbishop of Ravenna, 850-950** (Language: English)
Igor Santos Salazar

Session: **218** **Maurice Keyworth Building: Room 1.09**
Title: **THE LATE ANTIQUE EMPRESS, I: IMPERIAL WOMEN BETWEEN COURT POLITICS AND 'BARBARIAN' KINGS**
Sponsor: Women's Classical Committee / Medieval & Ancient Research Centre, University of Sheffield (MARCUS)
Organiser: Julia Hillner, Department of History, University of Sheffield and Victoria Leonard, Institute of Classical Studies, University of London
Moderator: Richard Flower, Department of Classics & Ancient History, University of Exeter
Paper 218-a: **Reviewing the Roles of 4th-Century Imperial Women: The Case of Justina** (Language: English)
Belinda Washington, Independent Scholar, Edinburgh
Paper 218-b: **Galla Placidia as 'Human Gold': Consent and Autonomy in the Early 5th-Century Western Mediterranean** (Language: English)
Victoria Leonard
Paper 218-c: **Return of the Confined Empress: The Burial of Verina** (Language: English)
Margarita Vallejo-Girvés, Departamento de Historia y Filosofía, Universidad de Alcalá de Henares, Madrid

Session: **219** **Social Sciences Building: Room 10.05**
Title: **URBAN LITERACY IN MEDIEVAL DENMARK**
Sponsor: Urban Literacy Research Network, Danish Research Council / Danish Centre for Urban History
Organiser: Jeppe B. Netterstrøm, Institut for Kultur og Samfund, Aarhus Universitet
Moderator: Jeppe B. Netterstrøm
Paper 219-a: **Runic Writing in Medieval Denmark** (Language: English)
Lisbeth Imer, National Museum of Denmark, København
Paper 219-b: **Urban Literacy in the Archaeological Record** (Language: English)
Morten Søvsø, Sydvestjyske Museer, Ribe
Paper 219-c: **Urban Vernacular Literacy in Denmark before 1400: A Marker of Ethnicity?** (Language: English)
Kasper H. Andersen, Afdeling for Historie og Klassiske Studier, Aarhus Universitet

Session: **220** **Social Sciences Building: Room 10.06**
Title: **WORDS, ORIGINS, AND TRADITIONS IN EARLIER MEDIEVAL ENGLISH TEXTS**
Organiser: IMC Programming Committee
Moderator: Katherine Miller, Institute for Medieval Studies, University of Leeds
Paper 220-a: **Reconstructing Memory: Digitising Mercian Dialect Analysis in *Beowulf*** (Language: English)
Berber Bossenbroek, Faculteit der Geesteswetenschappen, Universiteit Leiden
Paper 220-b: **The Old English Vocabulary of Sacrifice** (Language: English)
Roland Brennan, Department of English, University College London
Paper 220-c: **Synonyms for 'Man' and 'Warrior' in Laȝamon's 'Brut': A Memory of Tradition?** (Language: English)
Maria Volkonskaya, Faculty of Humanities, National Research University Higher School of Economics, Moscow

Session:	**221** **Charles Thackrah Building: 1.02**
Title:	**REMEMBERING THE TROUBADOURS IN THE CROWN OF ARAGON: MAPPING, MANUSCRIPTS, AND NARRATIVE**
Sponsor:	Association Internationale d'Études Occitanes (AIEO), Montpellier
Organiser:	Catherine E. Léglu, Graduate Centre for Medieval Studies, University of Reading
Moderator:	Catherine E. Léglu
Paper 221-a:	**Geopolitical Memory: Mapping the Catalan Chansonniers** (Language: English) Miriam Cabré, Institut de Llengua i Cultura Catalanes, Universitat de Girona
Paper 221-b:	**Remembering the 'Ancient' Troubadours: Memory and Interpretation of Troubadour Lyrics in Occitan Treatises** (Language: English) Sadurní Martí, Institut de Llengua i Cultura Catalanes, Universitat de Girona
Paper 221-c:	**Le Viatge al Purgatori de sanct Patrici par Ramon de Perelhos: une autobiographie restée dans les mémoires** (Language: Français) Marine Mazars, Département Lettres Modernes, Cinéma et Occitan, Université Toulouse-Jean Jaurès
Paper 221-d:	**A Remembrance of Things Past: Blandin de Cornoalha and the Armagnac Family** (Language: English) Wendy Pfeffer, Department of Classical & Modern Languages, University of Louisville, Kentucky / Centre d'Études Supérieures de la Renaissance, Tours

Session:	**222** **Maurice Keyworth Building: Room 1.32**
Title:	**MNEMONICS IN WORD AND IMAGE, I**
Sponsor:	Huygens ING, De Koninklijke Nederlandse Akademie van Wetenschappen
Organiser:	Seb Falk, Girton College, University of Cambridge, Amanda Gerber, Department of English, University of California, Los Angeles and Irene A. O'Daly, Huygens Instituut voor Nederlandse Geschiedenis, Koninklijke Nederlandse Academie van Wetenschappen (ING - KNAW), Amsterdam
Moderator:	Laura Cleaver, Department of History of Art & Architecture, Trinity College Dublin
Paper 222-a:	**Cues as Clues: Reconstructing the Use of Stemmatic Diagrams in the Medieval Classroom** (Language: English) Irene A. O'Daly
Paper 222-b:	**Verses to Remember and Diagrams to Forget: The Case of Aristotle's Figures** (Language: English) Ayelet Even-Ezra, Department of History, The Hebrew University of Jerusalem
Paper 222-c:	***Dispositio* and the Art of Memory in Sermons of Mikołaj of Błonie, c. 1400-c. 1448** (Language: English) Lidia Grzybowska, Faculty of Polish Studies, Jagiellonian University, Kraków

Session: **223** **Maurice Keyworth Building: Room 1.06**
Title: **RECLAIMING THE MIDDLE AGES FOR AFRICA, II: MEDIEVAL MALI AND THE INDIAN OCEAN**
Sponsor: Fakultät für Geschichtswissenschaft, Ruhr-Universität Bochum
Organiser: Verena Krebs, Historisches Institut, Ruhr-Universität Bochum and Adam Simmons, Department of History, Lancaster University
Moderator: Meseret Oldjira, Department of Art & Archaeology, Princeton University
Paper 223-a: **Human-Environment Interaction in Indian Ocean Africa, c. 800-c. 1300: A Neglected Theme in Global History** (Language: English)
Gwyn Campbell, Indian Ocean World Centre (IOWC), McGill University, Québec
Paper 223-b: **Timbuktu: A Forgotten Medieval Knowledge Centre** (Language: English)
Tahar Abbou, Departement d'Anglais, Université d'Adrar, Algeria
Paper 223-c: **'Per l'abondànçia de l'or': Metalwork Techniques and the Kingdom of Mali** (Language: English)
Sarah Guérin, Department of the History of Art, University of Pennsylvania

Session: **224** **Maurice Keyworth Building: Room 1.31**
Title: **MEMORY AND CONQUEST: THE NORMANS IN THE SOUTH**
Sponsor: Department of History, Lancaster University
Organiser: John Aspinwall, Department of History, Lancaster University
Moderator: John Aspinwall
Paper 224-a: **The Conquest of Sicily: From Memory to Written Record?** (Language: English)
Alex Metcalfe, Department of History, Lancaster University
Paper 224-b: **The Norman Conquest of Palermo: Gates and the Tradition of Remembrance** (Language: English)
Theresa Jäckh, Transkulturelle Studien, Ruprecht-Karls-Universität Heidelberg
Paper 224-c: **Muslim Soldiers in Roger II's Armies** (Language: English)
Aron Kecskes, School of History, University of St Andrews

Session: **225** **Michael Sadler Building: Room LG.19**
Title: **FROM MYTH TO MEMORY: THE LOST MEDIEVAL LIBRARIES OF CHARTRES**
Sponsor: Institut de Recherche et d'Histoire des Textes (IRHT), Centre National de la Recherche Scientifique (CNRS), Paris / Renaissance virtuelle des manuscrits brûlés de Chartres Project
Organiser: Joanna Frońska, Institut de Recherche et d'Histoire des Textes (IRHT), Centre National de la Recherche Scientifique (CNRS), Paris
Moderator: Isabelle Bretthauer, Centre de recherches archéologiques et historiques anciennes et médiévales (CRAHAM - UMR 6273), Université de Caen Normandie
Paper 225-a: **Remembering the Beginnings of a Lost Library: The Case of Saint-Père-en-Vallée** (Language: English)
Veronika Drescher, Institut d'Études Médiévales, Université de Fribourg
Paper 225-b: **The New Chapter Library of Chartres and the Binding Campaign of 1415** (Language: English)
Claudia Rabel, Institut de Recherche et d'Histoire des Textes (IRHT), Centre National de la Recherche Scientifique (CNRS), Paris
Paper 225-c: **Augustin Dupuy's Inventory of c. 1600: Imagining Space of the Chapter Library of Chartres** (Language: English)
Joanna Frońska

Session:	**226** **Social Sciences Building: Room 10.07**
Title:	**WOMEN'S STRATEGIES OF MEMORY, II: VISUAL STRUCTURES OF MEMORY**
Organiser:	Lucy Allen, Newnham College, University of Cambridge and Emma Bridget O'Loughlin Bérat, Institut für Anglistik, Amerikanistik und Keltologie, Rheinische Friedrich-Wilhelms-Universität Bonn
Moderator:	Lucy Allen
Paper 226-a:	**'Do not forget me if you live longer than me': Strategies of Memory in the Construction of a Prayerbook from Vadstena Abbey** (Language: English) David Carrillo-Rangel, Institut de Recerca de Cultures Medievals, Universitat de Barcelona
Paper 226-b:	**Cassandra's Reconstructed Memory: Page Design and Fatalism in *Troilus and Criseyde*** (Language: English) Ruen-chuan Ma, Department of English & Literature, Utah Valley University
Paper 226-c:	**Lamenting Susanna: Iconography, Sarcophagi, and the Art of Memorial** (Language: English) Catherine Gines Taylor, Department of Ancient Scripture, Brigham Young University, Utah

Session:	**227** **Baines Wing: Room 1.16**
Title:	**MEMORY IN TOLKIEN'S MEDIEVALISM, II**
Sponsor:	Cardiff Metropolitan University
Organiser:	Dimitra Fimi, Department of Humanities, Cardiff Metropolitan University
Moderator:	Andrew Higgins, Independent Scholar, Brighton
Paper 227-a:	**Tolkien Remembering Tolkien: Textual Memory in the 1977 *Silmarillion*** (Language: English) Gergely Nagy, Independent Scholar, Budapest
Paper 227-b:	**Remembering and Forgetting: National Identity Construction in Tolkien's Middle-Earth** (Language: English) Sara Brown, Independent Scholar, Conwy
Paper 227-c:	**Longing to Remember, Dying to Forget: Memory and Monstrosity** (Language: English) Penelope Holdaway, Department of Humanities, Cardiff Metropolitan University
Paper 227-d:	**'Forgot even the stones': Stone Monuments and Imperfect Cultural and Personal Memories in *The Lord of the Rings*** (Language: English) Kristine Larsen, Department of Geological Sciences, Central Connecticut State University

Session: **228** **Emmanuel Centre: Wilson Room**
Title: **BETWEEN MEMORY AND IMAGINATION, II: JEWISH ENGAGEMENTS FROM ETHIOPIA TO THE PERSIANATE WORLD**
Sponsor: Arc Humanities Press
Organiser: Alexandra F. C. Cuffel, Centrum für Religionswissenschaftliche Studien, Ruhr-Universität Bochum
Moderator: Irven Resnick, Department of Philosophy & Religion, University of Tennessee, Chattanooga
Paper 228-a: **The Attitude towards Christianity and Islam in the Early Judeo-Persian Bible Exegesis** (Language: English)
Ofir Haim, Mandel School for Advanced Studies / Department of Middle Eastern & Islamic Studies, Hebrew University of Jerusalem
Paper 228-b **Whose Persecution Is It Anyway?: The Death of Yazdgird in Persian, Jewish, and Syriac Christian Memory?** (Language: English)
Simcha Gross, Department of History, University of California, Irvine
Paper 228-c: **The Impact of Betä ɜsra'el (Ethiopian Jewish): Christian Interaction on the Development of Betä ɜsra'el Holy Sites in the Səmen Mountains** (Language: English)
Bar Kribus, Institute of Archaeology, Hebrew University of Jerusalem / Centrum für Religionswissenschaftliche Studien, Ruhr-Universität Bochum

Session: **229** **Michael Sadler Building: Room LG.10**
Title: **MEMORIES OF THE ANGLO-SAXON MISSION**
Organiser: Thijs Porck, Centre for the Arts in Society, Universiteit Leiden
Moderator: James Palmer, St Andrews Institute of Mediaeval Studies, University of St Andrews
Paper 229-a: **Willibrord's Companions: Remembering and Inventing Anglo-Saxon Missionaries on the Continent** (Language: English)
Thijs Porck
Paper 229-b: **Apostle, Preacher, Mentor, Martyr: Remembering Boniface in Medieval *Vitae*** (Language: English)
Shannon Godlove, Department of English, Columbus State University, Georgia
Paper 229-c: **The Anglo-Saxon Mission: Memory, Kinship, and the Motivations of History** (Language: English)
Harold C. Zimmerman, Department of English, Indiana University Southeast

Session:	**230**	**Charles Thackrah Building: 1.03**

Title: **MYSTICAL MEMORIES, II: IS THE MEMORY MYSTICAL? - REFLECTIONS ON MIND AND BODY**
Sponsor: Institute for the Study of Spirituality, KU Leuven / Ruusbroecgenootschap, Universiteit Antwerpen
Organiser: Rob Faesen, Institute for the Study of Spirituality, KU Leuven / Ruusbroecgenootschap, Universiteit Antwerpen
Moderator: John Arblaster, Institute for the Study of Spirituality, KU Leuven / Ruusbroecgenootschap, Universiteit Antwerpen
Paper 230-a: **The Making and Un-Making of the World: *Memoria*, Apophasis, and Pain in the Works of Ruusbroec** (Language: English)
Sander Vloebergs, Institute for the Study of Spirituality, KU Leuven
Paper 230-b: **Desire, Memory, and Hope in John of the Cross** (Language: English)
Edward William Howells, Heythrop College, University of London
Paper 230-c: **Memory as 'Inwardness' (*Er-innerung*): Neoplatonism (Plotin), Mysticism (Meister Eckhart), and Idealism (Hegel)** (Language: English)
Andrés Quero-Sánchez, Max-Weber-Kolleg für kultur- und sozialwissenschaftliche Studien, Universität Erfurt

---

Session:	**231**	**Maurice Keyworth Building: Room 1.05**

Title: **MEMORY AND COMMUNITY, II**
Sponsor: Centre d'Études Supérieures de Civilisation Médiévale (CESCM), Université de Poitiers / Centre Nationale de la Recherche Scientifique (CNRS), Institute for Medieval Studies, Leeds
Organiser: Estelle Ingrand-Varenne, Centre d'Études Supérieures de Civilisation Médiévale (CESCM), Université de Poitiers / Centre National de la Recherche Scientifique (CNRS), Paris
Moderator: Emilia Jamroziak, Institute for Medieval Studies / School of History, University of Leeds
Paper 231-a: **Singing Memory in Byzantium: The Duty of Liturgic Memorialisation in Cenobitic Monasteries, 9th-15th Centuries** (Language: English)
Marie-Emmanuelle Torres, Laboratoire d'archéologie médiévale et moderne en Méditerranée (LA3M - UMR 7298), Aix-Marseille Université / Centre National de la Recherche Scientifique (CNRS), Paris
Paper 231-b: **Collective Memory Loss and Shifting Heterodox Identities in Two Vernacular Textual Communities of the Late 12th Century** (Language: English)
Vladimir Agrigoroaei, Centre d'Études Supérieures de Civilisation Médiévale (CESCM), Université de Poitiers / Centre National de la Recherche Scientifique (CNRS), Paris
Paper 231-c: **Nuns on the Periphery?: Irish Dominican Sisters, Memory, History, and Assimilation in Late Medieval Lisbon** (Language: English)
Andrea Knox, Department of History, Northumbria University

Session: **232** **Social Sciences Building: Room 10.09**
Title: **BRITISH ARCHAEOLOGICAL ASSOCIATION, II: MONASTIC MEMORY - ARCHITECTURE AND ITS IMPORTANCE TO THE MONASTIC LIFE**
Sponsor: British Archaeological Association
Organiser: Harriet Mahood, Graduate Centre for Medieval Studies, University of Reading
Moderator: Lindy Grant, Department of History, University of Reading
Paper 232-a: **Performance and Commemoration in the Chapter House of Saint-Georges-de-Boscherville, I** (Language: English)
Kathleen Nolan, Wetherill Visual Arts Center, Hollins University, Virginia
Paper 232-b: **Performance and Commemoration in the Chapter House of Saint-Georges-de-Boscherville, II** (Language: English)
Susan L. Ward, Department of Art & Architectural History, Rhode Island School of Design
Paper 232-c: **Understanding the Monastic Life through 'La Sainte Abbaye'** (Language: English)
Harriet Mahood

Session: **233** **Leeds University Union: Room 2 - Elland Road**
Title: **REMEMBERING THE VIKING AGE AROUND THE IRISH SEA, II: ECCLESIASTICAL ENCOUNTERS**
Sponsor: ISMARN: The Irish Sea in the Middle Ages Research Network
Organiser: Lindy Brady, Department of English, University of Mississippi
Moderator: Alex Woolf, St Andrews Institute of Mediaeval Studies, University of St Andrews
Paper 233-a: **Remembering the Viking Age while It's Still Going On: The Gosforth Cross as an 11th-Century Antiquarian Exercise** (Language: English)
Victoria Whitworth, School of History, Classics & Archaeology, Newcastle University
Paper 233-b: **From the Land of Ice and Snow: Case Studies of Viking Settlement and Religious Interaction in the Irish Sea Area** (Language: English)
Danica Ramsey-Brimberg, Department of History, University of Liverpool
Respondent: Charles Insley, Department of History, University of Manchester

---

Session: **234** **Leeds University Union: Room 4 - Hyde Park**
Title: **HONOUR, FAMILY, AND COLLECTIVE MEMORY IN ENGLAND AND GERMANY, 1250-1500: THE COUNTRY AND THE CITY**
Sponsor: Department of History, Durham University
Organiser: Christian Liddy, Department of History, Durham University
Moderator: Craig D. Taylor, Centre for Medieval Studies, University of York
Paper 234-a: **Shields of Chivalry and History: Grants of Arms and the Visual Communication of Corporate Identity in England and Germany** (Language: English)
Marcus Meer, Department of History, Durham University
Paper 234-b: **The Scrope versus Grosvenor Controversy: A 'matter of common fame and report'** (Language: English)
Rhiannon Elizabeth Snaith, Department of History, Durham University
Paper 234-c: **Family, Lineage, and Dynasty in the Late Medieval City** (Language: English)
Christian Liddy

Session: **235** **Leeds University Union: Room 5 - Kirkstall Abbey**
Title: **MEMORY AND THE MATERIALITY OF MEDIEVAL TEXTS, II: BOOKS AND BEYOND**
Sponsor: Centre for Medieval Studies, University of Bristol
Organiser: Benjamin Pohl, Department of History, University of Bristol
Moderator: Leah Tether, Department of English, University of Bristol
Paper 235-a: **Creating Meanings beyond Words: Interplay of Pictorial Sources in Manuscripts of the *Estoire Del Saint Graal*, c. 1275-1315** (Language: English)
Miha Zor, Department of Art History, University of Ljubljana
Paper 235-b: **Stick Together around the King: Memory of the Coronation in the Time of Charles V** (Language: English)
Pamela Nourrigeon, Centre d'Études Supérieures de Civilisation Médiévale (CESCM), Université de Poitiers
Paper 235-c: **Trying to Remember Who Invented Perpendicular Architecture: The *Tabulae* of William Malvern, Abbot of Gloucester** (Language: English)
Richard Fisher, Faculty of Arts, University of Bristol

Session: **236** **Charles Thackrah Building: 1.04**
Title: **CONFLICTING MEMORIES: NAVIGATING CONFLICT AND CREATING CONSENSUS IN THE MEDIEVAL WORLD, I - REMEMBERING BODIES**
Organiser: Kieran Ball, Faculty of History, Trinity College, University of Oxford
Moderator: David Addison, Mansfield College, University of Oxford
Paper 236-a: **Memory, Warfare, and the Anglo-Saxon Landscape** (Language: English)
Andrew Holland, Queen's College, University of Oxford
Paper 236-b: **Recollecting Corineus's Contribution to the Founding of Britain** (Language: English)
Timothy J. Nelson, Department of English, University of Arkansas, Fayetteville
Paper 236-c: **In Script and Stone: A Bellicose Civic Lord and the (Re)Building of Memory and Reputation in Late 13th-Century Italy** (Language: English)
Lorenzo Caravaggi, Balliol College, University of Oxford

Session: **237** **Maurice Keyworth Building: Room 1.03**

Title: **REMEMBERING AND FORGETTING THE ANCIENT CITY, II: BEING A CITY**

Sponsor: ERC Project 'The Impact of the Ancient City'

Organiser: Javier Martínez-Jiménez, Faculty of Classics, University of Cambridge and Sam Ottewill-Soulsby, Faculty of Classics, University of Cambridge

Moderator: Caroline Goodson, Faculty of History, University of Cambridge

Paper 237-a: **Factors of Promotion and Demotion of Cities in Late Antique Spain** (Language: English)
Pablo C. Díaz Martínez, Departamento de Prehistoria, Historia Antigua y Arqueología, Universidad de Salamanca and Pablo Poveda Arias, Departamento de Prehistoria, Historia Antigua y Arqueología, Universidad de Salamanca

Paper 237-b: **'Civitatem Seguntinam? Madinat Šigūnsa?': Legends, Memories, and Archaeologies of a Current Town in Central Iberia during the Early Middle Ages** (Language: English)
Ricardo Barbas Nieto, Departamento de Geografía Humana, Universidad Complutense de Madrid and Guillermo García-Contreras, Facultad de Filosofía y Letras, Universidad de Granada

Paper 237-c: **Wealth and the City in 7th- to 9th-Century Rome and Ravenna** (Language: English)
Thomas Langley, Faculty of History, University of Cambridge

Session: **238** **Maurice Keyworth Building: Room 1.33**

Title: **EDUCATION AND SOCIETY: SCHOOLS, TEACHERS, AND PUPILS IN THE MEDIEVAL WORLD**

Organiser: Sarah Bridget Lynch, Department of History, Angelo State University, Texas

Moderator: Christine E. Meek, Department of History, Trinity College Dublin

Paper 238-a: **'Princeps erudire ac bonis moribus imbutere': Cultural, Moral, and Civic Education in Giorgio Valagussa's Elite Teaching Experience** (Language: English)
Federico Piseri, Dipartimento di Studi Umanistici, Università degli Studi di Pavia

Paper 238-b: **Educating Citizens: Grammar and Abacus Teaching in the Italian Cities from the 13th to the 15th Century** (Language: English)
Stefania Zucchini, Dipartimento di Lettere - Lingue, Letterature e Civiltà antiche e moderne, Università degli Studi di Perugia

Paper 238-c: **Education and Schooling in Late Medieval French Wills** (Language: English)
Sarah Bridget Lynch

Session: **239** **University House: Great Woodhouse Room**
Title: **Memory and the Construction of History**
Organiser: IMC Programming Committee
Moderator: Trevor Russell Smith, Institute for Medieval Studies, University of Leeds
Paper 239-a: **Constructing the Future and the Past: Prophecy and Memory in Adam Usk's *Chronicle*** (Language: English)
Henry Marsh, Department of History, University of Exeter
Paper 239-b: **Prophecy and Identity in Adam Usk's *Chronicle*** (Language: English)
Jennifer Ruggier, Faculty of History, University of Cambridge
Paper 239-c: **Gendered Body Politic and the Construction of Czech Historical Memory** (Language: English)
Věra Soukupová, Department of History, University of Ostrava / Department of Czech History, Univerzita Karlova, Praha
Paper 239-d: **Politics of Abduction and 'Sites of Memory' in the So-Called *Dalimil's Chronicle*** (Language: English)
Martin Šorm, Centre for Medieval Studies / Institute of Philosophy, Czech Academy of Sciences, Praha / Department of Czech History, Univerzita Karlova, Praha

Session: **240** **Leeds University Union: Room 6 - Roundhay**
Title: **Monarchy and Memory, II: Queenship and Memory in Western Europe**
Sponsor: Royal Studies Network
Organiser: Gabrielle Storey, Department of History, University of Winchester
Moderator: Chloë McKenzie, Department of History, University of Southampton
Paper 240-a: **Legacy through Religious Patronage: Philippa of Hainault and St Katherine's by the Tower** (Language: English)
Louise Tingle, School of History, Archaeology & Religion, Cardiff University
Paper 240-b: **Remembering Isabella: The Post-Medieval Creation of a She-Wolf** (Language: English)
Michael Evans, Faculty of Social Science, Delta College, Michigan
Paper 240-c: **Empress Adelheid, Queen Mathilda, and Abbess Mathilda of Quedlinburg: Ottonian Queens and the Creation of their Memories, Memoirs, and Memorials in Germany and Italy** (Language: English)
Penelope Joan Nash, Medieval & Early Modern Centre, University of Sydney
Paper 240-d: **The Two Bodies of the Monarch: Remembering Mary Stuart in Popular and Academic Media** (Language: English)
Cathleen Sarti, Historisches Seminar, Johannes Gutenberg-Universität Mainz

Session: **241** **Parkinson Building: Nathan Bodington Chamber**

Title: **REMEMBERING *ADMONITIO*: EPISCOPAL CRITICISM OF RULERS IN THE MIDDLE AGES, II**

Organiser: Ryan Kemp, Department of History & Welsh History, Aberystwyth University

Moderator: Jinty Nelson, Department of History, King's College London

Paper 241-a: **Admonishing Bishops in the Late 7th and the Early 9th Century: A Comparison** (Language: English)
Steffen Patzold, Seminar für Mittelalterliche Geschichte, Eberhard-Karls-Universität Tübingen

Paper 241-b: **'Tecum et propter te nobis est sermo, domne rex': Bishops Directly Addressing the King** (Language: English)
Dominik Waßenhoven, Historisches Institut, Universität zu Köln

Paper 241-c: **How to Admonish a King: Bishops as Critics in 11th-Century Germany and England** (Language: English)
Alheydis Plassmann, Institut für Geschichtswissenschaft, Rheinische Friedrich-Wilhelms-Universität Bonn

Respondent: Mayke de Jong, Utrecht Centre for Medieval Studies, Universiteit Utrecht

Session: **242** **Baines Wing: Room G.37**

Title: **FAME: PATRONS AND MEMORIES IN BYZANTIUM, II**

Organiser: Francisco Lopez-Santos Kornberger, Centre for Byzantine, Ottoman & Modern Greek Studies, University of Birmingham and Jessica Varsallona, Centre for Byzantine, Ottoman & Modern Greek Studies, University of Birmingham

Moderator: Francesca Dell'Acqua, Centre for Byzantine, Ottoman & Modern Greek Studies, University of Birmingham

Paper 242-a: **'We renewed the memory of the blessed founder': A Mausoleum for the Palaiologoi?** (Language: English)
Jessica Varsallona

Paper 242-b: **Cap in Hand: The Church of Jerusalem and the Pre-Crusader West** (Language: English)
Daniel K. Reynolds, Centre for Byzantine, Ottoman & Modern Greek Studies, University of Birmingham

Paper 242-c: **Short Memory?: The Use of Stucco Spolia in Late Byzantine Buildings of Mistra and the Epiros** (Language: English)
Flavia Vanni, Centre for Byzantine, Ottoman & Modern Greek Studies, University of Birmingham

Session: **243** **Stage@leeds: Stage 3**

Title: **CRUSADES AND MEMORY, II : ART AND MATERIAL CULTURE**

Organiser: Pagona Papadopoulou, School of History & Archaeology, Aristotle University of Thessaloniki

Moderator: Scott Redford, Department of History of Art & Archaeology, School of Oriental & African Studies, University of London

Paper 243-a: **Foundation Legends: Memory and Authority in the Art of the Latin Kingdom of Jerusalem** (Language: English)
Gil Fishhof, Department of Art History, University of Haifa

Paper 243-b: **Between Remembrance and Necessity in Crusader-Period Architecture** (Language: English)
Rebecca Darley, Department of History, Classics & Archaeology, Birkbeck, University of London

Paper 243-c: **Coins and Seals in the Crusader Period and Beyond** (Language: English)
Pagona Papadopoulou

Session: **244** **Fine Art Building: SR 1.10**
Title: **PILGRIM LIBRARIES, II: REMEMBERING PILGRIMAGE AND PILGRIMS**
Sponsor: Leverhulme International Research Network 'Pilgrim Libraries - Books & Reading on the Medieval Routes to Rome & Jerusalem'
Organiser: Philip Booth, Department of History, Politics & Philosophy, Manchester Metropolitan University
Moderator: Laura Grazia Di Stefano, Department of History, University of Nottingham
Paper 244-a: **Ricoldus de Monte Crucis and His Ideal Reader** (Language: English)
Martin M. Bauer, Institut für Sprachen und Literaturen, Universität Innsbruck
Paper 244-b: **Who Is This Guy?: Remembering Pilgrims in the Later Medieval Period** (Language: English)
Philip Booth

Session: **245** **Baines Wing: Room G.36**
Title: **MEMORY AND MIGRATIONS, I: IMPACT OF THE MEMORABLE**
Sponsor: MIGWEB: A Comparative Diachronic Analysis of Post-Byzantine Networks in Early Modern Europe (15th-18th Centuries), Department of History, Royal Holloway, University of London / Marie Skłodowska Curie Action Project
Organiser: Jonathan Harris, Department of History, Royal Holloway, University of London
Moderator: Felicitas Schmieder, Historisches Institut, FernUniversität Hagen
Paper 245-a: **Spectacle and Propaganda in the Visit of a Patriarch of Antioch to England, 1466-1467** (Language: English)
Jonathan Harris
Paper 245-b: **'Ignorant barbarians, infected by schism': Perceptions of Balkan Migrants in Italy, 15th-17th Centuries** (Language: English)
Niccolò Fattori, Department of History, Royal Holloway, University of London
Paper 245-c: **Starry-Eyed Tristram: *Tristrams saga*, Norse Astronomical Vocabulary, and Arab Astronomical Knowledge in 13th-Century Norway - Was It Just a Rumsfeldian 'known unknown'?** (Language: English)
Roderick McDonald, Independent Scholar, Sheffield
Respondent: Mihailo Popović, Institut für Mittelalterforschung, Abteilung Byzanzforschung, Österreichische Akademie der Wissenschaften, Wien

Session:	**246**	**Emmanuel Centre: Room 10**
Title:	**REMEMBERING JERUSALEM IN CENTRAL EUROPE**	
Organiser:	Lenka Panušková, Institute of Art History, Czech Academy of Sciences, Praha	
Moderator:	Sara Offenberg, Department of the Arts, Ben-Gurion University of the Negev, Beer-Sheva	
Paper 246-a:	**Old Czech Duke Ernst as a Quest for Surrogate Centre** (Language: English) Matouš Jaluška, Institute of Czech Literature, Czech Academy of Sciences, Praha	
Paper 246-b:	**How to Transfer the Holy Land Reality?: Pilgrim Accounts as Vehicles of Holy Land Transmission in the Late 15th Century** (Language: English) Jaroslav Svátek, Centre for Medieval Studies, Univerzita Karlova, Praha	
Paper 246-c:	**Heavenly Jerusalem as a Diagram: Symbolics in Devotional Practices** (Language: English) Lenka Panušková	
Paper 246-d:	**Memory of a Pilgrim: An Instrument of Urban Community Representation** (Language: English) Vojtěch Bažant, Institute of Philosophy, Czech Academy of Sciences, Praha / Faculty of Arts, Univerzita Karlova, Praha	

Session:	**247**	**Baines Wing: Room 2.15**
Title:	**AUGUSTINE AND ANSELM ON MEMORY, WILL, AND GOD**	
Sponsor:	Institute for Saint Anselm Studies, Saint Anselm College, New Hampshire / International Association for Anselm Studies	
Organiser:	Montague Brown, Department of Philosophy, Saint Anselm College, New Hampshire	
Moderator:	Montague Brown	
Paper 247-a:	**Augustine on God's Presence to Memory and Will** (Language: English) Montague Brown	
Paper 247-b:	**'Without which it is never free': Free Will and Justice in Anselm** (Language: English) Bernd Goebel, Lehrstuhl der Philosophie und Geschichte der Philosophie, Theologische Fakultät Fulda	
Paper 247-c:	**The Theological and Anthropological Function of Memory in Anselm's Thought** (Language: English) Ian Logan, Blackfriars Hall, University of Oxford	

Session: **248** **University House: St George Room**
Title: **MINOR ANNALS, I: ALTERNATIVE VOICES IN FRANKISH HISTORIOGRAPHY**
Organiser: Sören Kaschke, Historisches Institut, Universität zu Köln and Bart Jeremy van Hees, Departement Geschiedenis en Kunstgeschiedenis, Universiteit Utrecht
Moderator: Ricky Broome, Leeds Institute for Clinical Trials Research (LICTR), University of Leeds
Paper 248-a: **Documents of Saxon Violence: The Saxon Wars in the Frankish Minor Annals** (Language: English)
Robert Flierman, Utrecht Centre for Medieval Studies, Universiteit Utrecht
Paper 248-b: **Christian Language in the Frankish 'Minor' Annals: Reception and Rejection** (Language: English)
Robert A. H. Evans, Sidney Sussex College / Christ Church, University of Cambridge
Paper 248-c: **Minor Annals in a Major Historiographical Compendium: The Case of Rome, Biblioteca Apostolica Vaticana, Reg. Lat. 213** (Language: English)
Bart Jeremy van Hees

Session: **249** **University House: Cloberry Room**
Title: **RE-ENACTMENT AND MEDIEVAL STUDIES, II: PROBLEMS AND POTENTIAL**
Organiser: Melissa Venables, School of English, University of Nottingham
Moderator: Melissa Venables
Paper 249-a: **Commerce is a Foreign Country: Can Conflicting Imperatives Be Reconciled?** (Language: English)
Timothy Dawson, Independent Scholar, Leeds
Paper 249-b: **Persona Development: Experimental Micro-History in Medieval Recreation** (Language: English)
Marcello Napolitano, Department of History, Trinity College Dublin
Respondent: Sara L. Uckelman, Institute of Medieval & Early Modern Studies, Durham University

Session: **250** **Michael Sadler Building: Room LG.15**
Title: **SCIENTIFIC, EMPIRICAL, BIBLICAL, AND HAGIOGRAPHICAL KNOWLEDGE IN THE MIDDLE AGES, II: WATER AND SEA BETWEEN SCIENCE AND RELIGION**
Sponsor: School of Arts, English & Languages, Queen's University Belfast
Organiser: Marilina Cesario, School of Arts, English & Languages, Queen's University Belfast
Moderator: Sarah Baccianti, School of Arts, English & Languages, Queen's University Belfast
Paper 250-a: **One Ocean, Many Seas: Representing the Waters of the Earth on 11th-Century Maps** (Language: English)
Margaret Tedford, School of Arts, English & Languages, Queen's University Belfast
Paper 250-b: **The Sea in the Old English *Orosius*** (Language: English)
Helen Appleton, Balliol College, University of Oxford
Paper 250-c: **Baptism at the Red Sea: Exodus Echoes in Old English Poetry** (Language: English)
Elisa Ramazzina, School of Arts, English & Languages, Queen's University Belfast

Session: **251** **Emmanuel Centre: Room 11**

Title: **INTEGRATING THE SASANIANS, II: PAST, PRESENT, AND FUTURE IN LATE ANTIQUE AND MEDIEVAL IRAN**

Sponsor: MPS - Middle Persian Studies, Universidade de Brasília / Sonderforschungsbereiche Project 'Visions of Community', Österreichische Akademie der Wissenschaften, Universität Wien

Organiser: Otávio Luiz Vieira Pinto, Middle Persian Studies Project, Universidade de Brasília

Moderator: Mark Humphries, Centre for Medieval & Early Modern Research (MEMO), Swansea University

Paper 251-a: **Take a Seat: The Throne Image from the Achaemenids to the *Shahnameh*** (Language: English)
Eve MacDonald, School of History, Archaeology & Religion, Cardiff University

Paper 251-b: **For Love of the Gazelles: The Story of Adizeh and Bahram Gur between the Sasanians and the Mongols** (Language: English)
Lloyd Llewellyn-Jones, School of History, Archaeology & Religion, Cardiff University

Paper 251-c: **Sitting on the Throne of Yazdegird: Political Power and the Sassanian Legacy in the North-East Caucasus** (Language: English)
John Latham-Sprinkle, Department of History, School of Oriental & African Studies, University of London

Session: **252** **Stage@leeds: Stage 2**

Title: **ENGLAND AND SCOTLAND AT PEACE AND WAR IN THE LATER MIDDLE AGES, II**

Organiser: Claire Etty, Oxford English Dictionary, Oxford University Press and Andy King, Department of History, University of Southampton

Moderator: David Green, Centre for British Studies, Harlaxton College, University of Evansville

Paper 252-a: **A Chapter of Woe: The Anglo-Scots Battle of Myton, 1319** (Language: English)
Paul R. Dryburgh, The National Archives, Kew

Paper 252-b: **Rebels or National Enemy?: English Perceptions of the Status of Their Scottish Adversaries** (Language: English)
Andy King

Paper 252-c: **Affinities across the Border in the Reigns of Henry VIII and James V** (Language: English)
Claire Etty

Session:	**253** **Stage@leeds: Stage 1**
Title:	**CREATIVE MEMORIES: SHAPING IDENTITY IN MEDIEVAL CULTURE, II**
Sponsor:	Sächsische Akademie der Wissenschaften zu Leipzig / Forschungsstelle für Vergleichende Ordensgeschichte (FOVOG), Technische Universität, Dresden
Organiser:	Mirko Breitenstein, Sächsische Akademie der Wissenschaften zu Leipzig / Forschungsstelle für Vergleichende Ordensgeschichte (FOVOG), Technische Universität Dresden
Moderator:	Gert Melville, Forschungsstelle für Vergleichende Ordensgeschichte (FOVOG), Technische Universität Dresden
Paper 253-a:	**Making History: The Remembrance of the Beginnings within the Pauline Order** (Language: English) Mirko Breitenstein
Paper 253-b:	**Changing *Memoria*: Adapted Donor Portraits in Late Medieval Art** (Language: English) Johanna Scheel, Kunstgeschichtliches Institut, Philipps-Universität Marburg
Paper 253-c:	**Memories of Emotional Communities in the Medieval City** (Language: English) Katrin Rösler, Forschungsstelle für Vergleichende Ordensgeschichte (FOVOG), Technische Universität Dresden

Session:	**254** **Maurice Keyworth Building: Room G.02**
Title:	**TEACHING THE CRUSADES IN AN AGE OF WHITE NATIONALISM: A ROUND TABLE DISCUSSION**
Organiser:	Susanna A. Throop, Department of History, Ursinus College, Pennsylvania
Moderator:	David Perry, Department of History, University of Minnesota, Twin Cities
Purpose:	*In recent years, resurgent white nationalists have taken their message to the streets and online, directly invoking the Crusades as a historical precedent and inspiration. As a result, teaching the Middle Ages and the Crusades especially has become unavoidably infused with contemporary political overtones. In this round table, scholars from different disciplinary and institutional perspectives will discuss how the history of the Crusades is being harnessed by white nationalist movements, consider how this does and should affect the way we teach the Crusades, and suggest some ways to address these issues as well as to extend discussions of race, religion, and transcultural networks in the medieval world.* *Participants include Chris Chism (University of California, Los Angeles), Matthew Gabriele (Virginia Technical Institute), Basit Hammad Qureshi (Macalester College, Minnesota), Kristin Skottki (Universität Bayreuth), Carol Symes (University of Illinois, Urbana-Champaign), Susanna Throop (Ursinus College, Pennyslvania), and Cord Whitaker (Wellesley College, Massachusetts).*

TEA BREAK: 15.45-16.30

Tea and Coffee will be served at the following locations:

Maurice Keyworth Building: Foyer
Michael Sadler Building: Foyer
Parkinson Building: Bookfair
University Square: The Marquee

See Map 7, p. 44.

Session: **302** **Michael Sadler Building: Banham Theatre**
Title: **PAPERS IN HONOUR OF DEBBY BANHAM, III: ANGLO-SAXON MEDICINE - VOCABULARY, ANATOMY, AND CONDITIONS**
Organiser: Christine Voth, Seminar für Englische Philologie, Georg-August-Universität Göttingen
Moderator: Faith Wallis, Department of History & Classical Studies / Department of Social Studies of Medicine, McGill University, Québec
Paper 302-a: **The Anglo-Saxon Spleen** (Language: English)
Carole Biggam, School of Critical Studies (English Language), University of Glasgow
Paper 302-b: **Gut Feelings and Belly Aches: Internal Anatomy in Old English with Specific Reference to *Bald's Leechbook*** (Language: English)
Conan Turlough Doyle, Independent Scholar, Dublin
Paper 302-c: **Fertility and Infertility in Anglo-Saxon England** (Language: English)
Christine Voth

Session: **303** **Baines Wing: Room 2.13**
Title: **BYZANTINE THEOLOGY IN THE PALAIOLOGAN ERA: PALAMISM BEFORE, DURING, AND AFTER, II**
Organiser: Tikhon Pino, Department of Theology, Marquette University, Wisconsin
Moderator: Tikhon Pino
Paper 303-a: **The Divine Simplicity According to St Gregory Palamas** (Language: English)
Marcus Plested, Department of Theology, Marquette University, Wisconsin
Paper 303-b: **The Concept of Spiritual Perception in (Proto-)Hesychastic Thought: Diadochos of Photiki, Niketas Stethatos, and Gregory Palamas** (Language: English)
Mikonja Knežević, Faculty of Philosophy, University of Priština, Kosovska Mitrovica
Paper 303-c: **St Maximos the Confessor and the Theology of Hesychasm** (Language: English)
Maximos Constas, Department of Patristics, Hellenic College Holy Cross Greek Orthodox School of Theology, Massachusetts

Session: **304** **Baines Wing: Room 2.14**
Title: **AGE OF BEDE, II: COMMUNICATIVE INTERACTIONS**
Sponsor: wordpress.bedenet.com
Organiser: Peter Darby, Department of History, University of Nottingham and Máirín MacCarron, Department of History, University of Sheffield
Moderator: Rory Naismith, Department of History, King's College London
Paper 304-a: **The Letters of Bede** (Language: English)
Peter Darby
Paper 304-b: **Bede, the Papacy, and Justinian, II: Interactions between Sources in the Early 8th Century** (Language: English)
Sihong Lin, Department of History, University of Manchester
Paper 304-c: **Language, Identity, and Communication in the Age of Bede** (Language: English)
Francesca Tinti, Departamento de Historia Medieval, Moderna y de América, Universidad del País Vasco - Euskal Herriko Unibertsitatea, Vitoria-Gasteiz

Session: **305** **Fine Art Building: SR G.04**
Title: **SYMBOLISM AND CASTLES, II: LANDSCAPES OF CHIVALRY AND ROMANCE**
Sponsor: Institute of Medieval & Early Modern Studies, Durham University
Organiser: Heidi Richards, Department of Archaeology, Durham University
Moderator: David Rollason, Department of History, Durham University
Paper 305-a: **Castles and the Chivalric Landscape: Constructing Aristocratic Space between Image and Reality** (Language: English)
Oliver Creighton, Department of Archaeology, University of Exeter
Paper 305-b: **Peeking into the Privy Garden: Courtly Love, Romance, and Chivalry** (Language: English)
Heidi Richards
Paper 305-c: **Dunstanburgh: Stronghold or Symbol** (Language: English)
Al Oswald, Department of Archaeology, University of York

Session: **307** **Michael Sadler Building: Room LG.16**
Title: **REGIONAL HISTORY AS A DECISIVE INDICATOR OF SOCIAL CHANGE: FRANCONIA IN THE MIDDLE AGES**
Sponsor: Lehrstuhl für Fränkische Landesgeschichte, Julius-Maximilians-Universität Würzburg
Organiser: John D. Young, Department of Humanities, Flagler College, Florida
Moderator: Helmut Flachenecker, Institut für Geschichte, Julius-Maximilians-Universität Würzburg
Paper 307-a: **A Fruitful Partnership: Jews and the Canons of St Kilian in 12th-Century Würzburg** (Language: English)
John D. Young
Paper 307-b: **Outsiders and Locals: Urban Classes in the Imperial City of Rothenburg** (Language: English)
Markus Naser, Institut für Geschichte, Julius-Maximilians-Universität Würzburg
Paper 307-c: **Peasants and Citizens: The Peasants' War of 1525** (Language: English)
Benjamin Heidenreich, Institut für Geschichte, Julius-Maximilians-Universität Würzburg

---

Session: **308** **Fine Art Building: Studio Ground Floor**
Title: **DISABLED ANIMALS**
Sponsor: MAD (Medieval Animal Data Network)
Organiser: Alice Choyke, Department of Medieval Studies, Central European University, Budapest
Moderator: Gerhard Jaritz, Department of Medieval Studies, Central European University, Budapest
Paper 308-a: **Care or Neglect?: Medieval Animals and the Osteological Paradox** (Language: English)
László Bartosiewicz, Institutionen för arkeologi och antikens kultur, Stockholms universitet
Paper 308-b: **Peredur's Old Horse and Other Dysfunctional Animals in the *Mabinogion*: Reception, Adaptation, and Pedagogic Potential** (Language: English)
Anastasija Ropa, Faculty of Humanities, University of Latvia, Riga
Paper 308-c: **Appreciation of Disabled Animals: The Perception of Lame Horses in Song-Yuan China** (Language: English)
Zhexin Xu, Fachbereich Geschichte, Universität Salzburg

Session: **309** **Parkinson Building: Room 1.16**
Title: **TRANSCULTURAL APPROACHES TO THE BIBLE: EXEGESIS AND HISTORICAL WRITING IN THE MEDIEVAL WORLDS, III**
Sponsor: Bible & Historiography in Transcultural Iberian Societies, 8th-12th Centuries, Institut für Mittelalterforschung, Österreichische Akademie der Wissenschaften, Wien / FWF Project
Organiser: Matthias Martin Tischler, Institut d'Estudis Medievals, Universitat Autònoma de Barcelona
Moderator: Graeme Ward, Institut für Mittelalterforschung, Österreichische Akademie der Wissenschaften, Wien
Paper 309-a: **Vincentius the Mozarab and His Manuscript** (Language: English)
Geoffrey K. Martin, Department of History, College of Charleston, South Carolina
Paper 309-b: **Reframing Salvific History in a Transcultural Society: Iberian Bibles as Models of Historical, Prophetic, and Eschatological Writing** (Language: English)
Matthias Martin Tischler
Paper 309-c: **The Bible of Vic (1268) and the Disputation of Barcelona (1263): Textual and Theological Value of Its Hebrew Bible Glosses** (Language: English)
Eulàlia Vernet i Pons, Departament de Ciències de l'Antiguitat i de l'Edat Mitjana, Universitat Autònoma de Barcelona

Session: **310** **Maurice Keyworth Building: Room 1.04**
Title: **BEYOND THE *LEGENDA AUREA*: JACOPO DA VARAGINE AS PREACHER, HISTORIAN, AND ARCHBISHOP**
Sponsor: Hagiography Society
Organiser: Carrie Beneš, Division of Social Sciences, New College of Florida
Moderator: Paola Guglielmotti, Dipartimento di Antichità, Filosofia e Storia, Università degli studi di Genova
Paper 310-a: **Exempla for Sunday Preaching: An Edition of Jacopo da Varagine's *Sermones de tempore*** (Language: English)
Laura Mastrantuono, CIHAM - Histoire, archéologie, littératures des mondes chrétiens et musulmans médiévaux (UMR 5648), Université Lyon 2
Paper 310-b: **The *Chronica civitatis Ianuensis*: Rethinking Jacopo da Varagine's Genoa** (Language: English)
Denise Bezzina, Centro interuniversitario di ricerca di storia del notariato (NOTARIORUM ITINERA), Università degli Studi di Genova
Paper 310-c: **Between Hagiography and Local History: Jacopo da Varagine's Genoese Relic Treatises** (Language: English)
Carrie Beneš

Session: **311** **Baines Wing: Room 1.16**
Title: **'NEW' TOLKIEN: EXPANDING THE CANON**
Sponsor: Cardiff Metropolitan University
Organiser: Dimitra Fimi, Department of Humanities, Cardiff Metropolitan University
Moderator: Dimitra Fimi
Paper 311-a: **'I will give you a name': Sentient Objects in Tolkien's Fiction** (Language: English)
J. Patrick Pazdziora, College of Liberal Arts, Shantou University, China
Paper 311-b: **Tolkien's 'The Lay of Aotrou and Itroun' and *The Lay of Leithian*** (Language: English)
Yvette Kisor, Salameno School of Humanities and Global Studies, Ramapo College of New Jersey
Paper 311-c: **Invented Language and Invented Religion: Tolkien's Innovative Symbolic Systems and New Religious Movements** (Language: English)
Nathan Fredrickson, Department of Religious Studies, University of California, Santa Barbara
Paper 311-d: **The Grammar of Historical Memory in Tolkien's Legendarium: *The Tale of Beren and Lúthien*** (Language: English)
Christian F. Hempelmann, Department of Literature & Languages, Texas A&M University, Commerce and Robin Anne Reid, Department of Literature & Languages, Texas A&M University, Commerce

Session: **312** **Charles Thackrah Building: 1.01**
Title: **NETWORK ANALYSIS FOR MEDIEVAL STUDIES, III: NETWORKS OF MANUSCRIPTS, AUTHORS, AND AUTHORITIES**
Sponsor: Department for the Study of Religions, Masarykova univerzita, Brno
Organiser: David Zbíral, Department for the Study of Religions, Masarykova univerzita, Brno
Moderator: Johannes Preiser-Kapeller, Institut für Mittelalterforschung, Abteilung Byzanzforschung, Österreichische Akademie der Wissenschaften, Wien
Paper 312-a: **Glosses to the First Book of the *Etymologies* as a Case Study in Early Medieval Intellectual Networks** (Language: English)
Evina Steinová, Pontifical Institute of Mediaeval Studies, University of Toronto, Downtown
Paper 312-b: **Networks in the Czech Reformation: The Case of the Lay Chalice** (Language: English)
Petra Mutlová, Department of Classical Studies, Masarykova univerzita, Brno
Paper 312-c: **Metadata for the Middle Ages: A Network Analysis of Manuscriptorium.com** (Language: English)
Zdenko Vozár, Department for the Study of Religions, Masarykova univerzita, Brno

Session: **313** **Baines Wing: Room 1.15**
Title: **GENDER QUEERING THE MEDIEVAL: TRANS AND NON-BINARY NARRATIVES AND READINGS**
Sponsor: Society for the Study of Homosexuality in the Middle Ages
Organiser: Sophie Sexon, School of Critical Studies, University of Glasgow
Moderator: Blake Gutt, Department of French, University of Cambridge
Paper 313-a: **Cross-Dressing and Saintly Bodies in Ælfic's *Lives of Saints*** (Language: English)
Rachel Evans, School of English, University of Leicester
Paper 313-b: **Joan's Gender in Celluloid: The Filmic Joan of Arc as Transhistorical 'Transgender Warrior'** (Language: English)
Andrew Seager, Department of Film Studies, University of Dundee
Paper 313-c: **Transhistorical Absence: Applying Modern Theory to Bodies Missing from Memory** (Language: English)
Sophie Sexon

Session: **314** **Michael Sadler Building: Room LG.17**
Title: **GENDER, NETWORKS, AND COMMUNITY IN LEGAL SOURCES, III: AGENCY AND REPRESENTATION**
Organiser: Aysu Dinçer, Department of History, University of Warwick and Chiara Ravera, Department of History, University of Nottingham
Moderator: Anna Rich-Abad, Department of History, University of Nottingham
Paper 314-a: **Law and Gender: A Micro-Historical Approach to Women in Portuguese Legal Actions during Fernando I's Kingship, 1367-1383** (Language: English)
Francisco José Díaz Marcilla, Instituto de Estudos Medievais, Universidade Nova de Lisboa
Paper 314-b: **Women's Agency in Pisan Notarial Documents in the 14th Century** (Language: English)
Sylvie Duval, CIHAM - Histoire, archéologie, littératures des mondes chrétiens et musulmans médiévaux (UMR 5648), Université Lyon 2
Paper 314-c: **'How to catch a wife': Marriage and 'Unmarriage' in 15th-Century Famagusta** (Language: English)
Aysu Dinçer

Session: **315** **Michael Sadler Building: Rupert Beckett Theatre**
Title: **DISTAFF, III: ASPECTS OF MEMORY IN MEDIEVAL TEXTILES AND GARMENTS**
Sponsor: Discussion, Interpretation & Study of Textile Arts, Fabrics & Fashions (DISTAFF)
Organiser: Nahum Ben-Yehuda, Department of Land of Israel Studies & Archaeology, Bar-Ilan University, Ramat Gan and Gale R. Owen-Crocker, Department of English & American Studies, University of Manchester
Moderator: Nahum Ben-Yehuda
Paper 315-a: **Memory and Identity through Medieval Castilian Dress and Textiles** (Language: English)
María Barrigón, Departamento de Conservación, Palacio Real, Patrimonio Nacional, Madrid
Paper 315-b: **Patterns of Textile Consumption in Medieval Portugal** (Language: English)
Joana Isabel Sequeira, Centro de Investigação Transdisciplinar 'Cultura, Espaço e Memória' (CITCEM), Universidade do Porto
Paper 315-c: **Egyptian Monks and Nuns: Different Garments for Different Occasions in Late Roman, Byzantine, and Early Medieval Arab Periods** (Language: English)
Maria Mossakowska-Gaubert, Saxo-Instituttet, Københavns Universitet
Paper 315-d: **Construction and Reconstruction of the Past** (Language: English)
Git Skoglund, Independent Scholar, Göteborg

Session: **316** **University House: Little Woodhouse Room**
Title: **IMPERIAL PERSONNEL IN LATE ANTIQUITY: NEW DIRECTIONS**
Organiser: Jeroen W.P. Wijnendaele, Vakgroep Geschiedenis, Universiteit Gent
Moderator: Mark Humphries, Centre for Medieval & Early Modern Research (MEMO), Swansea University
Paper 316-a: **Towards a Prosopography of Roman Frontier Soldiers at the End of Antiquity** (Language: English)
Conor Whately, Department of Classics, University of Winnipeg, Manitoba
Paper 316-b: ***Agentes* of Control: The Roles and Authority of the *agentes in rebus*** (Language: English)
Stuart McCunn, Department of Classics, University of Nottingham
Paper 316-c: **'Quis custodiet ipsos custodes?': Bodyguards and Political Murder in Early Byzantium** (Language: English)
Jeroen W.P. Wijnendaele

Session: **317** **Baines Wing: Room 1.14**
Title: **CHANGE AND CONTINUITY IN 10TH-CENTURY WESTERN EUROPE, II: ARCHAEOLOGICAL RECORD AND HISTORIC EXPLANATION**
Sponsor: Instituto de Estudos Medievais, Universidade Nova de Lisboa
Organiser: Catarina Tente, Instituto de Estudos Medievais, Universidade Nova de Lisboa
Moderator: Catarina Tente
Paper 317-a: **Viking Elites in the 10th Century** (Language: English)
Frode Iversen, Kulturhistorisk museum, Universitetet i Oslo
Paper 317-b: **Assembly Practices in 10th-Century England: Continuities and Innovations in the Landscape of Governance** (Language: English)
Stuart Brookes, Institute of Archaeology, University College London
Paper 317-c: **Hay una arqueología del campesinado del siglo X?** (Language: Español)
Juan Antonio Quirós Castillo, Facultad de Letras, Universidad del País Vasco - Euskal Herriko Unibertsitatea, Vitoria-Gasteiz

Session: **318** **Maurice Keyworth Building: Room 1.09**
Title: **THE LATE ANTIQUE EMPRESS, II: HOW TO READ, WRITE, AND VIEW IMPERIAL WOMEN**
Sponsor: Women's Classical Committee / Medieval & Ancient Research Centre, University of Sheffield (MARCUS)
Organiser: Julia Hillner, Department of History, University of Sheffield and Victoria Leonard, Institute of Classical Studies, University of London
Moderator: Robin Whelan, Department of History, University of Liverpool
Paper 318-a: **Empress, Interrupted: Writing the Biography of a Late Antique Imperial Woman** (Language: English)
Julia Hillner
Paper 318-b: **Women on the Move: Representations of Imperial Women and Urban Space in Late Antique Rome and Constantinople** (Language: English)
Robert Heffron, Department of History, University of Sheffield
Paper 318-c: **Late Antique Empresses and the Queen of Heaven: On the Correlation between Sacred and Secular in the Imagery of a Female Potentate** (Language: English)
Maria Lidova, British Museum, London / Wolfson College, University of Oxford

Session: **319** **Social Sciences Building: Room 10.05**
Title: **ORALITY AND TEXT**
Organiser: IMC Programming Committee
Moderator: Anna Adamska, Onderzoeksinstituut voor Geschiedenis en Kunstgeschiedenis, Universiteit Utrecht
Paper 319-a: **Lacking Memory: Widukind of Corvey's Claim to Have Used Oral Tradition and Saxon Propagandistic Historiography** (Language: English)
Harald Kleinschmidt, Graduate School of International Political Economy, University of Tsukuba, Japan
Paper 319-b: **Hildegard's Botany: Literary Tradition, Oral Tradition, or Divine Inspiration?** (Language: English)
Helga Ruppe, Department of Modern Languages & Literatures, University of Western Ontario
Paper 319-c: **Distinguishing Orality through Emotions: The Textual Transmission of *Ami et Amile*** (Language: English)
Hailey Ogle, St Andrews Institute of Mediaeval Studies / School of Modern Languages, University of St. Andrews

Session: **320** — **Social Sciences Building: Room 10.06**
Title: **WEST MEETS EAST IN MIDDLE ENGLISH ROMANCE**
Organiser: IMC Programming Committee
Moderator: Amy Louise Morgan, School of Literature & Languages, University of Surrey
Paper 320-a: **The Romance of Gilbert and Matilda: Genre and Rhetoric in the *Life of Thomas Becket*** (Language: English)
Tristan B. Taylor, Department of English, University of Saskatchewan
Paper 320-b: **'Where the way is ful sondy': Memorialising the Levant in Middle English Romances** (Language: English)
Brandon Katzir, Department of English, Oklahoma City University
Paper 320-c: **Perceptions of *memoria viva* in the Romances of Medieval England and in the *Darüşşifa* of Gevher Nesibe** (Language: English)
Hülya Tafli Düzgün, School of English, Erciyes University, Turkey

Session: **321** — **Charles Thackrah Building: 1.02**
Title: **MEMORY AS ETHICAL REFASHIONING IN POETRY**
Organiser: IMC Programming Committee
Moderator: Catherine J. Batt, Institute for Medieval Studies, University of Leeds
Paper 321-a: **Memory, Will, and Ethics in Juan Ruiz's *Libro de Buen Amor*** (Language: English)
Kevin Poole, Department of Humanities, Pontifical College Josephinum, Ohio
Paper 321-b: **Powerlessness: Redeeming the Memory of Trauma in *Patience*** (Language: English)
Jane Beal, Department of English, University of La Verne, California
Paper 321-c: **Take Down That Statue?: Wrongful Collective Memory and Ugolino della Gherardesca** (Language: English)
Dena Arguelles, Department of English, Seton Hall University, New Jersey

Session: **322** — **Maurice Keyworth Building: Room 1.32**
Title: **MNEMONICS IN WORD AND IMAGE, II**
Sponsor: Huygens ING, De Koninklijke Nederlandse Akademie van Wetenschappen
Organiser: Seb Falk, Girton College, University of Cambridge, Amanda Gerber, Department of English, University of California, Los Angeles and Irene A. O'Daly, Huygens Instituut voor Nederlandse Geschiedenis, Koninklijke Nederlandse Academie van Wetenschappen (ING - KNAW), Amsterdam
Moderator: Philipp Nothaft, All Souls College, University of Oxford
Paper 322-a: **Drawn, Diagrammed, and Versified: The Various Guises of Scientific Mnemonics in Classical Commentaries** (Language: English)
Amanda Gerber
Paper 322-b: **Diagrams in Pseudo-Lullian Alchemy** (Language: English)
Marlis Hinckley, King's College, University of Cambridge
Paper 322-c: **Astronomical Mnemonics in Late Medieval Monasteries** (Language: English)
Seb Falk

Session: **323** **Baines Wing: Room 2.16**
Title: **REMEMBERING HOLY BODIES IN THE 12TH AND 13TH CENTURIES**
Sponsor: Prato Consortium for Medieval & Renaissance Studies, Monash University, Victoria
Organiser: Peter Francis Howard, Centre for Medieval & Renaissance Studies, Monash University, Victoria
Moderator: Peter Francis Howard
Paper 323-a: **Owning the Madonna: The Madonna of Le Puy and Political Control, 1000-1200** (Language: English)
Mimi Petrakis, Centre for Medieval & Renaissance Studies, Monash University, Victoria
Paper 323-b: **Lives of Saints and Landscapes: Strategic Uses of the Natural World in 12th-Century German Hagiography** (Language: English)
Hannah Ellen Skipworth, Centre for Medieval & Renaissance Studies, Monash University, Victoria
Paper 323-c: **The Political Use of a Provençal Saint's Body: Commemorating the Violence Done to Douceline of Digne, 1215-1274** (Language: English)
Jennifer Lord, Centre for Medieval & Renaissance Studies, Monash University, Victoria

Session: **324** **Maurice Keyworth Building: Room 1.31**
Title: **THE CHRONICLING OF CONQUEST IN THE NORMAN SOUTH**
Sponsor: Department of History, Lancaster University
Organiser: John Aspinwall, Department of History, Lancaster University
Moderator: Graham A. Loud, School of History, University of Leeds
Paper 324-a: **'From an ancient and corrupt hand': The Role of Memory in the Early Modern Manuscript Transmission of the *Cronica Roberti Biscardi*** (Language: English)
John Aspinwall
Paper 324-b: **The Norman Conquest in the Historiography of Post-Norman Southern Italy** (Language: English)
Jakub Kujawiński, Institute of History, Adam Mickiewicz University, Poznań / Department of History, University of Helsinki

Session: **325** **Michael Sadler Building: Room LG.19**
Title: **'SOMETHING WICKED THIS WAY COMES'?: MEMORIES OF MAGICIANS AND WITCHES**
Organiser: IMC Programming Committee
Moderator: Daisy Black, School of Humanities, University of Wolverhampton
Paper 325-a: **'Darke corners and garden allyes': London's Forgotten Magical Underworld** (Language: English)
Tabitha Stanmore, Department of History, University of Bristol
Paper 325-b: **The Cultural Construction of the Witch's Mind and Memory in Early America and Medieval England** (Language: English)
William Arguelles, Graduate Center, City University of New York

Session: **326** **Social Sciences Building: Room 10.07**
Title: **WOMEN'S STRATEGIES OF MEMORY, III: SHAPING THE POLITICAL LANDSCAPE**
Organiser: Lucy Allen, Newnham College, University of Cambridge and Emma Bridget O'Loughlin Bérat, Institut für Anglistik, Amerikanistik und Keltologie, Rheinische Friedrich-Wilhelms-Universität Bonn
Moderator: Theresa Earenfight, Department of History, Seattle University
Paper 326-a: **Women, Memory, Nostalgia, and the Translation of Byzantine Visual Culture after 1453** (Language: English)
Lana Sloutsky, Massachusetts College of Art & Design / Hellenic College Holy Cross Greek Orthodox School of Theology, Massachusetts / Museum of Fine Arts, Boston
Paper 326-b: **Forgetting Ælfthryth at Wherwell Abbey** (Language: English)
Cynthia Turner Camp, Department of English, University of Georgia, Athens
Paper 326-c: **Performing Dynastic Memory in 14th-Century France: Jeanne de Bourgogne (d. 1348) - Capetian Princess and Valois Queen** (Language: English)
Juliana Amorim Goskes, Department of History, New York University

---

Session: **327** **Maurice Keyworth Building: Room G.02**
Title: **CREATING THE MEDIEVAL STUDIES WE WANT TO REMEMBER: A ROUND TABLE DISCUSSION**
Organiser: Eva Frojmovic, Centre for Jewish Studies, University of Leeds and Catherine E. Karkov, School of Fine Art, History of Art & Cultural Studies, University of Leeds
Moderator: Catherine E. Karkov
Purpose: *While much important and paradigm-changing work has been done by medievalists on issues of race, gender, disability, ethics, postcolonial, and trauma theory, it is clear that we are experiencing a backlash against work on these and related topics, on the medievalists who work on them, and on our attempts to diversify our field. The problems are, of course, not limited to medieval studies, or even to academia. Medievalists have often been in the forefront of speaking out and working for change, and in this spirit we will discuss not only what is being done, but also what more we can do to work together to change our field and culture for the better.*

Participants include Roland Betancourt (University of California, Irvine), Eva Frojmovic (University of Leeds), Vincent van Gerven Oei (punctum books, Tirana), and Anna Klosowska (Miami University, Ohio).

Session: **328** **Emmanuel Centre: Wilson Room**
Title: **BETWEEN MEMORY AND IMAGINATION, III: JEWISH ENGAGEMENTS IN MEDIEVAL SOUTH INDIA**
Sponsor: Arc Humanities Press
Organiser: Alexandra F. C. Cuffel, Centrum für Religionswissenschaftliche Studien, Ruhr-Universität Bochum
Moderator: Ophira Gamliel, Centrum für Religionswissenschaftliche Studien, Ruhr-Universität Bochum
Paper 328-a: **'Till the sun and the moon remains': A Comparative Analysis of the Privileges Granted to Jewish and Non-Jewish Communities by the Cera Rulers of Kerala in the Early Medieval Period** (Language: English)
K. J. Tintu, Kuriakose Elias College, Mahatma Gandhi University, Kerala / Centre for Historical Studies, Jawaharlal Nehru University, New Delhi
Paper 328-b: **Transcending Boundaries: Investigating Jewish Material Culture in Relation to the Material Culture of Co-Existing Religious Communities in the Context of Kerala, South India** (Language: English)
Percy Arfeen, Centre for Historical Studies, Jawaharlal Nehru University, New Delhi
Paper 328-c: **Between the Heichal and the Synagogue Walls: An Exploration of Jewish Sacred Spaces in Kerela** (Language: English)
Malavika Binny, Centre for Historical Studies, Jawaharlal Nehru University, New Delhi

---

Session: **329** **Michael Sadler Building: Room LG.10**
Title: **DONATIONS OF THE FAITHFUL, CATHEDRAL FINANCING, AND MEMORIALISATION**
Organiser: Martina Saltamacchia, Department of History, University of Nebraska, Omaha
Moderator: David Lepine, Department of History, University of Exeter
Paper 329-a: ***Ad perpetuam memoriam*: The Cathedral of Milan's Patrons** (Language: English)
Martina Saltamacchia
Paper 329-b: **Remembered by the Brotherhood of Our Lady: The Late Medieval Patrons of Strasbourg Cathedral** (Language: English)
Charlotte Stanford, Department of Humanities, Classics & Comparative Literature, Brigham Young University, Utah
Paper 329-c: **Commissioning the Building of Chapels in a Finished Cathedral and Letting It Be Known: The Example of the Woad Sellers' Chapel at Amiens, End of the 13th Century** (Language: English)
Etienne Hamon, Institut de Recherches Historiques du Septentrion (IRHiS - UMR 8529), Université de Lille
Paper 329-d: **The Role of the Quest Collections in the Financing of Utrecht Cathedral** (Language: English)
Wim Vroom, Afdeling Geschiedenis, Universiteit van Amsterdam

Session: **330** **Charles Thackrah Building: 1.03**
Title: **MYSTICAL MEMORIES, III: HOW MYSTICS REMEMBER HAGIOGRAPHY AND LITERARY MOTIFS**
Sponsor: Mystical Theology Network
Organiser: Louise Nelstrop, St Benet's Hall, University of Oxford / Department of Theology & Religious Studies, York St John University
Moderator: Louise Nelstrop
Paper 330-a: ***Imitatio Francisci*: The Influence of Hagiographic Depictions of Francis of Assisi on the Mystical Writings of Angela of Foligno** (Language: English)
Michael Hahn, School of Divinity, University of St Andrews
Paper 330-b: **Mystics Remembering Each Other: Affection, Instruction, and Relationship in the *Vitae* of Beatrice of Nazareth and Ida of Nivelles** (Language: English)
Lydia Shahan, Institute for the Study of Spirituality, KU Leuven / Ruusbroecgenootschap, Universiteit Antwerpen
Paper 330-c: **Bernard's Belching Bride: Remembering the Inexpressible Love of the Soul for God with a Belch** (Language: English)
Philip Liston-Kraft, Department of Germanic Languages & Literatures, Harvard University

Session: **331** **Maurice Keyworth Building: Room 1.05**
Title: **MEMORY AND COMMUNITY, III**
Sponsor: Centre d'Études Supérieures de Civilisation Médiévale (CESCM), Université de Poitiers / Centre Nationale de la Recherche Scientifique (CNRS), Institute for Medieval Studies, Leeds
Organiser: Martin Aurell, Centre d'Études Supérieures de Civilisation Médiévale (CESCM), Université de Poitiers
Moderator: Estelle Ingrand-Varenne, Centre d'Études Supérieures de Civilisation Médiévale (CESCM), Université de Poitiers / Centre National de la Recherche Scientifique (CNRS), Paris
Paper 331-a: **The Last Will Forgotten: King Peter III of Aragón and Sicily** (Language: English)
Hans-Joachim Schmidt, Departement für Historische Wissenschaften, Universität Freiburg
Paper 331-b: **Excalibur, Curtana, Joyeuse, Durendal, Tizona: Swords in Epic and Genealogical Memory of Aristocratic Communities** (Language: English)
Martin Aurell
Paper 331-c: **Law as Collective Knowledge and Memory in Medieval Poland** (Language: English)
Piotr Górecki, Department of History, University of California, Riverside
Paper 331-d: **Forging Memories and Forgetting Divisions: The Role of Memory in Early 15th-Century Royal Processions in Paris** (Language: English)
Luke Giraudet, Department of History, University of York

Session:	**332** **Social Sciences Building: Room 10.09**
Title:	**BRITISH ARCHAEOLOGICAL ASSOCIATION, III: CONCEPTUAL MEMORY - REMEMBRANCE THROUGH OBJECTS, PAINTINGS, AND CHURCH ARCHITECTURE**
Sponsor:	British Archaeological Association
Organiser:	Harriet Mahood, Graduate Centre for Medieval Studies, University of Reading
Moderator:	Harriet Mahood
Paper 332-a:	**Material Mnemonics in Later Medieval England** (Language: English) Anna Boeles Rowland, Merton College, University of Oxford
Paper 332-b:	**Formal Memory: Commemorating John the Baptist** (Language: English) Ann Montgomery Jones, Sarum Seminar, California
Paper 332-c:	***Penetrale amplum et infinitum*: Memory as Metaphysical Refrain in English Medieval Architecture** (Language: English) Caroline Novak, Department of History of Art, University of Bristol

Session:	**333** **Leeds University Union: Room 2 - Elland Road**
Title:	**NEW PERSPECTIVES IN OLD NORSE MEMORY STUDIES**
Sponsor:	Memory & the Pre-Modern North Network
Organiser:	Simon Nygaard, Afdeling for Religionsvidenskab, Aarhus Universitet and Yoav Tirosh, Faculty of Icelandic & Comparative Cultural Studies, University of Iceland, Reykjavík
Moderator:	Yoav Tirosh
Paper 333-a:	**The Creation of Cultural Memory in the Paratexts of *Íslendingabók*** (Language: English) Lukas Rösli, Deutsches Seminar, Universität Zurich
Paper 333-b:	**Traumatic Memories: Writing The Violent Past in Medieval Iceland** (Language: English) Marion Poilvez, Faculty of Icelandic & Comparative Cultural Studies, University of Iceland, Reykjavík
Paper 333-c:	**Old Norse Memory Studies: Project Presentation** (Language: English) Jürg Glauser, Deutsches Seminar, Universität Zürich and Pernille Hermann, Afdeling for Nordiske Studier og Oplevelsesøkonomi, Aarhus Universitet

Session: **334** **Leeds University Union: Room 4 - Hyde Park**
Title: **FORGING COLLECTIVE MEMORIES: POWER, VIOLENCE, AND IDENTITIES IN MEDIEVAL SPAIN**
Sponsor: Cristianos y musulmanes en el medievo hispano, UCM Research Group 930.347
Organiser: Marisa Bueno, Departamento de Historia Medieval, Universidad Complutense de Madrid
Moderator: Iñaki Martín Viso, Departamento de Historia Medieval, Moderna y Contemporánea, Universidad de Salamanca
Paper 334-a: **Foundational Violence and Memory as Divine Power: Episcopal Historiography in Galicia during the Middle Ages** (Language: English)
Abel Lorenzo Rodríguez, Consejo Superior de Investigaciones Científicas, Universidade de Santiago de Compostela
Paper 334-b: **Death Violent and Sacred Memory: Historiography of Martyrdom and Cartography of Christian Identity in Medieval Spain** (Language: English)
Marisa Bueno
Paper 334-c: **'Iudicio Dei opprimuntur et asturorum regnum divina providentia exortitur': War and Divine Action in the Origin of Hispanic Historiography** (Language: English)
Gonzalo J. Escudero Manzano, Departamento de Historia Medieval, Universidad Complutense de Madrid
Paper 334-d: **A Justified Power?: Memory, Violence, and Jews during Castillian Civil War** (Language: English)
Gonzalo Pérez Castaño, Departamento de Historia Antigua y Medieval, Universidad de Valladolid

Session: **335** **Leeds University Union: Room 5 - Kirkstall Abbey**
Title: **MEMORY AND THE MATERIALITY OF MEDIEVAL TEXTS, III: (PSEUDO-) PROPHECIES AS FUTURE MEMORY IN MEDIEVAL HISTORIOGRAPHY AND HAGIOGRAPHY**
Sponsor: Fate, Freedom & Prognostication, Internationales Kolleg für Geisteswissenschaftliche Forschung (IKGF), Friedrich-Alexander-Universität Erlangen-Nürnberg
Organiser: Hans-Christian Lehner, Internationales Kolleg für Geisteswissenschaftliche Forschung (IKGF), Friedrich-Alexander-Universität Erlangen-Nürnberg
Moderator: Anke Holdenried, Department of History, University of Bristol
Paper 335-a: **Manipulated *Memoria*: How Andronikos I Survived in Historiographical Thought** (Language: English)
Michael Grünbart, Institut für Byzantinistik und Neogräzistik, Westfälische Wilhelms-Universität Münster
Paper 335-b: **(Pseudo-)Prophecies as Future Memory in Medieval Chronicles** (Language: English)
Hans-Christian Lehner
Paper 335-c: **Hagiography and Future Memory** (Language: English)
Klaus Herbers, Institut für Geschichte, Friedrich-Alexander-Universität Erlangen-Nürnberg

Session: **336** **Charles Thackrah Building: 1.04**
Title: **CONFLICTING MEMORIES: NAVIGATING CONFLICT AND CREATING CONSENSUS IN THE MEDIEVAL WORLD, II**
Organiser: Kieran Ball, Faculty of History, Trinity College, University of Oxford
Moderator: Andrew Holland, Queen's College, University of Oxford
Paper 336-a: **An 8th-Century Abbess in an 11th-Century World: Late Anglo-Saxon Spirituality in the Memories of St Mildrith** (Language: English)
Sumner Braund, St John's College, University of Oxford
Paper 336-b: **Disobedient Martyrs: Memory and Authority in the Visigothic Passions** (Language: English)
David Addison, Mansfield College, University of Oxford
Paper 336-c: **'It was a graveyard smash': Humour and the Dance of Death in the 15th-Century *Danse Macabre des Femmes* and Bergamo's Oratorio dei Disciplini** (Language: English)
Ariana Ellis, Centre for Medieval Studies, University of Toronto, Downtown

Session: **337** **Maurice Keyworth Building: Room 1.03**
Title: **REMEMBERING AND FORGETTING THE ANCIENT CITY, III: THE PHYSICAL CITY**
Sponsor: ERC Project 'The Impact of the Ancient City'
Organiser: Javier Martínez-Jiménez, Faculty of Classics, University of Cambridge and Sam Ottewill-Soulsby, Faculty of Classics, University of Cambridge
Moderator: Sam Ottewill-Soulsby
Paper 337-a: **Trier as 'Roma Secunda': The Roman Past of Trier in the Long 10th Century** (Language: English)
Lenneke Van Raaij, Department of History, University of Exeter
Paper 337-b: **Dismantling Roman Pasts: New Monuments and New Identities at the End of the Early Middle Ages in Southern Gaul** (Language: English)
Javier Martínez-Jiménez
Paper 337-c: **The Post-Classical Life of an Athenian Suburban Precinct: Radical Appropriation or Multi-Layered Simultaneity?** (Language: English)
Elizabeth Key Fowden, Faculty of Classics, University of Cambridge
Respondent: Andrew Wallace-Hadrill, Faculty of Classics, University of Cambridge

Session: **338** **Maurice Keyworth Building: Room 1.33**
Title: ***MEMORIA* (AND MEMO) IN PRACTICE**
Sponsor: Medieval Memoria Online Project (MeMO), Universiteit Utrecht
Organiser: Arnoud-Jan A. Bijsterveld, Department of Sociology, Tilburg University
Moderator: Truus van Bueren, Medieval Memoria Online Project (MeMO), Universiteit Utrecht
Paper 338-a: **Medieval Floor Slabs in the Netherlands: Iconography and Intentions** (Language: English)
Corinne van Dijk, Medieval Memoria Online Project (MeMO), Universiteit Utrecht
Paper 338-b: **Commemorating Ancestors: Chronicles of Noble Houses and *Memoria*** (Language: English)
Rolf de Weijert, Medieval Memoria Online Project (MeMO), Universiteit Utrecht
Paper 338-c: **Medieval Commemoration in Stained-Glass Windows** (Language: English)
Charlotte Dikken, Medieval Memoria Online Project (MeMO), Universiteit Utrecht

Session: **339** **University House: Great Woodhouse Room**
Title: **MEMORY IN THE ANGEVIN WORLD**
Sponsor: Angevin World Network
Organiser: Michael Staunton, School of History, University College Dublin
Moderator: Stephen Church, School of History, University of East Anglia
Paper 339-a: **Remembering the Conquest of Ireland in the Angevin World** (Language: English)
Colin Veach, School of Histories, Languages & Cultures, University of Hull
Paper 339-b: **Remembering Illness in the Angevin World: Variations of Familial Memory in the Miracle Accounts of Gilbert of Sempringham** (Language: English)
Krystal Carmichael, School of History, University College Dublin
Paper 339-c: **Remembering the Loss of Normandy** (Language: English)
Michael Staunton

Session: **340** **Leeds University Union: Room 6 - Roundhay**
Title: **MONARCHY AND MEMORY, III: REMEMBERING MONARCHS IN THE MODERN ERA**
Sponsor: Royal Studies Network
Organiser: Gabrielle Storey, Department of History, University of Winchester
Moderator: Elena Woodacre, Department of History, University of Winchester
Paper 340-a: **Early Reputation and Modern Scholarship: The Memory of Urraca of Castile-Leon and Her Sister Teresa of Portugal** (Language: English)
Lorena Fierro, Department of History, University of Exeter
Paper 340-b: **Forgetting Edward I's Daughters** (Language: English)
Kathleen Neal, Centre for Medieval & Renaissance Studies, Monash University, Victoria
Paper 340-c: **She-Wolf or Feminist Heroine: The Memory and Reputation of Margaret of Anjou** (Language: English)
Imogene Dudley, Department of History, University of Exeter

Session: **341** **Parkinson Building: Nathan Bodington Chamber**
Title: **REMEMBERING *ADMONITIO*: EPISCOPAL CRITICISM OF RULERS IN THE MIDDLE AGES, III**
Organiser: Ryan Kemp, Department of History & Welsh History, Aberystwyth University
Moderator: Katy Cubitt, School of History, University of East Anglia
Paper 341-a: **'Sancta tractabat arte': Lanfranc's 'Management' of King William the Conqueror as a Sacred Art** (Language: English)
Sally N. Vaughn, Department of History, University of Houston, Texas
Paper 341-b: **The Admonishing Bishop in 12th-Century England and Germany** (Language: English)
Ryan Kemp
Paper 341-c: **13th-Century Bishops of Auxerre Trying to Whip the Counts into Line** (Language: English)
Constance Bouchard, Department of History, University of Akron, Ohio

Session: **342** **Baines Wing: Room G.37**
Title: **FAME: PATRONS AND MEMORIES IN BYZANTIUM, III**
Organiser: Francisco Lopez-Santos Kornberger, Centre for Byzantine, Ottoman & Modern Greek Studies, University of Birmingham and Jessica Varsallona, Centre for Byzantine, Ottoman & Modern Greek Studies, University of Birmingham
Moderator: Daniel K. Reynolds, Centre for Byzantine, Ottoman & Modern Greek Studies, University of Birmingham
Paper 342-a: **Discreet Patrons: Hints of Komnenian Propaganda in the Continuation of Skylitzes** (Language: English)
Francisco Lopez-Santos Kornberger
Paper 342-b: **Pulcheria: A 5th-Century Role Model for the 9th Century?** (Language: English)
Maria Vrij, Centre for Byzantine, Ottoman & Modern Greek Studies / Barber Institute of Fine Arts, University of Birmingham
Paper 342-c: **Remnants of a Classical Past in Byzantine Attica: An Archbishop's Testimony** (Language: English)
Panagiota Mantouvalou, Centre for Byzantine, Ottoman & Modern Greek Studies, University of Birmingham

---

Session: **343** **Stage@leeds: Stage 3**
Title: **CRUSADES AND MEMORY, III : REMEMBERING THE CRUSADES**
Organiser: Pagona Papadopoulou, School of History & Archaeology, Aristotle University of Thessaloniki
Moderator: Doris Behrens-Abuseif, Department of History of Art & Archaeology, School of Oriental & African Studies, University of London
Paper 343-a: **In Search of Lost Jerusalem: Amnesia and Crusader Constantinople** (Language: English)
Nicholas Melvani, Department of Byzantine Research, National Hellenic Research Foundation (NHRF), Athens
Paper 343-b: **'O worthy Petro, kyng of Cipre, also, that Alisandre wan by heigh maistrie...': Commemorating Peter I's Italian Peregrinations in Material Culture, 1361-1369** (Language: English)
Anthi Andronikou, Seeger Center for Hellenic Studies, Princeton University
Paper 343-c: **Recapturing the Glory Days of the Lusignan Kingdom: Architectural Historicism in Venetian Cyprus** (Language: English)
Michalis Olympios, Department of History & Archaeology, University of Cyprus, Nicosia

---

Session: **344** **Fine Art Building: SR 1.10**
Title: **RELIGIOUS MEMORY IN EARLY MEDIEVAL EUROPE**
Organiser: IMC Programming Committee
Moderator: Julia M. H. Smith, Faculty of History, University of Oxford
Paper 344-a: **Pictures as Material Memory in the Carolingian Controversies about the Worship of Images** (Language: English)
Kristina Mitalaite, Laboratoire D'études sur les Monothéismes (LEM), Centre National de la Recherche Scientifique (CNRS), Paris
Paper 344-b: **Salvation by Memory: Early Christian Pilgrims and Their Visits of Holy Places** (Language: English)
Elisabeth Caroline Engler-Starck, Fachbereich Geschichts- und Kulturwissenschaften, Justus-Liebig-Universität Gießen
Paper 344-c: **Memory of Old Beliefs in the Newly Christianised World of the Early Middle Ages** (Language: English)
Beate Korntner, Institut für Geschichte, Universität Wien

Session: **345** **Baines Wing: Room G.36**

Title: **MEMORY AND MIGRATIONS, II: PLACES OF MEMORY**

Sponsor: MIGWEB: A Comparative Diachronic Analysis of Post-Byzantine Networks in the Early Modern Europe (15th-18th Centuries), Department of History, Royal Holloway, University of London / Marie Skłodowska Curie Action Project under Grant Agreement 747 857

Organiser: Nada Zečević, Department of History, Royal Holloway, University of London / Marie Sklodowska Curie Action Project

Moderator: Jonathan Harris, Department of History, Royal Holloway, University of London

Paper 345-a: **Something Old, Something New: Memory and Identity of Croatian and Slavonian Nobility in the Late Middle Ages** (Language: English)
Suzana Miljan, Institute of Historical & Social Sciences, Croatian Academy of Sciences & Arts, Zagreb

Paper 345-b: **Memories of Home in the Songs of Stratiotic Soldiers in the Adriatic and Southern Italy, 15th-17th Centuries** (Language: English)
Nada Zečević

Paper 345-c: **Tracing the Ancestors to the 'Reconquest': Historical Memory and Uses of the Past in Making Claims to Status in the Colonial Society of New Spain** (Language: English)
Karoline Cook, Department of History, Royal Holloway, University of London

Respondent: Mihailo Popović, Institut für Mittelalterforschung, Abteilung Byzanzforschung, Österreichische Akademie der Wissenschaften, Wien

---

Session: **346** **Emmanuel Centre: Room 10**

Title: **MEMORY AND *MEMORIA*: THE DEAD CAN'T DEFEND THEMSELVES OR, HOW ARCHIVES CREATE PORTRAITS OF PERSONALITIES**

Sponsor: Mittelhochdeutsche Begriffsdatenbank (MHDBDB) / Interdisziplinäres Zentrum für Mittelalter und Frühneuzeit (IZMF), Universität Salzburg

Organiser: Katharina Zeppezauer-Wachauer, Mittelhochdeutsche Begriffsdatenbank (MHDBDB) / Interdisziplinäres Zentrum für Mittelalter und Frühneuzeit (IZMF), Universität Salzburg

Moderator: Jutta Baumgartner, Zentrum für Gastrosophie, Universität Salzburg

Paper 346-a: **The Digital Archive: Data-Based (His-)Stories** (Language: English)
Katharina Zeppezauer-Wachauer and Peter Hinkelmanns, Mittelhochdeutsche Begriffsdatenbank (MHDBDB) / Interdisziplinäres Zentrum für Mittelalter und Frühneuzeit (IZMF), Universität Salzburg

Paper 346-b: **The Bishop on the Kermis: The Canonization of Bishop Virgil and Regional Cult in Salzburg** (Language: English)
Wolfgang Neuper, Archiv der Erzdiözese Salzburg

Paper 346-c: **Book-Donations in Blessed Memory of the Dead: Examples from the Library of the Archabbey of St Peter, Salzburg** (Language: English)
Sonja Führer, Bibliothek, Erzabtei St. Peter, Salzburg

Paper 346-d: **Of Books and Memories: Traces of Individuals in the Medieval Library of the Nonnberg Abbey in Salzburg** (Language: English)
Manuel Schwembacher, Interdisziplinäres Zentrum für Mittelalter und Frühneuzeit (IZMF), Universität Salzburg

Session: **347** **Baines Wing: Room 2.15**
Title: **MEMORY IN THOMAS AQUINAS**
Organiser: IMC Programming Committee
Moderator: Mark Wynn, School of Philosophy, Religion & History of Science, University of Leeds
Paper 347-a: **Aquinas: Is There Salvation for People with Bad Memory?** (Language: English)
Mariella Annika Asikanius, Senter for misjon og globale studier, VID vitenskapelige høgskole, Stavanger
Paper 347-b: **The Importance of the Exercise of Memory for Progressing in Science according to Thomas Aquinas** (Language: English)
Inês Bolinhas, Faculdade de Ciências Humanas, Universidade Católica Portuguesa, Lisboa
Paper 347-c: **The Theological and Mnemonic Structure of Aquinas' *Summa Theologiae*** (Language: English)
Anton ten Klooster, Thomas Instituut, Utrecht / Department of Systematic Theology & Philosophy, Tilburg University

---

Session: **348** **University House: St George Room**
Title: **MINOR ANNALS, II: PROBLEMS AND PERSPECTIVES**
Organiser: Sören Kaschke, Historisches Institut, Universität zu Köln and Bart Jeremy van Hees, Departement Geschiedenis en Kunstgeschiedenis, Universiteit Utrecht
Moderator: Jennifer R. Davis, Department of History, Catholic University of America, Washington DC
Paper 348-a: **Rewriting Histor(iograph)y: The *Annales Petaviani*** (Language: English)
Sören Kaschke
Paper 348-b: **Scriptural Cosmology, *Correctio*, and the Manuscripts of the So-Called *Annales Petaviani*** (Language: English)
Andrew Sorber, Corcoran Department of History, University of Virginia
Respondent: Helmut Reimitz, Department of History, Princeton University

---

Session: **349** **University House: Cloberry Room**
Title: **MAPPINGS, I: MAPS IN COMMUNICATION WITH (OTHER) TEXTS**
Organiser: Felicitas Schmieder, Historisches Institut, FernUniversität Hagen and Dan Terkla, Department of English, Illinois Wesleyan University
Moderator: Felicitas Schmieder
Paper 349-a: **Heart of Darkness: Antonio Fernandez's Exploration of the Southern African Interior in 1514 Revisited** (Language: English)
Thomas Wozniak, Seminar für Mittelalterliche Geschichte, Eberhard-Karls-Universität Tübingen
Paper 349-b: **Coastal Lines on Late Medieval Maps as Transitional Zones** (Language: English)
Gerda Brunnlechner, Historisches Institut, FernUniversität Hagen
Paper 349-c: **Maps and Their Materiality: Revisiting the Two Mappaemundi of London, British Library Add MS 28681** (Language: English)
LauraLee Brott, Department of Art History, University of Wisconsin-Madison and Heather Gaile Wacha, School of Library & Information Studies, University of Wisconsin-Madison

Session:	**350** **Michael Sadler Building: Room LG.15**
Title:	**SCIENTIFIC, EMPIRICAL, BIBLICAL, AND HAGIOGRAPHICAL KNOWLEDGE IN THE MIDDLE AGES, III: SAINTS, SCRIPTURE, AND LITURGY**
Sponsor:	School of Arts, English & Languages, Queen's University Belfast
Organiser:	Ciaran Arthur, School of Arts, English & Languages, Queen's University Belfast
Moderator:	Elisa Ramazzina, School of Arts, English & Languages, Queen's University Belfast
Paper 350-a:	**'You wished to vomit forth words which you had not swallowed down': Imitating Scriptural Obscurity in Early Medieval Texts** (Language: English) Ciaran Arthur
Paper 350-b:	**Old English in the Liturgy** (Language: English) Helen Gittos, Balliol College, University of Oxford
Paper 350-c:	**The Seven Sleepers in Anglo-Saxon England** (Language: English) Hugh Magennis, School of Arts, English & Languages, Queen's University Belfast

Session:	**351** **Emmanuel Centre: Room 11**
Title:	**INTEGRATING THE SASANIANS, III: RELIGIONS, IDEOLOGIES, AND MODES OF DIPLOMACY IN LATE ANTIQUE AND MEDIEVAL IRAN**
Sponsor:	MPS - Middle Persian Studies, Universidade de Brasília / Sonderforschungsbereiche Project 'Visions of Community', Österreichische Akademie der Wissenschaften, Universität Wien
Organiser:	Otávio Luiz Vieira Pinto, Middle Persian Studies Project, Universidade de Brasília
Moderator:	John Latham-Sprinkle, Department of History, School of Oriental & African Studies, University of London
Paper 351-a:	**Reflections on the Perspective of Sasanian 'Past' in Islamic Sources** (Language: English) Domiziana Rossi, Dipartimento di Storia Culture Civiltà, Università di Bologna
Paper 351-b:	**Early Christian Georgia and Sasanian Iran: Issues of Cultural Relations** (Language: English) Nino Silagadze, Institute of Art History & Theory, Ivane Javakhishvili State University, Georgia
Paper 351-c:	**The Role of the Nestorians in the Peace of 630 between the Byzantines and Sasanians** (Language: English) Mahnaz Babaee, Department of History, Islamic Azad University, Iran

Session: **352** **Stage@leeds: Stage 2**
Title: **ENGLAND AND SCOTLAND AT PEACE AND WAR IN THE LATER MIDDLE AGES, III**
Organiser: Claire Etty, Oxford English Dictionary, Oxford University Press and Andy King, Department of History, University of Southampton
Moderator: Andy King
Paper 352-a: **Piracy and Anglo-Scottish Relations during the Hundred Years War** (Language: English)
Thomas Heebøll-Holm, Institut for Historie, Syddansk Universitet, Odense
Paper 352-b: **Smashing the Nobility in the 14th and 15th Centuries?: An Anglo-Scottish Comparison** (Language: English)
Gordon McKelvie, Department of History, University of Winchester
Paper 352-c: **Manhood, Masculinity, and Marrying Your Enemies: A New Approach for Considering Late Medieval Anglo-Scottish Relations** (Language: English)
Lucinda Dean, Centre for History, University of the Highlands & Islands, Dornoch

Session: **353** **Stage@leeds: Stage 1**
Title: **SAVING AND TRANSFORMING SOUND MEMORIES: MOTIVATIONS, STRATEGIES, TECHNIQUES**
Sponsor: HERA Project 'Sound Memories - Uses of the Past'
Organiser: David Eben, Institute of Musicology, Univerzita Karlova, Praha
Moderator: Susan Rankin, Faculty of Music, Emmanuel College, University of Cambridge
Paper 353-a: **Same Songs, Different Opportunities: How Performance Affects Musical Forms** (Language: English)
Jan Ciglbauer, Institute of Musicology, Univerzita Karlova, Praha
Paper 353-b: **Preserving Sound Memories in Central Europe: The Polyphonic Song *Martir Christi insignitus*** (Language: English)
Antonio Chemotti, Institute of Art, Polish Academy of Sciences, Warszawa
Paper 353-c: **Re-Fashioning a Repertory: Experimentation and Re-Use in the Musical Culture of 13th-Century Paris** (Language: English)
Adam Mathias, Faculty of Music, University of Cambridge

Session: **354** **Maurice Keyworth Building: Room 1.06**
Title: **NEW RESEARCH PERSPECTIVES ON THE TRIPARTITE CODIFICATION OF STEPHAN DUŠAN: A ROUND TABLE DISCUSSION**
Sponsor: Department for Roman Law & Legal History, KU Leuven
Organiser: Paolo Angelini, Faculty of Law, KU Leuven
Moderator: Paolo Angelini
Purpose: *The aim of this round table is to bring together scholars who focus their research on the tripartite codification enacted by the Serbian emperor Stefan Dušan. We seek to examine some particular aspects of the civil, customary, penal, and public law, as well as the links between the* Code of Dušan *1349-1354, the* Abridged syntagma, *and the so-called* Law of the Emperor Justinian.

If, on the one hand, the Code of Dušan *is considered to be the most important Serbian medieval legislative text, on the other hand, the influence of the Byzantine (or Greco-Roman) law is evident. The analysis of the juridical contents will show how the Byzantine and Slav juridical institutions were included and combined in the tripartite codification enacted by the Serbian emperor.*

Participants include Nina Kršljanin (University of Belgrade), Valerio Massimo Minale (Università Bocconi, Milano), Tamara Matović (Serbian Academy of Sciences & Arts, Beograd), Srđan Šarkić (University of Novi Sad), and Miljana Todorović (University of Niš).

* * * * *

RECEPTION AT PARKINSON COURT

HOSTED BY
THE IMC ADMINISTRATION AND THE IMC EXHIBITORS

PARKINSON BUILDING: PARKINSON COURT
18.00-19.00

All delegates are very welcome to enjoy a glass of wine to celebrate the opening of the IMC 2018 and its Bookfair. The Bookfair will also remain open until 19.30 to allow you time to meet and network with colleagues, publishers, and booksellers.

* * * * *

DINNER

Meal Times

Refectory 18.00-20.00

See Map 9, p. 51.

---

* * * * *

RECEPTION AT MICHAEL SADLER BUILDING

HOSTED BY
MEDIEVAL ACADEMY OF AMERICA – GRADUATE STUDENT COMMITTEE

UNIVERSITY HOUSE: BEECHGROVE ROOM
18.30-19.00

Please join us for drinks, food, and insightful discussion with other Medieval Academy of America graduate students at the MAA-GSC Reception. Hope to see you there!

* * * * *

RECEPTION AT UNIVERSITY HOUSE

HOSTED BY
INTERNATIONAL MEDIEVAL BIBLIOGRAPHY

UNIVERSITY HOUSE: LITTLE WOODHOUSE ROOM
19.00-20.00

The *International Medieval Bibliography* (IMB) is the world's leading multidisciplinary bibliography of Medieval Studies. For over 50 years it has been produced by an editorial team based at Leeds, assisted by a network of contributors around the globe. The editors are looking for new contributors, both for national and regional history of specific countries and for many thematic areas. If you are interested in becoming a contributor (or if you are already associated with the IMB), please come along and meet the editorial team, who will be happy to explain new developments in the project and talk about how new contributors can become involved.

* * * * *

RECEPTION AT UNIVERSITY HOUSE

HOSTED BY
CENTRE FOR MEDIEVAL STUDIES, UNIVERSITY OF BRISTOL

UNIVERSITY HOUSE: GREAT WOODHOUSE ROOM
19.00-20.00

The Centre for Medieval Studies, University of Bristol is pleased to host a one-hour wine reception. Staff will be available to answer questions about the Centre such as its book series (Bristol Studies in Medieval Cultures, Boydell & Brewer), upcoming events, and postgraduate programmes (MA, MPhil, and PhD). For more information about Bristol's Centre for Medieval Studies, please see www.bristol.ac.uk/medieval/. We look forward to seeing you there to join us for a drink and an informal chat.

* * * * *

Session: **401** **Stage@leeds: Stage 3**
Title: **ANGLO-SAXON STUDIES AT IMC #25: LOOKING BACK, LOOKING FORWARD - A ROUND TABLE DISCUSSION**
Sponsor: Centre for Medieval & Renaissance Culture, University of Southampton
Organiser: Catherine A. M. Clarke, Faculty of Humanities, University of Southampton
Moderator: Catherine A. M. Clarke
Purpose: *This round table session takes the opportunity of the 25th International Medieval Congress to look back at Anglo-Saxon Studies over the past 25 years, and to look ahead to the future of the field. As a starting-point, members of the panel will each respond to a paper title from the first Leeds IMC in 1994. How has thinking in our disciplines changed or developed since then? What conversations are continuing, and where have agendas shifted? Our discussion will also focus on the future of Anglo-Saxon Studies, and the challenges and opportunities we face. How can we better foster inclusivity and diversity? What new conversations do we need to open up? Where do we hope to see the field in another 25 years? Anyone with an interest in Anglo-Saxon Studies is most welcome to attend and join the discussion, which will be followed by a drinks reception.*

Participants include Stewart J. Brookes (University of Cambridge), Megan Cavell (University of Birmingham), Peter Darby (University of Nottingham), Adam Miyashiro (Stockton University, New Jersey), Jennifer Neville (Royal Holloway, University of London), Daniel Thomas (University of Oxford), and Diane Watt (University of Surrey).

Session: **405** **Maurice Keyworth Building: Room 1.32**
Title: **SYMBOLISM AND CASTLES, III: GENDER, SPACE, AND TIME - A ROUND TABLE DISCUSSION**
Sponsor: Institute of Medieval & Early Modern Studies, Durham University
Organiser: Heidi Richards, Department of Archaeology, Durham University
Moderator: Heidi Richards
Purpose: *As the field of castle studies expands with fresh perspectives, gendered areas and concepts of privacy within the medieval castle have been somewhat left behind. This round table discussion explores the themes of female and masculine spaces within the castle and other secular elite structures, movement and liturgy within and around the castle, and the evolution and fluctuating importance of privacy from Anglo-Saxon England through the Late Middle Ages.*

Participants include Rachel Delman (University of Oxford), Pamela Graves (Durham University), Amanda Richardson (University of Chichester), David Rollason (Durham University), Audrey Thorstad (Bangor University), and Katherine Weikert (University of Winchester).

Session: **408** **Maurice Keyworth Building: Room 1.05**
Title: **BEARS: A ROUND TABLE DISCUSSION**
Sponsor: MAD (Medieval Animal Data Network)
Organiser: Alice Choyke, Department of Medieval Studies, Central European University, Budapest
Moderator: Gerhard Jaritz, Department of Medieval Studies, Central European University, Budapest
Purpose: *This year MAD has chosen bears as a subject of discussion. Bears occupy an important liminal space in medieval human thought. They were considered wild animals but nevertheless also conceived as sharing human characteristics. The round table will explore the many ways bears were used and regarded by medieval society.*

Participants include Floris Bernard (Central European University, Budapest), Alice Choyke (Central European University, Budapest), Irina Metzler (Swansea University), Anastasija Ropa (University of Latvia, Riga), and Mónica Ann Walker Vadillo (Old Operating Theatre Museum, London).

Session: **416** **Maurice Keyworth Building: Room 1.06**
Title: **LATE MEDIEVAL WILLS: DIRECTIONS FOR FUTURE RESEARCH - A ROUND TABLE DISCUSSION**
Sponsor: Institute for Medieval Research, University of Nottingham / Gender, Place & Memory, 1400-1900 Research Cluster, University of Hull
Organiser: Rob Lutton, Department of History, University of Nottingham
Moderator: Elisabeth Salter, Gender, Place & Memory, 1400-1900 Research Cluster, University of Hull
Purpose: *This round table brings together experts on late medieval wills and considers the potential for future research using this valuable source of evidence. Late medieval wills survive in huge numbers for locations all across England. There are some surviving records for Wales, Scotland, and Ireland, and many in other European countries. Wills provide extensive evidence for popular religious belief and practice, the construction of identity and memory, ownership and attitudes to material goods, literate activity, and much more. They also enable access to stories of our ancestors' lives and as such their contents have popular appeal. This round table will discuss the potential for future research looking qualitatively and quantitatively at this source and the ways we might enhance its accessibility for academic and public use.*

Participants include Cordelia Beattie (University of Edinburgh), Margriet Hoogvliet (Rijksuniversiteit Groningen), Lisa Howarth (University of Winchester), Alex Marchbank (University of Nottingham), and Marianne Wilson (The National Archives, Kew).

Session: **418** **Michael Sadler Building: Rupert Beckett Theatre**
Title: **ANNUAL *EARLY MEDIEVAL EUROPE* LECTURE: LIGHTS, POWER, AND THE MORAL ECONOMY OF EARLY MEDIEVAL EUROPE (LANGUAGE: ENGLISH)**
Sponsor: *Early Medieval Europe*
Speaker: Paul Fouracre, Department of History, University of Manchester
Introduction: Marios Costambeys, Department of History, University of Liverpool and Simon MacLean, School of History, University of St Andrews
Details: *From Antiquity, light has been associated with power. Taking on board the Old Testament injunction to keep a light burning before the tabernacle, the Christian Church required all churches to burn a light before the altar, and saints' shrines were also honoured with lights. As lighting was expensive it was initially the elite in society which made grants for lighting provision. It can be demonstrated that rulers made such grants at politically important moments. This lecture examines how the burden of providing for the lights spread into the wider population. In Francia this happened in two ways: precarial tenures created a class of rent payers (*censuales or cerocensuales*) whose rent was often designated for light provision, and, secondly, a proportion of the tithe was also assigned to the lights. From Carolingian legislation (capitularies, the canons of councils, and episcopal statutes) we can see a reform programme insisting on the maintenance of the lights. In the 10th century we see the first evidence of voluntary associations (guilds) forming for this purpose. Although the requirement to burn lights was universal, it is possible to identify significant differences in the way this requirement was met: top-down in West Francia, but by a growing class of ecclesiastical tributaries (the so-called *Zensualität*) in East Francia/Germany, by local arrangement in Italy and Spain, and apparently by quasi-taxation ('wax-scot') in England. The conjunction of religious belief, resource dedication, and social organisation is what makes up the moral economy here. The lecture seeks to understand the differences between the various regions of Europe and asks whether the subject of lighting can contribute to our understanding of social structuration in the Early Middle Ages.*

The journal Early Medieval Europe *(published by Wiley) is very pleased to sponsor the Annual* Early Medieval Europe *Lecture at the International Medieval Congress. By contributing a major scholarly lecture to the Congress programme, the journal aims to highlight the importance of the Congress to scholars working in early medieval European history and to support further research in this field.* Early Medieval Europe *is an interdisciplinary journal encouraging the discussion of archaeology, numismatics, palaeography, diplomatic, literature, onomastics, art history, linguistics, and epigraphy, as well as more traditional historical approaches. It covers Europe in its entirety, including material on Iceland, Ireland, the British Isles, Scandinavia, and Continental Europe (both west and east). Further information about the journal and details on how to submit material to it are available at http://eu.wiley.com (the full url is http://onlinelibrary.wiley.com/journal/10.1111/%28ISSN%291468-0254). All those attending are warmly invited to join members of the editorial board after the lecture for a glass of wine.*

Please note that admission to this event will be on a first-come, first-served basis as there will be no tickets for the event. Please ensure that you arrive as early as possible to avoid disapointment.

Session: **420** **Maurice Keyworth Building: Room 1.03**
Title: **LITERARY APPROACHES TO WITNESSING AND MEMORY: A ROUND TABLE DISCUSSION**
Sponsor: International Medieval Society, Paris - Société Internationale des Médiévistes, Paris
Organiser: Victoria Turner, School of Modern Languages - French, University of St Andrews
Moderator: Victoria Turner
Purpose: *Interest in the study of medieval memory continues to transform the way we think about relationships between writer and witness, witness and reader, narrative and event, and text and testimony in the Middle Ages. Acts of witnessing involve processes of recording, reconstructing, and commemorating information and experiences; may express mourning and trauma; and may reveal cross-generational ties in the shaping of collective memory. This round table unites scholars with different theoretical and methodological approaches (e.g. semiotics, gender, political history) and aims to explore what it meant to witness and be a witness in different genres of medieval writing. As a new collaboration between the French research network 'Questes' and the IMS, it will showcase current approaches to witnessing and memory that cross literary and historical disciplines.*

Participants include Viviane Griveau-Genest (Université Paris Nanterre), Simon Thomas Parsons (Royal Holloway, University of London), and Marie-Christine Payne (Université Paris III - Sorbonne Nouvelle).

Session: **430** **Maurice Keyworth Building: Room 1.09**
Title: **MYSTICAL MEMORIES, IV: MYSTICS, MEMORY, AND METHODOLOGY - A ROUND TABLE DISCUSSION**
Sponsor: Mystical Theology Network
Organiser: Louise Nelstrop, St Benet's Hall, University of Oxford / Department of Theology & Religious Studies, York St John University
Moderator: Louise Nelstrop
Purpose: *The round table will examine different methodological approaches to medieval mystics and memory. Focusing on late medieval Dutch and English mystics, this round table will explore theological, historical, feminist, neurological, and historiographical perspectives on how these writers understood the memory and are remembered.*

Participants include Rob Faesen (KU Leuven / Universiteit Antwerpen), Veerle Fraeters (Universiteit Antwerpen), Einat Klafter (Tel Aviv University), and Godelinde Gertrude Perk (Mittuniversitets, Sundsvall).

Session: **438** **Maurice Keyworth Building: Room 1.04**
Title: **THE FUTURE OF MEMO AND *MEMORIA* STUDIES - A ROUND TABLE DISCUSSION**
Sponsor: Medieval Memoria Online Project (MeMO), Universiteit Utrecht / Memoria & Remembrance Practices, Brepols
Organiser: Arnoud-Jan A. Bijsterveld, Department of Sociology, Tilburg University
Moderator: Arnoud-Jan A. Bijsterveld
Purpose: *In recent decades, several joint efforts have been undertaken to raise the study of medieval commemoration and of (religious) foundations to the academic fore. Some projects have finished or are finishing shortly, others are still underway. At Utrecht University, the Medieval Memoria Online Project (MeMO) ran between 2009 and 2018. This created a database of objects and texts that functioned in the medieval commemoration of the dead in the Netherlands until 1580. Also, MeMO has been publishing the online Medieval Memoria Research newsletter for 10 years now. Between 2012 and 2017, Professor Michael Borgolte (Humboldt-Universität zu Berlin) directed the ERC project FOUNDMED - Foundations in medieval societies. Cross-cultural comparisons. This got a follow-up in the new journal* Endowments Studies *(Brill). Since 2017, Brepols Publishers has published a series entitled Memoria and Remembrance Practices. This round table invites IMC delegates to discuss possible new research pathways for the study of medieval commemoration and ways to cooperate on the international level. What are relevant new research questions and ways to continue the fruitful work of recent years?*

Participants include Truus van Bueren (Universiteit Utrecht), Charlotte Dikken (Universiteit Utrecht), Tine Kondrup (Syddansk Universitet, Odense), Tillman Lohse (Humboldt-Universität zu Berlin), and Thomas Schilp (Ruhr-Universität Bochum).

Session: **440** **Leeds University Union: Room 6 - Roundhay**
Title: **MONARCHY AND MEMORY, IV: GONE BUT NOT FORGOTTEN? - A ROUND TABLE DISCUSSION**
Sponsor: Royal Studies Network
Organiser: Gabrielle Storey, Department of History, University of Winchester
Moderator: Zita Eva Rohr, Department of Modern History, Politics & International Relations, Macquarie University, Sydney
Purpose: *This round table will focus on the issues facing monarchy and memory on a global scale, with speakers presenting issues faced in Europe, Africa, and Asia. The round table will develop upon discussions raised by the strand, and invite debate as to whether we can draw upon common themes or distinctions between the ways countries commemorated and memoralised their monarchs. The round table will focus on both medieval and modern historiography and offer suggestions as to how future scholarship can overcome issues surrounding the remembrance of monarchs in a global context.*

Participants include Karl Alvestad (University of Winchester), Lucinda Dean (University of the Highlands & Islands, Dornoch), Maria Harvey (University of Cambridge), Melanie Maddox (Military College of South Carolina), Fatima Rhorchi (Université Moulay Ismaïl, Morocco), Levi Roach (University of Exeter), and Angus Stewart (University of St Andrews).

Session:	**451**	**Stage@leeds: Stage 1**

Title: **SPECIAL LECTURE: BLACK LEGENDS, BULLYING QUEENS, AND THE WONDERS OF MOORISHLAND - HOW SPAIN LIVES ITS MEDIEVAL PAST TODAY**
(Language: English)

Speaker: Giles Tremlett, *The Guardian / The Economist*

Introduction: Iona McCleery, Institute for Medieval Studies / School of History, University of Leeds

Sponsor: Instituto Cervantes / Centre for the History of Ibero-America, University of Leeds

Details: *From the charters of regional governments to the brochures of city tourism departments, medieval Spain remains remarkably visible. It is also a source of conflict. The ongoing confrontation in Catalonia, for example, includes references to a deep but disputed medieval 'national' past and identity - which has been referenced by architects, poets, and television scriptwriters. Politicians are surprisingly willing to scrap over Spain's medieval past. They have argued over everything from whether 'Moors' owe Spain an apology for invading it in the 8th century, to whether 10th-century Andalucians or Catalans could claim to have had the best hygiene. Some also loudly proclaim that a 'black legend', crafted by foreign writers and based on Christian Spain's treatment of Jews, Muslims, and conversos, still shapes the way in which the country is seen. And yet that 'black legend', which extends beyond the medieval period, has also had a huge impact on how - at historic low points - Spain has seen itself. Even now, the appropriation by Francoism of late medieval figures like Isabel of Castile - and their symbols - colours the ways in which they can be viewed.*

Please note that admission to this event will be on a first-come, first-served basis as there will be no tickets. Please ensure that you arrive as early as possible to avoid disappointment.

Session:	**452**	**Stage@leeds: Stage 2**

Title: **ENGLAND AND SCOTLAND AT PEACE AND WAR IN THE LATER MIDDLE AGES, IV: A ROUND TABLE DISCUSSION**

Sponsor: Department of History, University of Southampton

Organiser: Claire Etty, Oxford English Dictionary, Oxford University Press and Andy King, Department of History, University of Southampton

Moderator: Paul R. Dryburgh, The National Archives, Kew

Purpose: *This round table aims to provide a forum for the discussion of the themes and ideas arising from the 'England and Scotland at Peace and War in the Later Middle Ages' sessions in this and last year's Congresses and in Anglo-Scottish relations more generally. What were the issues which shaped these relations over the long durée, from 1286 until the Union of the Crowns, and what are the continuities and discontinuities across the period? Can we identify new approaches or gaps in the current scholarship? Has there been too much focus on war? What differing perspectives can historians of the two realms, and indeed of other European polities, offer to each other? And what can the study of Anglo-Scottish relations offer to medieval studies more generally?*

Participants include Stephen Boardman (University of Edinburgh), Andy King (University of Southampton), and Alastair Macdonald (University of Aberdeen).

Session: **453** **Maurice Keyworth Building: Room G.02**
Title: **FITTING THE BILL: NAVIGATING ACADEMIC JOB APPLICATIONS - A ROUND TABLE DISCUSSION**
Sponsor: HistoryLab+
Organiser: Marci Freedman, School of Arts, Languages & Cultures, University of Manchester
Moderator: Marci Freedman
Purpose: *The purpose of this round table is to gather together early career researchers and more established lecturers to offer their experiences and advice on the academic job market. They will speak about good practice for CVs and covering letters, both for teaching and research posts. It will specifically deconstruct 'essential' and 'desirable' criteria, and how to ensure that your application illustrates how you fit the post. The round table will also discuss the differences between European and North American applications and the variation of documents that are requested. Audience members will have the opportunity to ask our speakers about their own academic journeys, as well as share their concerns about academic employment.*

This round table discussion is sponsored by HistoryLab+, a network to support late-stage postgraduates, early career historians, and independent scholars by providing access to training, career development, and networking opportunities.

Participants include Catherine Fletcher (Swansea University), Laura L. Gathagan (State University of New York, Cortland), and Charlie Rozier (Swansea University).

Session: **454** **Maurice Keyworth Building: Room 1.33**
Title: **#disIMC: CURRENT CHALLENGES TO ACCESSIBILITY AND WAYS FORWARD - A ROUND TABLE DISCUSSION**
Sponsor: Medievalists with Disabilities Network
Organiser: Alexandra R. A. Lee, Department of Italian, University College London
Moderator: Alexandra R. A. Lee
Purpose: *At the IMC 2017, Medievalists with Disabilities hosted its first event. #disIMC was a 'bring your own lunch' affair, slotted into the timetable at the last minute. It was a great success and marked the beginning of the Medievalists with Disabilities (#dismed) network.*

This round table discussion will discuss accessibility in higher education and ways that we can address issues. We take the term disabilities in the broadest possible sense, incorporating invisible and visible conditions, chronic illness, and mental health, to name but a few. Panellists will address issues individuals have overcome in Higher Education, discuss what it is like to be in HE with a disability/chronic condition, and pinpoint issues that need further attention.

Participants include Kimm Curran (University of Glasgow), Edward Mills (University of Exeter), Emma Osborne (University of Glasgow), Alicia Spencer-Hall (University College London), and Therron Welstead (University of Wales Trinity Saint David).

* * * * *

'TO LERNE THE TRETIS OF THE ASTRELABIE': ASTROLABE WORKSHOP

DIRECTED BY
KRISTINE LARSEN

MAURICE KEYWORTH BUILDING: ROOM 1.31
19.00-20.30

This event is free of charge.

Most medieval scholars have heard of the astrolabe, part work of art and part personal computer. For centuries the instrument was used across both the Christian and Islamic worlds in order to calculate times of prayer, measure the height of the sun and stars above the horizon for navigation, and aid in surveying. It is a two-dimensional model of the three-dimensional heavens that you can hold in your hands.

Anyone who has ever tried to work their way through Chaucer's *Treatise on the Astrolabe* without a basic astronomical knowledge might have (understandably) given up after the first few steps, but the astrolabe is actually not a daunting device if you just have some basic background. This hands-on workshop is a step-by-step walk-through of selected computations from Chaucer's work, including computing the current local time from the apparent position of the sun and stars and finding one's latitude.

The workshop is presented by Kristine Larsen (Professor of Astronomy at Central Connecticut State University), who has made similar presentations at the International Medieval Congress at Western Michigan University for several years, as well as numerous other universities and educational centres. The first 50 attendees will receive a free cardboard astrolabe as well as an instruction sheet (both theirs to keep).

* * * * *

* * * * *

'ALL THY BEST PARTS BOUND TOGETHER': COPTIC BOOKBINDING WORKSHOP

DIRECTED BY
LINETTE WITHERS

CLOTHWORKERS BUILDING SOUTH: ROOM G.11B
19.00-21.00

PRICE: £28.50

In 1945, a collection of early Christian and Gnostic texts was discovered near the Egyptian town of Nag Hammadi. These leather-bound vellum codices, dating from the 3rd and 4th centuries, were sealed within a jar which was found by a local farmer. These volumes were written in the Coptic language and bound in a single-section Coptic style, with covers of soft leather that were stiffened by sheets of waste papyrus. The first true form of the codex, the Coptic style of binding continued to be used until the 11th century.

Participants in the workshop will recreate one of the types of Coptic bindings used in the Nag Hammadi finds with goat leather and papyrus covers and linen thread. The internal pages of the book will be blank sketch paper. All materials will be provided.

Linette Withers completed an MA in Medieval Studies at the University of Leeds before joining the IMC team as Senior Congress Officer. She has been binding books since 2005 and since 2012 has worked as a professional book binder, producing codices that are inspired by historical books. Recently one of her works was shortlisted for display at the Bodleian Library at the University of Oxford as part of their 'Redesigning the Medieval Book' competition and exhibition. She also regularly volunteers for library conservation projects and teaches binding techniques in her studio in Leeds.

This workshop can only accommodate a limited number of participants. Early booking is recommended.

* * * * *

MEDIEVAL SOCIETY PUB QUIZ

ORGANISED BY
LEEDS UNIVERSITY UNION MEDIEVAL SOCIETY

LEEDS UNIVERSITY UNION: OLD BAR
19.15-20.30

Come wind down after your first day of sessions with the annual Medieval Society Pub Quiz! The LUU Medieval Society will re-imagine the traditional British Pub Quiz by asking IMC delegates to form teams and answer questions posed by the Medieval Society quizmaster. Pool your knowledge with your colleagues for quiz topics such as: Name the Century, Latin Translation, and Match the Illuminations. Teams will be competing for everlasting glory and a small prize.

* * * * *

* * * * *

RECEPTION AT MICHAEL SADLER BUILDING

HOSTED BY
EARLY MEDIEVAL EUROPE

MICHAEL SADLER BUILDING: RUPERT BECKETT THEATRE
20.00-21.00

The journal *Early Medieval Europe* is pleased to sponsor a reception after its annual lecture at the International Medieval Congress in order to highlight the importance of the Congress to scholars working in early medieval European history and to support further research in this field. *Early Medieval Europe* is an interdisciplinary journal that covers Europe in its entirety, including material on Iceland, the British Isles, Scandinavia, and continental Europe. Further information about the journal and details on how to submit material to it are available at http://eu.wiley.com. All those attending are warmly invited to join members of the editorial board after the lecture for refreshment and conversation.

* * * * *

RECEPTION AT MICHAEL SADLER BUILDING

HOSTED BY
BRILL PUBLISHERS

MICHAEL SADLER BUILDING: ROOM LG.10
20.00-21.00

Brill Publishers of Leiden invites authors, friends of the press, and other conference participants to a wine reception. Drinks and nibbles will be provided. We look forward to seeing you there.

* * * * *

* * * * *

Music from the Ritson Manuscript

Performed by
The Clothworkers Consort of Leeds

Directed by
Bryan White

School of Music: Clothworkers Concert Hall
20.30-21.30

Price: £12.50

The Clothworkers Consort of Leeds performs music from the Ritson Manuscript (London, British Library, Add. 5665). This manuscript contains a diverse collection of carols, masses, Latin liturgical and devotional texts, sacred chant, and secular and religious songs in English, representing a compendium of vocal music from the mid-15th to early 16th centuries. This programme will explore the diversity of the collection including two large-scale works by Thomas Pack ('Lumen ad revelacionem gencium' and an English Te Deum), a setting of the prayer to the Blessed Virgin Mary against the plague, 'Stella celi extirpavit', the Marian antiphon 'Salve regina', and a range of carols and songs for small ensemble.

The Clothworkers Consort of Leeds (CCL) was formed in 2001 as a chamber choir which included the performance of sacred choral music in liturgical settings as one of its important aims. Since that time, it has developed into one of the finest choral ensembles in the north of England. The choir performs at services and gives concerts; it has collaborated with professional ensembles including Fretwork, QuintEssential Sackbut and Cornett Ensemble, Skipton Building Society Camerata, and Leeds Baroque Orchestra. The choir has performed in prestigious venues throughout the UK, including the Howard Assembly Room, St. Paul's London, York Minster, and 15 English cathedrals. It has toured to the Czech Republic, Germany, Italy, Poland, and Hungary, and recorded three CDs: *Songs of Praise: Music from the West Riding* (2004), *Vox Dei* (2006), and *No Man is an Island* (2008). The choir has staged performances of *Dido and Aeneas* at Temple Newsam House and joined with Rambert Dance Company and London Musici for performances of Howard Goodall's *Eternal Light* at the Grand Theatre in Leeds. The choir appeared on Corinne Bailey Rae's second album, *The Sea* (2010), and recorded Stephen Kilpatrick's title music for Michelle Lipton's play, *Amazing Grace*, broadcast on BBC Radio 4. CCL has been involved in modern premieres of Philip Hayes's *The Judgment of Hermes* (1783), with Skipton Camerata, and E. J. Loder's music for Lord Byron's *Manfred* at the Ilkley Literature Festival. In 2017 the choir made its Wigmore Hall debut in *Music on the Verge of Destruction*, subsequently broadcast on BBC Radio 3. This is the choir's third appearance at the IMC.

* * * * *

Today's Excursions
Kirkstall Abbey 13.30-17.00
See p. 454 for full details.

* * * * *

SECOND-HAND AND ANTIQUARIAN BOOKFAIR

LEEDS UNIVERSITY UNION: FOYER
08.00-17.00

This event is free of charge.

The IMC 2018 Exhibitions and Bookfairs (see pp. 472-474) will open with a three-day specialist Second-Hand and Antiquarian Bookfair. The following booksellers will be among those exhibiting:

Bennett & Kerr Books - Old, rare, and scholarly books on medieval studies.
Chevin Books - Books on most subjects, including archaeology, theology, art and architecture.
Northern Herald Books - Scholarly books on medieval studies, together with general economic and social history.
Pinwell Books - All aspects of the Middle Ages.
Salsus Books - Medieval and Byzantine Studies, Patristics, and general academic books.
Unsworth's Booksellers - Antiquarian and second-hand books on the Middle Ages.

* * * * *

Session: **501** **Parkinson Building: Room 1.16**
Title: **THE POLITICS OF TIME IN ANGLO-SAXON ENGLAND**
Organiser: Joana Marie Eileen Blanquer, School of English, Trinity College Dublin and Neville Mogford, Department of English, Royal Holloway, University of London
Moderator: Rebecca Stephenson, School of English, Drama, Film & Creative Writing, University College Dublin
Paper 501-a: **Quotidian Time in Anglo-Saxon Literary Culture** (Language: English)
Neville Mogford
Paper 501-b: **The Collective Stream of Consciousness: Creating the Ancestral Community in *Beowulf*** (Language: English)
Joana Marie Eileen Blanquer
Paper 501-c: **Temporal and Eternal Kingship in *Beowulf* and *Andreas*** (Language: English)
Francis Leneghan, Faculty of English Language & Literature, University of Oxford

Session: **502** **Baines Wing: Room 2.16**
Title: **MARKERS OF IDENTITY IN MEDIEVAL GEORGIA AND ARMENIA**
Organiser: IMC Programming Committee
Moderator: Beata Możejko, Zakład Historii Średniowiecza Polski i Nauk Pomocniczych Historii, Uniwersytet Gdański
Paper 502-a: **The Cross Emblem in Georgian Art: Echoes of Historical Events and Memories of Jerusalem** (Language: English)
Erga Shneurson, Independent Scholar, Petach Tikva, Israel
Paper 502-b: **The Marker of Identity in Medieval Georgia: Holy Kings** (Language: English)
Bejan Javakhia, Department of Medieval Studies, Ilia State University, Georgia
Paper 502-c: **'God save the Emperor': Utilisation of the *Book of Letters (Girk' T'łt'oc')* in Uxtanes' *History of Armenians*** (Language: English)
Kosuke Nakada, St Andrews Institute of Mediaeval Studies, University of St Andrews

Session: **503** **University House: Little Woodhouse Room**
Title: **CONSTRUCTING AND DECONSTRUCTING BYZANTINE ELEMENTS: PERCEPTIONS OF A MEDIEVAL WORLD IN THE LATE 19TH AND EARLY 20TH CENTURIES**
Organiser: Darlene Brooks Hedstrom, Department of History, Wittenberg University, Ohio
Moderator: E. T. Dailey, Amsterdam University Press / Arc Humanities Press / Medieval Institute Publications, Western Michigan University, Kalamazoo
Paper 503-a: **Misplacing Byzantine Egypt** (Language: English)
Darlene Brooks Hedstrom
Paper 503-b: **Mykhailo Hrushevsky and the Construction of a Non-Byzantine History of Rus'** (Language: English)
Christian Raffensperger, Department of History, Wittenberg University, Ohio
Paper 503-c: **Architectural Archaeology in Soviet Ukraine: The Creation of a Rus' City Center in Chernihiv** (Language: English)
Olenka Pevny, Fitzwilliam College, University of Cambridge

Session:	**504**	**Maurice Keyworth Building: Room 1.04**
Title:	**WATERWAYS IN THE AGE OF CHARLEMAGNE**	
Organiser:	Lukas Werther, Institut für Orientalistik, Indogermanistik und Ur- und Frühgeschichtliche Archäologie, Friedrich-Schiller-Universität Jena	
Moderator:	Stefan Esders, Friedrich-Meinecke-Institut, Freie Universität Berlin	
Paper 504-a:	**Waterways and Royal Power in the Age of Charlemagne** (Language: English) Ildar Garipzanov, Institutt for Arkeologi, Bevaring og Historie, Universitetet i Oslo	
Paper 504-b:	**Chronology, Chronological Memory, and the Setting of Charlemagne's Canal Project** (Language: English) Lukas Werther	
Paper 504-c:	**Charlemagne's 792/793 Canal Project: Craft, Nature, and Memory** (Language: English) Jinty Nelson, Department of History, King's College London	

Session:	**505**	**Fine Art Building: SR G.04**
Title:	**ME, MYSELF, AND I?: CONSTRUCTING THE SELF IN ART**	
Organiser:	IMC Programming Committee	
Moderator:	Gilbert Jones, Department of Art History & Art, Case Western Reserve University, Ohio	
Paper 505-a:	**Self-Observation: The Case of Philip the Good and His Book of Hours (The Hague, Koninklijke Bibliotheek, MS 76F2)** (Language: English) Dafna Nissim, Department of the Arts, Ben-Gurion University of the Negev, Beer-Sheva	
Paper 505-b:	**The Guardian of England: Shaping and Presenting Self-Identity in Two Personal Prayer Books of John of Lancaster, Duke of Bedford** (Language: English) Orly Amit, Department of Art History, Tel Aviv University	
Paper 505-c:	**Medieval Portrait as Object of Memory** (Language: English) Liya Okroshidze, Department of History of Art, Lomonosov Moscow State University	

Session:	**506**	**Michael Sadler Building: Room LG.16**
Title:	**TRACING THE JERUSALEM CODE, I: REMEMBERING JERUSALEM IN SCANDINAVIAN PARISH CHURCHES**	
Sponsor:	Research Council of Norway Project 'Tracing the Jerusalem Code: Christian Cultures in Scandinavia'	
Organiser:	Kristin B. Aavitsland, Det teologiske Menighetsfakultet, Oslo	
Moderator:	Kristin B. Aavitsland	
Paper 506-a:	**Jerusalem as an Architectural Cue: The Chancel Arches in 12th-Century Danish Churches** (Language: English) Line M. Bonde, Det teologiske Menighetsfakultet, Oslo	
Paper 506-b:	**A Wooden Golgotha: Jerusalem and Personal Commemoration in Torpo Stave Church** (Language: English) Linn Willetts Borgen, Institutt for arkeologi, konservering og historie, Universitetet i Oslo	
Paper 506-c:	**The Persistent Jerusalem: The Holy Cross of Borre across Confessional Cultures** (Language: English) Kaja Merete Haug Hagen, Det teologiske fakultet, Universitetet i Oslo	

Session: **507** **Michael Sadler Building: Room LG.17**
Title: **CHRISTIAN AND MUSLIM IDENTITY IN MEDIEVAL NORTHERN SPAIN**
Organiser: Victor Martínez, Department of Art History, Arkansas State University
Moderator: Scott de Brestian, Department of Art & Design, Central Michigan University
Paper 507-a: **Almofalla: On the Chronology of Arab Camps in Castile** (Language: English)
David Peterson, Departamento de Historia, Universidad de Burgos
Paper 507-b: **El misterio de Beato de Liebana: Completa lectura iconográfica del tímpano de Moradillo de Sedano a través de la epigrafía** (Language: Español)
Álvaro Castresana López, Archivo Histórico Provincial de Burgos, Junta de Castilla y León
Paper 507-c: **Style and Medieval Identity in the Funerary Stele from San Vicente del Valle, Burgos** (Language: English)
Victor Martínez

Session: **508** **Fine Art Building: Studio Ground Floor**
Title: **HORSES ACROSS EUROPE**
Organiser: Timothy Dawson, Independent Scholar, Leeds and Anastasija Ropa, Faculty of Humanities, University of Latvia, Riga
Moderator: Edgar Rops, Independent Scholar, Latvia
Paper 508-a: **The Typology of Horses in Burgundian Chronicles of the 15th Century** (Language: English)
Loïs Forster, Institut de Recherches Historiques du Septentrion (IRHiS - UMR 8529), Université de Lille
Paper 508-b: **'Hrafn ok Sleipnir, hestar ágætir': Horses of the Medieval North** (Language: English)
Rebecca Henderson, St Anne's College, University of Oxford
Paper 508-c: **Remembering Vegetius and Arrian: Cavalry Tactics and Training in the Early Middle Ages** (Language: English)
Jürg Gassmann, Independent Scholar, Bulgan
Paper 508-d: **Horses as Military Force Multipliers in Medieval Europe** (Language: English)
John Henry Gassmann, Independent Scholar, Bühler

Session: **509** **Baines Wing: Room 2.13**
Title: **NEW DIRECTIONS IN MEDIEVAL CONFESSION, I: LATIN CONFESSION**
Sponsor: Network for the Study of Late Antique & Early Medieval Monasticism
Organiser: Andrea Mancini, Institute for Medieval Studies, University of Leeds and Krista A. Murchison, Faculteit der Geesteswetenschappen, Universiteit Leiden
Moderator: Krista A. Murchison
Paper 509-a: **Pilgrimage and Exile in the Irish Penitentials** (Language: English)
Lane Springer, Centre for Medieval Studies, University of Toronto, Downtown
Paper 509-b: **The Introspective Roots of Confession** (Language: English)
Inbar Graiver, Theologische Fakultät, Humboldt-Universität zu Berlin
Paper 509-c: **The Education of Confessor in Nicholas of Osimo's Works, 1429-1444** (Language: English)
Andrea Mancini

Session:	**510** **Baines Wing: Room 1.13**
Title:	**NEW PERSPECTIVES ON THE USES OF BIBLICAL EXEGESIS**
Organiser:	IMC Programming Committee
Moderator:	Lydia Marie Walker, Department of History, University of Tennessee, Knoxville
Paper 510-a:	**The Perspective of the Kingdom of God in Gregory of Nyssa's Sermons on the Lord's Prayer in Comparison with the Analysis of the Same Prayer in the Writings of Ambrose of Milan and John Chrysostom** (Language: English) Eirini Artemi, School of Humanities, Hellenic Open University, Greece
Paper 510-b:	**Encyclopedic Memory: Hildegard of Bingen and Carolingian Exegesis** (Language: English) Hannah W. Matis, Department of Church History, Virginia Theological Seminary
Paper 510-c:	**Using Biblical Exegesis in Commentaries or in Sermons: Edification or Demonstration of Know-How? - The Readings of the Epistle of St James in the Iberian Peninsula at the End of the 12th Century** (Language: English) Amélie De Las Heras, Fondation Thiers, Paris / Institut de Recherche et d'Histoire des Textes (IRHT), Centre National de la Recherche Scientifique (CNRS), Paris

Session:	**511** **Baines Wing: Room 1.15**
Title:	**CEU 25, I: URBAN STUDIES - CENTRAL EUROPE AS AN URBAN REGION?**
Sponsor:	Department of Medieval Studies, Central European University, Budapest / Croatian Science Foundation (HRZZ/7235) / Medieval Central Europe Research Network (MECERN)
Organiser:	Katalin Szende, Department of Medieval Studies, Central European University, Budapest
Moderator:	Zoë Opačić, Department of History of Art, Birkbeck, University of London
Paper 511-a:	**Medieval Urban History in Croatia: Between Central Europe and the Mediterranean** (Language: English) Irena Benyovsky Latin, Department of Medieval History, Croatian Institute of History, Zagreb
Paper 511-b:	**Crown and Town: Royal and Princely Seats in Their Urban Setting in Late Medieval Central Europe** (Language: English) Leslie Carr-Riegel, Department of Medieval Studies, Central European University, Budapest
Paper 511-c:	**Coherence and Divergence in the Urbanisation of Central Europe** (Language: English) Katalin Szende

Session:	**512**	**Baines Wing: Room 1.14**
Title:	**FEMALE ABBATIAL AUTHORITY, I**	
Sponsor:	Haskins Society / John Rylands Research Institute, University of Manchester	
Organiser:	Laura Gathagan, Department of History, State University of New York, Cortland	
Moderator:	Charles Insley, Department of History, University of Manchester	
Paper 512-a:	**Chronicle of a Death Foretold: Hildegard of Bingen's Memory and Communal Identity at Rupertsberg** (Language: English) Andra-Nicoleta Alexiu, Historisches Seminar, Westfälische Wilhelms-Universität Münster	
Paper 512-b:	**Abbess Tiburga and the Rebranding of the Convent of St Catherine, Avignon** (Language: English) Christine Axen, Center for Medieval Studies, Fordham University, New York	
Paper 512-c:	**From Cash to Capons: How the Abbesses Established a Monastic Income at Saint-Amand, Rouen** (Language: English) Charlotte Cartwright, Department of History, Christopher Newport University, Virginia	

Session:	**513**	**Charles Thackrah Building: 1.01**
Title:	**MASCULINE JOURNEYS / JOURNEYING MASCULINITIES, I**	
Organiser:	Ruth Mazo Karras, Department of History, University of Minnesota, Twin Cities and Oded Zinger, Martin Buber Society of Fellows in the Humanities, Hebrew University of Jerusalem	
Moderator:	Oded Zinger	
Paper 513-a:	**'Eternal love I conceived for you': Traveling Jewish Men, Covenantal Bromances, and the Boundaries of Normative Jewish Masculinity in Two Late Medieval Hebrew Sources** (Language: English) Eyal Levinson, ERC Project Beyond the Elite, Hebrew University of Jerusalem	
Paper 513-b:	**Clothes Do Not Make the Man: Socially Reinforced Gender and Class in the *Libro de buen amor*** (Language: English) Benjamin Obernolte, Department of French & Italian, University of Minnesota, Twin Cities	
Paper 513-c:	**Masculinity and Travel in the Career of Robert of Sorbon** (Language: English) Tanya Stabler Miller, Department of History, Loyola University Chicago	

Session: **514** **University House: Beechgrove Room**
Title: **THE *SEVEN SAGES OF ROME* IN EUROPE: THE OLD FRENCH *ROMAN DES SEPT SAGES DE ROME* AND ITS TRANSLATIONS IN MEDIEVAL LATIN, ENGLISH, GERMAN, AND DUTCH, I**
Organiser: Anne Reynders, Faculty of Arts, KU Leuven and Remco Sleiderink, Departement Letterkunde, Universiteit Antwerpen
Moderator: Remco Sleiderink
Paper 514-a: **Anti-Feminism and the Trends of an European Success: The French Prose *Roman des Sept Sages de Rome*** (Language: English)
Yasmina Foehr-Janssens, Faculté des Lettres, Université de Genève
Paper 514-b: **The Dialectic of Misogyny: Comparing Early German and Latin Versions of the *Sieben weise Meister* from a Gender Perspective** (Language: English)
Bea Lundt, Fachbereich Geschichts- und Kulturwissenschaften, Freie Universität Berlin / Seminar für Geschichte und Geschichtsdidaktik, Europa Universität Flensburg
Paper 514-c: **Form and Life at Risk: Seriality and Framing in the *Seven Sages of Rome*** (Language: English)
Nico Kunkel, Fachbereich Literaturwissenschaft, Universität Konstanz

Session: **515** **Baines Wing: Room 1.16**
Title: **RE-THINKING THE ARISTOCRACY IN CAPETIAN FRANCE, I: ARISTOCRATIC IDENTITIES**
Sponsor: Society for the Study of French History (SSFH)
Organiser: Charlotte Crouch, Graduate Centre for Medieval Studies, University of Reading and Niall Ó Súilleabháin, Department of History, Trinity College Dublin
Moderator: Constance Bouchard, Department of History, University of Akron, Ohio
Paper 515-a: **The North Remembers: Religious Houses, Kinship, and Memory in Early Capetian France, c. 950-1050** (Language: English)
Jelle Lisson, Department of History, KU Leuven
Paper 515-b: **Aristocratic Childlessness in 12th- and 13th-Century France** (Language: English)
Charlotte Pickard, Centre for Continuing & Professional Education, Cardiff University
Paper 515-c: **A Crisis of Identity: Who Were the Nobles of 13th-Century Languedoc?** (Language: English)
Rachael Hardstaff, Department of History, University of York

Session: **516** **Michael Sadler Building: Rupert Beckett Theatre**

Title: **LEGAL TEXTS AND THEIR USERS, I: USING LAW IN MEDIEVAL EUROPE**
Sponsor: Iuris Canonici Medii Aevi Consociatio (ICMAC)
Organiser: Kathleen Cushing, Department of History, Keele University
Moderator: Anne J. Duggan, Department of History, King's College London
Paper 516-a: **A Tradition of Canon Law in Early Medieval Britain and Ireland?: A Case Study** (Language: English)
Roy Flechner, School of History, University College Dublin
Paper 516-b: **Using Canon Law in Late 9th-Century Italy** (Language: English)
Michael Heil, Department of History, University of Arkansas at Little Rock
Paper 516-c: **Thomas the Wolf versus Richard of Abingdon, c. 1292-94: A Case Study on Arguments Based in Written Law** (Language: English)
Sarah White, St Andrews Institute of Mediaeval Studies, University of St Andrews

Session: **517** **Social Sciences Building: Room 10.05**
Title: **CLERICS AND THEIR HOUSEHOLDS IN LATE ANTIQUITY, I**
Sponsor: Presbyters in the Late Antique West Project, Uniwersytet Warszawski
Organiser: Stanisław Adamiak, Instytut Historyczny, Uniwersytet Warszawski and Lisa Bailey, Department of Classics & Ancient History, University of Auckland
Moderator: Przemysław Nehring, Katedra Filologii Klasycznej, Uniwersytet Mikolaja Kopernika, Toruń
Paper 517-a: **The Canonical Legislation on the Families of Clergy, 4th-7th Centuries** (Language: English)
Stanisław Adamiak
Paper 517-b: **Enforcing Sexual Continence in the Households of Married Clergy** (Language: English)
David Hunter, Department of Modern & Classical Languages, Literatures & Cultures, University of Kentucky
Paper 517-c: **Two Major Threats for Clerics: Wine and Women, 4th-6th Centuries** (Language: English)
Bertrand Lançon, Département d'Histoire, Université de Limoges / Centre de recherche interdisciplinaire en histoire, histoire de l'art et musicologie, Université de Poitiers

Session: **518** **Stage@leeds: Stage 2**
Title: **TECHNOLOGY AND THE 'MEMORY' OF MEDIEVAL ART AND ARCHITECTURE, I: MATERIALS**
Sponsor: Index of Medieval Art, Princeton University
Organiser: Pamela A. Patton, Department of Art & Archaeology, Princeton University
Moderator: Pamela A. Patton
Paper 518-a: **Textile Studies in the Digital Age: The Medieval Textiles in Iberia and the Mediterranean Research Project** (Language: English)
María Judith Feliciano, Independent Scholar, New York
Paper 518-b: **From Textile Fragments to Luxury Garments: Reconstructing Medieval Textiles from Their Materiality** (Language: English)
Ana Cabrera-Lafuente, Victoria & Albert Museum, London
Paper 518-c: **Quantity, Memory, and the Parchment Inheritance** (Language: English)
Bruce Holsinger, Department of English, University of Virginia

Session: **519** **Charles Thackrah Building: 1.02**
Title: **GLOSSING BOOKS, I: GLIMPSES INTO THE MINDS OF READERS**
Organiser: Mariken Teeuwen, Huygens Instituut voor Nederlandse Geschiedenis, Koninklijke Nederlandse Academie van Wetenschappen (ING - KNAW), Amsterdam
Moderator: Evina Steinová, Pontifical Institute of Mediaeval Studies, University of Toronto, Downtown
Paper 519-a: **Glosses on Grammar: The Study of Priscian at Early Medieval Wissembourg** (Language: English)
Cinzia Grifoni, Institut für Mittelalterforschung, Österreichische Akademie der Wissenschaften, Wien
Paper 519-b: **Bede's Home for Peculiar Glosses** (Language: English)
Bernhard Bauer, Department of Early Irish, Maynooth University
Paper 519-c: **Of Bilingual Glosses and Those Who Copy Them** (Language: English)
Nike Stam, Departement Talen, Literatuur en Communicatie, Universiteit Utrecht

Session: **520** **University House: Great Woodhouse Room**
Title: **YOU'RE SO YWAIN (YOU PROBABLY THINK THIS ROMANCE IS ABOUT YOU): NEW APPROACHES TO THE MIDDLE ENGLISH *YWAIN AND GAWAIN***
Organiser: Danielle Howarth, School of Literatures, Languages & Cultures, University of Edinburgh
Moderator: Sarah Carpenter, School of Literatures, Languages & Cultures - English Literature, University of Edinburgh
Paper 520-a: **His Bark is Worse than His Bite: Trees and Ywain's Identity in *Ywain and Gawain*** (Language: English)
Danielle Howarth
Paper 520-b: **Why Is a Woman Like a Lion?: And Other Questions of Friendship in *Ywain and Gawain*** (Language: English)
Amy Brown, Département de langue et littérature anglaises, Université de Genève
Paper 520-c: **Affect, Authority, and Forgiveness in *Ywain and Gawain*** (Language: English)
Usha Vishnuvajjala, Department of Literature, American University, Washington DC

Session: **521** **Emmanuel Centre: Wilson Room**
Title: **ALLUSION, REFERENCE, AND MEMORY IN HIGH MEDIEVAL NARRATIVES, I**
Sponsor: Centre for Research in Historiography & Historical Cultures / Department of History & Welsh History, Aberystwyth University
Organiser: Caitlin Naylor, Department of History & Welsh History, Aberystwyth University
Moderator: Björn Weiler, Department of History & Welsh History, Aberystwyth University
Paper 521-a: **'So that readers can know exactly what happened': The Role of Allusions as a Means of Authority and Memory in 12th-Century Origin Stories** (Language: English)
Kiri Kolt, Department of History & Welsh History, Aberystwyth University

Paper 521-b: **The *Gesta Stephani*'s Atypical Use of Intertextual Figures** (Language: English)
Tom Forster, Selwyn College, University of Cambridge
Paper 521-c: **Why Did the British Burn Their Walking Dead?: Common Sense and Classical References in William of Newburgh's *Historia Rerum Anglicarum*** (Language: English)
Polina Ignatova, Department of History, Lancaster University

Session: **522** **Social Sciences Building: Room 10.06**
Title: **MNEMONIC VERSES AND DEVICES**
Organiser: IMC Programming Committee
Moderator: Lucie Doležalová, Institute of Greek & Latin Studies, Univerzita Karlova, Praha
Paper 522-a: **Making Mynde: Mnemonic Devices as Clues to the Audience of a Middle English Bible Summary** (Language: English)
Hannah Schuhle-Lewis, Faculty of English Language & Literature, University of Oxford
Paper 522-b: **'Unde versus': The Mnemonic Poetry of Leeds, Royal Armouries MS I.33** (Language: English)
Antti Ijäs, Department of World Cultures, University of Helsinki
Paper 522-c: **Acrostics and the Art of Memory in Poland and Silesia in the Late Middle Ages** (Language: English)
Rafał Wójcik, Section of Old Prints, University Library, Adam Mickiewicz University, Poznań
Paper 522-d: **Windy Wings and Burning Bellows: Evidence of Words and Images as Mnemonical Devices in the Macclesfield Psalter** (Language: English)
Angelo Maria Monaco, La Scuola di Pittura / La Scuola di Grafica, Accademia Belle Arti di Lecce

Session: **523** **Maurice Keyworth Building: Room 1.31**
Title: **COMMEMORATING SAINTS AND MARTYRS, I: TRANSFORMING IDENTITIES IN HAGIOGRAPHY**
Sponsor: MARTRAE Network
Organiser: Nicole Volmering, Department of Irish & Celtic Languages, Trinity College Dublin
Moderator: Ann Buckley, Trinity Medieval History Research Centre, Trinity College Dublin
Paper 523-a: **'To rente the flessch fro the bone': St Margaret, Mutilation, and Ungendering Divinity** (Language: English)
Gitana Deneff, Department of English, California State University, Long Beach
Paper 523-b: **Sacrifice for Virginity's Sake: The Case of St Cairech Dercáin and Her Charge in Dublin, Royal Irish Academy, Stowe MS B iv 2** (Language: English)
Kathryn O'Neill, Department of Celtic Languages & Literatures, Harvard University
Paper 523-c: **Óengus and His *Féilire*: Shaping Sanctity, Memory, and Commemoration** (Language: English)
Nicole Volmering

Session:	**524** **Michael Sadler Building: Room LG.19**
Title:	**MEMORY THEATRE, I: SHAPING MEMORY THROUGH THEATRE**
Sponsor:	Société internationale pour l'étude du théâtre médiéval (SITM)
Organiser:	Cora Dietl, Institut für Germanistik, Justus-Liebig-Universität Gießen
Moderator:	Cora Dietl
Paper 524-a:	**A Prince or a Pauper?: Staging Noble Lineage in the Coronation Order of Emperor Charles IV** (Language: English) Eliška Poláčková, Department of Theatre Studies, Masarykova univerzita, Brno / Centre for Classical Studies, Czech Academy of Sciences, Praha
Paper 524-b:	**Unreliable Witnesses: Foreign and Local Memories of the 1589 Florentine *Intermedi*** (Language: English) M. A. Katritzky, Department of English, Open University, Milton Keynes
Paper 524-c:	**Imagery, Memory, and Dynasties in Shakespeare's *Richard II*** (Language: English) Giorgia De Santis, Dipartimento di Storia, Patrimonio culturale, Formazione e Società, Università degli Studi di Roma 'Tor Vergata'

Session:	**525** **Maurice Keyworth Building: Room 1.06**
Title:	**MEMORY AND MYTH: REMEMBERING MEDIEVAL IRELAND AND ITS NEIGHBOURS, I - COMMUNITY IDENTITY**
Sponsor:	Medieval History Research Centre, Trinity College Dublin
Organiser:	Áine Foley, Medieval History Research Centre, Trinity College Dublin
Moderator:	Seán Duffy, Department of History, Trinity College Dublin
Paper 525-a:	***Brennu-Njáls saga* and the Memory of Ireland in Iceland** (Language: English) Annie Humphrey, Department of History, Trinity College Dublin
Paper 525-b:	**Early Irish Identity, c. 600-900: *Féni*, *Gael*, and the Manipulation of Memory** (Language: English) Brendan Meighan, Department of History, Trinity College Dublin
Paper 525-c:	**A New Book of Invasions?: The Historiography of Medieval Ireland** (Language: English) Clare Downham, Institute of Irish Studies, University of Liverpool

Session: **526** **Social Sciences Building: Room 10.07**
Title: **'DIANA AND ALL HER SECT': REMEMBERING WOMEN WARRIORS, I**
Sponsor: Society for Medieval Feminist Scholarship
Organiser: Sophie Harwood, Institute for Medieval Studies, University of Leeds, Roberta Magnani, Centre for Medieval & Early Modern Research (MEMO), Swansea University and Amy Louise Morgan, School of Literature & Languages, University of Surrey
Moderator: Amy Louise Morgan
Paper 526-a: **Reviving Dihya, the Once and Future Queen of the Berbers** (Language: English)
Rebecca Hill, Department of English, University of California, Los Angeles
Paper 526-b: **In the Family Way: Containing the Power of Female Japanese Warriors** (Language: English)
Kim Mc Nelly, Department of Asian Languages & Cultures, University of California, Los Angeles
Paper 526-c: **Judith as Jewish Heroine in the Medieval European Synagogue** (Language: English)
Gabriel Wasserman, Department of Hebrew Literature, The Hebrew University of Jerusalem
Paper 526-d: **Diana's Sect: Amazon Queens between East and West** (Language: English)
Roberta Magnani

Session: **527** **Michael Sadler Building: Banham Theatre**
Title: **MEMORIES OF NATION, MEDIEVAL AND MODERN, I: METHODS AND MEDIEVAL STUDIES**
Sponsor: Richard Bland College of William & Mary, Virginia
Organiser: Daniel Franke, Department of History, Richard Bland College of William & Mary, Virginia
Moderator: Daniel Franke
Paper 527-a: **The Problem of Anachronism in Nationalism Studies** (Language: English)
Caspar Hirschi, Fachbereich Geschichte, Universität St. Gallen
Paper 527-b: **Huizinga, Haskins, Pirenne: Contested Medievalisms on the Belgian Frontier** (Language: English)
Carol Symes, Department of History, University of Illinois, Urbana-Champaign
Paper 527-c: **Beyond 'Nationalism': Historical Terms, Analytical Categories, and Problems of Terminology** (Language: English)
Andrea Ruddick, Exeter College, University of Oxford

Session: **528** **Stage@leeds: Stage 3**
Title: ***ZIKARON/MEMORIA*: JEWISH MEMORY AND JEWISH COMMUNITY, I**
Organiser: IMC Programming Committee
Moderator: Eva Frojmovic, Centre for Jewish Studies, University of Leeds
Paper 528-a: **Christian Handling of Jewish Space after the Black Death Persecutions** (Language: English)
Franziska Kleybolte, Historisches Seminar, Ludwig-Maximilians-Universität München
Paper 528-b: **Torah-Binders and *Taufwindel* at a Time of Turmoil** (Language: English)
Annette Weber, Lehrstuhl für Jüdische Kunst, Hochschule für Jüdische Studien, Heidelberg

Session:	**529** **Maurice Keyworth Building: Room 1.05**
Title:	**REMEMBERING PENANCE, GHOSTS, AND EMOTIONS IN THE MIDDLE AGES**
Sponsor:	Oxford Handbook of the Merovingian World
Organiser:	Isabel Moreira, Department of History, University of Utah
Moderator:	Bonnie Effros, Department of History, University of Liverpool
Paper 529-a:	**Memorable Penance and Penitential Memory** (Language: English) Kevin Uhalde, Department of History, Ohio University
Paper 529-b:	**Purgatory, Intercession, and the Rise of Christian Ghosts** (Language: English) Isabel Moreira
Paper 529-c:	**Sensual Experience in Heaven and Hell** (Language: English) Eileen Gardiner, Italica Press, New York

Session:	**530** **Charles Thackrah Building: 1.03**
Title:	**MEMORY DEPICTED, I**
Sponsor:	Universiteit van Amsterdam
Organiser:	Wendelien A. W. Van Welie-Vink, Afdeling Kunst- en cultuurwetenschappen, Universiteit van Amsterdam
Moderator:	Julian Gardner, Department of the History of Art, University of Warwick
Paper 530-a:	**Remembering the Dead: Albert of Ouwater's *Raising of Lazarus* Revisited** (Language: English) Huib Iserief, Afdeling Kunst- en cultuurwetenschappen, Universiteit van Amsterdam
Paper 530-b:	**The Use of Holy Heads in Memory** (Language: English) Wendelien A. W. Van Welie-Vink
Paper 530-c:	**The Forgotten Iconography of St James: The Evolution of an Apostle Becoming a Warrior Saint and Pilgrim** (Language: English) Sophie de Boer, Faculteit der Geesteswetenschappen, Universiteit van Amsterdam

Session:	**531** **Charles Thackrah Building: 1.04**
Title:	**MATERIAL CULTURE AND LANDSCAPES, I: MEMORY AND MANUSCRIPTS**
Sponsor:	Forschungsportal Englische Geschichte und Britische Inseln (FEMBI)
Organiser:	Daniel Brown, Historisches Institut, Universität zu Köln and Stefanie Schild, Independent Scholar, Hilden
Moderator:	Benjamin Pohl, Department of History, University of Bristol
Paper 531-a:	**We Can Be Heroes: Material Culture and the Creation of Brythnoth** (Language: English) Katherine Weikert, Department of Archaeology / Department of History, University of Winchester
Paper 531-b:	**Remembering since the Creation: Universal History as a Manuscript in Torigni's *Liber Chronicorum*** (Language: English) Gabriele Passabì, Sidney Sussex College, University of Cambridge
Paper 531-c:	**Imagination, Identity, and Memory: *Le livre de chasse* as *Memoria*** (Language: English) Becky Pratt-Sturges, Department of Comparative Cultural Studies, Northern Arizona University

Session:	**532** **Social Sciences Building: Room 10.09**
Title:	**GRADUATE CENTRE FOR MEDIEVAL STUDIES, UNIVERSITY OF READING, I: MEMORY, SAINTS' CULTS, AND HEALING**
Sponsor:	Graduate Centre for Medieval Studies, University of Reading
Organiser:	Rebecca A. C. Rist, Graduate Centre for Medieval Studies, University of Reading
Moderator:	Rebecca A. C. Rist
Paper 532-a:	**Miracles, Monks, Memories, and the Cult of St Æbbe** (Language: English) Ruth Salter, Graduate Centre for Medieval Studies, University of Reading
Paper 532-b:	**Committing Madness to Memory: A Holy Fool and Four Demoniacs in the Foundation Legend of St Bartholomew's Priory and Hospital in London** (Language: English) Claire Trenery, School of History, University of Leeds
Paper 532-c:	**St Louis and St Peregrinus: The Role of the Leper in the Consecration Legend of Saint-Denis** (Language: English) Katie Phillips, Graduate Centre for Medieval Studies, University of Reading

Session:	**533** **Leeds University Union: Room 2 - Elland Road**
Title:	**COMMUNICATION AND THE EXPLOITATION OF KNOWLEDGE, I: COLLECTIVE MEMORY IN AND AROUND THE COURTROOM**
Sponsor:	Onderzoeksschool Mediëvistiek, Rijksuniversiteit Groningen
Organiser:	Nathan van Kleij, Afdeling Geschiedenis, Europese studies en Religiewetenschappen, Universiteit van Amsterdam
Moderator:	Mark Vermeer, Departement Geschiedenis en Kunstgeschiedenis, Universiteit Utrecht
Paper 533-a:	**Paintings, Space, and Collective Memory in the Late Medieval Urban Courtroom** (Language: English) Nathan van Kleij
Paper 533-b:	**Memory Politics of the Late Medieval Law Court: A Multimedial Analysis** (Language: English) Frans Camphuijsen, Center for Medieval & Renaissance Studies Amsterdam, Universiteit van Amsterdam
Paper 533-c:	**Ideological Poems and Political Memory in Late Medieval Town Halls** (Language: English) Minne de Boodt, Research Group for the History of the Middle Ages / Department of History, KU Leuven

Session:	**534**	**Leeds University Union: Room 4 - Hyde Park**
Title:	**NOTHING NEW!: HERITAGE, MEMORY, AND IDENTITY IN THE MIDDLE AGES, I**	
Sponsor:	Centre for Religion & Heritage, Rijksuniversiteit Groningen	
Organiser:	Mathilde van Dijk, Faculteit der Godgeleerdheid en Godsdienstwetenschap, Rijksuniversiteit Groningen and Andrew J. M. Irving, Faculteit der Godgeleerdheid en Godsdienstwetenschap, Rijksuniversiteit Groningen	
Moderator:	Charlie Rozier, Department of History, Swansea University	
Paper 534-a:	**The Saints of Northumbria and the Legacy of Bede in the 12th Century** (Language: English) Lauren L. Whitnah, Marco Institute for Medieval & Renaissance Studies, University of Tennessee, Knoxville	
Paper 534-b:	**Monastic Legacy and Identity Formation in Ottonian Female Monastic Communities** (Language: English) Jirki Thibaut, Vakgroep Geschiedenis, Universiteit Gent / KU Leuven	
Paper 534-c:	**'And St Augustine was her brother': Mnemonic Strategies and Hagiographic Heritage in the Sisterbooks of Diepenveen and Deventer** (Language: English) Godelinde Gertrude Perk, Avdelningen för Humaniora, Mittuniversitets, Sundsvall	
Respondent:	Mathilde van Dijk	

Session:	**535**	**Maurice Keyworth Building: Room 1.09**
Title:	**POWER, MEMORY, AND WRITTEN RECORD IN MEDIEVAL SPAIN, I: CREATION AND RECREATION OF MEMORY IN LOCAL COMMUNITIES AND TOWNS**	
Sponsor:	El ejercicio del poder: espacios, agentes y escrituras (siglos XI-XV), EJEPO Project	
Organiser:	Álvaro Jesús Sanz Martín, Departamento de Historia Antigua y Medieval, Universidad de Valladolid	
Moderator:	Alberto Navarro Baena, Facultad de Filosofía y Letras, Universidad de Valladolid	
Paper 535-a:	**Memories of the Past in 12th-Century Castile and Leon** (Language: English) Pascual Martínez Sopena, Facultad de Filosofía y Letras, Universidad de Valladolid	
Paper 535-b:	**Privileges, Copies, and Forgeries: Royal Confirmations of Town Charters in Castile and Leon, c. 1250-1500** (Language: English) Álvaro Jesús Sanz Martín	
Paper 535-c:	**Rewriting the Origins of Towns: Conflict, Memory, and Charters in Late Medieval Castile** (Language: English) Miguel Calleja Puerta, Departamento de Historia, Universidad de Oviedo	

Session: **536** **Leeds University Union: Room 5 - Kirkstall Abbey**
Title: **SAVE THE DATE!: CONFLICTING IDEAS ABOUT THE QUALITY OF TIME IN MEMORY AND FOR PROGNOSIS, I**
Organiser: Uta Heil, Institut für Kirchengeschichte, Christliche Archäologie und Kirchliche Kunst, Universität Wien
Moderator: Hans-Werner Goetz, Historisches Seminar, Universität Hamburg
Paper 536-a: **Save the Date!: The Sunday between the Memory of Salvation and Divine Punishment** (Language: English)
Uta Heil
Paper 536-b: **The Early Medieval Reception of Augustine on 'Wednesday'** (Language: English)
Immo Warntjes, Department of History, Trinity College Dublin
Paper 536-c: **Thursday in the Later Roman Empire** (Language: English)
Ilaria Bultrighini, Department of Hebrew & Jewish Studies, University College London

Session: **537** **Maurice Keyworth Building: Room 1.03**
Title: **REMEMBERING CONSTANTINOPLE IN THE 15TH CENTURY**
Sponsor: Society for the Promotion of Byzantine Studies
Organiser: Aslıhan Akışık-Karakullukçu, General Education Department, Bahçeşehir University, Istanbul / Department of Humanities & Social Sciences, Işık University, İstanbul
Moderator: Aslıhan Akışık-Karakullukçu
Paper 537-a: **From West to East: The Legacy of Constantinople in Bessarion's Literary Portrayal of Trebizond** (Language: English)
Annika Asp-Talwar, Centre for Byzantine, Ottoman & Modern Greek Studies, University of Birmingham
Paper 537-b: **Historical Memory and Constantinople in Isidore's Encomium of John VIII** (Language: English)
Aslıhan Akışık-Karakullukçu
Paper 537-c: **Literary Memory and Classicizing Discourse in John Dokeianos's Encomium of Constantine XI** (Language: English)
Anna Calia, Seeger Center for Hellenic Studies, Princeton University

Session: **538** **Michael Sadler Building: Room LG.10**
Title: **A DIGITAL KEY TO MATTHEW PARKER'S LEGACY: NEW CONTRIBUTIONS THROUGH *PARKER ON THE WEB 2.0***
Sponsor: Parker Library, Corpus Christi College, University of Cambridge
Organiser: Anne McLaughlin, Parker Library, Corpus Christi College, University of Cambridge
Moderator: Anne McLaughlin
Paper 538-a: **Matthew Parker's Library: 'The chief treasury of his manuscripts' as Research Collection and Digital Resource** (Language: English)
Alexander Devine, Parker Library, Corpus Christi College, University of Cambridge
Paper 538-b: **Marginalia, Memory, and Metadata in Cambridge: Cambridge, Corpus Christi College, MS 41** (Language: English)
Patricia O'Connor, School of English, University College Cork
Paper 538-c: **Cambridge, Corpus Christi College, MS 315 and the Transmission of Architectural Images in the 12th Century** (Language: English)
Karl Kinsella, Department of History of Art, University of York

Session:	**539** **Maurice Keyworth Building: Room 1.33**
Title:	**REMEMBERING THE PAST AFTER THE CAROLINGIAN EMPIRE, I: LITURGY AND *AUCTORITAS***
Sponsor:	After Empire: Using & Not Using the Past in the Crisis of the Carolingian World, c. 900-1050
Organiser:	Sarah Greer, St Andrews Institute of Mediaeval Studies, University of St Andrews
Moderator:	Erik Niblaeus, Department of History, Durham University
Paper 539-a:	**Different Models of Sanctity in Catalonia: Testimonies of the Transformation of the Post-Carolingian World** (Language: English) Ekaterina Novokhatko, Institut d'Estudis Medievals, Universitat Autònoma de Barcelona
Paper 539-b:	**Carolingian Music after the Carolingians: Writing, Memory, and the Struggle to Define Liturgical *Auctoritas*** (Language: English) Henry Parkes, Institute of Sacred Music, Yale University
Paper 539-c:	**I, Amalarius: Ademar of Chabannes and the Imitation of Carolingian Authority in 11th-Century Aquitaine** (Language: English) Graeme Ward, Institut für Mittelalterforschung, Österreichische Akademie der Wissenschaften, Wien

Session:	**540** **Parkinson Building: Nathan Bodington Chamber**
Title:	**MEMORIES OF EMPIRE**
Sponsor:	*Ceræ*: An Australasian Journal of Medieval & Early Modern Studies
Organiser:	Vanessa Wright, Institute for Medieval Studies, University of Leeds
Moderator:	Vanessa Wright
Paper 540-a:	**Sallust, Caution** (Language: English) Philippa Byrne, St John's College, University of Oxford
Paper 540-b:	**Magic and the Pagan World in the French Family of Reine Sébile Texts** (Language: English) Stephanie Hathaway, Faculty of Medieval & Modern Languages, University of Oxford
Paper 540-c:	**Maxen Wledig versus Beli Mawr?: Remembering Rome in Medieval Welsh Tradition** (Language: English) Celeste Andrews, Department of Celtic Languages & Literatures, Harvard University
Paper 540-d:	**The Malleable Roman Poet: Authorship, Authority, and Antiquity in the Misattributions of a Late Antique Text** (Language: English) Sean Tandy, Department of Classical Studies, Indiana University, Bloomington

Session: **541** **Baines Wing: Room G.36**
Title: **MEMORY AND *INQUISITIO*, I: MIRACLES, HEALINGS, AND MALEFACTORS**
Sponsor: Department for the Study of Religions, Masarykova univerzita, Brno
Organiser: David Zbíral, Department for the Study of Religions, Masarykova univerzita, Brno
Moderator: Sari Katajala-Peltomaa, School of Social Sciences & Humanities, University of Tampere
Paper 541-a: **Inquisition, Memory, and Miracle in the 15th Century: Examples from the Canonizations of Bernardino of Siena and Vincent Ferrer** (Language: English)
Laura Ackerman Smoller, Department of History, University of Rochester, New York
Paper 541-b: **Memories of Healing and Healers in Late Medieval Italian Canonization and Inquisition Protocols** (Language: English)
Jenni Kuuliala, School of Social Sciences & Humanities, University of Tampere
Paper 541-c: **Inquisitorial Processes in Italian Judicial Registers (*Libri Maleficiorum*) and Canonization Processes at the End of the Middle Ages: Changing Individual Reminiscences within Collective Memory** (Language: English)
Didier Lett, Laboratoire Identités, Cultures, Territoires (EA337), Université Paris Diderot - Paris 7 / Institut Universitaire de France, Paris

Session: **542** **Baines Wing: Room G.37**
Title: **FAME: PATRONS AND MEMORIES IN BYZANTIUM, IV**
Organiser: Francisco Lopez-Santos Kornberger, Centre for Byzantine, Ottoman & Modern Greek Studies, University of Birmingham and Jessica Varsallona, Centre for Byzantine, Ottoman & Modern Greek Studies, University of Birmingham
Moderator: Jonathan Shepard, Khalili Research Centre, University of Oxford
Paper 542-a: **Memory of Dynasty: The Byzantine Attitude to Their Ruling Imperial Families** (Language: English)
Joseph Parsonage, Centre for Byzantine, Ottoman & Modern Greek Studies, University of Birmingham
Paper 542-b: **Empresses on the Peripheries: Creating a *Basilissa* outside Byzantium** (Language: English)
Lauren A. Wainwright, Centre for Byzantine, Ottoman & Modern Greek Studies, University of Birmingham
Paper 542-c: **Faith, Memory, and Internalisation in Khazaria: The 'Return to Judaism' in the Schechter Text** (Language: English)
Alex Feldman, Centre for Byzantine, Ottoman & Modern Greek Studies, University of Birmingham

Session: **543** **Maurice Keyworth Building: Room 1.32**
Title: **THE MEMORY OF THE CRUSADES, I: GODFREY, LOUIS, AND THE SULTAN REMEMBERED**
Sponsor: Routledge
Organiser: Mike Horswell, Department of History, Royal Holloway, University of London
Moderator: Jonathan Phillips, Department of History, Royal Holloway, University of London
Paper 543-a: **'Au héros belge de la première croisade': The 1848 Equestrian Statue of Godfrey of Bouillon in the Place Royale, Brussels, and the Memory of the First Crusade in 19th-Century Belgium** (Language: English)
Simon A. John, Centre for Medieval & Early Modern Research (MEMO), Swansea University
Paper 543-b: **St Louis: A Crusader King and Hero for Victorian and First World War Britain and Ireland** (Language: English)
Elizabeth Siberry, Independent Scholar, London
Paper 543-c: **The Sultan, the Kaiser, the Colonel, and the Purloined Wreath** (Language: English)
Carole Hillenbrand, School of History, University of St Andrews

---

Session: **544** **Fine Art Building: SR 1.10**
Title: **CULTURAL MEMORY IN LATE ANTIQUITY, I: NEGOTIATING CHRISTIAN AND CLASSICAL MEMORY**
Organiser: Richard Flower, Department of Classics & Ancient History, University of Exeter and Robin Whelan, Department of History, University of Liverpool
Moderator: Robin Whelan
Paper 544-a: **Remembering a Christian Past in Didymus the Blind and the Tura Papyri** (Language: English)
Blossom Stefaniw, Theologische Fakultät, Martin-Luther-Universität Halle-Wittenberg
Paper 544-b: **Christianising the Romans of Rome: Exempla in Augustine, *City of God*, 1** (Language: English)
Teresa Röger, Faculty of Classics, University of Cambridge
Paper 544-c: **Re-Membering Rome: Biblical Sarcophagi in the Tradition of Roman Funerary Commemoration** (Language: English)
Miriam Hay, Department of Classics & Ancient History, University of Warwick

---

Session: **545** **Leeds University Union: Room 6 - Roundhay**
Title: **REMEMBERING TRAVELS, TRAVELLING IN MEMORIES, I**
Organiser: Jana Valtrová, Department for the Study of Religions, Masarykova univerzita, Brno
Moderator: Jana Valtrová
Paper 545-a: **Remembering Pilgrimage to Rome and Jerusalem: Analysing Eyewitness Testimony in Early Medieval Topographical Texts and Travel Accounts** (Language: English)
Rebecca Lawton, School of History, University of Leicester / British Library, London
Paper 545-b: ***Il Milione*: Marco Polo's Travel Memories?** (Language: English)
Felicitas Schmieder, Historisches Institut, FernUniversität Hagen
Paper 545-c: **Christopher Columbus and the Memory of the Middle Ages in the Early Modern Exploration** (Language: English)
Irene Malfatto, John Carter Brown Library, Rhode Island

Session: **546** **Emmanuel Centre: Room 10**
Title: **Traces of Memory in the Western Mediterranean, I: Landscape and Underground Memory**
Sponsor: Institut de Recerca en Cultures Medievals / Institución Milá y Fontanals (IMF), Consejo Superior de Investigaciones Científicas (CSIC) / Grup de Recerca en Estudis Medievals d'Art, Història, Paleografia i Arqueologia (MAHPA), Universitat de Barcelona
Organiser: Pau Castell-Granados, Departament d'Història i Arqueologia, Universitat de Barcelona and Marta Sancho i Planas, Institut de Recerca en Cultures Medievals, Universitat de Barcelona
Moderator: Pol Junyent Molins, Institució Milà i Fontanals (IMF), Consejo Superior de Investigaciones Científicas (CSIC), Barcelona
Paper 546-a: **The Underground Memory: Archaeological Traces of the Medieval Past in the Catalan Pyrenees** (Language: English)
Marta Sancho i Planas
Paper 546-b: **Textual, Archaeological, and Territorial Sources for the Study of Spiritual Landscape Memory** (Language: English)
Maria Soler-Sala, Departament d'Història Medieval, Paleografia i Diplomàtica, Universitat de Barcelona
Paper 546-c: **Landscapes as a Source: Using Territory to Study the Early Medieval Monasteries in the Catalan Counties** (Language: English)
Xavier Costa-Badia, Institut de Recerca en Cultures Medievals, Universitat de Barcelona

Session: **547** **Baines Wing: Room 2.14**
Title: **Memory and Knowledge in Petrus Hispanus**
Organiser: José Francisco Meirinhos, Departamento de Filosofia, Universidade do Porto
Moderator: José Francisco Meirinhos
Paper 547-a: **Sensible and Intellectual Memory in Petrus Hispanus' *Scientia libri de anima*** (Language: English)
Celia López Alcalde, Instituto de Filosofia, Universidade do Porto
Paper 547-b: **Memory and Free Choice in Petrus Hispanus' *Scientia libri de anima*** (Language: English)
João Rebalde, Instituto de Filosofia, Universidade do Porto
Paper 547-c: **Abstraction and Memory in Petrus Hispanus' Commentary on the *De anima*** (Language: English)
Ana Soares Ferreira, Instituto de Filosofia, Universidade do Porto

Session: **548** **University House: St George Room**
Title: **Jousts and *Pas d'Armes*, I: Armour, Equipment, and Costume**
Sponsor: Pas d'Armes Research Group
Organiser: Alan V. Murray, Institute for Medieval Studies, University of Leeds
Moderator: Ros Brown-Grant, School of Languages, Cultures & Societies - French, University of Leeds
Paper 548-a: **Armour and Dress for the *Pas d'Armes*: Real Playing for Roles** (Language: English)
Karen Watts, Institute for Medieval Studies, University of Leeds / Musée du Louvre, Paris
Paper 548-b: **Heraldic Horse Harness Pendants and Related Equipment Fittings** (Language: English)
David Harpin, Independent Scholar, Huddersfield
Paper 548-c: **Between a Monk and a Hard Place: Ulrich von Liechtenstein and the Invention of the Jousting Tour** (Language: English)
Alan V. Murray

Session: **549** **University House: Cloberry Room**
Title: **DISASTER MEMORY IN THE MIDDLE AGES, I**
Sponsor: Abteilung für Wirtschafts-, Sozial- und Umweltgeschichte, Universität Bern
Organiser: Christian Rohr, Historisches Institut, Universität Bern
Moderator: Martin Bauch, Leibniz-Institut für Geschichte und Kultur des östlichen Europa, Leipzig
Paper 549-a: **Disaster Memory in Norman Historiography, 1000-1550** (Language: English)
Chantal Camenisch, Historisches Institut, Universität Bern
Paper 549-b: **The Great Famine and the Cattle Plague and the Interest in Astrometeorology in 14th-Century England** (Language: English)
Kathleen Pribyl, Climatic Research Unit, University of East Anglia
Paper 549-c: **Flood Marks as Relics of Medieval Disaster Memory Cultures in Central Europe** (Language: English)
Christian Rohr

Session: **550** **Emmanuel Centre: Room 11**
Title: **CISTERCIANS, I: MEMORY, HOSPITALITY, AND BERNARD OF CLAIRVAUX**
Sponsor: *Cîteaux: Commentarii cistercienses*
Organiser: Terryl N. Kinder, *Cîteaux: Commentarii cistercienses*, Pontigny
Moderator: Terryl N. Kinder
Paper 550-a: **Echoing the Past: The Memory of Bernard of Clairvaux in the Anti-Heretical Polemic of Geoffrey of Auxerre** (Language: English)
Stamatia Noutsou, Department for the Study of Religions, Masarykova univerzita, Brno
Paper 550-b: **Human Reality Transcended: Gendered Imagery as Conveyor of the Supernatural in Bernard of Clairvaux's Letters** (Language: English)
Anna-Riina Hakala, Department of Church History, University of Helsinki
Paper 550-c: **Stricter Customs?: Remembering the Impact of Incorporation on Saints' Cults in the 12th Century** (Language: English)
Georgina Fitzgibbon, Department of History, University of Birmingham
Paper 550-d: **'Hospites tamquam Christus suscipiantur': Hospitality and the Pontigny Commentary in Its Cistercian Context** (Language: English)
Richard Thomason, Department of Classical & Archaeological Studies / Centre for Medieval & Early Modern Studies, University of Kent

Session: **551** **Baines Wing: Room 2.15**
Title: **MYTHICAL FIGURES, LEGENDARY CHARACTERS, AND GREAT MEN IN THE SO-CALLED OCCULT SCIENCES IN ARABIC, HEBREW, AND LATIN MEDIEVAL TEXTS**
Sponsor: Centre d'Etudes Orientales - Institut Orientaliste de Louvain / H37 - Histoire & Cultures Graphiques, Université catholique de Louvain, Louvain-la-Neuve
Organiser: Odile Dapsens, Faculté de Philosophie, Arts et Lettres, Université catholique de Louvain, Louvain-la-Neuve
Moderator: Paul Bertrand, Faculté de Philosophie, Arts et Lettres, Université catholique de Louvain, Louvain-la-Neuve
Paper 551-a: **The Figure of the Prince Khālid ibn Yazīd in Arabic Alchemy** (Language: English)
Marion Dapsens, Institut supérieur de philosophie, Université catholique de Louvain, Louvain-la-Neuve
Paper 551-c: **A Magic Book Attributed to Adam: The *Liber Razielis*** (Language: English)
Odile Dapsens
Paper 551-c: **Outstanding Alchemists: Great Men and Legendary Characters in Arabic Medieval Alchemy** (Language: English)
Sebastien Moureau, Warburg Institute, University of London

Session: **552** **Stage@leeds: Stage 1**
Title: **BASED ON HISTORICAL EVENTS?: TV MEDIEVALISM**
Organiser: IMC Programming Committee
Moderator: Sabina Rahman, Department of English, Macquarie University, Sydney
Paper 552-a: **Vikings in the Classroom: Popular Television as an Effective Tool for Teaching Old English and Icelandic Studies** (Language: English)
John C. Ford, Institut National Universitaire Champollion, Université Fédérale Toulouse Midi-Pyrénées
Paper 552-b: **The Medieval Memory through *Game of Thrones*** (Language: English)
Caitlyn Davis, Arizona Center for Medieval & Renaissance Studies (ACMRS), Tempe
Paper 552-c: ***In memoriam Ricardi Regis*: Rebuilding King Richard III's Historical Reputation in the TV Series *The White Queen*** (Language: English)
Cristina Mourón-Figueroa, Departamento de Filoloxía Inglesa e Alemá, Universidade de Santiago de Compostela

Session: **553** **Michael Sadler Building: Room LG.15**
Title: **MANUS-ON MANUSCRIPTS, I: VISUAL COLLATION - A WORKSHOP**
Sponsor: Schoenberg Institute for Manuscript Studies, University of Pennsylvania
Organiser: Dorothy Carr Porter, Schoenberg Institute for Manuscript Studies, University of Pennsylvania and Abigail G. Robertson, Department of English Language & Literature, University of New Mexico, Albuquerque
Tutor: Dorothy Carr Porter and Abigail G. Robertson
Purpose: *This first session, led by Dorothy Porter, Curator of Digital Research Services at the Schoenberg Institute for Manuscript Studies, will consist of an overview of digital collation resources and how they can be utilized when studying the codex and its foliation. Dorothy will demonstrate how her project, VisColl, works to help better understand the composition of codices, moving into a workshop where participants can use the project and familiarize themselves with how it works and how it could apply to their research.*

Session: **554** **Maurice Keyworth Building: Room G.02**
Title: **MONASTICON AQUITANIAE, THE MONT SAINT-MICHEL PROJECT, MILBRETEUR (L'AN MIL EN BRETAGNE ET EN EUROPE): THREE NEW COLLABORATIVE AND INTERDISCIPLINARY PROJECTS - A ROUND TABLE DISCUSSION**
Sponsor: Ancient Abbeys of Brittany Project
Organiser: Claude Lucette Evans, Department of Language Studies, University of Toronto, Mississauga
Moderator: Kenneth Paul Evans, School of Administrative Studies, York University, Ontario
Purpose: *The aim of this round table discussion is to present and discuss new collaborative and interdisciplinary projects concerning Aquitaine, Normandy, and Brittany. The aim of Monasticon Aquitaniae is to establish a comprehensive history of abbeys in southwestern France which will be made available electronically. The Mont Saint-Michel Project includes a reconsideration of the architecture of the site enhanced by the use of 3D scans and orthophotography, as well as a study (entitled* Ex monasterio sancti Michaelis in periculo maris*) and digitalisation of the well-preserved Mont Saint-Michel library. The MILBRETEUR Project focuses on religious, economic, and social life in early Brittany soon after the end of Scandinavian control. It relies on evidence from various sources: textual, linguistic, archaeological, and geological.*

Participants include Marie Bisson (Université de Caen Normandie), Yves Gallet (Université Bordeaux Montaigne), Christian Gensbeitel (Université Bordeaux Montaigne), and Joëlle Quaghebeur (Université de Bretagne-Sud).

COFFEE BREAK: 10.30-11.15

Coffee and Tea will be served at the following locations:

Maurice Keyworth Building: Foyer
Michael Sadler Building: Foyer
Parkinson Building: Bookfair
University Square: The Marquee

See Map 7, p. 44.

Session: **601** **Parkinson Building: Room 1.16**
Title: ***DRINCAN DRIHTINBEAG GEST*: IN SEARCH OF A LOST TIME OF A WARRIOR SOCIETY**
Organiser: Letizia Vezzosi, Dipartimento di Lingue, Letterature e Studi Interculturali, Università degli Studi di Firenze
Moderator: Roberta Manetti, Dipartimento di Lingue, Letterature e Studi Interculturali, Università degli Studi di Firenze
Paper 601-a: **Archaic Warrior's Practices of Fight: Evidence of a Prehistoric Continuity in Early Celtic, Germanic, and Romance Texts** (Language: English)
Francesco Benozzo, Dipartimento di Lingue, Letterature e Culture Moderne, Università di Bologna
Paper 601-b: **Features of a Warrior Society in the Kentish Legislation** (Language: English)
Daniela Fruscione, Institut für Rechtsgeschichte, Goethe-Universität, Frankfurt am Main
Paper 601-c: **Some Thoughts on the Lexicon of Memory in Old and Middle English Texts** (Language: English)
Letizia Vezzosi

Session: **602** **Baines Wing: Room 2.16**
Title: **LANDSCAPE TRANSFORMATION AND REPRESENTATION**
Organiser: IMC Programming Committee
Moderator: Hervin Fernández-Aceves, School of History / Institute for Medieval Studies, University of Leeds
Paper 602-a: **Continuities and Changes in the Landscape of the Visigoth Capital of Toletum, Spain: The Aristocratic Building of Los Hitos, 6th-8th Centuries** (Language: English)
Jorge Morín, Departamento de Arqueología, Paleontología y Recursos Culturales, Universidad Autónoma de Madrid and Isabel Sanchez Ramos, Departamento de Prehistoria y Arqueología, Universidad Autónoma de Madrid
Paper 602-b: **Space, Nature (and Landscape?) in the *Cantigas de Santa Maria*** (Language: English)
Manuel Magán, Departamento de Historia del Arte, Universidad Complutense de Madrid

Session: **603** **University House: Little Woodhouse Room**
Title: **EMPIRE AND GEOGRAPHY: THE BORDERS OF BYZANTIUM**
Organiser: IMC Programming Committee
Moderator: Shaun Tougher, School of History, Archaeology & Religion, Cardiff University
Paper 603-a: **The Gothic War and the Battle for Italy's Past** (Language: English)
Marco Cristini, Classe di Scienze Umane, Scuola Normale Superiore di Pisa
Paper 603-b: **The Landscape of an Imperial Frontier and Its Hinterland at the End of Antiquity** (Language: English)
Amy Wood, Department of Ancient History, Macquarie University, Sydney
Paper 603-c: **Travel Accounts in Philotheos Kokkinos' *Vitae* of Contemporary Saints** (Language: English)
Mihail Mitrea, School of History, Classics & Archaeology, Newcastle University

Session: **604** — **Baines Wing: Room 1.13**
Title: **NEW VOICES IN ANGLO-SAXON STUDIES, I**
Sponsor: International Society of Anglo-Saxonists
Organiser: Megan Cavell, Department of English Literature, University of Birmingham
Moderator: Damian Fleming, Department of English & Linguistics, Indiana University-Purdue University, Fort Wayne
Paper 604-a: **'Se bið mihtigre se ðe gæð þonne se þe crypð': Metaphoric Disability in the Old English *Boethius*** (Language: English)
Leah Pope Parker, Department of English, University of Wisconsin-Madison
Paper 604-b: **Women, Adornment, and Social Change: Necklaces in 7th-Century Anglo-Saxon England** (Language: English)
Katie Haworth, Department of Archaeology, Durham University
Paper 604-c: **The Body in Confession: Memory and Embodiment in Anglo-Saxon Confessional Prayer** (Language: English)
Kyle J. Williams, Department of English, University of Illinois, Urbana-Champaign / University of South Carolina, Aiken

---

Session: **605** — **Fine Art Building: SR G.04**
Title: **MEDIEVAL IMAGES AND THE MAKINGS OF SOCIAL IDENTITY**
Sponsor: Anthropologie historique du long Moyen Âge, Groupe d'Anthropologie Historique de l'Occident Médiéval (GAHOM-AHLOMA), l'École des Hautes Études en Sciences Sociales (EHESS), Paris
Organiser: Élise Haddad, Groupe d'Anthropologie Historique de l'Occident Médiéval (GAHOM), École des Hautes Études en Sciences Sociales (EHESS), Paris
Moderator: Chloé Maillet, Département d'Histoire de l'art, École Supérieure des Beaux-Arts Tours Angers Le Mans
Paper 605-a: **Stag-ing Oneself: Gender and Animality in Late Medieval Emblematic** (Language: English)
Clémentine Girault, Groupe d'Anthropologie Historique de l'Occident Médiéval (GAHOM), École des Hautes Études en Sciences Sociales (EHESS), Paris
Paper 605-b: **Makings of a Community in Eschatological Images: Romanesque Sculpture** (Language: English)
Élise Haddad

Session: **606** — **Michael Sadler Building: Room LG.16**
Title: **TRACING THE JERUSALEM CODE, II: TRAVELLING MEMORIES AND SACRALISATION OF LANDSCAPE**
Sponsor: Research Council of Norway Project 'Tracing the Jerusalem Code: Christian Cultures in Scandinavia'
Organiser: Maria H. Oen, Centrum för medeltidsstudier, Stockholms universitet / Institutt for lingvistiske og nordiske studier, Universitetet i Oslo
Moderator: Mia Münster-Swendsen, Institut for Kommunikation og Humanistisk Videnskab, Roskilde Universitet
Paper 606-a: **Connecting to the Navel of the World** (Language: English)
Kristin B. Aavitsland, Det teologiske Menighetsfakultet, Oslo
Paper 606-b: **Bringing Jerusalem Back Home: The Transfer of the Idea of Jerusalem to the North and of Crusader Institutions** (Language: English)
Kurt Villads Jensen, Historiska institutionen, Stockholms universitet
Paper 606-c: **Jerusalem and the Authority of Birgitta of Sweden** (Language: English)
Maria H. Oen

Session: **607** **Michael Sadler Building: Room LG.17**
Title: **THE MATERIALITY OF INTER-FAITH RELATIONS AND MEMORIES ACROSS AND BEYOND THE MEDITERRANEAN**
Organiser: IMC Programming Committee
Moderator: Marie Thérèse Champagne, Department of History, University of West Florida
Paper 607-a: **(An)Iconism in Turkish Islam: A Literary Genre and the Calligraphic Form of Depiction of the Prophet** (Language: English)
Isa Babur, Faculty of Theology, Igdir University, Turkey
Paper 607-b: **Construction and Reconstruction of the Past in the Mediterranean Basin, 350-800: Transformation of the Sacred Landscapes in the Name of the Utopian Ideals** (Language: English)
Leonela Fundic, Department of Ancient History, Macquarie University, Sydney
Paper 607-c: **Andalusian Mudejar: A Collective Memory of the Islamic Form between Christians, Jews, and Muslims in the Old and New World** (Language: English)
Hee Sook Lee-Niinioja, Independent Scholar, Helsinki

Session: **608** **Fine Art Building: Studio Ground Floor**
Title: **EQUESTRIAN EQUIPMENT**
Organiser: Timothy Dawson, Independent Scholar, Leeds and Anastasija Ropa, Faculty of Humanities, University of Latvia, Riga
Moderator: Annemarieke Willemsen, Rijksmuseum van Oudheden, Leiden
Paper 608-a: **Horsing Around at the Angevin Court of Naples: A Study of Two 14th-Century Enameled Horse Bits Preserved in New York and Turin** (Language: English)
Marina Viallon, Ecole Pratique des Hautes Etudes (EPHE), Université de Recherche Paris Sciences et Lettres
Paper 608-b: **La Selle de Senonches: Histoire d'une renaissance** (Language: Français)
Adeline Dumont, Institut de Recherches Historiques du Septentrion (IRHiS - UMR 8529), Université de Lille
Paper 608-c: **Elevation: The Key Issue in Understanding Medieval Knightly Riding Styles** (Language: English)
Tobias Capwell, Department of Arms & Armour, Wallace Collection, London

Session: **609** **Baines Wing: Room 2.13**
Title: **NEW DIRECTIONS IN MEDIEVAL CONFESSION, II: VERNACULAR CONFESSION**
Sponsor: Network for the Study of Late Antique & Early Medieval Monasticism
Organiser: Andrea Mancini, Institute for Medieval Studies, University of Leeds and Krista A. Murchison, Faculteit der Geesteswetenschappen, Universiteit Leiden
Moderator: Andrea Mancini
Paper 609-a: **The Depiction of Private Sins in the Anglo-Norman Version of Robert Grosseteste's *Perambulauit Iudas*, c. 1235** (Language: English)
Krista A. Murchison
Paper 609-b: **Conscience and Confession: Penitential Practice in the Kingship of Louis IX** (Language: English)
Emilie Lavallée, Faculty of History, St Cross College, University of Oxford
Paper 609-c: **Judgement, Judge, and Jury: A Posthumous Confession and Penance in St Erkenwald** (Language: English)
Dalicia Raymond, Department of English, University of New Mexico, Albuquerque

Session: **610** **Maurice Keyworth Building: Room 1.04**
Title: **25 YEARS OF HAGIOGRAPHICAL RESEARCH: PAST ACHIEVEMENTS AND FUTURE PERSPECTIVES, I**
Sponsor: Université Paris VIII - Vincennes-Saint-Denis / Université de Montréal
Organiser: Gordon Blennemann, Département d'histoire, Université de Montréal
Moderator: Gordon Blennemann
Paper 610-a: **25 Years of Hagiographical Studies at the IMC, Leeds** (Language: English)
Anne-Marie Helvétius, Département d'histoire, Université Paris VIII - Vincennes-Saint-Denis
Paper 610-b: **Hagiographical Studies in Early 21st-Century Italy: Turning Points, Problems, and Possibilities** (Language: English)
Francesco Veronese, Istituto Storico Italiano per il Medioevo, Roma
Paper 610-c: **Spanish and Portuguese Hagiography: Survey and New Perspectives** (Language: English)
Paulo Jorge Farmhouse Simões Alberto, Faculdade de Letras, Universidade de Lisboa

Session: **611** **Baines Wing: Room 1.15**
Title: **CEU 25, II: JEWISH STUDIES**
Sponsor: Department of Medieval Studies, Central European University, Budapest
Organiser: Carsten L. Wilke, Department of Medieval Studies, Central European University, Budapest
Moderator: Gerhard Jaritz, Department of Medieval Studies, Central European University, Budapest
Paper 611-a: **The Lady with the Book: Iconographical Peculiarities in a 15th-Century Ashkenazi Rylands Haggadah** (Language: English)
Zsófia Buda, British Library, London
Paper 611-b: **The Maid and Her Rescuer: Gendered Allegories of Exile in Andalusian Hebrew Poetry** (Language: English)
Carsten L. Wilke
Paper 611-c: **Blurred Memories: The Sufi Background of a Sephardi Myth of Origin** (Language: English)
Dora Zsom, Department of Semitic Philology & Arabic, Eötvös Loránd University, Budapest

Session: **612** **Baines Wing: Room 1.14**
Title: **FEMALE ABBATIAL AUTHORITY, II: GENDER, DOCUMENTARY CULTURE, AND MEMORY**
Sponsor: Haskins Society / John Rylands Research Institute, University of Manchester
Organiser: Laura Gathagan, Department of History, State University of New York, Cortland
Moderator: Amy Livingstone, Department of History, Wittenberg University, Ohio
Paper 612-a: **Managing a Cross-Channel Estate: The Uses of Literacy in a Great Anglo-Norman Nunnery - Holy Trinity, Caen, 11th-13th Centuries** (Language: English)
Catherine Letouzey-Réty, Laboratoire de Médiévistique Occidentale de Paris (LAMOP - UMR 8589), Université Paris I - Panthéon-Sorbonne
Paper 612-b: **Abbatial Tombs as Legal Evidence** (Language: English)
Katharina Holderegger, Institut für Kunstgeschichte, Universität Bern
Paper 612-c: **The Prioress, the Proctor, and the Arbiter: The Social Dynamics of Arbitration and Female Abbatial Authority in a Medieval Carthusian Nunnery** (Language: English)
Hollis Shaul, Department of History, Princeton University
Paper 612-d: **Female Abbatial Judicial Authority at Holy Trinity, Caen: Clues from the Beaumont Charters at the John Rylands Library** (Language: English)
Laura Gathagan

Session: **613** **Charles Thackrah Building: 1.01**
Title: **MASCULINE JOURNEYS / JOURNEYING MASCULINITIES, II**
Organiser: Ruth Mazo Karras, Department of History, University of Minnesota, Twin Cities and Oded Zinger, Martin Buber Society of Fellows in the Humanities, Hebrew University of Jerusalem
Moderator: Ruth Mazo Karras
Paper 613-a: **Interfaith Masculine Identities in the Riḥla of Ibn Jubayr** (Language: English)
Matthew King, Department of History, University of Minnesota, Twin Cities
Paper 613-b: **A Man on the Move: Prince Pedro of Portugal (1185-1240) and Male Freedom in Medieval Iberia** (Language: English)
Miriam Shadis, Department of History, Ohio University
Paper 613-c: **'Return to God and the brotherhood of good and excellent men': Competing Masculinities in the Jewish Communities of Medieval Egypt** (Language: English)
Oded Zinger

Session: **614** **University House: Beechgrove Room**
Title: **THE *SEVEN SAGES OF ROME* IN EUROPE: THE OLD FRENCH *ROMAN DES SEPT SAGES DE ROME* AND ITS TRANSLATIONS IN MEDIEVAL LATIN, ENGLISH, GERMAN, AND DUTCH, II**
Organiser: Anne Reynders, Faculty of Arts, KU Leuven and Remco Sleiderink, Departement Letterkunde, Universiteit Antwerpen
Moderator: Nico Kunkel, Fachbereich Literaturwissenschaft, Universität Konstanz
Paper 614-a: **Misogyny or Morality?: Women Readers, Conduct Texts, and the Auchinleck Manuscript's *Seven Sages of Rome*** (Language: English)
Emma Osborne, School of Critical Studies, University of Glasgow
Paper 614-b: **How Lonely Are Women in the Middle Dutch Versions of the *Seven Sages of Rome*?: An Analysis of the Resources and Networks of the Male and Female Characters** (Language: English)
Anne Reynders
Paper 614-c: **The *Sept Sages* in a Dutch Multi-Text Codex: Brussels, Koninklijke Bibliotheek van België, II 1171, c. 1325-50** (Language: English)
Remco Sleiderink

Session: **615** **Baines Wing: Room 1.16**
Title: **RE-THINKING THE ARISTOCRACY IN CAPETIAN FRANCE, II: ARISTOCRACY AND MONARCHY**
Sponsor: Society for the Study of French History (SSFH)
Organiser: Charlotte Crouch, Graduate Centre for Medieval Studies, University of Reading and Niall Ó Súilleabháin, Department of History, Trinity College Dublin
Moderator: Alice Taylor, Department of History, King's College London
Paper 615-a: **The Montforts and the Capetians in the 13th Century** (Language: English)
Lindy Grant, Department of History, University of Reading
Paper 615-b: **'I Will Survive!': Isabella of Angoulême and Negotiating [with] the Capetians in the 13th Century** (Language: English)
Sally Spong, School of History, University of East Anglia
Paper 615-c: **Taming the Diaspora: The French Crown and the Briennes, c. 1191-1356** (Language: English)
Guy Perry, Institute for Medieval Studies / School of History, University of Leeds

---

Session: **616** **Michael Sadler Building: Rupert Beckett Theatre**
Title: **LEGAL TEXTS AND THEIR USERS, II: PAST AND PRESENT IN MEDIEVAL CANONISTIC PROCEDURE**
Sponsor: Iuris Canonici Medii Aevi Consociatio (ICMAC)
Organiser: Bruce C. Brasington, Department of History, West Texas A&M University, Canyon
Moderator: Kathleen Cushing, Department of History, Keele University
Paper 616-a: **The Past, the Bible, and the Law: A 12th-Century Exegete's View on the Foundation of Law** (Language: English)
Reinhild Rössler, Institut für Geschichte, Universität Wien
Paper 616-b: **Rules to Remember: A 12th-Century Fragmentary Commentary on the *De regulis iuris* of the *Digest*** (Language: English)
Bruce C. Brasington
Paper 616-c: **The Use of the First Papal Laws** (Language: English)
David L. D'Avray, Department of History, University College London

Session: **617** **Social Sciences Building: Room 10.05**
Title: **CLERICS AND THEIR HOUSEHOLDS IN LATE ANTIQUITY, II**
Sponsor: Presbyters in the Late Antique West Project, Uniwersytet Warszawski
Organiser: Stanisław Adamiak, Instytut Historyczny, Uniwersytet Warszawski and Lisa Bailey, Department of Classics & Ancient History, University of Auckland
Moderator: David Hunter, Department of Modern & Classical Languages, Literatures & Cultures, University of Kentucky
Paper 617-a: **Slaves and Servants in Clerical Households in the Early Middle Ages** (Language: English)
Lisa Bailey
Paper 617-b: **Brothers in Blood, Brothers in Spirit: Clerical Siblings in Late Antique Inscriptions** (Language: English)
Isabelle Mossong, Kommission für Alte Geschichte und Epigraphik, Deutsches Archäologisches Institut, München
Paper 617-c: **Presbyters in the *Tituli* in 5th-Century Rome: Patrons and Clients** (Language: English)
Michele R. Salzman, Department of History, University of California, Riverside

Session: **618** **Stage@leeds: Stage 2**
Title: **TECHNOLOGY AND THE 'MEMORY' OF MEDIEVAL ART AND ARCHITECTURE, II: MODELS**
Sponsor: Index of Medieval Art, Princeton University
Organiser: Pamela A. Patton, Department of Art & Archaeology, Princeton University
Moderator: Pamela A. Patton
Paper 618-a: **Mapping Visual Memory: Networks of Artistic Contact in French Gothic Manuscripts** (Language: English)
Alex Brey, Department of the History of Art, Bryn Mawr College, Pennsylvania and Maeve Doyle, Department of Art & Art History, Eastern Connecticut State University
Paper 618-b: **Visualizing Anician Topographies of Power with SketchUp and QGIS** (Language: English)
Kaelin Jewell, Department of Art History, Temple University, Pennsylvania
Paper 618-c: **Recovering a Lost State: The 12th-Century East End at Sainte-Marie-Madeleine de Vézelay** (Language: English)
Kristine Tanton, Département d'histoire de l'art et d'études cinématographiques, Université de Montréal

Session: **619** **Charles Thackrah Building: 1.02**
Title: **GLOSSING BOOKS, II: TEACHERS AND STUDENTS ANNOTATING PAGES**
Organiser: Mariken Teeuwen, Huygens Instituut voor Nederlandse Geschiedenis, Koninklijke Nederlandse Academie van Wetenschappen (ING - KNAW), Amsterdam
Moderator: Irene A. O'Daly, Huygens Instituut voor Nederlandse Geschiedenis, Koninklijke Nederlandse Academie van Wetenschappen (ING - KNAW), Amsterdam
Paper 619-a: **Late Antique and Early Medieval Annotations to Augustine's *City of God*** (Language: English)
Jesse Miika Johannes Keskiaho, Department of Philosophy, History, Culture & Art Studies, University of Helsinki
Paper 619-b: **Reading Boethius in the 10th Century** (Language: English)
Mariken Teeuwen
Paper 619-c: **Annotating Textbooks: Page and Margin Layouts of Early 13th-Century University Books** (Language: English)
Erik Kwakkel, Centre for the Arts in Society, Universiteit Leiden

Session: **620** **University House: Great Woodhouse Room**
Title: **MEMORY AND MATERIAL CULTURE IN EARLIER MEDIEVAL ENGLISH TEXTS**
Organiser: IMC Programming Committee
Moderator: Francis Leneghan, Faculty of English Language & Literature, University of Oxford
Paper 620-a: **'Don't let it be forgot': How the Medieval Memory of King Æthelstan May Have Inspired the Creation of Geoffrey of Monmouth's *King Arthur*** (Language: English)
Lori A. Lehtola, Department of History, Houston Community College, Texas
Paper 620-b: **What Does Hrothgar 'Read' on the Giants' Sword-Hilt?** (Language: English)
Dorothy Lawrenson, Department of English, University of Edinburgh
Paper 620-c: **Memory and Mimicry in the Transmission of Practical Skills in Early Medieval England** (Language: English)
Debby Banham, Department of Anglo-Saxon, Norse & Celtic, University of Cambridge

Session:	**621** **Emmanuel Centre: Wilson Room**
Title:	**ALLUSION, REFERENCE, AND MEMORY IN HIGH MEDIEVAL NARRATIVES, II**
Sponsor:	Centre for Research in Historiography & Historical Cultures / Department of History & Welsh History, Aberystwyth University
Organiser:	Caitlin Naylor, Department of History & Welsh History, Aberystwyth University
Moderator:	Kiri Kolt, Department of History & Welsh History, Aberystwyth University
Paper 621-a:	**'I came...as an exile, unknown to all, knowing no one': Biblical Allusion and Self-Identification in the 12th-Century English Monastic Sphere** (Language: English) Abigail Monk, Department of History & Welsh History, Aberystwyth University
Paper 621-b:	**Referencing and Alluding to Bede in 12th-Century British Historiography** (Language: English) Jacqueline Burek, Department of English, George Mason University, Virginia
Paper 621-c:	**'I quote therefore I am': Hélinand of Froidmont and His Chronicle** (Language: English) Antoni Grabowski, Tadeusz Manteuffel Institute of History, Polish Academy of Sciences, Warszawa

Session:	**622** **Social Sciences Building: Room 10.06**
Title:	***MEMORIA*, MNEMONICS, AND THE MULTISENSORY IN BIRGITTINE MONASTICISM: OBSERVATIONS FROM NEUROSCIENCE**
Sponsor:	Extraordinary Sensescapes Working Group
Organiser:	Corine Schleif, School of Art, Arizona State University
Moderator:	Karin Strinnholm Lagergren, Institutionen för musik och bild, Linnéuniversitetet, Växjö
Paper 622-a:	**Color, Adrenalin, and Memory: The Birgittine Monastery as a Historical Laboratory** (Language: English) Corine Schleif
Paper 622-b:	**In Tact and in Sync: Birgittine Processional Chant and Memory** (Language: English) Volker Schier, Department of Musicology, KU Leuven
Paper 622-c:	**Memory Made 'Gestalt' through Archaeo-Artistic Sketching between Fragment and Entirety** (Language: English) Magali Ljungar-Chapelon, Institutionen för designvetenskaper, Lunds Universitet

Session: **623** **Maurice Keyworth Building: Room 1.31**
Title: **COMMEMORATING SAINTS AND MARTYRS, II: PRESENCE AND (RE)PRESENTATION AT WORSHIP**
Sponsor: MARTRAE Network
Organiser: Ann Buckley, Trinity Medieval History Research Centre, Trinity College Dublin
Moderator: Nicole Volmering, Department of Irish & Celtic Languages, Trinity College Dublin
Paper 623-a: **Baptism *ad sanctos*: Remembering the Saints in the Liturgy and Objects of Baptism in Early Medieval England** (Language: English)
Carolyn Twomey, Department of History, Boston College, Massachusetts
Paper 623-b: **Commemorating Saints through Chant Texts: Columba and Kentigern** (Language: English)
Andrew Bull, Department of Music, University of Glasgow
Paper 623-c: **Saints' Books as Secondary Relics in Early Medieval Ireland** (Language: English)
Austin Rushnell, Department of Early & Medieval Irish, University College Cork

Session: **624** **Michael Sadler Building: Room LG.19**
Title: **MEMORY THEATRE, II: THEATRICAL MEMENTO**
Sponsor: Société internationale pour l'étude du théâtre médiéval (SITM)
Organiser: Cora Dietl, Institut für Germanistik, Justus-Liebig-Universität Gießen
Moderator: M. A. Katritzky, Department of English, Open University, Milton Keynes
Paper 624-a: **Three *Memento mori* Plays on the Late Medieval Majorcan Stage** (Language: English)
Lenke Kovács, Departament de Filologia Catalana i Lingüística General, Universitat de les Illes Balears, Palma
Paper 624-b: ***Memento mori* on Swiss Stage: Johannes Kolross's *Spil von Fünfferley betrachtnussen zur Buß*** (Language: English)
Cora Dietl
Paper 624-c: **'And do not say 'tis superstition...': Shakespeare, Memory, and the Iconography of Death** (Language: English)
Lawrence Green, Centre for the Study of the Renaissance, University of Warwick

Session: **625** **Maurice Keyworth Building: Room 1.06**
Title: **MEMORY AND MYTH: REMEMBERING MEDIEVAL IRELAND AND ITS NEIGHBOURS, II - REPRESENTATION AND MISREMEMBERING**
Sponsor: Medieval History Research Centre, Trinity College Dublin
Organiser: Áine Foley, Medieval History Research Centre, Trinity College Dublin
Moderator: Clare Downham, Institute of Irish Studies, University of Liverpool
Paper 625-a: **How to Forget a King: Regicide in 12th-Century Ireland** (Language: English)
Ronan Mulhaire, Department of History, Trinity College Dublin
Paper 625-b: **Black Cats, Brewsters, and Broomsticks: Misrepresentation of Medieval Alewives in Modern Pop Culture** (Language: English) 
Christina Wade, Department of History, Trinity College Dublin
Paper 625-c: **'The Earth was flat and everyone died of plague': Remembering the Middle Ages in Modern Ireland** (Language: English)
Daryl Hendley Rooney, Department of History, Trinity College Dublin

Session:	**626** **Social Sciences Building: Room 10.07**
Title:	**'DIANA AND ALL HER SECT': REMEMBERING WOMEN WARRIORS, II**
Sponsor:	Society for Medieval Feminist Scholarship
Organiser:	Sophie Harwood, Institute for Medieval Studies, University of Leeds, Roberta Magnani, Centre for Medieval & Early Modern Research (MEMO), Swansea University and Amy Louise Morgan, School of Literature & Languages, University of Surrey
Moderator:	Natasha Ruth Hodgson, School of Arts & Humanities, Nottingham Trent University
Paper 626-a:	**Women as Knights: The Use of Disguise in Hispano-Hebrew and Romance Fiction from the 13th Century** (Language: English) Paulina Lorca Koch, Departamento de Estudios Semíticos, Universidad de Granada
Paper 626-b:	**Identity Crisis: The Polyvalency of Gender and Race in *Aucassin et Nicolette*** (Language: English) Alison Williams, Centre for Medieval & Early Modern Research (MEMO), Swansea University
Paper 626-c:	**Zenobia, East and West** (Language: English) Anna Klosowska, Department of French & Italian, Miami University, Ohio
Paper 626-d:	**What Are They Doing Here?: Ludie and Her Army of Women Warriors in *Anseÿs de Mes*** (Language: English) Sara Rychtarik, Graduate Center, City University of New York

Session:	**627** **Michael Sadler Building: Banham Theatre**
Title:	**MEMORIES OF NATION, MEDIEVAL AND MODERN, II: NATIONAL MEDIEVALISMS IN THE 20TH CENTURY**
Sponsor:	Richard Bland College of William & Mary, Virginia
Organiser:	Daniel Franke, Department of History, Richard Bland College of William & Mary, Virginia
Moderator:	Daniel Franke
Paper 627-a:	**Performing the Hindu Nation: Quotidian Simulations of Hindu Nationalism** (Language: English) Sushant Kishore, Department of Humanities & Social Sciences, Birla Institute of Technology & Science, Pilani University, Goa
Paper 627-b:	**Ibn 'Asakir and the Making of Modern Syrian Nationalisms** (Language: English) Suleiman A. Mourad, Department of Religion, Smith College, Massachusetts
Paper 627-c:	***Brabantia Nostra*: Appropriating the Medieval Past in Constructing a Brabantine Regional Identity, 1900-Present** (Language: English) Arnoud-Jan A. Bijsterveld, Department of Sociology, Tilburg University

Session: **628** **Stage@leeds: Stage 3**
Title: ***ZIKARON/MEMORIA*: JEWISH MEMORY AND JEWISH COMMUNITY, II**
Organiser: IMC Programming Committee
Moderator: Gabriel Wasserman, Department of Hebrew Literature, The Hebrew University of Jerusalem
Paper 628-a: **The Use of Collective Memory in Grounding New Institutions, 11th-13th Centuries** (Language: English)
Simha Goldin, Goldstein-Goren Diaspora Research Center, Tel Aviv University
Paper 628-b: **The Memory Book of the Jewish Community in Nuremberg in the Context of Christian Medieval Necrologies, 13th and 14th Centuries** (Language: English)
Rainer Josef Barzen, Institut für Jüdische Studien, Westfälische Wilhelms-Universität Münster
Paper 628-c: **The Theology of Memory in Ashkenaz** (Language: English)
Joseph Isaac Lifshitz, Goldstein-Goren Diaspora Research Center, Tel Aviv University / Shalem College, Jerusalem

Session: **629** **Maurice Keyworth Building: Room 1.05**
Title: **SAVING MEMORIES?: SALVATION AND REMEMBRANCE**
Organiser: IMC Programming Committee
Moderator: Rob Lutton, Department of History, University of Nottingham
Paper 629-a: **The Memory of the Cross and the Passion of Christ: The Connection between Salvation and Terrestrial Power since the Late Middle Ages** (Language: English)
Monika Veronika Eisenhauer, Independent Scholar, Koblenz
Paper 629-b: **Always Remember and Never Forget: The Cluniac Keys to Salvation** (Language: English)
Amanda Swinford, Department of History, Portland State University, Oregon
Paper 629-c: **Individual Experience, Collective Memory: Virtual Space and the Transmission of Salvation in Visions** (Language: English)
Sebastian Kleinschmidt, Graduiertenkolleg 1767 'Faktuales und fiktionales Erzählen', Albert-Ludwigs-Universität Freiburg

Session: **630** **Charles Thackrah Building: 1.03**
Title: **MEMORY DEPICTED, II**
Sponsor: Universiteit van Amsterdam
Organiser: Wendelien A. W. Van Welie-Vink, Afdeling Kunst- en cultuurwetenschappen, Universiteit van Amsterdam
Moderator: Wendelien A. W. Van Welie-Vink
Paper 630-a: **Theodoric the Great: Rome's Memory Returning in Ravenna** (Language: English)
Mathilde Van den Bosch, Faculteit der Geesteswetenschappen, Universiteit van Amsterdam
Paper 630-b: **Pagan Stories Remembered on Christian Churches** (Language: English)
Henry Dwarswaard, Afdeling Kunst-, Religie- und Cultuurwetenschappen, Universiteit van Amsterdam
Paper 630-c: **'May thy God remember thou': The Advocacy for Dirk II and Hildegard through Votive Gifts** (Language: English)
Judith Bruijn, Graduate School of Humanities, Universiteit van Amsterdam
Paper 630-d: **Reinventing the Cherubim Iconography: An Angel Lost from Memory** (Language: English)
Julia van Rosmalen, Capaciteitsgroep Kunstgeschiedenis, Universitet van Amsterdam

Session: **631** **Charles Thackrah Building: 1.04**
Title: **MATERIAL CULTURE AND LANDSCAPES, II: MEMORY AND THE SACRED**
Sponsor: Medieval Landscape/Seascape Research Group
Organiser: Daniel Brown, Historisches Institut, Universität zu Köln and Stefanie Schild, Independent Scholar, Hilden
Moderator: Kimm Curran, School of Critical Studies, University of Glasgow
Paper 631-a: ***Bene memoria*: Constructing a Christian History out of Cologne's Early Medieval Urban Landscape** (Language: English)
Daniel Brown
Paper 631-b: **Claiming Cuthbert: Durham Cathedral Priory and the Landscape of Northern Monasticism** (Language: English)
Ross McIntire, Centre for Medieval Studies, University of York
Paper 631-c: **Temple, Cornwall: The Legacy of the Military Orders on the English Landscape** (Language: English)
Thomas Hayes, Faculty of Humanities & Social Sciences, University of Winchester

Session:	**632** **Social Sciences Building: Room 10.09**
Title:	**GRADUATE CENTRE FOR MEDIEVAL STUDIES, UNIVERSITY OF READING, II: MEMORY, SAINTS' CULTS, AND MATERIAL CULTURE**
Sponsor:	Graduate Centre for Medieval Studies, University of Reading
Organiser:	Rebecca A. C. Rist, Graduate Centre for Medieval Studies, University of Reading
Moderator:	Rebecca A. C. Rist
Paper 632-a:	**Dante's Marian Devotion as a Secular Piety: Memory and Brotherhood** (Language: English) Michael Biasin, Department of Modern Languages & European Studies, University of Reading
Paper 632-b:	**Memory and Material Culture: St Margaret of Antioch and Her Devotees in Late Medieval England** (Language: English) Frances Cook, Graduate Centre for Medieval Studies, University of Reading
Paper 632-c:	**St Louis, Memory, and the Cult of the Most Holy French King** (Language: English) Olivier Sirjacq, Department of History, University of Reading

Session:	**633** **Leeds University Union: Room 2 - Elland Road**
Title:	**COMMUNICATION AND THE EXPLOITATION OF KNOWLEDGE, II: CHARTERS AS AN INSTRUMENT AND MIRROR OF COLLECTIVE MEMORY IN TRANSALPINE EUROPE - THE LOW COUNTRIES AND POLAND IN COMPARATIVE PERSPECTIVE**
Sponsor:	Onderzoeksschool Mediëvistiek, Rijksuniversiteit Groningen
Organiser:	Mark Vermeer, Departement Geschiedenis en Kunstgeschiedenis, Universiteit Utrecht
Moderator:	Beata Możejko, Zakład Historii Średniowiecza Polski i Nauk Pomocniczych Historii, Uniwersytet Gdański
Paper 633-a:	***Littera vel prothocolla*: The Legal Power of Charters and Registers in Late Medieval Rural Brabant** (Language: English) Mark Vermeer
Paper 633-b:	**Ideas about the Nature of Memory in the Preambles of Episcopal Charters in Late Medieval Poland** (Language: English) Zofia Wilk-Woś, Instytut Bezpieczeństwa Narodowego, Społeczna Akademia Nauk, Łódź
Paper 633-c:	**Digging in the Chests: Charters and Archives as Instruments of Political Claims in 15th-Century Poland** (Language: English) Anna Adamska, Onderzoeksinstituut voor Geschiedenis en Kunstgeschiedenis, Universiteit Utrecht
Respondent:	Herwig Weigl, Institut für Österreichische Geschichtsforschung / Institut für Geschichte, Universität Wien

Session: **634** **Leeds University Union: Room 4 - Hyde Park**
Title: **NOTHING NEW!: HERITAGE, MEMORY, AND IDENTITY IN THE MIDDLE AGES, II**
Sponsor: Centre for Religion & Heritage, Rijksuniversiteit Groningen
Organiser: Mathilde van Dijk, Faculteit der Godgeleerdheid en Godsdienstwetenschap, Rijksuniversiteit Groningen and Andrew J. M. Irving, Faculteit der Godgeleerdheid en Godsdienstwetenschap, Rijksuniversiteit Groningen
Moderator: Andrew J. M. Irving
Paper 634-a: **Thomas Becket: The Saint, the Shrine, and Their Owners** (Language: English)
John Jenkins, Centre for the Study of Christianity & Culture, University of York
Paper 634-b: **Papal Mass at St Peter's on 25 December 800** (Language: English)
John Romano, Department of History, Benedictine College, Kansas
Paper 634-c: **Religious Memory and Royal Piety: The Antwerp Commission of Christian II** (Language: English)
Ragnhild Marthine Bø, Institutt for arkeologi, konservering og historie, Universitetet i Oslo
Respondent: Mathilde van Dijk

Session: **635** **Maurice Keyworth Building: Room 1.09**
Title: **POWER, MEMORY, AND WRITTEN RECORD IN MEDIEVAL SPAIN, II: MEMORY AND RECORD KEEPING**
Sponsor: El ejercicio del poder: espacios, agentes y escrituras (siglos XI-XV), EJEPO Project
Organiser: Alberto Navarro Baena, Facultad de Filosofía y Letras, Universidad de Valladolid
Moderator: Soledad Morandeira de Paz, Departamento de Historia Antigua y Medieval, Universidad de Valladolid
Paper 635-a: **The Benefactors of the Cathedral Chapter of Leon in Its Necrologies and Cartularies** (Language: English)
Alberto Navarro Baena
Paper 635-b: **Escritura y poder en Castilla durante la Baja Edad Media: Escribir para el gobierno, escribir para la administración** (Language: Español)
Mauricio Herrero Jiménez, Facultad de Filosofía y Letras, Universidad de Valladolid
Paper 635-c: **The Memory of the Monastery of Santa María la Real de las Huelgas in Valladolid according to Their Diplomatic Codices** (Language: English)
María Herranz Pinacho, Facultad de Filosofía y Letras, Universidad de Valladolid

Session: **636** **Leeds University Union: Room 5 - Kirkstall Abbey**
Title: **SAVE THE DATE!: CONFLICTING IDEAS ABOUT THE QUALITY OF TIME IN MEMORY AND FOR PROGNOSIS, II**
Organiser: Uta Heil, Institut für Kirchengeschichte, Christliche Archäologie und Kirchliche Kunst, Universität Wien
Moderator: Miriam Czock, Historisches Institut, Universität Duisburg-Essen
Paper 636-a: **There Will Be Blood...: Deciding on the Best and Worst Days to Let Blood in Carolingian Times** (Language: English)
Ria Paroubek-Groenewoud, Departement Geschiedenis en Kunstgeschiedenis, Universiteit Utrecht
Paper 636-b: **Be Still and Wait for Better Times: Unlucky Days in Early Medieval Manuscripts** (Language: English)
Annemarie Veenstra, Departement Geschiedenis en Kunstgeschiedenis, Universiteit Utrecht
Paper 636-c: **As Sure as the Sun Will Rise?: Dealing with Conflicting Ideas about Days and Times in the Carolingian Period** (Language: English)
Carine van Rhijn, Departement Geschiedenis en Kunstgeschiedenis, Universiteit Utrecht

Session: **637** **Maurice Keyworth Building: Room 1.03**
Title: **MEMORIES OF JERUSALEM AND THE HOLY LAND IN MEDIEVAL BRITAIN**
Sponsor: Northern Network for the Study of the Crusades
Organiser: Kathryn Hurlock, Department of History, Politics & Philosophy, Manchester Metropolitan University
Moderator: Laura Julinda Whatley, College of Arts & Sciences, Auburn University at Montgomery, Alabama
Paper 637-a: **Finding Jerusalem in Late Medieval Wales?: The Case of the Stradlings of St Donat's** (Language: English)
Kathryn Hurlock
Paper 637-b: **'As you came from the Holy Land': Crusader Patronage and Marian Devotion at Walsingham** (Language: English)
Elisa Foster, Henry Moore Institute, Leeds
Paper 637-c: **Medieval Provenance and Holy Land Relics: Inventing Traditions in the 12th and 13th Centuries** (Language: English)
Liz Mylod, Independent Scholar, Edinburgh

Session: **638** **Baines Wing: Room G.36**
Title: **THE POLONSKY FOUNDATION ENGLAND AND FRANCE PROJECT: CONSTRUCTING MEMORY THROUGH MANUSCRIPTS, 8TH-12TH CENTURIES**
Sponsor: Bibliothèque nationale de France / British Library / Polonsky Foundation
Organiser: Francesco Siri, Bibliothèque nationale de France, Paris
Moderator: Joanna Frońska, Institut de Recherche et d'Histoire des Textes (IRHT), Centre National de la Recherche Scientifique (CNRS), Paris
Paper 638-a: **Constructing Memory through Liturgy** (Language: English)
Laura Albiero, Bibliothèque nationale de France, Paris
Paper 638-b: ***Imagines poetarum*: Manuscripts of Classical Authors and Their Decoration, England and France, 8th-12th Centuries** (Language: English)
Cristian Ispir, British Library, London
Paper 638-c: **The Use of Diagrams in the Transmission of Knowledge** (Language: English)
Francesco Siri

Session:	**639** **Maurice Keyworth Building: Room 1.33**
Title:	**REMEMBERING THE PAST AFTER THE CAROLINGIAN EMPIRE, II: LEARNING AND LITURGY**
Sponsor:	After Empire: Using & Not Using the Past in the Crisis of the Carolingian World, c. 900-1050
Organiser:	Sarah Greer, St Andrews Institute of Mediaeval Studies, University of St Andrews
Moderator:	Stefan Esders, Friedrich-Meinecke-Institut, Freie Universität Berlin
Paper 639-a:	**The Birth of the Breviary: Reorganising the Divine Office in the 11th Century** (Language: English) Erik Niblaeus, Department of History, Durham University
Paper 639-b:	**'What they should most understand': Educating the Pastoral Clergy in the Post-Carolingian World** (Language: English) Sarah M. Hamilton, Department of History, University of Exeter
Paper 639-c:	**Old Books in a New Age: The Reuse of Continental Manuscripts in 10th-Century England** (Language: English) Robert Gallagher, St Cross College, University of Oxford

Session:	**640** **Parkinson Building: Nathan Bodington Chamber**
Title:	**IMPERIAL MEMORY THEN AND NOW, I: PERSONAL AGENCY IN BYZANTINE MACEDONIA**
Sponsor:	Byzantino-Serbian Border Zones in Transition (1282-1355), FWF Project P 30384-G28
Organiser:	Mihailo Popović, Institut für Mittelalterforschung, Abteilung Byzanzforschung, Österreichische Akademie der Wissenschaften, Wien
Moderator:	Jonathan Shepard, Khalili Research Centre, University of Oxford
Paper 640-a:	**Memories are Made of This: Tracing Local Elites in Byzantine Macedonia** (Language: English) Mihailo Popović
Paper 640-b:	**Border Warlords as Founders and Donators: Memory-Keeping in Monasteries and Churches of Byzantine Macedonia** (Language: English) Vratislav Zervan, Institut für Mittelalterforschung, Abteilung Byzanzforschung, Österreichische Akademie der Wissenschaften, Wien
Paper 640-c:	**Digital Memory-Keeping of Border: Warlords in Byzantine Macedonia in the OpenAtlas Database** (Language: English) Bernhard Koschicek, Institut für Mittelalterforschung, Abteilung Byzanzforschung, Österreichische Akademie der Wissenschaften, Wien

Session: **641** **Michael Sadler Building: Room LG.10**
Title: **REGISTERING THE PAST: SOURCES AND METHODS FOR THE STUDY OF EPISCOPAL MEMORY AND MEMORIALIZATION**
Sponsor: EPISCOPUS: Society for the Study of Bishops & the Secular Clergy in the Middle Ages
Organiser: Evan Gatti, Department of Art & Art History, Elon University, North Carolina
Moderator: Katy Cubitt, School of History, University of East Anglia
Paper 641-a: **Bishops as Patrons in Carolingian *Gesta Episcoporum*** (Language: English)
Deborah Mauskopf Deliyannis, Department of History, Indiana University, Bloomington
Paper 641-b: **Bishops and Their Registers as Guardians of Public Memory in Late Medieval England** (Language: English)
Alison McHardy, Department of History, University of Nottingham
Paper 641-c: **Lapidary Virtues: Inscriptions and Epitaphs Commemorating Bishops, c. 900-1150** (Language: English)
John S. Ott, Department of History, Portland State University, Oregon

Session: **642** **Baines Wing: Room G.37**
Title: **CONSTRUCTION AND DECONSTRUCTION OF MEMORY IN BYZANTIUM**
Organiser: Michael Grünbart, Institut für Byzantinistik und Neogräzistik, Westfälische Wilhelms-Universität Münster and Paraskevi Toma, Institut für Byzantinistik und Neogräzistik, Westfälische Wilhelms-Universität Münster
Moderator: Michael Grünbart
Paper 642-a: **Memory and Patronage: Commemorating the Patron in Dedicatory Inscriptions of Macedonia in the Middle Byzantine Period** (Language: English)
Nectarios Zarras, Institut für Byzantinistik und Neogräzistik, Westfälische Wilhelms-Universität Münster
Paper 642-b: ***Memento mori*: The Remembrance of Death in the *Catecheses* of Theodore the Studite** (Language: English)
Paraskevi Toma
Paper 642-c: **The *Memoria* of Sin and Penance and the Byzantine Ruler Image** (Language: English)
Lutz Rickelt, Institut für Byzantinistik und Neogräzistik, Westfälische Wilhelms-Universität Münster

Session:	**643** **Maurice Keyworth Building: Room 1.32**
Title:	**THE MEMORY OF THE CRUSADES, II: NATIONAL MEMORIES, CRUSADING PROJECTIONS**
Sponsor:	Routledge
Organiser:	Mike Horswell, Department of History, Royal Holloway, University of London
Moderator:	Kristin Skottki, Lehrstuhl für Mittelalterliche Geschichte, Universität Bayreuth
Paper 643-a:	**The Memory and Perceptions of the Crusades and Crusaders in Egyptian Writings of the 19th and 20th Centuries** (Language: English) Ahmed Mohamed A. Sheir, Centrum für Nah- und Mittelost-Studien (CNMS), Philipps-Universität Marburg
Paper 643-b:	**Crusader Propaganda Strategies during the Gulf Crisis, c. 1990-1991** (Language: English) Sophia Menache, Department of History, University of Haifa
Paper 643-c:	**'An episode of the Crusades'?: Historiographical Debates on the Role of the Crusading Idea in the Formation of Portugal, c. 1915-1947** (Language: English) Pedro Alexandre Guerreiro Martins, Instituto de História Contemporânea, Universidade Nova de Lisboa

Session:	**644** **Fine Art Building: SR 1.10**
Title:	**CULTURAL MEMORY IN LATE ANTIQUITY, II: THE MEMORY OF PERSECUTION**
Organiser:	Richard Flower, Department of Classics & Ancient History, University of Exeter and Robin Whelan, Department of History, University of Liverpool
Moderator:	Veronika Wieser, Institut für Mittelalterforschung, Österreichische Akademie der Wissenschaften, Wien
Paper 644-a:	**The Memory of Persecution in Late Antique Polemical Literature** (Language: English) Samuel Cohen, Department of History, Sonoma State University, California
Paper 644-b:	**The 411 Conference of Carthage in Donatist Memory** (Language: English) Kevin Feeney, Department of History, Yale University
Paper 644-c:	**The Echo of the Martyrdom: Collective Memory in the First Greek *Life of St Pachomius*** (Language: English) Fabrizio Petorella, Dipartimento di Studi Umanistici, Università degli studi Roma Tre

Session: **645** **Leeds University Union: Room 6 - Roundhay**
Title: **REMEMBERING TRAVELS, TRAVELLING IN MEMORIES, II**
Organiser: Jana Valtrová, Department for the Study of Religions, Masarykova univerzita, Brno
Moderator: Rebecca Darley, Department of History, Classics & Archaeology, Birkbeck, University of London
Paper 645-a: **Looking for Tradition: Zoroastrian Travellers between Iran and India** (Language: English)
Ionuţ-Valentin Cucu, Institut für Iranistik, Freie Universität Berlin / Facultatea de Istorie, Universitatea din Bucureşti
Paper 645-b: **The Alan Christian Nobles at the Court of Great Khans** (Language: English)
Vladimír Liščák, Oriental Institute, Czech Academy of Sciences, Praha
Paper 645-c: **Remembering Franciscan Martyrs in Europe and Asia** (Language: English)
Jana Valtrová

Session: **646** **Emmanuel Centre: Room 10**
Title: **TRACES OF MEMORY IN THE WESTERN MEDITERRANEAN, II: MONASTIC MEMORY**
Sponsor: Institut de Recerca en Cultures Medievals / Institución Milá y Fontanals (IMF), Consejo Superior de Investigaciones Científicas (CSIC) / Grup de Recerca en Estudis Medievals d'Art, Història, Paleografia i Arqueologia (MAHPA), Universitat de Barcelona
Organiser: Núria Jornet-Benito, Departament de Biblioteconomia, Documentació i Comunicació Audiovisual / Institut de Recerca en Cultures Medievals, Universitat de Barcelona and Maria Soler-Sala, Departament d'Història Medieval, Paleografia i Diplomàtica, Universitat de Barcelona
Moderator: Xavier Costa-Badia, Institut de Recerca en Cultures Medievals, Universitat de Barcelona
Paper 646-a: **Archival Memory in the Medieval Monasteries: The Case of St Antoni i Sta Clara of Barcelona** (Language: English)
Núria Jornet-Benito
Paper 646-b: **Spaces, Chronicles, and Modern Narratives: The Constructed Memory of Iberian Poor Clares** (Language: English)
Araceli Rosillo-Luque, Arxiu-Biblioteca dels Franciscans de Catalunya / Departament d'Història Medieval, Paleografia i Diplomàtica, Universitat de Barcelona
Paper 646-c: ***Diversitas* and Memory on Liturgical Performance in Iberian Mendicant Nunneries** (Language: English)
Mercedes Pérez Vidal, Departament d'Història i Arqueologia / Institut de Recerca en Cultures Medievals, Universitat de Barcelona

Session: **647** **Baines Wing: Room 2.14**
Title: **Memory in Late Medieval Faculty Psychology**
Sponsor: Rationality in Perception: Transformations of Mind & Cognition, 1250-1550, ERC Project
Organiser: José Filipe Pereira da Silva, Department of Philosophy, History, Culture & Art Studies, University of Helsinki
Moderator: José Filipe Pereira da Silva
Paper 647-a: **Memory in Rational and Non-Rational Animals** (Language: English)
Annemieke Verboon, Department of Philosophy, University of Helsinki
Paper 647-b: **Two Types of Memory: Nicholas of Cusa on Remembering the Physical and the Non-Physical** (Language: English)
Christian Kny, Department of Philosophy, History, Culture & Art Studies, University of Helsinki
Paper 647-c: **Memory: Power or Function?** (Language: English)
José Filipe Pereira da Silva

Session: **648** **University House: St George Room**
Title: **Jousts and *Pas d'Armes*, II: Literary and Visual Sources**
Sponsor: Pas d'Armes Research Group
Organiser: Alan V. Murray, Institute for Medieval Studies, University of Leeds
Moderator: Alan V. Murray
Paper 648-a: **Representations of the *Pas d'Armes* in Burgundian Prose Romance and Chivalric Biography** (Language: English)
Ros Brown-Grant, School of Languages, Cultures & Societies - French, University of Leeds
Paper 648-b: **Writing the *Pas d'Armes*: The *Pas de Saumur*, 1446** (Language: English)
Cathy Blunk, School of Humanities, Drury University, Missouri
Paper 648-c: **Patrons, Participants, and Spectators in the *Pas de Saumur*, 1446** (Language: English)
Justin Sturgeon, Department of Art, University of West Florida

Session: **649** **University House: Cloberry Room**
Title: **Disaster Memory in the Middle Ages, II**
Sponsor: Abteilung für Wirtschafts-, Sozial- und Umweltgeschichte, Universität Bern
Organiser: Christian Rohr, Historisches Institut, Universität Bern
Moderator: Thomas Labbé, Archéologie, Terre, Histoire, Sociétés (ARTEHIS - UMR 6298), Université de Bourgogne
Paper 649-a: **'New Traditions' in Natural Disaster Rituals in Late Medieval Valencia** (Language: English)
Abigail Agresta, Department of History, Queen's University, Ontario
Paper 649-b: **Christopher of Bavaria and Climate-Related Crises in the Light of Memory of Nature** (Language: English)
Heli Huhtamaa, Departement Geschiedenis en Kunstgeschiedenis, Universiteit Utrecht
Respondent: Martin Bauch, Leibniz-Institut für Geschichte und Kultur des östlichen Europa, Leipzig

Session: **650** **Emmanuel Centre: Room 11**
Title: **CISTERCIANS, II: EXPLORING THE RELATIONSHIP TO THE SUN IN CISTERCIAN ABBEY CHURCHES OF THE UK AND IRELAND**
Sponsor: *Cîteaux: Commentarii cistercienses*
Organiser: Darrelyn Gunzburg, Sophia Centre for the Study of Cosmology in Culture, University of Wales Trinity Saint David and Terryl N. Kinder, *Cîteaux: Commentarii cistercienses*, Pontigny
Moderator: Terryl N. Kinder
Paper 650-a: **Skyscape: Cultural Astronomy and Its Impact on the Landscape** (Language: English)
Fabio Silva, Sophia Centre for the Study of Cosmology in Culture, University of Wales Trinity Saint David / Institut Català de Paleoecologia Humana i Evolució Social, Tarragona
Paper 650-b: **Cistercian Abbeys, Sky, and Landscape** (Language: English)
Darrelyn Gunzburg
Paper 650-c: **The Shifting Expression of the UK/Ireland Cistercian Template** (Language: English)
Bernadette Brady, Sophia Centre for the Study of Cosmology in Culture, University of Wales Trinity Saint David

Session: **651** **Baines Wing: Room 2.15**
Title: **SCIENTIFIC THOUGHT: MEDIEVAL AND MODERN**
Organiser: IMC Programming Committee
Moderator: Heide Estes, Department of English, Monmouth University, New Jersey
Paper 651-a: **The Halo Drawings in *Flores Historiarum* and *Chronica Majora*** (Language: English)
Ágnes Kiricsi, Department of Literary & Cultural Studies in English, Károli Gáspár University of the Reformed Church in Hungary, Budapest
Paper 651-b: **The Lost Memory of Some Sources of *Inferno*: Dante and Geothermy** (Language: English)
Antonio Raschi, Istituto di Biometeorologia, Consiglio Nazionale delle Ricerche, Firenze
Paper 651-c: **Medieval Alchemy: Early Metaphors for Collective Memory** (Language: English)
Roula-Maria Dib Nassif, Institute for Medieval Studies, University of Leeds

Session: **652** **Stage@leeds: Stage 1**
Title: **DO YOU REMEMBER THE FIRST TIME?: HISTORIOGRAPHIES OF MEMORY SINCE THE 1990S**
Sponsor: Centre for the Study of the Middle Ages (CeSMA), University of Birmingham
Organiser: Christopher P. Callow, Centre for the Study of the Middle Ages (CeSMA), University of Birmingham
Moderator: Chris Wickham, Faculty of History, University of Oxford
Paper 652-a: **A Thousand Material Memories: Relic-Cults and Memories of Miracles in 12th-Century England** (Language: English)
Simon Stuart Yarrow, Centre for the Study of the Middle Ages (CeSMA), University of Birmingham
Paper 652-b: **Memory in Medieval Scandinavia** (Language: English)
Christopher P. Callow
Paper 652-c: **Imagined Communities: Monasteries, Memory, and Monastic History** (Language: English)
Katharine Sykes, School of History & Cultures, University of Birmingham

Session: **653** **Michael Sadler Building: Room LG.15**
Title: **MANUS-ON MANUSCRIPTS, II: DIGITAL EDITING METHODS - A WORKSHOP**
Sponsor: Schoenberg Institute for Manuscript Studies, University of Pennsylvania
Organiser: Dorothy Carr Porter, Schoenberg Institute for Manuscript Studies, University of Pennsylvania and Abigail G. Robertson, Department of English Language & Literature, University of New Mexico, Albuquerque
Tutors: Anya Adair, Faculty of Arts & Social Sciences, University of Sydney and Abigail G. Robertson
Purpose: *This second session, led by Anya Adair, will consist of an overview of digital editing methods and how they can be utilized when studying the rolls and their representation on digital platforms. Anya will demonstrate how her digital project on manuscript rolls helps to better understand how to lead, organize, and implement projects to digitize and edit rolls and fragments, moving into a workshop where participants can use the project and familiarize themselves with how it works and how it could apply to their research.*

Session: **654** **Maurice Keyworth Building: Room G.02**
Title: **THE PEOPLE OF MEDIEVAL LONDON: A ROUND TABLE DISCUSSION**
Sponsor: *Medieval Prosopography*
Organiser: Caroline M. Barron, Department of History, Royal Holloway, University of London and Joel Rosenthal, Department of History, State University of New York, Stony Brook
Moderator: Caroline M. Barron
Purpose: *The four panellists have all carried out research into the guilds and companies of medieval London: the ironmongers, glovers, carpenters, and carters. The four speakers will bring to the round table their knowledge of four very different crafts, ranging from the ironmongers numbered among the 'Great Twelve' to the Carters who only formed themselves into a company in the early 16th century. The panel will work from a common agenda to discuss what can be determined about individual members of their crafts, their family life and household structures, and the role that their guild or company played in shaping their social, religious, and commercial lives. It is hoped that this discussion will throw light on how very different sets of records, created within a single geographical environment, can be used to answer common questions and issues and to analyse changing practices and priorities over time.*

Participants include Peter Brown (Independent Scholar, London), Doreen Leach (Royal Holloway, University of London), Claire Martin (Royal Holloway, University of London), and Leah Rhys (Royal Holloway, University of London).

LUNCH

Meal Times

Refectory	12.00-14.00
University Square: The Marquee	12.00-14.00

See Map 9, p. 51.

---

* * * * *

MEDIEVAL HIGHLIGHTS FROM LEEDS UNIVERSITY LIBRARY SPECIAL COLLECTIONS

PARKINSON BUILDING: TREASURES OF THE BROTHERTON GALLERY
12.00-14.00

Join us for a drop-in session to see medieval treasures from Special Collections at the University of Leeds. Special Collections staff will be in the Treasures of the Brotherton Gallery with a selection of highlights from the collections for delegates to examine close-up.

The collections at Leeds contain beautiful illuminated 15th-century French and Flemish books of hours, psalters, and prayer books, as well as German chained manuscripts from the 1450s. Some of these will be on show alongside examples from our fine collection of incunabula. The Library of Ripon Cathedral is held on long-term deposit in Special Collections at the University of Leeds and includes a Latin Bible from the 13th century. A highlight of the Yorkshire Archaeological and Historical Society Collection is the enormous series of surviving court rolls of the manor of Wakefield (1274-1925). Also for the first time at the IMC, we will be revealing examples from our extensive coin collection.

Special Collections houses over 200,000 rare books and 7 km of manuscripts and archives, including the celebrated Brotherton Collection. The Special Collections Reading Room is open from 09.00-17.00 during the IMC, and delegates are welcome to pursue their research and explore the collection. More details on how to search and use the collections can be found at https://library.leeds.ac.uk/special-collections.

* * * * *

Session:	**699** **Stage@leeds: Stage 1**
Title:	**KEYNOTE LECTURE 2018: HISTORICAL PRESENT: FAKE HISTORY, MATERIAL CULTURE, AND COLLECTIVE MISREMEMBERING** (Language: English)
Speaker:	Alixe Bovey, Courtauld Institute of Art, University of London
Introduction:	Lucie Doležalová, Institute of Greek & Latin Studies, Univerzita Karlova, Praha and Jan Čermák, Department of English, Univerzita Karlova, Praha
Details:	*We live in history, scurrying along streets with ancient names, past old buildings and historic landmarks, through protected landscapes, amidst plaques and statuary memorialising achievement and catastrophe. While the commemoration industry is focused on events that actually happened in the past - births, deaths, discoveries, battles, calamities - an important dimension of cultural memory concerns larger truths about origins and identities with a much looser connection to 'the facts of history'. The central example in this lecture is the complex legacy of the opening of Geoffrey of Monmouth's* Historia regum Britanniae, *which describes how Trojan refugees exterminated Albion's indigenous giants and founded the British nation. How and why have material things (manuscript illuminations, printed books, turf-cut chalk drawings, elaborate costumes, immense figures in papier-mâché, oak, wicker, and even latex) preserved and embellished the memory of this foundation myth, alongside centuries of destruction, ridicule, indifference, and misunderstanding? Memory loss, confusion, and destruction are, it will be argued, essential pretexts for invention and survival, and underpin the dynamic interaction between material things, mythic history, and cultural memory.* *Please note that admission to this event will be on a first-come, first-served basis as there will be no tickets. Please ensure that you arrive as early as possible to avoid disappointment.*

Session: **701** **Parkinson Building: Room 1.16**
Title: **EADMER OF CANTERBURY, I: EADMER'S MEMORY, MANUSCRIPTS, AND EVIDENCE**
Organiser: Charlie Rozier, Department of History, Swansea University and Sally N. Vaughn, Department of History, University of Houston, Texas
Moderator: Charlie Rozier
Paper 701-a: **Memory and Rhetoric in Eadmer's Histories** (Language: English)
Paul Hayward, Department of History, Lancaster University
Paper 701-b: **Eadmer and His Books: What Sort of Scribe Was He?** (Language: English)
Benjamin Pohl, Department of History, University of Bristol
Paper 701-c: **Uses of Evidence in Eadmer's *Historia novorum*** (Language: English)
Robert F. Berkhofer, Department of History, Western Michigan University, Kalamazoo
Respondent: Charlie Rozier

Session: **702** **Baines Wing: Room 2.16**
Title: **MEMORY AND IDENTITY IN MEDIEVAL MONASTERIES**
Organiser: IMC Programming Committee
Moderator: Steven Vanderputten, Vakgroep Geschiedenis, Universiteit Gent
Paper 702-a: **Manipulation des Gedächtnisses bei den ersten Zisterzienser?** (Language: Deutsch)
Iva Adamkova, Institute of Greek & Latin Studies, Univerzita Karlova, Praha
Paper 702-b: **Remembering Benefactors in the Cartulary of the Carthusian Charterhouse of Beauvale** (Language: English)
Kaan Vural Gorman, Institute for Medieval Studies, University of Leeds
Paper 702-c: **The Memory of the Monks: Disentangling the Life of the Medieval Documents from San Clodio Do Ribeiro** (Language: English)
Aránzazu Fernández Quintas, Facultade de Historia, Universidade de Vigo, Ourense

Session: **703** **University House: Little Woodhouse Room**
Title: **BEYOND THE ANGLO-NORMAN CONQUESTS: ALTERNATIVE NARRATIVES IN INSULAR HISTORY, I**
Organiser: Ben Guy, Department of Anglo-Saxon, Norse & Celtic, University of Cambridge and Rebecca Thomas, Department of Anglo-Saxon, Norse & Celtic, University of Cambridge
Moderator: Ben Guy
Paper 703-a: **Remembering the Welsh Citizens of Medieval Dublin** (Language: English)
Seán Duffy, Department of History, Trinity College Dublin
Paper 703-b: **International Dimensions to Identity in 12th-Century Wales: The Evidence of the *Vita Griffini*** (Language: English)
Rebecca Thomas
Paper 703-c: **Two Polities in Perspective: Gwynedd and the Kingdom of Man and the Isles** (Language: English)
Owain Wyn Jones, School of History, Welsh History & Archaeology, Bangor University

Session: **704** **Baines Wing: Room 1.13**
Title: **NEW VOICES IN ANGLO-SAXON STUDIES, II**
Sponsor: International Society of Anglo-Saxonists
Organiser: Megan Cavell, Department of English Literature, University of Birmingham
Moderator: Francesca Tinti, Departamento de Historia Medieval, Moderna y de América, Universidad del País Vasco - Euskal Herriko Unibertsitatea, Vitoria-Gasteiz
Paper 704-a: ***Rōmaji* and Runes: Literary Polygraphy and Societal Memories** (Language: English)
Jacob Runner, School of Cultures, Languages & Area Studies / School of English, University of Nottingham
Paper 704-b: **Remembering Uhtred: Naming and Collective Memory in Anglo-Saxon England** (Language: English)
James Chetwood, Department of History, University of Sheffield
Paper 704-c: **Soundscapes in the *Vitae* of St Guthlac** (Language: English)
Britton Elliott Brooks, Department of English, University of Hawai'i at Mānoa

---

Session: **705** **Fine Art Building: SR G.04**
Title: **GAMES AND VISUAL CULTURE, I**
Organiser: Elizabeth Lapina, Department of History, University of Wisconsin-Madison
Moderator: Elizabeth Lapina
Paper 705-a: **Cultural Transmissions: Gaming Pieces in Action** (Language: English)
Madeline Walsh, Department of Archaeology, University of York
Paper 705-b: **Children's Toys in Medieval Italy** (Language: English)
Annemarieke Willemsen, Rijksmuseum van Oudheden, Leiden

Session: **706** **Michael Sadler Building: Room LG.16**
Title: **MEMORY IN RUNES AND COMMUNITY**
Sponsor: Memory & the Pre-Modern North Network
Organiser: Simon Nygaard, Afdeling for Religionsvidenskab, Aarhus Universitet and Yoav Tirosh, Faculty of Icelandic & Comparative Cultural Studies, University of Iceland, Reykjavík
Moderator: Simon Nygaard
Paper 706-a: **Haraldr's Jelling: Cultivating a Collective Identity of the Danes** (Language: English)
Sophie Bønding, Afdeling for Religionsvidenskab, Aarhus Universitet
Paper 706-b: **Beyond the Banalities of Burial-Stones: Memory Studies and Old Nordic Monuments** (Language: English)
Jonas Koesling, School of Humanities, University of Iceland, Reykjavík
Paper 706-c: **Thoughts of Home: A Study of Cultural Memory and Heritage among Viking Age Rus'** (Language: English)
William Pidzamecky, School of English, University of Nottingham
Paper 706-d: **'All these stones': Runestone Monuments with Multiple Inscriptions** (Language: English)
Maja Bäckvall, Institutionen för nordiska språk, Uppsala Universitet

Session: **707** **Michael Sadler Building: Room LG.17**
Title: **ACCOUNTING AND BOOKKEEPING IN THE LATE MEDIEVAL CROWN OF ARAGON: A COMPARATIVE APPROACH - CATALONIA, SARDINIA, AND SICILY**
Sponsor: Irish Research Council Project 'Empire or Composite State?: Aragonese Rule over the Mediterranean in Later Middle Ages' (ID: GOIPD/2016/488)
Organiser: Alessandro Silvestri, School of Histories & Humanities, Trinity College Dublin
Moderator: Flocel Sabaté Curull, Departament d'Història, Universitat de Lleida
Paper 707-a: **The 'House of the Racional': A Repository for the Political Memory of Late Medieval Catalonia** (Language: English)
Pere Verdés-Pijuan, Departamento de Estudios Medievales, Consejo Superior de Investigaciones Científicas, Barcelona
Paper 707-b: **Accumulating Information and Examining the Accounts in the Kingdom of Sardinia during the Late Middle Ages** (Language: English)
Fabrizio Alias, Dipartimento di Storia, scienze dell'uomo e della formazione, Università degli Studi di Sassari
Paper 707-c: **Too Much to Account For: Recording, Budgeting, and Auditing in the 15th-Century Kingdom of Sicily** (Language: English)
Alessandro Silvestri

Session: **708** **Fine Art Building: Studio Ground Floor**
Title: **LA MÉMOIRE DES IMAGES: BEASTS AND ANIMALS CHANGING THROUGH CONTEXTS IN THE MIDDLE AGES**
Sponsor: Departamento de Historia Medieval, Universidad Complutense de Madrid
Organiser: Marisa Bueno, Departamento de Historia Medieval, Universidad Complutense de Madrid
Moderator: Gonzalo J. Escudero Manzano, Departamento de Historia Medieval, Universidad Complutense de Madrid
Paper 708-a: **The Prostitute on the Beast in the Turin Beatus: Visual Devices to Depict the Enemies of Christianity** (Language: English)
Nadia Mariana Consiglieri, Consejo Nacional de Investigaciones Científicas y Técnicas (CONICET) / Facultad de Filosofía y Letras, Universidad de Buenos Aires
Paper 708-b: **Images of Mouth of Hell in Oxford, Bodleian Library, MS Junius 11** (Language: English)
Gesner Las Casas Brito Filho, School of Fine Art, History of Art & Cultural Studies, University of Leeds
Paper 708-c: **The Origin of the Unicorn as Steed in Medieval Culture** (Language: English)
Adriana Gallardo Luque, Departamento de Historia Medieval, Universidad Complutense de Madrid
Paper 708-d: **The Rhetoric of Images: Memory and Ornamentation in Oxford, St John's College, MS 61** (Language: English)
Muriel Araujo Lima, Departamento de História, Universidade de São Paulo

Session: **709** **Baines Wing: Room 2.13**
Title: **THE FALL OF ANGELS IN ORTHODOX AND HETERODOX BIBLICAL EXEGESIS**
Sponsor: Department for the Study of Religions, Masarykova univerzita, Brno
Organiser: Rachel Ernst, Department of History, Georgia State University and David Zbíral, Department for the Study of Religions, Masarykova univerzita, Brno
Moderator: Delfi-Isabel Nieto-Isabel, Departament d'Història Medieval, Paleografia i Diplomàtica, Universitat de Barcelona
Paper 709-a: **Becoming Human: The Fall of Angels in the Christian Tradition** (Language: English)
Daniela Müller, Faculteit der Filosofie, Theologie en Religiewetenschappen, Radboud Universiteit Nijmegen
Paper 709-b: **The Lost Sheep, the House of Israel, and a Man Who Descended from Jerusalem: Mapping Exegetical Imagery of Fallen Angels in Anti-Heretical Polemic** (Language: English)
Rachel Ernst
Paper 709-c: **The Changing Biblical Foundations of the Cathar Myth of the Fall** (Language: English)
Piotr Czarnecki, Instytut Religioznawstwa, Uniwersytet Jagielloński, Kraków

Session: **710** **Maurice Keyworth Building: Room 1.04**
Title: **25 YEARS OF HAGIOGRAPHICAL RESEARCH: PAST ACHIEVEMENTS AND FUTURE PERSPECTIVES, II**
Sponsor: Université Paris VIII - Vincennes-Saint-Denis / Université de Montréal
Organiser: Anne-Marie Helvétius, Département d'histoire, Université Paris VIII - Vincennes-Saint-Denis
Moderator: Francesco Veronese, Istituto Storico Italiano per il Medioevo, Roma
Paper 710-a: **Recent Research on Medieval Cult of Saints in Central Europe** (Language: English)
Gábor Klaniczay, Department of Medieval Studies, Central European University, Budapest
Paper 710-b: ***Hagiographica Septentrionalia*** (Language: English)
Christian Krötzl, Department of History, University of Tampere
Paper 710-c: **Saints in Their Time and in Their Manuscripts: 25 Years of Hagiographical Studies in Belgium, France, and Germany** (Language: English)
Sylvie Joye, Département d'Histoire, Université de Reims Champagne-Ardenne

Session: **711** — **Baines Wing: Room 1.15**
Title: **CEU 25, III: BYZANTINE STUDIES - REACTIVATIONS OF KNOWLEDGE**
Sponsor: Department of Medieval Studies, Central European University, Budapest
Organiser: Floris Bernard, Department of Medieval Studies, Central European University, Budapest
Moderator: Alice Choyke, Department of Medieval Studies, Central European University, Budapest
Paper 711-a: **Interactive Reading of the Past: *Excerpta Constantiniana* and the *Suda*** (Language: English)
András Németh, Biblioteca Apostolica Vaticana, Vatican City
Paper 711-b: **Teaching and Learning Mathematics in 11th-Century Byzantium: The Case of the 'Anonymous Heiberg'** (Language: English)
Divna Manolova, Department of Philology, University of Silesia, Katowice
Paper 711-c: **Réactivation de savoirs comme stratégie de survie: les livres des migrants dans la Méditerranée du VIIe s.** (Language: Français)
Filippo Ronconi, Centre d'Études Byzantines, Néo-Helléniques et sud-est Européennes, École des Hautes Études en Sciences Sociales (EHESS), Paris

Session: **712** — **Baines Wing: Room 1.14**
Title: **DEVOTED TO THE BODY: DEVOTIONAL PRACTICES AND PERFORMANCES IN FEMININE SPIRITUALITY, I - TEXTUAL WITNESSES**
Organiser: Godelinde Gertrude Perk, Avdelningen för Humaniora, Mittuniversitets, Sundsvall and Lieke Andrea Smits, Centre for the Arts in Society, Universiteit Leiden
Moderator: Lieke Andrea Smits
Paper 712-a: **'Fair Lord, in your honour I have undertaken this battle': The Influence of St Catherine of Alexandria on Female Movement in the Late Middle Ages** (Language: English)
Jade Godsall, Department of Religion & Theology, University of Bristol / Department of English, University of Exeter
Paper 712-b: **Corpus Christi, or *Corpus Mariae*?: The Gendered Body as Devotional Ideal** (Language: English)
Joseph Morgan, Department of English, Indiana University, Bloomington
Paper 712-c: **The Carthusian Design of Female Piety in Late Medieval England: Literal Identification with Christ in Carthusian Prayers and Meditations Written for English Women** (Language: English)
Clarck Drieshen, British Library, London

Session: **713** — **Charles Thackrah Building: 1.01**
Title: **SLINGS AND ARROWS: HOMOSOCIAL NARRATIVES OF DESIRE, I**
Organiser: Kathryn Maude, Department of English, American University of Beirut
Moderator: Kathryn Maude
Paper 713-a: **Bondages of War: Homosociality, Warfare, and the Early Tudor Chivalric Ideal** (Language: English)
Audrey Thorstad, School of History, Welsh History & Archaeology, Bangor University
Paper 713-b: **Locker Room Talk: Homosocial Discourse in Late Medieval England** (Language: English)
Rachel E. Moss, Corpus Christi College, University of Oxford
Paper 713-c: **Homoeroticism and Heterosexuality in TV Fictions of the Renaissance** (Language: English)
Catherine Fletcher, Department of History, Swansea University

Session: **714** **University House: Beechgrove Room**
Title: **WOMEN AND JUSTICE, I: NEGOTIATING JURISDICTIONS**
Organiser: Emma Cavell, Department of History, University of Swansea
Moderator: Emma Cavell
Paper 714-a: **Disorderly Daughters?: Gender and Household in Borough Court Trespass Pleas** (Language: English)
Teresa Phipps, Centre for Medieval & Early Modern Research (MEMO), Swansea University
Paper 714-b: **Dower, Remarriage, and Lifecycle in Medieval English Ireland** (Language: English)
Sparky Booker, School of History, Anthropology, Philosophy & Politics, Queen's University Belfast
Paper 714-c: **'She hath no remedy by course of commyn law': Legal Options and Strategic Decision-Making in the Early Tudor Star Chamber** (Language: English)
Deborah Youngs, Centre for Medieval & Early Modern Research (MEMO), Swansea University

Session: **715** **Baines Wing: Room 1.16**
Title: **RE-THINKING THE ARISTOCRACY IN CAPETIAN FRANCE, III: REGULATING THE ARISTOCRACY**
Sponsor: Society for the Study of French History (SSFH)
Organiser: Charlotte Crouch, Graduate Centre for Medieval Studies, University of Reading and Niall Ó Súilleabháin, Department of History, Trinity College Dublin
Moderator: Daniel Power, Centre for Medieval & Early Modern Research (MEMO), Swansea University
Paper 715-a: **How Did the Peace of God Make Peace?** (Language: English)
Geoffrey Koziol, Department of History, University of California, Berkeley
Paper 715-b: **The Sires of Beaujeu as Crusaders, 1147-1250** (Language: English)
Jean H. Dunbabin, St Anne's College, University of Oxford
Paper 715-c: **Different Rules, Same Game?: Marriage as a Tool of Power for the Bourbon Family in Late 12th and 13th-Century France** (Language: English)
Charlotte Crouch

Session: **716** **Michael Sadler Building: Rupert Beckett Theatre**
Title: **LEGAL TEXTS AND THEIR USERS, III: LAW IN LEARNING AND PRACTICE IN THE LATER MIDDLE AGES**
Sponsor: Iuris Canonici Medii Aevi Consociatio (ICMAC)
Organiser: Kathleen Cushing, Department of History, Keele University
Moderator: Bruce C. Brasington, Department of History, West Texas A&M University, Canyon
Paper 716-a: **How Law Became 'New': The Decretal Collections and 'Old' Law in the Later 12th Century** (Language: English)
Danica Summerlin, Department of History, University of Sheffield
Paper 716-b: **The Early Transalpine Decretistic: Its Manuscript Transmission and Readers** (Language: English)
Tatsushi Genka, Faculty of Law, University of Tokyo
Paper 716-c: **The *Liber minoricarum decisionum* of Bartolus and Its Users in 15th-Century Italy: A Manuscript Belonging to St John of Capestrano** (Language: English)
Andrea Bartocci, Facoltà di Giurisprudenzia, Università degli Studi di Teramo

Session: **717** — **Social Sciences Building: Room 10.05**
Title: **THE ORIGINS, EFFECTS, AND MEMORY OF CAROLINE MINUSCULE, I**
Sponsor: Network for the Study of Caroline Minuscule
Organiser: Arthur Westwell, Kompetenzzentrum für elektronische Erschließungs- und Publikationsverfahren in den Geisteswissenschaften, Universität Trier
Moderator: Evina Steinová, Pontifical Institute of Mediaeval Studies, University of Toronto, Downtown
Paper 717-a: **Writing on the Edge of an Empire: The 9th-Century Scriptorium at Chieti** (Language: English)
Arthur Westwell
Paper 717-b: **Did a Veronese Caroline Minuscule Really Exist?** (Language: English)
Laura Pani, Dipartimento di Studi Umanistici, Università degli Studi di Udine
Paper 717-c: **Caroline Minuscule in Early Medieval Catalonia** (Language: English)
Anna Dorofeeva, School of History, University College Dublin

Session: **718** — **Stage@leeds: Stage 2**
Title: **RELATIONS BETWEEN CLERICS AND MONKS IN LATE ANTIQUITY AND EARLY MIDDLE AGES**
Sponsor: Presbyters in the Late Antique West Project, Uniwersytet Warszawski / Network for the Study of Late Antique & Early Medieval Monasticism
Organiser: Jerzy Szafranowski, Instytut Historyczny, Uniwersytet Warszawski
Moderator: Yaniv Fox, Department of General History, Bar-Ilan University, Ramat Gan
Paper 718-a: **Monasticism and Anti-Donatism in Augustine of Hippo** (Language: English)
Matheus Coutinho Figuinha, Departamento de História, Universidade Estadual de Campinas, Brazil
Paper 718-b: **Grounds for Clerical Ordinations of Monks in Late Antique Gaul** (Language: English)
Jerzy Szafranowski
Paper 718-c: **A Crisis of Identity: Canons, Monks, and the 9th-Century Reform of Saint-Denis** (Language: English)
Matthew Mattingly, Centre for Medieval Studies, University of Toronto, Downtown

---

Session: **719** — **Charles Thackrah Building: 1.02**
Title: **MEDIEVAL PUBLISHING**
Sponsor: Medieval Publishing from c. 1000-1500, ERC Starting Grant Project
Organiser: Samu K. Niskanen, Department of History, University of Helsinki
Moderator: Jakub Kujawiński, Institute of History, Adam Mickiewicz University, Poznań / Department of History, University of Helsinki
Paper 719-a: **Papal Authority and Publishing in the Late 11th Century** (Language: English)
Samu K. Niskanen
Paper 719-b: **Publishing and Disseminating Historical Works in the Anglo-Norman World** (Language: English)
Jaakko Tahkokallio, National Library of Finland, Helsinki
Paper 719-c: **Database of Literary Dedications and Commissions: Problems and Prospects** (Language: English)
Lauri Leinonen, Department of History, University of Helsinki

Session: **720** **University House: Great Woodhouse Room**
Title: ***MORTES*, MEMORY, AND RETRACTION**
Organiser: Karen Cherewatuk, Department of English, St Olaf College, Minnesota
Moderator: Karen Cherewatuk
Paper 720-a: **Forgetting to Remember in Malory's *Morte*** (Language: English)
Catherine J. Batt, Institute for Medieval Studies, University of Leeds
Paper 720-b: **Mourning and Memory in Malory** (Language: English)
Karen Cherewatuk
Paper 720-c: **Tricks of Memory: Malory and the Stock Phrase** (Language: English)
Joyce Coleman, Department of English, University of Oklahoma
Paper 720-d: **Memories of War: Retracting the Dominant Reading of the Alliterative *Morte Arthure*** (Language: English)
Fiona Tolhurst, Department of Language & Literature, Florida Gulf Coast University and Kevin S. Whetter, Department of English, Acadia University, Nova Scotia

Session: **721** **Emmanuel Centre: Wilson Room**
Title: **MEMORY STRATEGIES IN WOLFRAM VON ESCHENBACH**
Sponsor: Centro de Investigação Transdisciplinar 'Cultura, Espaço e Memória' (CITCEM) / German Literature in the German Middle Ages Research Unit (GLITEMA), Universidade do Porto
Organiser: John Greenfield, Centro de Investigação Transdisciplinar 'Cultura, Espaço e Memória' (CITCEM), Universidade do Porto
Moderator: Laura Auteri, Dipartimento di Scienze Umanistiche, Università degli Studi di Palermo
Paper 721-a: **Memory Themes in Wolfram's *Parzival*** (Language: English)
Mafalda Sofia Gomes, Faculdade de Letras, Universidade do Porto
Paper 721-b: **Narrative Times and Auctorial Memory in Wolfram's *Titurel*** (Language: English)
Paul Gross, Departamento de Estudos Germanísticos, Universidade do Porto
Paper 721-c: **Recollection and Memory in Wolfram's Dawn Songs** (Language: English)
J. Carlos Teixeira, Centro de Investigação Transdisciplinar 'Cultura, Espaço e Memória' (CITCEM), Universidade do Porto

Session: **722** **Social Sciences Building: Room 10.06**
Title: **THE ART OF MEMORY, I**
Organiser: IMC Programming Committee
Moderator: Kimberly Rivers, Department of History, University of Wisconsin-Oshkosh
Paper 722-a: **El *Ars memorativa* de I. Publicius: una aproximación a la historia del texto** (Language: Español)
Merino Jerez Luis, Departamento de Ciencias de la Antigüedad, Universidad de Extremadura, Cáceres
Paper 722-b: ***Per cola et commata*: *Mise-en-page* and Medieval Memorisation** (Language: English)
Astrid Khoo, Department of Classics, King's College London
Paper 722-c: **The Commemorative Function of the *divisiones thematis* as a Key to Orientation in Late Scholastic Preaching Texts: The Example of the Sermons of Henry of Wildenstein** (Language: English)
Vojtěch Večeře, Department of Greek & Latin Studies, Univerzita Karlova, Praha

Session: **723** **Maurice Keyworth Building: Room 1.31**
Title: **Remembering the Northern English Saints, I: Buildings and Bodies**
Sponsor: Late Medieval Devotion to Northern English Saints, Swiss National Science Foundation Project
Organiser: Christiania Whitehead, Faculté des lettres, Université de Lausanne
Moderator: Denis Renevey, Faculté des lettres, Université de Lausanne
Paper 723-a: **Reusing the Cathedral: Space, Ritual, and Community in Late Medieval Durham** (Language: English)
Euan McCartney Robson, Department of History of Art, University College London
Paper 723-b: **Keeping it in the *Familia*: Creating and Recreating the Cult of Saints in Northern England, 1300-1500** (Language: English)
Emma J. Wells, Centre for Lifelong Learning / Department of History, University of York
Paper 723-c: **Flesh, Bone, and Text: Reading Relics in Anglo-Norman Saints' Lives** (Language: English)
Jane Sinnett-Smith, Department of French, University of Warwick

Session: **724** **Michael Sadler Building: Room LG.19**
Title: **Writing and Performing Memory**
Organiser: IMC Programming Committee
Moderator: Cora Dietl, Institut für Germanistik, Justus-Liebig-Universität Gießen
Paper 724-a: **The Lethe River as a Metaphor in the *Comoedia Babionis* and in Osbern Pinnock's *Derivationes*** (Language: English)
Klementyna Aura Glińska, Bibliothèque nationale de France, Paris
Paper 724-b: **The Written and the Performed: The Metonymic Memory in Croxton *Play of the Sacrament*** (Language: English)
Jia Liu, Département de langue et littérature anglaises, Université de Genève
Paper 724-c: **Music and Memory: Politics and National Identity in the Late Medieval Carol** (Language: English)
Louise McInnes, Department of Music, University of Sheffield

Session: **725** **Maurice Keyworth Building: Room 1.06**
Title: **Memory and Myth: Remembering Medieval Ireland and Its Neighbours, III - Crafting Administrative Memory**
Sponsor: Medieval History Research Centre, Trinity College Dublin
Organiser: Áine Foley, Medieval History Research Centre, Trinity College Dublin
Moderator: David Ditchburn, Department of History, Trinity College Dublin
Paper 725-a: **To 'summon up remembrance of things past': The Importance and Limitations of Memory in Late Medieval Irish and English Court Cases** (Language: English)
Áine Foley
Paper 725-b: **False Memory of Medieval Ireland** (Language: English)
Stephen Hewer, Department of History, Trinity College Dublin
Paper 725-c: **'In all times within memory': Conservative Language, Radical Ideas, and Assembly Politics in Late Medieval Ireland and Scotland** (Language: English)
Lynn Kilgallon, Department of History, Trinity College Dublin

Session: **726** **Social Sciences Building: Room 10.07**
Title: **'DIANA AND ALL HER SECT': REMEMBERING WOMEN WARRIORS, III**
Sponsor: Society for Medieval Feminist Scholarship
Organiser: Sophie Harwood, Institute for Medieval Studies, University of Leeds, Roberta Magnani, Centre for Medieval & Early Modern Research (MEMO), Swansea University and Amy Louise Morgan, School of Literature & Languages, University of Surrey
Moderator: Roberta Magnani
Paper 726-a: **Ulrich von Liechtenstein: A Very Different Woman Warrior** (Language: English)
Natalie Anderson, Institute for Medieval Studies, University of Leeds
Paper 726-b: **Strategies of Integration, Strategies of Annihilation: Amazons and Their Ends in Middle High German Literature** (Language: English)
Christopher Liebtag Miller, School of Modern Languages - German, University of St Andrews
Paper 726-c: **Weaponed Women, Warrior Women?: Female Skeletons with 'Masculine' Objects in Early Anglo-Saxon England** (Language: English)
Katherine Fliegel, School of Arts, Languages & Cultures, University of Manchester

---

Session: **727** **Michael Sadler Building: Banham Theatre**
Title: **MEMORIES OF NATION, MEDIEVAL AND MODERN, III: 19TH-CENTURY NATIONALISM AND THE MIDDLE AGES**
Sponsor: Richard Bland College of William & Mary, Virginia
Organiser: Daniel Franke, Department of History, Richard Bland College of William & Mary, Virginia
Moderator: Helen Birkett, Department of History, University of Exeter
Paper 727-a: **Creating a Golden Age for Italy: Medieval Histories and Historians in the Age of Nationalism** (Language: English)
Laura K. Morreale, Center for Medieval Studies, Fordham University, New York
Paper 727-b: **From the Golden Horns to Gunnar Hámundarson: Medievalism in the Danish and Icelandic Nationalist Movements** (Language: English)
Vanessa Iacocca, Department of English, Purdue University
Paper 727-c: **Anti-Enlightenment, Nationalism, and Medieval Studies** (Language: English)
Daniel Wollenberg, Department of English & Writing, University of Tampa, Florida

Session:	**728**	**Stage@leeds: Stage 3**
Title:	**REMEMBERING AND MISREMEMBERING THE ISLAMIC WORLD, I**	
Organiser:	Ann R. Christys, Independent Scholar, Leeds	
Moderator:	Hugh Kennedy, Department of the Languages & Cultures of the Near & Middle East, School of Oriental & African Studies, University of London	
Paper 728-a:	**The Umayyads in the *Kitab al-Aghani*** (Language: English) Andrew Marsham, Faculty of Asian & Middle Eastern Studies, University of Cambridge	
Paper 728-b:	**Truncated Memories: Historiographical Agency in the Arabic *Mukhtaṣar* of *Ta'rīkh* (Historical Digest)** (Language: English) Fozia Bora, School of Languages, Cultures & Societies - Arabic, Islamic & Middle Eastern Studies, University of Leeds	
Paper 728-c:	**Early Hijazi Governors, Stewards, and Scholars: Personal History Set in Stone** (Language: English) Ghali Adi, Independent Scholar, Manchester	

Session:	**729**	**Maurice Keyworth Building: Room 1.05**
Title:	**CLERICS, PARISHIONERS, AND THEIR BOOKS IN LATE MEDIEVAL ENGLAND**	
Organiser:	IMC Programming Committee	
Moderator:	John Jenkins, Centre for the Study of Christianity & Culture, University of York	
Paper 729-a:	**Who Remembered the Rememberers?: Clergy Probate and Memory, 1340-1440** (Language: English) Gary Brannan, Borthwick Institute for Archives, University of York	
Paper 729-b:	**'...fro þe time þat ȝe were boȝ in-to þis tyme': Memory and Confession in a 15th-Century English Confessor's Manual, Cambridge, St John's College, MS S. 35** (Language: English) Maria Luisa Maggioni, Dipartimento di Scienze linguistiche e letterature straniere, Università Cattolica del Sacro Cuore, Milano	
Paper 729-c:	**John Mirk's Instructions for Parish Priests and the Aesthetics of Medieval Massbooks** (Language: English) Christine Kozikowski, School of English Studies, University of The Bahamas	

Session: **730** **Charles Thackrah Building: 1.03**
Title: **MEMORY AS A TOOL IN MEDIEVAL ART: CREATION, DEPICTION, AND HERITAGE**
Sponsor: Institute of History of Art & Culture, Pontifical University of John Paul II, Kraków
Organiser: Dariusz Tabor, Institute of History of Art & Culture, Pontifical University of John Paul II, Kraków
Moderator: Arnold Otto, Erzbischöfliches Generalvikariat Erzbistumsarchiv, Paderborn
Paper 730-a: **Memory of Scripture and Church Fathers in the Iconophile Polemics: The Case of *Chresis*** (Language: English)
Piotr Łukasz Grotowski, Institute of History of Art & Culture, Pontifical University of John Paul II, Kraków
Paper 730-b: **The Flowers of Memory: (Re)Collecting the Church Fathers' Thought in Medieval *Florilegia*** (Language: English)
Justyna Słowik, Institute of History of Art & Culture, Pontifical University of John Paul II, Kraków
Paper 730-c: **The Memorial of St Hedvig (and Duke Henry): Sainthood from Heroic Death or Sainthood from Virtuous Life - Reinterpreting Miniatures from Hedvig Codex (Malibu, CA, J. P. Getty Museum 83. MN. 126)** (Language: English)
Dariusz Tabor
Paper 730-d: **Against Tragic Memory: Allegory and Historiosophy in 19th-Century Polish Historical Painting - The Example of Jan Matejko's *Defeat at Legnica - Revival*** (Language: English)
Barbara Ciciora, Institute of History of Art & Culture, Pontifical University of John Paul II, Kraków

---

Session: **731** **Charles Thackrah Building: 1.04**
Title: **MATERIAL CULTURE AND LANDSCAPES, III: REMEMBERING PAST DEEDS**
Sponsor: Medieval Landscape/Seascape Research Group
Organiser: Daniel Brown, Historisches Institut, Universität zu Köln and Stefanie Schild, Independent Scholar, Hilden
Moderator: Karl Christian Alvestad, Department of History, University of Winchester
Paper 731-a: **'The tilt of the torn heath': Landscape and Memory in Early Medieval Warfare** (Language: English)
Tom J. T. Williams, British Museum, London
Paper 731-b: **'Such guardian or defiant tombs': Memorialisation of Burial Mounds by Early and Post-Conquest Poets and Chroniclers** (Language: English)
Lily Alice Gwendoline Hawker-Yates, Centre for Kent History & Heritage, Canterbury Christ Church University
Paper 731-c: **'Now we're going back to the 21st century': Remembering Early Medieval Places, Poems, and Objects in Performances at Sutton Hoo** (Language: English)
Fran Allfrey, Department of English / Centre for Late Antique & Medieval Studies, King's College London

Session:	**732** **Social Sciences Building: Room 10.09**
Title:	**MEMORY AND HOSPITALS, I: BIOGRAPHIES, POLITICS, AND IDEOLOGIES OF CHARITY**
Sponsor:	Alle origini del welfare (XIII-XVI secolo), PRIN 2015 / New Communities of Interpretation, ISCH COST Action IS1301
Organiser:	Marina Gazzini, Dipartimento di Discipline Umanistiche, Sociali e delle Imprese Culturali, Università degli Studi di Parma
Moderator:	Thomas Frank, Dipartimento di Studi Umanistici, Università degli Studi di Pavia
Paper 732-a:	**Promoters and Protectors of Hospitals: The Memory of the Hospital of the Holy Cross in the Municipal Documentation of the City of Barcelona** (Language: English) Pol Bridgewater Mateu, Departament d'Història i Arqueologia / Institut de Recerca en Cultures Medievals, Universitat de Barcelona
Paper 732-b:	**Heart and Spirit United: The Cusanus-Library at the St Nikolaus-Hospital in Bernkastel-Kues as a Memorial Site** (Language: English) Marco Brösch, Institut für Cusanus-Forschung, Universität Trier
Paper 732-c:	**Charity and Memories of Men and Women: A Survey on Central and Northern Italian Medieval Hospitals** (Language: English) Marina Gazzini

Session:	**733** **Leeds University Union: Room 2 - Elland Road**
Title:	**COMMUNICATION AND THE EXPLOITATION OF KNOWLEDGE, III: COLLECTIVE MEMORY AND PREACHING**
Sponsor:	Onderzoeksschool Mediëvistiek, Rijksuniversiteit Groningen
Organiser:	Pieter Boonstra, Afdeling Geschiedenis, Rijksuniversiteit Groningen
Moderator:	Theo Lap, Afdeling Geschiedenis, Rijksuniversiteit Groningen
Paper 733-a:	**Lenten Sermon Collections: Mnemonic Strategies to Order Knowledge** (Language: English) Pietro Delcorno, School of Languages, Cultures & Societies, University of Leeds / School of Literature, Language & Media, University of the Witwatersrand
Paper 733-b:	**Combining Religious Knowledge and Collective Memory in the Modern Devout *Collatio*** (Language: English) Pieter Boonstra
Paper 733-c:	**Collective Imagery in the Middle Dutch *Jhesus collacien* (Jesus's Sermons)** (Language: English) Thom Mertens, Ruusbroecgenootschap, Universiteit Antwerpen

Session: **734** **Leeds University Union: Room 4 - Hyde Park**
Title: **GRAPHIC AND TEXTUAL COMMUNITIES: BETWEEN MEMORY AND IDENTITY, I**
Sponsor: H37 - Histoire & Cultures Graphiques, Université catholique de Louvain, Louvain-la-Neuve
Organiser: Paul Bertrand, Faculté de Philosophie, Arts et Lettres, Université catholique de Louvain, Louvain-la-Neuve
Moderator: Nicolas Ruffini-Ronzani, Département d'Histoire, Université de Namur
Paper 734-a: **Graphic Communities: Towards a New Conceptual Approach** (Language: English)
Paul Bertrand
Paper 734-b: **Matching Copies: The Making of Chirographs - Northern France and Southern Low Countries, 12th and 13th Centuries** (Language: English)
Emilie Mineo, Département d'Histoire, Université de Namur
Paper 734-c: **Epistolography at Savoy Court during the 15th Century: Between Private and State Matters** (Language: English)
Laura Gaffuri, Dipartimento di Studi storici, Università degli Studi di Torino

---

Session: **735** **Maurice Keyworth Building: Room 1.09**
Title: **POWER, MEMORY, AND WRITTEN RECORD IN MEDIEVAL SPAIN, III: THE CONSTRUCTION AND TRANSMISSION OF ROYAL MEMORY IN CASTILE**
Sponsor: El ejercicio del poder: espacios, agentes y escrituras (siglos XI-XV), EJEPO Project
Organiser: Fernando Arias Guillén, Facultad de Filosofía y Letras, Universidad de Valladolid
Moderator: Álvaro Jesús Sanz Martín, Departamento de Historia Antigua y Medieval, Universidad de Valladolid
Paper 735-a: ***A honra del rey et de su sennorio*: Royal Privileges and the Construction of Royal Memory in Castile, c. 1158-1350** (Language: English)
Fernando Arias Guillén
Paper 735-b: **Memoria y legitimidad: la transmisión de los testamentos de Alfonso X en la historiografía castellana del primer XIV** (Language: Español)
Carmen Benítez Herrero, Facultad de Geografía e Historia, Universidad de Sevilla
Paper 735-c: **The Literary Works of Juan Manuel: Familial Memory and Ideological Discourse of a Castilian Magnate in the First Half of the 14th Century** (Language: English)
Laura Rodríguez Martín, Facultad de Filosofía y Letras, Universidad de Valladolid

Session: **736** **Leeds University Union: Room 5 - Kirkstall Abbey**
Title: **TIME IN MEDIEVAL EUROPE, I: THE ENGLISH PERSPECTIVE**
Sponsor: Centre for Research in Historiography & Historical Cultures / Department of History & Welsh History, Aberystwyth University
Organiser: Caitlin Naylor, Department of History & Welsh History, Aberystwyth University
Moderator: Hans-Werner Goetz, Historisches Seminar, Universität Hamburg
Paper 736-a: **Bede and Vulgate Chronology** (Language: English)
Máirín MacCarron, Department of History, University of Sheffield
Paper 736-b: **Writing History, Writing Time: Temporality in the Works of William of Malmesbury** (Language: English)
Caitlin Naylor
Paper 736-c: **Representing Time in the *Historia Regum Britanniae* of Geoffrey of Monmouth** (Language: English)
Jennifer Farrell, Department of History, University of Exeter

Session: **737** **Maurice Keyworth Building: Room 1.03**
Title: **JERUSALEM LOST: THE MEMORY OF 1187**
Organiser: IMC Programming Committee
Moderator: Ane L. Bysted, Institut for Kultur og Samfund, Aarhus Universitet
Paper 737-a: ***In memoriam crucis Christi*: The Loss of the True Cross in 1187 and Its Meaning in the Latin West** (Language: English)
Alexander Marx, Institut für Geschichte, Universität Wien / Österreichische Akademie der Wissenschaften, Wien
Paper 737-b: **Near and Distant Past: A Double Memory of the Fall of Jerusalem in Scripture and in 1187** (Language: English)
Katrine Funding Højgaard, Saxo-Instituttet, Københavns Universitet
Paper 737-c: **Exegesis of a Disaster: Remembering the Fall of Jerusalem in 1187 at Coggeshall Abbey** (Language: English)
James Henry Kane, Medieval & Early Modern Centre, University of Sydney

Session: **738** **Baines Wing: Room G.36**
Title: **NOTHING MORE THAN FEELINGS?: THE HISTORY OF EMOTIONS IN RELATION TO CHILDREN, ROYALTY, AND WALTER HILTON**
Organiser: IMC Programming Committee
Moderator: Annie Blachly, Centre for Medieval & Renaissance Studies, Monash University, Victoria
Paper 738-a: **Reforming Feelings: Walter Hilton's Emotional Programme** (Language: English)
Olli Lampinen-Enqvist, Faculty of Theology, University of Helsinki
Paper 738-b: **'Son if yu list to understand': Memory and the Culture of Children in Late Medieval England** (Language: English)
Jenny Weeks, Department of History, Royal Holloway, University of London
Paper 738-c: **Staging Royal Emotions in the Time of Troubles, c. 1598-1613** (Language: English)
Nailya Shamgunova, Churchill College, University of Cambridge

Session: **739** **Maurice Keyworth Building: Room 1.33**
Title: **REMEMBERING THE PAST AFTER THE CAROLINGIAN EMPIRE, III: MEMORIES OF RULE, ACTS OF AUTHORITY**
Sponsor: After Empire: Using & Not Using the Past in the Crisis of the Carolingian World, c. 900-1050
Organiser: Sarah Greer, St Andrews Institute of Mediaeval Studies, University of St Andrews
Moderator: Sarah Greer
Paper 739-a: **A Memory in Between: Using or Not Using the Carolingian Past in 10th-Century Nonantola's Abbey** (Language: English)
Edoardo Manarini, Deutsches Historisches Institut, Roma
Paper 739-b: **'Zum Raum wird hier die Zeit': Place, Memory, and Text in the *Annals of Quedlinburg*** (Language: English)
Stuart Airlie, School of Humanities (History), University of Glasgow
Paper 739-c: **What's in a Name?: Royal and Imperial Appellations in Royal Diplomata from Conrad I to Henry II** (Language: English)
Alice Hicklin, Friedrich-Meinecke-Institut, Freie Universität Berlin

---

Session: **740** **Parkinson Building: Nathan Bodington Chamber**
Title: **IMPERIAL MEMORY THEN AND NOW, II: THE AFTERMATH OF IMPERIAL LANDSCAPES**
Sponsor: Digital Clusterproject 'Digitising Patterns of Power (DPP): Peripherical Mountains in the Medieval World', Institut für Mittelalterforschung, Österreichische Akademie der Wissenschaften, Wien
Organiser: Stefan Eichert, Institut für Mittelalterforschung, Österreichische Akademie der Wissenschaften, Wien
Moderator: Simon MacLean, School of History, University of St Andrews
Paper 740-a: **Macedonian Memories: How to Expand *Tabula Imperii Byzantini* 11 in a Digital Age?** (Language: English)
Veronika Polloczek, Institut für Mittelalterforschung, Österreichische Akademie der Wissenschaften, Wien
Paper 740-b: **Emperor Theoderic?: Imperial Policy of the King of the Goths** (Language: English)
David Schmid, Institut für Mittelalterforschung, Österreichische Akademie der Wissenschaften, Wien
Paper 740-c: **Frontier, Contact Zone, or No Man's Land?: The Morava-Thaya Region from the Early to the High Middle Ages** (Language: English)
Stefan Eichert
Paper 740-d: **A New Project on Galician Medieval Heritage: Planning the Paths for Cultural Outreach** (Language: English)
Javier Castiñeiras López, Departamento de Historia da Arte, Universidade de Santiago de Compostela

Session: **741** **Michael Sadler Building: Room LG.10**
Title: **THE LIVES OF THE MEDIEVAL POPES: MEMORY AND CONSTRUCTION**
Sponsor: Paul Maria Baumgarten Institut für Papsttumsforschung, Bergische Universität Wuppertal
Organiser: Jochen Johrendt, Lehrstuhl für Mittelalterliche Geschichte, Bergische Universität Wuppertal
Moderator: Jochen Johrendt
Paper 741-a: ***Life of Pope Leo IX*: Memory of a Saint and Apology of a Zealous Reformer** (Language: English)
Francesco Massetti, Fakultät für Geistes und Kulturwissenschaften - Historisches Seminar, Bergische Universität Wuppertal / Dipartimento di Storia, culture, religioni, Università degli Studi di Roma 'La Sapienza'
Paper 741-b: **The Righteous Must Suffer: History and Legitimation in Cardinal Boso's *Life of Alexander III*** (Language: English)
Stephan Pongratz, Historisches Seminar, Ludwig-Maximilians-Universität München
Paper 741-c: ***Respublica* and *Ecclesia Sancti Petri*: Holy Roman Empire in the *Liber Pontificalis*** (Language: English)
Longguo Li, Department of History, Peking University
Paper 741-d: **Construction of the Enemy: Frederick II in the Anonymous *Vita Gregorii IX*** (Language: English)
Wendan Li, Friedrich-Meinecke-Institut, Freie Universität Berlin

Session: **742** **Baines Wing: Room G.37**
Title: **DESIGNING THE PAST**
Organiser: IMC Programming Committee
Moderator: Jeff Rider, Department of Romance Languages & Literatures, Wesleyan University, Connecticut
Paper 742-a: **Mingled Memories: The Chronicle of Victor of Tunnuna, 565/575** (Language: English)
Antje Klein, Institut für Kirchengeschichte, Christliche Archäologie und Kirchliche Kunst, Universität Wien
Paper 742-b: **La construction de la mémoire dans *l'Historia Calamitatum*** (Language: Français)
Rafael Bosch, Instituto de Filosofia e Ciências Humanas, Universidade Estadual de Campinas, Brazil
Paper 742-c: **Faultless Memory in Medieval Iberian Literature: Ibn al-Khatib and Ibn Khaldun** (Language: English)
Sherif Abdelkarim, Department of English, University of Virginia

Session:	**743** **Maurice Keyworth Building: Room 1.32**
Title:	**THE MEMORY OF THE CRUSADES, III: HISTORIOGRAPHICAL ECHOES**
Sponsor:	Routledge
Organiser:	Mike Horswell, Department of History, Royal Holloway, University of London
Moderator:	Guy Perry, Institute for Medieval Studies / School of History, University of Leeds
Paper 743-a:	**Medieval Atlit in the Historiography of Incarceration** (Language: English) Yvonne Friedman, Department of History, Bar-Ilan University, Ramat Gan
Paper 743-b:	**Crusading Historiography in the Early Modern Age: The Question of the Normans of Southern Italy** (Language: English) Luigi Russo, Dipartimento di Scienza Storiche, Università Europea di Roma
Paper 743-c:	**Muslim Ideological Responses to the Crusades: From Al-Sulami to Ibn Taymiyya** (Language: English) Mabrouka Kamel, Faculty of Education, Damanhour University, Egypt

Session:	**744** **Fine Art Building: SR 1.10**
Title:	**CULTURAL MEMORY IN LATE ANTIQUITY, III: CREATION OF MEMORY IN WESTERN SUCCESSOR KINGDOMS**
Organiser:	Richard Flower, Department of Classics & Ancient History, University of Exeter and Robin Whelan, Department of History, University of Liverpool
Moderator:	Mark Humphries, Centre for Medieval & Early Modern Research (MEMO), Swansea University
Paper 744-a:	**Apocalypse Avoided: Historiographical Rehabilitation from Gregory the Great to Paul the Deacon** (Language: English) Shane Bjornlie, Department of History, Claremont McKenna College, California
Paper 744-b:	***Expeditio Gallicana*: The Frankish-Gothic War in 507/508 and the *Variae* of Flavius Magnus Aurelius Cassiodorus Senator** (Language: English) Christian Stadermann, Historisches Seminar - Alte Geschichte, Johannes Gutenberg-Universität Mainz
Paper 744-c:	**Cultural Memory in the Gothic Migration** (Language: English) Viola Gheller, Istituto Italiano per la Storia Antica, Università degli Studi di Trento

Session: **745** **Leeds University Union: Room 6 - Roundhay**
Title: **(Mis)Remembering First Encounter, I: The 'New World'**
Organiser: Claudia Rogers, School of History, University of Leeds
Moderator: Adam Simmons, Department of History, Lancaster University
Paper 745-a: **Misremembering or Misrepresenting Ritual: How Can We Access Pre-Hispanic Nahua Religious Behaviour from Colonial Missionaries' Writings?** (Language: English)
Harriet Smart, Department of History, University of Sheffield
Paper 745-b: **For Their Own Good: Re-Writing the Conquest of Mexico** (Language: English)
Amy Fuller, Department of History, Languages & Global Culture, Nottingham Trent University
Paper 745-c: **'Come! Come to see the people from Heaven!': Deconstructing the Myth of the White Gods in Christopher Columbus's Accounts of His First Voyage to the New World, 1492-1493** (Language: English)
Claudia Rogers

Session: **746** **Emmanuel Centre: Room 10**
Title: **Traces of Memory in the Western Mediterranean, III: Public and Private Memory**
Sponsor: Institut de Recerca en Cultures Medievals / Institución Milá y Fontanals (IMF), Consejo Superior de Investigaciones Científicas (CSIC) / Grup de Recerca en Estudis Medievals d'Art, Història, Paleografia i Arqueologia (MAHPA), Universitat de Barcelona
Organiser: Pol Junyent Molins, Institució Milà i Fontanals (IMF), Consejo Superior de Investigaciones Científicas (CSIC), Barcelona and Laura Miquel Milian, Institució Milà i Fontanals (IMF), Consejo Superior de Investigaciones Científicas (CSIC), Barcelona
Moderator: Jaume Marcé Sánchez, Institut de Recerca en Cultures Medievals, Universitat de Barcelona
Paper 746-a: **Memory in Catalan Cities: Notaries, Scribes, and Chroniclers** (Language: English)
Daniel Piñol, Departament d'Història i Arqueologia, Universitat de Barcelona
Paper 746-b: **The Construction of Memory within a Noble Catalan Family: The Marc from Eramprunyà, 14th and 15th Centuries** (Language: English)
Mireia Comas, Departament d'Història i Arqueologia, Universitat de Barcelona
Paper 746-c: **La costruzione della memoria: la geneaologia della Casa d'Arborea** (Language: Italiano)
Giacomo Floris, Departament d'Història Medieval, Paleografia i Diplomàtica, Universitat de Barcelona

Session: **747** **Baines Wing: Room 2.14**

Title: **MEMORISING AND REMEMBERING IN THE MIDDLE AGES: PHILOSOPHICAL APPROACHES**

Sponsor: Groupe de Recherches Antiquité, Moyen-Âge, Transmission Arabe (GRAMATA), Université Paris I - Panthéon-Sorbonne / Representation & Reality Research Programme, Göteborgs Universitet

Organiser: Véronique Decaix, UFR de Philosophie, Université Paris I - Panthéon-Sorbonne

Moderator: Véronique Decaix

Paper 747-a: **Mémoire, représentation et signification chez Aristote (arabe) et Averroès** (Language: Français)
Carla Di Martino, Laboratoire Savoir, Textes, Langage (UMR 8163), Université Charles-de-Gaulle - Lille 3

Paper 747-b: **Aristotle and His Early Latin Commentators on Motion and Memory in Sleep** (Language: English)
Christina Thomsen Thörnqvist, Institutionen för filosofi, lingvistik och vetenskapsteori, Göteborgs Universitet

---

Session: **748** **University House: St George Room**

Title: **HISTORICAL EUROPEAN MARTIAL ARTS STUDIES: PRACTICES, CONTEXTS, AND NARRATIVES**

Sponsor: Society for Historical European Martial Arts Studies

Organiser: Iason-Eleftherios Tzouriadis, Institute for Medieval Studies, University of Leeds

Moderator: Jacob H. Deacon, Institute for Medieval Studies, University of Leeds

Paper 748-a: **Learning the Sword: Fighting Manuals and Pedagogy** (Language: English)
Robert W. Jones, Advanced Studies in England, Franklin & Marshall College, Pennsylvania

Paper 748-b: **Practices of Fighting in the Late Middle Ages: A Praxiographic Case Study on the Imperial City of Nuremberg, c. 1350-1550** (Language: English)
Eric Burkart, Abteilung Mittelalterliche Geschichte, Universität Trier

Paper 748-c: **Fighting in a Banquet in the Mid-16th Century: The Fantastic Exchange of Gioan Girolamo and Mutio under the Pen of the Fencing Master Marc'Antonio Pagano** (Language: English)
Daniel Jaquet, Musée militaire, Château de Morges / Centre d'Etudes Supérieures de la Renaissance, Université François-Rabelais, Tours

Session: **749** **University House: Cloberry Room**
Title: **TOLKIEN: MEDIEVAL ROOTS AND MODERN BRANCHES, I**
Sponsor: Cardiff Metropolitan University
Organiser: Thomas Honegger, Institut für Anglistik, Friedrich-Schiller-Universität Jena
Moderator: Brad Eden, Christopher Center for Library & Information Resources, Valparaiso University, Indiana
Paper 749-a: **Some Boethian Themes as Tools of Characterization in J. R. R. Tolkien's *Lord of the Rings*** (Language: English)
Andrzej Wicher, Zakład Dramatu i Dawnej Literatury Angielskiej, Uniwersytet Łódzki
Paper 749-b: **Eldest: Tom Bombadil and Fintan Mac Bóchra** (Language: English)
Kris Swank, Northwest Campus Library, Pima Community College, Arizona
Paper 749-c: **Under the Wings of Shadow: Mental Health and the Price of Civilization in *The Lord of the Rings*** (Language: English)
Hilary Justice, Ernest Hemingway Collection, John F. Kennedy Presidential Library, Boston, Massachusetts
Paper 749-d: **Hobbits: The Un-Recorded People of Middle-Earth** (Language: English)
Aurélie Brémont, Centre d'Études Médiévales Anglaises (CEMA), Université Paris IV - Sorbonne

Session: **750** **Emmanuel Centre: Room 11**
Title: **CISTERCIANS, III: CISTERCIANS IN ENGLAND AND WALES**
Sponsor: *Cîteaux: Commentarii cistercienses*
Organiser: Terryl N. Kinder, *Cîteaux: Commentarii cistercienses*, Pontigny
Moderator: David N. Bell, Department of Religious Studies, Memorial University of Newfoundland
Paper 750-a: **13th-Century English Cistercian Nunneries and their Cartularies: Focusing on Nun Cotham Priory** (Language: English)
Elizabeth Freeman, School of Humanities, University of Tasmania
Paper 750-b: **Stability or Mobility?: Movement between Cistercian Houses in Late Medieval England and Wales** (Language: English)
David E. Thornton, Department of History, Bilkent University, Turkey
Paper 750-c: **The Property of Sallay Abbey in the Wharfe Valley, North Yorkshire: Its Purpose and Development** (Language: English)
Stephen Anthony Moorhouse, Institute for Medieval Studies, University of Leeds

Session: **751** **Baines Wing: Room 2.15**
Title: **MEDIEVAL ICELANDIC FARMING, I: MILKING THE LANDSCAPE?**
Sponsor: University of Iceland / National Museum of Iceland
Organiser: Bernadette McCooey, Independent Scholar, Birmingham
Moderator: Bernadette McCooey
Paper 751-a: **Manor Formation in Early Iceland** (Language: English)
Axel Kristinsson, Reykjavík Academy, Iceland
Paper 751-b: **The Cultural Landscape of Milk** (Language: English)
Árni Daníel Júlíusson, National Museum of Iceland, Reykjavík
Paper 751-c: **Infrastructure Re-Use and Persistence of Place in the Icelandic Agricultural Landscape** (Language: English)
Kathryn Catlin, Department of Anthropology, Northwestern University, Illinois

Session: **752** **Stage@leeds: Stage 1**
Title: **GRAND NARRATIVES AND BIG PICTURE MEDIEVALISM**
Organiser: IMC Programming Committee
Moderator: Paul B. Sturtevant, PublicMedievalist.com
Paper 752-a: **Forging a Saga for Canada: Interpretations, Illusions, and Memories** (Language: English)
Brianna Bosgraaf, Institute of Women & Gender Studies, University of Toronto, Downtown
Paper 752-b: **Historical Re-Creation: On Reconstructing, Living, Re-Enacting, and Roleplaying Medieval Pasts** (Language: English)
Stefan Nyzell, Historical Studies, Department of Society, Culture & Identity, Malmö University
Paper 752-c: **Decline and Fall: The End of Rome and the Modern World** (Language: English)
Jonathan Theodore, Department of Culture, Media & Creative Industries, King's College London
Paper 752-d: **The Black Death and Historical Change: (Mis)Remembering the Great Pestilence in the 20th and 21st Centuries** (Language: English)
Ben Dodds, Department of History, Florida State University

Session: **753** **Michael Sadler Building: Room LG.15**
Title: **MANUS-ON MANUSCRIPTS, III: DIGITAL PLATFORMS AS PEDAGOGICAL AND RESEARCH TOOLS - A WORKSHOP**
Sponsor: Schoenberg Institute for Manuscript Studies, University of Pennsylvania
Organiser: Dorothy Carr Porter, Schoenberg Institute for Manuscript Studies, University of Pennsylvania and Abigail G. Robertson, Department of English Language & Literature, University of New Mexico, Albuquerque
Tutor: Abigail G. Robertson
Purpose: *This third session, led by Abigail G. Robertson, will consist of an overview of digital research and drafting platforms and how they can be utilised in data collection and the classroom. Abigail will demonstrate how she uses digital platforms in her own research and those that she uses to teach medieval studies courses and then will move into a workshop where participants can use the projects and familiarise themselves with how they work and how it could apply to their research and classroom methods.*

Session:	**754** **Maurice Keyworth Building: Room G.02**
Title:	**TROUBLING CONCEPTS OF MEDIEVAL EUROPE: A ROUND TABLE DISCUSSION**
Sponsor:	Historisches Institut, FernUniversität Hagen / Centre for Medieval Literature, University of York and University of Odense
Organiser:	Felicitas Schmieder, Historisches Institut, FernUniversität Hagen
Moderator:	Elizabeth M. Tyler, Department of English & Related Literature, University of York
Purpose:	*This round table discussion looks at contemporary and modern ideas of medieval Europe in order to consider how we study medieval Europe without reifying or essentialising its make-up, its borders, and its character.* *Participants include Stavroula Constantinou (University of Cyprus), Shazia Jagot (University of Surrey), Christian Raffensperger (Wittenberg University, Ohio), and Julia Verkholantsev (University of Pennsylvania).*

TEA BREAK: 15.45-16.30

Tea and Coffee will be served at the following locations:

Maurice Keyworth Building: Foyer
Michael Sadler Building: Foyer
Parkinson Building: Bookfair
University Square: The Marquee

See Map 7, p. 44.

Session: **801** **Parkinson Building: Room 1.16**
Title: **EADMER OF CANTERBURY, II: EADMER'S MEMORIES OF ANSELM'S ETHICS, EXAMPLE, AND THEOLOGY**
Organiser: Charlie Rozier, Department of History, Swansea University and Sally N. Vaughn, Department of History, University of Houston, Texas
Moderator: Paul Hayward, Department of History, Lancaster University
Paper 801-a: **Anselm as Ethicist and as Example in Eadmer's *Vita Anselmi*** (Language: English)
Tomas Ekenberg, Filosofiska Institutionen, Uppsala Universitet
Paper 801-b: **'A higher consideration': Eadmer beyond Anselm on the Immaculate Conception** (Language: English)
Michael Magree, Department of Theology, University of Notre Dame, Indiana
Respondent: Charlie Rozier and Sally N. Vaughn

Session: **802** **Baines Wing: Room 2.16**
Title: **HOUSES AND HOUSEHOLDS**
Organiser: IMC Programming Committee
Moderator: Jitske Jasperse, Instituto de Historia, Consejo Superior de Investigaciones Científicas (CSIC), Madrid
Paper 802-a: **Special Drinking Vessels and Late Medieval English Households: Objects of Memory** (Language: English)
Chris Woolgar, Department of History, University of Southampton
Paper 802-b: **Forgotten over Time: Survival and Demolition among Late Medieval Brick Houses** (Language: English)
David H. Kennett, Independent Scholar, Shipston-on-Stour
Paper 802-c: **Women in Grobiņa: Only Wives and Passive Members of the Household?** (Language: English)
Santa Jansone, Faculty of History & Philosophy, University of Latvia, Riga

Session: **803** **University House: Little Woodhouse Room**
Title: **BEYOND THE ANGLO-NORMAN CONQUESTS: ALTERNATIVE NARRATIVES IN INSULAR HISTORY, II**
Organiser: Ben Guy, Department of Anglo-Saxon, Norse & Celtic, University of Cambridge and Rebecca Thomas, Department of Anglo-Saxon, Norse & Celtic, University of Cambridge
Moderator: Patrick Wadden, Department of History, Belmont Abbey College, North Carolina
Paper 803-a: **The Welsh Conquest of North-Western Mercia in the 12th Century** (Language: English)
Ben Guy
Paper 803-b: **Gerald of Wales on Henry II and the Third Crusade in the *Expugnatio Hibernica*'s Narrative of Irish History** (Language: English)
Diarmuid Scully, School of History, University College Cork
Paper 803-c: **Missives and Messages in Britain's 12th-Century Chronicles** (Language: English)
Emily A. Winkler, St Edmund Hall, University of Oxford / Department of History, University College London

Session: **804** **Baines Wing: Room 1.13**
Title: **REFRAMING THE LEGAL AND HISTORICAL PAST IN LATE MEDIEVAL SCOTLAND**
Sponsor: AHRC Project 'The Community of the Realm in Scotland, 1249-1424: History, Law & Charters in a Recreated Kingdom'
Organiser: Alice Taylor, Department of History, King's College London
Moderator: Alice Taylor
Paper 804-a: **A New Chronicle of the Wars of Independence** (Language: English)
Dauvit Broun, School of Humanities (History), University of Glasgow
Paper 804-b: **Defenders of the Realm or Wolves of War?: Condemnation of Magnate Violence in 14th-Century Scotland** (Language: English)
Stephen Boardman, School of History, Classics & Archaeology, University of Edinburgh
Paper 804-c: ***Regiam Maiestatem*: The Manuscript Tradition of Scotland's Earliest Legal Treatise** (Language: English)
John Reuben Davies, School of Humanities (History), University of Glasgow

Session: **805** **Fine Art Building: SR G.04**
Title: **GAMES AND VISUAL CULTURE, II**
Organiser: Elizabeth Lapina, Department of History, University of Wisconsin-Madison
Moderator: Vanina Kopp, Deutsches Historisches Institut, Paris
Paper 805-a: **Liturgical Book, Reliquary, or Memorial?: Chess as the Central Motif on the Book Cover of Duke Otto the Mild of Braunschweig** (Language: English)
Anna Schubert, Institut für Kunstwissenschaft und Historische Urbanistik, Technische Universität Berlin
Paper 805-b: **'The lot is cast into the lap, but its every decision is by the Lord': Gaming's Role in Representations of the Passion** (Language: English)
Lisa Mahoney, Department of the History of Art & Architecture, DePaul University, Illinois
Paper 805-c: **Playing Memory: Thomas Murner's Didactical Games as Material-Discursive Practices** (Language: English)
Michael A. Conrad, Kunsthistorisches Institut, Universität Zürich

Session: **806** **Michael Sadler Building: Room LG.16**
Title: **ADAPTING CANON LAW IN MEDIEVAL SCANDINAVIA**
Organiser: Ane L. Bysted, Institut for Kultur og Samfund, Aarhus Universitet and Anthony Perron, Department of History, Loyola Marymount University, California
Moderator: Bertil Nilsson, Institutionen för litteratur, idéhistoria och religion, Göteborgs Universitet
Paper 806-a: **What Did Archbishop Eskil Do as Papal Legate?** (Language: English)
Mia Münster-Swendsen, Institut for Kommunikation og Humanistisk Videnskab, Roskilde Universitet
Paper 806-b: **The Cathedral Chapter of Lund and Archepiscopal Appointments: Canonical Elections under Pressure, 14th Century** (Language: English)
Ane L. Bysted
Paper 806-c: **The Landscape of Canon Law: Custom and Environment in Medieval Scandinavia** (Language: English)
Anthony Perron

Session: **807** **Michael Sadler Building: Room LG.17**
Title: **LAW, FINANCE, AND THE WRITTEN RECORD IN THE WESTERN MEDITERRANEAN**
Organiser: IMC Programming Committee
Moderator: Maria João Branco, Instituto de Estudos Medievais, Universidade Nova de Lisboa
Paper 807-a: **The Power of Writing in Memory: Lisbon Notary and the Document** (Language: English)
Ana Pereira Ferreira, Centro de História, Universidade de Lisboa
Paper 807-b: **Animosity Against the 'Drowning in Debt': An Analysis of a Fatwa in 14th-Century Fez** (Language: English)
Tomoaki Shinoda, Department of Islamic Studies, University of Tokyo
Paper 807-c: **Tributes Paid by the Nasri Kingdom of Granada, 1246-1464** (Language: English)
Adrian Elias Negro Cortés, Facultad de Filosofía y Letras, Universidad de Extremadura, Cáceres
Paper 807-d: **Collective Memory in Alphonse X's Legal Texts: Justifications Based on Analogies, Etymologies, and Exempla** (Language: English)
Maria Clara Barros, Centro de Linguística, Universidade do Porto

---

Session: **808** **Fine Art Building: Studio Ground Floor**
Title: **HORSES IN COURTLY LITERATURE**
Organiser: Timothy Dawson, Independent Scholar, Leeds and Anastasija Ropa, Faculty of Humanities, University of Latvia, Riga
Moderator: Anastasija Ropa
Paper 808-a: **Horse Descriptions in the Unedited Prose *Rinaldo da Montalbano* (Florence, Biblioteca Laurenziana MS Pluteus 42, codex 37)** (Language: English)
Gloria Allaire, Department of Modern & Classical Languages, Literatures & Cultures, University of Kentucky
Paper 808-b: **Horses as Status Indicators in Wolfram's *Parzival*** (Language: English)
Anna-Lena Lange, Institut für Skandinavistik, Frisistik und Allgemeine Sprachwissenschaft (ISFAS), Christian-Albrechts-Universität zu Kiel
Paper 808-c: **Unbridled Horses and Knights Errant** (Language: English)
Gavina Luigia Guiseppina Cherchi, Dipartimento di Storia, scienze dell'uomo e della formazione, Università degli Studi di Sassari
Paper 808-d: **Dead Horses in Arthurian Romance (and Beyond)** (Language: English)
Luise Borek, Germanistik - Computerphilologie und Mediävistik, Technische Universität Darmstadt

Session: **809** **Baines Wing: Room 2.13**
Title: **EXEGESIS AND POLEMICS IN LATE ANTIQUITY: THE LETTERS (AND WRITINGS) OF JEROME AND AUGUSTINE**
Organiser: Joseph Grabau, Faculty of Theology & Religious Studies, KU Leuven
Moderator: Przemysław Nehring, Katedra Filologii Klasycznej, Uniwersytet Mikolaja Kopernika, Toruń
Paper 809-a: **Purging the Prophet's Lips: Jerome's Shifting Exegesis of Isaiah 6** (Language: English)
Angela Zielinski Kinney, Institut für Klassische Philologie, Mittel- und Neulatein, Universität Wien / Centre for Advanced Welsh & Celtic Studies, University of Wales, Aberystwyth
Paper 809-b: **The Use of Biblical Exempla in Augustine's Epistolary Polemic with the Donatists** (Language: English)
Rafał Toczko, Katedra Filologii Klasycznej, Uniwersytet Mikołaja Kopernika, Toruń
Paper 809-c: **Johannine Citation in the Anti-Donatist and Anti-Pelagian Letters of Augustine** (Language: English)
Joseph Grabau

Session: **810** **Maurice Keyworth Building: Room 1.04**
Title: **25 YEARS OF HAGIOGRAPHICAL RESEARCH: PAST ACHIEVEMENTS AND FUTURE PERSPECTIVES, III**
Sponsor: Université Paris VIII - Vincennes-Saint-Denis / Université de Montréal
Organiser: Anne-Marie Helvétius, Département d'histoire, Université Paris VIII - Vincennes-Saint-Denis
Moderator: Anne-Marie Helvétius
Paper 810-a: **Hagiography and the Cult of Relics in Lotharingia** (Language: English)
Anne Wagner, Centre de Recherche Universitaire Lorrain d'Histoire (CRULH), Université de Lorraine / Département d'histoire, Université de Franche-Comté
Paper 810-b: **Hagiography and Liturgy in the Early Middle Ages** (Language: English)
Gordon Blennemann, Département d'histoire, Université de Montréal
Respondent: Julia M. H. Smith, Faculty of History, University of Oxford

Session: **811** **Baines Wing: Room 1.15**
Title: **CEU 25, IV: ETHNIC IDENTITIES IN SOUTH-EASTERN EUROPE, 9TH-15TH CENTURIES**
Sponsor: Department of Medieval Studies, Central European University, Budapest
Organiser: Daniel Ziemann, Department of Medieval Studies, Central European University, Budapest
Moderator: Francesco Dall'Aglio, Department of Medieval History of Bulgaria, Institute for Historical Studies, Bulgarian Academy of Sciences
Paper 811-a: **The Genesis of the Imperial Idea among Bulgarians as a Factor in the Evolution of Their Ethnic Identity, 9th-10th Century** (Language: English)
Angel Nikolov, Department of the History of Bulgaria, Sofia University 'St. Kliment Ohridski'
Paper 811-b: **Shifting Identities in the Late Medieval Balkans: The Case of Albania and Bosnia** (Language: English)
Panos Sophoulis, Department for Slavic Studies, National & Kapodistrian University of Athens
Paper 811-c: **Identities on the Move: The Problem of Ethnicity in the Second Bulgarian Empire and Its Neighbours in the 13th Century** (Language: English)
Daniel Ziemann

Session: **812** **Baines Wing: Room 1.14**
Title: **DEVOTED TO THE BODY: DEVOTIONAL PRACTICES AND PERFORMANCES IN FEMININE SPIRITUALITY, II - VISUAL CULTURE**
Organiser: Godelinde Gertrude Perk, Avdelningen för Humaniora, Mittuniversitets, Sundsvall and Lieke Andrea Smits, Centre for the Arts in Society, Universiteit Leiden
Moderator: Godelinde Gertrude Perk
Paper 812-a: **'She often sweetly kissed the feet of the Lord's image': Sanctifying the Senses in Devotional Practices of the Low Countries** (Language: English)
Lieke Andrea Smits
Paper 812-b: **The Cell on the Threshold: The Role of the Cell in Meditation Practice Visualised by the Housebook Master** (Language: English)
Sandra Kaden, Institut für Kunst- und Musikwissenschaft, Technische Universität Dresden
Paper 812-c: **A 17th-Century Booklet as Source for Research into the Continuity of Medieval Devotional Practices of (Semi-)Religious Women** (Language: English)
Evelyne Verheggen, Ruusbroecgenootschap, Universiteit Antwerpen

---

Session: **813** **Charles Thackrah Building: 1.01**
Title: **SLINGS AND ARROWS: HOMOSOCIAL NARRATIVES OF DESIRE, II**
Organiser: Rachel E. Moss, Corpus Christi College, University of Oxford
Moderator: Catherine Fletcher, Department of History, Swansea University
Paper 813-a: **Sex and/or Death: Re-Reading the Plague Saints, Roche and Sebastian** (Language: English)
Patricia Cullum, Department of History, University of Huddersfield
Paper 813-b: **'Seye hise bludi wundes': Penetrating Men in Medieval English Devotional Song** (Language: English)
Lisa Colton, School of Music, Humanities & Media, University of Huddersfield
Paper 813-c: **'Martyrdoms and Butchers' Boys': Reading Male-Male Relationships in Saints' Lives** (Language: English)
Kathryn Maude, Department of English, American University of Beirut

Session: **814** **University House: Beechgrove Room**
Title: **WOMEN AND JUSTICE, II: NEGOTIATING VICTIMHOOD**
Organiser: Emma Cavell, Department of History, University of Swansea
Moderator: Deborah Youngs, Centre for Medieval & Early Modern Research (MEMO), Swansea University
Paper 814-a: **Jewish Women and Violence in the Court of the Exchequer of the Jews, 1218-1290** (Language: English)
Emma Cavell
Paper 814-b: **The Perils of Pursuing Dower: The Abduction of Eleanor de Ferrers, d. c. 1326** (Language: English)
Harriet Kersey, School of Humanities, Canterbury Christ Church University
Paper 814-c: **The Legal Actions of Abducted Women in the Late Medieval Low Countries** (Language: English)
Chanelle Delameillieure, Middle Ages Research Group, KU Leuven

Session: **815** **Baines Wing: Room 1.16**
Title: **KINGSHIP, COURT, AND SOCIETY: THE REIGN OF HENRY VII, 1485-1509**
Sponsor: Project 'Kingship, Court & Society: The Chamber Books of Henry VII & Henry VIII', University of Winchester
Organiser: James Ross, Department of History, University of Winchester
Moderator: Elena Woodacre, Department of History, University of Winchester
Paper 815-a: **The Chamber Books of Henry VII: An Overview** (Language: English)
Samantha Harper, Department of History, University of Winchester
Paper 815-b: **Rumours and Remembrances: Connecting Gossip, Information, and Policy in the Early Tudor Court and Household, 1485-1521** (Language: English)
Sean Cunningham, The National Archives, Kew
Paper 815-c: **Revolution, Evolution, or *plus ça change*?: Henry VII and the Gentry** (Language: English)
James Ross

Session: **816** **Michael Sadler Building: Rupert Beckett Theatre**
Title: **LEGAL TEXTS AND THEIR USERS, IV: LAW AS SOCIAL PRACTICE**
Sponsor: Iuris Canonici Medii Aevi Consociatio (ICMAC)
Organiser: Cornelia Scherer, Deutsche Forschungsgemeinschaft ANR-Projekt 'Epistola', Friedrich-Alexander-Universität Erlangen-Nürnberg
Moderator: Simon Teuscher, Historisches Seminar, Universität Zürich
Paper 816-a: **Eternal Law?: Situational Law-Making and Its Representation in Visigothic Law Codes** (Language: English)
Cornelia Scherer
Paper 816-b: **Multiple Jurisdictions and Their Accessibility through Legal Practice in England, c. 1200-1400** (Language: English)
Silke Schwandt, Fakultät für Geschichtswissenschaft, Philosophie und Theologie, Universität Bielefeld
Paper 816-c: **Roman, Canon, Merchants' Law: Merchants' Representation in Late Medieval Antwerp** (Language: English)
Ulla Kypta, Departement Geschichte, Universität Basel

Session:	**817** **Social Sciences Building: Room 10.05**
Title:	**THE ORIGINS, EFFECTS, AND MEMORY OF CAROLINE MINUSCULE, II**
Sponsor:	Network for the Study of Caroline Minuscule
Organiser:	Arthur Westwell, Kompetenzzentrum für elektronische Erschließungs- und Publikationsverfahren in den Geisteswissenschaften, Universität Trier
Moderator:	Anna Dorofeeva, School of History, University College Dublin
Paper 817-a:	**I Won't Learn This!: The First Generation of Caroline Minuscule Scribes in North-Western Iberia** (Language: English) Ainoa Castro Correa, Departamento de Historia Medieval, Universidad de Salamanca
Paper 817-b:	**Reading and Writing Philadelphia, University of Pennsylvania LJS 101, c. 850–1100** (Language: English) Dorothy Carr Porter, Schoenberg Institute for Manuscript Studies, University of Pennsylvania
Paper 817-c:	**Optical Character Recognition for Caroline Minuscule** (Language: English) Antonia Karaisl, Warburg Institute, University of London

Session:	**818** **Stage@leeds: Stage 2**
Title:	**TRANSFORMATIONS OF POWER: SESSIONS IN HONOUR OF PAUL FOURACRE, I - FROM THE MEROVINGIANS TO THE CAROLINGIANS**
Sponsor:	Centre for Medieval & Early Modern Studies, University of Manchester
Organiser:	Katherine Fliegel, School of Arts, Languages & Cultures, University of Manchester, Ryan T. Goodman, Department of History, University of Manchester and Sihong Lin, Department of History, University of Manchester
Moderator:	Charles Insley, Department of History, University of Manchester
Paper 818-a:	**Eternal Light and Earthly Images: Lighting Churches and the Struggle for Power in 8th-Century Rome** (Language: English) Marios Costambeys, Department of History, University of Liverpool
Paper 818-b:	**Comparing Resources: Reading Carolingian Political Economy through the Merovingians** (Language: English) Jennifer R. Davis, Department of History, Catholic University of America, Washington DC
Paper 818-c:	**Merovingian to Carolingian Justice** (Language: English) Alice Rio, Department of History, King's College London

Session:	**819** **Charles Thackrah Building: 1.02**
Title:	**NEWSGATHERING AND HISTORY IN THE HIGH TO LATE MIDDLE AGES**
Sponsor:	Centre for Historiography & Historical Culture, Aberystwyth University
Organiser:	Nathan Greasley, Department of History & Welsh History, Aberystwyth University
Moderator:	Björn Weiler, Department of History & Welsh History, Aberystwyth University
Paper 819-a:	**Chronicling Disaster in 1187** (Language: English) Helen Birkett, Department of History, University of Exeter
Paper 819-b:	**Getting News from the Government: Revisiting Matthew Paris and the Red Book of the Exchequer** (Language: English) Nathan Greasley
Paper 819-c:	**The Reception of Written News in Late Medieval Manuscripts from St Albans Abbey, c. 1370-c. 1440** (Language: English) Elisa Mantienne, Campus Lettres et Sciences Humaines, Université de Lorraine

Session: **820** **University House: Great Woodhouse Room**
Title: **MEMORY IN MALORY AND RELATED ROMANCES**
Organiser: IMC Programming Committee
Moderator: Zoë Eve Enstone, Lifelong Learning Centre, University of Leeds
Paper 820-a: **Sir Lancelot in Queen Guenivere's Mind: Her Personal and Forbidden Memory of Him, through Exclusion and Remembrance in Thomas Malory's *Le Morte Darthur*** (Language: English)
Hanneli Seppänen, Faculty of Arts / Faculty of Theology, University of Helsinki
Paper 820-b: **The Necessary Bastard: Inversions, Paradoxes, and the Characterization of Mordred in Thomas Malory's *Morte Darthur*** (Language: English)
Peter Valenti, School of Liberal Studies, New York University
Paper 820-c: **'He had forgotten his lemon': The Lady of the Fountain as *Fides* Forgotten** (Language: English)
Rebekah Fowler, Department of English, University of Wisconsin-La Crosse

Session: **821** **Emmanuel Centre: Wilson Room**
Title: **REMEMBERING ROMANCE**
Organiser: IMC Programming Committee
Moderator: Catherine E. Léglu, Graduate Centre for Medieval Studies, University of Reading
Paper 821-a: **Tensión y *anagnórisis* en la *Historia Apollonii Regis Tyri*** (Language: Español)
María Florencia Saracino, Departamento de Letras, Universidad de Buenos Aires / Dipartimento di Scienze dell'Antichità, Università degli Studi di Roma 'La Sapienza'
Paper 821-b: **Funny Memories: The Art of Citation in *Flamenca*** (Language: English)
Giulia Boitani, Department of French, University of Cambridge
Paper 821-c: **La memoria come libro: un excursus sulla tradizione manoscritta della letteratura antico-provenzale** (Language: Italiano)
Susanna Barsotti, Dipartimento di Studi linguistici e letterari, Università degli Studi di Padova

Session: **822** **Social Sciences Building: Room 10.06**
Title: **THE ART OF MEMORY, II**
Organiser: IMC Programming Committee
Moderator: Alixe Bovey, Courtauld Institute of Art, University of London
Paper 822-a: **The 'Memory Brothel': The Role of Sex in Medieval and Early Modern Mnemonics** (Language: English)
Leon Jacobowitz Efron, Department of Humanistic Studies, Shalem College, Jerusalem
Paper 822-b: **'Me, patriam et dulces cara cum coniuge natos': Dynastic Memory and Marian Devotion in Lorenzo Costa's *Enthroned Madonna with the Bentivoglio Family*** (Language: English)
Gloria de Liberali, School of Art, Art History & Design, University of Washington
Paper 822-c: **Mnemonic Functions of Late Medieval Monumental Paintings** (Language: English)
Jan Dienstbier, Fakulta Humanitních Studií, Univerzity Karlova, Praha

Session: **823** **Maurice Keyworth Building: Room 1.31**
Title: **REMEMBERING THE NORTHERN ENGLISH SAINTS, II: TEXT AND GENDER**
Sponsor: Late Medieval Devotion to Northern English Saints, Swiss National Science Foundation Project
Organiser: Christiania Whitehead, Faculté des lettres, Université de Lausanne
Moderator: Christiania Whitehead
Paper 823-a: **The Absence of the Middle English Lives of St Hild of Whitby** (Language: English)
Mami Kanno, Faculty of Foreign Language Studies, Kanazawa University, Japan
Paper 823-b: **Northern Saints and Southern Sisters: Unlocking a Late Medieval Benedictine Mystery** (Language: English)
Christina Carlson, Department of English, Iona College, New York
Paper 823-c: **Flower of York: Region and Nation in Late Medieval Devotion to St Robert of Knaresborough** (Language: English)
Hazel Blair, Faculté des lettres, Université de Lausanne

Session: **824** **Michael Sadler Building: Room LG.19**
Title: **MEMORY IN PERFORMANCE**
Sponsor: Memory & the Pre-Modern North Network
Organiser: Simon Nygaard, Afdeling for Religionsvidenskab, Aarhus Universitet and Yoav Tirosh, Faculty of Icelandic & Comparative Cultural Studies, University of Iceland, Reykjavík
Moderator: Jürg Glauser, Deutsches Seminar, Universität Zürich
Paper 824-a: **Cultural Memory in Oral Contexts: Ritual Reproduction and Ritual Specialists in Pre-Christian Nordic Religion** (Language: English)
Simon Nygaard
Paper 824-b: **Remembering Heathen Women: Female Keepers of Memory in Medieval Icelandic Literature** (Language: English)
Ann Sheffield, Department of Chemistry, Allegheny College, Pennsylvania
Paper 824-c: **Heart Is Up: Seats of Memory in Kenning Metaphors** (Language: English)
Flavia Cornelia Teoc, Facultatea de Litere, Universitatea Babeș-Bolyai, Cluj-Napoca
Paper 824-d: **An Ugly Head and a Beautiful Mind: The Memories of 'Höfuðlausn'** (Language: English)
Anna Solovyeva, Faculty of Icelandic & Comparative Cultural Studies, University of Iceland, Reykjavík

Session: **825** **Maurice Keyworth Building: Room 1.06**
Title: **MEMORY AND MYTH: REMEMBERING MEDIEVAL IRELAND AND ITS NEIGHBOURS, IV - HISTORIOGRAPHY ON THE BORDERS**
Sponsor: Medieval History Research Centre, Trinity College Dublin
Organiser: Áine Foley, Medieval History Research Centre, Trinity College Dublin
Moderator: Sparky Booker, School of History, Anthropology, Philosophy & Politics, Queen's University Belfast

Paper 825-a: **The Interface between Hagiography and History in Medieval Wales** (Language: English)
Barry James Lewis, School of Celtic Studies, Dublin Institute of Advanced Studies

Paper 825-b: **Family Memory on the Welsh Frontier: Reconstructing the Past in Marcher Chronicles and Genealogies** (Language: English)
Georgia Henley, Department of English / Center for Spatial and Textual Analysis, Stanford University

Paper 825-c: **Community Reading in English Ireland: Memory and Vernacular Didactic texts** (Language: English)
Caoimhe Whelan, Department of History, Trinity College Dublin

---

Session: **826** **Social Sciences Building: Room 10.07**
Title: **'DIANA AND ALL HER SECT': REMEMBERING WOMEN WARRIORS, IV**
Sponsor: Society for Medieval Feminist Scholarship
Organiser: Sophie Harwood, Institute for Medieval Studies, University of Leeds, Roberta Magnani, Centre for Medieval & Early Modern Research (MEMO), Swansea University and Amy Louise Morgan, School of Literature & Languages, University of Surrey
Moderator: Liz Herbert McAvoy, Centre for Medieval & Early Modern Research (MEMO), Swansea University

Paper 826-a: **The Honest Androgyne: The Queer Virtues of Queen Pantsylla in Lydgate's *Troy Book*** (Language: English)
Barbara Ellen Logan, Department of History, University of Wyoming

Paper 826-b: **The Position of Women Warriors in Layamon's *Brut*** (Language: English)
Natalie Whitaker, Department of English, Saint Louis University, Missouri

Paper 826-c: **Lagertha and St Theodora of Vasta: Medieval Warrior Women in Folk Tradition and Pop Culture** (Language: English)
Maria Zygogianni, Centre for Medieval & Early Modern Research (MEMO), Swansea University

Paper 826-d: ***Freoðuwebbe* or *Friðusibb*? That is the Question: Expanding the Role of Women in *Beowulf*** (Language: English)
Jillian Sutton, Center for Medieval & Renaissance Studies, California State University, Long Beach

Session: **827** **Michael Sadler Building: Banham Theatre**
Title: **MEMORIES OF NATION, MEDIEVAL AND MODERN, IV: MEDIEVAL NATIONALISMS**
Sponsor: Richard Bland College of William & Mary, Virginia
Organiser: Daniel Franke, Department of History, Richard Bland College of William & Mary, Virginia
Moderator: Craig M. Nakashian, Department of History, Texas A&M University, Texarkana
Paper 827-a: **Aelred of Rievaulx, the Battle of the Standard, and the English** (Language: English)
Richard Vert, Department of History, Durham University
Paper 827-b: **The Danish Usurper: National Discourse in a 13th-Century Saga?** (Language: English)
Barbora Davídková, Independent Scholar, Correvon
Paper 827-c: **Dismembering Bodies, Producing England: *The Siege of Jerusalem*** (Language: English)
Carolyn B. Anderson, Department of English, University of Wyoming

Session: **828** **Stage@leeds: Stage 3**
Title: **REMEMBERING AND MISREMEMBERING THE ISLAMIC WORLD, II**
Organiser: Ann R. Christys, Independent Scholar, Leeds
Moderator: Harry Munt, Department of History, University of York
Paper 828-a: **The Modern Arabian Horse and Memories from Medieval Literature** (Language: English)
Hylke Hettema, School of Middle Eastern Studies, Universiteit Leiden
Paper 828-b: **Was the Umayyad Caliphate of al-Andalus as Strong as the Arab Chroniclers Said?** (Language: English)
Josep Suñé, Departament d'Història i Arqueologia, Universitat de Barcelona
Paper 828-c: **Ibn Khaldun Misremembers the Umayyad Dynasty in al-Andalus** (Language: English)
Ann R. Christys

Session: **829** **Maurice Keyworth Building: Room 1.05**
Title: **'AVE MARIA GRATIA PLENA': REMEMBERING THE VIRGIN MARY**
Organiser: IMC Programming Committee
Moderator: Amy Devenney, Institute for Medieval Studies, University of Leeds
Paper 829-a: **The *Camisa* of the Virgin at Chartres: A Memory Re-Modelled** (Language: English)
Julia Watson, Independent Scholar, Oxford
Paper 829-b: **Mary as *perfectissima roboratrix* in the Latter Years of Her Life?** (Language: English)
Mary Dzon, Department of English, University of Tennessee, Knoxville
Paper 829-c: **Mary and the Apocrypha: The Nativity and Presentation at the Temple between Hagiographic Collections and Church Representations** (Language: English)
Andrea-Bianka Znorovszky, Trivent Publishing, Budapest

Session: 830 — **Charles Thackrah Building: 1.03**
Title: **VISUAL MEMORY IN THE LATE ANTIQUE AND BYZANTINE WORLD**
Organiser: Nicole Paxton Sullo, Department of the History of Art, Yale University
Moderator: Nicole Paxton Sullo
Paper 830-a: **Commenting on Aristotelian Memory: Towards a Byzantine Interpretation** (Language: English)
Daphne Argyri, Department of History & Philosophy of Science, National & Kapodistrian University of Athens
Paper 830-b: **The Memory of Inscriptions in Later Byzantium** (Language: English)
Foteini Spingou, Ioannou Centre for Classical & Byzantine Studies, University of Oxford

---

Session: 831 — **Charles Thackrah Building: 1.04**
Title: **MATERIAL CULTURE AND LANDSCAPES, IV: MEMORY AND HOUSES OF WORSHIP**
Sponsor: Medieval Landscape/Seascape Research Group
Organiser: Daniel Brown, Historisches Institut, Universität zu Köln and Stefanie Schild, Independent Scholar, Hilden
Moderator: James Michael Harland, Department of Arts, Design & Social Sciences, Northumbria University
Paper 831-a: **England's Medieval Jews: Remembering a Materially Absent Community** (Language: English)
Toni Griffiths, Department of Theology, Religion & Philosophy, University of Winchester
Paper 831-b: **The Medieval Cage Chantry and the Accuracy of Memory** (Language: English)
Cindy Wood, Department of History, University of Winchester
Paper 831-c: **Pop Culture Pilgrimages: Conspiracies and Codes in the Carvings at Rosslyn** (Language: English)
Lizzie Swarbrick, School of Art History, University of Edinburgh

---

Session: 832 — **Social Sciences Building: Room 10.09**
Title: **MEMORY AND HOSPITALS, II: ARCHIVES, WRITTEN RECORDS, ICONOGRAPHIC EVIDENCES**
Sponsor: Alle origini del welfare (XIII-XVI secolo), PRIN 2015 / New Communities of Interpretation, ISCH COST Action IS1301
Organiser: Thomas Frank, Dipartimento di Studi Umanistici, Università degli Studi di Pavia
Moderator: Marina Gazzini, Dipartimento di Discipline Umanistiche, Sociali e delle Imprese Culturali, Università degli Studi di Parma
Paper 832-a: **Memory and Images: Iconographic Sources for the Study of Hospital Architecture in the Middle Ages** (Language: English)
Antoni Conejo da Pena, Departament d'Història de l'Art, Universitat de Barcelona
Paper 832-b: **Notaries and Hospital Memory in Barcelona and Naples** (Language: English)
Salvatore Marino, Istituto di Studi sulle Società del Mediterraneo, Consiglio Nazionale delle Ricerche, Napoli
Paper 832-c: **The Institutional Memory of a Hospital and Confraternity: The Archives of Santa Maria dei Battuti in Treviso, Italy** (Language: English)
Thomas Frank

Session: **833** **Leeds University Union: Room 2 - Elland Road**
Title: **COMMUNICATION AND THE EXPLOITATION OF KNOWLEDGE, IV: SHAPING MEMORIES THROUGH LETTER COLLECTIONS**
Sponsor: Onderzoeksschool Mediëvistiek, Rijksuniversiteit Groningen
Organiser: Theo Lap, Afdeling Geschiedenis, Rijksuniversiteit Groningen
Moderator: Pieter Boonstra, Afdeling Geschiedenis, Rijksuniversiteit Groningen
Paper 833-a: **One Voice, One Memory, One Identity?: The Creation and Use of Letter Collections in Late Medieval Convents** (Language: English)
Lena Vosding, Institut für Geschichtswissenschaften, Heinrich-Heine-Universität Düsseldorf
Paper 833-b: **Blurred Memories: Letter Collections and the Future - Bernard versus Abelard** (Language: English)
Wim Verbaal, Vakgroep Romaanse Talen, Universiteit Gent
Paper 833-c: **The Meme of a Lifetime: Exemplary Knowledge in High Medieval Letter Collections** (Language: English)
Theo Lap
Paper 833-d: **The Threshold of the Reader: Does the Monastic Rule Represent the Ending of Abelard and Heloise's Letter Collection?** (Language: English)
Babette Hellemans, Afdeling Geschiedenis, Rijksuniversiteit Groningen / Wolfson College, University of Oxford

---

Session: **834** **Leeds University Union: Room 4 - Hyde Park**
Title: **GRAPHIC AND TEXTUAL COMMUNITIES: BETWEEN MEMORY AND IDENTITY, II**
Sponsor: H37 - Histoire & Cultures Graphiques, Université catholique de Louvain, Louvain-la-Neuve
Organiser: Paul Bertrand, Faculté de Philosophie, Arts et Lettres, Université catholique de Louvain, Louvain-la-Neuve
Moderator: Sébastien Barret, Institut de Recherche et d'Histoire des Textes (IRHT), Centre National de la Recherche Scientifique (CNRS), Paris
Paper 834-a: **Mapping the City: Graphic Community in Nantes, Brittany, in the Late Middle Ages - Tool or Category of Analysis?** (Language: English)
Aurore Denmat-Leon, UFR d'Histoire, Centre Roland Mousnier, Université Paris IV - Sorbonne
Paper 834-b: **The Chirographs of Nivelles: Witnesses of a Mutation in Urban Politics at the Beginning of the 14th Century** (Language: English)
Mathilde Rivière, Fonds de la Recherche Scientifique (FRS-FNRS), Université Catholique de Louvain, Louvain-la-Neuve
Paper 834-c: **The Diffusion of *ars dictaminis* Treatises in Medieval Low Countries** (Language: English)
Nicolas Michel, Faculté de philosophie et lettres, Université de Namur

Session: **835** **Maurice Keyworth Building: Room 1.09**
Title: **POWER, MEMORY, AND WRITTEN RECORD IN MEDIEVAL SPAIN, IV: CONFLICTING MEMORIES AND THE APPROPRIATION OF THE PAST**
Sponsor: El ejercicio del poder: espacios, agentes y escrituras (siglos XI-XV), EJEPO Project
Organiser: Carlos Reglero de la Fuente, Facultad de Filosofía y Letras, Universidad de Valladolid
Moderator: Fernando Arias Guillén, Facultad de Filosofía y Letras, Universidad de Valladolid
Paper 835-a: **St Jacob Apostle, the Toletum Church, and a Big Fish: Iberian Peninsula Memory in the 'Commentary on the Apocalypse' of Burgo de Osma Mappa Mundi** (Language: English)
Soledad Morandeira de Paz, Departamento de Historia Antigua y Medieval, Universidad de Valladolid
Paper 835-b: **Dompnus Petrus, infans Portugalie et regni Maioricarum dominus: Memoria y poder** (Language: Español)
Inés Calderón Medina, Facultad de Filosofía y Letras, Universitat de les Illes Balears, Palma
Paper 835-c: **Memory and Power in Sahagun: Judicial Inquiries during the 15th Century** (Language: English)
Carlos Reglero de la Fuente

Session: **836** **Leeds University Union: Room 5 - Kirkstall Abbey**
Title: **TIME IN MEDIEVAL EUROPE, II: THE CONTINENTAL PERSPECTIVE - REMEMBERING THE FUTURE, 11TH AND 12TH CENTURIES**
Organiser: Miriam Czock, Historisches Institut, Universität Duisburg-Essen and Amalie Fößel, Historisches Institut, Universität Duisburg-Essen
Moderator: Amalie Fößel
Paper 836-a: **Future Deaths and Present Occupations in Hélinand of Froidmont's Work** (Language: English)
Anja B. Rathmann-Lutz, Departement Geschichte, Universität Basel
Paper 836-b: **Ascertaining Uncertainty?: Concepts of Mutability in the 12th Century** (Language: English)
David Passig, Historisches Institut, Universität Duisburg-Essen
Paper 836-c: **Sacramental Security?: Discussing the Eucharist between the Last Supper and the Heavenly Wedding Meal in the 12th Century** (Language: English)
Jörg Bölling, Seminar für Mittlere und Neuere Geschichte, Georg-August-Universität Göttingen / Institut für Katholische Theologie, Universität Hildesheim
Paper 836-d: **No Time like the Present of the Past to Face the Future: Rupert of Deutz's Explanation of the Liturgy** (Language: English)
Miriam Czock

Session:	**837** **Maurice Keyworth Building: Room 1.03**
Title:	**CREATING MEMORIES USING CHARTERS, CARTULARIES, AND ARCHIVES**
Organiser:	IMC Programming Committee
Moderator:	Christine E. Meek, Department of History, Trinity College Dublin
Paper 837-a:	**Identity Memories of Some Urban Communities in Guyenne in the Late Middle Ages** (Language: English) Nathalie Crouzier-Roland, Ausonius (UMR 5607), Université Bordeaux Montaigne
Paper 837-b:	**Archivio come memoria e identità della città: il caso degli archivi comunali di Forlì, Cesena e Rimini nel Medioevo** (Language: Italiano) Gianluca Braschi, Archivio di Stato, Forlì-Cesena
Paper 837-c:	**The Golden Bulls of Sicily: Memories of the Past that Did Not Exist** (Language: English) Martin Wihoda, Department of History, Masarykova univerzita, Brno

Session:	**838** **Baines Wing: Room G.36**
Title:	**RELATIONSHIPS BETWEEN PEASANTS AND LORDS**
Organiser:	IMC Programming Committee
Moderator:	Balázs Nagy, Department of Medieval Studies, Central European University, Budapest
Paper 838-a:	**Between Memory and Written Record: Land Management and Peasant Obligations in Medieval Tuscany, 12th and 13th Centuries** (Language: English) Lorenzo Tabarrini, Faculty of History, University of Oxford
Paper 838-b:	**Lords, Peasants, and Labour Services in the Late Medieval Low Countries, c. 1250-1500** (Language: English) Thijs Lambrecht, Vakgroep Geschiedenis, Universiteit Gent
Paper 838-c:	**Peasant Food and High Cuisine in Italy, 14th and 15th Centuries** (Language: English) Filippo Ribani, Dipartimento di Storia Culture Civiltà, Università di Bologna

Session:	**839** **Maurice Keyworth Building: Room 1.33**
Title:	**REMEMBERING THE PAST AFTER THE CAROLINGIAN EMPIRE, IV: MYTHS AND MEMORIES**
Sponsor:	After Empire: Using & Not Using the Past in the Crisis of the Carolingian World, c. 900-1050
Organiser:	Sarah Greer, St Andrews Institute of Mediaeval Studies, University of St Andrews
Moderator:	Stuart Airlie, School of Humanities (History), University of Glasgow
Paper 839-a:	**Beyond the Cadaver Synod: Myths of Pope Formosus and the Late Anglo-Saxon Church's Sense of Its Past** (Language: English) Benjamin Savill, Wadham College, University of Oxford
Paper 839-b:	**'Last in the order of kings': Prior Kings and Ideas about Kingship in the West Frankish kingdom, c. 1000** (Language: English) Fraser McNair, School of History, University of Leeds
Paper 839-c:	**'Pro spe futurae remunerationis': Queens, Memorialization, and the Hope for a Better Future in the Ottonian Empire** (Language: English) Megan Welton, Medieval Institute, University of Notre Dame, Indiana

Session:	**840** **Parkinson Building: Nathan Bodington Chamber**
Title:	**IMPERIAL MEMORY THEN AND NOW, III: EMPIRE, GEOGRAPHY, AND DIGITAL HUMANITIES**
Sponsor:	Institut für Geographie und Regionalforschung, Universität Wien
Organiser:	Karel Kriz, Institut für Geographie und Regionalforschung, Universität Wien
Moderator:	David Rollason, Department of History, Durham University
Paper 840-a:	**Representing Historical Landscapes: An Interactive Map-Based Solution** (Language: English) Markus Breier, Institut für Geographie und Regionalforschung, Universität Wien
Paper 840-b:	**From Past to Future: Interactive Geographic (Hi)Storytelling of Historical Landscapes** (Language: English) Alexander Pucher, Institut für Geographie und Regionalforschung, Universität Wien
Paper 840-c:	**OpenAtlas: How to Grow Software for Historians** (Language: English) Alexander Watzinger, Institut für Mittelalterforschung, Österreichische Akademie der Wissenschaften, Wien
Paper 840-d:	**A New Project on Galician Medieval Heritage, II: GIS as a Work Tool** (Language: English) Mariña Bermúdez Beloso, Departamento de Historia, Universidade de Santiago de Compostela

Session:	**841** **Michael Sadler Building: Room LG.10**
Title:	**'DON'T YOU (FORGET ABOUT ME)': REMEMBERING THE FOUNDERS OF EREMITICAL ORDERS**
Sponsor:	Cartusiana
Organiser:	Tom Gaens, Faculteit der Letteren, Rijksuniversiteit Groningen and Stephen J. Molvarec, Department of History, Marquette University, Wisconsin
Moderator:	Emilia Jamroziak, Institute for Medieval Studies / School of History, University of Leeds
Paper 841-a:	**A Controversial Memory: The Order of Grandmont and the 12th-Century Lives of St Stephen of Muret and Hugo Lacerta** (Language: English) Daniela Bianca Hoffmann, Historisches Institut, Universität Mannheim
Paper 841-b:	**Abandoning *La Chartreuse*: Memory, Identity, and Narrative Discontinuity among Early Carthusians** (Language: English) Stephen J. Molvarec
Paper 841-c:	**Remembering Romualdian Reforms in the *Vita Romualdi*** (Language: English) Kathryn L. Jasper, Department of History, Illinois State University

Session: **842** **Baines Wing: Room G.37**
Title: **POLITICAL STRUGGLES, POLITICAL MEMORIES**
Organiser: IMC Programming Committee
Moderator: Thomas Heebøll-Holm, Institut for Historie, Syddansk Universitet, Odense
Paper 842-a: ***Regnum Sardiniae* Catalan-Aragonese and the District of Arborea in the 14th Century: Peter IV of Aragon versus Marianus IV of Arborea and the Construction of the Myth of a Rebellious Subject** (Language: English)
Alessandra Cioppi, Istituto di Storia dell'Europa Mediterranea (ISEM), Consiglio Nazionale delle Ricerche, Roma
Paper 842-b: **Social Memory and Revolt: How Political Remembrances Engaged with Public Opinion in Late Medieval England, c. 1450-1509** (Language: English)
Wesley Correa, Faculty of History, University of Oxford
Paper 842-c: **Celebrating the Memory of Victory: Memorial Manifestations of the Battle of Brunkeberg, 1471** (Language: English)
Margaretha Nordquist, Historiska institutionen, Stockholms universitet
Paper 842-d: **'Crónica Geral de Espanha de 1344': The Avis Court and the Reconstruction of the Past** (Language: English)
Catarina Martins Tibúrcio, Instituto de Estudos Medievais, Universidade Nova de Lisboa

Session: **843** **Maurice Keyworth Building: Room 1.32**
Title: **THE MEMORY OF THE CRUSADES, IV: REPUTATION AND DIFFUSION**
Sponsor: Routledge
Organiser: Mike Horswell, Department of History, Royal Holloway, University of London
Moderator: Adam Knobler, Centrum für Religionswissenschaftliche Studien, Ruhr-Universität Bochum
Paper 843-a: **Getting Away with Murder: Conrad of Montferrat's (Character) Assassination** (Language: English)
Marianne M. Gilchrist, Independent Scholar, Hull
Paper 843-b: **Blame it on the Templar: The Representation of the Knights Templar in Ridley Scott's *Kingdom of Heaven*** (Language: English)
Patrick Masters, School of Media & Performing Arts, University of Portsmouth
Recipient of a 2018 Templar Heritage Trust Bursary
Paper 843-c: **Depictions of the Crusades in Philately** (Language: English)
Rachael Pymm, Independent Scholar, Surrey
Recipient of a 2018 Templar Heritage Trust Bursary

Session: **844** **Fine Art Building: SR 1.10**
Title: **CULTURAL MEMORY IN LATE ANTIQUITY, IV: BUILDING LATE ANTIQUE COMMUNITIES THROUGH MEMORY**
Organiser: Richard Flower, Department of Classics & Ancient History, University of Exeter and Robin Whelan, Department of History, University of Liverpool
Moderator: Adrastos Omissi, School of Humanities (Classics), University of Glasgow
Paper 844-a: **Embodying Community through Late Antique Ritual** (Language: English)
Heather Hunter-Crawley, Independent Scholar, Bristol
Paper 844-b: **The Onomastics of Ancestry in the Self-Celebrating Strategies of the Late Antique Aristocracy: The Case of the Valeri** (Language: English)
Mara Mudu, Independent Scholar, Cagliari
Paper 844-c: **Making Memory from Silence: John of Damascus on Inter-Ecclesiastical Disputes and the Shaping of Church Memory** (Language: English)
Maria Dolores Casero Chamorro, Centro de Ciencias Humanas y Sociales, Consejo Superior de Investigaciones Científicas (CSIC), Madrid and Petros Tsagkaropoulos, Department of Classics, King's College London

Session: **845** **Leeds University Union: Room 6 - Roundhay**
Title: **(MIS)REMEMBERING FIRST ENCOUNTER, II: WEST AFRICA**
Organiser: Claudia Rogers, School of History, University of Leeds and Adam Simmons, Department of History, Lancaster University
Moderator: Verena Krebs, Historisches Institut, Ruhr-Universität Bochum
Paper 845-a: **Memories of Meals: The Role of Food Encounters in European Narratives of West Africa and the Western Atlantic Islands in the 15th and Early 16th Centuries** (Language: English)
Iona McCleery, Institute for Medieval Studies / School of History, University of Leeds
Paper 845-b: **The Concept of the Exotic in First Encounters on the 'Gold Coast'** (Language: English)
Holly Atkinson, School of Arts, Languages & Cultures, University of Manchester
Paper 845-c: **First First Encounters: Interacting, Understanding, and Evolving before the Traditional Narrative** (Language: English)
Adam Simmons
Respondent: David Abulafia, Gonville & Caius College, University of Cambridge

Session: **846** **Emmanuel Centre: Room 10**
Title: **TRACES OF MEMORY IN THE WESTERN MEDITERRANEAN, IV: INSTITUTIONAL MEMORY**
Sponsor: Institut de Recerca en Cultures Medievals / Institución Milá y Fontanals (IMF), Consejo Superior de Investigaciones Científicas (CSIC) / Grup de Recerca en Estudis Medievals d'Art, Història, Paleografia i Arqueologia (MAHPA), Universitat de Barcelona
Organiser: Giacomo Floris, Departament d'Història Medieval, Paleografia i Diplomàtica, Universitat de Barcelona and Jaume Marcé Sánchez, Institut de Recerca en Cultures Medievals, Universitat de Barcelona
Moderator: Mireia Comas, Departament d'Història i Arqueologia, Universitat de Barcelona
Paper 846-a: **Memory of War: The North-African Campaigns of Alfonso the Magnanimous** (Language: English)
Pol Junyent Molins, Institució Milà i Fontanals (IMF), Consejo Superior de Investigaciones Científicas (CSIC), Barcelona
Paper 846-b: **The Memory of the City: Barcelona's Registers in the 15th Century** (Language: English)
Laura Miquel Milian, Institució Milà i Fontanals (IMF), Consejo Superior de Investigaciones Científicas (CSIC), Barcelona
Paper 846-c: **Models in Motion: Economic Memory in Late Medieval Hospitals** (Language: English)
Jaume Marcé Sánchez

Session: **847** **Baines Wing: Room 2.14**
Title: **POLITICAL AND LITURGICAL MEMORY IN THE CENTRAL MIDDLE AGES**
Sponsor: Politics, Society and Liturgy in the Middle Ages (PSALM) Network
Organiser: Pieter Byttebier, Vakgroep Geschiedenis, Universiteit Gent
Moderator: Sarah M. Hamilton, Department of History, University of Exeter
Paper 847-a: **Liturgy, History, and Memory in the Medieval Mediterranean** (Language: English)
Sean Griffin, Department of History / Department of Russian, Dartmouth College
Paper 847-b: **Liturgy in Historical Writing from Medieval Southern Italy: Lay and Monastic Perspectives** (Language: English)
Andrew J. M. Irving, Faculteit der Godgeleerdheid en Godsdienstwetenschap, Rijksuniversiteit Groningen
Paper 847-c: **Liturgical Realpolitik, Historiographical Memory, and the Restoration(s) of the Medieval Polish Kingdom** (Language: English)
Paweł Figurski, Instytut Historyczny, Uniwersytet Warszawski

Session: **848** **University House: St George Room**
Title: **MEMORY AND *INQUISITIO*, II: RECOLLECTING AND RECORDING**
Sponsor: Trivium - Tampere Centre for Classical, Medieval & Early Modern Studies
Organiser: Sari Katajala-Peltomaa, School of Social Sciences & Humanities, University of Tampere
Moderator: Gábor Klaniczay, Department of Medieval Studies, Central European University, Budapest
Paper 848-a: **'It happened when we had that reddish-brown cow': Levels of Recollection and Narration in the Canonization Process of Thomas Cantilupe, 1307** (Language: English)
Sari Katajala-Peltomaa
Paper 848-b: **Shaping Memory: Limoux Nègre and the Apostles' Creed, 1326-1329** (Language: English)
Louisa A. Burnham, Department of History, Middlebury College, Vermont
Paper 848-c: **The Evaluation of Evidence and Memory in Concluded Canonisation and Heresy Cases** (Language: English)
Derek Hill, Independent Scholar, Harrow Weald

Session: **849** **University House: Cloberry Room**
Title: **TOLKIEN: MEDIEVAL ROOTS AND MODERN BRANCHES, II**
Sponsor: Cardiff Metropolitan University
Organiser: Thomas Honegger, Institut für Anglistik, Friedrich-Schiller-Universität Jena
Moderator: Thomas Honegger
Paper 849-a: **Longing for Death: Tolkien and *Sehnsucht*** (Language: English)
Anna Vaninskaya, School of Literatures, Languages & Cultures, University of Edinburgh
Paper 849-b: **Tolkien's Agrarianism in Its Time** (Language: English)
Joshua Richards, Faculty of English, Williams Baptist College, Arkansas
Paper 849-c: **Frodo Surrealist: André Breton and J. R. R. Tolkien on Dreams** (Language: English)
Claudio Antonio Testi, Independent Scholar, Modena
Paper 849-d: **A Man of His Time?: Tolkien and the Edwardian Worldview** (Language: English)
Brad Eden, Christopher Center for Library & Information Resources, Valparaiso University, Indiana

Session: **850** **Emmanuel Centre: Room 11**
Title: **CISTERCIANS, IV: TRAVELLING CISTERCIANS**
Sponsor: Instituto de Estudos Medievais, Universidade Nova de Lisboa
Organiser: Terryl N. Kinder, *Cîteaux: Commentarii cistercienses*, Pontigny
Moderator: David N. Bell, Department of Religious Studies, Memorial University of Newfoundland
Paper 850-a: **Portuguese Cistercian Abbesses and Nuns Travelling in the 13th and 14th Centuries** (Language: English)
Luís Miguel Rêpas, Instituto de Estudos Medievais, Universidade Nova de Lisboa
Paper 850-b: **The Centrality of the Practice of Travel in the Reformist Action of Frei Estêvão De Aguiar as Abbot of the Cistercian Monastery of Santa Maria De Alcobaça, 1431-1446** (Language: English)
Paulo Catarino Lopes, Instituto de Estudos Medievais / Centro de História d'Aquém e d'Além-Mar, Universidade Nova de Lisboa
Paper 850-c: **The Circulation of Manuscripts and Monks from Alcobaça** (Language: English)
Catarina Fernandes Barreira, Instituto de Estudos Medievais, Universidade Nova de Lisboa

Session: **851** **Baines Wing: Room 2.15**
Title: **MEDIEVAL ICELANDIC FARMING, II: REMEMBER THE WORKERS!**
Sponsor: University of Iceland / National Museum of Iceland
Organiser: Bernadette McCooey, Independent Scholar, Birmingham
Moderator: Árni Daníel Júlíusson, National Museum of Iceland, Reykjavík
Paper 851-a: **I Can't Believe It's Not Battle!: Skyr-Making and Memory in Medieval Iceland** (Language: English)
Bethany Rogers, Department of Humanities, University of Iceland, Reykjavík
Paper 851-b: **Remembering the Work of Animals in Old Norse-Icelandic Textual Sources** (Language: English)
Harriet Jean Evans, Centre for Medieval Studies, University of York
Paper 851-c: ***Búalög*: The Lesser Remembered Icelandic Legal Text** (Language: English)
Bernadette McCooey

Session: **852** **Stage@leeds: Stage 1**
Title: **RACISM AND MEDIEVALISM BEYOND THE CONTEMPORARY US**
Sponsor: IMC Programming Committee
Organiser: Bettina Bildhauer, School of Modern Languages - German, University of St Andrews
Moderator: Bettina Bildhauer
Paper 852-a: **Confederate Gothic: Medievalism, Memory, and the American Civil War** (Language: English)
Josh Davies, Department of English Language & Literature, King's College London
Paper 852-b: **Eurocentricity, Racism, and Intangible Cultural Heritage** (Language: English)
Heather Maring, Department of English, Arizona State University
Paper 852-c: **Race and Medievalism in Gilberto Freyre's Mozarabic Brazil** (Language: English)
Nadia Altschul, School of Modern Languages & Cultures (Hispanic Studies), University of Glasgow
Paper 852-d: **Fragile Masculinity and Beleaguered Womanhood: The Construction of White Gender in Some Swedish Asatru Groups** (Language: English)
Kristina Hildebrand, Akademin för lärande, humaniora och samhälle, Högskolan i Halmstad

Session: **853** **Michael Sadler Building: Room LG.15**
Title: **MEMORY: THE CARMEN READING ROOM - A WORKSHOP**
Sponsor: CARMEN: The Worldwide Medieval Network
Organiser: Catherine A. M. Clarke, Faculty of Humanities, University of Southampton
Moderator: Catherine A. M. Clarke
Purpose: *This drop-in workshop session is sponsored by CARMEN: The Worldwide Medieval Network, and reflects CARMEN's distinctive mission as an international forum for scholars at all levels to exchange ideas, build partnerships, and develop collaborative research. The session presents an opportunity to engage with key sources, theories, and approaches relating to the special thematic strand of this year's IMC: Memory. Materials for discussion have been selected by leading scholars in the field and by plenary speakers at this year's conference; a short reading pack is downloadable before the conference from the CARMEN website (www.carmen-medieval.net/), or just come along and pick up a hand-out at the session (no pre-reading is necessary). Scholars from any discipline are warmly invited to join this informal discussion.*

Participants include Lisa Fagin Davis (Medieval Academy of America, Massachusetts), and Simon Forde (ARC Humanities Press, Leeds).

Session: **854** **Maurice Keyworth Building: Room G.02**
Title: **MEMORY, LANDSCAPE, AND HERITAGE: ENCOUNTERING THE MEDIEVAL IN THE PRESENT - A ROUND TABLE DISCUSSION**
Sponsor: Medieval Landscape/Seascape Research Group / Landscape Research Group
Organiser: Kimm Curran, School of Critical Studies, University of Glasgow
Moderator: Kimm Curran
Purpose: *Experiencing medieval places in the present can often act as mnemonic tools of the interactions between culture and the environment of the past. Heritage, community archaeology, experiential, and experimental approaches to place, as well as critical analysis of memorial sites, have provided opportunities for us to engage more profoundly with views of the medieval past. This round table discussion will bring together a chance to discuss how medievalists are using landscape and heritage to engage with the past in the present. It offers opportunities to encounter the varied approaches used by medievalists in discovering landscapes of the past and re-remembering them for the future.*

Participants include Karl Christian Alvestad (University of Winchester), Michael Bintley (Canterbury Christ Church University), David Carrillo-Rangel (Universitat de Barcelona), Linsey F. Hunter (University of the Highlands & Islands, Dornoch), and Chloë McKenzie (University of Southampton).

DINNER

Meal Times

Refectory 18.00-20.00

See Map 9, p. 51.

---

* * * * *

INTERNATIONAL MEDIEVAL FILM FESTIVAL: *THE LITTLE HOURS* (2017)

HYDE PARK PICTURE HOUSE
18.00

This event is free of charge.

Presented by LUU Medieval Society as part of the fourth International Medieval Film Festival, *The Little Hours* (2017) has been described as 'one of the most faithful adaptations of a piece of medieval literature yet put to screen'. When a handsome fugitive pretends to be deaf and without speech and takes up refuge in a convent, the bored young nuns are delighted to have such an attractive man in their midst. Jeff Baena's (*Life After Beth*) latest comedy adapts a tale from *The Decameron* into an alternatively hilarious and heartbreaking film.

After the film the panel will discuss the film and take questions from the audience.

Entry is free for IMC delegates. For more details and the full programme of LUU Medieval Society events please see p. 470.

* * * * *

RECEPTION AT PARKINSON BUILDING

HOSTED BY
UNIVERSITY OF WALES PRESS

PARKINSON BUILDING: BOOKFAIR
18.00-18.30

Join the University of Wales Press to celebrate the publication of *Gerald of Wales: New Perspectives on a Medieval Writer and Critic*.

* * * * *

RECEPTION AT PARKINSON BUILDING

HOSTED BY
WALTER DE GRUYTER

PARKINSON BUILDING: BOOKFAIR
18.00-18.30

We would like to celebrate with you the book launch of our *Handbook of Pre-Modern Nordic Memory Studies*. Be our guest, join us at our booth for a reception, and meet the editors Juerg Glauser and Pernille Hermann. We look forward to welcoming you!

* * * * *

* * * * *

RECEPTION AT UNIVERSITY HOUSE

HOSTED BY
CENTRE FOR THE STUDY OF THE MIDDLE AGES, UNIVERSITY OF BIRMINGHAM

UNIVERSITY HOUSE: ST GEORGE ROOM
18.30-19.30

The Centre for the Study of the Middle Ages, University of Birmingham, invites all delegates to a wine reception.

We particularly welcome graduate students considering further study. Academic staff from the Centre will be on hand to discuss our new provisions for MA and PhD programmes in Medieval Studies, including our interdisciplinary pathways in History and Literature.

For any advance queries, please contact Victoria Flood (v.flood@bham.ac.uk) (Literature) or Kate Sykes (k.sykes@bham.ac.uk) (History).

* * * * *

RECEPTION AT UNIVERSITY HOUSE

HOSTED BY
BRITISH ARCHAEOLOGICAL ASSOCIATION

UNIVERSITY HOUSE: LITTLE WOODHOUSE ROOM
18.30-19.30

The British Archaeological Association invites you to come along and raise a glass to the IMC.

* * * * *

RECEPTION AT MICHAEL SADLER BUILDING

HOSTED BY
NATIONAL MUSEUMS SCOTLAND & THE GLENMORANGIE COMPANY

MICHAEL SADLER BUILDING: ROOM LG.15
18.30-19.30

Join National Museums Scotland for a dram as we celebrate ten years of the Glenmorangie Research Project on Medieval Scotland and look forward to an exciting new phase of research. Supported by The Glenmorangie Company.

* * * * *

Session: **901** **Michael Sadler Building: Rupert Beckett Theatre**
Title: **NEW VOICES LECTURE: TRANSGENDER LIVES IN BYZANTIUM** (Language: English)
Speaker: Roland Betancourt, Department of Art History, University of California, Irvine
Introduction: Shaun Tougher, School of History, Archaeology & Religion, Cardiff University
Details: *From the 5th to the 9th century, there are a series of saints'* Lives *composed in the Greek-speaking Mediterranean that detail the lives of individuals assigned female at birth, who for a variety of reasons choose to live most of their lives as monks, usually presenting as male and passing as eunuchs within monastic communities. This talk takes these* Lives *and their popularity in later centuries as a starting point to consider the role of transgender and non-binary figures across the Late Antique and Byzantine world, covering the Greek, Coptic, and Syriac traditions. Weaving together saints'* Lives*, rhetorical treatises, letters, and medical textbooks, this talk focuses on the host of bodily and medical practices deployed in the Byzantine world to alter or affirm a person's gender identity. And, secondly, on Byzantine authors' eloquent descriptions of non-binary and transgender identity, both for themselves and others. The figures discussed throughout this talk push against expectations of gender identity in the medieval world, rubbing against our own anachronistic notions of a binary gender construct, and demanding a revaluation of what transgender subjectivities could have looked like in Late Antiquity and the Middle Ages.*

Session: **908** **Leeds University Union: Room 5 - Kirkstall Abbey**
Title: **RECONSTRUCTING THE MEDIEVAL HORSE: A ROUND TABLE DISCUSSION**
Organiser: Anastasija Ropa, Faculty of Humanities, University of Latvia, Riga
Moderator: Anastasija Ropa
Purpose: *Can we ever understand what the horse meant for people in the Middle Ages and what medieval horses were like? In this round table, we interpret the issue of 'reconstructing' the medieval horse very broadly, going beyond the physical reality of a four-hoofed animal used to perform a number of tasks in pre-industrial society. The contributions range from the practicalities of medieval equitation, including the possibilities of reconstructing equipment and riding styles through a combination of source study and experimental approaches, to the critical analysis of visual and textual sources, from romances to legal treatises, with the view of 'reconstructing' both the real animals behind the representation and the contemporary ideas about horses that informed source production and consumption.*

Participants include Gloria Allaire (University of Kentucky), Timothy Dawson (Independent Scholar, Leeds), Adeline Dumont (Université Charles-de-Gaulle - Lille 3), John C. Ford (Université Fédérale Toulouse Midi-Pyrénées), John Henry Gassmann (Independent Scholar, Bühler), and Edgar Rops (Independent Scholar, Latvia).

Session: **911** **Stage@leeds: Stage 1**

Title: **INTERNATIONAL MEDIEVAL CONGRESS AND CENTRAL EUROPEAN UNIVERSITY, BEING 25: NETWORKS OF MEDIEVAL STUDIES AND THEIR FUTURE - A ROUND TABLE DISCUSSION**

Sponsor: Department of Medieval Studies, Central European University, Budapest / International Medieval Congress

Organiser: Gerhard Jaritz, Department of Medieval Studies, Central European University, Budapest

Moderator: Marco Mostert, Utrecht Centre for Medieval Studies, Universiteit Utrecht

Purpose: *The Leeds International Medieval Congress as well as the Department of Medieval Studies at Central European University (Budapest) celebrate their 25th birthday in 2018. In their activities, both institutions have concentrated on establishing multidisciplinary networks of research into the Middle Ages and communication referring to it on an international basis. They have been successful in these enterprises to promote and stimulate Medieval Studies. This round table discussion will deal with ideas, possibilities, and difficulties in continuing such network endeavours and strengthening the co-operation of researchers and research groups among each other: to offer, at least with regard to comparative study and analysis, new approaches towards the 'global' aspects of the Middle Ages.*

Participants include Emilia Jamroziak (University of Leeds), Gábor Klaniczay (Central European University, Budapest), Axel E.W. Müller (University of Leeds), and Mária Vargha (Central European University, Budapest).

Session: **914** **Maurice Keyworth Building: Room 1.06**

Title: **NEW PERSPECTIVES ON WOMEN AND JUSTICE: A ROUND TABLE DISCUSSION**

Sponsor: Centre for Medieval & Early Modern Research (MEMO), Swansea University

Organiser: Emma Cavell, Department of History, University of Swansea

Moderator: Teresa Phipps, Centre for Medieval & Early Modern Research (MEMO), Swansea University

Purpose: *Scholarship on medieval women's experiences of justice has expanded over past decades. It now spans a wide range of jurisdictions across medieval Europe, as well as a range of legal actions, from petty trading complaints to cases of serious violence and abuse. This research is characterised by debates about agency, legal knowledge, the construction of gendered narratives, and women's capabilities and limitations as litigants. This round table will examine the state of the field and will explore new directions for further scholarship. Participants include those researching women's experiences of the law across several jurisdictions in medieval Britain and beyond, allowing for comparisons to be drawn across contexts.*

Participants include Cordelia Beattie (University of Edinburgh), Sara Butler (Ohio State University), Jeremy Goldberg (University of York), Michaela Antonín Malaníková (Palacký University, Olomouc), Llinos Beverley Smith (Aberystwyth University), and Deborah Youngs (Swansea University).

Session: **915** — **Stage@leeds: Stage 3**
Title: **Re-Thinking the Aristocracy in Capetian France, IV: A Round Table Discussion**
Sponsor: Society for the Study of French History (SSFH)
Organiser: Charlotte Crouch, Graduate Centre for Medieval Studies, University of Reading and Niall Ó Súilleabháin, Department of History, Trinity College Dublin
Moderator: Niall Ó Súilleabháin
Purpose: *The aristocracy has been the cornerstone of many studies of French medieval history, but have often been viewed from a regionally or chronologically limited perspective. Moreover, the aristocracy has traditionally been characterised solely by its relationships to the Capetian monarchy, either as over-mighty vassals or as loyal centralisers. This round table discussion will move towards bringing together the themes explored across the preceding sessions (aristocracy and monarchy, aristocratic identity, and control) into a more nuanced and holistic view of the French aristocracy across the longue durée of the Capetian kingdom. By allowing scholars working on different regions, themes, and chronological periods to engage in conversations, reflections, and comparisons, it hopes to begin a larger conversation about the complex development, significance, and experience of the aristocracy of Capetian France.*

Participants include Constance Brittain Bouchard (University of Akron, Ohio), Geoffrey Koziol (University of California, Berkeley), Daniel Power (Swansea University), and Alice Taylor (King's College London).

Session: **923** — **Maurice Keyworth Building: Room 1.32**
Title: **Remembering the Northern English Saints, III: A Round Table Discussion**
Sponsor: Late Medieval Devotion to Northern English Saints, Swiss National Science Foundation Project
Organiser: Christiania Whitehead, Faculté des lettres, Université de Lausanne
Moderator: Hazel Blair, Faculté des lettres, Université de Lausanne
Purpose: *Despite widespread interest in the cults of northern English saints in the early Middle Ages (pre-1200), comparatively little work has been done on the degree to which and the ways in which these early northern saints were remembered (or occasionally obscured) in the post-1300 period. This round table presents a number of case studies of northern cults: the tension between northern and national identity in late medieval textual references to St John of Beverley, the imbalance between Aelred of Rievaulx's memorialisation as saint and as spiritual guidance writer, the geographical fluidity of St Bega's cult from Hartlepool to Copeland, and a new digital model challenging traditional understandings of pilgrim access to the shrine of St Cuthbert at Durham. Jocelyn Wogan-Browne will offer a response to the round table discussion and two related panel sessions, followed by general exchanges.*

Participants include Cynthia Turner Camp (University of Georgia, Athens), John Jenkins (University of York), Denis Renevey (Université de Lausanne), and Jocelyn Wogan-Browne (Fordham University, New York).

Session: **926** **Maurice Keyworth Building: Room 1.05**

Title: **MODERN AND MEDIEVAL TRANS AND GENDERQUEER SUBJECTS: TOUCHING ACROSS TIME - A ROUND TABLE DISCUSSION**

Sponsor: Hagiography Beyond Tradition, Amsterdam University Press

Organiser: Blake Gutt, Department of French, University of Cambridge

Moderator: Alicia Spencer-Hall, School of Languages, Linguistics & Film, Queen Mary University of London

Purpose: *In her work on queer temporalities, Carolyn Dinshaw discusses 'the possibility of touching across time, collapsing time through affective contact', and suggests that 'with such queer historical touches we could form communities across time'. This round table, whose participants are contributors to the forthcoming volume* Trans and Genderqueer Subjects in Medieval Hagiography *(Amsterdam University Press, 2019), discusses the personal and political importance of trans and genderqueer readings of medieval texts. In answer to the conference theme of 'Memory', the session explores the unfortunately still controversial question of recognition and familiarity between queer subjects, past and present, and considers what it means for the community of trans and genderqueer medievalists also to be in community with the historical and literary characters their work addresses. Short presentations will be followed by discussion between participants and with the audience.*

Participants include Lee Colwill (University of Iceland, Reykjavík), Blake Gutt (University of Cambridge), and Sophie Sexon (University of Glasgow).

Session: **927** **Michael Sadler Building: Banham Theatre**

Title: **MEMORIES OF NATION, MEDIEVAL AND MODERN, V: A ROUND TABLE DISCUSSION**

Sponsor: Richard Bland College of William & Mary, Virginia

Organiser: Daniel Franke, Department of History, Richard Bland College of William & Mary, Virginia

Moderator: Daniel Franke

Purpose: *How people collectively remember their past creates or reshapes the political realities of the present, and nowhere perhaps is this better displayed than in the contentious question of 'the nation' and its origins. On the one hand, as Michelle Warren has written, countries have not hesitated to invoke the medieval European past as the 'cradle' of the 19th-century states forged through violence, colonialism, and the demarcation of bodies as included or excluded from their communities. On the other hand, only more recently has work by Susan Reynolds, Caspar Hirschi, and others argued effectively that 'nationalism' as such did indeed exist in the European Middle Ages, though not perhaps as templates of 19th-century nationalism, nor in ways that correspond to most modern theories of nationalism.*

Meanwhile, whether in the breakup of Yugoslavia in the 1990s, white nationalist terror attacks in 2011 and 2017, the Islamic State's terror attacks, the European debates over immigration and refugees after 2012, or even the re-emergence of the central European 'Visegrad Conference', the appropriation of the (global) Middle Ages in current nationalistic discourse continues unabated. Indeed, with the ever-growing invocation of the medieval past as a warrant for white nationalist fantasies of nation, and the resurgence of the struggle between nationalism and globalism in Europe, America, and elsewhere in the world, the issue of national medievalisms and medieval nationalisms needs discussion more than ever.

The final event on this thread is a round table, in which the participants are asked to draw together the threads of what has been discussed in the sessions, and to reflect broadly on modern uses of the premodern past and what this means for academics in their research, in the classroom, and in public outreach.

Participants include Barbora Davídková (Independent Scholar, Correvon), Suleiman A. Mourad (Smith College, Massachusetts), Craig M. Nakashian (Texas A&M University, Texarkana), Andrea Ruddick (University of Oxford), and Daniel Wollenberg (University of Tampa, Florida).

Session: **938** **Leeds University Union: Room 4 - Hyde Park**
Title: **THE POLONSKY FOUNDATION ENGLAND AND FRANCE PROJECT: MANUSCRIPTS FROM THE BRITISH LIBRARY AND THE BIBLIOTHÈQUE NATIONALE DE FRANCE, 700-1200 - A ROUND TABLE DISCUSSION**
Sponsor: Bibliothèque nationale de France / British Library / Polonsky Foundation
Organiser: Francesco Siri, Bibliothèque nationale de France, Paris
Moderator: Laura Albiero, Bibliothèque nationale de France, Paris
Purpose: *Thanks to the patronage of The Polonsky Foundation, the Bibliothèque nationale de France and the British Library started an unedited partnership aiming at cataloguing, digitising, and showcasing a corpus of 800 illuminated manuscripts, produced in France or England between the 8th and 12th centuries. The two libraries are working to give access to this corpus to a large public, digitising 400 manuscripts from each library collection, cataloguing them, and partially restoring them. The Bibliothèque nationale de France will create a new tri-lingual website in order to collect all selected manuscripts and to allow digital comparison among them. The British Library will create a bilingual website intended for a general audience that will feature highlights from the most important of these manuscripts and articles commissioned by leading experts in the field.*

At Leeds IMC, we would like to introduce our project, focusing on presenting the plans, the expectations, and the targeted outputs of the project; the challenges we are meeting concerning the cataloguing and the conservation aspects; and finally, the digitisation process and publicity.

Participants include Tuija Ainonen (British Library, London), Alison Ray (British Library, London), and Francesco Siri (Bibliothèque nationale de France, Paris).

Session: **943** **Maurice Keyworth Building: Room G.02**
Title: **CRUSADER MEDIEVALISM: A ROUND TABLE DISCUSSION**
Sponsor: Routledge
Organiser: Kristin Skottki, Lehrstuhl für Mittelalterliche Geschichte, Universität Bayreuth
Moderator: Kristin Skottki
Purpose: *'Crusader medievalism' - the modern use of crusading rhetoric, imagery, and ideology - is, as other sessions have demonstrated, all around us, forming a part of the contemporary social imaginary. Key scholars of the crusades and their post-medieval receptions will reflect and discuss the advantages and challenges of the concept of crusader medievalism in regards to a) crusade studies and b) modern history, culture, and politics.*

Participants include Mike Horswell (Royal Holloway, University of London), Adam Knobler (Ruhr-Universität Bochum), Jonathan Phillips (Royal Holloway, University of London), and Elizabeth Siberry (Independent Scholar, London).

Session: **945** **Leeds University Union: Room 6 - Roundhay**
Title: **MEMORY AND FIRST ENCOUNTERS: A ROUND TABLE DISCUSSION**
Organiser: Claudia Rogers, School of History, University of Leeds and Adam Simmons, Department of History, Lancaster University
Moderator: Claudia Rogers
Purpose: *Considering the IMC's 2018 thematic strand on 'Memory' - and in conjunction with the IMC's new strand of Global Medieval Studies - this round table session will explore the challenges faced by scholars studying the memory of first encounters, both in terms of local and global diaspora, between indigenous peoples and others in and across the Atlantic. Thinking about how early cultural encounters are (mis)remembered and/or (mis)represented (both in historical sources and modern scholarship), the session will ask how scholars can effectively approach areas of research involving non-European peoples and geographies. Accordingly, a particular focus of the session will be given to issues surrounding Eurocentrism, selective and manipulative memory/forgetting, and 'reading' different visions of the past.*

Participants include David Abulafia (University of Cambridge), Toby Green (King's College London), and Iona McCleery (University of Leeds).

Session: **947** **Maurice Keyworth Building: Room 1.04**
Title: **THE MILITARISATION OF EARLY MEDIEVAL SOCIETIES: A ROUND TABLE DISCUSSION**
Sponsor: Fritz Thyssen Stiftung, Köln
Organiser: Guido M. Berndt, Friedrich-Meinecke-Institut, Freie Universität Berlin and Laury Sarti, Historisches Seminar, Albert-Ludwigs-Universität Freiburg
Moderator: Stefan Esders, Friedrich-Meinecke-Institut, Freie Universität Berlin
Purpose: *Since the end of Antiquity, the societies of Western Europe underwent a continual process of militarisation. This process intensified during the early Middle Ages, and came to be a defining characteristic of the period. Militarisation can be identified by criteria like the lack of demarcation between the martial and civil spheres of the population, weapons becoming increasingly widespread, and warlike attributes, activities, and values being widely recognised and respected. Furthermore, militarisation also impacted how contemporaries perceived their own world. This round table aims to conclude a triennial research project conducted in Berlin and funded by the Fritz Thyssen Foundation by discussing the use of the concept of 'militarisation' for the study of early medieval societies and possible approaches. The speakers include specialists in Anglo-Saxon, Frankish, Lombard, Viking, and Byzantine military history.*

Participants include Ellora Bennett (Freie Universität Berlin), Guido Berndt (Freie Universität Berlin), Simon Coupland (University of Cambridge), Edward James (University College Dublin), Ryan Lavelle (University of Winchester), Philip Rance (Freie Universität Berlin), Philipp von Rummel (Deutsches Archäologisches Institut, Berlin), Laury Sarti (Albert-Ludwigs-Universitat Freiburg), and Thomas Scharff (Technische Universität Braunschweig).

Session: **949** **Maurice Keyworth Building: Room 1.09**
Title: **TOLKIEN IN CONTEXT(S): A ROUND TABLE DISCUSSION**
Sponsor: Cardiff Metropolitan University
Organiser: Dimitra Fimi, Department of Humanities, Cardiff Metropolitan University
Moderator: Dimitra Fimi
Purpose: *This round table discussion will provide a forum to explore different approaches to Tolkien's work via various frameworks and contexts, from Tolkien's medieval scholarship and his social/historical/intellectual milieu, to worldbuilding, science, linguistics, and theory.*

Participants include Yvette Kisor (Ramapo College of New Jersey), Kristine Larsen (Central Connecticut State University), Irina Metzler (Swansea University), Gergely Nagy (Independent Scholar, Budapest), and Sara L. Uckelman (Durham University).

Session: **953** **Maurice Keyworth Building: Room 1.03**
Title: **THE ACADEMIC WORK-LIFE IMBALANCE: TIPS AND TECHNIQUES FOR MANAGING GRADUATE SCHOOL AND YOUR PERSONAL LIFE - A ROUND TABLE DISCUSSION**
Sponsor: Medieval Academy of America Graduate Student Council
Organiser: Courtney Krolikoski, Department of History & Classical Studies, McGill University, Québec
Moderator: Lucy Christine Barnhouse, Department of English / Department of History, College of Wooster, Ohio
Purpose: *As the MAA-GSC's mission is to voice the concerns of young scholars, this round table discussion will bring together three or more recent PhDs and established academics to discuss the work/life imbalance that arises from the competing, often demanding, commitments of graduate school. We will call upon participants to discuss the importance of balance in completing their doctoral studies and how they were able to do so successfully while being mindful of their wellbeing. We hope that such a panel will advance the growing discussion around mental health and the work/life imbalance that persists within academia, and, in turn, give graduate students the tools and resources to complete their degree and excel in their field and future careers.*

Participants include Anna Peterson (Independent Scholar, Valladolid), Abigail G. Robertson (University of New Mexico, Albuquerque), and Faith Wallis (McGill University, Québec).

Session: **954** **Maurice Keyworth Building: Room 1.33**

Title: **RETHINKING REFORM: NEW INTERPRETATIONS OF ECCLESIASTICAL REFORM, 900-1150 - A ROUND TABLE DISCUSSION**

Sponsor: University of East Anglia

Organiser: Julia Steuart Barrow, Institute for Medieval Studies, University of Leeds

Moderator: Steven Vanderputten, Vakgroep Geschiedenis, Universiteit Gent

Purpose: *How should we conceptualise the programme of institutional change which swept the western church 900-1150? The now-universal label 'reform' is essentially a modern creation going back to c. 1800, and its frequent use in modern writings contrasts with the sparse occurrence of* reformare *in sources 900-1150. This round table will introduce findings from the Leverhulme-funded 'Rethinking Reform' international network, which has so far investigated the vocabulary and narratives of reform and which is about to explore modern historical writing about reform in the western church in the Middle Ages. We invite challenges and responses.*

Participants include Julia Steuart Barrow (University of Leeds), Katy Cubitt (University of East Anglia), Kathleen Cushing (Keele University), Anne-Marie Helvétius (Université Paris VIII, Vincennes-Saint-Denis) and Ludger Körntgen (Johannes Gutenberg-Universität Mainz).

Tuesday 03 July 2018

* * * * *

Art of the Sofer: Jewish Calligraphy Workshop

Directed by
Joseph Isaac Lifshitz

Clothworkers Building South: Room G.11B
19.00-20.30

Price: £7.50

Were all the skies parchment,
And all the reeds pens,
And all the oceans ink,
And all who dwell on earth scribes,
God's grandeur could not be told.

Akdamut Millan, Rabbi Meir Ben Isaac Nehorai (died c. 1095)

'Sofer' is the Hebrew word for a scribe who can copy out the Torah, tefillin, and mezuzot, as well as other religious writings according to the laws of 'sofrut'. If these laws are not followed, the text is not deemed to be valid. A sofer would be also responsible for preparing the *kulmus* (quill), *klaf* (parchment), and *d'yo* (ink) according to traditional methods.

In this workshop, Joseph Isaac Lifshitz will demonstrate the techniques of the medieval sofer. Participants will also learn to write medieval Hebrew characters with a quill on parchment. All materials will be provided.

Joseph Isaac Lifshitz is an expert on Jewish philosophy and history, with an emphasis on the philosophy of Ashkenaz in the high Middle Ages. He received his rabbinical ordination from Rabbis Yitzhak Kulitz and David Nesher. He earned his PhD in Jewish Thought from Tel Aviv University, and holds an MA in Jewish history from Touro College. Author of numerous books, most recently *Judaism, Law & The Free Market* (Acton, 2012), he has written both scholarly and popular articles on subjects related to Judaism and economics. He is also a qualified Hebrew scribe.

This workshop can only accommodate a limited number of participants. Early booking is recommended.

* * * * *

* * * * *

RECEPTION AT UNIVERSITY HOUSE

HOSTED BY
PRATO CONSORTIUM FOR MEDIEVAL & RENAISSANCE STUDIES, MONASH UNIVERSITY

UNIVERSITY HOUSE: BEECHGROVE ROOM
20.00-21.00

The Prato Consortium for Medieval & Renaissance Studies (PCMRS) and the Centre for Medieval & Renaissance Studies at Monash University (CMRS) invites and welcomes all delegates to the IMC to a reception. Wine and canapes will be served and attendees will have an opportunity to learn more about the PCMRS, meet individuals from member institutions, and engage first-hand with the 'Bodies in the City, 1100-1800' research project and its Routledge publication series. Delegates will be able to meet the speakers and engage in discussion about themes and ideas emerging from PCMRS/CMRS sponsored sessions.

* * * * *

RECEPTION AT MICHAEL SADLER BUILDING

HOSTED BY
ST ANDREWS INSTITUTE OF MEDIAEVAL STUDIES

MICHAEL SADLER BUILDING: ROOM LG.19
20.00-22.00

All delegates are warmly invited to join the St Andrews Institute of Mediaeval Studies (SAIMS) for a glass of wine. SAIMS embraces all disciplines and fields, and looks forward to welcoming friends new and old! We will also announce the winner of the 2018 SAIMS/TMJ prize, awarded in collaboration with *The Mediaeval Journal*.

* * * * *

RECEPTION AT MICHAEL SADLER BUILDING

HOSTED BY
MEDIÄVISTENVERBAND

MICHAEL SADLER BUILDING: ROOM LG.10
20.15-21.15

The Association of Medievalists (Mediävistenverband) was founded in 1983 to provide a forum for all disciplines concerned with the Middle Ages. Today it is the largest association of medievalists in Europe, with over 1100 members from different countries representing a spectrum of subjects ranging from archaeology to theology, history, and philologies. Medievalists from Germany and German-speaking countries warmly invite you to enjoy a glass of wine, hoping to strengthen ties among medievalists from all disciplines and countries. For more information please check www.mediaevistenverband.de.

* * * * *

* * * * *

DETOUR TO PARADISE: OSWALD VON WOLKENSTEIN AND THE COUNCIL OF CONSTANCE (1414-1418)

PERFORMED AND STAGED BY
SILVAN WAGNER

STAGE@LEEDS: STAGE 2
20.30-21.30

PRICE: £12.00

Oswald von Wolkenstein (1376/77-1445), the travelling knight and courtly singer, paid several visits to Constance, the city of the famous Council. In his poetry, he praised the city as 'wünnikliches paradis'. Indeed, one area of the city, the site of a former monastery for Poor Clares, was called Paradies (literally 'paradise').

In 1415, Oswald visited Constance before joining the crusading army gathered by King John I in Portugal for the 'Reconquista' of Ceuta in North Africa. In contrast to the glories of Constance, this expedition, like so many of the other journeys that he had undertaken since his early years, greeted him with hardship and pain rather than paradisiacal pleasure. Recalling his many travels in his poetry, Oswald frequently invokes the sufferings he had to endure in other parts of the world from Europe to Africa and further east to Asia. From this perspective, the city of Constance in Germany, not far from Oswald's home county Tyrol, offers a brief detour to Paradise.

Silvan Wagner, who has a PhD in medieval German literature from the University of Bayreuth, has gained a rich experience as a professional musician directing and producing multimedia dramas featuring the texts and illustrations of medieval love poetry and courtly epics. His productions bring together the musical principles of historically informed performance with acting medieval narrative literature, making him the ideal person to perform the music and poetry of Oswald von Wolkenstein. Accompanying himself with gittern and drum, he will bring the cosmopolitan knight to life in a programme that features the Council of Constance, its city, and its world in songs full of realistic detail, sparkling with wit, irony, and humor.

The International Medieval Congress and the Oswald von Wolkenstein-Gesellschaft are proud to sponsor this unique musical event, creating new aesthetic means of bringing medieval poetry to life.

* * * * *

Today's Excursions
York Minster 13.30-19.00
See p. 455 for full details.

Session: **1001** **Michael Sadler Building: Room LG.17**
Title: **THE ANGLO-SAXON POETIC TRADITION, I**
Sponsor: A Consolidated Library of Anglo-Saxon Poetry
Organiser: Colleen Curran, Faculty of English Literature & Language, University of Oxford
Moderator: Robert Gallagher, St Cross College, University of Oxford
Paper 1001-a: **Remembering the Canticles in Old English Verse** (Language: English)
Emily V. Thornbury, Department of English, University of California, Berkeley
Paper 1001-b: **Inscribing the Saints at York: Alcuin and the Roman Epigraphic Tradition** (Language: English)
Christopher Scheirer, Medieval Institute, University of Notre Dame, Indiana
Paper 1001-c: **Beyond the Bible: Anglo-Saxon Influence on the Old English *Judith*** (Language: English)
Andy Orchard, Pembroke College, University of Oxford

Session: **1002** **Baines Wing: Room 1.13**
Title: **REMEMBERING THE 'OTHER' VIRTUES: THE IMPORTANCE OF NON-CARDINAL AND NON-THEOLOGICAL VIRTUES IN MEDIEVAL LIFE**
Organiser: Claire Macht, Faculty of History, University of Oxford
Moderator: Hannah Skoda, St John's College, University of Oxford
Paper 1002-a: **Meekness as the 'Mother' of All Virtues** (Language: English)
Merridee Lee Bailey, Faculty of History, University of Oxford
Paper 1002-b: **Peacemaking: Excelling as an Abbot in Medieval England** (Language: English)
Claire Macht
Paper 1002-c: **Domestication as a Virtue in the Human-Animal Relation** (Language: English)
Lesley MacGregor, Oriel College, University of Oxford

Session: **1003** **Baines Wing: Room 2.16**
Title: **MOVING BYZANTIUM, I: METHODS, TOOLS, AND CONCEPTS ACROSS DISCIPLINES**
Sponsor: Moving Byzantium: Mobility, Microstructures & Personal Agency, Österreichische Akademie der Wissenschaften, Universität Wien / FWF Wittgenstein-Prize Project
Organiser: Claudia Rapp, Institut für Byzantinistik & Neogräzistik, Universität Wien / Österreichische Akademie der Wissenschaften, Wien
Moderator: Claudia Rapp
Paper 1003-a: **Mapping Byzantine Mobility: Digital Tools and Analytical Concepts** (Language: English)
Johannes Preiser-Kapeller, Institut für Mittelalterforschung, Abteilung Byzanzforschung, Österreichische Akademie der Wissenschaften, Wien
Paper 1003-b: **Digital Mobility: Byzantine Prosopography, Networks, and Space** (Language: English)
Ekaterini Mitsiou, Institut für Byzantinistik & Neogräzistik, Universität Wien
Paper 1003-c: **Pottery Traditions 'beyond' Byzantium: Production and Supply in Rural and Urban Contexts within the Frankish Duchy of Athens and Thebes** (Language: English)
Florence Liard, Fitch Laboratory, British School at Athens
Paper 1003-d: **Rethinking Sites of Production for Early Byzantine Visual Culture** (Language: English)
Elizabeth Bolman, Department of Art History & Art, Case Western Reserve University, Ohio

---

Session: **1004** **Fine Art Building: SR G.04**
Title: **NEW DIRECTIONS IN CRUSADE STUDIES, I**
Sponsor: Center for Medieval & Renaissance Studies, Saint Louis University, Missouri / Royal Holloway, University of London
Organiser: Jonathan Phillips, Department of History, Royal Holloway, University of London
Moderator: Thomas F. Madden, Center for Medieval & Renaissance Studies, Saint Louis University, Missouri
Paper 1004-a: **'Whether we live or whether we die': Battle Rhetoric in Narratives of the Third Crusade** (Language: English)
Connor Wilson, Department of History, Royal Holloway, University of London
Paper 1004-b: **The Redemption of Crusaders' Vows in England** (Language: English)
Daniel Edwards, Department of History, Royal Holloway, University of London
Paper 1004-c: ***Et hostes superare*: The Remembrance of Crusading in the Liturgies of Medieval Iberia** (Language: English)
Edward Holt, Department of History, Saint Louis University, Missouri

Session: **1005** **Michael Sadler Building: Room LG.16**
Title: **TOWARDS MARKET INTEGRATION: CENTRAL CONCEPTS IN PRE-MODERN ECONOMIC HISTORY**
Organiser: Emil Skaarup, Saxo-Instituttet, Københavns Universitet
Moderator: Angela Huang, Forschungsstelle für die Geschichte der Hanse und des Ostseeraums, Lübeck
Paper 1005-a: **Prospect Theory and Subsistence Economies** (Language: English)
Emil Skaarup
Paper 1005-b: **Different Conceptions of the Meaning of the Word 'Capitalism' in Economic History** (Language: English)
Nicolai Bagger, Saxo-Instituttet, Københavns Universitet
Paper 1005-c: **Specialisation and Modes of Production in Medieval Northern Europe: A Study of Beer Production** (Language: English)
Johanne Steensgaard, Saxo-Instituttet, Københavns Universitet

Session: **1006** **Parkinson Building: Room 1.16**
Title: **ANGLO-SAXON RIDDLES, III: SELVES AND THINGS**
Sponsor: The Riddle Ages: An Anglo-Saxon Riddle Blog
Organiser: Megan Cavell, Department of English Literature, University of Birmingham and Jennifer Neville, Department of English, Royal Holloway, University of London
Moderator: Megan Cavell
Paper 1006-a: **Beating the Bounds of the Riddle Creature** (Language: English)
Amy Clark, English Department, University of California, Berkeley
Paper 1006-b: **Manifestations of Alterity in the Exeter Book Riddles** (Language: English)
Karin E. Olsen, Afdeling Engelse Taal en Cultuur, Rijksuniversiteit Groningen
Paper 1006-c: **Translating the Nonhuman: Anglo-Saxon 'Things' across Medieval and Modern Verse** (Language: English)
James Antonio Paz, School of Arts, Languages & Cultures, University of Manchester

Session: **1007** **Fine Art Building: Studio Ground Floor**
Title: **THE 'CONTI' POPES IN ACTION**
Organiser: IMC Programming Committee
Moderator: Brenda M. Bolton, University of London
Paper 1007-a: **The Pope and the King: Innocent III's Rewriting of Portuguese History during the Reign of Sancho I (1185-1211)** (Language: English)
Francesco Renzi, Centro de Investigação Transdisciplinar 'Cultura, Espaço e Memória' (CITCEM), Universidade do Porto
Paper 1007-b: **The Pope and the University at Paris: Gregory IX and the Condemnation of 1241-1244** (Language: English)
Deborah Grice, Faculty of History, University of Oxford
Paper 1007-c: **Pope Alexander IV, King Henry III, and the Treaty of Paris (1258-1259): Papal Mediation in 13th-Century Europe** (Language: English)
Philippa Mesiano, Centre for Medieval & Early Modern Studies, University of Kent

Session: **1008** **Maurice Keyworth Building: Room 1.04**
Title: **SCHOLASTIC MEDICINE**
Organiser: IMC Programming Committee
Moderator: Elma Brenner, Wellcome Library, London
Paper 1008-a: **Old Age and the Radical Moisture: The Rise and Fall of Scholastic Bio-Gerontology** (Language: English)
Chris Gilleard, Faculty of Brain Sciences, University College London
Paper 1008-b: **'Propter quam causam rememoramur rem absentem quae non est praesens, potius quam passionem praesentes?': The Scientific Account of Memory in Albertus Magnus** (Language: English)
Evelina Miteva, Philosophisches Seminar, Universität zu Köln
Paper 1008-c: **Source Memory and Authoritative Citations** (Language: English)
Elise Williams, Faculty of the History & Philosophy of Science, University of Cambridge

Session: **1009** **Baines Wing: Room 2.13**
Title: **HERESY, CRIME, AND FORGOTTEN WOMEN**
Organiser: IMC Programming Committee
Moderator: Laura Marie Grimes, Sophia Catholic Communion, San Jose
Paper 1009-a: **1600 Years a Heretic: Assessing the Impact of Pelagius** (Language: English)
Ali Bonner, Department of Anglo-Saxon, Norse & Celtic, University of Cambridge
Paper 1009-b: **A Comparative Study of Mother Crime in High Society in the Middle Ages** (Language: English)
Salah Hadi Mustafa Al-Haideri, Department of History, University of Soran, Iraq
Paper 1009-c: **Remembering Phoebe in the 12th Century: The Forgotten Deacon in Paul's Letter to Romans** (Language: English)
Anne Clark, Department of Religion, University of Vermont

Session: **1010** **Baines Wing: Room 1.16**
Title: **THE AFTERLIFE OF ANTIQUE PAGAN AND CHRISTIAN RELIGION IN ASIA MINOR AND BEYOND DURING THE BYZANTINE PERIOD**
Organiser: IMC Programming Committee
Moderator: Robin Whelan, Department of History, University of Liverpool
Paper 1010-a: **Ganymede in Phrygia: The Readaptation of a Myth between Identity-Related Memory and Eschatological Hopes** (Language: English)
Elisa Nuria Merisio, Dipartimento di Scienze dell'Antichità, Università degli Studi di Roma 'La Sapienza'
Paper 1010-b: **Remembering the Past?: Amphitrite in Byzantine Iconography of the Last Judgement - Change or Continuity of the Ancient Motif?** (Language: English)
Aleksandra Krauze-Kołodziej, Faculty of Humanities, John Paul II Catholic University, Lublin
Paper 1010-c: **'For the glory of the faithful': The *Mandylion* of Edessa as a Remembrance of War** (Language: English)
Mary Grace DuPree, Department of History, Emory University

Session: **1011** **Baines Wing: Room 1.15**
Title: **THE CENTRE AND THE PERIPHERY: ASPECTS OF CORRELATION AND CO-DEPENDENCY OF RELIGIOUS, POLITICAL, AND CULTURAL MATTERS, I**
Sponsor: Ben-Gurion University of the Negev, Beer-Sheva
Organiser: Daniel Varga, Israel Antiquities Authority, Omer
Moderator: Dimitri Tarat, Department of History, Ben-Gurion University of the Negev, Beer-Sheva
Paper 1011-a: **Beit Naqquba: A Byzantine Site along the Ancient Road between Jerusalem and Jaffa** (Language: English)
Annette Landes-Nagar, Israel Antiquities Authority, Jerusalem
Paper 1011-b: **A Nestorian Monastery in Hura and Its Regional Context** (Language: English)
Daniel Varga
Paper 1011-c: **'Surviving the flood': Traces of Monastic Communities in the Palestina III Salutaris Province in the Late Byzantine and Early Islamic (Umayyad) Periods** (Language: English)
Tali Erickson, Israel Antiquities Authority, Omer

Session: **1012** **University House: Little Woodhouse Room**
Title: **MUSIC AND LITURGY IN THE EARLY MIDDLE AGES**
Organiser: IMC Programming Committee
Moderator: Henry Parkes, Institute of Sacred Music, Yale University
Paper 1012-a: **Late Antique Consular Diptychs as Technologies of Medieval Memory** (Language: English)
Nicole Pulichene, Department of History of Art & Architecture, Harvard University
Paper 1012-b: ***Ordo Romanus Primus*: The Origins and Early History of the Text** (Language: English)
Peter Jeffery, Department of Music & Sacred Music, University of Notre Dame, Indiana
Paper 1012-c: **Shaping a Memory for the Lost Latin *Cherubikon*** (Language: English)
Geert Maessen, Independent Scholar, Amstelveen
Paper 1012-d: **The Designed Past: Layers of Time and Their Function in the Carolingian *Libri memoriales*** (Language: English)
Eva-Maria Butz, Historisches Institut, Technische Universität Dortmund

Session: **1013** **University House: Beechgrove Room**
Title: **WOMEN AND SURVEILLANCE IN MEDIEVALIST TELEVISION AND CINEMA**
Organiser: Sabina Rahman, Department of English, Macquarie University, Sydney
Moderator: Usha Vishnuvajjala, Department of Literature, American University, Washington DC
Paper 1013-a: **Surveillance and the 'Other'** (Language: English)
Sabina Rahman
Paper 1013-b: **The Little Hours: Surveillance and Sexual Libertarianism in Medievalist Farce** (Language: English)
Louise D'Arcens, Department of English, Macquarie University, Sydney
Paper 1013-c: **Rape and Pillage: Surveillance, Sexual Violence, and Historical Revision in *Vikings*** (Language: English)
Kate Lister, Department of English, Leeds Trinity University

Session: **1014** **Charles Thackrah Building: 1.01**
Title: **ROYAL MARRIAGES, I: ROYAL MARRIAGES IN PERSPECTIVE - PERMANENCIES AND CHANGES THROUGH TIME AND SPACE**
Organiser: Manuela Santos Silva, Departamento de História, Universidade de Lisboa
Moderator: Ana Maria S. A. Rodrigues, Centro de História, Universidade de Lisboa
Paper 1014-a: **Monarchy and Marriage: A Glance at the Iberian Legislation on the Concepts of Monarchy, Royal Marriage, and Royal Family** (Language: English)
Manuela Santos Silva
Paper 1014-b: **A Trial of Affective Piety in *The Wedding of Sir Gawain and Dame Ragnelle*** (Language: English)
Shelby Preston, Department of English, University of Rochester, New York
Paper 1014-c: **The Constant and the Changed in the Traditions of Royal Marriage in Morocco: The Alawi Dynasty, 1672-Present** (Language: English)
Fatima Rhorchi, Department of History, Moulay Ismail University, Morocco

Session: **1015** **Michael Sadler Building: Room LG.19**
Title: **MATERIALITY AND RELIGIOUS PRACTICE IN MEDIEVAL DENMARK**
Organiser: Sarah Croix, Afdeling for Arkaeologi og Kulturarvsstudier, Aarhus Universitet
Moderator: Bertil Nilsson, Institutionen för litteratur, idéhistoria och religion, Göteborgs Universitet
Paper 1015-a: **Materiality of Memory: The Use and Significance of Wax in Late Medieval Devotion** (Language: English)
Laura Kathrine Skinnebach, Institut for Kunsthistorie, Aarhus Universitet
Paper 1015-b: **Outer Markers and Inner Meanings: Personal Objects and Religious Materiality** (Language: English)
Mette Højmark Søvsø, Department of Collections, Sydvestjyske Museer, Ribe
Paper 1015-c: **Miraculous Materiality in Medieval Denmark** (Language: English)
Mads Vedel Heilskov, Centre for Scandinavian Studies, University of Aberdeen
Paper 1015-d: **Materiality in Medieval Burials** (Language: English)
Jakob Tue Christensen, Department of Cultural Heritage & Archaelogy, Odense Bys Museer, Denmark

Session: **1016** **Michael Sadler Building: Rupert Beckett Theatre**
Title: **14TH-CENTURY ENGLAND, I: LATE MEDIEVAL MILITARY SERVICE - THEORY AND PRACTICE**
Sponsor: Society for 14th Century Studies
Organiser: David Green, Centre for British Studies, Harlaxton College, University of Evansville
Moderator: Andy King, Department of History, University of Southampton
Paper 1016-a: **The Rise and Decline of Military Pardons in 14th-Century England** (Language: English)
Quentin Verreycken, Centre d'histoire du droit et de la justice (CHDJ), Université catholique de Louvain, Louvain-la-Neuve / Centre de recherches en histoire du droit et des institutions (CRHiDI), Université Saint-Louis, Bruxelles
Paper 1016-b: **'It's not what you have but the way that you use it': The Arms, Armour, and Ordnance of Lionel of Clarence in Ireland, 1361-1369** (Language: English)
Malcolm Mercer, Royal Armouries, London
Paper 1016-c: **Chivalry and Nobility in the Works of John Gower** (Language: English)
David Green

Session: **1017** **Social Sciences Building: Room 10.05**
Title: **EARLY MEDIEVAL MILAN: A METROPOLIS AND ITS HINTERLAND**
Sponsor: University of Nottingham
Organiser: Michele Baitieri, Department of History, University of Nottingham
Moderator: Roberta Cimino, Department of History, University of Nottingham
Paper 1017-a: **Early Medieval Milan: Micro-Exchanges and the Formation of a Hinterland** (Language: English)
Ross Balzaretti, Institute for Medieval Research, University of Nottingham
Paper 1017-b: **Local Priests in the Ecclesiastical Province of Milan, 9th and 10th Centuries** (Language: English)
Michele Baitieri
Paper 1017-c: **Popular Politics and Market Economies in the Medieval Metropolis: Milan and Rome in the 11th Century** (Language: English)
James Norrie, Dipartimento di Scienze Storiche, Geografiche e dell'Antichità, Università degli Studi di Padova / Humanities Research Programme, British School at Rome

Session: **1018** **Michael Sadler Building: Banham Theatre**
Title: **TRANSFORMATIONS OF POWER: SESSIONS IN HONOUR OF PAUL FOURACRE, II - THE POWER OF SAINTS**
Sponsor: Centre for Medieval & Early Modern Studies, University of Manchester
Organiser: Katherine Fliegel, School of Arts, Languages & Cultures, University of Manchester, Ryan T. Goodman, Department of History, University of Manchester and Sihong Lin, Department of History, University of Manchester
Moderator: Sarah M. Hamilton, Department of History, University of Exeter
Paper 1018-a: **Hagiography and Memory: Revisiting the *Vita Rigoberti*** (Language: English)
Edward Roberts, School of History, University of Kent
Paper 1018-b: **The Material Inheritance of Martin** (Language: English)
Julia M. H. Smith, Faculty of History, University of Oxford
Paper 1018-c: **St Wilfrid, Archbishop Theodore, and the Council of London** (Language: English)
Katy Cubitt, School of History, University of East Anglia

Session: **1019** **Maurice Keyworth Building: Room 1.09**
Title: **CITIES OF READERS, I: SHARED DEVOTIONAL CULTURE**
Sponsor: NWO Project 'Cities of Readers', Rijksuniversiteit Groningen
Organiser: Johanneke Uphoff, Afdeling Geschiedenis, Rijksuniversiteit Groningen
Moderator: Pieter Boonstra, Afdeling Geschiedenis, Rijksuniversiteit Groningen
Paper 1019-a: **About 'Amor Dei': Texts and Experiences across Laity and Religious in Late Medieval Italy, 14th and 15th Centuries** (Language: English)
Isabella Gagliardi, Dipartimento di Storia, Archeologia, Geografia, Arte, Spettacolo, Università degli Studi di Firenze
Paper 1019-b: **Belief in Business: The Role of Gerard Leeu's (active 1477-1492) Incunabula in the Spirituality of the Late Medieval Low Countries** (Language: English)
Anna Dlabačová, Centre for the Arts in Society, Universiteit Leiden
Paper 1019-c: **Bequeathing Books: Book Donation and Shared Devotional Culture between Lay and Religious in the Late Medieval Low Countries** (Language: English)
Johanneke Uphoff

Session: **1020** **Charles Thackrah Building: 1.02**
Title: **REMEMBERING TROY IN THE MIDDLE AGES, I: ORIGIN STORIES AND IDENTITY FORMATION**
Organiser: Sabine Heidi Walther, Abteilung für Skandinavische Sprachen und Literaturen, Rheinische Friedrich-Wilhelms-Universität Bonn and N. Kıvılcım Yavuz, Den Arnamagnæanske Samling, Københavns Universitet
Moderator: Ralph Mathisen, Department of History, University of Illinois, Urbana-Champaign
Paper 1020-a: **Invented Memories: Imagining Trojan Nations** (Language: English)
Thomas J. MacMaster, Department of History, Morehouse College, Georgia / School of History, Classics & Archaeology, University of Edinburgh

Paper 1020-b: **Heroes and Villains: Memories of Troy in Medieval Britain** (Language: English)
Helen Fulton, Department of English, University of Bristol
Paper 1020-c: **Who Is Brutus in Late Medieval England?** (Language: English)
Julia Marvin, Program of Liberal Studies, University of Notre Dame, Indiana

Session: **1021** **Social Sciences Building: Room 10.06**
Title: **MEMORY IN CHRÉTIEN DE TROYES**
Organiser: IMC Programming Committee
Moderator: Martin Šorm, Centre for Medieval Studies / Institute of Philosophy, Czech Academy of Sciences, Praha / Department of Czech History, Univerzita Karlova, Praha
Paper 1021-a: **Losing Sight of Guinevere: Memory and Its Relationship to the Senses of Sight and Touch in Chrétien de Troyes's *The Knight and the Cart*** (Language: English)
Rosann Gage, Department of English, Kent State University, Ohio
Paper 1021-b: **Grail Rider: The Genealogy of Memory in Chrétien's *Perceval*** (Language: English)
Geneviève Young, Department of French & Italian, University of Minnesota, Twin Cities
Paper 1021-c: **Memory Loss and the Circular Trajectory of the Hero in Chretien de Troyes's *Yvain*** (Language: English)
Rebecca Ellen Newby, School of English, Communication & Philosophy, Cardiff University / School of Humanities, University of Bristol
Paper 1021-d: **Identity, Memory, and the Cart** (Language: English)
Michael C. Sloan, Department of Classical Languages, Wake Forest University, North Carolina

Session: **1022** **Baines Wing: Room 1.14**
Title: **THOSE FIRST LESSONS: REMEMBERING SCHOOLING AND EDUCATION IN THE MIDDLE AGES**
Organiser: Sarah Bridget Lynch, Department of History, Angelo State University, Texas
Moderator: Sarah Bridget Lynch
Paper 1022-a: **In the Lines and between the Lines of the *civita sapientiarum*: Memory in the Relationship between Masters and Disciples in the Pedagogy of the 11th and 12th Centuries** (Language: English)
Carlile Lanzieri Júnior, Departamento de História, Universidade Federal de Mato Grosso, Brazil
Paper 1022-b: **Alphabets and Memory in Early Medieval Schoolbooks** (Language: English)
Elizabeth P. Archibald, Department of History, University of Pittsburgh
Paper 1022-c: **Schooling Carthage: Remembering Teacher and School in the Vandal City** (Language: English)
Mark Lewis Tizzoni, Department of History, Angelo State University, Texas
Paper 1022-d: **Erasmus and His Education** (Language: English)
Ad Tervoort, Afdeling Kunst en Cultuur, Geschiedenis, Oudheid, Vrije Universiteit Amsterdam

Session: **1023** **Maurice Keyworth Building: Room 1.31**
Title: **REMEMBERING THE SAINTS, I: THE FORMATION AND REVISION OF MEMORY**
Sponsor: Cult of Saints Project, University of Oxford
Organiser: Bryan Ward-Perkins, Faculty of History, University of Oxford
Moderator: Ian N. Wood, School of History, University of Leeds
Paper 1023-a: **Holy Time in a Holy Place: Annual Miracles at the Feasts of Saints in Late Antiquity** (Language: English)
Robert Wiśniewski, Instytut Historyczny, Uniwersytet Warszawski
Paper 1023-b: **Paradigm, Platonism, and Memory in the Cult of the Saints, c. 500-1100** (Language: English)
David Defries, Department of History, Kansas State University
Paper 1023-c: **Adapting Memory in Byzantine Hagiography** (Language: English)
Anne P. Alwis, Department of Classical & Archaeological Studies, University of Kent

Session: **1024** **Charles Thackrah Building: 1.04**
Title: **NAMES AS MEMORIALS, I: PLACE-NAMES AND GENEALOGIES**
Sponsor: Dictionary of Medieval Names from European Sources
Organiser: Sara L. Uckelman, Institute of Medieval & Early Modern Studies, Durham University
Moderator: Sara L. Uckelman
Paper 1024-a: **Remembering Past Events: Commemoration and Invention in Scottish Place-Names** (Language: English)
Sofia Evemalm, School of Humanities, University of Glasgow
Paper 1024-b: **Remembering the Deviant Dead: The Place of the Outcast in Medieval England** (Language: English)
Rebecca Gregory, School of Critical Studies, University of Glasgow
Paper 1024-c: **Memory and Truth in the Construction of the Early Medieval Anglo-Saxon and Irish Genealogies** (Language: English)
Catherine Maria Bromhead, Department of History, Trinity College Dublin

Session: **1025** **Maurice Keyworth Building: Room 1.06**

Title: **MEMORY, IMAGES, AND MAGIC IN 15TH-CENTURY ART AND HUMANISTIC THOUGHT**

Sponsor: Images of Learned Magic - Formation, Continuity & Transmutations Project (IMAFOR), University of Jyväskylä

Organiser: Lauri Ockenström, Department of Music, Art & Culture Studies, University of Jyväskylä

Moderator: Katja Fält, Department of Music, Art & Culture Studies, University of Jyväskylä

Paper 1025-a: **Muses, Virtues, and Arts: The Construction of Pictorial Cycles for Divine Contemplation and Education in 15th-Century Italy** (Language: English)
Mauricio Oviedo Salazar, Independent Scholar, Maastricht

Paper 1025-b: **Humanism and the Revivals of Medieval Image Magic and Pagan Antiquity at the End of the 15th Century** (Language: English)
Lauri Ockenström

Paper 1025-c: **Mercurial Talismans: Magic and Memory in Marsilio Ficino's *De Vita*** (Language: English)
Susanne Kathrin Beiweis, Department of Philosophy (Zhuhai), Sun Yat-sen University, China

---

Session: **1026** **University House: Great Woodhouse Room**

Title: **NORMAN WOMEN RULERS, I: MEMORY, MYTH, AND DAMNATION**

Sponsor: Institute for Medieval Studies, University of Leeds

Organiser: Francesca Petrizzo, Institute for Medieval Studies, University of Leeds

Moderator: Rachael Gillibrand, Institute for Medieval Studies, University of Leeds

Paper 1026-a: **Emma of Normandy and Her Legacy: The *Encomium Emmae Reginae* and the Anglo-Saxon Chronicles, 1035-1044** (Language: English)
Florence Scott, Institute for Medieval Studies, University of Leeds

Paper 1026-b: **William of Tyre and the Problem of the Antiochene Princesses** (Language: English)
Andrew David Buck, School of History, Queen Mary University of London

Paper 1026-c: **Memories of Norman Sicily in 17th-Century Palermo: The Cult of Santa Rosalia in Its Historical Context** (Language: English)
Dawn Marie Hayes, Department of History, Montclair State University, New Jersey

Session: **1027** **Social Sciences Building: Room 10.07**
Title: **Place and Memory: The St Thomas Way Project and Medieval Pilgrimage Today**
Sponsor: Centre for Medieval & Renaissance Culture, University of Southampton
Organiser: Catherine A. M. Clarke, Faculty of Humanities, University of Southampton
Moderator: Marianne O'Doherty, Department of English / Centre for Medieval & Renaissance Culture, University of Southampton
Paper 1027-a: **Walking into Memory: The Progress of the St Thomas Way** (Language: English)
Chloë McKenzie, Department of History, University of Southampton
Paper 1027-b: **Re-Thinking Place and Time: Folded Temporalities and the St Thomas Way** (Language: English)
Catherine A. M. Clarke
Paper 1027-c: **Archives as Commemoration / Pilgrimage as Interpretation: Hereford Cathedral, the St Thomas Way Project, and Cantilupe 2020** (Language: English)
Bethany J. Hamblen, Library & Archives, Hereford Cathedral
Paper 1027-d: **Changing Roles of Pilgrimage: Retreating, Remembering, Re-Enacting** (Language: English)
Jonathan Wooding, School of Literature, Art & Media, University of Sydney

Session: **1028** **Baines Wing: Room G.37**
Title: **Remembering the Other in Islamic History**
Organiser: IMC Programming Committee
Moderator: Fozia Bora, School of Languages, Cultures & Societies - Arabic, Islamic & Middle Eastern Studies, University of Leeds
Paper 1028-a: **Arabic Voices and the Memory of the Byzantine Expansion in the East: Evidence of Military Effectiveness in the 10th Century** (Language: English)
Georgios Theotokis, Department of Italian Language & Literature, National & Kapodistrian University of Athens
Paper 1028-b: **Memorizing *Zindiqs*: The Making of Biographies of Some Poets** (Language: English)
Yuko Tanaka, School of Oriental & African Studies, University of London
Paper 1028-c: **The Elite Islamic Discourse in the Construction of the 'Other' during the Mamluk-Ilkhanid Mongol War, 13th-14th Century** (Language: English)
Mehdi Berriah, Histoire de l'islam médiéval, Orient et Méditerranée (UMR 8167), Université Paris I - Panthéon-Sorbonne / UFR de Langues Étrangères, Université Grenoble-Alpes / L'Institut de Recherche Stratégique de l'École Militaire (IRSEM), Paris

Session: **1029** **Charles Thackrah Building: 1.03**
Title: ***THE MEDITATIONES VITAE CHRISTI* AND VISUAL CONSTRUCTIONS OF MEMORY, I**
Organiser: Renana Bartal, Department of Art History, Tel Aviv University and Holly Flora, School of Liberal Arts, Tulane University, Louisiana
Moderator: Holly Flora
Paper 1029-a: **San Gimignano as a Context for the Meditations: Fra Jacopo in the Archives** (Language: English)
Donal Cooper, Department of History of Art, University of Cambridge
Paper 1029-b: **Remembering Birth and Death: Mary under the Cross in an Illuminated *Meditationes*, Oxford, Corpus Christi College, MS 410** (Language: English)
Renana Bartal
Paper 1029-c: **Textual and Visual Meditations on the Passion: The Frescoes of the Santa Maria Donnaregina of Naples and the Written Evidence** (Language: English)
Dávid Falvay, Department of Italian Studies, Eötvös Loránd University, Budapest

Session: **1030** **Social Sciences Building: Room 10.09**
Title: **TEXTS AND ARTEFACTS IN EARLY CHRISTIAN BRITAIN AND IRELAND**
Organiser: IMC Programming Committee
Moderator: Lenka Panušková, Institute of Art History, Czech Academy of Sciences, Praha
Paper 1030-a: **Church Organisation in Early Christian Ireland: The Evidence of High Crosses** (Language: English)
Megan Henvey, Department of History of Art, University of York
Paper 1030-b: **The Elements of Traditional Celtic Cultures in the British Hagiography (on the Examples of the Lives of St Kentigern and St David of Wales)** (Language: English)
Anna Gusakova, Department of Medieval History, Lomonosov Moscow State University
Paper 1030-c: **The Cover of the Faddan More Psalter and the Practice of Ornament in the Early Middle Ages** (Language: English)
Christine Bachman, Department of Art History, University of Delaware

Session: **1031** **Maurice Keyworth Building: Room 1.05**
Title: **THE CASTELLANIES OF MEDIEVAL SAVOY AND THEIR ROLLS OF ACCOUNTS**
Sponsor: Universitatea din București
Organiser: Ionuț Epurescu-Pascovici, Humanities Division, Research Institute of the University of Bucharest
Moderator: Divna Manolova, Department of Philology, University of Silesia, Katowice
Paper 1031-a: **The Savoyard Castellany Accounts as Dialogical Texts** (Language: English)
Ionuț Epurescu-Pascovici
Paper 1031-b: **Justice and Its Administration in the Savoyard *Computi*** (Language: English)
Aude Wirth-Jaillard, Humanities Division, Research Institute of the University of Bucharest
Paper 1031-c: **War and Its Financing in Late Medieval Savoy** (Language: English)
Roberto Biolzi, Faculté des lettres, Université de Lausanne / Humanities Division, Research Institute of the University of Bucharest

Session: **1032** **Parkinson Building: Nathan Bodington Chamber**
Title: **MONUMENTS AND MEMORY: NEW RESEARCH AT ENGLISH HERITAGE**
Organiser: Michael Carter, Curatorial Department, English Heritage, London
Moderator: Karen Stöber, Departament d'Història, Universitat de Lleida
Paper 1032-a: **Tintagel Castle: Preliminary Analysis of a Five-Year Research Project** (Language: English)
Win Scutt, Curatorial Department, English Heritage, London
Paper 1032-b: **Constable's Gate, Dover Castle: Form and Planning** (Language: English)
Roy Porter, Curatorial Department, English Heritage, London
Paper 1032-c: **Furness Abbey: Death and Memory** (Language: English)
Michael Carter

Session: **1033** **Leeds University Union: Room 2 - Elland Road**
Title: **INVENTING HEROES, REVERSING LEGENDS, CONSTRUCTING FACTS: THE DYNAMICS OF IDENTITY SHAPING, I - MEDIEVAL ASPECTS**
Sponsor: Lise-Meitner Project, Institut für Mittelalterforschung, Österreichische Akademie der Wissenschaften, Wien / Department of Auxiliary Historical Sciences & Archive Studies, Masarykova univerzita, Brno
Organiser: Klara Hübner, Department of Auxiliary Historical Sciences & Archive Studies, Masarykova univerzita, Brno and David Kalhous, Institut für Mittelalterforschung, Österreichische Akademie der Wissenschaften, Wien
Moderator: Klara Hübner
Paper 1033-a: **Creating the Identity of the *gens Boemorum* through the Holy Days of Czech Patrons in the Narrative Sources of Early Premyslid Bohemia, until 1198** (Language: English)
Ludmila Luňáková, Institute of History, Masarykova univerzita, Brno
Paper 1033-b: **Remembering the Competition: Benedictines and New Religious Orders in the 12th-Century Czech Lands from a Contemporary and Modern View** (Language: English)
Josef Šrámek, Museum of East Bohemia, Hradec Králové
Paper 1033-c: **Canon Law as *lieu de mémoire*?: Identity-Building in 13th-Century Bohemia** (Language: English)
Lukáš Führer, Institute of Auxiliary Historical Sciences & Archive Studies, Masarykova univerzita, Brno
Paper 1033-d: **'Neronior Nerone?': Patriarch John of Moravia (1387-1394) between *damnatio memoriae* and *fama sanctitatis*** (Language: English)
Ondřej Schmidt, Department of Auxiliary Historical Sciences & Archive Studies, Masarykova univerzita, Brno

---

Session: **1034** **Maurice Keyworth Building: Room 1.33**
Title: **TEXTUAL MEMORIES: EXPLORING IDENTITY IN LATE MEDIEVAL WILLS**
Organiser: Hannah Ward, Department of History, University of Nottingham
Moderator: Marianne Wilson, Department of Collections Expertise & Engagement, The National Archives, Kew
Paper 1034-a: **Bristolian Burgesses: Urban Piety in 15th-Century Testamentary Evidence** (Language: English)
Esther Lewis, Department of History, University of Nottingham
Paper 1034-b: **Gowns, Rings, and Other Shiny Things: Personal Possessions in Late Medieval London Wills** (Language: English)
Hannah Ward
Paper 1034-c: **Strategies of Memory and Identity in Late Medieval Women's Wills** (Language: English)
Alex Marchbank, Department of History, University of Nottingham

Session: **1035** **Leeds University Union: Room 4 - Hyde Park**
Title: **ARCHIVAL MEMORY: INSTITUTIONS, TEXTS, AND SHAPES, I**
Sponsor: Institut de Recherche et d'Histoire des Textes (IRHT), Centre National de la Recherche Scientifique (CNRS), Paris
Organiser: Sébastien Barret, Institut de Recherche et d'Histoire des Textes (IRHT), Centre National de la Recherche Scientifique (CNRS), Paris
Moderator: Dominique Stutzmann, Institut de Recherche et d'Histoire des Textes (IRHT), Centre National de la Recherche Scientifique (CNRS), Paris
Paper 1035-a: **The Cartulary of Egmond Abbey, c. 1420** (Language: English)
Jan W. J. Burgers, Huygens Instituut voor Nederlandse Geschiedenis, Koninklijke Nederlandse Academie van Wetenschappen (ING - KNAW), Amsterdam / Capaciteitsgroep Geschiedenis, Universiteit van Amsterdam
Paper 1035-b: **Active Scribes and Active Memory in Late Medieval Scottish Cartularies** (Language: English)
Joanna Tucker, School of Humanities (History), University of Glasgow
Paper 1035-c: **Recording, Administrating, and Claiming Rights: One Example of the Archival Work in Saint-Germain-Des-Prés** (Language: English)
Louis Genton, Institut d'études culturelles et internationales (IECI), Université Paris-Saclay

Session: **1036** **Leeds University Union: Room 5 - Kirkstall Abbey**
Title: **VOICES OF LAW, I: MEMORY, LAW, AND PRECEDENT**
Sponsor: Voices of Law: Language, Text & Practice / Iuris Canonici Medii Aevi Consociatio (ICMAC)
Organiser: Matthew McHaffie, Department of History, King's College London and Danica Summerlin, Department of History, University of Sheffield
Moderator: Helle Vogt, Center for Retskulturelle Studier, Det Juridiske Fakultet, Københavns Universitet
Paper 1036-a: **Pleading, Proof, and Precedent in Norman Lawsuits, c. 1000-c. 1144** (Language: English)
Mark Hagger, School of History, Welsh History & Archaeology, Bangor University
Paper 1036-b: **Fabricating and Forgetting Facts: Communal Attempts to Conceal Criminality at Trial in 13th-Century England** (Language: English)
Kenneth F. Duggan, Huron University College, Western University, Ontario
Paper 1036-c: **The Legal Memory of Eastern Married Clerics in Two Anglo-Norman Decretists** (Language: English)
Maroula Perisanidi, School of History, University of Leeds

Session: **1037** **Emmanuel Centre: Wilson Room**
Title: **INVESTING IN MEMORY: CIVIC ENDOWMENTS, MATERIAL CULTURE, AND URBAN COMMUNITIES, I**
Sponsor: Institut für Österreichische Geschichtsforschung (IÖG), Universität Wien / Interdisziplinäres Zentrum für Mittelalter und Frühneuzeit (IZMF), Universität Salzburg
Organiser: Elisabeth Gruber, Institut für Realienkunde des Mittelalters und der frühen Neuzeit, Universität Salzburg and Judit Majorossy, Institut für Geschichte, Universität Wien
Moderator: Anna Adamska, Onderzoeksinstituut voor Geschiedenis en Kunstgeschiedenis, Universiteit Utrecht
Paper 1037-a: **Joining Common Memory: The Town's Elites and Their Chapels as Places of Political Self-Presentation in Central Europe** (Language: English)
Elisabeth Gruber
Paper 1037-b: **Buying Memory: Hospital Endowments in Southern Germany and Austria** (Language: English)
Herwig Weigl, Institut für Österreichische Geschichtsforschung / Institut für Geschichte, Universität Wien
Paper 1037-c: **For the Sake of Souls and Sisterhood: Founding Nunneries by Noble Women of Zadar (Zara)** (Language: English)
Zrinka Nikolić Jakus, Department of History, University of Zagreb

Session: **1038** **Michael Sadler Building: Room LG.10**
Title: **COLLECTIVE MEMORY IN MONTPELLIER'S *PETIT THALAMUS*: DIGITAL HUMANITIES, LANGUAGE, AND THE MAPPING OF THE PAST**
Sponsor: Association Internationale d'Études Occitanes (AIEO), Montpellier
Organiser: Catherine E. Léglu, Graduate Centre for Medieval Studies, University of Reading
Moderator: Wendy Pfeffer, Department of Classical & Modern Languages, University of Louisville, Kentucky / Centre d'Études Supérieures de la Renaissance, Tours
Paper 1038-a: **Production documentaire, pouvoir consulaire et identité urbaine dans le *Petit Thalamus*** (Language: Français)
Gilda Caïti-Russo, Équipe Langues, Littératures, Arts et Cultures des Suds, Université Paul-Valéry Montpellier III
Paper 1038-b: **Reconstructing Urban Cartography Using Geo-Annotations** (Language: English)
Francesca Frontini, Institut des Technosciences de l'Information et de la Communication (ITIC), Université Paul-Valéry Montpellier 3
Paper 1038-c: **Mémoire civique et choix linguistiques, entre occitan and latin** (Language: Français)
Hervé Lieutard, Équipe Langues, Littératures, Arts et Cultures des Suds, Université Paul-Valéry Montpellier III
Paper 1038-d: **Memory and Becoming in the Construction of the Lyrical Ego of the Trobairitz** (Language: English)
Rosa Maria Medina Granda, Departamento de Filología Clásica y Románica, Universidad de Oviedo

Session:	**1039**	**Maurice Keyworth Building: Room 1.03**
Title:	**THE PRESENT OF THE PAST: THE MEROVINGIAN AND CAROLINGIAN LEGACY IN THE LATER MIDDLE AGES**	
Organiser:	Daisy Delogu, Department of Romance Languages & Literatures, University of Chicago, Illinois	
Moderator:	Craig D. Taylor, Centre for Medieval Studies, University of York	
Paper 1039-a:	**Primat's *Roman aux roys* and the Vernacularization of History in 13th-Century Saint-Denis** (Language: English) Anne-Hélène Miller, Department of Modern Foreign Languages & Literatures, University of Tennessee, Knoxville	
Paper 1039-b:	**Promoting Merovingian Memory under the First Valois: Using the Example of the *Miracle de Clovis*, mid-14th Century** (Language: English) Sarah Olivier, Unité d'histoire médiévale, Université de Genève	
Paper 1039-c:	**Charlemagne and the University of Paris in the Later Middle Ages** (Language: English) Daisy Delogu	

Session:	**1040**	**Michael Sadler Building: Room LG.15**
Title:	**MEMORIES OF ROYAL POWER**	
Organiser:	IMC Programming Committee	
Moderator:	Karl Christian Alvestad, Department of History, University of Winchester	
Paper 1040-a:	**Norman Sicily and the Fatimid Royal Correspondence, 1137** (Language: English) Maher Hasan, Department of History, University of Tobruk, Libya	
Paper 1040-b:	**'And let these tears, distilling from mine eyes, / Be witness of my grief and innocency': Commemoration of Edward II as a Political Tool** (Language: English) Daniel Oliver, School of Humanities (History), University of Glasgow	
Paper 1040-c:	**Memories of Royal Power in the Legal Tradition of Late Medieval Iceland: Evidence of Narrative and Legal Sources** (Language: English) Marta Miller, St Andrews Institute of Mediaeval Studies, University of St Andrews	

Session: **1041** **Stage@leeds: Stage 2**
Title: **BIRGITTINE ACTS OF MEMORY, I: COMMUNITIES AND MANUSCRIPTS**
Sponsor: Institut de Recerca de Cultures Medievals (IRCVM), Universitat de Barcelona / Centrum för teologi och religionsvetenskap, Lunds universitet
Organiser: David Carrillo-Rangel, Institut de Recerca de Cultures Medievals (IRCVM), Universitat de Barcelona and Erik Claeson, Centrum för teologi och religionsvetenskap, Lunds universitet
Moderator: Erik Claeson
Paper 1041-a: **St Bridget in a Norwegian Legal Manuscript: *Codex Hardenbergensis*** (Language: English)
Helen F. Leslie-Jacobsen, Institutt for lingvistiske, litterære og estetiske studier, Universitetet i Bergen
Paper 1041-b: **Donations as Manifestations of Imagined Communities around Birgittine Monasteries on the Baltic Rim** (Language: English)
Anna-Stina Hägglund, Department of History, Åbo Akademi University, Turku
Paper 1041-c: **The Community of the Living and the Dead at Syon Abbey: Evidence from Three Necrologies, c. 1415-1650** (Language: English)
Virginia Bainbridge, Department of History, University of Exeter

Session: **1042** **Stage@leeds: Stage 3**
Title: **TEXTS AND THE TRANSMISSION OF SCIENTIFIC AND BIBLICAL KNOWLEDGE**
Organiser: IMC Programming Committee
Moderator: Matthias Martin Tischler, Institut d'Estudis Medievals, Universitat Autònoma de Barcelona
Paper 1042-a: **Vincent de Beauvais and the *Physiologus*** (Language: English)
Ilya Dines, Library of Congress, Washington DC
Paper 1042-b: **La transmisión textual de los *Excerpta Taionis*** (Language: Español)
Joel Varela Rodríguez, Facultade de Filoloxía, Universidade de Santiago de Compostela
Paper 1042-c: **Peter Lombard's *Collectanea*: Tracing Patterns of the Marginal Rubrics in Manuscripts Made in France, c. 1200** (Language: English)
Nina Baker, Department of History of Art & Architecture, Trinity College Dublin
Paper 1042-d: **The Memory of Colours** (Language: English)
Robert Fuchs, Institut für Restaurierungs- und Konservierungswissenschaft, Technische Hochschule Köln and Doris Oltrogge, Institut für Restaurierungs- und Konservierungswissenschaft, Technische Hochschule Köln

Session: **1043** **Emmanuel Centre: Room 10**
Title: **REMEMBERING THE CRUSADES: THE LEGACY OF THE BALTIC CRUSADES IN THE LATE MIDDLE AGES**
Sponsor: University of Tartu / Universität Hamburg
Organiser: Anti Selart, Institute of History & Archaeology, University of Tartu
Moderator: Torben Kjersgaard Nielsen, Institut for Kultur og Globale Studier, Aalborg Universitet
Paper 1043-a: **The Baltic Crusades as *lieu de mémoire* in 15th-Century Prussia** (Language: English)
Sebastian Kubon, Historisches Seminar, Universität Hamburg
Paper 1043-b: **Politicisation of the Remembrance of the Crusades in Late Medieval Livonia** (Language: English)
Mihkel Mäesalu, Institute of History & Archeology, University of Tartu
Paper 1043-c: **History and Its Uses: The Presence of the Baltic Crusades in the Late Middle Ages** (Language: English)
Kristjan Kaljusaar, Institute of History & Archaeology, University of Tartu

---

Session: **1044** **Fine Art Building: SR 1.10**
Title: **IMPERIAL MEMORIES IN LATE ANTIQUITY, I: THE MEMORY OF ROMAN EMPERORS**
Organiser: Adrastos Omissi, School of Humanities (Classics), University of Glasgow
Moderator: Richard Flower, Department of Classics & Ancient History, University of Exeter
Paper 1044-a: **Two Letters of the Usurper Magnus Maximus (383-388): The Contested Memory of an Orthodox Christian and a Political Heretic** (Language: English)
Adrastos Omissi
Paper 1044-b: **Imperial Archetypes in Cultural Memory** (Language: English)
Rebecca Usherwood, School of Classics, University of St Andrews
Paper 1044-c: **'Thou hast conquered, Galilean!': Julian's Death Narratives** (Language: English)
Victoria Hughes, School of History, Classics & Archaeology, Newcastle University

---

Session: **1045** **Maurice Keyworth Building: Room 1.32**
Title: **AT THE CUTTING EDGE OF DIGITAL MEMORY: THE ONLINE CORPUS OF ROMANESQUE SCULPTURE IN BRITAIN AND IRELAND - POST-CONQUEST CARVING AT YOUR FINGERTIPS, I**
Sponsor: Corpus of Romanesque Sculpture in Britain & Ireland (CRSBI)
Organiser: Jill A. Franklin, Corpus of Romanesque Sculpture in Britain & Ireland (CRSBI), London
Moderator: Ron Baxter, Corpus of Romanesque Sculpture in Britain & Ireland (CRSBI), London
Paper 1045-a: **Architecture and Memory: The Re-Use of Romanesque Sculptural Fragments** (Language: English)
Toby J. Huitson, School of History, University of Kent
Paper 1045-b: **Spot the Altar: Locating the Liturgy in the Romanesque Parish Church** (Language: English)
James Alexander Cameron, Corpus of Romanesque Sculpture in Britain & Ireland (CRSBI), London
Paper 1045-c: **Baptismal Fonts, I: Ornament as Monument - A Family of Elaborately Decorated Romanesque Fonts in Victorian Churches in Norfolk** (Language: English)
Jill A. Franklin

Session: **1046** **Leeds University Union: Room 6 - Roundhay**
Title: **REMEMBERING CHIVALRY, I: SPECTACLE AND DISPLAY**
Sponsor: Institute for Medieval Studies, University of Leeds
Organiser: Jeri Smith-Cronin, School of English, University of Leeds
Moderator: James Titterton, Institute for Medieval Studies, University of Leeds
Paper 1046-a: **The Art of Chivalry: Pageantry and Display in the Cabinet Miniatures of Nicholas Hilliard** (Language: English)
Elizabeth Goldring, Centre for the Study of the Renaissance, University of Warwick
Paper 1046-b: **Remembering Elizabethan Chivalry in Thomas Dekker's *The Whore of Babylon*** (Language: English)
Jeri Smith-Cronin
Paper 1046-c: **Medieval Heraldry: An *aide-memoire*?** (Language: English)
Adrian Ailes, Centre for Medieval Studies, University of Bristol

Session: **1047** **Baines Wing: Room 2.14**
Title: **REPUTATION, EMOTION, AND REMEMBERING DEATH AND ILLNESS**
Sponsor: Prato Consortium for Medieval & Renaissance Studies, Monash University, Victoria
Organiser: Peter Francis Howard, Centre for Medieval & Renaissance Studies, Monash University, Victoria
Moderator: John Henderson, Department of History, Classics & Archaeology, Birkbeck, University of London / School of Philosophy, History & International Studies, Monash University
Paper 1047-a: **Recording a Place of Emotions and Violence: Mapping the Coronial Deaths of Medieval Oxfordshire** (Language: English)
Annie Blachly, Centre for Medieval & Renaissance Studies, Monash University, Victoria
Paper 1047-b: **The *Insania* and Piety of Herimann of Nevers: Remembering a Mentally Ill Carolingian Bishop** (Language: English)
Rachel Stone, Department of History, King's College London / Learning Resources and Service Excellence, University of Bedfordshire
Paper 1047-c: ***Medical Memory of Sense and Emotion* by Baverio de'Bonetti (d. 1480): A Physician of Bologna** (Language: English)
Gordon Whyte, School of Philosophical, Historical & International Studies, Monash University, Victoria

Session: **1048** **University House: St George Room**
Title: **TIME, SCIENCE, AND THE BODY IN THE ANGLO-NORMAN WORLD: DURHAM, CATHEDRAL LIBRARY, MS HUNTER 100 AND ITS CONTEXTS, I - NETWORKS AND CONNECTIONS**
Sponsor: Department of History, Durham University
Organiser: Giles E. M. Gasper, Department of History, Durham University
Moderator: Jay Diehl, Department of History, Long Island University, New York
Paper 1048-a: **Networks and Borders in the Anglo-Norman World** (Language: English)
Anne Lawrence-Mathers, Graduate Centre for Medieval Studies, University of Reading
Paper 1048-b: **From the Wye to the Wear: Hereford, Durham, and Communities of Learning in England, c. 1090-1130** (Language: English)
Giles E. M. Gasper
Paper 1048-c: **The 12th-Century Severn Valley: A Culture of Inquiry** (Language: English)
Kathy Bader, Department of History, Durham University

Session: **1049** **Stage@leeds: Stage 1**
Title: **'SING AND CRY, "VALHALLA, I AM COMING!"': NATIONALISM AND INTERNATIONALISM IN VIKING METAL MUSIC**
Organiser: IMC Programming Committee
Moderator: Katherine J. Lewis, Department of History, University of Huddersfield
Paper 1049-a: **'Nata vimpi curmi da': Linguistic Atavism and the Construction of Primordial Nationalisms in Folk Metal Music** (Language: English)
Simon Trafford, Institute of Historical Research, University of London
Paper 1049-b: **Beyond Viking Shores: The Uses and Abuses of Cultural Memory in Heavy Metal** (Language: English)
Kathryn Ania Haley-Halinski, Department of Anglo-Saxon, Norse & Celtic, University of Cambridge

---

Session: **1050** **Baines Wing: Room 2.15**
Title: **CANONIZE YOURSELF!, I: HOW TO BECOME A SECULAR CANON IN A MEDIEVAL SCANDINAVIAN CHAPTER**
Sponsor: Erzbistum Paderborn / Universitetet i Tromsø - Norges Arktiske Universitetet
Organiser: Arnold Otto, Erzbischöfliches Generalvikariat Erzbistumsarchiv, Paderborn
Moderator: Arnold Otto
Paper 1050-a: **Chapters in Northern Norway and How to Enter in the Later Middle Ages** (Language: English)
Sigrun Høgetveit Berg, Institutt for historie og religionsvitenskap, Universitetet i Tromsø - Norges Arktiske Universitetet
Paper 1050-b: **On Cathedral Chapters, Canons, and Careers in Denmark, c. 1070-1225** (Language: English)
Anna Minara Ciardi, Centrum för Teologi och Religionsvetenskap, Lunds Universitet
Paper 1050-c: **To be a Canon, or Not to Be?: Papal Provisions to the Medieval Cathedral Chapter of Turku versus Local Appointment Policy** (Language: English)
Kirsi Salonen, Department of Finnish History, University of Turku

---

Session: **1051** **Baines Wing: Room G.36**
Title: **ARCHITECTURE AS A MEANS OF REMEMBRANCE**
Organiser: IMC Programming Committee
Moderator: Przemysław Waszak, Katedra Historii Sztuki i Kultury, Uniwersytet Mikołaja Kopernika, Toruń
Paper 1051-a: **Architecture as a Living Memory: The Chapel of the Cypress in Samos** (Language: English)
Estefanía López Salas, Departamento de Proyectos Arquitectónicos, Urbanismo y Composición, Universidade da Coruña
Paper 1051-b: **Architectures of Memory: Reconstructing the Past through Spolia in the Byzantine Middle Ages** (Language: English)
Ufuk Serin, Department of Architecture, Middle East Technical University, Ankara
Paper 1051-c: **Architectual Decoration in Cistercian Monasteries in Poland: The Motives of the Decoration and Their Origin** (Language: English)
Julia Falat, Institute of Art, Polish Academy of Sciences, Warszawa

Session: **1052** **University House: Cloberry Room**
Title: **MEDIEVAL ETHIOPIA, I: MUSLIMS AND JEWS**
Sponsor: Fakultät für Geschichtswissenschaft, Ruhr-Universität Bochum
Organiser: Vincent van Gerven Oei, punctum books, Tirana and Verena Krebs, Historisches Institut, Ruhr-Universität Bochum
Moderator: Verena Krebs
Paper 1052-a: **The Ethiopian Sultanate of Awfāt, Its Capital, and the Walasma' Necropolis, 14th Century** (Language: English)
Amélie Chekroun, Institut de Recherches et d'Etudes sur le Monde Arabe et Musulman (UMR 7310) / Horneast, European Research Council, Aix-Marseille Université
Paper 1052-b: **Mamluk Models in the Qur'ans of Harar as Evidence of a Longue Durée Red Sea Manuscript Culture** (Language: English)
Sana Mirza, Institute of Fine Arts, New York University
Paper 1052-c: **A Historical Look at the Presence and Influence of Jews in Ethiopia: Aksumite to 'Solomonic' Dynasties, 6th-14th Centuries** (Language: English)
Afework Beyene, Department of Historical Studies, Ethiopian Graduate School of Theology, Addis Ababa

Session: **1053** **Emmanuel Centre: Room 11**
Title: **VISIONS OF CRUSADING AND THE HOLY LAND IN MEDIEVAL ENGLAND**
Sponsor: Northern Network for the Study of the Crusades
Organiser: Kathryn Hurlock, Department of History, Politics & Philosophy, Manchester Metropolitan University
Moderator: Kathryn Hurlock
Paper 1053-a: **Visualising Jerusalem in Anglo-Saxon England** (Language: English)
Meg Boulton, Department of History of Art, University of York
Paper 1053-b: **Imagining and Reimagining the Holy Land in 12th- and Early 13th-Century Wall Painting** (Language: English)
John Munns, Department of History of Art, University of Cambridge
Paper 1053-c: **Apocalypse Manuscripts and the Crusade Spirituality of Women in Medieval England** (Language: English)
Laura Julinda Whatley, College of Arts & Sciences, Auburn University at Montgomery, Alabama

Session: **1054** **Maurice Keyworth Building: Room G.02**

Title: **RE-CONSTRUCTING A FRAGMENTARY INTER-SCANDINAVIAN LIBRARY: NORDIC AND INTERNATIONAL COLLABORATION IN PARCHMENT FRAGMENT RESEARCH - A ROUND TABLE DISCUSSION**

Sponsor: National Library of Finland, Helsinki

Organiser: Sara Ellis Nilsson, Historical Studies, Department of Society, Culture & Identity, Malmö University

Moderator: Jaakko Tahkokallio, National Library of Finland, Helsinki

Purpose: *The Nordic fragment collections provide us, among other things, with a unique view of one of the least well-preserved corners of medieval book culture: liturgical parish books. This round table discussion will address the work that still needs to be done to make these unique sources accessible to international scholarship. Some issues that will be raised are the benefits of a digital format for re-stitching/reconstructing books, the void that exists in scholarship due to uneven access to the fragments, as well as artefact survival and its influence on collective memory. Finally, the importance of a greater collaboration will be discussed.*

Participants include Olli-Pekka Kasurinen (University of Helsinki), Synnøve Myking (Universitetet i Bergen), Erik Niblaeus (Durham University), Sara Ellis Nilsson (Malmö Högskola), and Åslaug Ommundsen (Universitetet i Bergen).

COFFEE BREAK: 10.30-11.15

Coffee and Tea will be served at the following locations:

Maurice Keyworth Building: Foyer
Michael Sadler Building: Foyer
Parkinson Building: Bookfair
University Square: The Marquee

See Map 7, p. 44.

---

* * * * *

MEDIEVAL CRAFT FAIR

LEEDS UNIVERSITY UNION: FOYER
10.30-19.30

This event is free of charge.

A one-day craft fair will take place in the Leeds University Union Foyer showcasing a variety of handmade items using and inspired by medieval craft techniques. Come see the range of unique items on offer! The exhibitors will include:

Anachronalia - Accessories and hand-bound books inspired by the past, present, and possible futures.
Ana Period Shoes - Historic footwear from 1000 BC to 1500 AD. Museum-grade made-to-measure reproductions and ready-made shoes in standard sizes.
Corium Artificium - Medieval-style leather bags and pouches, candlesticks, drinking horns, and cast jewellery made using traditional techniques.
D-Art Francisca - Artistic jewellery.
Early Music Shop - A selection of historical musical instruments.
FiftyEleven - Hand-tooled, lovingly crafted, historically inspired woodwork and pyrography.
Gemmeus - Handcrafted historical, classical, and revival jewellery, created in sterling silver, gold, and natural gemstones and pearls.
Hare and Tabor - Clothing, greetings cards, postcards, and jewellery inspired by folklore and folk traditions.
John Hudson Claypotter - Medieval and post-medieval reproduction pottery.
The Mulberry Dyer - Naturally dyed fibres, yarn, and cloth, as well as small textile tools and related items.
Pen to Press - Tea towels, coasters, cocktail napkins, matches with images from medieval and early modern manuscripts and incunabula.
Pretender to the Throne - Historically inspired, hand-made soft furnishings and ceramics.
Runesmith - Jewellery and a variety of other items inspired by Viking and early medieval designs.
Tanya Bentham - Embroidery, embroidery kits, and related merchandise.
Tillerman Beads handmade by Mike Poole - Handmade glass lampwork beads based on originals from archaeological reports and museum artefacts.
Trinity Court Potteries - Replica medieval pottery from original sources.

* * * * *

Session: **1101** **Michael Sadler Building: Room LG.17**
Title: **THE ANGLO-SAXON POETIC TRADITION, II**
Sponsor: A Consolidated Library of Anglo-Saxon Poetry
Organiser: Colleen Curran, Faculty of English Literature & Language, University of Oxford
Moderator: Francis Leneghan, Faculty of English Language & Literature, University of Oxford
Paper 1101-a: **More than Just Words: Influence and Inspiration in Old English Poetry** (Language: English)
Daniel Thomas, Faculty of English Language & Literature, University of Oxford
Paper 1101-b: **Memorialising St Wilfrid: The Poetic Act of Memory in Frithegod's *Breviloquium Vitae Wilfridi*** (Language: English)
Colleen Curran
Paper 1101-c: **'Like unto Eternity': Remembering the Heroic Past in Anglo-Saxon Poetry** (Language: English)
Patrick McBrine, Department of English, Bishop's University, Quebec

Session: **1102** **Baines Wing: Room 1.13**
Title: **THROUGH A MIRROR DARKLY: LATE MEDIEVAL ENGLISH DREAM VISIONS**
Organiser: IMC Programming Committee
Moderator: Rosanne Gasse, Department of English, Brandon University, Manitoba
Paper 1102-a: **Metaphysical Presentation of the Dream Visions in *Piers Plowman*** (Language: English)
Tomonori Matsushita, Department of English, Senshu University, Tokyo
Paper 1102-b: **Remembering Melting Authors' Names: *The House of Fame*'s Mountain of Ice** (Language: English)
Kathleen Cawsey, Department of English, Dalhousie University, Nova Scotia

Session: **1103** **Baines Wing: Room 2.16**
Title: **MOVING BYZANTIUM, II: THE MOVEMENT OF MANUSCRIPTS**
Sponsor: Moving Byzantium: Mobility, Microstructures & Personal Agency, Österreichische Akademie der Wissenschaften, Universität Wien / FWF Wittgenstein-Prize Project
Organiser: Claudia Rapp, Institut für Byzantinistik & Neogräzistik, Universität Wien / Österreichische Akademie der Wissenschaften, Wien
Moderator: Matthew Kinloch, Institut für Mittelalterforschung, Abteilung Byzanzforschung, Österreichische Akademie der Wissenschaften, Wien
Paper 1103-a: **From West to East: Evidence for Southern Italian Manuscript Culture in St Catherine's Monastery in the Sinai** (Language: English)
Giulia Rossetto, Institut für Byzantinistik & Neogräzistik, Universität Wien
Paper 1103-b: **Moving Byzantium to the West: Greek Manuscripts from Byzantine Constantinople to the Italian Cities in the 15th Century** (Language: English)
Elias Petrou, Thesaurus Linguae Graecae, University of California, Irvine
Paper 1103-c: **Books Travelling within and beyond the Byzantine Empire** (Language: English)
Giuseppe Pascale, Dipartimento di Scienze religiose, Università Cattolica del Sacro Cuore, Milano
Paper 1103-d: **Between Byzantium and the Mongols: A Rare Description of 13th-Century Anatolia** (Language: English)
Bruno De Nicola, Department of History, Goldsmiths, University of London / Institut für Iranistik, Österreichischen Akademie der Wissenschaften, Wien

Session: **1104** **Fine Art Building: SR G.04**
Title: **NEW DIRECTIONS IN CRUSADE STUDIES, II**
Sponsor: Center for Medieval & Renaissance Studies, Saint Louis University, Missouri / Royal Holloway, University of London
Organiser: Thomas F. Madden, Center for Medieval & Renaissance Studies, Saint Louis University, Missouri
Moderator: Jonathan Phillips, Department of History, Royal Holloway, University of London
Paper 1104-a: **At War in the Monastery: Praying for the Crusades in the Cistercian Houses of the Papal States** (Language: English)
Richard Allington, Department of History, Saint Louis University, Missouri
Paper 1104-b: **Papal Legates: The Role of James Pantaleon, Thomas of Lentino, and William II of Agen** (Language: English)
Hannah Strathern, Royal Holloway, University of London
Paper 1104-c: **The Battle of Párkány 1683: Polish Acts of Spiritual Rededication and the First Crusade** (Language: English)
Philip James, Department of History, Royal Holloway, University of London

Session: **1105** **Michael Sadler Building: Room LG.16**
Title: **THE GERMAN HANSE: WELL-REMEMBERED, LITTLE UNDERSTOOD**
Sponsor: Forschungsstelle für die Geschichte der Hanse und des Ostseeraums (FGHO), Europäische Hansemuseum, Lübeck
Organiser: Angela Huang, Forschungsstelle für die Geschichte der Hanse und des Ostseeraums, Lübeck
Moderator: Ulla Kypta, Departement Geschichte, Universität Basel
Paper 1105-a: **What Is the Hanse?** (Language: English)
Angela Huang
Paper 1105-b: **Material Culture and the Hanse** (Language: English)
Ulrich Müller, Institut für Ur- und Frühgeschichte, Christian-Albrechts-Universität zu Kiel
Paper 1105-c: **Showcasing an Immaterial Phenomenon** (Language: English)
Franziska Evers, Europäisches Hansemuseum, Lübeck

Session: **1106** **Parkinson Building: Room 1.16**
Title: **GENTRY IDENTITY AND LEGACY, I: ADMINISTRATION AND GENTILITY**
Organiser: Katie Bridger, Centre for English Local History, University of Leicester and Matthew Ward, School of History, University of Nottingham
Moderator: Raluca Radulescu, Institute for Medieval & Early Modern Studies, Bangor University
Paper 1106-a: **Identity and Public Authority: The Gentry of Wakefield, 1300-1347** (Language: English)
Susanna Markert, Faculty of History, University of Oxford
Paper 1106-b: **Centre and Periphery: The Local Gentry and the Enforcement of the Early Reformation in the South-West of England** (Language: English)
Thomas J. Morrissey, Department of History, University of Liverpool
Paper 1106-c: **The Problem of the Gentry: How to Identify a Gentleman in 15th-Century England** (Language: English)
Kristin Pinyan, Department of History, Rutgers University, New Jersey

---

Session: **1107** **Fine Art Building: Studio Ground Floor**
Title: **THE 'GREY POPES': LUCIUS III (1181-1185), URBAN III (1185-1187), GREGORY VIII (1187), AND CLEMENT III (1187-1191), I**
Sponsor: Center for Medieval & Renaissance Studies, Saint Louis University, Missouri
Organiser: Damian Smith, Department of History, Saint Louis University, Missouri
Moderator: Damian Smith
Paper 1107-a: **The Separation of Canon Law from Theology** (Language: English)
Christoph Egger, Institut für Österreichische Geschichtsforschung, Universität Wien
Paper 1107-b: **The Grey Popes and the Law** (Language: English)
Anne J. Duggan, Department of History, King's College London
Paper 1107-c: **The Grey Popes and the Commune** (Language: English)
Kathleen Walkowiak, Department of History, Saint Louis University, Missouri

Session: **1108** **Maurice Keyworth Building: Room 1.04**
Title: **SANCTIFYING THE CRIP, CRIPPING THE SACRED: DISABILITY, HOLINESS, AND EMBODIED KNOWLEDGE**
Sponsor: Hagiography Society
Organiser: Alicia Spencer-Hall, School of Languages, Linguistics & Film, Queen Mary University of London
Moderator: Alicia Spencer-Hall
Paper 1108-a: **Hildegard of Bingen's Hagiography: The Community of Heaven and Earth and the Social Model of Disability** (Language: English)
Stephen Marc D'Evelyn, School for Policy Studies, University of Bristol
Paper 1108-b: **Translations of (Dis)Ability, Disease, and Digestion in *The Book of Margery Kempe*** (Language: English)
Katherine Gubbels, Department of English, Memphis College of Art, Tennessee
Paper 1108-c: **Disability and Power in the Early Lives of St Francis of Assisi** (Language: English)
Donna Trembinski, Department of History, St. Francis Xavier University, Nova Scotia
Paper 1108-d: **Bodily Arithmetic: Physical and Sacred Identity in *Tristan de Nanteuil*** (Language: English)
Blake Gutt, Department of French, University of Cambridge

Session: **1109** **Baines Wing: Room 2.13**
Title: **HETERODOXY AND APOCALYPSE**
Organiser: IMC Programming Committee
Moderator: Daniel Ziemann, Department of Medieval Studies, Central European University, Budapest
Paper 1109-a: **Religious Identities: Collective and Individual Memory in Waldensian Treatises** (Language: English)
Joanna Poetz, Department of French / Centre for Medieval & Renaissance Studies, Trinity College Dublin
Paper 1109-b: **The Influence of John Wyclif in Jan Hus's Criticism of the Antichrist** (Language: English)
Lucie Mazalová, Department of Classical Studies, Masarykova univerzita, Brno
Paper 1109-c: **The Taborites in the Christian Apocalyptic Tradition** (Language: English)
Martin Pjecha, Department of History, Central European University, Budapest

Session: **1110** **Baines Wing: Room 1.16**
Title: **RETHINKING AGENCY, I: READING WOMEN**
Sponsor: *Medieval Prosopography*
Organiser: Charlotte Pickard, Centre for Continuing & Professional Education, Cardiff University and Rebecca Searby, Centre for Medieval Studies, University of York
Moderator: Amy Livingstone, Department of History, Wittenberg University, Ohio
Paper 1110-a: **Queen or Puppet Lady?: Æthelflaed's Agency in the Politics, Power, and Identity of Mercia** (Language: English)
Melanie C. Maddox, Department of History, The Citadel, Military College of South Carolina
Paper 1110-b: **Agency beyond the Record: Female Friendship and Advocacy in Late Anglo-Saxon England** (Language: English)
Kieran Ball, Faculty of History, Trinity College, University of Oxford
Paper 1110-c: **Rethinking Female Agency and the Formal Expression of Female Power in 13th-Century Royal Letters** (Language: English)
Anaïs Waag, Department of History, King's College London
Paper 1110-d: **Rethinking Agency: Adela of Blois, Penelope, and the Rejection of Suitors** (Language: English)
Natasha Amendola, Centre for Medieval & Renaissance Studies, Monash University, Victoria

Session: **1111** **Baines Wing: Room 1.15**
Title: **THE CENTRE AND THE PERIPHERY: ASPECTS OF CORRELATION AND CO-DEPENDENCY OF RELIGIOUS, POLITICAL, AND CULTURAL MATTERS, II**
Sponsor: Ben-Gurion University of the Negev, Beer-Sheva
Organiser: Dimitri Tarat, Department of History, Ben-Gurion University of the Negev, Beer-Sheva
Moderator: Lukas Bothe, Sonderforschungsbereich 700 'Governance in Areas of Limited Statehood', Freie Universität Berlin
Paper 1111-a: **A Swarm from the Blessed Hive: The Social Networks of the Jura Monasteries** (Language: English)
Yaniv Fox, Department of General History, Bar-Ilan University, Ramat Gan
Paper 1111-b: **The Abbey of Corbie: A Center and a Periphery of the Carolingian Empire** (Language: English)
Dimitri Tarat
Paper 1111-c: **Have You Heard the Good News?: The Adaptation of the Missionary Message in Kievan Rus'** (Language: English)
Asya Bereznyak, Department of History, Hebrew University of Jerusalem
Paper 1111-d: **Marginal Centrality: Portraying Nobility in Jewish Medieval Visual Culture** (Language: English)
Sara Offenberg, Department of the Arts, Ben-Gurion University of the Negev, Beer-Sheva

Session: **1112** **University House: Little Woodhouse Room**
Title: **ADAPTATION OF BYZANTINE HYMNOGRAPHY IN THE MEDIEVAL WORLD: EAST AND WEST**
Organiser: Victoria Legkikh, Institut für Slawistik, Universität Wien
Moderator: Victoria Legkikh
Paper 1112-a: **Adaptation of One Byzantine *Kontakion* in Medieval Rus'** (Language: English)
Victoria Legkikh
Paper 1112-b: **The Textual Tradition of the *Missa Graeca* Chants** (Language: English)
Nina-Maria Wanek, Institut für Byzantinistik & Neogräzistik, Universität Wien
Paper 1112-c: **The Canon of the Nativity of Christ at the Frontier of East and West: The Case of the Irmologia of Byzantine-Slavonic Tradition in the Carpathians** (Language: English)
Mária Prokipčáková, Jan Stanislav Institute of Slavistics, Slovak Academy of Sciences, Bratislava

Session: **1113** **University House: Beechgrove Room**
Title: **DISRUPTIVE GENDERS IN OLD AND MIDDLE ENGLISH LITERATURE**
Organiser: IMC Programming Committee
Moderator: Lucy Allen, Newnham College, University of Cambridge
Paper 1113-a: **Veterans Inciting Queerness: The Specter of the Dead in *Beowulf*** (Language: English)
Christopher Vaccaro, Department of English, University of Vermont
Paper 1113-b: **Women and Cultural Memory in Chaucer's *Legend of Good Women*** (Language: English)
Huriye Reis, Department of English Language & Literature, Hacettepe University, Turkey
Paper 1113-c: **Chaucer and Affirmation of Karma: A Case of *Wife of Bath's Tale*** (Language: English)
Koichi Kano, Department of Cross-Cultural Studies, Koeki University, Japan
Paper 1113-d: **Gendering Memory: The Depiction of Women in Medieval Mystery Plays** (Language: English)
Zahra Alamri, School of Humanities - English, University of Dundee

Session: **1114** **Charles Thackrah Building: 1.01**
Title: **ROYAL MARRIAGES, II: THE LONG PATH TO A PROPER ROYAL WEDDING**
Organiser: Manuela Santos Silva, Departamento de História, Universidade de Lisboa
Moderator: Manuela Santos Silva
Paper 1114-a: **The Long Path to a Proper Royal Wedding: Isabella and King Alphonse V of Portugal** (Language: English)
Ana Maria S. A. Rodrigues, Centro de História, Universidade de Lisboa
Paper 1114-b: **When the King Marries Off His Son: The Case of Afonso, 1st Duke of Bragança** (Language: English)
Beatriz van Zeller, Departamento da história, Universidade de Lisboa
Paper 1114-c: **The Meeting of Jagiellon and Habsburg House: How Polish King Casimir IV Married Elizabeth of Austria** (Language: English)
Beata Możejko, Zakład Historii Średniowiecza Polski i Nauk Pomocniczych Historii, Uniwersytet Gdański

Session:	**1115** **Michael Sadler Building: Room LG.19**
Title:	**PEWTER, PARCHMENT, AND PIXELS: NEW PERSPECTIVES ON PILGRIM AND SECULAR BADGES**
Sponsor:	Rijksmuseum van Oudheden, Leiden / Radboud Universiteit Nijmegen
Organiser:	Hanneke van Asperen, Vakgroep Kunstgeschiedenis, Radboud Universiteit Nijmegen and Annemarieke Willemsen, Rijksmuseum van Oudheden, Leiden
Moderator:	Jos Koldeweij, Vakgroep Kunstgeschiedenis, Radboud Universiteit Nijmegen
Paper 1115-a:	**The Polyfunctionality of Script on Medieval Badges** (Language: English) Ann Marie Rasmussen, Department of Germanic & Slavic Studies, University of Waterloo, Ontario
Paper 1115-b:	**Badges of Our Lady of Grace: New Sources on the Early Pilgrimages to Scheut** (Language: English) Hanneke van Asperen
Paper 1115-c:	**A Hood of Cherries: A New Interpretation of a Enigmatic Badge** (Language: English) Amy Jeffs, Department of History of Art, University of Cambridge

Session:	**1116** **Michael Sadler Building: Rupert Beckett Theatre**
Title:	**14TH-CENTURY ENGLAND, II: LOYALTY AND ALLEGIANCE IN 14TH CENTURY ENGLAND**
Sponsor:	Society for 14th Century Studies
Organiser:	David Green, Centre for British Studies, Harlaxton College, University of Evansville
Moderator:	Gwilym Dodd, Department of History, University of Nottingham
Paper 1116-a:	**A Forgotten Brotherhood: Investigating the Knightly Following of Thomas Beauchamp, Earl of Warwick, 1330-1369** (Language: English) Pierre Gaite, School of History, Archaeology & Religion, Cardiff University
Paper 1116-b:	**Ludlow and the Palmers' Guild: Networks and Spaces** (Language: English) Rachel Clare Harkes, Department of History, Durham University
Paper 1116-c:	**Remembering the Battle of Crécy: The Great East Window of Gloucester Cathedral** (Language: English) Netta Clavner, Department of History, Classics & Archaeology, Birkbeck, University of London

Session: **1117** **Social Sciences Building: Room 10.05**
Title: **THE LOMBARD WARRIOR RECONSIDERED**
Sponsor: Fritz Thyssen Stiftung, Köln
Organiser: Guido M. Berndt, Friedrich-Meinecke-Institut, Freie Universität Berlin
Moderator: Christopher Heath, Department of History, Politics & Philosophy, Manchester Metropolitan University
Paper 1117-a: **Lombard Warriors: Facts and Fiction** (Language: English)
Guido M. Berndt
Paper 1117-b: **Warrior Equals Man?: Masculinity and Weapons in the Written, Iconographic, and Archaeological Sources of the Lombard Period** (Language: English)
Giulia Vollono, Independent Scholar, Rome
Paper 1117-c: **Representation and Reality: A Beneventan Warrior Elite, 8th-9th Century** (Language: English)
Giulia Zornetta, Dipartimento di Studi Storici, Geografici e Antropologici, Università degli Studi di Padova / School of History, University of St Andrews

Session: **1118** **Michael Sadler Building: Banham Theatre**
Title: **TRANSFORMATIONS OF POWER: SESSIONS IN HONOUR OF PAUL FOURACRE, III - COMMUNICATION, CONSENSUS, AND EXCHANGE**
Sponsor: Centre for Medieval & Early Modern Studies, University of Manchester
Organiser: Katherine Fliegel, School of Arts, Languages & Cultures, University of Manchester, Ryan T. Goodman, Department of History, University of Manchester and Sihong Lin, Department of History, University of Manchester
Moderator: Chris Wickham, Faculty of History, University of Oxford
Paper 1118-a: **Tangled Transactions in Desiderius of Cahors** (Language: English)
Danuta Shanzer, Institut für Klassische Philologie, Mittel- und Neulatein, Universität Wien
Paper 1118-b: **Revisiting Breton Disputes** (Language: English)
Wendy Davies, Independent Scholar, Woolstone
Paper 1118-c: **Consensus in Merovingian Politics: An Assessment of the Validity of the Concept of Consensus for Understanding 7th-Century Francia** (Language: English)
Ian N. Wood, School of History, University of Leeds

Session: **1119** **Maurice Keyworth Building: Room 1.09**
Title: **CITIES OF READERS, II: THE PERFORMANCE OF WRITING**
Sponsor: NWO Project 'Cities of Readers', Rijksuniversiteit Groningen
Organiser: Sabrina Corbellini, Afdeling Geschiedenis, Rijksuniversiteit Groningen
Moderator: Johanneke Uphoff, Afdeling Geschiedenis, Rijksuniversiteit Groningen
Paper 1119-a: **The Manuscripts of the 'Coutume de Normandie': Between Legal Uses and Religious Consciousness** (Language: English)
Isabelle Bretthauer, Centre de recherches archéologiques et historiques anciennes et médiévales (CRAHAM - UMR 6273), Université de Caen Normandie
Paper 1119-b: **Performing Scribal Identity in Medieval English Devotional Manuscripts** (Language: English)
Wendy Scase, Department of English Literature, University of Birmingham
Paper 1119-c: **'Scripto per me': The Performance of Writing in Late Medieval Italy** (Language: English)
Sabrina Corbellini

Session: **1120** **Charles Thackrah Building: 1.02**
Title: **REMEMBERING TROY IN THE MIDDLE AGES, II: SOCIO-POLITICAL CONSIDERATIONS**
Organiser: Sabine Heidi Walther, Abteilung für Skandinavische Sprachen und Literaturen, Rheinische Friedrich-Wilhelms-Universität Bonn and N. Kıvılcım Yavuz, Den Arnamagnæanske Samling, Københavns Universitet
Moderator: Mia Münster-Swendsen, Institut for Kommunikation og Humanistisk Videnskab, Roskilde Universitet
Paper 1120-a: **Dares Phrygius in Context: Text, Textual Apparatus, and the Corpus of Associated Works in Manuscripts of the *De excidio Troiae historia*** (Language: English)
Louis Faivre d'Arcier, Archives Municipales de Lyon
Paper 1120-b: **Dares in Verse** (Language: English)
Marek Thue Kretschmer, Institutt for historiske studier, Norges teknisk-naturvitenskapelige universitet, Trondheim
Paper 1120-c: **Les traductions de Guido delle Colonne en français, constantes et variantes** (Language: Français)
Catherine Croizy-Naquet, Centre d'Études du Moyen-Âge (CEMA), Université de la Sorbonne Nouvelle - Paris III
Paper 1120-d: **Describing the City of Troy, or How to Shape 'Good Governement'?** (Language: English)
Anne Rochebouet, Institut d'Etudes Culturelles et Internationales, Université de Versailles Saint-Quentin-en-Yvelines

Session: **1121** **Social Sciences Building: Room 10.06**
Title: **'FAKE' MEMORIES, CROSS REFERENCES, AND INCONSISTENCIES IN HEROIC EPICS AND ARTHURIAN ROMANCES**
Organiser: IMC Programming Committee
Moderator: Sieglinde Hartmann, Oswald von Wolkenstein-Gesellschaft, Frankfurt am Main
Paper 1121-a: **Memory, Allegory, and Retrospective Characterisation in *Erec et Enide* and *Perceval*** (Language: English)
Caitlin Watt, Department of English & Comparative Literature, University of North Carolina, Chapel Hill
Paper 1121-b: **Kriemhild's 'Fake' Memory in *Das Nibelungenlied*** (Language: English)
John Greenfield, Centro de Investigação Transdisciplinar 'Cultura, Espaço e Memória' (CITCEM), Universidade do Porto
Paper 1121-c: **Mind the Gap: Inconsistencies and the Importance of Recollections in Later Medieval Arthurian Romances** (Language: English)
Sabrina Niederelz, Gutenberg Lehrkolleg, Johannes Gutenberg-Universität Mainz

Session: **1122** **Baines Wing: Room 1.14**
Title: **MASTERS AND DISCIPLES: LEARNING, MEMORISING, REMEMBERING**
Organiser: IMC Programming Committee
Moderator: Farkas Gabor Kiss, Department for Early Hungarian Literature, Eötvös Loránd University, Budapest
Paper 1122-a: **Le livre universitaire, un instrument mémoriel à vocation mémoriale?** (Language: Français)
Frédérique Cahu, UFR d'Histoire de l'Art et Archéologie, Université Paris IV - Sorbonne
Paper 1122-b: **'Non stude respiciendo in librum declive': The Use of Textbooks in Medieval Manuals for Successful Study** (Language: English)
Jan Odstrčilík, Institut für Mittelalterforschung, Österreichische Akademie der Wissenschaften, Wien
Paper 1122-c: **El ámbito de recepción del *Libro de Alexandre*: entre el *Speculum principium* y el arte verbal de clerecía** (Language: Español)
Jaime González Álvarez, Independent Scholar, London

Session: **1123** **Maurice Keyworth Building: Room 1.31**
Title: **REMEMBERING THE SAINTS, II: FORGOTTEN AND EPHEMERAL SAINTS**
Sponsor: Cult of Saints Project, University of Oxford
Organiser: Bryan Ward-Perkins, Faculty of History, University of Oxford and Robert Wiśniewski, Instytut Historyczny, Uniwersytet Warszawski
Moderator: David Hunter, Department of Modern & Classical Languages, Literatures & Cultures, University of Kentucky
Paper 1123-a: **How to Tell the Story of Obscure Martyrs?: Eupsychius, Mamas, and Gordius at Caesarea in Cappadocia** (Language: English)
Aude Busine, Département d'Histoire, Arts et Archéologie, Université Libre de Bruxelles
Paper 1123-b: **Forgetting Saints from the Martyrology of Jerome: Manuscript Evidence** (Language: English)
Marijana Vuković, Instytut Historyczny, Uniwersytet Warszawski
Paper 1123-c: **Syrian and Byzantine Saints in a 12th-Century Syriac Manuscript** (Language: English)
Christian Sahner, Faculty of Oriental Studies, University of Oxford

Session: **1124** **Charles Thackrah Building: 1.04**
Title: **NAMES AS MEMORIALS, II: SAINTS, PILGRIMS, AND CHILDREN**
Sponsor: Dictionary of Medieval Names from European Sources
Organiser: Sara L. Uckelman, Institute of Medieval & Early Modern Studies, Durham University
Moderator: Sofia Evemalm, School of Humanities, University of Glasgow
Paper 1124-a: **A Tale of Four Roberts: Pilgrimage and Penance in 11th-Century Normandy and Flanders** (Language: English)
Brad Phillis, Department of History, University of Tennessee, Knoxville
Paper 1124-b: **Legendary Landscapes and Mythical Memories: The Interrelationship between Popular History, Megalithic Sites, and Medieval Brunhilde Toponyms** (Language: English)
Karel Fraaije, Department of English, University College London
Paper 1124-c: **Augurative and Commemorative Personal Names in Early 14th-Century Imola** (Language: English)
Sara L. Uckelman

Session: **1125** **Maurice Keyworth Building: Room 1.06**
Title: **'ONCE UPON A TIME...': VEILED MEMORIES AND VANISHED POWERS**
Sponsor: Rikkyo University, Tokyo / Universität Basel
Organiser: Jessika Nowak, Departement Geschichte, Universität Basel and Minoru Ozawa, College of Arts, Rikkyo University, Tokyo
Moderator: Andreas Karg, Abteilung 'Forschung & Nachwuchs', Goethe-Universität, Frankfurt am Main
Paper 1125-a: **Commemoration Strategy of the Jelling Dynasty in the 10th and 11th Centuries** (Language: English)
Minoru Ozawa
Paper 1125-b: **The Saxons** (Language: English)
Caspar Ehlers, Max-Planck-Gesellschaft zur Förderung der Wissenschaften, Institut für Europäische Rechtsgeschichte, Frankfurt am Main
Paper 1125-c: **Gone and Forgotten?: The *damnatio memoriae* of the Kingdom of Burgundy** (Language: English)
Jessika Nowak
Paper 1125-d: **Created to Be Conquered: Gerald of Wales's Construction of a Foundational Myth for Ireland** (Language: English)
Fabienne Schwizer, Departement Geschichte, Universität Basel

Session: **1126** **University House: Great Woodhouse Room**
Title: **NORMAN WOMEN RULERS, II: COUNTESSES TO QUEENS IN SOUTHERN ITALIAN MEMORY**
Sponsor: Institute for Medieval Studies, University of Leeds
Organiser: Francesca Petrizzo, Institute for Medieval Studies, University of Leeds
Moderator: Joanna Phillips, School of History, University of Leeds
Paper 1126-a: **Alberada Reconsidered** (Language: English)
Valeria DiClemente, Struttura Didattica Speciale di Lingue e letterature straniere, Università degli Studi di Catania
Paper 1126-b: ***De mobilitate mulierum*?: The Countesses' Role amid the Italo-Norman Nobility and the Sicilian Monarchy** (Language: English)
Hervin Fernández-Aceves, School of History / Institute for Medieval Studies, University of Leeds
Paper 1126-c: **Victims or Vixens?: The Last Three Queens of Norman Sicily, 1177-1198** (Language: English)
Paula Hailstone, Department of History, Royal Holloway, University of London

Session: **1127** **Social Sciences Building: Room 10.07**
Title: **MEDIEVALISM IN 18TH- AND 19TH-CENTURY LITERATURE IN ENGLISH**
Organiser: IMC Programming Committee
Moderator: Louise D'Arcens, Department of English, Macquarie University, Sydney
Paper 1127-a: **'Enlightened Medievalism' and National Identity in Clara Reeve's *The Old English Baron*** (Language: English)
Hi Kyung Moon, Department of English, Korea University, South Korea
Paper 1127-b: **Memory in Matthew Lewis's *The Monk*** (Language: English)
Maria Margarita Rivera Santiago, Department of Curriculum & Instruction, Pennsylvania State University
Paper 1127-c: **Moral Chaucer?: Remembering Medieval Fabliaux in the 19th Century** (Language: English)
Natalie Hanna, Department of English, University of Liverpool
Paper 1127-d: **'Echoes from Mist-Land': The Anglophone *Nibelungenlied* in the 19th Century** (Language: English)
Mary Boyle, Department of German, Maynooth University

Session: **1128** **Baines Wing: Room G.37**
Title: **EXPERIENCE AND MEMORY IN MEDIEVAL CHRISTIAN POLEMICS AGAINST ISLAM**
Sponsor: Centrum för medeltidsstudier, Stockholms universitet
Organiser: Kurt Villads Jensen, Historiska institutionen, Stockholms universitet
Moderator: Martin M. Bauer, Institut für Sprachen und Literaturen, Universität Innsbruck
Paper 1128-a: **Experience as Evidence in the 15th-Century Theological Debate on Islam** (Language: English)
Davide Scotto, Conversion, Overlapping Religiosities, Polemics, Interaction (CORPI) Project, Consejo Superior de Investigaciones Científicas, Madrid
Paper 1128-b: **Experience and Memory in Dominican Missionary Strategies** (Language: English)
Rita George-Tvrtković, Department of History, Philosophy & Religion, Benedictine University, Lisle, Illinois
Paper 1128-c: **Reworking and Remembering Riccoldo: The Use of Riccoldo de Monte di Croce's *Contra legem saracenorum* in Later Anti-Islam Treatises** (Language: English)
Jacob Langeloh, Institut für Katholische Theologie, Universität Koblenz-Landau

---

Session: **1129** **Charles Thackrah Building: 1.03**
Title: ***THE MEDITATIONES VITAE CHRISTI* AND VISUAL CONSTRUCTIONS OF MEMORY, II**
Organiser: Renana Bartal, Department of Art History, Tel Aviv University and Holly Flora, School of Liberal Arts, Tulane University, Louisiana
Moderator: Renana Bartal
Paper 1129-a: **The Writer as Viewer: Recollecting Art in the Text of the *Meditationes*** (Language: English)
Joanna Cannon, Courtauld Institute of Art, University of London
Paper 1129-b: **Memory and Female Agency in Illustrated Manuscripts of the *Meditationes*** (Language: English)
Holly Flora
Paper 1129-c: **The *Meditationes Vitae Christi* in a New Light** (Language: English)
Péter Tóth, British Library, London

Session: **1130** **Social Sciences Building: Room 10.09**
Title: **VISUAL REMEMBRANCE**
Organiser: IMC Programming Committee
Moderator: Kateřina Horníčková, Sonderforschungsbereich Project 'Visions of Community', Universität Wien / Southern Bohemian University, České Budějovice
Paper 1130-a: **Mapping Knowledge: The Mosaic Floor of Otranto Cathedral, 1163-1165** (Language: English)
Nurit Golan, Cohn Institute for the History & Philosophy of Science & Ideas, Tel Aviv University
Paper 1130-b: **Visual Indexing in Medieval England: Memory, Mind, and Information** (Language: English)
Yin Liu, Department of English, University of Saskatchewan
Paper 1130-c: **Remembering through Bodies: Memory and Visual Culture in Late Medieval Finland** (Language: English)
Katja Fält, Department of Music, Art & Culture Studies, University of Jyväskylä

Session: **1131** **Maurice Keyworth Building: Room 1.05**
Title: **MEMORY, SETTLEMENT, AND LANDSCAPE, I: LANDSCAPE AND MEMORY**
Sponsor: Medieval Settlement Research Group
Organiser: Duncan Berryman, School of Geography, Archaeology & Palaeoecology, Queen's University Belfast, Susan Kilby, Centre for English Local History, University of Leicester and Eddie Procter, Department of Archaeology, University of Exeter
Moderator: Duncan Berryman
Paper 1131-a: **Fields of Vision: Memorising the Medieval Rural Landscape** (Language: English)
Susan Kilby
Paper 1131-b: **Medieval Landscape and Memory: How Do Traditional Societies Remember?** (Language: English)
Mark Gardiner, School of History & Heritage, University of Lincoln
Paper 1131-c: **Little Flanders beyond Wales: A Landscape Archaeological Research on the Memory of Flemish Settlement Landscapes in the British Isles** (Language: English)
Gerben Verbrugghe, Vakgroep Archeologie, Universiteit Gent

Session: **1132** **Baines Wing: Room G.36**
Title: **WORLD HERITAGE AS MEMORY OF THE MIDDLE AGES**
Sponsor: Zentrum für Mittelalterstudien (Zemas), Otto-Friedrich-Universität Bamberg
Organiser: Ingrid Bennewitz, Lehrstuhl für Deutsche Philologie des Mittelalters, Otto-Friedrich-Universität Bamberg
Moderator: Christof Rolker, Institut für Geschichtswissenschaften und Europäische Ethnologie, Otto-Friedrich-Universität Bamberg
Paper 1132-a: **Memory as Category in Art History** (Language: English)
Stephan Albrecht, Institut für Archäologische Wissenschaften, Denkmalwissenschaften und Kunstgeschichte, Otto-Friedrich Universität Bamberg
Paper 1132-b: **The Memory of an Emperor: The Manuscripts of Emperor Henry II (1014-1024) at the Staatsbibliothek Bamberg** (Language: English)
Bettina Wagner, Staatsbibliothek Bamberg
Paper 1132-c: **The Stolen Lance: The Medieval Bamberg World Heritage for Kids** (Language: English)
Detlef Goller, Zentrum für Mittelalterstudien, Otto-Friedrich-Universität Bamberg and Linda Wolters, Fränkisches Freilandmuseum, Fladungen

Session: **1133** **Leeds University Union: Room 2 - Elland Road**
Title: **INVENTING HEROES, REVERSING LEGENDS, CONSTRUCTING FACTS: THE DYNAMICS OF IDENTITY SHAPING, II - THE MIRROR OF HISTORIOGRAPHY**
Sponsor: Lise-Meitner Project, Institut für Mittelalterforschung, Österreichische Akademie der Wissenschaften, Wien / Department of Auxiliary Historical Sciences & Archive Studies, Masarykova univerzita, Brno
Organiser: Klara Hübner, Department of Auxiliary Historical Sciences & Archive Studies, Masarykova univerzita, Brno and David Kalhous, Institut für Mittelalterforschung, Österreichische Akademie der Wissenschaften, Wien
Moderator: Walter Pohl, Institut für Mittelalterforschung, Österreichische Akademie der Wissenschaften, Wien
Paper 1133-a: **'In the cradle with Germany': Creating a Modern Nation in/through the Middle Ages** (Language: English)
David Kalhous
Paper 1133-b: **The Big History of Small Noblemen: Swiss Rural Elites Struggling for a Noble Ancestry** (Language: English)
Heinrich Speich, Independent Scholar, Switzerland
Paper 1133-c: **The Medieval Heroes of Swedish Romantic Nationalism** (Language: English)
Christian Oertel, Historisches Seminar, Universität Erfurt

Session: **1134** **Maurice Keyworth Building: Room 1.33**
Title: **PERCEPTIONS OF IDENTITY IN MEDIEVAL CHRONICLES**
Organiser: IMC Programming Committee
Moderator: Anti Selart, Institute of History & Archaeology, University of Tartu
Paper 1134-a: **The Kings of León and the Kings of Castile in Lucas of Tuy's *Chronicon mundi*** (Language: English)
Diego Rodríguez-Peña Sainz de la Maza, Departamento de Historia Antigua, Historia Medieval y Paleografía y Diplomática, Universidad Autónoma de Madrid
Paper 1134-b: **Half-Remembered Grievances: Guelfs, Ghibellines, and the Pisans in Giovanni Sercambi's *Chronicle of Lucca*** (Language: English)
Daniel Jamison, Centre for Medieval Studies, University of Toronto, Downtown
Paper 1134-c: **Construction of the Past in the *Chronicle of the Grand Duchy of Lithuania and Samogitia*** (Language: English)
Miraslau Shpakau, Department of Medieval Studies, Central European University, Budapest

Session: **1135** **Leeds University Union: Room 4 - Hyde Park**
Title: **ARCHIVAL MEMORY: INSTITUTIONS, TEXTS, AND SHAPES, II**
Sponsor: Institut de Recherche et d'Histoire des Textes (IRHT), Centre National de la Recherche Scientifique (CNRS), Paris
Organiser: Dominique Stutzmann, Institut de Recherche et d'Histoire des Textes (IRHT), Centre National de la Recherche Scientifique (CNRS), Paris
Moderator: Sébastien Barret, Institut de Recherche et d'Histoire des Textes (IRHT), Centre National de la Recherche Scientifique (CNRS), Paris
Paper 1135-a: **'Memories false and real': Memorial Aspects of Episcopal Charters from 13th-Century Livonia** (Language: English)
Edgar Rops, Independent Scholar, Latvia
Paper 1135-b: **Preserving Missives at Metz during the 15th Century: An Administrative Memory of Legal Practices?** (Language: English)
Amélie Marineau-Pelletier, Department of History, University of Ottawa / Centre de Recherches Historiques, École des Hautes Études en Sciences Sociales (EHESS), Paris
Paper 1135-c: **An Imaginary Frailty?: Memory Discourses in Charters, 7th-13th Centuries** (Language: English)
Nicolas Perreaux, Sonderforschungsbereich 1095 'Schwächediskurse und Ressourcenregime', Goethe-Universität, Frankfurt am Main / Laboratoire de médiévistique occidentale de Paris (LaMOP), Université de la Sorbonne, Paris

Session: **1136** **Leeds University Union: Room 5 - Kirkstall Abbey**
Title: **VOICES OF LAW, II: MEMORY, ORALITY, AND LEGAL PERFORMANCE**
Sponsor: Voices of Law: Language, Text & Practice
Organiser: Jenny Benham, School of History, Archaeology & Religion, Cardiff University
Moderator: Jenny Benham
Paper 1136-a: **Compurgation as Legal Performance in 13th-Century Norway** (Language: English)
Ole-Albert Rønning, Institutt for Arkeologi, Bevaring og Historie, Universitetet i Oslo
Paper 1136-b: **A Performance of Forgetting: Exploring Legal Stigmas in Early Medieval Scandinavia** (Language: English)
Keith Ruiter, Centre for Scandinavian Studies, University of Aberdeen
Paper 1136-c: **Traces of Orality and Literacy in the Old Frisian Laws** (Language: English)
Han Nijdam, Fryske Akademy, De Koninklijke Nederlandse Akademie van Wetenschappen, Leeuwarden

Session:	**1137** **Emmanuel Centre: Wilson Room**
Title:	**INVESTING IN MEMORY: CIVIC ENDOWMENTS, MATERIAL CULTURE, AND URBAN COMMUNITIES, II**
Sponsor:	Institut für Österreichische Geschichtsforschung (IÖG), Universität Wien / Interdisziplinäres Zentrum für Mittelalter und Frühneuzeit (IZMF), Universität Salzburg
Organiser:	Elisabeth Gruber, Institut für Realienkunde des Mittelalters und der frühen Neuzeit, Universität Salzburg and Judit Majorossy, Institut für Geschichte, Universität Wien
Moderator:	Anu Mänd, Institute of History, Archaeology & Art History, Tallinn University
Paper 1137-a:	**Practical Memory: Supporting Church Building Funds in West-Hungarian Towns** (Language: English) Judit Majorossy
Paper 1137-b:	**Remembering Papal Rome: Aspects of the Popes' Representation in Exile in Avignon, 1309–1377** (Language: English) Tanja Hinterholz, Interdisziplinäres Zentrum für Mittelalter und Frühneuzeit (IZMF), Universität Salzburg
Paper 1137-c:	**Ways to Heaven: Spousal Attitudes to Memory among the Elite Citizens of Late Medieval Dubrovnik (Ragusa)** (Language: English) Zrinka Pešorda Vardić, Department of Medieval History, Croatian Institute of History, Zagreb
Paper 1137-d:	**Commemorative Strategies in Medieval Moravian Wills from a Gender Perspective** (Language: English) Michaela Antonín Malaníková, Department of History, Palacký University, Olomouc

Session:	**1138** **Michael Sadler Building: Room LG.10**
Title:	**MONUMENTS AND MITRES**
Sponsor:	EPISCOPUS: Society for the Study of Bishops & the Secular Clergy in the Middle Ages
Organiser:	Evan Gatti, Department of Art & Art History, Elon University, North Carolina
Moderator:	John S. Ott, Department of History, Portland State University, Oregon
Paper 1138-a:	**Re-Writing Episcopal Memory in Old St Paul's Cathedral** (Language: English) David Harry, Department of History & Archaeology, University of Chester
Paper 1138-b:	**The Bishop in Santa Croce: John Catterick and His Tomb** (Language: English) Christian Steer, Department of History, University of York
Paper 1138-c:	**Bishop Fleming's Chantry in Lincoln Cathedral: Image and Text in Episcopal Commemoration** (Language: English) David Lepine, Department of History University of Exeter

Session:	**1139** **Maurice Keyworth Building: Room 1.03**
Title:	**MODES OF REMEMBRANCE IN HIGH MEDIEVAL GERMANY**
Organiser:	Johanna Dale, Department of History, University College London
Moderator:	Alheydis Plassmann, Institut für Geschichtswissenschaft, Rheinische Friedrich-Wilhelms-Universität Bonn
Paper 1139-a:	**Abbot Herman of Niederaltaich's Rent Book and Cartulary: From Memory to Written Record or Phantoms of Remembrance?** (Language: English) Jonathan Lyon, Department of History, University of Chicago, Illinois
Paper 1139-b:	**The Karlsschrein in Aachen: *Cui bono*?** (Language: English) Vedran Sulovsky, Faculty of History, University of Cambridge
Paper 1139-c:	**How and Why Was a 7th-Century Northumbrian King Remembered in High Medieval Germany?** (Language: English) Johanna Dale

Session:	**1140** **Michael Sadler Building: Room LG.15**
Title:	**MEMORIES OF CLOVIS**
Organiser:	Birgit Kynast, Historisches Seminar, Johannes Gutenberg-Universität Mainz
Moderator:	Dominik Waßenhoven, Historisches Institut, Universität zu Köln
Paper 1140-a:	***Rex Francorum*: Clovis and the Charisma of Merovingian Kings** (Language: English) Ludger Körntgen, Historisches Seminar, Johannes Gutenberg-Universität Mainz
Paper 1140-b:	**Clovis: King, Consul, or Even Emperor?** (Language: English) Roland Zingg, Historisches Seminar, Johannes Gutenberg-Universität Mainz
Paper 1140-c:	**Sicamber, Constantine, Silvester?: The Baptism of Clovis** (Language: English) Birgit Kynast

Session:	**1141** **Stage@leeds: Stage 2**
Title:	**BIRGITTINE ACTS OF MEMORY, II: REMEMBERING AND FORGETTING**
Sponsor:	Institut de Recerca de Cultures Medievals (IRCVM), Universitat de Barcelona / Centrum för teologi och religionsvetenskap, Lunds universitet
Organiser:	David Carrillo-Rangel, Institut de Recerca de Cultures Medievals (IRCVM), Universitat de Barcelona and Erik Claeson, Centrum för teologi och religionsvetenskap, Lunds universitet
Moderator:	David Carrillo-Rangel
Paper 1141-a:	**Remembering Birgitta with Music** (Language: English) Karin Strinnholm Lagergren, Institutionen för musik och bild, Linnéuniversitetet, Växjö
Paper 1141-b:	**Strategies for Remembering St Birgitta in Sermons from Vadstena Abbey, c. 1400-1510** (Language: English) Erik Claeson
Paper 1141-c:	**God's Ambassadress: Commemorations of St Bridget of Sweden by the Syon Bridgettines, 1861-1961** (Language: English) Carmen M. Mangion, Department of History, Classics & Archaeology, Birkbeck, University of London

Session: **1142** **Stage@leeds: Stage 3**
Title: **RECOLLECTING MEDIEVAL ARTEFACTS: A GLOBAL PERSPECTIVE**
Sponsor: International Center of Medieval Art, The Met Cloisters, New York
Organiser: Jitske Jasperse, Instituto de Historia, Consejo Superior de Investigaciones Científicas, Madrid
Moderator: Wendelien A. W. Van Welie-Vink, Afdeling Kunst- en cultuurwetenschappen, Universiteit van Amsterdam
Paper 1142-a: **Texts from Tombs: Buried Biography in Medieval China and Its Reception in Modern Times** (Language: English)
Timothy Davis, Independent Scholar, Utah
Paper 1142-b: **Buried Coins and Seals: Making the Invisible Visible?** (Language: English)
Jitske Jasperse
Paper 1142-c: **Hidden Presence: Miracle-Working Objects in Medieval Buildings** (Language: English)
Minou Schraven, Department of Humanities, Amsterdam University College

---

Session: **1143** **Emmanuel Centre: Room 10**
Title: **LAY MEMORIES OF CRUSADING**
Organiser: James Doherty, School of Modern Languages, University of Bristol
Moderator: Katherine J. Lewis, Department of History, University of Huddersfield
Paper 1143-a: **Memory and Literary Influences on the Lay Authorship of Crusade Narratives** (Language: English)
Natasha Ruth Hodgson, School of Arts & Humanities, Nottingham Trent University
Paper 1143-b: **Constructing a Legacy: Crusading and Kingship in the Long 12th Century** (Language: English)
Matthew Mesley, School of Music, Humanities & Media, University of Huddersfield
Paper 1143-c: **Remembering Lay Initiative in Crusade Instigation** (Language: English)
James Doherty

Session: **1144** **Fine Art Building: SR 1.10**
Title: **IMPERIAL MEMORIES IN LATE ANTIQUITY, II: COMMUNAL MEMORY OF LATE ANTIQUE CITIES**
Organiser: Adrastos Omissi, School of Humanities (Classics), University of Glasgow
Moderator: Julia Hillner, Department of History, University of Sheffield
Paper 1144-a: **Remembering the Past in Former Roman *sedes imperii*** (Language: English)
Markus Löx, DFG-Graduiertenkolleg 2337 'Metropolität in der Vormoderne', Universität Regensburg
Paper 1144-b: **Commemorating War in the 5th-Century West** (Language: English)
Glenn McDorman, Department of History, Princeton University
Paper 1144-c: **Trauma, Memory, and Authority in Late Antique Antioch: the Case of the Sack of Antioch in 252-253** (Language: English)
Laurent Cases, Department of History, Pennsylvania State University

Session: **1145** **Maurice Keyworth Building: Room 1.32**
Title: **AT THE CUTTING EDGE OF DIGITAL MEMORY: THE ONLINE CORPUS OF ROMANESQUE SCULPTURE IN BRITAIN AND IRELAND - POST-CONQUEST CARVING AT YOUR FINGERTIPS, II**
Sponsor: Corpus of Romanesque Sculpture in Britain & Ireland (CRSBI)
Organiser: Karen Impey, Corpus of Romanesque Sculpture in Britain & Ireland (CRSBI), London
Moderator: Eric Campbell Fernie, Courtauld Institute of Art, University of London
Paper 1145-a: **Baptismal Fonts, II: The Romanesque Coleby Font Group - A Design, Distribution, and Iconographic Analysis** (Language: English)
Thomas E. Russo, Department of Fine & Performing Arts, Drury University, Missouri
Paper 1145-b: **For the Record: Putting the Romanesque Sculpture of Wales Online** (Language: English)
David M. Robinson, Independent Scholar, London
Paper 1145-c: **Baptismal Fonts, III: Magnates in the Midlands** (Language: English)
Susan Nettle, Independent Scholar, Teddington

Session: **1146** **Leeds University Union: Room 6 - Roundhay**
Title: **REMEMBERING CHIVALRY, II: BATTLEFIELD CONDUCT**
Sponsor: Institute for Medieval Studies, University of Leeds
Organiser: James Titterton, Institute for Medieval Studies, University of Leeds
Moderator: Trevor Russell Smith, Institute for Medieval Studies, University of Leeds
Paper 1146-a: **'Por les granz biens e por l'onor, qu'il orront de lor anseisor': Memorialisation and Emulation as Key Facets in Developing a Chivalric Culture** (Language: English)
Matthew Bennett, Department of History, University of Winchester
Paper 1146-b: **The Boldness of the Knights in the Battles: Study and Evolution of a Commonplace of the Medieval Chronicles** (Language: English)
Pierre Courroux, British Academy / Department of History, University of Southampton
Paper 1146-c: **A Chivalrous Trickster?: Remembering Cunning in the *History of William Marshal*** (Language: English)
James Titterton

Session: **1147** **Baines Wing: Room 2.14**
Title: **NEW PERSPECTIVES ON MEDIEVAL COMBAT AND WEAPONRY**
Organiser: IMC Programming Committee
Moderator: Kelly DeVries, Department of History, Loyola University Maryland
Paper 1147-a: **European and Middle Eastern Armor: Similarity and Divergence** (Language: English)
Doran Tucker, College of Earth & Mineral Sciences, Pennsylvania State University
Paper 1147-b: **Crossbow Classification: The Need for a More Diverse Understanding of Medieval Europe's Iconic Weapon** (Language: English)
Stuart Gorman, Independent Scholar, Dublin
Paper 1147-c: **Augmented Memory and the Visualisation of Single Combat** (Language: English)
Michael Ovens, Department of English & Cultural Studies, University of Western Australia

Session:	**1148** **University House: St George Room**
Title:	**TIME, SCIENCE, AND THE BODY IN THE ANGLO-NORMAN WORLD: DURHAM, CATHEDRAL LIBRARY, MS HUNTER 100 AND ITS CONTEXTS, II - SCIENCE, HISTORY, AND IMAGINATION**
Sponsor:	Department of History, Durham University
Organiser:	Giles E. M. Gasper, Department of History, Durham University
Moderator:	Sigbjorn Sonnesyn, Department of History, Durham University
Paper 1148-a:	**Computus as 'Scientific Literacy': Insights from Durham MS Hunter 100** (Language: English) Faith Wallis, Department of History & Classical Studies / Department of Social Studies of Medicine, McGill University, Québec
Paper 1148-b:	**An Arithmetical Case Study in Abbo of Fleury's *Commentary on Calculus*** (Language: English) Clelia Crialesi, Dipartimento di Studi letterari, Filosofici e Storia dell'arte, Università degli Studi di Roma 'Tor Vergata' / École Pratique des Hautes Études (EPHE), Paris
Paper 1148-c:	**Frameworks of Time: The Easter-Table Annals of Durham MS Hunter 100 and Other Contemporary Durham Manuscripts** (Language: English) Charlie Rozier, Department of History, Swansea University

Session:	**1149** **Stage@leeds: Stage 1**
Title:	**THE WHOLE IS MORE THAN THE SUM OF ITS PARTS: STUDYING MEDIEVAL LEGAL COMPILATIONS**
Organiser:	Daniela Schulz, Graduiertenkolleg 2196 'Dokument - Text - Edition', Bergische Universität Wuppertal
Moderator:	Stefan Esders, Friedrich-Meinecke-Institut, Freie Universität Berlin
Paper 1149-a:	**'Ein zusammengestoppeltes elendes Machwerk': Some Views on Wolfenbüttel, Herzog August Bibliothek, Cod. Guelf. 97 Weiss** (Language: English) Daniela Schulz
Paper 1149-b:	**Tracing the Origins of Capitulary Collections: The Manuscript Evidence** (Language: English) Britta Mischke, Historisches Institut, Universität zu Köln
Paper 1149-c:	**'There's a manuscript for that': Assembling a Legal Dossier in the 10th Century** (Language: English) Ian Ward, Department of History, Princeton University
Paper 1149-d:	**Norman Customaries and Their Manuscripts** (Language: English) Thomas Roche, Archives départementales de l'Eure / Groupe de Recherche d'Histoire (GRHis), Université de Rouen Normandie

Session: **1150** **Baines Wing: Room 2.15**
Title: **CANONIZE YOURSELF!, II: HOW TO BECOME A CANON IN A MEDIEVAL CENTRAL EUROPEAN CHAPTER**
Sponsor: Erzbistum Paderborn / Universitetet i Tromsø - Norges Arktiske Universitetet
Organiser: Arnold Otto, Erzbischöfliches Generalvikariat Erzbistumsarchiv, Paderborn
Moderator: Anna Pobog-Lenartowicz, Instytut Historii, Uniwersytet Opolski
Paper 1150-a: **Career Paths among the Clergy of the Collegiate Chapters in the Medieval Archdiocese of Gniezno** (Language: English)
Anna Kowalska-Pietrzak, Instytut Historii, Uniwersytet Łódzki
Paper 1150-b: **Collectors or Hunters of Benefices?: The Question of Accumulation and Some Extreme Examples from Late Medieval Silesia** (Language: English)
Stanislaw Jujeczka, Instytut Historyczny, Uniwersytet Wrocławski
Paper 1150-c: **Getting a Prebend in the Cathedral Chapter of Paderborn in the 15th and 16th Century** (Language: English)
Jörg Wunschhofer, Projekt 'Germania Sacra', Akademie der Wissenschaften zu Göttingen

Session: **1152** **University House: Cloberry Room**
Title: **MEDIEVAL ETHIOPIA, II: CHRISTIANS AND PAGANS**
Sponsor: Fakultät für Geschichtswissenschaft, Ruhr-Universität Bochum
Organiser: Vincent van Gerven Oei, punctum books, Tirana and Adam Simmons, Department of History, Lancaster University
Moderator: Meseret Oldjira, Department of Art & Archaeology, Princeton University
Paper 1152-a: **The Zagwe Church of Yemrehanna Krestos: A Contemporary of the Rock-Hewn Churches of Lalibala** (Language: English)
Michael Gervers, 'Documents of Early England Dataset' Project, University of Toronto, Downtown
Paper 1152-b: **Pagan Religious Practices in Medieval Ethiopia: Development and Resistance of the Christian Kingdom, 1434–1468** (Language: English)
Solomon Gebreyes Beyene, Hiob Ludolf Centre for Ethiopian Studies, Universität Hamburg
Paper 1152-c: **Northern Ethiopia as the Last Refuge of King Lebna Dengel (1508-1540): Evaluation of Manuscript Evidence from Tigray** (Language: English)
Denis Nosnitsin, Hiob Ludolf Centre for Ethiopian Studies, Universität Hamburg

Session:	**1153**	**Emmanuel Centre: Room 11**
Title:	**MINING THE MOTHER LODE: MAKING NEW USE OF REGESTS AND REGISTERS**	
Sponsor:	Akademie der Wissenschaften und Literatur, Mainz	
Organiser:	Gerhard Lubich, Historisches Institut, Ruhr-Universität Bochum	
Moderator:	Dirk Jäckel, Lehrstuhl für die Geschichte des Frühmittelalters, Ruhr-Universität Bochum / *Regesta Imperii*, Akademie der Wissenschaften und Literatur, Mainz	
Paper 1153-a:	**New Tools for Old Fools?: History and Digital Humanities - The State of Their Union** (Language: English) Gerhard Lubich	
Paper 1153-b:	**Transforming Registers into Entangled Entities: Why and How to Use Graphs in History** (Language: English) Andreas Kuczera, Historisches Institut, Justus-Liebig Universität Gießen	
Paper 1153-c:	**The Simple Art of Register and Regesta: A How-To Guide** (Language: English) Lisa Klocke, Lehrstuhl für die Geschichte des Frühmittelalters, Ruhr-Universität Bochum / *Regesta Imperii*, Akademie der Wissenschaften und Literatur, Mainz and Matthias Weber, Lehrstuhl für die Geschichte des Frühmittelalters, Ruhr-Universität Bochum / *Regesta Imperii*, Akademie der Wissenschaften und Literatur, Mainz	

Session:	**1154**	**Maurice Keyworth Building: Room G.02**
Title:	**TEACHING THE EUROPEAN MIDDLE AGES OUTSIDE THE GLOBAL WEST - A ROUND TABLE DISCUSSION**	
Sponsor:	BABEL working group	
Organiser:	Sjoerd Levelt, Program in Cultures, Civilizations & Ideas, Bilkent University, Ankara and Kathryn Maude, Department of English, American University of Beirut	
Moderator:	Dorothy Kim, Department of English, Vassar College, New York	
Purpose:	*This round table discussion brings together scholars of literature, history, and art history to think through the challenges and opportunities that teaching the European Middle Ages outside the traditional academic geographies brings. How does teaching the canon of western medieval literature function differently in a postcolonial setting? What meanings do western medieval art and philosophy have for students outside North America and Europe? What comparative perspectives can be brought to bear on these texts and histories when teaching in non-western settings? By attempting to answer some of these questions we shall contribute to ongoing discussions of medievalism and the global Middle Ages, and of race, inclusivity, and diversity in medieval studies.* *Participants include Paulo Henrique de Carvalho Pachá (Universidade Federal Fluminense, Rio de Janeiro), René Hernández Vera (Universidad Santo Tomás, Bogotá), Sjoerd Levelt (Bilkent University, Ankara), Kathryn Maude (American University of Beirut), and Idette Noomé (University of Pretoria).*	

LUNCH

Meal Times

Refectory	12.00-14.00
University Square: The Marquee	12.00-14.00

See Map 9, p. 51.

*   *   *   *   *

MEDIEVAL HIGHLIGHTS FROM LEEDS UNIVERSITY LIBRARY SPECIAL COLLECTIONS

PARKINSON BUILDING: TREASURES OF THE BROTHERTON GALLERY
12.00-14.00

Join us for a drop-in session to see medieval treasures from Special Collections at the University of Leeds. Special Collections staff will be in the Treasures of the Brotherton Gallery with a selection of highlights from the collections for delegates to examine close-up.

The collections at Leeds contain beautiful illuminated 15th-century French and Flemish books of hours, psalters, and prayer books, as well as German chained manuscripts from the 1450s. Some of these will be on show alongside examples from our fine collection of incunabula. The Library of Ripon Cathedral is held on long-term deposit in Special Collections at the University of Leeds and includes a Latin Bible from the 13th century. A highlight of the Yorkshire Archaeological and Historical Society Collection is the enormous series of surviving court rolls of the manor of Wakefield (1274-1925). Also for the first time at the IMC, we will be revealing examples from our extensive coin collection.

Special Collections houses over 200,000 rare books and 7 km of manuscripts and archives, including the celebrated Brotherton Collection. The Special Collections Reading Room is open from 09.00-17.00 during the IMC, and delegates are welcome to pursue their research and explore the collection. More details on how to search and use the collections can be found at https://library.leeds.ac.uk/special-collections.

*   *   *   *   *

Session:	**1199**	**Stage@leeds: Stage 1**
Title:	**Keynote Lecture 2018:** **I Can't Remember the Middle Ages** (Language: English)	
Speaker:	Jeff Rider, Department of Romance Languages & Literatures, Wesleyan University, Connecticut	
Introduction:	Lucie Doležalová, Institute of Greek & Latin Studies, Univerzita Karlova, Praha and Jan Čermák, Department of English, Univerzita Karlova, Praha	
Details:	*Because we remember our personal past, it is not surprising that we think of our imagination of the past in terms of memory. But memory is always personal and incommunicable. I cannot remember things I did not perceive, and I cannot communicate my memories to another person. I have to imagine any past other than my own. My memories of my past do, however, play an essential role in imagining pasts other than my own since they provide the material I use to imagine those pasts. When I imagine a past other than my own, I rearrange the stuff of my memories in new ways and this leads to new insights into my world of everyday experience and my place in it.* *Please note that admission to this event will be on a first-come, first-served basis as there will be no tickets. Please ensure that you arrive as early as possible to avoid disappointment.*	

Session: **1201** **Michael Sadler Building: Room LG.17**
Title: **LEME, I: THE MAKING OF SPACE IN THE EARLY MEDIEVAL WEST**
Sponsor: Laboratório de Estudos Medievais (LEME), Cidade Universitária São Paulo
Organiser: Hervin Fernández-Aceves, School of History / Institute for Medieval Studies, University of Leeds
Moderator: Otávio Luiz Vieira Pinto, Middle Persian Studies Project, Universidade de Brasília
Paper 1201-a: **Places of Power, Economic Networks, and Space Control in Carolingian Aquitaine** (Language: English)
Adrien Bayard, Faculdade de Filosofia, Letras e Ciências Humanas, Universidade de São Paulo
Paper 1201-b: **The Making of Space in Adomnán of Iona's *Vita Columbae*** (Language: English)
Gabriel Barth Tarifa, Faculdade de Filosofia, Letras e Ciências Humanas, Universidade de São Paulo
Paper 1201-c: **Perceptions of Property in Early Medieval France and Historical Memory** (Language: English)
Igor Filippov, Faculty of History, Lomonosov Moscow State University

Session: **1202** **Baines Wing: Room 1.13**
Title: **BOOKS AND TEXTS: PRESENTATION AND READERSHIP**
Sponsor: Onderzoeksschool Mediëvistiek, Rijksuniversiteit Groningen
Organiser: Rob Meens, Departement Geschiedenis en Kunstgeschiedenis, Universiteit Utrecht
Moderator: Rob Meens
Paper 1202-a: **Reading and Studying the *Moralia in Iob*: Marginal Scholarship in Utrecht, Universiteitsbibliotheek, HS. 86 from the Utrecht Abbey of St Paul** (Language: English)
Nick Pouls, Departement Geschiedenis en Kunstgeschiedenis, Universiteit Utrecht
Paper 1202-b: **Political Language during the Wars of the Roses: The *Somnium Vigilantis* and Sir John Fortescue's *Declaration* in London, British Library, Royal MS 17 D.XV** (Language: English)
Aline Douma, Afdeling Engelse Taal en Cultuur, Rijksuniversiteit Groningen
Paper 1202-c: **Fortune Favours the Bold: Books of Fate and Human Agency in the Late Medieval Low Countries** (Language: English)
Sander Ootjers, Afdeling Geschiedenis, Rijksuniversiteit Groningen

Session:	**1203**	**Baines Wing: Room 2.16**
Title:	**MOVING BYZANTIUM, III: THE GEOGRAPHIC MOBILITY OF PEOPLE, OBJECTS, AND IDEAS**	
Sponsor:	Moving Byzantium: Mobility, Microstructures & Personal Agency, Österreichische Akademie der Wissenschaften, Universität Wien / FWF Wittgenstein-Prize Project	
Organiser:	Claudia Rapp, Institut für Byzantinistik & Neogräzistik, Universität Wien / Österreichische Akademie der Wissenschaften, Wien and Dirk Hoerder, Institut für Geschichtswissenschaft, Universität Bremen / Department of History, Arizona State University	
Moderator:	Nicholas Evans, Clare College, University of Cambridge	
Paper 1203-a:	**A Network for Pilgrims at Late Antique Ephesus: The Case Study of a Newly Explored Pilgrimage Church at the Harbor Canal** (Language: English) Katinka Sewing, Institut für Byzantinische Archäologie und Kunstgeschichte, Ruprecht-Karls-Universität Heidelberg	
Paper 1203-b:	**The Making of the Armenian Church in Historical Memory of the Armenians: Mobility of Persons, Theologies, and Missions** (Language: English) Emilio Bonfiglio, Institut für Byzantinistik & Neogräzistik, Universität Wien	
Paper 1203-c:	**The Chalcedonian Armenians and Moving Borders in Isauria and Pamphylia, 1176-1226** (Language: English) Samvel Grigoryan, Centre d'Études Médiévales, Paul-Valery Université de Montpellier	
Paper 1203-d:	**Traveling and the Geographies of Disorientation: Exile in Late Byzantium** (Language: English) Florin Leonte, Department of the Classics, Palacký University, Olomouc	

Session:	**1204**	**Maurice Keyworth Building: Room 1.32**
Title:	**NEW APPROACHES TO THE THIRD CRUSADE, I**	
Sponsor:	Past & Present Society / Third Crusade Research Network	
Organiser:	Beth Spacey, School of History & Cultures, University of Birmingham and Stephen Spencer, Institute of Historical Research, University of London	
Moderator:	Andrew David Buck, School of History, Queen Mary University of London	
Paper 1204-a:	**Interpreting Signs at the Time of the Third Crusade** (Language: English) Beth Spacey	
Paper 1204-b:	**Rewriting the Third Crusade: Ralph of Coggeshall's *Chronicon Anglicanum*** (Language: English) Stephen Spencer	
Paper 1204-c:	**The Troubadours, the Third Crusade, and Richard the Lionheart** (Language: English) Linda Paterson, Department of French Studies, University of Warwick	

Session: **1205** **Michael Sadler Building: Room LG.16**
Title: **LEGITIMACY THROUGH WEALTH AND DISPLAYS OF WEALTH IN MEDIEVAL EUROPE**
Organiser: IMC Programming Committee
Moderator: Daniel Piñol, Departament d'Història i Arqueologia, Universitat de Barcelona
Paper 1205-a: **Swank Scraps?: Gilding Waste Parchment in a *Statuta Angliæ* Manuscript** (Language: English)
Stephanie Jane Lahey, Department of English, University of Victoria, British Columbia
Paper 1205-b: **Books and Bricks: Dynasty and Memory in Quattrocento Farnese Cultural Politics** (Language: English)
Loek Luiten, New College, University of Oxford
Paper 1205-c: **Founding and Financing the Medieval Portuguese University: Two Sides of the Same Coin** (Language: English)
Rui Miguel Rocha, Centro de História, Universidade de Lisboa

Session: **1206** **Parkinson Building: Room 1.16**
Title: **MEDIEVAL BODIES IGNORED, I: HUMANS AND ANIMALS**
Sponsor: Institute for Medieval Studies, University of Leeds
Organiser: Sunny Harrison, Institute for Medieval Studies, University of Leeds
Moderator: Rose A. Sawyer, Institute for Medieval Studies, University of Leeds
Paper 1206-a: **Beast, Heal Thyself: Animals Treating Animals in Late Medieval Illustrated Veterinary Treatises** (Language: English)
Sunny Harrison
Paper 1206-b: **Man's Best Friend: Animals as Mobility Aids in Late Medieval Art** (Language: English)
Rachael Gillibrand, Institute for Medieval Studies, University of Leeds
Paper 1206-c: **Animals on Trial: The Beastly Problem of Criminal Culpability** (Language: English)
Irina Metzler, Centre for Medieval & Early Modern Research (MEMO), Swansea University

Session: **1207** **Fine Art Building: Studio Ground Floor**
Title: **THE 'GREY POPES': LUCIUS III (1181-1185), URBAN III (1185-1187), GREGORY VIII (1187), AND CLEMENT III (1187-1191), II**
Sponsor: Center for Medieval & Renaissance Studies, Saint Louis University, Missouri
Organiser: Damian Smith, Department of History, Saint Louis University, Missouri
Moderator: Anne J. Duggan, Department of History, King's College London
Paper 1207-a: **Pope Lucius III and the Monastic World** (Language: English)
Enrico Veneziani, St Andrews Institute of Mediaeval Studies, University of St Andrews
Paper 1207-b: ***Audita Tremendi*, the Grey Popes, and the Crusades** (Language: English)
Thomas William Smith, Institute for Medieval Studies, University of Leeds
Paper 1207-c: **The Grey Popes and France** (Language: English)
Pascal Montaubin, UFR d'histoire et de géographie, Université de Picardie Jules Verne

Session:	**1208** **Maurice Keyworth Building: Room 1.04**
Title:	**EARLY ENGLISH LIFE CYCLES: CORPORA AND CORPSES**
Organiser:	Thijs Porck, Centre for the Arts in Society, Universiteit Leiden and Harriet Soper, Department of Anglo-Saxon, Norse & Celtic, University of Cambridge
Moderator:	Christina Lee, School of English, University of Nottingham
Paper 1208-a:	**'Weapon-Boys' and 'Once-Maidens': A Study of Old English Vocabulary for Stages of Life** (Language: English) Daria Izdebska, Department of English, Liverpool Hope University
Paper 1208-b:	**Life Cycles in the Soul's Address to the Body** (Language: English) Terri Sanderson, Centre for Medieval Studies, University of Toronto, Downtown
Paper 1208-c:	**Incorruptible Saint: The Holy Corpses of Anglo-Saxon Women** (Language: English) Jessica Troy, Department of English Language & Literature, University of New Mexico, Albuquerque

Session:	**1209** **Baines Wing: Room 2.13**
Title:	**THE SELF IN SOCIAL SPACES: REPRESENTATIONS AND CONCEPTUALISATIONS IN TEXTUAL AND MATERIAL CULTURE OF MEDIEVAL SCANDINAVIA**
Organiser:	Stefka G. Eriksen, Norsk institutt for kulturminneforskning, Oslo
Moderator:	Stefka G. Eriksen
Paper 1209-a:	**A Personality Set in Stone: Portrayals of Self in Medieval Epigraphic Texts** (Language: English) Karen Langsholt Holmqvist, Institutt for lingvistiske og nordiske studier, Universitetet i Oslo / Norsk institutt for kulturminneforskning, Oslo
Paper 1209-b:	**Materialising the Self: Clothing and Appearances in Urban Spaces** (Language: English) Bjørn Bandlien, Institutt for økonomi, historie og samfunnsvitenskap, Høgskolen i Sørøst-Norge
Paper 1209-c:	**Representations of the Self in Old Norse Sagas** (Language: English) Stefka G. Eriksen

Session:	**1210** **Baines Wing: Room 1.16**
Title:	**RETHINKING AGENCY, II: READING JEWS**
Sponsor:	*Medieval Prosopography*
Organiser:	Charlotte Pickard, Centre for Continuing & Professional Education, Cardiff University and Rebecca Searby, Centre for Medieval Studies, University of York
Moderator:	Lindy Grant, Department of History, University of Reading
Paper 1210-a:	**The Agency of the 13th-Century Anglo-Jewess** (Language: English) Dean A. Irwin, School of Humanities, Canterbury Christ Church University
Paper 1210-b:	**The Tale of Two Tolranas: Jewish Women's Agency and Conversion in Late Medieval Girona** (Language: English) Alexandra Guerson, Department of History, University of Toronto, New College and Dana Wessell Lightfoot, Department of History, University of Northern British Columbia
Paper 1210-c:	**The Problems and Possibilities of Reading Jewish Agency in English Common Law** (Language: English) Rebecca Searby

Session:	**1211** **Baines Wing: Room 1.15**
Title:	**Mind over Matter: Debates about Relics as Sacred Objects, c. 350-c. 1150**
Sponsor:	Mind over Matter: Debates about Relics as Sacred Objects, c. 350-c. 1150, NWO-VIDI Project
Organiser:	Janneke Raaijmakers, Departement Geschiedenis en Kunstgeschiedenis, Universiteit Utrecht
Moderator:	Julia M. H. Smith, Faculty of History, University of Oxford
Paper 1211-a:	**Material for Thought: Relic Veneration in the Earlier Middle Ages - Devotion, Reflection, and Doubt** (Language: English) Janneke Raaijmakers
Paper 1211-b:	**Inscribing Sanctity: An Epigraphic Approach to the Material Culture of the Cult of Relics in Western Christianity, c. 800-c. 1150** (Language: English) Elisa Pallottini, Departement Geschiedenis en Kunstgeschiedenis, Universiteit Utrecht
Paper 1211-c:	**What Kind of Virtu(e)s?: Alcuin and Thiofrid on Sanctity and Relics, c. 800-1100** (Language: English) Jelle Visser, Departement Geschiedenis en Kunstgeschiedenis, Universiteit Utrecht

Session:	**1212** **University House: Little Woodhouse Room**
Title:	**Music, History, and Representation in the 13th and 14th Centuries**
Organiser:	IMC Programming Committee
Moderator:	Rachel McNellis, Department of Music, Case Western Reserve University, Ohio
Paper 1212-a:	**Bunnies at Play: Music in the Marginalia** (Language: English) Samantha Chang, Graduate Department of Art, University of Toronto, St. George
Paper 1212-b:	**Music and Poetry of the Troubadours at the Latin Kingdom of Thessalonica after 1204** (Language: English) Menelaos-Dimitris Kountouras, Department of Music, Science & Art, University of Macedonia, Thessaloniki
Paper 1212-c:	**Literary Tradition as a Form of Cultural Memory: Reassessing the Importance of Literature for an Occitan Sense of Regional Identity through the *Song of the Albigensian Crusade* and the Academy of the Floral Games** (Language: English) Jodie Miller, Department of Modern Foreign Languages & Literatures, University of Tennessee, Knoxville
Paper 1212-d:	**Music and Memory in Chaucer's *Boece*, London, British Library Add. MS 10340** (Language: English) Juliana Chapman, Department of Comparative Literature, Pennsylvania State University

Session: **1213** **University House: Beechgrove Room**
Title: **NEW PERSPECTIVES ON WOMEN IN MEDIEVAL ROMANCE, I: REDISCOVERING FORGOTTEN WOMEN**
Organiser: Anum Dada, Institute of Medieval & Early Modern Studies, Durham University and Hannah Piercy, Institute of Medieval & Early Modern Studies, Durham University
Moderator: Alice Stamataki, Institute of Medieval & Early Modern Studies, Durham University
Paper 1213-a: **(Re)Inventing Medieval Romance in Iceland: Representing Women and Their Relationships in *Dámusta saga* and *Sigurðar saga turnara*** (Language: English)
Sheryl McDonald Werronen, Den Arnamagnæanske Samling, Københavns Universitet
Paper 1213-b: **Gender, Age, Status, and Ethnicity: Methods of Marginalisation in Byzantine Romance** (Language: English)
Stephanie Novasio, Centre for Byzantine, Ottoman & Modern Greek Studies, University of Birmingham
Paper 1213-c: **Fictional Saracen Women?: Remembering Muslim Women in Medieval Romance** (Language: English)
Anum Dada
Paper 1213-d: **'Hit waried, hit wayment, as a woman': Missing Manuscripts and the Ghosts of the Women Who Read Them** (Language: English)
Rebecca Pope, Centre for Medieval & Early Modern Studies, University of Kent

Session: **1214** **Charles Thackrah Building: 1.01**
Title: **ROYAL MARRIAGES, III: POLITICAL STRATEGY AND DIPLOMACY THROUGH ROYAL MARRIAGES**
Organiser: Manuela Santos Silva, Departamento de História, Universidade de Lisboa
Moderator: Manuela Santos Silva
Paper 1214-a: **Yaroslav the Wise and the Network of Marriages in Medieval Europe: State Policy and Legacy in Modern Historiography** (Language: English)
Oleksandr Okhrimenko, Department of Ancient & Medieval History, Taras Shevchenko National University of Kyiv
Paper 1214-b: **Advance Queens: Placing Your Pieces on the Checker-Board of 12th-Century International Politics - Sancho I of Portugal and the Marriage Strategies for His Offspring** (Language: English)
Maria João Branco, Instituto de Estudos Medievais, Universidade Nova de Lisboa
Paper 1214-c: **The Marriage of Isabel of Portugal with Emperor Charles V: Diplomatic Aspects, Geostrategic, and Affectionate** (Language: English)
Vitor Pinto, Departamento de História e de Estudos Políticos e Internacionais, Universidade do Porto

Session: **1215** **Michael Sadler Building: Room LG.19**
Title: **CULTURAL MEMORY AND MATERIALITY IN THE CULT OF SAINTS**
Sponsor: Department of Medieval Studies, Central European University, Budapest
Organiser: Gábor Klaniczay, Department of Medieval Studies, Central European University, Budapest
Moderator: Gábor Klaniczay
Paper 1215-a: **Re-Shaping Cultural Memory: The Cult of Slavonic Saints in 14th-Century Bohemia** (Language: English)
Zoë Opačić, Department of History of Art, Birkbeck, University of London
Paper 1215-b: **Household Objects as Memorials to St Margaret's Ordinary and Extraordinary Powers** (Language: English)
Ildikó Csepregi, Department of Medieval Studies, Central European University, Budapest
Paper 1215-c: **Saints and Spolia: Cult of the Saints as (a Form of) Cultural Memory in Medieval Dalmatia** (Language: English)
Trpimir Vedriš, Faculty of Humanities & Social Sciences, University of Zagreb
Respondent: Kateřina Horníčková, Sonderforschungsbereich Project 'Visions of Community', Universität Wien / Southern Bohemian University, České Budějovice

---

Session: **1216** **Michael Sadler Building: Rupert Beckett Theatre**
Title: **14TH-CENTURY ENGLAND, III: PLANTAGENET POWER AT HOME AND ABROAD**
Sponsor: Society for 14th Century Studies
Organiser: David Green, Centre for British Studies, Harlaxton College, University of Evansville
Moderator: Chris Given-Wilson, St Andrews Institute of Mediaeval Studies, University of St Andrews
Paper 1216-a: **English Colonial Enterprises in the 14th Century: Practice and Theory** (Language: English)
Brendan Smith, Department of History, University of Bristol
Paper 1216-b: **Centre and Region: The 'Political North' at the End of the 14th Century** (Language: English)
Mark E. Arvanigian, Department of History, California State University, Fresno
Paper 1216-c: **The Royal Lancastrian Affinity and the Governance of the Realm, 1399-1413** (Language: English)
Douglas Biggs, Department of History, University of Nebraska, Kearney

---

Session: **1217** **Social Sciences Building: Room 10.05**
Title: **THE TRANSFORMATION OF THE CAROLINGIAN WORLD, I**
Sponsor: Transformation of the Carolingian World Network
Organiser: Richard Corradini, Institut für Mittelalterforschung, Österreichische Akademie der Wissenschaften, Wien
Moderator: Stefan Esders, Friedrich-Meinecke-Institut, Freie Universität Berlin
Paper 1217-a: **Prelates in Royal Service under the Ottonian Kings of Germany** (Language: English)
David Bachrach, Department of History, University of New Hampshire
Paper 1217-b: **Money on the Move: Changing Patterns of Coin Circulation and the 'Transformation of the Carolingian Empire'** (Language: English)
Elina Screen, Trinity College, University of Oxford
Paper 1217-c: **From *Gens* to Territory?: Territorial Foundations of Power in the East Frankish Kingdom** (Language: English)
Hans-Werner Goetz, Historisches Seminar, Universität Hamburg

Session: **1218** **Michael Sadler Building: Banham Theatre**
Title: **TRANSFORMATIONS OF POWER: SESSIONS IN HONOUR OF PAUL FOURACRE, IV - BEYOND FRANCIA**
Sponsor: Centre for Medieval & Early Modern Studies, University of Manchester
Organiser: Katherine Fliegel, School of Arts, Languages & Cultures, University of Manchester, Ryan T. Goodman, Department of History, University of Manchester and Sihong Lin, Department of History, University of Manchester
Moderator: Helmut Reimitz, Department of History, Princeton University
Paper 1218-a: **The Age of Charles Martel and Liutprand: Cultures of Governance in the 8th-Century West** (Language: English)
Christopher Heath, Department of History, Politics & Philosophy, Manchester Metropolitan University
Paper 1218-b: **The Frankish Connection: Lombard and Byzantine Involvement in Merovingian Gaul, c. 662-680** (Language: English)
Thomas Brown, School of History, Classics & Archaeology, University of Edinburgh
Paper 1218-c: **History and Biography in Visigothic Iberia: Byzantines, Goths and Romans** (Language: English)
Jamie Wood, School of History & Heritage, University of Lincoln

Session: **1219** **Maurice Keyworth Building: Room 1.09**
Title: **CITIES OF READERS, III: THE PERFORMANCE OF TEXT**
Sponsor: NWO Project 'Cities of Readers', Rijksuniversiteit Groningen
Organiser: Bart Ramakers, Oudere Nederlandse Letterkunde, Rijksuniversiteit Groningen
Moderator: Margriet Hoogvliet, Vakgroep Mediaevistiek, Rijksuniversiteit Groningen
Paper 1219-a: **Deguilleville in the Convent: Pilgrimage, Poem, and Play-Script** (Language: English)
Olivia Robinson, Département des langues et littératures, Université de Fribourg
Paper 1219-b: **Experiencing Comedy in Early English Biblical Drama** (Language: English)
Sarah Brazil, Département de langue et littérature anglaises, Université de Genève
Paper 1219-c: **A Miracle Staged: Performative Didactics in Cornelis Everaert's *Play of Mary's Chaplet*** (Language: English)
Bart Ramakers

Session: **1220** **Charles Thackrah Building: 1.02**
Title: **REMEMBERING TROY IN THE MIDDLE AGES, III: (RE)NARRATING HEROES**
Organiser: Sabine Heidi Walther, Abteilung für Skandinavische Sprachen und Literaturen, Rheinische Friedrich-Wilhelms-Universität Bonn and N. Kıvılcım Yavuz, Den Arnamagnæanske Samling, Københavns Universitet
Moderator: N. Kıvılcım Yavuz
Paper 1220-a: **Mémoire de Troie à la cour de Bourgogne** (Language: Français)
Florence Tanniou, Département de Lettres Modernes, Université Paris Nanterre
Paper 1220-b: **A New Light on the Story of the Trojan War's Tapestries** (Language: English)
Anne-Sophie Laruelle, Département des Sciences Historiques, Université de Liège
Paper 1220-c: **Importing Ideals from Burgundy?: On Late Medieval Icelandic Elites and Their Cultural Contacts** (Language: English)
Sabine Heidi Walther

Session: **1221** **Social Sciences Building: Room 10.06**
Title: **LATE MEDIEVAL AND EARLY MODERN ARISTOCRATIC MEMOIRS**
Organiser: IMC Programming Committee
Moderator: Przemysław Wiszewski, Wydział Nauk Historycznych i Pedagogicznych, Uniwersytet Wrocławski
Paper 1221-a: **'(T)here it is a beautiful place': Remembering and Un-Remembering *Patria* and Lineage in Three Generations of the Strozzi** (Language: English)
Lisa Di Crescenzo, School of History, Queen Mary University of London
Paper 1221-b: ***Ex Romana Gente*: Constructing the Memory of Ancient Origin of the House of Hunyadi** (Language: English)
Tomáš Homoľa, Institute of History, Slovak Academy of Sciences, Bratislava
Paper 1221-c: **Knight's Tale: Memoirs of Christopher of Týn** (Language: English)
Jan Boukal, Department of Czech History, Univerzita Karlova, Praha

Session: **1222** **Baines Wing: Room 1.14**
Title: **HORRIFIC MEMORIES FOR DIDACTIC REASONS**
Organiser: IMC Programming Committee
Moderator: Irene A. O'Daly, Huygens Instituut voor Nederlandse Geschiedenis, Koninklijke Nederlandse Academie van Wetenschappen (ING - KNAW), Amsterdam
Paper 1222-a: **Cannibalism and Identity in the First Mouth of Hell** (Language: English)
Han Tame, Centre for Medieval & Early Modern Studies, University of Kent
Paper 1222-b: **Learning with the Devil** (Language: English)
Arina Zaytseva, Department of Medieval Studies, Central European University, Budapest
Paper 1222-c: **The Worm of Conscience: Medieval Moral Psychology and Damnation as Remembrance** (Language: English)
Gustav Zamore, Historiska institutionen, Stockholms universitet

Session:	**1223** **Maurice Keyworth Building: Room 1.31**
Title:	**Remembering the Saints, III: Creating and Adapting Memory in the Late Antique Mediterranean**
Sponsor:	Cult of Saints Project, University of Oxford
Organiser:	Bryan Ward-Perkins, Faculty of History, University of Oxford and Robert Wiśniewski, Instytut Historyczny, Uniwersytet Warszawski
Moderator:	Bonnie Effros, Department of History, University of Liverpool
Paper 1223-a:	**Le culte des saints en Afrique vandale: Entre Catholiques et Ariens** (Language: Français) Mohamed-Arbi Nsiri, Département d'histoire, Université Paris Nanterre
Paper 1223-b:	**The Transformations of the Legend of Athenogenes of Pedachthoe** (Language: English) Efthymios Rizos, Faculty of History, University of Oxford
Paper 1223-c:	**Remembering St Febronia: The Textual Cult of a Nun Martyr** (Language: English) Stavroula Constantinou, Department of Byzantine & Modern Greek Studies, University of Cyprus, Nicosia

Session:	**1224** **Charles Thackrah Building: 1.04**
Title:	**Remembering Our Prayers in Old and Middle English**
Organiser:	IMC Programming Committee
Moderator:	Krista A. Murchison, Faculteit der Geesteswetenschappen, Universiteit Leiden
Paper 1224-a:	**Memory and Catechism in *Speculum vitae*** (Language: English) Kathryn Vulic, Department of English, Western Washington University
Paper 1224-b:	**'In one ABC': Tracing the Alphabet in Medieval Devotional Literature** (Language: English) Stacie Vos, Department of Literature, University of California, San Diego
Paper 1224-c:	**Innovation and Continuity in Medieval English Prayers: The Case of *Pater noster*** (Language: English) Monika Maria Opalinska, Instytut Anglistyki, Uniwersytet Warszawski

Session:	**1225** **Maurice Keyworth Building: Room 1.06**
Title:	**Practical Medicine: Assuming and Aiding Memory**
Organiser:	Lucy Christine Barnhouse, Department of English / Department of History, College of Wooster, Ohio
Moderator:	Elma Brenner, Wellcome Library, London
Paper 1225-a:	**Diagrams, Mnemonics, and Identity in Three Late Medieval English Surgical Manuscripts** (Language: English) Sara Öberg Strådal, Science Museum, London
Paper 1225-b:	**Inclusions and Exclusions: Directions in Recipes for Women's Healthcare in England** (Language: English) Kristin Uscinski, Department of History, State University of New York, Purchase
Paper 1225-c:	**Just Give Me the Highlights: Color Washes as Finding Aids in Early Beneventan Manuscripts** (Language: English) Jeffrey Doolittle, Department of History, Fordham University, New York

Session: **1226** **University House: Great Woodhouse Room**
Title: **WOMEN, MEMORY, AND MATERIAL CULTURE**
Sponsor: Society for Medieval Feminist Scholarship
Organiser: Erin Jordan, Department of History, Old Dominion University, Virginia
Moderator: Wendy Marie Hoofnagle, Department of Languages & Literatures, University of Northern Iowa
Paper 1226-a: **Hero or Heretic: Remembering Marguerite Porete** (Language: English)
Danielle Dubois, Department of Religion, University of Manitoba
Paper 1226-b: **'In good memory of...': The Significance of Familial Commemorations in the Seals of Scottish Countesses in Late Medieval Scotland, c. 1300-1450** (Language: English)
Rachel Meredith Davis, School of History, Classics & Archaeology, University of Edinburgh
Paper 1226-c: **To Lie beside the Virgin: The Funerary Chapel of Queen Melisende of Jerusalem** (Language: English)
Erin Jordan

Session: **1227** **Social Sciences Building: Room 10.07**
Title: **MEDIEVALISM IN 20TH-CENTURY LITERATURE**
Organiser: IMC Programming Committee
Moderator: Nadia Altschul, School of Modern Languages & Cultures (Hispanic Studies), University of Glasgow
Paper 1227-a: **Journeys of Discovery: C.S. Lewis's *Space Trilogy* as Medieval Voyages of Wonder** (Language: English)
Nathan E. H. Fayard, J. William Fulbright College of Arts & Sciences, University of Arkansas, Fayetteville
Paper 1227-b: **Mélusine, Memory, and Reconstruction of the Past in *El unicornio* by Manuel Mugica Láinez** (Language: English)
Juan Manuel Lacalle, Instituto de Filología y Literaturas Hispánicas 'Dr. Amado Alonso', Universidad de Buenos Aires

---

Session: **1228** **Fine Art Building: SR G.04**
Title: **RELIGIOUS KNOWLEDGE AND MEMORY, I: ACTUALISATION OF RELIGIOUS KNOWLEDGE**
Organiser: Michael Neumaier, Graduiertenkolleg 1662 'Religiöses Wissen im vormodernen Europa (800–1800)', Eberhard-Karls-Universität Tübingen
Moderator: Steffen Patzold, Seminar für Mittelalterliche Geschichte, Eberhard-Karls-Universität Tübingen
Paper 1228-a: **Learning the Lord's Prayer: Variation in Educational Texts Found in 9th- and 10th-Century Clerical Manuscripts** (Language: English)
Bastiaan Waagmeester, Graduiertenkolleg 1662 'Religiöses Wissen im vormodernen Europa (800–1800)', Eberhard-Karls-Universität Tübingen
Paper 1228-b: **Rethinking the Idea(l) of 'Hohe Minne': Religious Knowledge in the Later Minnesang** (Language: English)
Isabell Väth, Graduiertenkolleg 1662 'Religiöses Wissen im vormodernen Europa (800–1800)', Eberhard-Karls-Universität Tübingen
Paper 1228-c: **Memorising Anselm of Canterbury?: The Satisfaction Theory of Atonement in Medieval Religious Plays** (Language: English)
Michael Neumaier

Session: **1229** **Charles Thackrah Building: 1.03**
Title: **REMEMBERING CHRIST'S LIFE IN THE 15TH-CENTURY LOW COUNTRIES**
Sponsor: Birkbeck, University of London / Institute for Religion & Critical Inquiry, Australian Catholic University
Organiser: Matthew S. Champion, Department of History, Classics & Archaeology, Birkbeck, University of London / Institute for Religion & Critical Inquiry, Australian Catholic University
Moderator: Seb Falk, Girton College, University of Cambridge
Paper 1229-a: ***Ad memoriam utile et ad pietatem proficiens*: Mnemonic Devices and Gospel Harmonies** (Language: English)
Serena Masolini, De Wulf-Mansion Centre for Ancient, Medieval & Renaissance Philosophy, KU Leuven
Paper 1229-b: **Dismembering a Gospel Harmony** (Language: English)
Matthew S. Champion
Paper 1229-c: **Remembering the Passion: Chronological Debates** (Language: English)
Philipp Nothaft, All Souls College, University of Oxford

Session: **1230** **Social Sciences Building: Room 10.09**
Title: **CULTURAL MEMORY AND VISUAL STRATEGY IN INSULAR ART**
Organiser: Colleen Thomas, Independent Scholar, Dublin
Moderator: Jennifer Gleeson, Independent Scholar, Dublin
Paper 1230-a: **Memory and Making: Early Christian Insular Glass Studs** (Language: English)
Jennifer Gleeson
Paper 1230-b: **Visual Strategies in Early Medieval 'Pocket' Gospels** (Language: English)
Colleen Thomas
Paper 1230-c: **Designing Cultural Memory: Celtic Revival Metalwork and Manuscripts in Ireland, 1840-1890** (Language: English)
Tara Kelly, Independent Scholar, Dublin

Session: **1231** **Maurice Keyworth Building: Room 1.05**
Title: **MEMORY, SETTLEMENT, AND LANDSCAPE, II: BUILDINGS AND MEMORY**
Sponsor: Medieval Settlement Research Group
Organiser: Duncan Berryman, School of Geography, Archaeology & Palaeoecology, Queen's University Belfast, Susan Kilby, Centre for English Local History, University of Leicester and Eddie Procter, Department of Archaeology, University of Exeter
Moderator: Susan Kilby
Paper 1231-a: **A House of Wood or Stone: A Practical Choice or a Link from the Late Medieval Peoples to their Ancestral Roots** (Language: English)
Laura Patrick, School of Natural & Built Environment, Queen's University Belfast
Paper 1231-b: **Finding Common Ground: Comparative Landscape Analysis and Re-Building Home and Memory in Medieval Armenian Cilicia** (Language: English)
Aurora E. Camaño, Department of Archaeology / The Stavros Niarchos Foundation Centre for Hellenic Studies, Simon Fraser University, British Columbia
Paper 1231-c: **Living in the Past?: Continuity and Change in Medieval Manorial Sites** (Language: English)
Duncan Berryman

Session: **1232** **Baines Wing: Room G.36**
Title: **CONTESTED MEDIEVAL SITES IN MODERN NATIONAL AND LOCAL POLITICS**
Organiser: IMC Programming Committee
Moderator: Renée Michelle Ward, School of English & Journalism, University of Lincoln
Paper 1232-a: **The Medieval Synagogue in Worms: A Case Study on Its Reconstruction Post-Shoah - Motifs and Interests, Visitors and Narratives** (Language: English)
Susanne Urban, SchUM-Städte e.V., Worms
Paper 1232-b: ***Lieux de mémoire*: The Politics and Ethics of Medieval War Memorials** (Language: English)
Ellen Caldwell, Department of Humanities & Social Sciences, Clarkson University, Potsdam
Paper 1232-c: **Memory and Loss at Saint-Denis in the Reign of Louis-Philippe** (Language: English)
Sarah Thompson, School of Art, Rochester Institute of Technology, New York
Paper 1232-d: **Sources, Archives, and Power: Constructing the Finnish Medieval Past** (Language: English)
Taina Saarenpää, Department of Finnish History, University of Turku

Session: **1233** **Leeds University Union: Room 2 - Elland Road**
Title: **REMEMBERING COMMUNITIES IN EARLY MEDIEVAL EUROPE, I: MEMORY AND AUTHORITY**
Sponsor: Kısmet Press
Organiser: Ricky Broome, Leeds Institute for Clinical Trials Research (LICTR), University of Leeds
Moderator: Ian N. Wood, School of History, University of Leeds
Paper 1233-a: **The Memory of the Origins of the First 'Duchy' of Aquitaine in the 7th Century** (Language: English)
Julien Bellarbre, UFR Lettres et Sciences Humaines, Université de Cergy-Pontoise / Faculté des Lettres et des Sciences Humaines, Université de Limoges
Paper 1233-b: **St Willibrord's Heirs: Remembering the Missionaries in Early Medieval Frisia** (Language: English)
Ricky Broome
Paper 1233-c: **Spiritual Genealogies for the Anglo-Saxon Church: Episcopal Lists and Their Communities** (Language: English)
Miriam Adan Jones, Faculteit der Godgeleerdheid, Vrije Universiteit Amsterdam

Session: **1234** **Maurice Keyworth Building: Room 1.33**
Title: **FORGING FAMILY IDENTITIES**
Sponsor: School of Histories & Humanities, Trinity College Dublin
Organiser: Caoimhe Whelan, Department of History, Trinity College Dublin
Moderator: Sparky Booker, School of History, Anthropology, Philosophy & Politics, Queen's University Belfast
Paper 1234-a: **Dynastic Creation, Memory, and the Irish in the Early Middle Ages** (Language: English)
Finn Tobin, Department of History, Trinity College Dublin
Paper 1234-b: **Brokering Ethnicity: Examining Fosterage in Practice and Local Memory** (Language: English)
Dawn Klos, Department of History, Trinity College Dublin
Paper 1234-c: **The Marches as Family Business in 13th-Century Ireland** (Language: English)
Eoghan Keane, Medieval History Research Centre, Trinity College Dublin

---

Session: **1235** **Leeds University Union: Room 4 - Hyde Park**
Title: **PROPRIETARY MEMORIES: *NOTITIAE*-INVENTORIES IN EARLY MEDIEVAL IBERIA, I**
Sponsor: Instituto de Estudos Medievais, Universidade Nova de Lisboa
Organiser: Álvaro Carvajal Castro, Departamento de Geografía, Prehistoria y Arqueología, Universidad del País Vasco - Euskal Herriko Unibertsitatea and André Evangelista Marques, Instituto de Estudos Medievais, Universidade Nova de Lisboa
Moderator: Wendy Davies, Independent Scholar, Woolstone
Paper 1235-a: **Why Make an Inventory (in 10th-Century Catalonia)?** (Language: English)
Jonathan Jarrett, Institute for Medieval Studies, University of Leeds
Paper 1235-b: **The Functions of an 11th-Century Inventory of Tithes from the Central Pyrenees** (Language: English)
Guillermo Tomás Faci, Departamento de Historia Medieval, Ciencias y Técnicas Historiográficas y Estudios Árabes e Islámicos, Universidad de Zaragoza
Paper 1235-c: **When Lists Are Claims: Using Inventories in and outside Court in 9th- to 11th-Century Portugal** (Language: English)
André Evangelista Marques

Session: **1236** **Leeds University Union: Room 5 - Kirkstall Abbey**
Title: **VOICES OF LAW, III: MEMORY, TEXTUALITY, AND THE RECORDING OF THE LAW**
Sponsor: Voices of Law: Language, Text & Practice
Organiser: Jenny Benham, School of History, Archaeology & Religion, Cardiff University
Moderator: Matthew McHaffie, Department of History, King's College London
Paper 1236-a: **The Use of Memory in Law of Gulaþing** (Language: English)
Miriam Tveit, Faculty of Social Sciences, Nord University, Bodø
Paper 1236-b: **Pragmatism and Intertextual Dependencies in the Revisions of Frankish Law, 6th-9th Centuries** (Language: English)
Lukas Bothe, Sonderforschungsbereich 700 'Governance in Areas of Limited Statehood', Freie Universität Berlin
Paper 1236-c: **Early Kentish Law and the Development of the Kingdom of Kent** (Language: English)
Courtnay Konshuh, Department of History, St Thomas More College, University of Saskatchewan

Session: **1237** **Emmanuel Centre: Wilson Room**
Title: **GLOBAL PRACTICES OF MEMORY AND EXCHANGE, I: MARITIME TRANSFER AND COMMUNICATION IN THE MEDITERRANEAN AND THE INDIAN OCEAN, C. 1200-1550**
Sponsor: Sonderforschungsbereich Project 'Visions of Community', Österreichische Akademie der Wissenschaften, Universität Wien / FWF Project F42
Organiser: Károly Goda, Sonderforschungsbereich Project 'Visions of Community', Institut für Geschichte, Universität Wien and Fabian Kümmeler, Sonderforschungsbereich Project 'Visions of Community' / Institut für Osteuropäische Geschichte, Universität Wien
Moderator: Roxani Eleni Margariti, Department of Middle Eastern & South Asian Studies, Emory University
Paper 1237-a: **'The King of China believes that all people are his slaves': Diplomatic and Commercial Contacts between Yemen and China in the 14th and 15th Centuries** (Language: English)
Johann Heiss, Institut für Sozialanthropologie, Österreichische Akademie der Wissenschaften, Wien
Paper 1237-b: **Beyond the Sea: Cross-Cultural Interaction in Ethiopian Medieval Art** (Language: English)
Lenka Vrlíková, Faculty of Arts, Masarykova univerzita, Brno
Paper 1237-c: **Watching the Sea: Communicating Memory and Exchanging News via Venetian Dalmatia, 15th-Century** (Language: English)
Fabian Kümmeler

Session: **1238** **Michael Sadler Building: Room LG.10**
Title: **EDIBLE MEMORY**
Sponsor: Zentrum für Gastrosophie, Universität Salzburg
Organiser: Gerhard Ammerer, Zentrum für Gastrosophie, Universität Salzburg
Moderator: Marlene Ernst, Zentrum für Gastrosophie, Universität Salzburg
Paper 1238-a: **When the Elected Go Marching In: Ceremonial Entrances as Places of Commemoration** (Language: English)
Simon Edlmayr, Zentrum für Gastrosophie, Universität Salzburg
Paper 1238-b: **Feasts as Representation: A Part of Remembrance of Bourgeois Self-Determination** (Language: English)
Dominik Maislinger, Zentrum für Gastrosophie, Universität Salzburg
Paper 1238-c: **Edible Salzburg: Gastronomy and Its Commemorative Memory** (Language: English)
Jutta Baumgartner, Zentrum für Gastrosophie, Universität Salzburg

Session: **1239** **Maurice Keyworth Building: Room 1.03**
Title: **SIX HUNDRED YEARS, 1418-2018: THRILLING MEMORIES OF OSWALD VON WOLKENSTEIN AND THE COUNCIL OF CONSTANCE**
Sponsor: Oswald von Wolkenstein-Gesellschaft
Organiser: Sieglinde Hartmann, Oswald von Wolkenstein-Gesellschaft, Frankfurt am Main
Moderator: David John Wallace, Department of English, University of Pennsylvania
Paper 1239-a: **Oswald von Wolkenstein in the Service of King Sigismund during the Time of the Council: Facts and Fiction** (Language: English)
Sieglinde Hartmann
Paper 1239-b: **Depictions of Oswald von Wolkenstein in Illustrated Copies of Ulrich von Richental's *Chronicle of the Council of Constance*** (Language: English)
Irma Trattner, Abteilung für Bildnerische Erziehung, Kunstuniversität Linz
Paper 1239-c: **The City of Constance as *lieu de mémoire* in the Writings of Viennese Theologians: Peter von Pulkau, Kaspar Maiselstein, Nikolaus von Dinkelsbühl** (Language: English)
Klaus Wolf, Abteilung Deutsche Sprache und Literatur des Mittelalters, Universität Augsburg

Session: **1240** **Michael Sadler Building: Room LG.15**
Title: **REMEMBERING CHARLEMAGNE AND MEROVINGIAN QUEENS IN MEDIEVAL AND MODERN HISTORIOGRAPHY**
Organiser: IMC Programming Committee
Moderator: Ingrid Schlegl, Institut für Geschichte, Karl-Franzens-Universität Graz
Paper 1240-a: **Shaping Memory with the Voice of an Angel: Narrations of Alien Consciousness and Their Functions in Medieval Chronicles** (Language: English)
Florian Michael Schmid, Institut für Deutsche Philologie, Ernst-Moritz-Arndt-Universität Greifswald
Recipient of the 2018 Sieglinde Hartmann Prize for German Language & Literature
Paper 1240-b: **The Cloister and the Cornfield: Henry Bradshaw's *Lyfe of Saynte Radegunde*** (Language: English)
Nancy Atkinson, Department of English, University of North Alabama
Paper 1240-c: **Remembering the Merovingian Queens in France** (Language: English)
Heta Aali, Department of Cultural History, University of Turku

Session: **1241** **Stage@leeds: Stage 2**
Title: **MONASTIC MEMORIES AND NARRATIVES: REMEMBERING, RECORDING, RE-INTERPRETING**
Sponsor: Department of Medieval Studies, Central European University, Budapest
Organiser: József Laszlovszky, Department of Medieval Studies, Central European University, Budapest
Moderator: József Laszlovszky
Paper 1241-a: **Models for Memory: Peter the Hermit and Inserted Allusions in the Benedictine Revisions of the First Crusade Narrative** (Language: English)
James Plumtree, Department of General Education, American University of Central Asia, Bishkek
Paper 1241-b: ***Epistolae ab ora*: The Matter of the Mongols in Matthew Paris's Narrative** (Language: English)
Zsuzsanna Papp Reed, Department of Medieval Studies, Central European University, Budapest
Paper 1241-c: **Language and Writing: Communication and Monastic Record Keeping in the Franciscan and Pauline Monasteries of Medieval Northern Dalmatia** (Language: English)
Kristian Bertović, Department of Medieval Studies, Central European University, Budapest

Session: **1242** **Stage@leeds: Stage 3**
Title: **MEANS AND METHODS OF REMEMBRANCE**
Organiser: IMC Programming Committee
Moderator: Luigi Campi, Dipartimento di Filosofia, Università degli Studi di Milano
Paper 1242-a: **Scrittura e Memoria nel Basso Medioevo** (Language: Italiano)
Chiara Baldestein, Dipartimento di Storia, Università degli Studi di Roma 'La Sapienza'
Paper 1242-b: **Early Medieval Architecture of Royal Seats of Piasts and Przemyslids as an Example of Creating Memory** (Language: English)
Kamila Oleś, Faculty of Arts, Univerzita Karlova, Praha / Faculty of Historical Studies, Adam Mickiewicz University, Poznań
Paper 1242-c: **Memory and Testaments in Late Medieval Bohemia** (Language: English)
Anna Vrtálková, Department of Ecclesiastical History & Patrology, Univerzita Karlova, Praha

Session: **1243** **Baines Wing: Room G.37**
Title: **MEDIEVAL MODELS: KINGS AND CRUSADERS IN MEDIEVAL ENGLAND**
Organiser: Kathryn Hurlock, Department of History, Politics & Philosophy, Manchester Metropolitan University
Moderator: Laura Julinda Whatley, College of Arts & Sciences, Auburn University at Montgomery, Alabama
Paper 1243-a: **The Defence of Royal Power and the Critique of Royal Power in Angevin England** (Language: English)
Katie Hodges-Kluck, Marco Institute for Medieval & Renaissance Studies, University of Tennessee, Knoxville
Paper 1243-b: **Remembering Richard: The Representation of the Crusades in Latin and French Accounts of the Expedition of Richard I** (Language: English)
Marianne J. Ailes, Department of French, University of Bristol
Paper 1243-c: **A Royal Crusade Chronicle: Visual Narrative in King Edward IV's Royal *Eracles* (London, British Library, Royal MS 15 E. I)** (Language: English)
Erin Donovan, Dr. Jörn Günther Rare Books, Stalden
Paper 1243-d: **Godfrey, Richard, and Edward: Representing Crusade Leaders in Early 16th-Century England** (Language: English)
Katherine J. Lewis, Department of History, University of Huddersfield

Session: **1244** **Fine Art Building: SR 1.10**
Title: **MEMORY AND 6TH-CENTURY GAUL, I: REMEMBERING THE SAINTS**
Organiser: Tamar Rotman, Department of General History, Ben-Gurion University of the Negev, Beer-Sheva
Moderator: Yaniv Fox, Department of General History, Bar-Ilan University, Ramat Gan
Paper 1244-a: **Remembering Holiness: The Commemoration of Saints in Gregory of Tours and Venantius Fortunatus** (Language: English)
Pia Bockius, Friedrich-Meinecke-Institut, Freie Universität Berlin
Paper 1244-b: ***In cordis membrana*: Memory, Writing, and Living Tradition in the Prose Lives of Venantius Fortunatus** (Language: English)
Kent E. Navalesi, Department of History, University of Illinois, Urbana-Champaign
Paper 1244-c: **The Memory of Praise in Venantius Fortunatus's *Life of St Martin*** (Language: English)
Lorenzo Livorsi, Department of Classics, University of Reading

Session: **1245** **Emmanuel Centre: Room 10**
Title: **CONTINUITY AND CONQUEST IN ENGLAND AND NORMANDY, I: SOCIETY AND MEMORY IN 11TH-CENTURY ENGLAND**
Sponsor: Haskins Society
Organiser: Stuart Pracy, Department of History, University of Manchester
Moderator: Julia Crick, Department of History, King's College London
Paper 1245-a: **What's in a Name?: Naming Practices in Defining Continuity** (Language: English)
Jeremy Piercy, School of History, Classics & Archaeology, University of Edinburgh
Paper 1245-b: **'Each according to his rank'?: Remembering and Constructing Status in 11th-Century England** (Language: English)
Stuart Pracy
Paper 1245-c: **Archaeologies of the Norman Conquest** (Language: English)
Aleksandra McClain, Department of Archaeology, University of York and Naomi Sykes, Department of Archaeology, University of Nottingham

Session: **1246** **Leeds University Union: Room 6 - Roundhay**
Title: **Remembering Chivalry, III: Faith and Faithfulness**
Sponsor: Institute for Medieval Studies, University of Leeds
Organiser: Eleanor Jayne Wilkinson-Keys, Institute for Medieval Studies, University of Leeds
Moderator: Craig M. Nakashian, Department of History, Texas A&M University, Texarkana
Paper 1246-a: **Objectifying Love: Chivalry, Courtly Love, and the Cult of Saints in Chrétien de Troyes** (Language: English)
Lydia Hayes, St Andrews Institute of Mediaeval Studies, University of St Andrews
Paper 1246-b: **Chivalric Remembrance: Form and Function of Funerary Achievements** (Language: English)
Eleanor Jayne Wilkinson-Keys
Paper 1246-c: **The Ambiguous Portrayal of Deserters from the First Crusade in 12th-Century Latin Sources** (Language: English)
Adam Sitár, Department of General History, Comenius University, Bratislava

---

Session: **1247** **Baines Wing: Room 2.14**
Title: **'Remember me when I am gone': Methods of Personal Commemoration**
Organiser: IMC Programming Committee
Moderator: Věra Soukupová, Department of History, University of Ostrava / Department of Czech History, Charles University, Prague
Paper 1247-a: **Communal and Personal Commemoration on East Anglian Screens** (Language: English)
Lucy Wrapson, Hamilton Kerr Institute, University of Cambridge
Paper 1247-b: **Jordan Fantosme / Jordan de Sandford: The Personal Memory of War** (Language: English)
Fletcher Crowe, Independent Scholar, Florida
Paper 1247-c: **Personal Memory through Notarial Sources** (Language: English)
Miquel Faus, Departament d'Història Medieval, Història Moderna i Ciències i Tècniques Historiogràfiques, Universitat de València
Paper 1247-d: **What Must Be Remembered: The Notarial Register as a Source for Studying Social and Political Memory?** (Language: English)
Javier Fajardo Paños, Departament d'Història Medieval, Història Moderna i Ciències i Tècniques Historiogràfiques, Universitat de València

Session: **1248** **University House: St George Room**
Title: **TIME, SCIENCE, AND THE BODY IN THE ANGLO-NORMAN WORLD: DURHAM, CATHEDRAL LIBRARY, MS HUNTER 100 AND ITS CONTEXTS, III - ILLUSTRATION BY DESIGN**
Sponsor: Institute of Medieval & Early Modern Studies, Durham University
Organiser: Giles E. M. Gasper, Department of History, Durham University
Moderator: Eric M. Ramírez-Weaver, McIntire Department of Art, University of Virginia
Paper 1248-a: **Authoring Nature: MS Hunter 100 and the Problem of Textual Authority at Durham** (Language: English)
Jay Diehl, Department of History, Long Island University, New York
Paper 1248-b: **Sin, Correction, and Learning: MS Hunter 100 and the Romanesque Sculpture of Durham Cathedral, c. 1120-c. 1140** (Language: English)
Jonathan Turnock, Department of History, Durham University
Paper 1248-c: **Illuminated Manuscripts and the Status of Science in 12th-Century England** (Language: English)
Laura Cleaver, Department of History of Art & Architecture, Trinity College Dublin

Session: **1249** **Stage@leeds: Stage 1**
Title: **PUBLIC MEDIEVALISM AND *THE PUBLIC MEDIEVALIST***
Sponsor: PublicMedievalist.com
Organiser: Paul B. Sturtevant, PublicMedievalist.com
Moderator: Robert Houghton, Department of History, University of Winchester
Paper 1249-a: **Public Medievalism as a Force for Change** (Language: English)
Paul B. Sturtevant
Paper 1249-b: **What's 'Impact' for a Public Medievalist?** (Language: English)
Richard J. Utz, School of Literature, Media & Communication, Georgia Institute of Technology, Atlanta
Paper 1249-c: **Going Public** (Language: English)
Amy S. Kaufman, PublicMedievalist.com

Session: **1250** **Baines Wing: Room 2.15**
Title: **CANONIZE YOURSELF!, III: HOW TO BECOME A CANON IN A MEDIEVAL CHAPTER ON THE SOUTH SIDE OF THE ALPS**
Sponsor: Erzbistum Paderborn / Universitetet i Tromsø - Norges Arktiske Universitetet
Organiser: Arnold Otto, Erzbischöfliches Generalvikariat Erzbistumsarchiv, Paderborn
Moderator: Cristina Andenna, Forschungsstelle für Vergleichende Ordensgeschichte (FOVOG), Technische Universität Dresden
Paper 1250-a: **Political Balance and Personal Ambition: Canons and Cathedral Chapter of Trento in the 14th and 15th Centuries** (Language: English)
Emanuele Curzel, Dipartimento di Lettere e Filosofia, Università degli Studi di Trento
Paper 1250-b: **Canonical Careers in the Angevin Southern Italy** (Language: English)
Antonio Antonetti, Dipartimento di Scienze del Patrimonio Culturale, (DISPAC), Università degli Studi di Salerno
Paper 1250-c: **The Chapter of St Peter in Rome: A Noble Institution?** (Language: English)
Jochen Johrendt, Lehrstuhl für Mittelalterliche Geschichte, Bergische Universität Wuppertal
Respondent: Arnold Otto

Session: **1252** **University House: Cloberry Room**
Title: **MEDIEVAL ETHIOPIA, III: RELIGIOUS MATERIAL CULTURE IN ETHIOPIA**
Sponsor: Fakultät für Geschichtswissenschaft, Ruhr-Universität Bochum
Organiser: Meseret Oldjira, Department of Art & Archaeology, Princeton University and Adam Simmons, Department of History, Lancaster University
Moderator: Verena Krebs, Historisches Institut, Ruhr-Universität Bochum
Paper 1252-a: **Ethiopia at the Crossroads: The African Art of a Christian Nation** (Language: English)
Christine Sciacca, Walters Art Museum, Baltimore
Paper 1252-b: **Evangelist Portraits in Ethiopic Gospel Books** (Language: English)
Jacopo Gnisci, Hiob Ludolf Centre for Ethiopian Studies, Universität Hamburg
Paper 1252-c: **On the Shape of the Lower End of Ethiopian Hand and Processional Crosses: A Tentative Interpretation of the Lower End of the Vertical Beam and Its Comparison to Armenian *Khatshk'ars*** (Language: English)
Dorothea McEwan, Warburg Institute, University of London

Session: **1253** **Emmanuel Centre: Room 11**
Title: ***PER CORPORA*: WHAT CORPUS FOR MEDIEVAL STUDIES?**
Sponsor: ANR Velum, Institut de Recherche et d'Histoire des Textes (IRHT), Centre National de la Recherche Scientifique (CNRS), Paris
Organiser: Bruno Bon, Institut de Recherche et d'Histoire des Textes (IRHT), Centre National de la Recherche Scientifique (CNRS), Paris
Moderator: Krzysztof Nowak, Institute of Polish Language, Polish Academy of Sciences, Kraków
Paper 1253-a: **A Reference Corpus for Medieval Latin: Chances and Challenges of a New Project** (Language: English)
Tim Geelhaar, Historisches Seminar, Goethe-Universität, Frankfurt am Main
Paper 1253-b: **Le corpus idéal : une somme de tous les états de tous les textes - l'exemple de la *Règle de saint Benoît*** (Language: Français)
Renaud Alexandre, Institut de Recherche et d'Histoire des Textes (IRHT), Centre National de la Recherche Scientifique (CNRS), Paris
Paper 1253-c: **Velum: Visualisation, exploration, et liaison de resources innovantes pour le latin médiéval** (Language: Français)
Bruno Bon

Session: **1254** **Maurice Keyworth Building: Room G.02**
Title: **THE SOCIAL SIGNIFICANCE OF *MEMORIA*: COMMEMORATION OF THE DEAD IN URBAN AND NOBLE ENVIRONMENTS**
Sponsor: Medieval Memoria Online Project (MeMO), Universiteit Utrecht / Memoria & Remembrance Practices, Brepols
Organiser: Arnoud-Jan A. Bijsterveld, Department of Sociology, Tilburg University
Moderator: Tillmann Lohse, Institut für Geschichtswissenschaften, Humboldt-Universität zu Berlin
Paper 1254-a: ***Memoria* in the Late Medieval Town: Formation of an Urban Society through Commemorative Foundations** (Language: English)
Thomas Schilp, Lehrstuhl für die Geschichte des Frühmittelalters, Ruhr-Universität Bochum
Paper 1254-b: **Taking Care of One's Memory: Noble Representation and Memory Culture in Denmark, 1400-1537** (Language: English)
Tine Kondrup, Institut for Historie, Syddansk Universitet, Odense
Paper 1254-c: ***Memoria* Culture in the 16th-Century Low Countries: Between Commemoration of the Dead and the Abolition of Death** (Language: English)
Arjan van Dixhoorn, Faculty of Arts & Humanities, University College Roosevelt / Faculteit Geesteswetenschappen, Universiteit Utrecht

---

TEA BREAK: 15.45-16.30

Tea and Coffee will be served at the following locations:

Maurice Keyworth Building: Foyer
Michael Sadler Building: Foyer
Parkinson Building: Bookfair
University Square: The Marquee

See Map 7, p. 44.

Session: **1301** **Michael Sadler Building: Room LG.17**
Title: **LEME, II: THINKING 'CRISIS' IN THE MEDIEVAL WEST**
Sponsor: Laboratório de Estudos Medievais (LEME), Cidade Universitária São Paulo
Organiser: Hervin Fernández-Aceves, School of History / Institute for Medieval Studies, University of Leeds
Moderator: Hervin Fernández-Aceves
Paper 1301-a: **The Making of Justice in the Carolingian Capitularies: Rethinking the 'Crisis' Approach** (Language: English)
Marcelo Moreira Ferrasin, Faculdade de Filosofia, Letras e Ciências Humanas, Universidade de São Paulo
Paper 1301-b: **'Crisis' and 'Governance' in Mercian Royal Charters** (Language: English)
Fábio de Souza Duque, Faculdade de Filosofia, Letras e Ciências Humanas, Universidade de São Paulo
Paper 1301-c: **Re-Evaluating 'Turbulence' in the Lordship of Ireland, c. 1189-1318: A Complex Systems Approach** (Language: English)
Vinicius Marino Carvalho, Faculdade de Filosofia, Letras e Ciências Humanas, Universidade de São Paulo

Session: **1302** **Baines Wing: Room 1.13**
Title: **WRITERS AND THEIR AUDIENCES IN THE MIDDLE AGES**
Sponsor: Onderzoeksschool Mediëvistiek, Rijksuniversiteit Groningen
Organiser: Rob Meens, Departement Geschiedenis en Kunstgeschiedenis, Universiteit Utrecht
Moderator: Marco Mostert, Utrecht Centre for Medieval Studies, Universiteit Utrecht
Paper 1302-a: **Transforming Memories: 'The Arian' in the Works of Victor of Vita and Gregory of Tours** (Language: English)
Rolf Lommerde, Departement Geschiedenis en Kunstgeschiedenis, Universiteit Utrecht
Paper 1302-b: **Damsels in Drag: Crossdressing Adventurers in Medieval Literature and Modern Fantasy** (Language: English)
Luke Schouwenaars, Onderzoeksgroep Comparative Literature, Universiteit Utrecht
Paper 1302-c: **The Letters and the Spirit: Writing as Performance in Late Medieval Italy** (Language: English)
Giulia Biagioni, Afdeling Geschiedenis, Rijksuniversiteit Groningen

Session: **1303** **Baines Wing: Room 2.16**
Title: **MOVING BYZANTIUM, IV: SOCIAL MOBILITY AND THE BYZANTINE WORLD**
Sponsor: Moving Byzantium: Mobility, Microstructures & Personal Agency, Österreichische Akademie der Wissenschaften, Universität Wien / FWF Wittgenstein-Prize Project
Organiser: Claudia Rapp, Institut für Byzantinistik & Neogräzistik, Universität Wien / Österreichische Akademie der Wissenschaften, Wien and Paraskevi Sykopetritou, Institut für Byzantinistik & Neogräzistik, Universität Wien
Moderator: Ioannis Stouraitis, Institut für Byzantinistik & Neogräzistik, Universität Wien / Österreichische Akademie der Wissenschaften, Wien
Paper 1303-a: **Towards the Upper Echelon: Agency and Social Ascent in Late Byzantium** (Language: English)
Christos Malatras, Research Centre for Byzantine & Post-Byzantine Art, Academy of Athens
Paper 1303-b: **Moving/Transforming Paristrion: From Byzantine Border Province to Heartland of the 'Second Bulgarian Kingdom'** (Language: English)
Francesco Dall'Aglio, Department of Medieval History of Bulgaria, Institute for Historical Studies, Bulgarian Academy of Sciences
Paper 1303-c: **Moving in Exalted Circles: Balkan Elites, Shifting Loyalties, and Social Mobility in Byzantium, 11th-13th Centuries** (Language: English)
Christos Makrypoulias, Institute of Byzantine Research, Athens and Angeliki Papageorgiou, Department of Russian Language & Literature of Slavic Studies, National & Kapodistrian University of Athens
Paper 1303-d: **Incoming Governor: The Narrative of Visiting Provincial Administrators and Its Function in the Byzantine Epistolography in the 'Long' 12th Century** (Language: English)
Márton Rózsa, Department of Medieval & Early Modern History, Eötvös Loránd University, Budapest

Session: **1304** **Maurice Keyworth Building: Room 1.32**
Title: **NEW APPROACHES TO THE THIRD CRUSADE, II**
Sponsor: Past & Present Society / Third Crusade Research Network
Organiser: Beth Spacey, School of History & Cultures, University of Birmingham and Stephen Spencer, Institute of Historical Research, University of London
Moderator: Natasha Ruth Hodgson, School of Arts & Humanities, Nottingham Trent University
Paper 1304-a: **More than Memories?: Representations of Kingship and Masculinity in the *Itinerarium Peregrinorum et Gesta Regis Ricardi*** (Language: English)
Mark McCabe, Department of History, University of Huddersfield
Paper 1304-b: **The Crusade of Baldwin of Forde, Archbishop of Canterbury** (Language: English)
Helen J. Nicholson, School of History, Archaeology & Religion, Cardiff University
Paper 1304-c: **Reconsidering the Acre Massacre during the Third Crusade** (Language: English)
Tom Asbridge, School of History, Queen Mary University of London

Session: **1305** **Michael Sadler Building: Room LG.16**
Title: **MOVING GOODS AND PEOPLE IN MEDIEVAL ENGLAND AND FRANCE**
Organiser: IMC Programming Committee
Moderator: Anna Rich-Abad, Department of History, University of Nottingham
Paper 1305-a: **The Memory of a Profitable Union: Anglo-Gascon Trade at the Close of the Hundred Years War, 1435–1465** (Language: English)
Robert Blackmore, Department of History, University of Southampton
Paper 1305-b: **Aliens and the Late Medieval Court of Chancery: Immigrant Choices and Options** (Language: English)
Joshua Ravenhill, Department of History, University of York
Paper 1305-c: **Precedent and Memory in Borough Customary Law** (Language: English)
Esther Liberman Cuenca, Department of History, Fordham University, New York

---

Session: **1306** **Parkinson Building: Room 1.16**
Title: **MEDIEVAL BODIES IGNORED, II: THE SUFFERING BODY**
Sponsor: Institute for Medieval Studies, University of Leeds
Organiser: Rose A. Sawyer, Institute for Medieval Studies, University of Leeds
Moderator: Sunny Harrison, Institute for Medieval Studies, University of Leeds
Paper 1306-a: **Broken and Remade: The Bodily Experience of Medieval War** (Language: English)
Joanna Phillips, School of History, University of Leeds
Paper 1306-b: **Incorporating the Physical: An Interdisciplinary Approach to Early Medieval Bodies** (Language: English)
Claire Burridge, Faculty of History, University of Cambridge
Paper 1306-c: **The Devil at Your Breast: Representations of Nursemaids' Exhausted Bodies in Changeling Hagiography** (Language: English)
Rose A. Sawyer

Session: **1307** **Fine Art Building: Studio Ground Floor**
Title: **DECLINE AND FALL IN THE MEDIEVAL MIDDLE EAST**
Organiser: Deborah Tor, Department of History, University of Notre Dame, Indiana
Moderator: Hugh Kennedy, Department of the Languages & Cultures of the Near & Middle East, School of Oriental & African Studies, University of London
Paper 1307-a: **Why Did the Sāsānids Fall?: *Ibn Shihāb al-Zuhrī* (d. c. 744) and the Construction of the Past in Late Umayyad Syria** (Language: English)
Sean W. Anthony, Department of Near Eastern Languages & Cultures, Ohio State University
Paper 1307-b: **Authoritative Memories of Decline and Fall: Pre-Islamic Inscriptions 'Translated' into Arabic** (Language: English)
Harry Munt, Department of History, University of York
Paper 1307-c: **The Eclipse of Khurāsān in the 1[illegible]th Century: Decline or Fall?** (Language: English)
Deborah Tor

Session: **1308** **Maurice Keyworth Building: Room 1.04**
Title: **MAMMARIES AND MEMORY: BREASTS IN MEDIEVAL CULTURE AND SOCIETY**
Organiser: Kim M. Phillips, Department of History, University of Auckland
Moderator: Katherine J. Lewis, Department of History, University of Huddersfield
Paper 1308-a: **The Maternal Breast and Male Shame in Ælfric's *Life of St Agatha*** (Language: English)
Alice D. Jorgensen, School of English, Trinity College Dublin
Paper 1308-b: **Female Bodies and Reproductive Memory in Late Medieval England** (Language: English)
Bronach Kane, School of History, Archaeology & Religion, Cardiff University
Paper 1308-c: **'Woman's Milk' as Medicine in Medieval Herbals and Handbooks** (Language: English)
Kim M. Phillips

Session: **1309** **Baines Wing: Room 2.13**
Title: **GENTRY IDENTITY AND LEGACY, II: LANDSCAPE AND ARCHITECTURE**
Organiser: Katie Bridger, Centre for English Local History, University of Leicester and Matthew Ward, School of History, University of Nottingham
Moderator: Philip J. Morgan, Research Institute for the Humanities, Keele University
Paper 1309-a: **Love Thy Neighbour?: Geographical Proximity and Gentry Identity in Leicestershire, c. 1460-1540** (Language: English)
Katie Bridger
Paper 1309-b: **Tattershall and Beyond: Elite Architecture in Late Medieval England** (Language: English)
James Wright, Department of Archaeology, University of Nottingham
Respondent: Matthew Ward

Session: **1310** **Baines Wing: Room 1.16**
Title: **RETHINKING AGENCY, III: A ROUND TABLE DISCUSSION**
Sponsor: *Medieval Prosopography*
Organiser: Charlotte Pickard, Centre for Continuing & Professional Education, Cardiff University and Rebecca Searby, Centre for Medieval Studies, University of York
Moderator: Charlotte Pickard
Purpose: *Detecting 'agency' in the medieval world, in recent years, has shaped the research of historians searching for the lesser voices of the past. It is a term often attributed to unusual 'action' or 'will' beyond the scope of societal expectation. Given its vast application, there is a pressing need to consider how we detect, define, and interpret agency across medieval record collections. Are we reading moments of individual will or is this a more complicated process that requires renewed appreciation? This round table discussion aims to consider how we can tackle the complicated subject of 'agency' in future research.*

Participants include Lindy Grant (University of Reading), Amy Livingstone (Wittenberg University, Ohio), Kathleen Nolan (Hollins University, Virginia), and Paul Webster (Cardiff University).

Session: **1311** **Baines Wing: Room 1.15**
Title: **NEW APPROACHES TO A CLIMATE HISTORY OF THE 13TH AND 14TH CENTURY: TIPPING POINTS AND EXTREME EVENTS**
Organiser: Martin Bauch, Leibniz-Institut für Geschichte und Kultur des östlichen Europa, Leipzig
Moderator: Chantal Camenisch, Historisches Institut, Universität Bern
Paper 1311-a: **The Onset of the Little Ice Age in 14th-Century Central Europe: Evidence from Narrative Sources and Deliberations about the Utility of Other Source Types** (Language: English)
Annabell Engel, Leibniz-Institut für Geschichte und Kultur des östlichen Europa, Leipzig
Paper 1311-b: **Economic and Social Impact of Climate in Northern Alpine Regions, c. 1280-1330** (Language: English)
Thomas Labbé, Archéologie, Terre, Histoire, Sociétés (ARTEHIS - UMR 6298), Université de Bourgogne
Paper 1311-c: **A Decade of Flooding: Infrastructural and Institutional Responses to Extreme Precipitation in Bologna between 1309 and 1321** (Language: English)
Martin Bauch

Session: **1312** **University House: Little Woodhouse Room**
Title: **MUSIC, MANUSCRIPTS, AND PRACTICE IN THE 14TH AND 15TH CENTURIES**
Organiser: IMC Programming Committee
Moderator: William T. Flynn, Institute for Medieval Studies, University of Leeds
Paper 1312-a: **A Discussion of the Function of Music Notation in Secular Manuscripts, c. 1300** (Language: English)
Frieda van der Heijden, Department of Music, Royal Holloway, University of London
Paper 1312-b: **Reconstructing Philippe de Vitry's *Ars nova*** (Language: English)
John Douglas Gray, Independent Scholar, Boulder, Colorado
Paper 1312-c: **Marchetto's *Lucidarium in arte musice plane* and Possible Philological Relations of the Italian Concept of Mode in the 14th and 15th Centuries** (Language: English)
Carlos Iafelice, Departamento de Música, Universidade Estadual Paulista, São Paulo

Session: **1313** **University House: Beechgrove Room**
Title: **NEW PERSPECTIVES ON WOMEN IN MEDIEVAL ROMANCE, II: MEMORY AND LINEAGE**
Organiser: Kirsty A. S. Bolton, Centre for Medieval & Renaissance Culture / Department of English, University of Southampton
Moderator: Grace Timperley, School of Arts, Languages & Cultures, University of Manchester
Paper 1313-a: **'From the Devil we came': Founding Fiction and the Taming of the Demon Mother of Europe** (Language: English)
Lauren E. Wood, Department of History, California State University, Fullerton
Paper 1313-b: **Loving *par amours*: Lexical Lineage and Medieval Romance in Translation** (Language: English)
Grace Catherine Greiner, Department of English, Cornell University
Paper 1313-c: **The Lady Commemorated: The Dame de Fayel's Secret Gift in Jakemes's *Châtelain de Coucy*** (Language: English)
Mimi Zhou, Department of French Literature, Thought & Culture, New York University

Session: **1314** **Charles Thackrah Building: 1.01**
Title: **ROYAL MARRIAGES, IV: ROYAL MARRIAGES AND MEMORY**
Organiser: Manuela Santos Silva, Departamento de História, Universidade de Lisboa
Moderator: Ana Maria S. A. Rodrigues, Centro de História, Universidade de Lisboa
Paper 1314-a: **Monastic Politics of a Royal Matrimony: Enrique II of Castile and Juana Manuel - Crown's Memory and Networks** (Language: English)
Maria del Mar Graña Cid, Departamento de Sagrada Escritura y de Historia de la Iglesia, Universidad Pontificia Comillas, Madrid
Paper 1314-b: **Constructing Memory as a Mechanism of Power: The Marriages of Isabel and Beatriz of Portugal** (Language: English)
Maria Barreto Dávila, Centro de Humanidades, Universidade Nova de Lisboa
Paper 1314-c: **Peripheral Marriages?: The Lost Memory of Infanta Beatrice's Wedding in Lisbon and Nice, 1521** (Language: English)
Carla Alferes Pinto, Centro de Humanidades, Universidade Nova de Lisboa

Session: **1315** **Michael Sadler Building: Room LG.19**
Title: **BASE METAL, SILVER, AND GOLD COINS: EXPLORING THE MEANINGS OF MEMORY THROUGH NUMISMATIC EVIDENCE**
Sponsor: University of Nottingham
Organiser: Marco Panato, Department of History, University of Nottingham and Mariele Valci, Department of History, University of Nottingham
Moderator: Alan M. Stahl, Department of Rare Books & Special Collections, Firestone Library, Princeton University
Paper 1315-a: **Between Two Worlds: Northern Italy and the Mint of Venice in Carolingian Times, 8th-9th Centuries** (Language: English)
Marco Panato
Paper 1315-b: **Popes, Senators, Pilgrims, and Creditors: The Rome Commune as Told by Black Money** (Language: English)
Mariele Valci
Paper 1315-c: **The Gold Florin of Florence between Memory, Fiction, and Performance** (Language: English)
Stefano Locatelli, Department of History, University of Manchester

Session: **1316** **Michael Sadler Building: Rupert Beckett Theatre**
Title: **14TH-CENTURY ENGLAND, IV: THE BOUNDARIES OF ROYAL POWER IN LATER MEDIEVAL ENGLAND - LAW AND THE CHURCH**
Sponsor: Society for 14th Century Studies
Organiser: David Green, Centre for British Studies, Harlaxton College, University of Evansville
Moderator: Mark E. Arvanigian, Department of History, California State University, Fresno
Paper 1316-a: **The Bishops and the Ordinances of 1311** (Language: English)
Samuel Lane, Christ Church, University of Oxford
Paper 1316-b: **Henry IV and the Friars: Speaking Truth to Power** (Language: English)
Chris Given-Wilson, St Andrews Institute of Mediaeval Studies, University of St Andrews
Paper 1316-c: **The Impact of Legislation in Late Medieval England** (Language: English)
Gwilym Dodd, Department of History, University of Nottingham

Session: **1317** **Social Sciences Building: Room 10.05**
Title: **THE TRANSFORMATION OF THE CAROLINGIAN WORLD, II**
Sponsor: Transformation of the Carolingian World Network
Organiser: Richard Corradini, Institut für Mittelalterforschung, Österreichische Akademie der Wissenschaften, Wien
Moderator: Stuart Airlie, School of Humanities (History), University of Glasgow
Paper 1317-a: **Historiography, Time Tables, Poetics: Some Observations on the Diversification of Knowledge** (Language: English)
Richard Corradini
Paper 1317-b: **Commemorating - or Not - Queens and Common Women in the Verses of the Carolingian Poet Ermoldus Nigellus, fl. 826** (Language: English)
Carey Fleiner, Department of History, University of Winchester
Paper 1317-c: **Abbo of Saint-Germain-des-Prés's Poetics of Martyrdom** (Language: English)
Matthew Bryan Gillis, Department of History, University of Tennessee, Knoxville

---

Session: **1318** **Michael Sadler Building: Banham Theatre**
Title: **VISIONS OF COMMUNITY, I: ADVENTURES IN COMPARISON**
Sponsor: Sonderforschungsbereich Project 'Visions of Community', Österreichische Akademie der Wissenschaften, Universität Wien / FWF Project F42
Organiser: Rutger Kramer, Institut für Mittelalterforschung, Österreichische Akademie der Wissenschaften, Wien and Walter Pohl, Institut für Mittelalterforschung, Österreichische Akademie der Wissenschaften, Wien
Moderator: Chris Wickham, Faculty of History, University of Oxford
Paper 1318-a: **Visions of Community: An Adventure in Comparison** (Language: English)
Walter Pohl
Paper 1318-b: **Trying to Define the Global Middle Ages: Collaborative Methods from an AHRC Network** (Language: English)
Naomi Standen, Centre for the Study of the Middle Ages, University of Birmingham
Paper 1318-c: **Comparing Power and Institutions in Medieval Islam and Christendom** (Language: English)
Ana Rodríguez, Departamento de Historia Medieval, Consejo Superior de Investigaciones Científicas, Madrid

Session: **1319** **Maurice Keyworth Building: Room 1.09**
Title: **CITIES OF READERS, IV: THE PERFORMANCE OF READING - TEXTS, OBJECTS, SPACES, AND PRACTICES**
Sponsor: NWO Project 'Cities of Readers', Rijksuniversiteit Groningen
Organiser: Joanka van der Laan, Oudere Nederlandse Letterkunde, Rijksuniversiteit Groningen
Moderator: Bart Ramakers, Oudere Nederlandse Letterkunde, Rijksuniversiteit Groningen
Paper 1319-a: **Having Christ as a Companion: The Significance of Daily Movement in Middle Dutch Devotional Texts** (Language: English)
Joanka van der Laan
Paper 1319-b: **The Impact of Catholic Reform on Domestic Devotional Art in the Southern Low Countries: Case Studies and Avenues for Research** (Language: English)
Sarah Joan Moran, Departement Geschiedenis en Kunstgeschiedenis, Universiteit Utrecht
Paper 1319-c: **Conceptualising the *vita activa* as a Space for Religious Life** (Language: English)
Margriet Hoogvliet, Vakgroep Mediaevistiek, Rijksuniversiteit Groningen

Session: **1320** **Charles Thackrah Building: 1.02**
Title: **REMEMBERING TROY IN THE MIDDLE AGES, IV: CULTURAL MEMORY BEYOND BORDERS**
Organiser: Sabine Heidi Walther, Abteilung für Skandinavische Sprachen und Literaturen, Rheinische Friedrich-Wilhelms-Universität Bonn and N. Kıvılcım Yavuz, Den Arnamagnæanske Samling, Københavns Universitet
Moderator: Sabine Heidi Walther
Paper 1320-a: **Temporality and Materiality in the Medieval Matter of Troy** (Language: English)
Marilynn Desmond, Department of English, State University of New York, Binghamton
Paper 1320-b: **'This whole great universe serves as a theatre': Pan-European Trojan Origins** (Language: English)
Peter Látka, Department of English, Trent University, Ontario
Paper 1320-c: **Travelling Images: The Illustrations in the First Printed Stories of Troy in Germany and Spain** (Language: English)
María Sanz Julián, Departamento de Filología Inglesa y Alemana, Universidad de Zaragoza
Paper 1320-d: **The Story of Troy: Facts and Figures, or Texts and Manuscripts** (Language: English)
N. Kıvılcım Yavuz

Session: **1321** **Social Sciences Building: Room 10.06**
Title: **'Libro de la mia memoria': Memory in Dante**
Organiser: IMC Programming Committee
Moderator: Federica Pich, School of Languages, Cultures & Societies - Italian, University of Leeds
Paper 1321-a: **'Conforti la memoria mia': Suicide and the Manipulation of Memory in Dante's *Commedia*** (Language: English)
Emma Louise Barlow, Department of Italian Studies, University of Sydney
Paper 1321-b: **Affective Memory in Dante's Works** (Language: English)
Xiaoyi Zhang, Medieval Institute, University of Notre Dame, Indiana
Paper 1321-c: **'The pricking of memory': Recollection as Punishment in Dante's *Inferno*** (Language: English)
Leonardo Chiarantini, Department of Romance Languages & Literatures, University of Michigan

Session: **1322** **Baines Wing: Room 1.14**
Title: **Memories Have Gone to Our Heads: Constructing Memory around the Figures of the Medieval Head and Skull**
Organiser: Lauren Rozenberg, Department of History of Art, University College London
Moderator: Eduardo Correia, Department of English, King's College London
Paper 1322-a: ***In memoriam Æschere*: A Head Full of Worry** (Language: English)
Sander Stolk, Faculteit der Geesteswetenschappen, Universiteit Leiden
Paper 1322-b: ***Virtus memorativa*: Diagramming the Brain in Late Medieval Medical Treatises** (Language: English)
Lauren Rozenberg
Paper 1322-c: **Memorialising Sanctity: Deconstructing the Textile Skull Reliquaries of Cologne's 11,000 Holy Virgins** (Language: English)
Cher Casey, Department of History of Art, University of York

Session: **1323** **Maurice Keyworth Building: Room 1.31**
Title: **Remembering the Saints, IV: Creating and Adapting Memory in Early Medieval England and Wales**
Sponsor: Cult of Saints Project, University of Oxford
Organiser: Bryan Ward-Perkins, Faculty of History, University of Oxford and Robert Wiśniewski, Instytut Historyczny, Uniwersytet Warszawski
Moderator: Bertrand Lançon, Département d'Histoire, Université de Limoges / Centre de recherche interdisciplinaire en histoire, histoire de l'art et musicologie, Université de Poitiers
Paper 1323-a: **Manipulating Memory: St Ælfgifu of Shaftesbury's 'Resurrection' and the Politics of Sanctity** (Language: English)
Rachel S. Anderson, Department of English, Grand Valley State University, Michigan
Paper 1323-b: **Remembering St Germanus in 9th-Century Wales** (Language: English)
Paweł Derecki, Instytut Historyczny, Uniwersytet Warszawski
Paper 1323-c: **Reworking Corporate Memory: St Calais (Carilefus) and St Cuthbert** (Language: English)
Margaret Coombe, Lady Margaret Hall, University of Oxford

Session: **1324** **Charles Thackrah Building: 1.04**
Title: ***MEMORIA* AND METAPHOR**
Organiser: IMC Programming Committee
Moderator: Jan Čermák, Department of English, Univerzita Karlova, Praha
Paper 1324-a: ***Memoria* and Its Metaphors: A Corpus Study** (Language: English)
Krzysztof Nowak, Institute of Polish Language, Polish Academy of Sciences, Kraków
Paper 1324-b: **Body Metaphors of Memory in *De Noe* by Ambrose of Milan** (Language: English)
Lidia Raquel Miranda, Consejo Nacional de Investigaciones Científicas y Técnicas (CONICET) / Facultad de Ciencias Humanas, Universidad Nacional de La Pampa, Argentina
Paper 1324-c: **The Mnemonic Metaphor of the Wound in the Italian and Latin Works of Petrarch** (Language: English)
Andrea Torre, Classe di Lettere, Scuola Normale Superiore di Pisa

Session: **1325** **Maurice Keyworth Building: Room 1.06**
Title: **MEDICAL RECOLLECTIONS IN MANUALS AND MANUSCRIPTS**
Organiser: IMC Programming Committee
Moderator: Flocel Sabaté Curull, Departament d'Història, Universitat de Lleida
Paper 1325-a: **Forgotten Authorities: Sources in the Recipe Miscellanies in St Gallen, Stiftsbibliothek, Cod. Sang. 751** (Language: English)
Nora Thorburn, Centre for Medieval Studies, University of Toronto, Downtown
Paper 1325-b: **Memorias de al-Andalus: Averroes y la medicina en el Medioevo Latín** (Language: Español)
Sara Lenzi, Departamento de Filosofía Teórica e Historia de la Filosofía, Universidad Complutense de Madrid
Paper 1325-c: **Facts to Remember: Some Annotations in Late Medieval Medical Manuscripts** (Language: English)
Rebeca Cubas-Peña, York Minster
Paper 1325-d: **Constructing Authority through Paratext and Personalisation: The Case of Printed Dutch Herbals** (Language: English)
Andrea van Leerdam, Departement Talen, Literatuur en Communicatie, Universiteit Utrecht

Session: **1326** **University House: Great Woodhouse Room**
Title: **WOMEN, MEMORY, AND LITERACY: NEW APPROACHES**
Organiser: Einat Klafter, Cohn Institute for the History & Philosophy of Science & Ideas, Tel Aviv University
Moderator: Catherine J. Batt, Institute for Medieval Studies, University of Leeds
Paper 1326-a: **Memorizing Mercy: Reading and Remembering Margaret of York's *Benois seront les misericordieux*** (Language: English)
Erica Blair O'Brien, Department of History of Art, University of Bristol
Paper 1326-b: **Look, No Hands!: Literary Production through Memory and Memorization in *The Book of Margery Kempe*** (Language: English)
Einat Klafter
Paper 1326-c: **Assessing Roles in the Production and Acquisition of Liturgical Books in the Dominican Nunneries of Late Medieval Portugal** (Language: English)
Paula Freire Cardoso, Instituto de Estudos Medievais, Universidade Nova de Lisboa

Session: **1327** **Social Sciences Building: Room 10.07**
Title: **MEDIEVALISM: MEMORIES OF MEDIEVAL LITERARY MOTIFS, FIGURES, AND REQUISITES IN (POST) MODERN MEDIA**
Sponsor: Interdisziplinäres Zentrum für Mittelalter und frühe Neuzeit (IZMF), Universität Salzburg
Organiser: Siegrid Schmidt, Interdisziplinäres Zentrum für Mittelalter und Frühneuzeit (IZMF), Universität Salzburg
Moderator: Wolfgang Neuper, Archiv der Erzdiözese Salzburg
Paper 1327-a: **Winter is Everywhere: *Game of Thrones* in Popular Culture** (Language: English)
Marlene Ernst, Zentrum für Gastrosophie, Universität Salzburg
Paper 1327-b: **Medieval Russian History on Film: 'Anna Jaroslavna, Queen of France'** (Language: English)
Ursula Bieber, Fachbereich Slawistik / Interdisziplinäres Zentrum für Mittelalter und Frühneuzeit (IZMF), Universität Salzburg
Paper 1327-c: **Harry Mulisch: 'Siegfried' - Adolf and Eva's Son** (Language: English)
Siegrid Schmidt
Paper 1327-d: **Foreign Friends: Unexpected Encounters with the Middle Ages in the Works of Franz Fühmann, Christoph Hein, and Orhan Pamuk** (Language: English)
Ingrid Bennewitz, Lehrstuhl für Deutsche Philologie des Mittelalters, Otto-Friedrich-Universität Bamberg

Session: **1328** **Fine Art Building: SR G.04**
Title: **RELIGIOUS KNOWLEDGE AND MEMORY, II: 'FALSE' AND 'FAKE' REMEMBRANCE**
Organiser: Michael Neumaier, Graduiertenkolleg 1662 'Religiöses Wissen im vormodernen Europa (800–1800)', Eberhard-Karls-Universität Tübingen
Moderator: Volker Leppin, Institut für Spätmittelalter und Reformation, Eberhard-Karls-Universität Tübingen
Paper 1328-a: **Places of Memory, Places of Oblivion: Gardens in Medieval Literature** (Language: English)
Alexandra Becker, Graduiertenkolleg 1662 'Religiöses Wissen im vormodernen Europa (800–1800)', Eberhard-Karls-Universität Tübingen
Paper 1328-b: **Interpreting Memory: Eadmer's Anselm between Historiography and Hagiography** (Language: English)
Sven Gröger, Graduiertenkolleg 1662 'Religiöses Wissen im vormodernen Europa (800–1800)', Eberhard-Karls-Universität Tübingen
Paper 1328-c: **Re-Memorising the Truth in the High Middle Ages: History and Authorities in the Context of Resistance** (Language: English)
Maximilian Nix, Graduiertenkolleg 1662 'Religiöses Wissen im vormodernen Europa (800–1800)', Eberhard-Karls-Universität Tübingen

Session: **1329** — **Charles Thackrah Building: 1.03**
Title: **RELIGIOUS MEMORY IN LATE MEDIEVAL UTRECHT**
Organiser: Jerem van Duijl, Instituut voor Geschiedenis, Universiteit Leiden
Moderator: Frans Camphuijsen, Center for Medieval & Renaissance Studies Amsterdam, Universiteit van Amsterdam
Paper 1329-a: **How to Create a Meaningful Personal Network: The Religious and Social Life of Alderman and Mayor Dirck Borre van Amerongen, c. 1438-1528** (Language: English)
Cora Zwart, Faculteit der Letteren, Rijksuniversiteit Groningen
Paper 1329-b: **Enhancing Social Standing through Memory: Donations to the Utrecht Commandry of the Teutonic Order in the 13th Century** (Language: English)
Jerem van Duijl
Paper 1329-c: **The Lost Memorial Registers of Utrecht: How Administration Hampered Remembrance** (Language: English)
Bram van den Hoven van Genderen, Departement Geschiedenis en Kunstgeschiedenis, Universiteit Utrecht

Session: **1330** — **Social Sciences Building: Room 10.09**
Title: **THE CONSTRUCTION OF SACRED MEMORY IN GOTHIC SPACES**
Sponsor: Centre for Medieval and Early Modern Studies (MEMS), University of Kent
Organiser: Roisin Astell, Centre for Medieval & Early Modern Studies (MEMS), University of Kent
Moderator: Emily Davenport Guerry, School of History, University of Kent
Paper 1330-a: **Past, Present, and Future: The Construction of Sacred Time and Memory in the Decorative Programme of the Sainte-Chapelle, Paris** (Language: English)
Roisin Astell
Paper 1330-b: **Remembering St Faith at Westminster Abbey** (Language: English)
Katherine Toussaint-Jackson, Centre for Medieval & Early Modern Studies (MEMS), University of Kent
Paper 1330-c: **If Stones Could Speak: The Foliate Heads of Gothic Chartres Cathedral** (Language: English)
Cassandra Harrington, Centre for Medieval & Early Modern Studies (MEMS), University of Kent

Session: **1331** — **Maurice Keyworth Building: Room 1.05**
Title: **MEMORY, SETTLEMENT, AND LANDSCAPE, III: PEOPLE, PLACES, AND MEMORY**
Sponsor: Medieval Settlement Research Group
Organiser: Duncan Berryman, School of Geography, Archaeology & Palaeoecology, Queen's University Belfast and Eddie Procter, Department of Archaeology, University of Exeter
Moderator: Eddie Procter
Paper 1331-a: **'It's the way I tell 'em': Memories of Medieval Charnwood Forest as Expressed in Post-Medieval Land Disputes** (Language: English)
Ann Stones, Centre for English Local History, University of Leicester
Paper 1331-b: **Layers of Legend, Lordship, and Landscape: A Fresh Interdisciplinary and Multi-Period Approach to Understanding Medieval Caernarfon in Gwynedd, Wales** (Language: English)
Rachel Elizabeth Swallow, Department of History & Archaeology, University of Chester

Session: **1332** **Baines Wing: Room G.36**
Title: **SHARING SPACES: USES AND FUNCTIONS OF MEDIEVAL BUILDINGS AND MONUMENTS**
Organiser: IMC Programming Committee
Moderator: Audrey Thorstad, School of History, Welsh History & Archaeology, Bangor University
Paper 1332-a: **HeRstory: Constructing an Holistic Account of Medieval Castles** (Language: English)
Karen Dempsey, School of Archaeology, Geography & Environmental Science, University of Reading
Paper 1332-b: **Set in Stone (and Wood)?: Non-Natural Theory, Conceptions of Medicine and Society, and the Archaeology of the Medieval Hospitals of England** (Language: English)
Martin Huggon, Department of Archaeology, University of Sheffield
Paper 1332-c: **Remembering the Patriarchs in Crusader Hebron: Making and Marking a Multi-Faith Monument** (Language: English)
Megan Boomer, Department of the History of Art, University of Pennsylvania
Paper 1332-d: **'Teeming with venerable memories': Functions, Associations, and Recollections at Old St Peter's in the Vatican** (Language: English)
Charles McClendon, Department of Fine Arts, Brandeis University, Massachusetts

Session: **1333** **Leeds University Union: Room 2 - Elland Road**
Title: **REMEMBERING COMMUNITIES IN EARLY MEDIEVAL EUROPE, II: MEMORY AND GEOGRAPHY**
Sponsor: Kısmet Press
Organiser: Ricky Broome, Leeds Institute for Clinical Trials Research (LICTR), University of Leeds
Moderator: Ricky Broome
Paper 1333-a: **Early Medieval Urban Communities in Britain and Remembering the Roman Past** (Language: English)
Mateusz Fafinski, Friedrich-Meinecke-Institut, Freie Universität Berlin
Paper 1333-b: **Monks and Missionaries on the Move: Mobility as a Memory or a Motif** (Language: English)
Helen Lawson, School of History, Classics & Archaeology, University of Edinburgh
Paper 1333-c: **Why Jordanes Claimed that the Franks Were Inhabitants of the Lands of the Germans** (Language: English)
Robert Kasperski, Tadeusz Manteuffel Institute of History, Polish Academy of Sciences, Warszawa

Session:	**1334** **Maurice Keyworth Building: Room 1.33**
Title:	**REPRESENTATIONS OF MEMORY, IDENTITY, AND NOBILITY IN MEDIEVAL EUROPE**
Sponsor:	Department of History, Texas A&M University, Texarkana
Organiser:	Craig M. Nakashian, Department of History, Texas A&M University, Texarkana
Moderator:	Craig M. Nakashian
Paper 1334-a:	**Memory and the West March: Identity in the *Lanercost Chronicle*** (Language: English) Jeff Hass, Department of History & Anthropology, Franciscan University of Steubenville, Ohio
Paper 1334-b:	**Reading between the Lines: The Cid of the *Cantar* and His Nobility** (Language: English) Marija Blašković, Institut für Romanistik, Universität Wien
Paper 1334-c:	**A Warrior Identity?: Late Anglo-Saxon Bishops and the Battlefield** (Language: English) Mary Blanchard, Department of History, Ave Maria University, Florida

Session:	**1335** **Leeds University Union: Room 4 - Hyde Park**
Title:	**PROPRIETARY MEMORIES: *NOTITIAE*-INVENTORIES IN EARLY MEDIEVAL IBERIA, II**
Sponsor:	Instituto de Estudos Medievais, Universidade Nova de Lisboa
Organiser:	Álvaro Carvajal Castro, Departamento de Geografía, Prehistoria y Arqueología, Universidad del País Vasco - Euskal Herriko Unibertsitatea and André Evangelista Marques, Instituto de Estudos Medievais, Universidade Nova de Lisboa
Moderator:	Julio Escalona, Instituto de Historia, Centro de Ciencias Humanas y Sociales, Consejo Superior de Investigaciones Científicas (CSIC), Madrid
Paper 1335-a:	**Property Inventories from an Archaeological Perspective: The Case of the Monastic Landscapes of Samos, North-West Spain, 8th-11th Centuries** (Language: English) Fernández Ferreiro Marcos, Facultade de Xeografía e Historia, Universidade de Santiago de Compostela and José Carlos Sánchez-Pardo, Facultade de Xeografía e Historia, Universidade de Santiago de Compostela
Paper 1335-b:	**Traces of Absent Inventories: References to *Notitiae* in the Charters from North-West Iberia, 9th-11th Centuries** (Language: English) Álvaro Carvajal Castro
Paper 1335-c:	***Sub censuario iugo*: The Census and Inventories in the First Decades of al-Andalus, c. 711-754** (Language: English) Jesús Lorenzo Jiménez, Departamento de Historia Medieval, Moderna y de América, Universidad del País Vasco - Euskal Herriko Unibertsitatea, Vitoria-Gasteiz

Session: **1336** **Leeds University Union: Room 5 - Kirkstall Abbey**
Title: **VOICES OF LAW, IV: MEMORY, LANGUAGE, AND THE (RE)DISCOVERY OF LAW**
Sponsor: Voices of Law: Language, Text & Practice
Organiser: Jenny Benham, School of History, Archaeology & Religion, Cardiff University
Moderator: Paul Russell, Department of Anglo-Saxon, Norse & Celtic, University of Cambridge
Paper 1336-a: **The Resonance of Church Law in Norwegian Legislation: Some Selected Examples** (Language: English)
Torstein Jørgensen, Fakultet for teologi, diakoni og ledelsesfag, VID vitenskapelige høgskole, Stavanger
Paper 1336-b: **Words from Ancient Times or New?: On the Ecclesiastical Terminology in the Early Norwegian Provincial Laws** (Language: English)
Bertil Nilsson, Institutionen för litteratur, idéhistoria och religion, Göteborgs Universitet
Paper 1336-c: **The Stability of Language in the Anglo-Saxon Laws, c. 890-1020** (Language: English)
Ingrid Ivarsen, School of History, University of St Andrews

Session: **1337** **Emmanuel Centre: Wilson Room**
Title: **GLOBAL PRACTICES OF MEMORY AND EXCHANGE, II: ACTS OF REMEMBERING IN CENTRAL EUROPEAN TOWNS AND CITIES, C. 1200-1550**
Sponsor: Sonderforschungsbereich Project 'Visions of Community', Österreichische Akademie der Wissenschaften, Universität Wien / FWF Project F42
Organiser: Károly Goda, Sonderforschungsbereich Project 'Visions of Community', Institut für Geschichte, Universität Wien and Fabian Kümmeler, Sonderforschungsbereich Project 'Visions of Community' / Institut für Osteuropäische Geschichte, Universität Wien
Moderator: Emilia Jamroziak, Institute for Medieval Studies / School of History, University of Leeds
Paper 1337-a: **Reminding Merchants of Their Christian Duty: 'Papal Embargo' in 15th-Century Central European Towns** (Language: English)
Alexandra Kaar, Institut für Österreichische Geschichtsforschung, Universität Wien
Paper 1337-b: **Patron Saints and Constructions of Cultural Memory in Bohemian Towns** (Language: English)
Kateřina Horníčková, Sonderforschungsbereich Project 'Visions of Community', Universität Wien / Southern Bohemian University, České Budějovice
Paper 1337-c: **Source of Love and Weapon of God: Staging the Eucharist in Late Medieval Buda and Cracow** (Language: English)
Károly Goda

Session: **1338** **Michael Sadler Building: Room LG.10**
Title: **ARCHITECTURE AND THE MEMORY OF OTHERNESS ON THE IBERIAN PENINSULA**
Organiser: Michael A. Conrad, Kunsthistorisches Institut, Universität Zürich and Maria Portmann, Kunsthistorisches Institut, Universität Zürich
Moderator: Michael A. Conrad and Maria Portmann
Paper 1338-a: **Walls of Silk: Parietal Decoration and Textiles in al-Andalus** (Language: English)
Asunción Lavesa, Departamento de Prehistoria y Arqueología, Universidad Autónoma of Madrid
Paper 1338-b: **The Memory of al-Andalus: The Islamic Perspective** (Language: English)
April Najjaj, Department of History, Texas A&M University, San Antonio
Paper 1338-c: **Sacred Places: The 'Cubas' from Southern Portugal** (Language: English)
Luís Duarte Ferro, Centro de História de Arte e Investigação Artística (CHAIA), Universidade de Évora / Faculdade de Arquitectura, Universidade do Porto / Calouste Gulbenkian Foundation, Portugal
Paper 1338-d: **Remembering Architecture of al-Andalus and Sefarad in Spanish Paintings around 1400** (Language: English)
Maria Portmann

Session: **1339** **Maurice Keyworth Building: Room 1.03**
Title: **MANIPULATING MEMORY: CHRONICLES AS RECONSTRUCTIONS OF THE PAST**
Organiser: Kari North, Department of History, University of Toronto, Downtown
Moderator: Elise Williams, Faculty of the History & Philosophy of Science, University of Cambridge
Paper 1339-a: **Misremembering Defeat: Leo IX and the Battle of Civitate** (Language: English)
Eduardo Fabbro, Department of History & Classical Studies, McGill University, Québec
Paper 1339-b: **Berengaria: The Forgotten Angevin Queen?** (Language: English)
Gabrielle Storey, Department of History, University of Winchester
Paper 1339-c: **Distorting the Past: The Kings of Majorca in the Chronicle of Pere the Ceremonious** (Language: English)
Kari North

Session: **1340** **Michael Sadler Building: Room LG.15**
Title: **MATERIALITY AND THE MEMORY OF CHARLEMAGNE IN MEDIEVAL ENGLAND**
Sponsor: Charlemagne: A European Icon (www.charlemagne-icon.ac.uk)
Organiser: Marianne J. Ailes, Department of French, University of Bristol and James Doherty, School of Modern Languages, University of Bristol
Moderator: Helen Fulton, Department of English, University of Bristol
Paper 1340-a: **Aligning the Text: *Mise-en-page* in Manuscripts of Middle English Charlemagne Romances** (Language: English)
Phillipa M. Hardman, Department of English Language & Literature, University of Reading
Paper 1340-b: **The Once and Future King: Charlemagne and Remembering the Past in the London, British Library, Cotton Caligula A.ix Manuscript** (Language: English)
Wendy Marie Hoofnagle, Department of Languages & Literatures, University of Northern Iowa
Paper 1340-c: **Remembering Charlemagne through Saracen Eyes** (Language: English)
Elizabeth Munro, Department of Religions & Philosophies, School of Oriental & African Studies, University of London

Session: **1341** **Stage@leeds: Stage 2**
Title: **MEDIEVAL MONASTIC MEMORY IN WORD AND STONE: A NEW LOOK AT RELIGIOUS COMMUNITIES IN ENGLAND AND IRELAND**
Sponsor: Journal of Medieval Monastic Studies, Brepols
Organiser: Janet Burton, School of Archaeology, History & Anthropology, University of Wales Trinity Saint David and Karen Stöber, Departament d'Història, Universitat de Lleida
Moderator: Karen Stöber
Paper 1341-a: **The Churches of the Premonstratensian Canons in Ireland** (Language: English)
Miriam Clyne, Monastic Ireland, Landscape & Settlement Project, Trinity College Dublin
Paper 1341-b: **'For the solace of his advanced years': The *Quondam* in Late Medieval England** (Language: English)
Martin Heale, Department of History, University of Liverpool
Paper 1341-c: **Record-Keeping at Fountains Abbey: Shaping Archival Memory** (Language: English)
Mike Spence, Institute for Medieval Studies, University of Leeds

Session: **1342** **Stage@leeds: Stage 3**
Title: **POWER AND AUTHORITY: THE REMEMBRANCE, LEGITIMISATION, AND EXERCISE OF POWER IN THE NORMAN SOUTH**
Sponsor: Department of History, Lancaster University
Organiser: John Aspinwall, Department of History, Lancaster University
Moderator: Alex Metcalfe, Department of History, Lancaster University
Paper 1342-a: **Abbot Peter of Cava and the Paradox of Memory** (Language: English)
Graham A. Loud, School of History, University of Leeds
Paper 1342-b: **'Let us recount these things worthy of memory': Hagiography and the Politics of Memory in the Norman Conquest of the Italian South** (Language: English)
Kalina Yamboliev, Department of History, University of California, Santa Barbara
Paper 1342-c: **Looking Behind the Veil of Remembrance: Some Considerations on How Muslims Did Contribute to the Norman Conquest of Sicily** (Language: English)
Kordula Wolf, Abteilung Mittelalterliche Geschichte, Deutsches Historisches Institut, Roma

Session: **1343** **Baines Wing: Room G.37**
Title: **CRUSADING HISTORIOGRAPHY**
Organiser: IMC Programming Committee
Moderator: Elizabeth Siberry, Independent Scholar, London
Paper 1343-a: **Claiming the Holy Land: On the Christian Appropriation of Jerusalem in Latin *Itineraria* and the *Gesta Francorum*** (Language: English)
Ana Celia Núñez, Department of History, University of Cambridge
Paper 1343-b: **Crusade Narratives: The Cause and Effect of Remembrance** (Language: English)
Jamie Griffin, Arizona Center for Medieval & Renaissance Studies (ACMRS), Tempe
Paper 1343-c: **Angevine England and the Iberian *Reconquista*** (Language: English)
Lucas Villegas-Aristizábal, Bader International Study Centre, Herstmonceux Castle, Queen's University, Ontario

Session: **1344** **Fine Art Building: SR 1.10**
Title: **Memory and 6th-Century Gaul, II: Remembering the Merovingians**
Organiser: Tamar Rotman, Department of General History, Ben-Gurion University of the Negev, Beer-Sheva
Moderator: Yitzhak Hen, Department of History, Ben-Gurion University of the Negev, Beer-Sheva
Paper 1344-a: **For Future Reference: Traits of Auto-Hagiography in the Writings of Gregory of Tours** (Language: English)
Tamar Rotman
Paper 1344-b: **Reading Merovingian Authors in the Middle Ages** (Language: English)
Hope Williard, Library, University of Lincoln
Respondent: Yaniv Fox, Department of General History, Bar-Ilan University, Ramat Gan

Session: **1345** **Emmanuel Centre: Room 10**
Title: **Continuity and Conquest in England and Normandy, II: Memory in 12th-Century Monastic Communities**
Sponsor: Haskins Society
Organiser: Dan Talbot, School of History, University of East Anglia
Moderator: Emily A. Winkler, St Edmund Hall, University of Oxford / Department of History, University College London
Paper 1345-a: **Days of Gloom and Darkness: Memories of Donations Lost** (Language: English)
Ethan Birney, School of History, University of St Andrews
Paper 1345-b: **Forgetting the Norman Kings?: Cultivating a Useful Past at Selby Abbey** (Language: English)
Dan Talbot
Paper 1345-c: **Fighting the Last War: Remembering the Norman Conquest during the Anarchy** (Language: English)
Jennifer Paxton, Department of History, Catholic University of America, Washington DC

Session: **1346** **Leeds University Union: Room 6 - Roundhay**
Title: **Remembering Chivalry, IV: Forgetting Chivalric Selves and Sites**
Sponsor: Institute for Medieval Studies, University of Leeds
Organiser: Jack Litchfield, Institute for Medieval Studies, University of Leeds
Moderator: Gordon McKelvie, Department of History, University of Winchester
Paper 1346-a: **The Function of Memory within the Idealised Construction of Medieval Chivalric Identity** (Language: English)
Erwann Hollevoet, Centre for the History of Medicine, University of Warwick
Paper 1346-b: **Proud Flesh: Wounding and Memory in 15th-Century English Chivalric Culture** (Language: English)
Jack Litchfield
Paper 1346-c: **Where Chivalry Died: Finding Agincourt** (Language: English)
Michael Livingston, Department of English, The Citadel, Military College of South Carolina

Session: **1347** **Baines Wing: Room 2.14**
Title: **THE MEMORY OF WAR IN HUNGARY**
Organiser: IMC Programming Committee
Moderator: Przemysław Wiszewski, Wydział Nauk Historycznych i Pedagogicznych, Uniwersytet Wrocławski
Paper 1347-a: **'Cum Teutonicis beluina feritate rugientibus et cum Latinis yrundinum garrulitate murmurantibus': The Concept and Memory of 'Otherness' in the Medieval Hungarian Historiography** (Language: English)
Gábor Bradács, 'Hungary in Medieval Europe' Lendület Research Group (MTA-DE), Hungarian Academy of Sciences, Budapest / Department of History, University of Debrecen
Paper 1347-b: **From Zero to Hero: Creative Reports of War Experiences in Medieval Hungary** (Language: English)
Angelika Herucová, Institute of History, Slovak Academy of Sciences, Bratislava
Paper 1347-c: **Reception of the 'Turk' in Later Medieval Hungary** (Language: English)
Attila Bárány, 'Hungary in Medieval Europe' Lendület Research Group (MTA-DE), Hungarian Academy of Sciences, Budapest / Department of History, University of Debrecen

Session: **1348** **University House: St George Room**
Title: **TIME, SCIENCE, AND THE BODY IN THE ANGLO-NORMAN WORLD: DURHAM CATHEDRAL LIBRARY, MS HUNTER 100 AND ITS CONTEXTS, IV - MODELS AND MODES**
Sponsor: Institute of Medieval & Early Modern Studies, Durham University
Organiser: Giles E. M. Gasper, Department of History, Durham University
Moderator: Charlie Rozier, Department of History, Swansea University
Paper 1348-a: **Coordinating Classical Traditions and Medieval Visions in the Star Pictures of Durham MS Hunter 100** (Language: English)
Eric M. Ramírez-Weaver, McIntire Department of Art, University of Virginia
Paper 1348-b: **Collaboration and Competition: The Early 12th-Century Scriptorium at Durham** (Language: English)
Sarah Gilbert, Department of History, Durham University
Paper 1348-c: ***Lectio Divina* and Durham MS Hunter 100** (Language: English)
Sigbjorn Sonnesyn, Department of History, Durham University

Session: **1349** **Stage@leeds: Stage 1**
Title: **MONSTROUS MEDIEVALISM: TOXIC APPROPRIATIONS OF THE MIDDLE AGES IN MODERN POPULAR CULTURE AND THOUGHT**
Sponsor: Monsters: The Experimental Association for the Research of Cryptozoology through Scholarly Theory & Practical Application (MEARCSTAPA)
Organiser: Renée Michelle Ward, School of English & Journalism, University of Lincoln
Moderator: Renée Michelle Ward
Paper 1349-a: **'Die, defenceless, primitive natives!': Colonialism and Genocide in *The Legacy of Heorot*** (Language: English)
Alison Elizabeth Killilea, School of English, University College Cork
Paper 1349-b: **'Mordred the Jew': Perpetuating the Judas Archetype in Medievalisms** (Language: English)
Tirumular (Drew) Narayanan, Department of Art & Art History, California State University, Chico
Paper 1349-c: **Paul Kingsnorth's *The Wake* and Anglo-Saxonism in Contemporary Political Discourse** (Language: English)
Shela Raman, Independent Scholar, Port Chester

Session: **1352** **University House: Cloberry Room**
Title: **THE MEAD OF MEMORY AND THE MEMORY OF MEAD**
Sponsor: Medieval Brewers Guild (USA)
Organiser: Stephen C. Law, Department of Humanities & Philosophy, University of Central Oklahoma
Moderator: Nuri Creager, Department of Foreign Languages & Literatures, Oklahoma State University
Paper 1352-a: **Mead, Memory, and Meter** (Language: English)
Stephen Pollington, Independent Scholar, Basildon
Paper 1352-b: **Remembrance of Meads Past: Intoxication and Toxicology** (Language: English)
Stephen C. Law

Session: **1353** **Emmanuel Centre: Room 11**
Title: **PRINCES AND EARLS: ASPECTS OF LORDSHIP AND THE REALITIES OF POWER IN THE 13TH CENTURY**
Organiser: Rodolphe Billaud, Independent Scholar, Tonbridge
Moderator: Paul R. Dryburgh, The National Archives, Kew
Paper 1353-a: **The Affinity of the de Lacy Constables of Chester and Earls of Lincoln in the 13th Century: A Demonstration of Aristocratic Prowess** (Language: English)
Andrew David Connell, Department of History, Canterbury Christ Church University
Paper 1353-b: **A Forgotten Island?: The Lord Edward's Lordship of Ireland, 1254-72** (Language: English)
Rodolphe Billaud
Paper 1353-c: **To Forgive and Forget: Lordship, Richard of Cornwall, and the Reconciliation Process in Post-Evesham England** (Language: English)
Adrian Jobson, School of Humanities, Canterbury Christ Church University

Session: **1354** **Maurice Keyworth Building: Room G.02**
Title: **RE-ENACTMENT AND MEDIEVAL STUDIES, III: PROBLEMS AND POTENTIAL - A ROUND TABLE DISCUSSION**
Sponsor: School of English, University of Nottingham
Organiser: Melissa Venables, School of English, University of Nottingham
Moderator: Melissa Venables
Purpose: *What is the relationship between medieval studies and re-enactment? There are many kinds of re-enactors with many different agendas, and the same re-enactment group may have different purposes at different times. Likewise, there are many academic approaches to the Middle Ages, to the point where defining 'medieval studies' itself is up for debate. But ultimately the core goal of re-enactment is the same as that of the most traditional academic researcher: to achieve some greater understanding of the past. Building on themes discussed in a series of two panel sessions focusing on medieval combat and examining re-enactment in specific case studies, this round table discussion will explore the problems and potential in developing the relationship between re-enactment and the academic study of the Middle Ages.*

Participants include Timothy Dawson (Independent Scholar, Leeds), Sam Just (University of Nottingham), Marcella Napolitano (Trinity College Dublin), and Sara L. Uckelman (Durham University).

DINNER

Meal Times

Refectory 18.00-20.00

See Map 9, p. 51.

UNIVERSITY OF LEEDS RECEPTION

HOSTED BY
THE UNIVERSITY OF LEEDS

UNIVERSITY SQUARE AND MARQUEE
18.00-19.00

All delegates are invited to enjoy a glass of wine to celebrate the 25th Congress. The Vice-Chancellor of the University of Leeds and the Lord Mayor of the City of Leeds have been invited to attend.

RECEPTION AT MICHAEL SADLER BUILDING

HOSTED BY
CENTRE FOR MEDIEVAL & EARLY MODERN STUDIES, UNIVERSITY OF KENT

MICHAEL SADLER BUILDING: ROOM LG.10
18.30-19.30

You are cordially invited to the drinks reception hosted by Centre for Medieval & Early Modern Studies, University of Kent. Come and meet our staff and students and share a glass.

RECEPTION AT PARKINSON BUILDING

HOSTED BY
CHARLEMAGNE: A EUROPEAN ICON – UNIVERSITY OF BRISTOL

PARKINSON BUILDING: PARKINSON COURT NORTH
18.30-19.30

You are invited to join us at 18:30 on Wednesday evening for the first of several events taking place in summer 2018 to showcase the work of the Leverhulme International Network Charlemagne: A European Icon. Over the past three years, our international teams have published a number of books and brought together a community of scholars working on various aspects of the Charlemagne legend. This reception is also an exhibition of medieval and early modern Charlemagne materials. On display will be items from the enigmatic Bayard's Colts collection (including the Charlemagne head), and they will feature alongside reproductions of some of the magnificent manuscripts and wall paintings related to the Charlemagne legend that survive in England. Come and join us for a chance to discuss the legend of the emperor, have a glass of wine, and see some remarkable but little-known artefacts of Charlemagne.

Session:	**1401** **Michael Sadler Building: Rupert Beckett Theatre**
Title:	**ANNUAL MEDIEVAL ACADEMY LECTURE: HISTORY AND VISUAL MEMORY IN THE LIBRARY OF KING CHARLES V OF FRANCE** (Language: English)
Speaker:	Anne D. Hedeman, Department of Art History, University of Kansas
Introduction:	Sif Ríkharðsdóttir, Faculty of Icelandic & Comparative Cultural Studies, University of Iceland, Reykjavík
Sponsor:	Medieval Academy of America
Details:	*Medieval libraries were sites of memory that served to preserve knowledge, give access to the past, and establish both individual and group identity. When library collections moved through time, expanding in size and acquiring new readers, they shaped the memory of different social, personal, and political pasts. In this lecture I consider how the illustrations in books forming these collections participated in reshaping memories, enabling associations between texts that may not have been associated previously. This phenomenon is especially visible in the library founded and expanded by King Charles V in the Louvre. By considering diverse relationships established between his growing royal collection and the* Grandes chroniques de France *(Paris, Bibliothèque nationale, Ms. fr. 2813), one of Charles' most treasured manuscripts, as it was made, disbound, extended with newly-written text, rebound, disbound, and expanded again with purely visual additions, I will show how visual relationships associated texts in order to create and sharpen particularly distinctive memories of the history of France.* *The Medieval Academy is pleased once again to host the Annual Medieval Academy Lecture, an opportunity for the Academy to showcase some of the important work being done by scholars in North America. We hope you will join us for a reception immediately following the lecture, where members of the Medieval Academy staff will be available to answer questions about the Academy and its work. For more information about the Academy, please see http://www.medievalacademy.org. All those attending are warmly invited to join members of the Medieval Academy after the lecture for a glass of wine.* *Please note that admission to this event will be on a first-come, first-served basis as there will be no tickets. Please ensure that you arrive as early as possible to avoid disappointment.*

Session: **1414** **Stage@leeds: Stage 2**
Title: **MARGINALISATION AND THE LAW: AN INTERDISCIPLINARY PERSPECTIVE - A ROUND TABLE DISCUSSION**
Sponsor: Institute for Medieval Studies, University of Leeds
Organiser: Maroula Perisanidi, School of History, University of Leeds
Moderator: Melanie Brunner, Institute for Medieval Studies, University of Leeds
Purpose: *This round table discussion aims to review some preliminary results of the White Rose-funded project 'Marginalisation and the Law: Medieval and Modern', which brings together medievalists and scholars of contemporary socio-legal theory in order to examine the key elements that have underpinned legal processes of marginalisation in medieval and modern societies. Topics will include: heretics, religious minorities, and women.*

As part of the session we will also bring our findings into conversation with work conducted by the AHRC-funded project 'Women Negotiating the Boundaries of Justice', exploring the related topic of women's access to justice in late medieval England.

Our main focus will be methodological: how can interdisciplinary approaches help us to understand marginalising processes in the Middle Ages as well as to create a more inclusive modern world?

Participants include Harry Munt (University of York), Maroula Perisanidi (University of Leeds), Teresa Phipps (Swansea University), and Danica Summerlin (University of Sheffield).

Session: **1418** **Michael Sadler Building: Banham Theatre**
Title: **NEW DIRECTIONS IN FRANKISH STUDIES: IN HONOUR OF PAUL FOURACRE - A ROUND TABLE DISCUSSION**
Sponsor: Centre for Medieval & Early Modern Studies, University of Manchester
Organiser: Katherine Fliegel, School of Arts, Languages & Cultures, University of Manchester, Ryan T. Goodman, Department of History, University of Manchester and Sihong Lin, Department of History, University of Manchester
Moderator: Ryan T. Goodman
Purpose: *Over his long career, Professor Paul Fouracre's books and essays on the complexity of Frankish legal, episcopal, and political institutions have significantly strengthened our understanding of early medieval Francia. More recently, new approaches to Frankish hagiography, gender, and the 'global turn' have brought renewed interest to the Merovingian and Carolingian worlds, bringing with them new interpretations and challenges to the field. The study of institutional power, in all its forms, nonetheless remains crucial to understanding Frankish history, and this round table discussion will consider how Frankish studies today builds on Professor Fouracre's work, as well as the future directions of the field.*

Participants include Paul Fouracre (University of Manchester), Jamie Kreiner (University of Georgia, Athens), Sihong Lin (University of Manchester), James Palmer (University of St Andrews), Alice Rio (King's College London), and Rachel Stone (King's College London / University of Bedfordshire).

Session: **1435** **Leeds University Union: Room 4 - Hyde Park**
Title: **PROPRIETARY MEMORIES: *NOTITIAE*-INVENTORIES IN EARLY MEDIEVAL IBERIA, III - A ROUND TABLE DISCUSSION**
Sponsor: Instituto de Estudos Medievais, Universidade Nova de Lisboa
Organiser: Álvaro Carvajal Castro, Departamento de Geografía, Prehistoria y Arqueología, Universidad del País Vasco - Euskal Herriko Unibertsitatea and André Evangelista Marques, Instituto de Estudos Medievais, Universidade Nova de Lisboa
Moderator: Wendy Davies, Independent Scholar, Woolstone
Purpose: *Early medieval inventories are commonly found among northern Iberian archival holdings, both as single-sheets and cartulary copies. However, notwithstanding the extensive use that has sometimes been made of their contents, Spanish and Portuguese historians have largely failed to address the problems that this particular type of record poses, although some recent work is changing this picture. The aim of this round table is to evaluate the potential of inventories as a source for the study of early medieval Iberian societies, to assess connections with other early medieval inventory practices and traditions, and to establish a framework within which further collaborative work on this topic can develop.*

Participants include Graham Barrett (University of Lincoln), David Peterson (Universidad de Burgos), Robert Portass (University of Lincoln), and Igor Santos Salazar (Universidad del País Vasco / Euskal Herriko Unibertsitatea).

Session: **1446** **Leeds University Union: Room 6 - Roundhay**
Title: **REMEMBERING CHIVALRY, V: CHIVALRY IN MODERN SCHOLARSHIP - A ROUND TABLE DISCUSSION**
Sponsor: Institute for Medieval Studies, University of Leeds
Organiser: Jack Litchfield, Institute for Medieval Studies, University of Leeds, James Titterton, Institute for Medieval Studies, University of Leeds and Eleanor Jayne Wilkinson-Keys, Institute for Medieval Studies, University of Leeds
Moderator: Alan V. Murray, Institute for Medieval Studies, University of Leeds
Purpose: *This round table will bring together scholars of different periods and subjects to discuss the importance of 'remembering chivalry' in scholarship. Discussion will consider the place of chivalry in contemporary military, social, and cultural historiography, fruitful future approaches to an interdisciplinary study of chivalry, and how scholars can use their research to engage with, and challenge, the predominantly 'anti-chivalric' narrative trend in popular medievalism.*

Participants include Matthew Bennett (University of Winchester), Kelly DeVries (Loyola University Maryland), Michael Livingston (The Citadel, Military College of South Carolina), and Karen Watts (University of Leeds / Musée du Louvre, Paris).

Session: **1450** **Stage@leeds: Stage 3**

Title: **PAULINE STAFFORD'S *QUEENS, CONCUBINES, AND DOWAGERS* 35 YEARS LATER: A ROUND TABLE DISCUSSION**

Sponsor: Medieval & Early Modern Centre, University of Sydney / *Medieval Prosopography*

Organiser: Penelope Joan Nash, Medieval & Early Modern Centre, University of Sydney

Moderator: Elena Woodacre, Department of History, University of Winchester

Purpose: *We are now able to celebrate and review changes in the study of the king's wife in the early Middle Ages since the publication of Pauline Stafford's* Queens, Concubines, and Dowagers *(1983, repr. 2000). Few books have had more lasting influence within the fields of women's history, early medieval history, family history, the history of power, and medieval prosopography. Stafford's book looked across traditional geographic and political divides in the early medieval era. A focused round table will enable a lively discussion of achievements and disenchantments in the intervening 35 years. Today's round table is a continuance in some ways of round tables on women and power at the IMC Leeds 2014 and ICMS Kalamazoo 2014 and 2015. This round table complements the one celebrating the same anniversary of Stafford's book at the recent ICMS Kalamazoo 2018.*

Participants include Valerie Garver (Northern Illinois University), Simon MacLean (University of St Andrews), Penelope Nash (University of Sydney), Jinty Nelson (King's College London), Katherine Weikert (University of Winchester), and Megan Welton (University of Notre Dame, Indiana).

Session: **1454** **Stage@leeds: Stage 1**

Title: **RACISM AND NATIONALISM IN MEDIEVAL STUDIES AND IN MEDIEVALISM: A ROUND TABLE DISCUSSION**

Sponsor: Gender & Medieval Studies Group / International Medieval Congress / Medievalists of Colour Collective / Society for Medieval Feminist Scholarship

Organiser: Roberta Magnani, Centre for Medieval & Early Modern Research (MEMO), Swansea University

Moderator: Bettina Bildhauer, School of Modern Languages - German, University of St Andrews

Purpose: *In a recent statement the Fellowship of Medievalists of Colour has pointed out that 'medieval studies is increasingly acknowledging realities of race and racism in the profession'. In response to bruising controversies which became apparent during the 2017 IMC, not only has the Fellowship denounced pernicious practices of marginalisation of scholars of colour and of scholarship offering global perspectives on the Middle Ages, but they have also advocated for inclusive and affirming academic communities. Over the summer of 2017 a number of other voices have addressed these pressing issues and have urged scholars of the Middle Ages to rethink the way in which questions of race are addressed in a variety of academic and non-academic contexts, such as our classrooms, social media, the formulation of calls for papers, conference organisation (from devising codes of conduct to promoting inclusivity at all levels), and our citational practices, to name a few. Furthermore, the marginalisation of scholars of colour and global scholarly perspectives is very closely tied to the marginalisation of women and feminist studies which has also continued unchecked in the profession for many years.*

Participants include Carolyn B. Anderson (University of Wyoming), Gabriela Cavalheiro (King's College London), Louise D'Arcens (University of Wollongong, New South Wales), Dorothy Kim (Vassar College, New York), Felice Lifshitz (University of Alberta), Adam Miyashiro (Stockton University, New Jersey), and Lisa Perfetti (Whitman College, Washington).

* * * * *

DEAD SISTERS DO TELL TALES: A THEATRICAL READING OF MODERN DEVOUT SISTER-BOOKS

WRITTEN AND PRODUCED BY
MARLY TERWISSCHA VAN SCHELTINGA, UNIVERSITEIT ANTWERPEN
LIEKE SMITS, UNIVERSITEIT LEIDEN
GODELINDE GERTRUDE PERK, MITTUNIVERSITETS, SUNDSVALL

CLOTHWORKERS BUILDING SOUTH: ROOM G.11B
19.00-20.00

This event is free of charge.

On a winter's day, in the Dutch city of Deventer, a group of semi-religious women, all Sisters of the Common Life, start telling each other devotional tales, but their storytelling soon reveals that being a Sister does not make you a saint...

Retelling biographies from two collections from Modern Devout Sisters' Houses, this theatrical reading in English reconstructs a medieval reading experience, including the modern audience in the community of holy women. We would like to welcome you to Master Geert's House: join the Sisters as they wish to hear 'edifying points of our elder Sisters', but cannot agree on the most spiritually exemplary and enjoyable tale. At the same time, each Sister strives to tell the story of her own life, trying to fit into the community by adapting and adopting Modern Devout narrative conventions. Whose story will be heard and whose forgotten?

This performance brings to life the Sister-Books of Deventer and Diepenveen, two female-authored Middle Dutch texts. Originating from the bookish *Devotio Moderna*, a late-medieval religious movement encompassing both monastic and semi-monastic communities, these *vitae* are brimming with unforgettable scenes and local colour. Written and read in the very same Sisters' House in which the narratives are set, these 15th-century texts not only recount Sisters' lives; they also prompt the Sisters to overlay their lives with those of their predecessors and stage the departed Sisters' devotional feats in the spaces inhabited by the living Sisters.

This theatrical reading explores how the Sister-Books construct the very community they describe, investigating how the Sister-Books surround the living Sisters with the presence of those gone before them. According to the Deventer Sister-Book, hearing these lives makes the departed Sisters 'seem alive after death'; this research-by-performance event therefore also examines how the text includes and engages its audience. Ultimately, this performance illuminates medieval reading practices, the effect of aurality on text and reception, and medieval women's literary activity. After the 45-minute performance, there will be time for discussion.

* * * * *

* * * * *

REMEMBER DEATH: JOHANNES KOLROSS'S *SPIL VON FÜNFFERLEY BETRACHTNUSSEN ZUR BUSS* (*PLAY OF FIVE TABLEAUX ABOUT REPENTANCE*), 1532

PERFORMED BY
THEATERGRUPPE DES INSTITUTS FÜR GERMANISTIK, JUSTUS-LIEBIG-UNIVERSITÄT, GIESSEN

DIRECTED BY
CORA DIETL

LIVE MUSIC PROVIDED BY
PETER BULL

BEECH GROVE PLAZA
19.00-20.30

This event is free of charge.

'Always be awake, and pray, / That I will not find you asleep in sin', says Death, warning a young man, whom he had just struck down in the midst of a sinful dance. The youth begs for pardon, and Death allows him some extra time to repent before he finally has to die. 'Memento mori' is the central message of the play that the Reformed School teacher Johannes Kolross performed with his pupils in Bâle. The youth is quickly converted to a holy life, but will he succeed? The 'Friends of World' and Devil try to lead him into temptation, but he firmly holds onto his new way. Devil and his Seven Deadly Sins, though, are successful in convincing others, and thus the epilogue can only repeat the call to remember death.

The aesthetics of the play are very different from those of 16th-century comedies that are often influenced by Terence. It can sometimes resemble an extended sermon, which can be unfamiliar to a 21st-century audience. The theatre group of the University of Giessen's German Department stages the play as part of the international research project 'Theatres of Persuasion', which focuses upon European morality plays of the 16th-century and uses experimental performances of these plays (preferably full length) in order to examine the theatrical potential of the seemingly merely rhetorical texts, once visual and acoustic effects are added, which are not recorded in the texts.

The Theatregruppe was founded by Cora Dietl in 2007, and has since been staging two medieval or early modern plays per year. The performances are always part of seminar courses in German literature, running from April until June/July or from October until December, with 50% new students each term, but with constant success, see: www.staff.uni-giessen.de/~g91159/archiv.htm

This production will be performed in German.

* * * * *

RECEPTION AT MICHAEL SADLER BUILDING

HOSTED BY
INTERNATIONAL CENTER OF MEDIEVAL ART (ICMA)

MICHAEL SADLER BUILDING: ROOM LG.19
19.00-21.00

The International Center of Medieval Art (ICMA) welcomes friends of medieval art to our reception. The ICMA is an international member-based organization headquartered in New York City. The ICMA publishes *Gesta*, sponsors many international sessions and lectures, and awards grants benefiting medieval scholars and students. Join us at our reception and find out more! www.medievalart.org

Our reception coincides with our session: Recollecting Medieval Artefacts: A Global Perspective, held earlier in the day on Wednesday 04 July 2018 at 11.15-12.45.

* * * * *

RECEPTION AT MICHAEL SADLER BUILDING

HOSTED BY
MEDIEVAL ACADEMY OF AMERICA

MICHAEL SADLER BUILDING: RUPERT BECKETT THEATRE
20.00-21.00

The Medieval Academy of America is pleased to once again host the Annual Medieval Academy Lecture, an opportunity for the Academy to showcase some of the important work being done by scholars in North America. We hope you will join us for a reception immediately following the lecture, where members of the Medieval Academy staff will be available to answer questions about the Academy and its work.

For more information about the Academy, please see www.medievalacademy.org.

* * * * *

* * * * *

OPEN MIC NIGHT

EMMANUEL CENTRE: CLAIRE CHAPEL
20.00-22.00

This event is free of charge.

Not with an actual microphone (that would be silly!), the IMC Open Mic Night offers a variety of fare from poetry readings to music, song, even dance sometimes. We have had music from the troubadours, Viking sagas, medieval poetry, and a variety of musical instruments. Medieval contributions are particularly welcome, but it is an opportunity to share anything you always wanted to perform with the international audience the IMC provides. Whether you come to perform or listen you will find the ambience of the Emmanuel Centre Claire Chapel and emcee Robin Fishwick's famous spiced fruit punch unforgettable.

Robin Fishwick is the Quaker Chaplain at the Universities Chaplaincy where he runs the Inspired Open Mic Nights. He is a bit of a singer/songwriter and plays a variety of instruments (some of them quite weird!).

* * * * *

IMC DANCE

LEEDS UNIVERSITY UNION: STYLUS

21.30-02.00

This event is free of charge

This year a local DJ will provide the entertainment.

* * * * *

Today's Excursions
Southwell Minster and Town 09.00-19.00
Conisbrough Castle 13.30-19.00
See pp. 456-458 for full details.

Session: **1501** **Baines Wing: Room 1.13**
Title: **LITERARY LINGUISTIC APPROACHES TO OLD ENGLISH TEXTS**
Organiser: Katrina Wilkins, School of English, University of Nottingham
Moderator: Katrina Wilkins
Paper 1501-a: **Irony and Old English Poetry** (Language: English)
Elise Louviot, UFR Lettres et Sciences Humaines, Université de Reims Champagne-Ardenne
Paper 1501-b: **Parentheses in *Beowulf*** (Language: English)
Taro Ishiguro, School of Commerce, Meiji University, Japan
Paper 1501-c: **Remembering and Curating Old English Style** (Language: English)
Rachel Fletcher, School of Critical Studies, University of Glasgow

Session: **1502** **Michael Sadler Building: Room LG.17**
Title: **HORSES IN THE ORIENT**
Organiser: Anastasija Ropa, Faculty of Humanities, University of Latvia, Riga
Moderator: Timothy Dawson, Independent Scholar, Leeds
Paper 1502-a: **The Role of the Horse in Tangut Society** (Language: English)
Romain Lefebvre, Centre de recherche Textes et Cultures, Université d'Artois, Arras
Paper 1502-b: **City of the Cavalrymen and House of the Rider: 'Landscaped Hippodromes' and Stable-Palaces in Mamlûk Cairo** (Language: English)
Agnès Carayon, Independent Scholar, Paris
Paper 1502-c: **Information of Middle Byzantine Hagiographical Texts about Horses** (Language: English)
Alexia-Foteini Stamouli, Independent Scholar, Patras

Session: **1503** **Michael Sadler Building: Room LG.16**
Title: **BYZANTINE STUDIES IN CHINA, I: STUDIES IN BYZANTINE LAW IN CHINA**
Organiser: Li Qiang, Institute for the History of Ancient Civilisations, Northeast Normal University, China
Moderator: Rebecca Darley, Department of History, Classics & Archaeology, Birkbeck, University of London
Paper 1503-a: **The Research Program on Byzantine Laws in China** (Language: English)
Jia-ling Xu, Institute for the History of Ancient Civilizations, Northeast Normal University, China
Paper 1503-b: **The Byzantine Legislation on the Sexual Crimes in the 8th Century** (Language: English)
Xiao-Bo Wang, School of Humanities, Kaili University, China
Paper 1503-c: **A Study on the Reasons of 'Humanization' in the Byzantine Law *Ecloga*** (Language: English)
Ji-rong Li, School of History & Politics, Guizhou Normal University, China

Session:	**1504** **Fine Art Building: SR G.04**
Title:	**A FRENCHMAN IN PORTUGAL: BISHOP HUGH OF PORTO AND THE TRANSFORMATIONS OF THE NORTH-WESTERN IBERIAN PENINSULA IN THE 12TH CENTURY, 1112-1136**
Sponsor:	Centro de Investigação Transdisciplinar 'Cultura, Espaço e Memória' (CITCEM), Universidade do Porto
Organiser:	Francesco Renzi, Centro de Investigação Transdisciplinar 'Cultura, Espaço e Memória' (CITCEM), Universidade do Porto
Moderator:	Francesco Renzi
Paper 1504-a:	**The Ecclesiastical Geography of Northern Portugal, 11th and 12th Centuries** (Language: English) Luís Carlos Amaral, Centro de Investigação Transdisciplinar 'Cultura, Espaço e Memória' (CITCEM), Universidade do Porto
Paper 1504-b:	**Oporto versus Coimbra and Braga: Bishop Hugo's Struggle for Diocesan Frontiers** (Language: English) Andrea Mariani, Centro de Investigação Transdisciplinar 'Cultura, Espaço e Memória' (CITCEM) / Faculdade de Letras, Universidade do Porto
Paper 1504-c:	**The Birth of a Chancery: The Role of Bishop Hugo in the Diocese of Porto** (Language: English) Maria João de Oliveira e Silva, Centro de Investigação Transdisciplinar 'Cultura, Espaço e Memória' (CITCEM), Universidade do Porto

Session:	**1505** **Parkinson Building: Room 1.16**
Title:	**MARGINS AND THE MARGINALISED IN MEDIEVAL MANUSCRIPTS**
Organiser:	IMC Programming Committee
Moderator:	Annemarieke Willemsen, Rijksmuseum van Oudheden, Leiden
Paper 1505-a:	**Marginal Deer in the 'forest adventurous' of the Manuscript Border** (Language: English) Anna Milon, Centre for Medieval Studies, University of York
Paper 1505-b:	**'I shall pray for my husband's salvation every single day': Personal Memory in the Service of Gender Inequality** (Language: English) Margo Stroumsa-Uzan, Department of the Arts, Ben-Gurion University of the Negev, Beer-Sheva
Paper 1505-c:	**Madrid, Biblioteca Nacional, MS Vitrina 24/3 and the Textual Tradition of the Parisian 'Danse Macabre'** (Language: English) Alina Zvonareva, Institut für Romanistik, Alpen-Adria-Universität, Klagenfurt

Session:	**1506** **Michael Sadler Building: Rupert Beckett Theatre**
Title:	**THE AFTER-LIVES OF MEDIEVAL MANUSCRIPTS: NEW DIGITAL APPROACHES**
Sponsor:	Mapping Manuscript Migrations Project
Organiser:	Toby Burrows, Oxford e-Research Centre, University of Oxford
Moderator:	Toby Burrows
Paper 1506-a:	**Mapping the Migrations of Medieval Manuscripts** (Language: English) Toby Burrows
Paper 1506-b:	**Manuscript Histories and Provenance: New Digital Environments** (Language: English) Lynn Ransom, Schoenberg Institute for Manuscript Studies, University of Pennsylvania
Paper 1506-c:	**Historic Collections, Provenance, and Medieval Text Transmission** (Language: English) Hanno Wijsman, Institut de Recherche et d'Histoire des Textes (IRHT), Centre National de la Recherche Scientifique (CNRS), Paris

Session: **1507** **Fine Art Building: Studio Ground Floor**
Title: **MEDIEVAL PROVENÇAL AND SEPHARDI TEXTS BETWEEN SECULAR CULTURE AND RELIGION, I**
Organiser: IMC Programming Committee
Moderator: Oded Zinger, Martin Buber Society of Fellows in the Humanities, Hebrew University of Jerusalem
Paper 1507-a: **Provencal Science in Mamluk Palestine: The Case of Ashtori Ha-Parchi** (Language: English)
Amichay Schwartz, Department of Israel Heritage, Ariel University, Israel
Paper 1507-b: **From Judaism to Islam and Back: A 14th-Century Autobiography of a Relapsed Convert** (Language: English)
Moshe Yagur, Center for the Study of Conversion & Inter-Religious Encounters, University of Haifa
Paper 1507-c: **Stating Constancy in a Time of Changes: Encyclopaedism between the 13th and 14th Century - Alfonso the Wise and Ibn Khaldoun** (Language: English)
Emilio González Ferrín, Departamento de Estudios Árabes e Islámicos, Universidad de Sevilla

Session: **1508** **Baines Wing: Room 2.13**
Title: **PEACE, POWER, AND PORTRAYAL: KINGSHIP IN THE 12TH AND 13TH CENTURIES**
Organiser: Thomas Tollefsen, School of History, Archaeology & Religion, Cardiff University
Moderator: Helle Vogt, Center for Retskulturelle Studier, Det Juridiske Fakultet, Københavns Universitet
Paper 1508-a: **Our Man in Bethune: Writing about Rulers in the *Histoire des ducs de Normandie et des rois d'Angleterre*** (Language: English)
Paul Webster, School of History, Archaeology & Religion, Cardiff University
Paper 1508-b: **Remembering the Kingmakers: Consolidation of Power and Minorities in Scandinavia** (Language: English)
Thomas Tollefsen
Paper 1508-c: **The 'Special Friend': Portraying the Arbitrating King** (Language: English)
Jenny Benham, School of History, Archaeology & Religion, Cardiff University

Session:	**1509**	**Baines Wing: Room 2.16**
Title:	**EDITING TEXTS FROM LATER MEDIEVAL ENGLAND**	
Sponsor:	AHRC Project 'Towards a New Edition of the Wycliffite Bible'	
Organiser:	Daniel Sawyer, Faculty of English Language & Literature, University of Oxford	
Moderator:	Anne Hudson, Faculty of English Language & Literature, University of Oxford	
Paper 1509-a:	**Editing the Wycliffite Old Testament Lectionary** (Language: English) Cosima Gillhammer, Faculty of English Language & Literature, University of Oxford	
Paper 1509-b:	**21st-Century Edition Design: The Wycliffite Bible in Print and Online** (Language: English) Daniel Sawyer	
Paper 1509-c:	**Butler, Palmer, Ullerston: An Oxford Debate on Biblical Language, c. 1400** (Language: English) Elizabeth Solopova, Faculty of English Language & Literature, University of Oxford	

Session:	**1510**	**Baines Wing: Room 1.16**
Title:	**MEMORIES OF CHRISTIAN TEXTS IN MEDIEVAL HAGIOGRAPHY AND THEOLOGY**	
Organiser:	IMC Programming Committee	
Moderator:	Sylvie Joye, Département d'Histoire, Université de Reims Champagne-Ardenne	
Paper 1510-a:	**Testi monastici antichi nella memoria delle prime traduzioni medievali** (Language: Italiano) Antonella Micolani, Dipartimento di Storia Società e Studi sull'Uomo, Università del Salento, Lecce	
Paper 1510-b:	***Auditus fidei* dans l'herméneutique théologique de l'abbaye de Saint-Victor à Paris au XIIe siècle** (Language: Français) Radomír Bužek, Centre for Patristic, Medieval & Renaissance Texts, Palacký University, Olomouc	
Paper 1510-c:	**Speaking Scripture in Early Medieval Rules and Saints' Lives** (Language: English) Katie Menendez, Centre for Medieval Studies, University of Toronto, Downtown	

Session: **1511** **Baines Wing: Room 1.15**
Title: **TO LEAVE A MARK IN MEMORY: POLISH AND POMERANIAN DUCHESSES IN THE STRUGGLE FOR POLITICAL INFLUENCE AND POWER IN THE MIDDLE AGES**
Sponsor: Uniwersytet Gdański / Akademia Pomorska, Słupsk
Organiser: Beata Możejko, Zakład Historii Średniowiecza Polski i Nauk Pomocniczych Historii, Uniwersytet Gdański
Moderator: Anna Adamska, Onderzoeksinstituut voor Geschiedenis en Kunstgeschiedenis, Universiteit Utrecht
Paper 1511-a: **Was It Possible that Agatha, the Wife of Edward the Exile, Hailed from Eastern Europe?** (Language: English)
Jędrzej Szerle, Zakład Historii Średniowiecza Polski i Nauk Pomocniczych Historii, Uniwersytet Gdański
Paper 1511-b: **Stepmother and Stepson: Duchess Matilda in the Power Struggle after the Death of Her Husband Barnim I, the Pomeranian Duke** (Language: English)
Mariola Freza-Olczyk, Instytut Historii, Uniwersytet Gdański
Paper 1511-c: **Medieval Duchesses as Regents in the Polish Lands: In Memory of Sources - Chronicles, Seals, and Documents** (Language: English)
Angieszka Teterycz-Puzio, Institute of History & Political Science, Pomeranian Academy, Gdansk

Session: **1513** **University House: Beechgrove Room**
Title: **NEW PERSPECTIVES ON WOMEN IN MEDIEVAL ROMANCE, III: (DIS)ABLING BODIES**
Sponsor: Institute of Medieval & Early Modern Studies, Durham University
Organiser: Olivia Colquitt, Department of English, University of Liverpool, Rachel Fennell, Institute of Medieval & Early Modern Studies, Durham University and Hannah Piercy, Institute of Medieval & Early Modern Studies, Durham University
Moderator: Amy Louise Morgan, School of Literature & Languages, University of Surrey
Paper 1513-a: **Psychosomatic Heredity: Forging Dynasty and Destiny through the Female Body in *Mélusine*** (Language: English)
Olivia Colquitt
Paper 1513-b: **'In all hur nobul ryche arraye': Visual Memory and Identity in *Le Bone Florence of Rome*** (Language: English)
Alice Stamataki, Institute of Medieval & Early Modern Studies, Durham University
Paper 1513-c: **(Dis)Ability in the 14th-Century Text *La Belle Hélène de Constantinople*** (Language: English)
Stephanie Grace-Petinos, Institute for Research in the Humanities, University of Wisconsin-Madison
Paper 1513-d: **Desire and the Corpse in Medieval Romance** (Language: English)
Rachel Fennell

Session: **1514** **Charles Thackrah Building: 1.01**
Title: **REBELLION AND RECONCILIATION IN ANGEVIN FAMILY POLITICS, C. 1103-1152**
Sponsor: Haskins Society / Battle Conference on Anglo-Norman Studies
Organiser: Amy Livingstone, Department of History, Wittenberg University, Ohio
Moderator: Robert F. Berkhofer, Department of History, Western Michigan University, Kalamazoo
Paper 1514-a: **Keeping the Peace: Countess Ermengarde's Role in Angevin Family Politics** (Language: English)
Amy Livingstone
Paper 1514-b: ***Consilio et ammonitione*: The Intercessory Agency of Queen Bertrade in Angevin Familial Politics, 1106-1119** (Language: English)
Basit Hammad Qureshi, Department of History, Macalester College, Minnesota
Paper 1514-c: **Fraternal Rebellions and the Comital Family in 12th-Century Anjou** (Language: English)
Kathryn Dutton, Department of History, University of Manchester

Session: **1515** **Maurice Keyworth Building: Room 1.33**
Title: **ENACTING AND DEPICTING QUEENSHIP**
Organiser: IMC Programming Committee
Moderator: Cordelia Beattie, School of History, Classics & Archaeology, University of Edinburgh
Paper 1515-a: **Evoking Queenship: The King's Widow and Memorial Practice** (Language: English)
Anne Foerster, Historisches Institut, Universität Paderborn
Paper 1515-b: **Eleanor of Aquitaine at the Interstices of History and Fiction** (Language: English)
Karen Sullivan, Division of Languages & Literature, Bard College, New York
Paper 1515-c: **Remembering Queens as Land-Holders: A Reappraisal of Medieval Queenship in Economic Terms** (Language: English)
Michele Seah, School of Humanities & Social Sciences, University of Newcastle, New South Wales

Session: **1516** **Maurice Keyworth Building: Room 1.04**
Title: **THE MEDIEVAL LAW COURTS, I: LONDON LITIGATION**
Sponsor: The Honourable Society of Gray's Inn
Organiser: Daniel F. Gosling, Department of Archives, The Honourable Society of Gray's Inn, London
Moderator: Daniel F. Gosling
Paper 1516-a: **Commoners and Common Pleas: Litigants and Social Status in the 15th Century** (Language: English)
Louisa Foroughi, Department of History, Fordham University, New York
Paper 1516-b: **Court Procedures for Pregnancy Diagnosis in Later Medieval England** (Language: English)
Zosia Edwards, Department of History, Royal Holloway, University of London
Paper 1516-c: **'In novo casu, novum remedium': The Origins of the Court of the Exchequer Chamber as a Court of Appeal in England, 1370-1420** (Language: English)
Edward Powell, Independent Scholar, Cambridge

Session: **1517** **Social Sciences Building: Room 10.05**
Title: **SHAPING THE PAST AFTER THE CAROLINGIAN EMPIRE, I: REGINO OF PRÜM**
Sponsor: After Empire: Using & Not Using the Past in the Crisis of the Carolingian World, c. 900-1050
Organiser: Alice Hicklin, Friedrich-Meinecke-Institut, Freie Universität Berlin
Moderator: Graeme Ward, Institut für Mittelalterforschung, Österreichische Akademie der Wissenschaften, Wien
Paper 1517-a: **Advice for a King in an Age of Crisis: Regino of Prüm and Louis the Child** (Language: English)
Eric J. Goldberg, Department of History, Massachusetts Institute of Technology
Paper 1517-b: **The Oath in the Chronicle of Regino of Prüm** (Language: English)
Heiko Behrmann, Freidrich-Meinecke-Institut, Freie Universität Berlin
Paper 1517-c: **Straining after Effect: Regino of Prüm, the Death of Charles the Fat, and the Hungarians** (Language: English)
Maximilian Diesenberger, Institut für Mittelalterforschung, Österreichische Akademie der Wissenschaften, Wien

Session: **1518** **Michael Sadler Building: Room LG.10**
Title: **VISIONS OF COMMUNITY, II: COMPARATIVE PERSPECTIVES ON MEDIEVAL BIOGRAPHICAL COLLECTIONS**
Sponsor: Sonderforschungsbereich Project 'Visions of Community', Österreichische Akademie der Wissenschaften, Universität Wien / FWF Project F42
Organiser: Rutger Kramer, Institut für Mittelalterforschung, Österreichische Akademie der Wissenschaften, Wien and Veronika Wieser, Institut für Mittelalterforschung, Österreichische Akademie der Wissenschaften, Wien
Moderator: Jamie Kreiner, Department of History, University of Georgia, Athens
Paper 1518-a: **A Comparative Approach to Medieval Biographical Collections from Rasulid South Arabia** (Language: English)
Daniel Mahoney, Abteilung für Geschichte, Universität Wien
Paper 1518-b: **Constructing a Mediterranean Church Community: Reading Gennadius' Continuation of Jerome's *De Viris Illustribus*** (Language: English)
Veronika Wieser
Paper 1518-c: **A Community Redone: The *Gesta Sanctorum Rotonensium* in a Comparative Context** (Language: English)
Rutger Kramer
Paper 1518-d: **The Eminent Life: Collected Stories in the 6th Century from Gregory of Tours to Hui Jiao of Jiaxiang Monastery** (Language: English)
James Palmer, St Andrews Institute of Mediaeval Studies, University of St Andrews

Session: **1519** **Baines Wing: Room 1.14**
Title: **MEDIEVAL POWER AND LETTERS, I: RELIGION AND LETTERS**
Sponsor: Centre for Medieval & Renaissance Research, University of Winchester
Organiser: Gordon McKelvie, Department of History, University of Winchester
Moderator: Gordon McKelvie
Paper 1519-a: **A King and His Letters: The Case of King Richard I and the Canterbury Election of 1193** (Language: English)
James Barnaby, School of History, University of East Anglia
Paper 1519-b: **Agents or Emissaries?: The Devolution of Papal Power in the East** (Language: English)
James Hill, Institute for Medieval Studies, University of Leeds
Paper 1519-c: **Gender and Power in Bishop Benzo of Alba's Letters to Adelaide of Turin** (Language: English)
Alison Creber, Department of History, King's College London

Session: **1520** **Charles Thackrah Building: 1.02**
Title: **REMEMBERING (AND FORGETTING) IN CHAUCERIAN AND POST-CHAUCERIAN VERSE**
Organiser: IMC Programming Committee
Moderator: Huriye Reis, Department of English Language & Literature, Hacettepe University, Turkey
Paper 1520-a: **The Trauma of Remembrance and the Pleasure of Forgetting: Anachronism in Chaucer's *Book of the Duchess*** (Language: English)
Gillian Adler, Department of English, Saint Peter's University, New Jersey
Paper 1520-b: **Chaucer's Pardoner: Motivations behind the Pardoner's Self-Revelations in His Prologue and Tale** (Language: English)
Mary Jean Miller, Department of English, University of Missouri-Kansas City
Paper 1520-c: **The Role of Memory in Post-Chaucerian Verse: Memory as a Literary Device in George Ashby's *Complaint of a Prisoner in the Fleet*, 1463** (Language: English)
Joanna Monika Bukowska, Faculty of Pedagogy & Fine Arts, Adam Mickiewicz University, Poznań

Session: **1521** **Social Sciences Building: Room 10.06**
Title: **THE CONSTRUCTION AND USE OF MEMORY IN MEDIEVAL SCANDINAVIAN NARRATIVES**
Organiser: Ralf Palmgren, Department of Philosophy, History, Culture & Art Studies, University of Helsinki
Moderator: Alaric Hall, School of English, University of Leeds
Paper 1521-a: **Legitimising a Bishopric in Medieval Sweden: The Legend of St Sigfrid** (Language: English)
Ralf Palmgren
Paper 1521-b: **'And each side dealt many blows on the other': The Construction of Battle Narratives in the Histories of the Norwegian *Borgerkrigene*** (Language: English)
Philip Walter Line, Independent Scholar, Helsinki
Paper 1521-c: **Myth and Memory in Medieval Swedish Historiography** (Language: English)
Anja Ute Blode, Institut für Skandinavistik / Fennistik, Universität zu Köln

Session: **1522** **University House: Cloberry Room**
Title: **PERAMBULATING THE BOOK: 'MANUSCRIPT ARCHITECTURE' AND MEMORY**
Sponsor: Sonderforschungsbereich 950 'Manuskriptkulturen in Asien, Afrika und Europa', Universität Hamburg
Organiser: Hanna M. Wimmer, Sonderforschungsbereich 950 'Manuskriptkulturen in Asien, Afrika und Europa' / Kunstgeschichtliches Seminar, Universität Hamburg
Moderator: Cornelius Berthold, Sonderforschungsbereich 950 'Manuskriptkulturen in Asien, Afrika und Europa', Universität Hamburg
Paper 1522-a: **'Manuscript Architecture' and Its Functions** (Language: English)
Hanna M. Wimmer
Paper 1522-b: **Animating the Mind: Manuscript Architecture and Literal Illustrations as Part of the Reading Experience** (Language: English)
Karin Becker, Sonderforschungsbereich 950 'Manuskriptkulturen in Asien, Afrika und Europa', Universität Hamburg
Paper 1522-c: **Indexing Music in Late Medieval Manuscripts** (Language: English)
Andreas Janke, Sonderforschungsbereich 950 'Manuskriptkulturen in Asien, Afrika und Europa', Universität Hamburg

---

Session: **1523** **Emmanuel Centre: Wilson Room**
Title: **MEMORY AND THE CONSTRUCTION OF MENDICANT SANCTITY**
Organiser: IMC Programming Committee
Moderator: Melanie Brunner, Institute for Medieval Studies, University of Leeds
Paper 1523-a: **Memorise and Forget: The Virtues of Francis of Assisi as a Tool for Controlling Franciscans in Capetian France in the 13th Century** (Language: English)
Elena Kravtsova, Department of Manuscripts & Rare Books, State Museum of the History of Religion, St Petersburg
Paper 1523-b: **Memory and the Politics of St Catherine of Siena's Canonization** (Language: English)
Lisa Vitale, Department of World Languages & Literatures, Southern Connecticut State University
Paper 1523-c: **The Hagiographic Representation of St Francis of Assisi in the Sermons of Antonio Vieira** (Language: English)
Thiago Maerki de Oliveira, Instituto de Estudos da Linguagem, Universidade Estadual de Campinas, Brazil

---

Session: **1524** **Charles Thackrah Building: 1.04**
Title: ***CAROLINGIAN CIVILIZATION* 25 YEARS LATER: IN HONOR OF PAUL EDWARD DUTTON, I**
Organiser: Matthew Gabriele, Department of Religion & Culture, Virginia Tech
Moderator: Matthew Gabriele
Paper 1524-a: **Louis the Pious's Theater of Illusions: Restagings from Fichtenau to Dutton and Beyond** (Language: English)
Courtney Booker, Department of History, University of British Columbia
Paper 1524-b: **Fictions of the Colossus: The Politics of Carolingian Panegyric** (Language: English)
Andrew Romig, Gallatin School of Individualized Study, New York University
Paper 1524-c: **Making Rain and the Politics of Magic in the Carolingian World** (Language: English)
Martha Rampton, Department of History, Pacific University, Oregon

Session: **1525** **Michael Sadler Building: Banham Theatre**
Title: **PAIN AND MEMORY IN THE MIDDLE AGES**
Organiser: Aisling Reid, School of Arts, English & Language, Queen's University Belfast
Moderator: Duncan Berryman, School of Geography, Archaeology & Palaeoecology, Queen's University Belfast
Paper 1525-a: **Pain, Sight, and Memory** (Language: English)
Aisling Reid
Paper 1525-b: **'Di viel dú arme har nider under die verhangenen und under die verworhten selen und dunkte ir alze gůt': Expressing and exploiting the memory of pain in Mechthild von Magdeburg's *Fließendes Licht der Gottheit*.** (Language: English)
Catherine Coffey, School of Arts, English & Language, Queen's University Belfast
Paper 1525-c: **'Contemplate the Lord and kiss His wounds': Reading Christ's Wounds and Pastoral Care in the *Visiones cuiusdam Virgines*** (Language: English)
Amanda Langley, School of History, Queen Mary University of London

Session: **1526** **Social Sciences Building: Room 10.07**
Title: **GENDER, MEMORY, AND WORSHIP: THE HELFTA THEOLOGIANS INTERPRETING AND INTERPRETED**
Organiser: Laura Marie Grimes, Sophia Catholic Communion, San Jose
Moderator: Rebecca Stephenson, School of English, Drama, Film & Creative Writing, University College Dublin
Paper 1526-a: **Beggar Maid and Baptist as Priestly Prophets: Mechthild of Magdeburg's Subversive Mystical Mass** (Language: English)
Laura Marie Grimes
Paper 1526-b: **Liturgical *ars-memoria* and the Function of Memory-Anamnesis** (Language: English)
Ann Marie Caron, Department of Religious Studies, University of Saint Joseph, Connecticut
Paper 1526-c: **Martin Luther and the Cistercian Spirit: Luther's Heritage from Bernard of Clairvaux and Mechthild of Hackeborn** (Language: English)
Else Marie Wiberg Pedersen, Afdeling for Teologi, Aarhus Universitet

Session: **1527** **Maurice Keyworth Building: Room 1.32**
Title: **EARLY SAINTS IN MODERN TIMES**
Sponsor: Cult of Saints Project, University of Oxford
Organiser: Robert Wiśniewski, Instytut Historyczny, Uniwersytet Warszawski
Moderator: Gábor Klaniczay, Department of Medieval Studies, Central European University, Budapest
Paper 1527-a: **Reviving the Cults of Perpetua and Felicity: Alfred-Louis Delattre and Christian Archaeology in Late 19th- and Early 20th-Century Carthage** (Language: English)
Bonnie Effros, Department of History, University of Liverpool
Paper 1527-b: **Between Adaptation and Oblivion: Cinematic Sanctification and the World of Late Antiquity** (Language: English)
Felice Lifshitz, Department of Women's & Gender Studies, University of Alberta
Paper 1527-c: **Remembering the Saints in a 21st-Century Database** (Language: English)
Bryan Ward-Perkins, Faculty of History, University of Oxford

Session:	**1528** **Maurice Keyworth Building: Room G.02**
Title:	**Memories of Heresy and Counter-Heresy, I: Time and Place**
Sponsor:	Department for the Study of Religions, Masarykova univerzita, Brno / Medieval Heresy & Dissent Research Network, University of Nottingham
Organiser:	Claire Taylor, Department of History, University of Nottingham
Moderator:	Claire Taylor
Paper 1528-a:	**Remembering Heresy: Place, Space, and Memory in Late 13th-Century Inquisition Records** (Language: English) Elinor French, School of Philosophical, Historical & International Studies, Monash University, Victoria
Paper 1528-b:	**Trigger Warning: Timelessness and Temporal Markers in 14th-Century Inquisition Records** (Language: English) Delfi-Isabel Nieto-Isabel, Departament d'Història Medieval, Paleografia i Diplomàtica, Universitat de Barcelona
Paper 1528-c:	**'Multi anni elapsi, multi fratres mortui': Time, Distance, and Self-Defense of the Interrogated Knights Templar** (Language: English) František Novotný, Department for the Study of Religions, Masarykova univerzita, Brno *Recipient of a 2018 Templar Heritage Trust Bursary*

Session:	**1529** **Maurice Keyworth Building: Room 1.06**
Title:	**Total Recall: Bishops Remembered in Medieval Practice and Modern Historiography**
Sponsor:	EPISCOPUS: Society for the Study of Bishops & the Secular Clergy in the Middle Ages
Organiser:	Evan Gatti, Department of Art & Art History, Elon University, North Carolina
Moderator:	John S. Ott, Department of History, Portland State University, Oregon
Paper 1529-a:	**Pope Leo IX: Bishop of Rome?** (Language: English) Andrew Smith, School of Humanities (History), University of Glasgow
Paper 1529-b:	**Fulcaricus of Tongres-Maastricht: 'He is only a name and a title that appear'** (Language: English) Jean-Noël Rolland, Département d'histoire, Université de Montréal / Département des Sciences historiques, Université de Liège
Paper 1529-c:	**Arnulf of Lisieux and the Need to Be Remembered Well** (Language: English) Matthew Leeper, Department of History, University of Glasgow

Session: **1530** **Charles Thackrah Building: 1.03**
Title: **INTERPRETATIONS AND PERMANENCE IN MEDIEVAL ART HISTORY RESEARCH**
Sponsor: Katedra Historii Sztuki i Kultury, Wydział Nauk Historycznych, Uniwersytet Mikołaja Kopernika, Toruń
Organiser: Ryszard Mączyński, Katedra Historii Sztuki i Kultury, Uniwersytet Mikołaja Kopernika, Toruń
Moderator: Irena Dżurkowa-Kossowska, Katedra Historii Sztuki i Kultury, Uniwersytet Mikołaja Kopernika, Toruń
Paper 1530-a: **Memory of Idea and Memory of Form: Tomb-Altars in Polish Art from the Middle Ages to the 18th and 19th Centuries** (Language: English)
Ryszard Mączyński
Paper 1530-b: **Neo-Medievalism of the 1920s and 1930s: Eric Gill and Wiktoria Goryńska** (Language: English)
Irena Dżurkowa-Kossowska
Paper 1530-c: **How a Work of Art Focuses on Itself the Memory of Generations from the Time When It Came into Existence till the Present Day** (Language: English)
Przemysław Waszak, Katedra Historii Sztuki i Kultury, Uniwersytet Mikołaja Kopernika, Toruń
Paper 1530-d: **The Sacred, Empty, and Black Portal: A Remembrance of Jerusalem and the Temple in Late Antique and Medieval Art** (Language: English)
Magdalena Maciudzińska-Kamczycka, Katedra Historii Sztuki i Kultury, Uniwersytet Mikołaja Kopernika, Toruń

Session: **1531** **Maurice Keyworth Building: Room 1.05**
Title: **MEMORY, THE MATERIAL, AND THE MIDDLE AGES, I**
Sponsor: National Museums Scotland
Organiser: Katie Stevenson, St Andrews Institute of Mediaeval Studies, University of St Andrews
Moderator: Alex Woolf, St Andrews Institute of Mediaeval Studies, University of St Andrews
Paper 1531-a: **Memory, Monuments, and the Prehistoric Past in Early Medieval Scotland** (Language: English)
Martin Goldberg, Department of Scottish History & Archaeology, National Museums Scotland, Edinburgh
Paper 1531-b: **Remembering and Remaking the Monymusk Reliquary** (Language: English)
Alice Blackwell, Department of Scottish History & Archaeology, National Museums Scotland, Edinburgh
Paper 1531-c: **Learning by Heart: Books, Boxes, and Breast-Hoards** (Language: English)
Heather Pulliam, Edinburgh College of Art, University of Edinburgh

Session: **1532** **Social Sciences Building: Room 10.09**
Title: **AT THE CROSSROADS OF EMPIRES: SANT'AMBROGIO AT MONTECORVINO ROVELLA - A *LOCUS MEMORIAE* IN SOUTHERN LOMBARDY, I**
Organiser: Francesca Dell'Acqua, Centre for Byzantine, Ottoman & Modern Greek Studies, University of Birmingham
Moderator: Walter Pohl, Institut für Mittelalterforschung, Österreichische Akademie der Wissenschaften, Wien
Paper 1532-a: **Sant'Ambrogio of Montecorvino Rovella: Past Excavations, the Geophysical Survey, and New Archaeological Perspectives** (Language: English)
Chiara M. Lambert, Dipartimento di Scienze del Patrimonio Culturale (DISPAC), Università degli Studi di Salerno
Paper 1532-b: **On Mary's Side: The Memory of St Ambrose of Milan in Southern Langobardia** (Language: English)
Ivan Foletti, Centre for Early Medieval Studies, Masarykova univerzita, Brno
Paper 1532-c: **Frankish Aspirations in the South and the 'Division' of the Principality of Benevento in the Mid-9th Century** (Language: English)
Clemens Gantner, Institut für Mittelalterforschung, Österreichische Akademie der Wissenschaften, Wien

Session: **1533** **Baines Wing: Room G.36**
Title: **IN HONOUR OF RICHARD HOLT, I: AN ENGLISHMAN IN NORWAY**
Sponsor: 'Creating the New North' Research Programme, Universitetet i Tromsø - Norges Arktiske Universitetet
Organiser: Stefan Figenschow, Institutt for historie og religionsvitenskap, Universitetet i Tromsø - Norges Arktiske Universitetet
Moderator: Miriam Tveit, Faculty of Social Sciences, Nord University, Bodø
Paper 1533-a: **A British Medievalist Describes a Dangerous World: Richard of Beccles's Views on the Norwegian Middle Ages and Historiography in the 20th and 21st Centuries** (Language: English)
Stefan Figenschow
Paper 1533-b: **The Ice Giant Cometh: Tracing Norwegian Origin Myths through Frost and Snow** (Language: English)
Eleanor Rosamund Barraclough, Department of History, Durham University
Paper 1533-c: **The Military Revolution in Norway that Never Was: An Analysis of Norwegian *Sonderweg* in 13th and 14th Centuries** (Language: English)
Erik Opsahl, Institutt for historiske studier, Norges teknisk-naturvitenskapelige universitet, Trondheim
Paper 1533-d: ***Sincere dilectionis affectum*: Anglo-Norwegian Friendship in the Central Middle Ages** (Language: English)
Ian Peter Grohse, Institutt for historie, Universitetet i Tromsø - Norges Arktiske Universitetet

Session: **1534** **Leeds University Union: Room 2 - Elland Road**
Title: **REMEMBERING SHARED RITUALS AND IDENTITIES IN THE MEDIEVAL MEDITERRANEAN AND AFRICA**
Sponsor: Mary Jaharis Center for Byzantine Art & Culture, Hellenic College Holy Cross, Massachusetts
Organiser: Andrea Achi, Institute of Fine Arts, New York University
Moderator: Andrea Achi and Meseret Oldjira, Department of Art & Archaeology, Princeton University
Paper 1534-a: **Devotional Graffiti: Writing, Ritual, and Remembrance in East Christian Churches** (Language: English)
Heather Badamo, History of Art & Architecture, University of California, Santa Barbara
Paper 1534-b: **Antony and Macarius: The Desert Fathers - Myths and Reconstruction of the Ethiopian Monastic 'Genesis'** (Language: English)
Martina Ambu, Laboratoire de rattachement 'Orient et Méditerranée: Mondes sémitiques' (UMR 8167), Université Paris I - Panthéon-Sorbonne
Paper 1534-c: **Egyptian Memory Layers in the Ethiopic Maṣḥafa Berhān** (Language: English)
Vince Bantu, Covenant Theological Seminary, St Louis, Missouri

Session: **1535** **Maurice Keyworth Building: Room 1.09**
Title: **RECORD, MEMORY, AND THE MAKING OF HISTORY, I: RELIGION ON THE RECORD**
Sponsor: The National Archives
Organiser: Abigail Dorr, School of History & Heritage, University of Lincoln and Rebecca Searby, Centre for Medieval Studies, University of York
Moderator: Paul R. Dryburgh, The National Archives, Kew
Paper 1535-a: **Recording for Posterity's Sake: Comparing the Constructed Characterisations of St Bridget of Sweden** (Language: English)
Sara Mederos, School of History & Heritage, University of Lincoln
Paper 1535-b: **Memories of Persecution and the Making of History: John Foxe and the Heresy Trial Records of Early 16th-Century Kent** (Language: English)
Rob Lutton, Department of History, University of Nottingham
Paper 1535-c: **Constructing Commemoration Narratives in Late Medieval Stanford** (Language: English)
Sheila Sweetinburgh, Centre for Kent History & Heritage, Canterbury Christ Church University

Session: **1536** **Leeds University Union: Room 4 - Hyde Park**
Title: **REMEMBERING, REMINDING, FORGETTING: LEGAL MEMORY IN EUROPEAN WRITING**
Organiser: Arendse Lund, Department of English, University College London and Agata Zielinska, Department of History, University College London
Moderator: Arendse Lund
Paper 1536-a: **Faulty Memories: When Is a Tort Not Wrong?** (Language: English)
Lindsey McNellis, Department of History, West Virginia University
Paper 1536-b: **Passing Memory: Borrowed Mnemonics in the Medieval Nordic Laws** (Language: English)
Seán Vrieland, Den Arnamagnæanske Samling, Københavns Universitet
Paper 1536-c: **Memory, Property, Pastoral Care: Polish Episcopal *Arengae* in the 13th and 14th Centuries** (Language: English)
Agata Zielinska

Session:	**1537** **Leeds University Union: Room 5 - Kirkstall Abbey**
Title:	**MEMORY, COMMUNITY, AND AUTHORITY IN MEDIEVAL IBERIA: FROM PERIPHERIES TO CITIES**
Sponsor:	Kısmet Press
Organiser:	Ricky Broome, Leeds Institute for Clinical Trials Research (LICTR), University of Leeds
Moderator:	Patrick Marschner, Institut für Mittelalterforschung, Österreichische Akademie der Wissenschaften, Wien
Paper 1537-a:	**Catalonia as a Carolingian Frontier** (Language: English) Cullen Chandler, Department of History, Lycoming College, Pennsylvania
Paper 1537-b:	**Memory, Territory, and Unity: Ecclesiastical Geography and the Integration Process in the Visigothic Kingdom of Toledo** (Language: English) Paulo Pachá, Departamento de História, Universidade Federal Fluminense, Rio de Janeiro
Paper 1537-c:	**Rights and Memory to Run a City: Coimbra's City Council Archive in Late Medieval Times** (Language: English) Leonor Zozaya-Montes, Departamento de Ciencias Históricas, Universidad de Las Palmas de Gran Canaria
Respondent:	Jonathan Jarrett, Institute for Medieval Studies, University of Leeds

Session:	**1538** **Michael Sadler Building: Room LG.15**
Title:	**THE CONTEXTS OF FUNERAL MONUMENTS**
Sponsor:	Department of Medieval Studies, Central European University, Budapest
Organiser:	Gerhard Jaritz, Department of Medieval Studies, Central European University, Budapest
Moderator:	Gerhard Jaritz
Paper 1538-a:	***Pro memoria animae*: Unknown Marble Tombs in Angevin Basilicata** (Language: English) Marcello Mignozzi, Dipartimento Lettere Lingue Arti. Italianistica e Culture Comparate, Università degli studi di Bari Aldo Moro
Paper 1538-b:	**Commemorating an Individual and an Institution: Grave Slabs of Teutonic Knights in Livonia** (Language: English) Anu Mänd, Institute of History, Archaeology & Art History, Tallinn University
Paper 1538-c:	**Funeral Monuments for the Elites of 16th-Century Saxon Towns in Transylvania** (Language: English) Dóra Mérai, Department of Medieval Studies, Central European University, Budapest

Session:	**1539** **Maurice Keyworth Building: Room 1.03**
Title:	**MEMORY IN 11TH-CENTURY HISTORIOGRAPHY**
Organiser:	IMC Programming Committee
Moderator:	Julie A. Hofmann, Department of History, Shenandoah University, Virginia
Paper 1539-a:	**Hariulf and the Reconstruction of the Past of the Abbey of Saint-Riquier, End of the 11th Century** (Language: English) Thomas Ledru, Institut de Recherches Historiques du Septentrion (IRHiS - UMR 8529), Université de Lille
Paper 1539-b:	**Recent Past and Memory in Historical Writing: The Example of the 11th-Century Chronicles** (Language: English) Vasilina Sidorova, Institute for Information Transmission Problems of the Russian Academy of Sciences / State Academic University for the Humanities, Moscow
Paper 1539-c:	**From Archive to Historical Memory: (Re)Construction of the Past in Central Italian Monastic Historiography, 11th-12th Centuries** (Language: English) Lari Ahokas, Department of Philosophy, History, Culture & Art Studies, University of Helsinki

Session:	**1540** **Stage@leeds: Stage 3**
Title:	**ANCESTRAL ROOTS: MEMORY AND ARBOREAL IMAGERY ACROSS CULTURES, I - KINSHIP**
Sponsor:	Trames Arborescentes Project
Organiser:	Pippa Salonius, School of Philosophical, Historical & International Studies, Monash University, Victoria and Naïs Virenque, Centre d'Études Supérieures de la Renaissance, Université François Rabelais, Tours
Moderator:	Naïs Virenque
Paper 1540-a:	**The Classical Ancestors of Medieval Genealogical Trees?: An Overview of Botanical Depictions of Kinship in Ancient Greece and Rome** (Language: English) Alessandro Buccheri, Centro Antropologia del Mondo Antico, Università di Siena / Centre Anthropologie et Histoire des Mondes Antiques (ANHIMA - UMR 8210), Paris
Paper 1540-b:	**Birth and Vegetal Growth: Two Metaphors of the Mnemonic Experience of Reading *The Stromata* by Clement of Alexandria** (Language: English) Antoine Paris, Université Paris-Sorbonne, Paris / Université de Montréal, Québec
Paper 1540-c:	**Learning from the Tree: How Medieval Europeans and Māori Remembered Their Ancestors** (Language: English) Pippa Salonius

Session: **1541** **Stage@leeds: Stage 2**
Title: **HERMITS, MONKS, FRIARS: NEW STUDIES ON MEDIEVAL MONASTICISM IN CENTRAL EUROPE**
Sponsor: Department of Medieval Studies, Central European University, Budapest
Organiser: József Laszlovszky, Department of Medieval Studies, Central European University, Budapest
Moderator: Beatrix F. Romhányi, 'Hungary in Medieval Europe', Lendület Research Group (MTA-DE), University of Debrecen / Hungarian Academy of Sciences, Budapest
Paper 1541-a: **Royal Burials in Cistercian Monasteries: Local Pattern or European Trend?** (Language: English)
József Laszlovszky
Paper 1541-b: **Marian Cult Places and Monastic Traditions in Late Medieval Central Europe** (Language: English)
Karen Stark, Department of Medieval Studies, Central European University, Budapest
Paper 1541-c: **The Bosnian Vicary as the First Observant Jurisdiction to Embrace the Reform: According to 16th-Century *Cronica*** (Language: English)
Paweł Cholewicki, Department of Medieval Studies, Central European University, Budapest

Session: **1542** **Stage@leeds: Stage 1**
Title: **POWER, MERCY, AND MEMORY: ROYAL AND PRINCELY PARDONS IN THE LATE MIDDLE AGES**
Organiser: Rudi Beaulant, Archéologie, Terre, Histoire, Sociétés (ARTEHIS - UMR 6298), Université Bourgogne, Dijon and Quentin Verreycken, Centre d'histoire du droit et de la justice (CHDJ), Université catholique de Louvain, Louvain-la-Neuve / Centre de recherches en histoire du droit et des institutions (CRHiDI), Université Saint-Louis, Bruxelles
Moderator: Quentin Verreycken
Paper 1542-a: **L'espace de la grâce ducale: L'invention d'un langage princier en Bretagne sous le règne de Jean IV** (Language: Français)
David Dominé-Cohn, Groupe D'anthropologie Historique de l'Occident Médiéval (GAHOM), École des Hautes Études en Sciences Sociales (EHESS), Paris
Paper 1542-b: **The Good, the Bad, and the Pardoned: The Evolution of the Pardon Procedure in Burgundy in the 14th and 15th Centuries** (Language: English)
Rudi Beaulant
Paper 1542-c: **To Forgive and To Forget?: The Use of Abolition Letters for Rebel Cities by King of France Louis XI, 1461-1483** (Language: English)
Adrien Carbonnet, Center Roland Mousnier, Université Paris IV - Sorbonne

Session: **1543** **Leeds University Union: Room 6 - Roundhay**
Title: **BRINGING THE MEMORY OF THE FIRST CRUSADE BACK TO LIFE: A NEW PROJECT TO EDIT THE *SIEGE D'ANTIOCHE***
Sponsor: University of Warwick / Fordham University
Organiser: Carol Elizabeth Sweetenham, School of Modern Languages & Cultures, University of Warwick / Royal Holloway, University of London
Moderator: Linda Paterson, Department of French Studies, University of Warwick
Paper 1543-a: **Putting the *Siege d'Antioche* Online: A Collaborative Approach** (Language: English)
Stephen Powell, Center for Medieval Studies, Fordham University, New York
Paper 1543-b: **The *Siege d'Antioche* as a Crusade Text** (Language: English)
Simon Thomas Parsons, Department of History, Royal Holloway, University of London
Paper 1543-c: **Literary Influences on the *Siege d'Antioche*** (Language: English)
Carol Elizabeth Sweetenham

Session: **1544** **Fine Art Building: SR 1.10**
Title: **MEMORIES OF MARTYRDOM IN LATE ANTIQUITY**
Organiser: IMC Programming Committee
Moderator: Péter Tóth, British Library, London
Paper 1544-a: **The Memory of the Governors of the Egyptian Provinces in Later Hagiographical Sources about the Great Persecution** (Language: English)
Giulia Agostini, Dipartimento di Scienze dell'Antichità, Università degli Studi di Roma 'La Sapienza' and Anna Salsano, Dipartimento di Scienze dell'Antichità, Università degli Studi di Roma 'La Sapienza'
Paper 1544-b: **Shaping Past Martyrdom in the Middle Ages: Hagiographical Record of Irenaeus of Sirmium** (Language: English)
Marijana Vukovic, Instytut Historyczny, Uniwersytet Warszawski
Paper 1544-c: **Building Memory in Stone and Rebuilding It through Texts: The Case of Sanctus Mantius** (Language: English)
André Carneiro, Departamento de História, Universidade de Évora

Session: **1545** **Michael Sadler Building: Room LG.19**
Title: **CONTINUITY AND CONQUEST IN ENGLAND AND NORMANDY, III: THE IMPACT OF CONQUEST ON 12TH-CENTURY THOUGHT**
Sponsor: Haskins Society
Organiser: Isaac Boothroyd, Department of History, University of Manchester
Moderator: Charlie Rozier, Department of History, Swansea University
Paper 1545-a: **A Tale of Two Conquests: Remembering 1016 and 1066 through Narratives of Divine Vengeance** (Language: English)
Abigail Steed, Department of History, Durham University
Paper 1545-b: **English Identity or English Identities?: The Multiplication and Stratification of English Identity in the 12th Century** (Language: English)
Isaac Boothroyd
Paper 1545-c: **Where Are the Women?: Women and Ethnic Discourse in Normandy and England, c. 1016-1142 - Paradox, Exclusion, and Commemoration** (Language: English)
Tom Chadwick, Centre for Medieval Studies, University of Exeter

Session: **1546** **Emmanuel Centre: Room 10**
Title: **TYPOLOGIES OF CONFLICT IN HIGH MEDIEVAL EUROPE, I**
Sponsor: Centre for Advanced Studies, Norwegian Academy of Science and Letters, Oslo
Organiser: Louisa Taylor, Institutt for arkeologi, konservering og historie, Universitetet i Oslo
Moderator: Richard E. Barton, Department of History, University of North Carolina, Greensboro
Paper 1546-a: **1199: Civil War, Rebellion, or Succession Dispute?** (Language: English)
Stephen Church, School of History, University of East Anglia
Paper 1546-b: **Kings, Authority, and Conflict: A Comparative Study of 'Civil War' in High Medieval England and Iceland** (Language: English)
Louisa Taylor
Paper 1546-c: **Opponent or Enemy?: Relationships across Factions in the Norwegian 'Civil Wars'** (Language: English)
Hilde Andrea Nysether, Institutt for arkeologi, konservering og historie, Universitetet i Oslo

Session: **1547** **Baines Wing: Room 2.14**
Title: **CONFLICTED OR COMPLEMENTARY MEMORIES?: VISIONS FROM THE INSIDE - DIFFERENT PASTS OF MEDIEVAL MULTIETHNIC SOCIETIES**
Sponsor: Uniwersytet Wrocławski
Organiser: Przemysław Wiszewski, Wydział Nauk Historycznych i Pedagogicznych, Uniwersytet Wrocławski
Moderator: Przemysław Wiszewski
Paper 1547-a: **Jews and Muslims as Targets in the Medieval *pontificia corpora* Sent to Military Orders in Portugal** (Language: English)
Joana Lencart, Faculdade de Letras, Universidade do Porto and Paula Pinto-Costa, Faculdade de Letras, Universidade do Porto
Paper 1547-b: **Multiethnicity in Memories of Medieval Transylvania** (Language: English)
Cosmin Popa-Gorjanu, Departamentul de Istorie, Arheologie si Muzeologie, Universitatea 1 Decembrie 1918, Alba Iulia
Paper 1547-c: **Catalans and Sardinians: Memories through the Centuries, 12th-17th Centuries** (Language: English)
Luciano Gallinari, Istituto di Storia dell'Europa Mediterranea (ISEM), Consiglio Nazionale delle Ricerche, Cagliari

Session: **1548** **University House: St George Room**
Title: **ENGAGING THE CRUSADES, I: PREACHING AND RECEIVING THE CRUSADES**
Sponsor: Routledge
Organiser: Kristin Skottki, Lehrstuhl für Mittelalterliche Geschichte, Universität Bayreuth
Moderator: Mike Horswell, Department of History, Royal Holloway, University of London
Paper 1548-a: **Urban's Modern Successors: Preaching the Modern Crusades** (Language: English)
Adam Knobler, Centrum für Religionswissenschaftliche Studien, Ruhr-Universität Bochum
Paper 1548-b: **Reception of the Crusades in the Contemporary Catholic Church: 'Purification of Memory' or Medieval Nostalgia?** (Language: English)
Marco Giardini, Independent Scholar, Ferrara
Paper 1548-c: **Different Perspectives on the Crusades: An International Comparison** (Language: English)
Felix Hinz, Historisches Institut, Universität Paderborn and Johannes Meyer-Hamme, Historisches Institut, Universität Paderborn

---

Session: **1549** **Parkinson Building: Nathan Bodington Chamber**
Title: **LEGAL AND FINANCIAL RIGHTS IN LATE MEDIEVAL ENGLAND**
Organiser: IMC Programming Committee
Moderator: Karen Stöber, Departament d'Història, Universitat de Lleida
Paper 1549-a: **The Crown's Ecclesiastical Creditors: State Loans from the English Church, 1307-1377** (Language: English)
Robin McCallum, School of History & Anthropology, Queen's University Belfast
Paper 1549-b: **Memory, Identity, and Power: The Pursuit of Self-Government in the Monastic Town of Reading, 1253-1539** (Language: English)
Joe Chick, Department of History, University of Warwick
Paper 1549-c: **Henry III, Edward I, and the Rule of Law** (Language: English)
Paulette Barton, Department of Modern Languages & Classics / Department of History, University of Maine

Session: **1550** **Maurice Keyworth Building: Room 1.31**
Title: **MEMORY AND THE BOLSTERING OF POLITICAL AND ECCLESIASTICAL AUTHORITY**
Organiser: IMC Programming Committee
Moderator: Anne J. Duggan, Department of History, King's College London
Paper 1550-a: **Bolesław the Forgotten and Cursed Dukes in Polish Historiography: Excommunication and Condemnation of Memory in Medieval Legal Culture** (Language: English)
Paweł Dziwiński, Faculty of Law & Administration, Jagiellonian University, Kraków
Paper 1550-b: **Republicanism and Radical Theology in the Roman Revolution, 1143-1155** (Language: English)
Peter J. A. Jones, School of Advanced Studies, University of Tyumen, Russia
Paper 1550-c: **Remembering the Schism of 1159: Alexander III and Victor IV in Contemporary Sources** (Language: English)
Kristýna Strnadová, Department of Greak & Latin Studies, Univerzita Karlova, Praha
Paper 1550-d: **Conflicting Memories and Memories of a Conflict: Clashing Memorial Cultures of the Teutonic Order and the Church of Riga in Late Medieval Livonia** (Language: English)
Gustavs Strenga, School of Humanities, Tallinn University

Session: **1551** **Baines Wing: Room 2.15**
Title: **LIVING BY THE SEA: CULTURE AND ECONOMY IN THE LATER MIDDLE AGES**
Organiser: Miriam Müller, Centre for the Study of the Middle Ages, University of Birmingham
Moderator: Michael Evans, Faculty of Social Science, Delta College, Michigan
Paper 1551-a: **The Consequences of the Black Death for the Populations along the Northern Sea and Atlantic Coast of Norway** (Language: English)
Arnved Nedkvitne, Institutt for arkeologi, konservering og historie, Universitetet i Oslo
Paper 1551-b: **Culture and the Sea: Living and Working in a Coastal Community in Later Medieval Norfolk** (Language: English)
Miriam Müller
Paper 1551-c: **The Crisis of a 'Golden Age': The Evolving Social Position of Wage Earners in the Coastal Area of Flanders, 13th-16th Centuries** (Language: English)
Sam Geens, Centrum voor Stadsgeschiedenis, Universiteit Antwerpen

Session: **1552** **University House: Great Woodhouse Room**
Title: **COMMUNICATING MEDIEVAL HERITAGE**
Sponsor: Arc Humanities Press
Organiser: Simon Forde, Arc Humanities Press, Leeds
Moderator: Anne Nolan, Arc Humanities Press / Medieval Institute Publications, Western Michigan University, Kalamazoo
Paper 1552-a: **The Medieval Jewish Heritage of Erfurt: Strategies of Investigation and Communication** (Language: English)
Maria Stürzebecher, Kulturdirektion, Landeshauptstadt Erfurt
Paper 1552-b: **The Rural Militia in the Battle of Visby, 1361: Contrasts between Sources and Narrative** (Language: English)
Thomas Neijman, Institutionen för mediestudier, Stockholms universitet

Session:	**1553**	**Emmanuel Centre: Room 11**
Title:	**HONOUR IN MEDIEVAL LITERATURE**	
Organiser:	Christopher Liebtag Miller, School of Modern Languages - German, University of St Andrews	
Moderator:	Kathrin Gollwitzer-Oh, Institut für Deutsche Philologie, Ludwig-Maximilians-Universität München	
Paper 1553-a:	**Honourable Violence: The Construct of Appropriate Aggression in Medieval Japanese War Tales** (Language: English) Morten Oxenboell, Department of East Asian Languages & Cultures, Indiana University, Bloomington	
Paper 1553-b:	**Constructing Honour: Richard I and Saladin** (Language: English) Karli Grazman, Medieval Studies Program, University of Connecticut	
Paper 1553-c:	**The Knights of Middle English Romance: Exemplars of Dishonor?** (Language: English) James T. Stewart, Department of English, University of Tennessee, Knoxville	

Session:	**1554**	**Baines Wing: Room G.37**
Title:	**EXPLORING MUSIC AND LATE MEDIEVAL EUROPEAN COURT CULTURES: THE MALMECC PROJECT AT THE UNIVERSITY OF OXFORD**	
Sponsor:	Music and Late Medieval European Court Cultures Project (MALMECC), The Oxford Research Centre in the Humanities (TORCH), University of Oxford	
Organiser:	Karl Kügle, Wadham College, University of Oxford	
Moderator:	Karl Kügle	
Paper 1554-a:	**Philippa of Hainault and Her Manuscripts** (Language: English) Laura Slater, Faculty of Music, University of Oxford	
Paper 1554-b:	**Organising Sound in Salzburg under Archbishop Pilgrim II** (Language: English) David Murray, The Oxford Research Centre in the Humanities (TORCH), University of Oxford	
Paper 1554-c:	**Courtly Feasts in Avignon, 1378–1403: Cultural Displays as Political Scripts** (Language: English) Christophe Masson, Faculty of Music, University of Oxford	

COFFEE BREAK: 10.30-11.15

Coffee and Tea will be served at the following locations:

Maurice Keyworth Building: Foyer
Michael Sadler Building: Foyer
Parkinson Building: Bookfair
University Square: The Marquee

See Map 7, p. 44.

MAKING LEEDS MEDIEVAL

LEEDS UNIVERSITY UNION, UNIVERSITY SQUARE, AND THE MARQUEE
10.30-18.00

This event is free of charge.

As the IMC 2018 draws to a close, join us in and around University Square for a range of activities, including a market featuring local produce and historical craft demonstrations. The Medieval Craft Fair will once again be extended to include a second day of trading during 'Making Leeds Medieval'. Come and browse a range of hand-crafted items including hand-bound books, historically-inspired woodwork, haberdashery, historic beads, and jewellery.

The Historical and Archaeological Societies Fair will be scheduled to coincide with 'Making Leeds Medieval', providing a unique opportunity to find out more about some of the many independent groups within the UK actively involved in preserving local and national history.

Similar to previous years, 'Making Leeds Medieval' will also feature a birds of prey display, live music, and combat displays.

*   *   *   *   *

* * * * *

HISTORICAL AND ARCHAEOLOGICAL SOCIETIES FAIR

UNIVERSITY SQUARE: THE MARQUEE
10.30-18.00

This event is free of charge

Scheduled to coincide with 'Making Leeds Medieval', the Historical and Archaeological Societies Fair will add a further dimension to the very popular end-of-Congress celebration events. The fair offers delegates the unique opportunity to discover more about some of the many independent groups within the UK who are actively involved in preserving local and national history.

The following organisations are amongst those currently confirmed as exhibiting at the Historical and Archaeological Societies Fair:

British Brick Society - The study of brick-making and brick buildings in their social, economic, and political contexts.

Church Monuments Society - The Church Monuments Society is dedicated to the study and preservation of church monuments. We produce an annual peer-reviewed journal, together with a newsletter, and have a varied programme of events through the year.

The Corpus of Romanesque Sculpture (CRSBI) - The Corpus of Romanesque Sculpture is a complete online record of all the surviving Romanesque sculpture in the British Isles and the Irish Republic. Freely available to all, it acts as both a record of a precious heritage and as an exciting new tool for researchers. Through its interactive capabilities, we are able to resolve old problems and ask new questions.

Friends of Stank Hall (FOSH) - The Friends of Stank Hall are a volunteer community group dedicated to saving and restoring the historic Stank Hall and Barn in South Leeds from dereliction. The site, consisting of Stank Old Hall (formerly a royal hunting lodge with garderobe dating back to c. 1280), Stank New Hall (built in 1590), and Stank Hall Barn (dating back to c. 1480), is owned by Leeds City Council.

Leeds Symposium on Food History - An organised annual symposium on a topic relating to food history and traditions with resulting papers published.

Thoresby Society, the Historical Society for Leeds & District - The Thoresby Society publishes original research on aspects of Leeds history and will be displaying copies of its publications, particularly those relating to Kirkstall Abbey and the Manor of Leeds.

Yorkshire Vernacular Buildings Study Group (YVBSG) - The study and recording of vernacular buildings in (and around) Yorkshire. Our Journal *Yorkshire Buildings* is published annually.

Yorkshire Archaeological & Historical Society - The Yorkshire Archaeological & Historical Society exists to promote the study of Yorkshire's history through events, lectures, and outings. The society publishes the Yorkshire Archaeological Journal annually, as well as a Record Series, and volumes such as the Wakefield Court Rolls.

* * * * *

Session: **1601** **Baines Wing: Room 1.13**
Title: **ALFREDIAN VOICES, I: REVOICING GREGORY, AUGUSTINE, AND BOETHIUS**
Organiser: Francis Leneghan, Faculty of English Language & Literature, University of Oxford
Moderator: Francis Leneghan
Paper 1601-a: **The Middle-Most Man: Calcidius's Latin Commentary in the Alfredian *Boethius*** (Language: English)
Karmen Lenz, Department of English, Middle Georgia State University
Paper 1601-b: **The Old English *Soliloquies*: The Soul's Memory of the Earthly Life** (Language: English)
Amy Faulkner, Faculty of English Language & Literature, University of Oxford
Paper 1601-c: **Voicing Wonder in Alfredian Dialogues** (Language: English)
Nicole Guenther Discenza, Department of English, University of South Florida

Session: **1602** **Michael Sadler Building: Room LG.17**
Title: **MEDIEVAL ARABIC SCHOLARSHIP**
Organiser: Sally Hany Abed, English Language & Literature Department, Alexandria University and Maha Baddar, Department of Writing, Pima Community College, Arizona
Moderator: Kris Swank, Northwest Campus Library, Pima Community College, Arizona
Paper 1602-a: **A Hybrid Theory of Style in Ibn Sina's Long Commentary on Aristotle's *Rhetoric*** (Language: English)
Maha Baddar
Paper 1602-b: **The Monstrous in Medieval Western versus Medieval Arabic Writings** (Language: English)
Sally Hany Abed
Paper 1602-c: ***Al-Ziyad ibn 'Amir al-Kinani* and the Production of Literary Space** (Language: English)
Jessica Zeitler, Department of Languages & the Arts, Pima Community College, Arizona

Session: **1603** **Michael Sadler Building: Room LG.16**
Title: **BYZANTINE STUDIES IN CHINA, II: ON THE SEA ROUTE OF THE SILK ROAD**
Organiser: Lin Ying, Department of History, Sun Yat-sen University, China
Moderator: Stefanos Kordosis, Department of Hellenic Civilizaton, Hellenic Open University, Greece
Paper 1603-a: **Suvarnabhumi and the Empires in the Mediterranean World in 100-900, Centring on Numismatic Evidence** (Language: English)
Lin Ying
Paper 1603-b: **The Daqin Lamp and Chinese Sources on the Contact between South-East Asia and Late Roman Empire** (Language: English)
Xue-fei Han, Department of History, Sun Yat-sen University, China
Respondent: Rebecca Darley, Department of History, Classics & Archaeology, Birkbeck, University of London

Session: **1604** **Fine Art Building: SR G.04**
Title: **RELIGIOUS PRAXIS AND PASTORAL CARE IN EARLY MEDIEVAL IBERIA, I: LITURGY**
Sponsor: Presbyters in the Late Antique West Project, Uniwersytet Warszawski
Organiser: Kati Ihnat, Afdeling Geschiedenis, Radboud Universiteit Nijmegen, Marta Szada, Instytut Historyczny, Uniwersytet Warszawski and Jamie Wood, School of History & Heritage, University of Lincoln
Moderator: Ian N. Wood, School of History, University of Leeds
Paper 1604-a: **The Best Faith: Showing Christian Superiority through Liturgy in 5th-Century Iberia** (Language: English)
Purificación Ubric, Departamento de Historia Antigua, Universidad de Granada
Paper 1604-b: **Effective Experience: Religious Orthodoxy, Ritual Performance, and Contacting the Divine in 7th-Century Iberia** (Language: English)
Molly Lester, Department of History, United States Naval Academy, Maryland
Paper 1604-c: **Space, Cult, and Community in Early Medieval Iberia** (Language: English)
Jeffrey A. Bowman, Department of History, Kenyon College, Ohio

Session: **1605** **Parkinson Building: Room 1.16**
Title: **VISUAL MEMORY: ART AS A REMINDER OF THE PAST**
Sponsor: Universität Zürich
Organiser: Zofia Jackson, Kunsthistorisches Institut, Universität Zürich
Moderator: Zofia Jackson
Paper 1605-a: **Sprouting out of Legends: National Genealogical Identity Rooted in the Trojan War Expressed in Art** (Language: English)
Zofia Jackson
Paper 1605-b: **Cloths of Honour: A Visual and Functional Memory of the Gold-Ground** (Language: English)
Sabrina Schmid, Independent Scholar, Günsberg
Paper 1605-c: **The Use of the Epic in Iran's National Memory: The *Book of Kings*** (Language: English)
Laura Castro Royo, School of Art History / School of Modern Languages, University of St Andrews

Session: **1606** **Michael Sadler Building: Rupert Beckett Theatre**
Title: **NEW STUDIES ON HISTORIOGRAPHICAL MANUSCRIPTS, I: HISTORIANS AT WORK**
Sponsor: H37 - Histoire & Cultures Graphiques, Université catholique de Louvain, Louvain-la-Neuve
Organiser: Antoine Brix, Département d'histoire, Université catholique de Louvain, Louvain-la-Neuve
Moderator: Antoine Brix
Paper 1606-a: **A 13th-Century Historian at Work: Giles of Orval and the Autograph of the *Gesta episcoporum Leodiensium*** (Language: English)
Nicolas Ruffini-Ronzani, Département d'histoire, Université de Namur
Paper 1606-b: **Étienne Maleu: A French Historian and His Sources at the Beginning of the 14th Century** (Language: English)
Pauline Bouchaud, École Pratique des Hautes Études (EPHE), Université de Recherche Paris Sciences et Lettres
Paper 1606-c: **Embarrassment of Riches or Hobson's Choice?: A Burgundian Historiographer's Journey into the Distant Past** (Language: English)
Elena Koroleva, Département de Lettres Modernes, Université de Lille / Département de Lettres Modernes, Université de Rouen Normandie

Session: **1607** **Fine Art Building: Studio Ground Floor**
Title: **MEDIEVAL PROVENÇAL AND SEPHARDI TEXTS BETWEEN SECULAR CULTURE AND RELIGION, II**
Organiser: IMC Programming Committee
Moderator: Sara Offenberg, Department of the Arts, Ben-Gurion University of the Negev, Beer-Sheva
Paper 1607-a: **Israel and Its Speaking Tombstones** (Language: English)
Elíshabá Mata, Department of Spanish Language, University of Salamanca
Paper 1607-b: **Parody, Ritual, and Function: The Medieval Parodies for Purim and Their History of Reception** (Language: English)
Roni Cohen, School of Jewish Studies, Tel Aviv University
Paper 1607-c: **Digitising the Memory of Iberian Jews: Virtual Museum of Sefarad** (Language: English)
Anna Katarzyna Dulska, Instituto Cultura y Sociedad, Universidad de Navarra, Pamplona

Session: **1608** **Baines Wing: Room 2.13**
Title: **RESIDUAL ORALITY IN MEDIEVAL EASTERN EUROPEAN CHRISTIAN EPIC POETRY: PATTERNS OF COMPOSITION AND TRANSMISSION**
Sponsor: Center for Byzantine, Modern Greek & Cypriot Studies, Granada
Organiser: Matilde Casas Olea, Departamento de Filología Griega y Filología Eslava, Universidad de Granada
Moderator: Simón J. Suárez Cuadros, Facultad de Traducción e Interpretación, Universidad de Granada
Paper 1608-a: **Elements of Orality in Byzantine Popular Poetry** (Language: English)
Maila García Amorós, Facultad de Filosofía y Letras, Universidad de Granada
Paper 1608-b: **The Epic Element in the East Slavic Spiritual Chants in Commemoration of the Martyred Princes Boris and Gleb** (Language: English)
Enrique Santos Marinas, Departamento de Filología Griega y Lingüística Indoeuropea, Universidad Complutense de Madrid
Paper 1608-c: **Orality and Literacy in the Epic Tradition about St George** (Language: English)
Matilde Casas Olea

Session: **1609** **Baines Wing: Room 2.16**
Title: **THE PREMONSTRATENSIANS AND SCRIPTURE**
Sponsor: Society for the Study of the Bible in the Middle Ages
Organiser: William P. Hyland, School of Divinity, University of St Andrews
Moderator: William P. Hyland
Paper 1609-a: **12th-Century Premonstratensian *lectio divina*: Perspectives on Study, Sacred Reading, and Contemplation** (Language: English)
Beatrise Bandeniece, School of Divinity, University of St Andrews
Paper 1609-b: **Prémontré or St Victor?: Adam of Dryburgh's *De Triplice Tabernaculo*** (Language: English)
Peter Damian Grint, School of History, University of St Andrews
Paper 1609-c: **Lazarus and the White Canons** (Language: English)
Carol Neel, Department of History, Colorado College

Session: **1610** **Baines Wing: Room 1.16**
Title: **MYSTICISM AND HAGIOGRAPHY**
Organiser: IMC Programming Committee
Moderator: Dávid Falvay, Department of Italian Studies, Eötvös Loránd University, Budapest
Paper 1610-a: **Being Her Own 'Creature': Memory and *The Book of Margery Kempe*** (Language: English)
Azime Pekşen Yakar, Department of English Language & Literature, Hacettepe University, Turkey
Paper 1610-b: **Oh God, She's a Woman: Contextualizing Julian of Norwich** (Language: English)
Katharine Beaulieu, Independent Scholar, Ontario
Paper 1610-c: **Liquid Memories** (Language: English)
Sarah Alison Miller, Department of Classics, Duquesne University, Pennsylvania

Session:	**1611**	**Baines Wing: Room 1.15**
Title:	**CREATING AND SHAPING IDENTITIES IN THE MEDIEVAL BALTIC**	
Organiser:	IMC Programming Committee	
Moderator:	Beata Możejko, Zakład Historii Średniowiecza Polski i Nauk Pomocniczych Historii, Uniwersytet Gdański	
Paper 1611-a:	**Livonian Hospitality: The *Livonian Rhymed Chronicle* and the Formation of Identities on the 13th-Century Baltic Frontier** (Language: English) Wojtek Jezierski, Institutionen för historiska studier, Göteborgs Universitet	
Paper 1611-b:	**'Thus does Riga always water the nations!': The Use of Past to Justify the Future in Livonian Conversion** (Language: English) Teemu Korpijärvi, Interdisciplinary Research Training Group (IRTG), Baltic Borderlands, Universität Greifswald / Department of Geographical & Historical Studies, University of Eastern Finland	
Paper 1611-c:	**The Haunting Memories of Forgotten Kings: Recollection of the Past and Oblivion in the Late Medieval Grand Duchy of Lithuania** (Language: English) Vladimir Kananovich, Independent Scholar, Minsk	

Session:	**1613**	**University House: Beechgrove Room**
Title:	**NEW PERSPECTIVES ON WOMEN IN MEDIEVAL ROMANCE, IV: FEMALE DESIRE AND QUEER IDENTITIES**	
Organiser:	Hannah Piercy, Institute of Medieval & Early Modern Studies, Durham University	
Moderator:	Kirsty A. S. Bolton, Centre for Medieval & Renaissance Culture / Department of English, University of Southampton	
Paper 1613-a:	**Going Between or Coming Between?: Go-Betweens, Agency, and Female Desire in Later Middle English Romance** (Language: English) Hannah Piercy	
Paper 1613-b:	**The Woman Knight and the Princess: Two Italian Medieval Tales of Female Same-Sex Desire** (Language: English) Anna Lisa Somma, Department of Italian Studies, University of Birmingham / Medici Archive Project, Firenze	
Paper 1613-c:	**'A lady that dwelled in that foreyste': Malory's Lady Huntress and Queering Medieval Romance** (Language: English) Amy Louise Morgan, School of Literature & Languages, University of Surrey	

Session: **1614** **Charles Thackrah Building: 1.01**
Title: **THE SIGNIFICANCE OF THE MIDDLE AGES FOR THE CONSTRUCTION OF MASCULINITY IN THE 19TH AND EARLY 20TH CENTURY**
Sponsor: Karl-Franzens-Universität Graz / Oswald von Wolkenstein-Gesellschaft
Organiser: Käthe Sonnleitner, Institut für Geschichte, Karl-Franzens-Universität Graz
Moderator: Sieglinde Hartmann, Oswald von Wolkenstein-Gesellschaft, Frankfurt am Main
Paper 1614-a: **What Is Wrong with Emperor Henry IV's Masculinity?** (Language: English)
Käthe Sonnleitner
Paper 1614-b: **Examples to Be Followed!: The Crusading Leopold V as a Paragon of Military Virtue for the Habsburg Monarchy** (Language: English)
Ingrid Schlegl, Institut für Geschichte, Karl-Franzens-Universität Graz
Paper 1614-c: **The Significance of Knightly Ideals for the Genesis of Austrian-Hungarian War Heroes during World War I** (Language: English)
Nicole Goll, Institut für Geschichte, Karl-Franzens-Universität Graz

---

Session: **1615** **Maurice Keyworth Building: Room 1.33**
Title: **COLLECTIVE DISPLAY: MEDIEVAL OBJECTS OUT OF ISOLATION, I**
Sponsor: Meadows Museum, Southern Methodist University, Dallas
Organiser: Amanda W. Dotseth, Meadows Museum, Southern Methodist University, Dallas
Moderator: Therese Martin, Instituto de Historia, Consejo Superior de Investigaciones Científicas (CSIC), Madrid
Paper 1615-a: **Storing Sacred Treasures: The Medieval *Wunderkammer*** (Language: English)
Lesley Milner, Institute of Historical Research, University of London
Paper 1615-b: **A Woman's Agency Reflected in Objects: The Identities of Queen Sancha of León and Castile** (Language: English)
Zaellotius A. Wilson, School of Art, Arizona State University
Paper 1615-c: **Memory as a Treasury / The Treasury as Memory: Medieval Networks of Collection - Inventories, Labels, and Inscribed Objects** (Language: English)
Amanda Luyster, Department of Visual Arts, College of the Holy Cross, Massachusetts

---

Session: **1616** **Maurice Keyworth Building: Room 1.04**
Title: **THE MEDIEVAL LAW COURTS, II: LAW IN THE LOCALITIES**
Sponsor: The Honourable Society of Gray's Inn
Organiser: Daniel F. Gosling, Department of Archives, The Honourable Society of Gray's Inn, London
Moderator: Zosia Edwards, Department of History, Royal Holloway, University of London
Paper 1616-a: **Crisis, Corruption, and the Commissions of Oyer and Terminer in Early 14th-Century England** (Language: English)
Jack Newman, Centre for Medieval & Early Modern Studies, University of Kent
Paper 1616-b: **Court Leets and Jurisdictional Conflict in Late Medieval England** (Language: English)
Alex Gibbs, Faculty of History, University of Cambridge
Paper 1616-c: **Ports, Markets, Forests, Mines: Local Courts in Comparative Perspective in Late Medieval England** (Language: English)
Tom Johnson, Department of History, University of York

Session: **1617** — **Social Sciences Building: Room 10.05**
Title: **SHAPING THE PAST AFTER THE CAROLINGIAN EMPIRE, II: IDEALS, PLACE, AND SPACE**
Sponsor: After Empire: Using & Not Using the Past in the Crisis of the Carolingian World, c. 900-1050
Organiser: Alice Hicklin, Friedrich-Meinecke-Institut, Freie Universität Berlin
Moderator: Sarah Greer, St Andrews Institute of Mediaeval Studies, University of St Andrews

Paper 1617-a: **Legacies of Empire: Rethinking the Dynamics of the Dano-Saxon-Slav Border in the Late 10th Century** (Language: English)
Paul Gazzoli, Department of Scandinavian Studies, University College London

Paper 1617-b: **Roman Law as a Bad Custom in 10th-Century Raetia Curiensis** (Language: English)
Stefan Esders, Friedrich-Meinecke-Institut, Freie Universität Berlin

Paper 1617-c: **Remembering the Carolingian Past in 10th-Century Italy: The *Libellus de imperatoria potestate in urbe Roma*** (Language: English)
Roberta Cimino, Department of History, University of Nottingham

---

Session: **1618** — **Michael Sadler Building: Room LG.10**
Title: **VISIONS OF COMMUNITY, III: TALES OF TWO CITIES - URBAN IDENTITIES AND BIOGRAPHICAL COLLECTIONS IN THE HIGH MIDDLE AGES**
Sponsor: Sonderforschungsbereich Project 'Visions of Community', Österreichische Akademie der Wissenschaften, Universität Wien / FWF Project F42
Organiser: Rutger Kramer, Institut für Mittelalterforschung, Österreichische Akademie der Wissenschaften, Wien and Veronika Wieser, Institut für Mittelalterforschung, Österreichische Akademie der Wissenschaften, Wien
Moderator: Jonathan Lyon, Department of History, University of Chicago, Illinois

Paper 1618-a: **Shaping a Christian Capital: Milan through the Lives of Its Early Bishops** (Language: English)
Giorgia Vocino, Dipartimento di Studi Umanistici, Università Ca' Foscari Venezia

Paper 1618-b: **A Place Apart?: The *Liber de sanctis Iuvavensibus* between Admont and Salzburg** (Language: English)
Diarmuid Ó Riain, Institut für Geschichte, Universität Wien

Paper 1618-c: **From Medieval Memories to a Modern Legendary: Wilhelm Wattenbach, *Monumenta Germaniae Historica* SS XI, and the Deeds of the Archbishops of Salzburg** (Language: English)
John Eldevik, Department of History, Hamilton College, New York

Session:	**1619** **Baines Wing: Room 1.14**
Title:	**MEDIEVAL POWER AND LETTERS, II: PLANTAGENET POWER IN THE 13TH CENTURY**
Sponsor:	Centre for Medieval & Renaissance Research, University of Winchester
Organiser:	Gabrielle Storey, Department of History, University of Winchester
Moderator:	Gabrielle Storey
Paper 1619-a:	**The Letters of Berengaria of Navarre and Her Fight for a Queen's Dower** (Language: English) Beth Thomas, Independent Scholar, St Andrews
Paper 1619-b:	***Dictamen*, Diplomacy, and Kingship during the Personal Rule of Henry III, 1230-1250** (Language: English) Lucy Hennings, Exeter College, University of Oxford
Paper 1619-c:	**'A son tres haut seignor, e a son tres cher pere': The Letters of Henry III and His Daughter, Beatrice** (Language: English) Abby Armstrong, School of Humanities, Canterbury Christ Church University

Session:	**1620** **Charles Thackrah Building: 1.02**
Title:	**REMEMBERING ROBIN HOOD: REPRESENTATION AND ADAPTATION IN THE POST-MEDIEVAL OUTLAW TRADITION**
Sponsor:	International Association for Robin Hood Studies
Organiser:	Stephen Basdeo, School of Arts & Communication, Leeds Trinity University
Moderator:	Hörður Barðdal, Independent Scholar, Wachtebeke
Paper 1620-a:	**Crafting Christmastime Memories in the Post-Medieval Robin Hood Tradition** (Language: English) Alexander L. Kaufman, Honors College / Department of English, Ball State University, Indiana
Paper 1620-b:	**Wat Tyler as Robin Hood in Victorian Fiction** (Language: English) Stephen Basdeo
Paper 1620-c:	**The Once and Future Thief: When King Arthur and Robin Hood Meet** (Language: English) Justine Breton, Centre de recherche Textes, Représentations, Archéologie, Autorité et Mémoires de l'Antiquité à la Renaissance (TRAME), Université de Picardie Jules Verne

Session:	**1621** **Social Sciences Building: Room 10.06**
Title:	**MEMORY IN OLD NORSE LITERATURE**
Sponsor:	Memory & the Pre-Modern North Network
Organiser:	Simon Nygaard, Afdeling for Religionsvidenskab, Aarhus Universitet and Yoav Tirosh, Faculty of Icelandic & Comparative Cultural Studies, University of Iceland, Reykjavík
Moderator:	Lukas Rösli, Deutsches Seminar, Universität Zurich
Paper 1621-a:	**Poetic Memory in the *Fornaldarsögur*** (Language: English) Timothy Rowbotham, Centre for Medieval Studies / Department of English & Related Literature, University of York
Paper 1621-b:	**Remembering Haraldr Hardráði, Forgetting Óláfr Kyrri: The Partisan Cultural Memory of *Morkinskinna*** (Language: English) Tom Morcom, Faculty of English Language & Literature, University of Oxford
Paper 1621-c:	**Myths of the Foremother Auðr/Unnr Re-Interpreted in Icelandic Literature during the 'Era of Memory'** (Language: English) Sofie Vanherpen, Faculteit Letteren en Wijsbegeerte, Universiteit Gent

Session: **1622** **University House: Cloberry Room**
Title: **'I CANNOT LIVE WITHOUT BOOKS': PERSONAL LIBRARIES AND MANUSCRIPTS**
Organiser: IMC Programming Committee
Moderator: Mariken Teeuwen, Huygens Instituut voor Nederlandse Geschiedenis, Koninklijke Nederlandse Academie van Wetenschappen (ING - KNAW), Amsterdam
Paper 1622-a: **Václav Koranda the Younger: Utraquist Tradition and Memory** (Language: English)
Jindřich Marek, Faculty of Arts, Univerzita Karlova, Praha
Paper 1622-b: **'Ce livre fut a feu madame agnes': Memorial Inscriptions in Women's Books in Late 15th-Century France** (Language: English)
S. C. Kaplan, Center for Languages & Intercultural Communication, Rice University, Texas
Paper 1622-c: **Individual Memory as Source and Subject in Patriarch Photius's *Bibliotheca* (Βιβλιοθήκη)** (Language: English)
Umut Var, Graduate School of Social Sciences, Istanbul Medeniyet University, Turkey

Session: **1623** **Emmanuel Centre: Wilson Room**
Title: **HAGIOGRAPHY, LANDSCAPE, AND MEMORY IN MEDIEVAL EAST ANGLIA AND SCANDINAVIA**
Organiser: Rebecca Pinner, School of Literature & Creative Writing, University of East Anglia
Moderator: Rebecca Pinner
Paper 1623-a: **Shifts in the Sanctified Cultural Landscape: New Local Saints in Early Medieval Scandinavia** (Language: English)
Sara Ellis Nilsson, Historical Studies, Department of Society, Culture & Identity, Malmö University
Paper 1623-b: **A Place of Her Own: The Role of Sacred Landscape in the Cult of St Æthelthryth** (Language: English)
John Black, Department of English, Moravian College, Pennsylvania
Paper 1623-c: **Saints and Wetlands in Medieval East Anglia** (Language: English)
Rebecca Pinner

Session: **1624** **Charles Thackrah Building: 1.04**
Title: ***CAROLINGIAN CIVILIZATION* 25 YEARS LATER: IN HONOR OF PAUL EDWARD DUTTON, II**
Organiser: Matthew Gabriele, Department of Religion & Culture, Virginia Tech
Moderator: Matthew Bryan Gillis, Department of History, University of Tennessee, Knoxville
Paper 1624-a: **Charles the Bald's Splendid Attire and the Politics of Clothing** (Language: English)
Valerie Garver, Department of History, Northern Illinois University
Paper 1624-b: **Disastrous Triumph: Divine Visions and the Invention of Carolingian Victory in Spain** (Language: English)
Anne Latowsky, Department of World Languages, University of South Florida
Paper 1624-c: **The Glimmering Gold of Memory and the Rust of Discontentment: The Chosen People Remember in the Late 9th Century** (Language: English)
Matthew Gabriele
Respondent: Paul E. Dutton, Department of Humanities, Simon Fraser University, British Columbia

Session: **1625** **Michael Sadler Building: Banham Theatre**
Title: **MEMORY OF TRAUMA AND DISEASE**
Sponsor: Department of Medieval Studies, Central European University, Budapest
Organiser: Gerhard Jaritz, Department of Medieval Studies, Central European University, Budapest
Moderator: Anu Mänd, Institute of History, Archaeology & Art History, Tallinn University
Paper 1625-a: **Bearing It in Mind: Teaching Medicine in Late Antiquity between Experience and Self-Promotion** (Language: English)
Iuliana Soficaru, Department of Medieval Studies, Central European University, Budapest
Paper 1625-b: **Memory and Remembrance: The Treatment of Stressful Events in a Medieval Community** (Language: English)
Matea Laginja, Department of Medieval Studies, Central European University, Budapest

---

Session: **1626** **Social Sciences Building: Room 10.07**
Title: **GENDER, SEXUALITY, AND MEMORY**
Organiser: IMC Programming Committee
Moderator: Anne Foerster, Historisches Institut, Universität Paderborn
Paper 1626-a: **Richard the Lionheart, Contested Queerness, and Crusading Memory** (Language: English)
Hilary Rhodes, Institute for Medieval Studies, University of Leeds
Paper 1626-b: **Cherishing the Memory of a Trebizond Emperor: The Case of Empress Eudokia Palaiologina Komnene** (Language: English)
Mila Krneta, Department of History, University of Banja Luka

Session: **1627** **Maurice Keyworth Building: Room 1.32**
Title: **REMAKING THE PAST IN 1483 AND 1951: CURSING, CAXTON, AND THE YORK CYCLE DRAMA**
Organiser: IMC Programming Committee
Moderator: Joyce Coleman, Department of English, University of Oklahoma
Paper 1627-a: **'Bloody Hell!': Breaking a Quintissentially British Swear Word** (Language: English)
Emily Reed, School of English, University of Sheffield
Paper 1627-b: **Saluting Classical Rome in William Caxton's *The Golden Legend*** (Language: English)
Judy Ann Ford, Department of History, Texas A&M University, Commerce
Paper 1627-c: **Remembering the Past and Looking to the Future: The 1951 Revival of the York Mystery Play Cycle** (Language: English)
Eleanor Margaret Bloomfield, Department of English & Drama, University of Auckland

Session: **1628** **Maurice Keyworth Building: Room G.02**
Title: **MEMORIES OF HERESY AND COUNTER-HERESY, II: LEGAL RECORDS**
Sponsor: Department for the Study of Religions, Masarykova univerzita, Brno / Medieval Heresy & Dissent Research Network, University of Nottingham
Organiser: David Zbíral, Department for the Study of Religions, Masarykova univerzita, Brno
Moderator: Lucy Sackville, Department of History, University of York
Paper 1628-a: **Selective Memory: Inquisitors and Deponents at Toulouse, 1245-1246** (Language: English)
Jean-Paul Rehr, CIHAM - Histoire, archéologie, littératures des mondes chrétiens et musulmans médiévaux (UMR 5648), Université Lyon 2
Paper 1628-b: **Memories of Hearsay in 13th-Century Inquisition Registers from Languedoc** (Language: English)
Saku Pihko, Trivium - Tampere Centre for Classical, Medieval & Early Modern Studies, University of Tampere
Paper 1628-c: **What Prompted Memories of Heresy?: Examples from Italian Inquisition Records, c. 1300** (Language: English)
Jill Moore, Department of History, Classics & Archaeology, Birkbeck, University of London

Session: **1629** **Maurice Keyworth Building: Room 1.06**
Title: **REMEMBERING GIFTS**
Sponsor: New College of the Humanities, London
Organiser: Lars Kjær, Department of History, New College of the Humanities, London
Moderator: Erik Niblaeus, Department of History, Durham University
Paper 1629-a: **'To remember a gift is to repay it': Memory and Reciprocity in Classical Literature** (Language: English)
Lars Kjær
Paper 1629-b: **Remembering a Generous Bishop: Bishop Sven in the *Øm Abbey Chronicle*** (Language: English)
Gunvor Helene Platou, Faculty of History, University of Cambridge
Paper 1629-c: **Unsolvable Disputes: Religious Donations and the Restructuring of the Social Order in High Medieval Denmark** (Language: English)
Emil Lauge Christensen, Institut for Kultur og Globale Studier, Aalborg Universitet

Session: **1630** **Charles Thackrah Building: 1.03**
Title: **CULTURAL MEMORY IN EARLY ENGLAND: CONTINUITIES AND CHANGE IN CULTURAL CONTACT EVENTS**
Sponsor: Flinders University
Organiser: Erin Sebo, Department of English, Creative Writing & Australian Studies, Flinders University, Adelaide
Moderator: Daniel Anlezark, Medieval & Early Modern Centre, University of Sydney
Paper 1630-a: **Cultural Memory in the Diaspora: The Development of the Ship Burial** (Language: English)
Erin Sebo
Paper 1630-b: **Memorialising and Anonymising Anglo-Saxon Women** (Language: English)
Gale R. Owen-Crocker, Department of English & American Studies, University of Manchester
Paper 1630-c: **Memory across the Longue Durée: Early Anglo-Saxon Landholdings in 13th-Century Fenland** (Language: English)
Susan Oosthuizen, Institute of Continuing Education, University of Cambridge

Session: **1631** **Maurice Keyworth Building: Room 1.05**
Title: **MEMORY, THE MATERIAL, AND THE MIDDLE AGES, II**
Sponsor: National Museums Scotland
Organiser: Katie Stevenson, St Andrews Institute of Mediaeval Studies, University of St Andrews
Moderator: Martin Goldberg, Department of Scottish History & Archaeology, National Museums Scotland, Edinburgh
Paper 1631-a: **Self, Status, and Cultural Memory: An Analysis of Identity and Self-Representation in Medieval Small Finds** (Language: English)
Stuart Campbell, Treasure Trove Unit, National Museums Scotland, Edinburgh
Paper 1631-b: **Memory of the Unseen: Visual Accounts and Material Traces of Unicorns in Western Europe, 13th-16th Centuries** (Language: English)
Xavier Dectot, Department of Art & Design, National Museums Scotland, Edinburgh
Paper 1631-c: **Lost and Found: The Material Culture of Religion in Medieval Scotland** (Language: English)
Adrienne Hynes, Department of Scottish History & Archaeology, National Museums Scotland, Edinburgh / School of History, Classics & Archaeology, University of Edinburgh

Session: **1632** **Social Sciences Building: Room 10.09**
Title: **AT THE CROSSROADS OF EMPIRES: SANT'AMBROGIO AT MONTECORVINO ROVELLA - A *LOCUS MEMORIAE* IN SOUTHERN LOMBARDY, II**
Organiser: Francesca Dell'Acqua, Centre for Byzantine, Ottoman & Modern Greek Studies, University of Birmingham
Moderator: Francesca Dell'Acqua
Paper 1632-a: ***Locus memoriae*: Sant'Ambrogio at Montecorvino Rovella in Its Cultural Landscape - The Building and Its Painted Decoration** (Language: English)
John Burnett Mitchell, School of World Art Studies & Museology, University of East Anglia
Paper 1632-b: **Veneers of Sophistication: The Painted Decoration of Sant'Ambrogio at Montecorvino Rovella** (Language: English)
Beatrice Leal, Department of Art History & World Art Studies, University of East Anglia
Paper 1632-c: **Seen in a New Light: The Incomparable Murals of Sant'Ambrogio at Montecorvino Rovella** (Language: English)
Rubén Montoya González, School of Archaeology & Ancient History, University of Leicester

Session:	**1633** **Baines Wing: Room G.36**
Title:	**IN HONOUR OF RICHARD HOLT, II: TOWNSCAPES AND URBAN SHAPES**
Sponsor:	'Creating the New North' Research Programme, Universitetet i Tromsø - Norges Arktiske Universitetet
Organiser:	Stefan Figenschow, Institutt for historie og religionsvitenskap, Universitetet i Tromsø - Norges Arktiske Universitetet
Moderator:	Sigrun Høgetveit Berg, Institutt for historie og religionsvitenskap, Universitetet i Tromsø - Norges Arktiske Universitetet
Paper 1633-a:	**Transforming Townscapes in 12th-Century England** (Language: English) Nigel Baker, School of Geography, Earth & Environmental Sciences, University of Birmingham
Paper 1633-b:	**New Light on the Town of Birmingham in the Middle Ages** (Language: English) Christopher Dyer, Centre for English Local History, University of Leicester
Paper 1633-c:	**Ribe's First Dwellers and the Beginnings of the Urbanisation of Scandinavia** (Language: English) Sarah Croix, Afdeling for Arkaeologi og Kulturarvsstudier, Aarhus Universitet
Paper 1633-d:	**Medieval Norway's Urbanisation in a Danish Perspective** (Language: English) Olav Elias Gundersen, Institut for Kultur og Samfund, Afdeling for Historie og Klassiske Studier, Aarhus Universitet

Session:	**1634** **Leeds University Union: Room 2 - Elland Road**
Title:	**MEMORY, IDENTITY, AND EMOTIONS IN MEDIEVAL WELSH MONASTERIES**
Sponsor:	Monastic Wales Project
Organiser:	Janet Burton, School of Archaeology, History & Anthropology, University of Wales Trinity Saint David and Karen Stöber, Departament d'Història, Universitat de Lleida
Moderator:	Emilia Jamroziak, Institute for Medieval Studies / School of History, University of Leeds
Paper 1634-a:	**English or Welsh?: The Struggle for Dore Abbey** (Language: English) Ian Bass, Department of History, Politics & Philosophy, Manchester Metropolitan University
Paper 1634-b:	**Memory and History: St Padarn, Llanbadarn Fawr, and the Monks of Gloucester** (Language: English) Janet Burton
Paper 1634-c:	**Mourning Monks in Medieval Wales** (Language: English) Karen Stöber

Session: **1635** **Maurice Keyworth Building: Room 1.09**
Title: **RECORD, MEMORY, AND THE MAKING OF HISTORY, II: LAW AND ADMINISTRATION**
Sponsor: The National Archives
Organiser: Abigail Dorr, School of History & Heritage, University of Lincoln and Rebecca Searby, Centre for Medieval Studies, University of York
Moderator: Sean Cunningham, The National Archives, Kew
Paper 1635-a: **Going on the Record: Memory and the Law Courts in Late Medieval England** (Language: English)
Euan Roger, The National Archives, Kew
Paper 1635-b: **Some Records Are Worth More than Others: The Perception, Use, and Reception of Final Concords Made in the Court of John, Count of Mortain** (Language: English)
Richard Daines, School of History, University of East Anglia
Paper 1635-c: **Off the Record: Prosecuting a London Riot in 1517** (Language: English)
Shannon McSheffrey, Department of History, Concordia University, Montréal

---

Session: **1636** **Leeds University Union: Room 4 - Hyde Park**
Title: ***FIAT IUSTITIA*: THE PRACTICE OF LAW INSIDE AND OUTSIDE THE COURTS**
Organiser: IMC Programming Committee
Moderator: Matthew McHaffie, Department of History, King's College London
Paper 1636-a: **Remembering Rape in the Courts of 13th- and 14th-Century Ireland** (Language: English)
Bridgette Slavin, Department of Interdisciplinary Studies, Medaille College, New York
Paper 1636-b: **Between the Tactics of the Weak and the Technology of Power: Memory in a Florentine Criminal Court, c. 1343-1363** (Language: English)
Joseph Figliulo-Rosswurm, Department of History, University of California, Santa Barbara
Paper 1636-c: **Legal Business outside the Courts: Private and Public Houses as Spaces of Law in the 15th Century** (Language: English)
Edda Frankot, Research Institute of Irish & Scottish Studies, University of Aberdeen

---

Session: **1637** **Leeds University Union: Room 5 - Kirkstall Abbey**
Title: **COLLECTIVE MEMORY AND MEMORIAL CULTURE IN PARISH, TOWN, AND GUILD**
Organiser: Claire Kennan, Department of History, Royal Holloway, University of London
Moderator: Marianne Wilson, Department of Collections Expertise & Engagement, The National Archives, Kew
Paper 1637-a: **For the Good of the Soul: Memory and Remembrance in Parish Guilds** (Language: English)
Claire Kennan
Paper 1637-b: **'From time immemorial...': An Examination of Memory, Discourse, and Legal Consciousness in the 1388 Guild Petitions** (Language: English)
Daniella Gonzalez, Centre for Medieval & Early Modern Studies, University of Kent
Paper 1637-c: **Common Profit Books and Memorial Culture in 15th-Century London** (Language: English)
Ryan Perry, Centre for Medieval & Early Modern Studies, University of Kent

Session: **1638** **Michael Sadler Building: Room LG.15**
Title: **MAPPINGS, II: FUNCTIONS OF MEMORY ON MAPS**
Organiser: Felicitas Schmieder, Historisches Institut, FernUniversität Hagen and Dan Terkla, Department of English, Illinois Wesleyan University
Moderator: Dan Terkla
Paper 1638-a: **Memories of Antiquity: How Medieval Texts and Maps Remembered the Ancient Origin of the Concept of Continents** (Language: English)
Christoph Mauntel, Graduiertenkolleg 1662 'Religiöses Wissen im vormodernen Europa (800–1800)', Eberhard-Karls-Universität Tübingen
Paper 1638-b: **The Ancient World on Medieval Maps: Cultural Memory at Work?** (Language: English)
Monika Schuol, Lehrstuhl für Alte Geschichte, Katholische Universität Eichstätt-Ingolstadt
Paper 1638-c: **The *Monstra* of *Herzog Ernst* B as Foundation of Ambiguous Storytelling and Remembrance** (Language: English)
Olivia Kobiela, Promotionsverbund 'Die andere Ästhetik', Eberhard-Karls-Universität Tübingen

Session: **1639** **Maurice Keyworth Building: Room 1.03**
Title: **REMEMBERING THE ANGLO-SAXON PAST: PLACES, PEOPLE, LEGACIES**
Organiser: IMC Programming Committee
Moderator: Christiania Whitehead, Faculté des lettres, Université de Lausanne
Paper 1639-a: **The Memory of Mercia in the 9th- and 10th-Century Charters and Coins** (Language: English)
Yuta Uchikawa, Department of Occidental History, University of Tokyo
Paper 1639-b: **Remembering Bede in the 10th Century: An All-Monastic Church?** (Language: English)
Christopher Riedel, Department of History, Albion College, Michigan
Paper 1639-c: **St Hild: Her Monastery and Her Legacy** (Language: English)
Christiane Kroebel, Independent Scholar, Whitby

Session: **1640** **Stage@leeds: Stage 3**
Title: **ANCESTRAL ROOTS: MEMORY AND ARBOREAL IMAGERY ACROSS CULTURES, II - THE CHRISTIAN TRADITION**
Sponsor: Trames Arborescentes Project
Organiser: Pippa Salonius, School of Philosophical, Historical & International Studies, Monash University, Victoria and Naïs Virenque, Centre d'Études Supérieures de la Renaissance, Université François Rabelais, Tours
Moderator: Antoine Paris, Université Paris-Sorbonne, Paris / Université de Montréal, Québec
Paper 1640-a: **Beyond Eden: Arboreal Images in Female Mystical Literature** (Language: English)
Sergi Sancho Fibla, Temps, Espaces, Langages, Europe Méridionale - Méditerranée, Aix-Marseille Université
Paper 1640-b: **Apulian Trees and the Democritean Tradition of the Art of Memory: At the Crossroads of Latin and Graeco-Byzantine Rhetoric in 14th-Century Franciscan Culture** (Language: English)
Naïs Virenque
Paper 1640-c: **Back to the Garden** (Language: English)
Guita Lamsechi, Centre for Reformation & Renaissance Studies, University of Toronto, Downtown

Session: **1641** **Stage@leeds: Stage 2**
Title: ***DAMNATIO MEMORIAE*: WHAT WE CHOOSE TO FORGET**
Organiser: IMC Programming Committee
Moderator: Rebecca Usherwood, School of Classics, University of St Andrews
Paper 1641-a: **Reconsidering Gregory of Tours's *damnatio memoriae* of King Chilperich I (561-584)** (Language: English)
Michael Naidos, Department of History, Ionian University, Corfu
Paper 1641-b: **'In the Company of Demons': Condemnation of Constantine V as a Unique Case of *damnatio memoriae* in Post-Iconoclast Byzantium** (Language: English)
Ivan Marić, School of History, Classics & Archaeology, University of Edinburgh
Paper 1641-c: **Forgetting the Heretic: The Emperor Heraclius in the Byzantine Liturgical Tradition** (Language: English)
Anastasiia Sirotenko, Institut für Byzantinistik, Byzantinische Kunstgeschichte und Neogräzistik, Ludwig-Maximilians-Universität München

Session: **1642** **Stage@leeds: Stage 1**
Title: **MEMORIES OF WAR: UNDERSTANDING MEDIEVAL MILITARY HISTORY**
Sponsor: De Re Militari
Organiser: John France, Department of History, Swansea University
Moderator: David Bachrach, Department of History, University of New Hampshire
Paper 1642-a: **The Three Orders Reconsidered** (Language: English)
John France
Paper 1642-b: **Technology and Medieval Warfare** (Language: English)
Kelly DeVries, Department of History, Loyola University Maryland
Paper 1642-c: **The Right of Self-Defence and Its Implications** (Language: English)
Lawrence Duggan, Department of History, University of Delaware

Session: **1643** **Leeds University Union: Room 6 - Roundhay**
Title: **SHARP THINKING, I: EARLY MEDIEVAL SWORDS LAID TO REST**
Sponsor: Rijksmuseum van Oudheden, Leiden
Organiser: Annemarieke Willemsen, Rijksmuseum van Oudheden, Leiden
Moderator: Nelleke IJssennagger, Faculteit der Letteren, Rijksuniversiteit Groningen / Archaeological & Medieval Collections, Frisian Museum, Leeuwarden
Paper 1643-a: **Right by My Side: The Placement of Swords in Anglo-Saxon Graves** (Language: English)
Sue Brunning, British Museum, London
Paper 1643-b: **'As if a snake runs from the point and up to the hilt': The Ring-Sword from the 'Royal Grave' at Krefeld-Gellep Reconstructed** (Language: English)
Ulrich Lehmann, Landschaftsverband Westfalen-Lippe (LWL) - Archäologie für Westfalen, Münster
Paper 1643-c: **In the Right Place: The Placement of Carolingian Swords in Rivers** (Language: English)
Dušan Maczek, Faculteit Archeologie, Universiteit Leiden

Session: **1644** **Fine Art Building: SR 1.10**
Title: **ROME IN THE EARLY MEDIEVAL MEMORY**
Sponsor: Quaestiones Medii Aevi Novae
Organiser: Maksymilian Sas, Instytut Historyczny, Uniwersytet Warszawski
Moderator: Clemens Gantner, Institut für Mittelalterforschung, Österreichische Akademie der Wissenschaften, Wien

Paper 1644-a: **Rewrite Memory, Rebuild the City: The Narration about the City of Rome in the First Redactions of the *Liber Pontificalis*** (Language: English)
Andrea Antonio Verardi, Dipartimento di Storia, Università degli Studi di Roma 'La Sapienza' / Facoltà di Storia e Beni Culturali della Chiesa, Pontificia Università Gregoriana, Roma

Paper 1644-b: **King Caedwalla of Wessex in Rome: The Significance of the Cult of St Peter the Apostle for the Anglo-Saxons, c. 600-800** (Language: English)
Maksymilian Sas

Paper 1644-c: **Byzantine Rome in the Eyes of 9th-Century Romans** (Language: English)
Philipp Winterhager, Institut für Geschichtswissenschaften, Humboldt-Universität zu Berlin

---

Session: **1645** **Michael Sadler Building: Room LG.19**
Title: **CONTINUITY AND CONQUEST IN ENGLAND AND NORMANDY, IV: THE LOSS OF NORMANDY**
Sponsor: Haskins Society
Organiser: Alex Hurlow, Department of History, University of Manchester
Moderator: Leonie V. Hicks, School of Humanities, Canterbury Christ Church University

Paper 1645-a: **Remembering and Forgetting the 'Loss of Normandy'** (Language: English)
Daniel Power, Centre for Medieval & Early Modern Research (MEMO), Swansea University

Paper 1645-b: **Kingship and Continuity: Royal Authority after Conquest and Loss in 12th- and 13th-Century English Literature** (Language: English)
Charlotte Liebelt, School of Humanities, Canterbury Christ Church University

Paper 1645-c: **Memories of the Ducal Past: Identities in 13th-Century Normandy** (Language: English)
Alex Hurlow

Session:	**1646** **Emmanuel Centre: Room 10**
Title:	**TYPOLOGIES OF CONFLICT IN HIGH MEDIEVAL EUROPE, II**
Sponsor:	Centre for Advanced Studies, Norwegian Academy of Science and Letters, Oslo
Organiser:	Louisa Taylor, Institutt for arkeologi, konservering og historie, Universitetet i Oslo
Moderator:	Arnoud-Jan A. Bijsterveld, Department of Sociology, Tilburg University
Paper 1646-a:	**Re-Thinking 'War' in Medieval England** (Language: English) Stephen D. White, Department of History, Emory University
Paper 1646-b:	**How to Distinguish between Internal (Civil) and External Wars in Medieval Scandinavia** (Language: English) Hans Jacob Orning, Institutt for arkeologi, konservering og historie, Universitetet i Oslo
Paper 1646-c:	**Regicide, Fratricide, and Blinding: Eliminating Rival Kings and Contenders** (Language: English) Max Naderer, Institutt for arkeologi, konservering og historie, Universitetet i Oslo

Session:	**1647** **Baines Wing: Room 2.14**
Title:	**BURIALS AND MEMORY IN CONTEXT: FROM DISTURBED GRAVES TO BURIAL MONUMENTS**
Sponsor:	Department of Medieval Studies, Central European University, Budapest
Organiser:	József Laszlovszky, Department of Medieval Studies, Central European University, Budapest
Moderator:	Alice Choyke, Department of Medieval Studies, Central European University, Budapest
Paper 1647-a:	**Disturbed Graves and Bad Memories: Deviant Burials in the Northern Balkan Region and Their Archaeological, Religious, and Legal Context** (Language: English) Petar Parvanov, Department of Medieval Studies, Central European University, Budapest
Paper 1647-b:	**Desacred Memory: A Medieval Crime Unveiled - Disturbed Burials of Monks from the Cistercian Grange of Pomáz-Nagykovácsi** (Language: English) Mária Vargha, Department of Medieval Studies, Central European University, Budapest
Paper 1647-c:	**Loss of Memory: Thoughts on the Duration of Medieval Tombs** (Language: English) Robert Marcoux, Département d'histoire, Université Laval, Québec

Session:	**1648** **University House: St George Room**
Title:	**ENGAGING THE CRUSADES, II: PLAYING CRUSADERS**
Sponsor:	Routledge
Organiser:	Kristin Skottki, Lehrstuhl für Mittelalterliche Geschichte, Universität Bayreuth
Moderator:	Felix Hinz, Historisches Institut, Universität Paderborn
Paper 1648-a:	**A Sacred Task, No Cross Required: The Image of Crusading in Non-Christian Fantasy and Science Fiction Settings** (Language: English) Roland Wenskus, Independent Scholar, Bovenden
Paper 1648-b:	**Reimagining Crusaders in Fantasy Video Games** (Language: English) Victoria Cooper, School of English, University of Leeds
Paper 1648-c:	**Crusader Kings Too?: Representing the Crusades in Grand Strategy Computer Games** (Language: English) Robert Houghton, Department of History, University of Winchester

Session: **1649** **Parkinson Building: Nathan Bodington Chamber**
Title: **MEDIEVAL ECOCRITICISMS, I: WIND, WATER, WEATHER**
Sponsor: Medieval Ecocriticisms
Organiser: Heide Estes, Department of English, Monmouth University, New Jersey
Moderator: Heide Estes
Paper 1649-a: **'Westron Wynde': Blustery Emotions in Middle English Lyrics** (Language: English)
Michael J. Warren, Department of English, Royal Holloway, University of London
Paper 1649-b: **The Hydrosocial Medieval: Water, Weather, and Texts** (Language: English)
Bethany Whalley, Department of English Language & Literature, King's College London
Paper 1649-c: **When There Is No Weather: An Ecocritical Reading of Climate in *The Phoenix*** (Language: English)
Corinne Dale, Department of English, Royal Holloway, University of London

---

Session: **1650** **Maurice Keyworth Building: Room 1.31**
Title: **THE BODY PERFORMED AND DISCIPLINED: DOMINICAN PREACHING ON PENANCE IN THE CITY**
Sponsor: Prato Consortium for Medieval & Renaissance Studies, Monash University, Victoria
Organiser: Peter Francis Howard, Centre for Medieval & Renaissance Studies, Monash University, Victoria
Moderator: Holly Johnson, Department of English, Mississippi State University
Paper 1650-a: **The Preacher's Narrative Body: Teaching Confession through Performance to the Community** (Language: English)
Anne Holloway, Centre for Medieval & Renaissance Studies, Monash University, Victoria
Paper 1650-b: **Whipping the Masses: The Discourse on Flagellation in de Bertis's Public Sermons** (Language: English)
Stephanie Jury, School of Philosophical, Historical & International Studies, Monash University, Victoria
Paper 1650-c: ***Convertimini*: Preaching and Penance in Renaissance Florence** (Language: English)
Peter Francis Howard

Session: **1651** **Baines Wing: Room 2.15**
Title: **LAND AND SEA IN ITALY**
Organiser: IMC Programming Committee
Moderator: Luciano Gallinari, Istituto di Storia dell'Europa Mediterranea (ISEM), Consiglio Nazionale delle Ricerche, Cagliari
Paper 1651-a: **Navires et navigation en Sicile à l époque de la conquête normande** (Language: Français)
Philippe Tisseyre, Soprintendenza del Mare, Palermo
Paper 1651-b: **Measuring Space and Memorising Place in Late Medieval Florence** (Language: English)
Anna Pomierny-Wąsińska, Tadeusz Manteuffel Institute of History, Polish Academy of Sciences, Warszawa
Paper 1651-c: **Coping with the Crisis: The Sienese State and the Development of Transhumance in Late Middle Ages, Southern Tuscany, 1353-1419** (Language: English)
Davide Cristoferi, Vakgroep Geschiedenis, Universiteit Gent

Session:	**1653**	**Emmanuel Centre: Room 11**
Title:	**LOOKING BACK ON CLASSICAL MYTHS IN DANTE AND BOCCACCIO**	
Organiser:	IMC Programming Committee	
Moderator:	Matthew Treherne, School of Languages, Cultures & Societies - Italian / Leeds Centre for Dante Studies, University of Leeds	
Paper 1653-a:	**La riscrittura di un mito classico: l'amore tragico di Didone in Dante** (Language: Italiano) Ginetta De Trane, Dipartimento di Studi Umanistici, Università del Salento, Lecce	
Paper 1653-b:	**Dido in Boccaccio: Reception and Poetic Memory of a Tragic Myth** (Language: English) Sabina Tuzzo, Dipartimento di Studi Umanistici, Università del Salento, Lecce	
Paper 1653-c:	**Conceptions of Mythological History in Boccaccio's *Genealogy of the Pagan Gods*** (Language: English) Jon Solomon, Department of the Classics, University of Illinois, Urbana-Champaign	

Session:	**1654**	**Baines Wing: Room G.37**
Title:	**MUSIC AND MEMORY IN MONASTIC CONTEXTS**	
Organiser:	IMC Programming Committee	
Moderator:	Peter Jeffery, Department of Music & Sacred Music, University of Notre Dame, Indiana	
Paper 1654-a:	**The Ripoll's Tonary: The Use of Memory and Mnemonics to Learn Music in the Year 1000** (Language: English) Joan Maria Martí Mendoza, Institut de Ciències de l'Educació, Universitat Autònoma de Barcelona	
Paper 1654-b:	**Apophatic Theology and Silent Memory in Late Medieval Singing** (Language: English) Eliza Jane Cassey, Faculty of Music, University of Toronto, Downtown	
Paper 1654-c:	**Memory and Liturgy: Transformative Remembering in Bernard of Clairvaux** (Language: English) Line Cecilie Engh, Istituto di Norvegia, Roma / Institutt for filosofi, ide- og kunsthistorie og klassiske språk, Universitetet i Oslo	

LUNCH

Meal Times

Refectory	12.00-14.00
University Square: The Marquee	12.00-14.00

See Map 9, p. 51.

MEDIEVAL HIGHLIGHTS FROM LEEDS UNIVERSITY LIBRARY SPECIAL COLLECTIONS

PARKINSON BUILDING: TREASURES OF THE BROTHERTON GALLERY
12.00-14.00

Join us for a drop-in session to see medieval treasures from Special Collections at the University of Leeds. Special Collections staff will be in the Treasures of the Brotherton Gallery with a selection of highlights from the collections for delegates to examine close-up.

The collections at Leeds contain beautiful illuminated 15th-century French and Flemish books of hours, psalters, and prayer books, as well as German chained manuscripts from the 1450s. Some of these will be on show alongside examples from our fine collection of incunabula. The Library of Ripon Cathedral is held on long-term deposit in Special Collections at the University of Leeds and includes a Latin Bible from the 13th century. A highlight of the Yorkshire Archaeological and Historical Society Collection is the enormous series of surviving court rolls of the manor of Wakefield (1274-1925). Also for the first time at the IMC, we will be revealing examples from our extensive coin collection.

Special Collections houses over 200,000 rare books and 7 km of manuscripts and archives, including the celebrated Brotherton Collection. The Special Collections Reading Room is open from 09.00-17.00 during the IMC, and delegates are welcome to pursue their research and explore the collection. More details on how to search and use the collections can be found at https://library.leeds.ac.uk/special-collections.

ANNUAL MEETING IN STAGE@LEEDS

HOSTED BY
DE RE MILITARI

STAGE@LEEDS: STAGE 1
13.00-14.00

Begun in 1992, De Re Militari is the Society for the Study of Medieval Military History. We would like to invite our members and all interested delegates to attend our annual meeting, which will take place after its session 'Memories of War: Understanding Medieval Military History'.

Session:	**1701** **Baines Wing: Room 1.13**
Title:	**ALFREDIAN VOICES, II: ENGLISH PROSE BEFORE AND AFTER ALFRED**
Organiser:	Francis Leneghan, Faculty of English Language & Literature, University of Oxford
Moderator:	Courtnay Konshuh, Department of History, St Thomas More College, University of Saskatchewan
Paper 1701-a:	**A Choir of Alfredian Voices: Exploring the Construction of Royal Authority in Alfred's *Domboc* and some Peripheral Works** (Language: English) Matthew Gillis, Faculty of English Language & Literature, University of Oxford
Paper 1701-b:	**Early Sources of the *Anglo-Saxon Chronicle*: A Reconsideration** (Language: English) John Quanrud, Independent Scholar, London
Paper 1701-c:	**Boethius and St Eustace in Anglo-Saxon England: The Reception of the Old English *Boethius* and the Old English *Passio Sancti Eustachii*** (Language: English) James McIntosh, Department of Anglo-Saxon, Norse & Celtic, University of Cambridge

Session:	**1702** **Michael Sadler Building: Room LG.17**
Title:	**THE SICULO-NORMAN LEGACY: ARCHAEOLOGY, ART, AND ARCHITECTURE**
Sponsor:	Department of History, Lancaster University
Organiser:	John Aspinwall, Department of History, Lancaster University
Moderator:	Theresa Jäckh, Transkulturelle Studien, Ruprecht-Karls-Universität Heidelberg
Paper 1702-a:	**The Norman Conquest of Malta: An Analysis of Its Rural Landscape Transformation Process** (Language: English) Keith Buhagiar, Department of Archaeology & Classics, University of Malta
Paper 1702-b:	**The Siculo-Norman Imprint on Malta's Muslim Medina** (Language: English) Charlene Vella, Department of Art & Art History, Faculty of Arts, University of Malta
Paper 1702-c:	**False Memories?: The Transformation of Norman Culture during and after the Conquest of Sicily as Showcased by the Archaeological Evidence** (Language: English) Nicole Mölk, Institut für Archäologien, Universität Innsbruck

Session:	**1703** **Michael Sadler Building: Room LG.16**
Title:	**BYZANTINE STUDIES IN CHINA, III: ON THE LAND ROUTE OF THE SILK ROAD**
Organiser:	Stefanos Kordosis, Department of Hellenic Civilization, Hellenic Open University, Greece
Moderator:	Lin Ying, Department of History, Sun Yat-sen University, China
Paper 1703-a:	**On Byzantine Bracteate Coins Found in China** (Language: English) Yun-yan Guo, School of History, Hebei University, China
Paper 1703-b:	**The Tibetan Title *Dru gu Gesar* (Caesar of the Turks) in the Northern Branch of the Silk Route and the Role of the Khazars** (Language: English) Stefanos Kordosis
Paper 1703-c:	**Reconsideration on the Embassies between Byzantium and Western Turks** (Language: English) Li Qiang, Institute for the History of Ancient Civilisations, Northeast Normal University, China

Session: **1704** **Fine Art Building: SR G.04**
Title: **RELIGIOUS PRAXIS AND PASTORAL CARE IN EARLY MEDIEVAL IBERIA, II: LEARNING**
Sponsor: Presbyters in the Late Antique West Project, Uniwersytet Warszawski
Organiser: Kati Ihnat, Afdeling Geschiedenis, Radboud Universiteit Nijmegen, Marta Szada, Instytut Historyczny, Uniwersytet Warszawski and Jamie Wood, School of History & Heritage, University of Lincoln
Moderator: Robert Wiśniewski, Instytut Historyczny, Uniwersytet Warszawski
Paper 1704-a: **Do You Need a Priest to Be a Christian?: Pastoral Care and Lay Piety in Visigothic Spain** (Language: English)
Marta Szada
Paper 1704-b: **Learning by Example?: Commemoration of Saints in Early Medieval Iberia** (Language: English)
Kati Ihnat
Paper 1704-c: **Canons without Councils in Early Medieval Iberia** (Language: English)
Graham Barrett, School of History & Heritage, University of Lincoln

---

Session: **1705** **Parkinson Building: Room 1.16**
Title: **BIBLIOPHILES AND WORKSHOPS: ILLUMINATED BOOKS OF HOURS FROM 15TH-CENTURY PARIS**
Sponsor: Chester Beatty Library, Dublin Castle / Trinity College Dublin
Organiser: Jill Unkel, Chester Beatty Library, Dublin Castle
Moderator: Laura Cleaver, Department of History of Art & Architecture, Trinity College Dublin
Paper 1705-a: **The Admiral and the Bastard: Their Prayer-Books Contrasted** (Language: English)
Richard Gameson, Department of History, Durham University
Paper 1705-b: **Between Paris and Persia: 15th-Century Manuscript Materiality in Europe and the Islamic World** (Language: English)
Kristine Rose-Beers, Chester Beatty Library, Dublin Castle
Paper 1705-c: **Inhabiting the Margins: The Coëtivy Hours Marginalia** (Language: English)
Jill Unkel

Session: **1706** **Michael Sadler Building: Rupert Beckett Theatre**
Title: **NEW STUDIES ON HISTORIOGRAPHICAL MANUSCRIPTS, II: READERS AND USERS**
Sponsor: H37 - Histoire & Cultures Graphiques, Université catholique de Louvain, Louvain-la-Neuve
Organiser: Antoine Brix, Département d'histoire, Université catholique de Louvain, Louvain-la-Neuve
Moderator: Paul Bertrand, Faculté de Philosophie, Arts et Lettres, Université catholique de Louvain, Louvain-la-Neuve
Paper 1706-a: **In Search of Burgundian Historiography: A Tour of Philip the Good's Library** (Language: English)
Antoine Brix
Paper 1706-b: **The Second Life of the *Dalimil's Chronicle*, 1309-1314: Textual Flow and New Publics in the 14th and 15th Centuries** (Language: English)
Éloïse Adde, Institut d'Histoire, Université du Luxembourg, Belval
Paper 1706-c: **Who Read the *Fleur des Histoires* by Jean Mansel?** (Language: English)
Anh Thy Nguyen, Département des langues et lettres françaises et romanes, Université catholique de Louvain, Louvain-la-Neuve

Session: **1707** **Fine Art Building: Studio Ground Floor**
Title: **CONTRA IUDAEOS, CONTRA CHRISTIANOS**
Organiser: IMC Programming Committee
Moderator: Eva Frojmovic, Centre for Jewish Studies, University of Leeds
Paper 1707-a: **Contra 'Christianos-Contra-Iudaeos': *Sefer Yosippon*'s Response to *Pseudo-Hegesippus*** (Language: English)
Carson Bay, Department of Religion, Florida State University
Paper 1707-b: **'The Blood cries out...': 13th-Century Ritual Murder Narrative(s) and Anti-Jewish Polemic** (Language: English)
Irven Resnick, Department of Philosophy & Religion, University of Tennessee, Chattanooga
Paper 1707-c: **The Croxton *Play of the Sacrament* and Collective Memory** (Language: English)
Maija Birenbaum, Department of Languages & Literatures, University of Wisconsin-Whitewater

Session: **1708** **Baines Wing: Room 2.13**
Title: **NARRATIVE AND PERSUASIVE TOOLS IN LATE ANTIQUE POETRY**
Organiser: IMC Programming Committee
Moderator: Danuta Shanzer, Institut für Klassische Philologie, Mittel- und Neulatein, Universität Wien
Paper 1708-a: **Time, Cultural Memory, and Persuasion: Some Observations on Dracontius's *Satisfactio*** (Language: English)
Maria Jennifer Falcone, Institut für Alte Sprachen - Klassische Philologie, Friedrich-Alexander-Universität Erlangen-Nürnberg
Paper 1708-b: ***Nec mora*: Delay in Biblical Epic** (Language: English)
Amy Oh, Department of Classics, Skidmore College, New York
Paper 1708-c: **Ausonius *Epistula* 6: *Monstrum illud semigraecum*** (Language: English)
Willum Westenholz, Institut für Klassische Philologie, Mittel- und Neulatein, Universität Wien

Session: **1709** **Baines Wing: Room 2.16**
Title: **SCRUTINISING SCRIPTURE: SACRED AND SEMINAL**
Sponsor: Society for the Study of the Bible in the Middle Ages
Organiser: Gail Lesley Blick, Independent Scholar, Monmouth
Moderator: William P. Hyland, School of Divinity, University of St Andrews
Paper 1709-a: **Reading the Bible and Seeing Christ Coincidentally: Nicholas of Cusa's Use of the Bible** (Language: English)
Joshua Hollmann, Department of Theology, Concordia College, New York
Paper 1709-b: **Reading the Bible with Joan of Arc** (Language: English)
Nancy J. Shaffer, Department of Communications, Design & Culture, California University of Pennsylvania
Paper 1709-c: **All in the Mind?: The Memory Topos, the Bible, and Women's Education** (Language: English)
Gail Lesley Blick

Session: **1710** **Baines Wing: Room 1.16**
Title: **ROYAL SAINTS IN POST-REFORMATION HISTORIOGRAPHY**
Sponsor: Nexus Nidaros
Organiser: Magne Njåstad, Institutt for historiske studier, Norges teknisk-naturvitenskapelige universitet, Trondheim
Moderator: Erik Opsahl, Institutt for historiske studier, Norges teknisk-naturvitenskapelige universitet, Trondheim
Paper 1710-a: **St Olaf in 16th- to 18th-Century Norwegian Historiography** (Language: English)
Magne Njåstad
Paper 1710-b: **St Erik in Swedish Historiography from Reformation to Enlightenment** (Language: English)
Henrik Ågren, Historiska Institutionen, Uppsala Universitet
Paper 1710-c: **St Stephen in Early Modern Hungarian Historiography** (Language: English)
Gergely Tóth, Department of History, Hungarian Academy of Sciences, Budapest

Session: **1711** **Baines Wing: Room 1.15**
Title: **IDENTITY IN THE MEDIEVAL ADRIATIC REGION**
Organiser: IMC Programming Committee
Moderator: Zrinka Nikolić Jakus, Department of History, University of Zagreb
Paper 1711-a: **Queen Jelena between Two Worlds: The Icon of St Peter and St Paul** (Language: English)
Marija Mihajlovic Shipley, Courtauld Institute of Art, University of London
Paper 1711-b: **Ritual and Text: Narrative Strategies of Thomas of Split's *Historia Salonitana*** (Language: English)
Dušan Zupka, Institute of History, Slovak Academy of Sciences, Bratislava
Paper 1711-c: **Forging the 'Shield of the Dominant': The Istrian Peninsula in Medieval Venetian Chronicles** (Language: English)
Josip Banic, Department of Medieval Studies, Central European University, Budapest

Session: **1713** **University House: Beechgrove Room**
Title: **POETS, WARRIORS, AND VIRGINS: REMEMBERING WOMEN IN MEDIEVALIST LITERATURE**
Organiser: Anna McKay, School of Literatures, Languages & Cultures - English Literature, University of Edinburgh
Moderator: Sarah Dunnigan, School of Literatures, Languages & Cultures, University of Edinburgh
Paper 1713-a: **'There is no friend like a sister': Rewriting the Medieval Minstrelsy Tradition in Christina Rossetti's 'Goblin Market' and Adelaide Procter's 'A Legend of Provence'** (Language: English)
Anna McKay
Paper 1713-b: **'But no living man am I!': Constructing and Empowering the Female Voice in J. R. R. Tolkien's Legendarium** (Language: English)
Anahit Behrooz, School of Literatures, Languages & Cultures - English Literature, University of Edinburgh
Paper 1713-c: **Evading Capture: Reinventing the Life of Christine Carpenter, Anchoress of Shere, in Popular Culture** (Language: English)
Joanna Witkowska, Department of English Literature, University of Edinburgh

Session: **1714** **Charles Thackrah Building: 1.01**
Title: **CONTESTED SCHOLASTICISM**
Organiser: Robert Porwoll, School of Divinity, University of Chicago, Illinois
Moderator: Jonathan Lyon, Department of History, University of Chicago, Illinois
Paper 1714-a: **The Cup of Demons: Walter of St Victor's *Contra quatuor labyrinthos Franciae*** (Language: English)
Jennifer Timmons, Department of History, University of Chicago, Illinois
Paper 1714-b: **John of Salisbury and the Neo-Abelardian Method** (Language: English)
Robert Porwoll
Paper 1714-c: **Bradwardine and Valla: The Post-Scholastic Intersection of Predestination and the Philosophy of Time** (Language: English)
Sean Hannan, Department of Humanities, MacEwan University, Alberta
Paper 1714-d: **Scholasticism Deconstructed: Nicholas de Clamanges' *De studio theologico*** (Language: English)
Matthew Vanderpoel, Divinity School, University of Chicago, Illinois / Histoire de la philosophie médiévale, Collège de France

Session: **1715** **Maurice Keyworth Building: Room 1.33**
Title: **COLLECTIVE DISPLAY: MEDIEVAL OBJECTS OUT OF ISOLATION, II**
Sponsor: Meadows Museum, Southern Methodist University, Dallas
Organiser: Amanda W. Dotseth, Meadows Museum, Southern Methodist University, Dallas
Moderator: Ana Cabrera-Lafuente, Victoria & Albert Museum, London
Paper 1715-a: **The More the Mary-er: Collections of Marian Sculptures and Castilian Marian Poetry** (Language: English)
Maeve Marta O'Donnell-Morales, Department of Art History, Courtauld Insitute of Art, University of London
Paper 1715-b: **Beloved Diamonds and Bedside Statues: Aesthetic Appreciation and Affection in the Late Medieval Collection** (Language: English)
Marguerite A. Keane, Department of Art History, Drew University, New Jersey
Paper 1715-c: **The Virgin and Child of Jeanne d'Evreux: Old Treasury or Modern Masterpiece?** (Language: English)
Diane Antille, Institut d'histoire de l'art et de muséologie, Université de Neuchâtel

Session: **1716** **Maurice Keyworth Building: Room 1.04**
Title: **THE MEDIEVAL LAW COURTS, III: THE INNS OF COURT**
Sponsor: The Honourable Society of Gray's Inn
Organiser: Daniel F. Gosling, Department of Archives, The Honourable Society of Gray's Inn, London
Moderator: Euan Roger, The National Archives, Kew
Paper 1716-a: **Proto-Political Clubs?: The Inns of Court and Parliament in the 15th Century** (Language: English)
Hannes Kleineke, History of Parliament Trust, London
Paper 1716-b: **Engendering Erudition: Masculinity and Legal Authority in the Inns of Court, c. 1350-1550** (Language: English)
E. Amanda McVitty, School of Humanities, Massey University, New Zealand
Paper 1716-c: **Medieval Memory at the Inns of Court: The Legal Precedents Cited in Burdett versus Abbot, 1811** (Language: English)
Daniel F. Gosling

Session: **1717** **Social Sciences Building: Room 10.05**
Title: **SHAPING THE PAST AFTER THE CAROLINGIAN EMPIRE, III: MATERIAL CULTURE AND RULERSHIP**
Sponsor: After Empire: Using & Not Using the Past in the Crisis of the Carolingian World, c. 900-1050
Organiser: Alice Hicklin, Friedrich-Meinecke-Institut, Freie Universität Berlin
Moderator: Alice Hicklin
Paper 1717-a: **The Transformation of the European Monetary Economy in the 10th and 11th Centuries** (Language: English)
Rory Naismith, Department of History, King's College London
Paper 1717-b: **Embodying the Past: Remembering the Merovingians at their Burial Sites in the 10th and 11th Centuries** (Language: English)
Sarah Greer, St Andrews Institute of Mediaeval Studies, University of St Andrews
Paper 1717-c: **Pasts and Presents in the Lothar Crystal** (Language: English)
Simon MacLean, School of History, University of St Andrews

Session: **1718** **Michael Sadler Building: Room LG.10**
Title: ***VOM MITTELALTERLICHEN KRIEGE*: CLAUSEWITZIAN APPROACHES IN REGARDS TO MEDIEVAL WAR**
Sponsor: Centrum för medeltidsstudier, Stockholms universitet
Organiser: Hörður Barðdal, Independent Scholar, Wachtebeke
Moderator: Kurt Villads Jensen, Historiska institutionen, Stockholms universitet
Paper 1718-a: **Remembering the Medieval(ist): Clausewitzian (Mis)Conceptions of Medieval Warfare** (Language: English)
Hörður Barðdal
Paper 1718-b: **Military Cohesion on the Third Crusade** (Language: English)
Stephen Bennett, Queen Mary, University of London
Paper 1718-c: **On (Medieval) War: Pierre Dubois, Strategy, and Statecraft at the Dawn of the 14th Century** (Language: English)
Daniel Franke, Department of History, Richard Bland College of William & Mary, Virginia

Session: **1719** **Baines Wing: Room 1.14**
Title: **MEDIEVAL POWER AND LETTERS, III: DANISH KINGSHIP AND ENGLISH ROYAL WOMEN**
Sponsor: Centre for Medieval & Renaissance Research, University of Winchester
Organiser: Gordon McKelvie, Department of History, University of Winchester
Moderator: Karl Christian Alvestad, Department of History, University of Winchester
Paper 1719-a: **Long Live the King, the King is Dead!: The Usage of Titular Kingship in Letters during the Danish Royal War in 1250** (Language: English)
Kerstin Hundahl, Historiska Institutionen, Lunds Universitet
Paper 1719-b: **'I may labor a gwd and loweng vay be twxst you': Mediating Anglo-Scottish Diplomacy in the Letters of Margaret Tudor, Queen of Scots, 1489-1541** (Language: English)
Helen Newsome, School of English, University of Sheffield
Paper 1719-c: **'To forgeve and pardonn me my greatt and haynusse crym': Understanding the Elizabethan Succession Crisis through the Letters of Ladies Katherine and Mary Grey** (Language: English)
Lynsey Wood, Department of History, University of Lancaster

Session: **1720** — **Charles Thackrah Building: 1.02**
Title: **JUSTICE, RIGHTS, AND TRADE IN NORTHERN EUROPE**
Organiser: IMC Programming Committee
Moderator: Igor Filippov, Faculty of History, Lomonosov Moscow State University
Paper 1720-a: **Labor, Community Memory, and Malicious Interpretation** (Language: English)
Alexis Becker, Society of Fellows in the Liberal Arts, University of Chicago, Illinois
Paper 1720-b: **Rules and Common Practice at the Market: Comparing Medieval Laws in Northern Europe** (Language: English)
Sofia Gustafsson, Institutionen för studier av samhällsutveckling och kultur, Linköpings Universitet
Paper 1720-c: **The Yeoman Quest in the Robin Hood Ballads** (Language: English)
Megan Woosley-Goodman, Department of English, Francis Marion University, South Carolina

---

Session: **1721** — **Social Sciences Building: Room 10.06**
Title: **MEMORABILIA OF ANTIQUITY: REMEMBERING ANCIENT WRITINGS IN MEDIEVAL TEXTS**
Organiser: IMC Programming Committee
Moderator: N. Kıvılcım Yavuz, Den Arnamagnæanske Samling, Københavns Universitet
Paper 1721-a: **Memory of the Ancient Philosophers in Late Medieval Bohemia: Jan Hus and His Personal Introductions to the Quodlibetal Dispute** (Language: English)
Martin Dekarli, Institut für Mittelalterforschung, Österreichische Akademie der Wissenschaften, Wien / Filozofická Fakulta, Univerzita Hradec Králové
Paper 1721-b: **Medieval Medical Memory: Remembering the Ancients** (Language: English)
Mujeeb Khan, Department of Area Studies, University of Tokyo

Session: **1722** — **University House: Cloberry Room**
Title: **NEW PERSPECTIVES ON THE STUDY OF ICELANDIC SAGAS AND MANUSCRIPTS**
Organiser: IMC Programming Committee
Moderator: Philip Cardew, Leeds Beckett University / Institute for Medieval Studies, University of Leeds
Paper 1722-a: **Old Norse-Latin Bilingualism in Arnamagnæan Manuscripts** (Language: English)
Astrid Maria Katharina Marner, Nordisk Forskningsinstitut, Københavns Universitet
Paper 1722-b: **Jarl Sigvaldi's Memory Gap in *Jómsvíkinga saga*: A Chance to What?** (Language: English)
Michael Irlenbusch-Reynard, Abteilung für Skandinavische Sprachen und Literaturen, Rheinische Friedrich-Wilhelms-Universität Bonn

Session: **1723** **Emmanuel Centre: Wilson Room**
Title: **REMEMBERING SAINTS IN TEXT AND IMAGE**
Organiser: IMC Programming Committee
Moderator: Julian Gardner, Department of the History of Art, University of Warwick
Paper 1723-a: **Odard's Circumcision: The Memory of St William of Norwich Explored through Secular Sources** (Language: English)
Julia Tomlinson Czesnik, Centre for Medieval Studies, University of Toronto, Downtown
Paper 1723-b: **Creating the Memory of the Early Augustinian Saints** (Language: English)
Krisztina Ilko, Pembroke College, University of Cambridge
Paper 1723-c: **The Memory of St Thomas Aquinas in Illuminated Manuscripts** (Language: English)
Mie Kuroiwa, College of Intercultural Communication, Rikkyo University, Tokyo

Session: **1724** **Charles Thackrah Building: 1.04**
Title: **FRAMING MURDER IN THE EARLY MEDIEVAL LEGAL IMAGINATION**
Sponsor: Institut für Mittelalterforschung, Österreichische Akademie der Wissenschaften, Wien
Organiser: Thomas Gobbitt, Institut für Mittelalterforschung, Österreichische Akademie der Wissenschaften, Wien
Moderator: Alice Rio, Department of History, King's College London
Paper 1724-a: **Legal Prologues and the Justification of Anglo-Saxon Law Codes** (Language: English)
Arendse Lund, Department of English, University College London
Paper 1724-b: **Murder, Killing, and Intent in the Lombard Laws** (Language: English)
Thomas Gobbitt
Paper 1724-c: **'Cantus de fontibus romanis': Roman Legal Thought on *Caedes, Homicidium, Dolus,* and *Culpa*** (Language: English)
Jaqueline Bemmer, Institut für Römisches Recht und Antike Rechtsgeschichte, Universität Wien

Session: **1725** **Michael Sadler Building: Banham Theatre**
Title: **MEMORY AND MENTAL HEALTH**
Sponsor: Premodern Health, Disease & Disability, Amsterdam University Press
Organiser: Tyler Cloherty, Amsterdam University Press
Moderator: Christina Lee, School of English, University of Nottingham
Paper 1725-a: **Memory and Forgetfulness in Monastic Communities in Medieval Normandy** (Language: English)
Elma Brenner, Wellcome Library, London
Paper 1725-b: **Bad Memory as a Pedagogical Tool in the *Conde Lucanor*** (Language: English)
Vivian Mills, Department of Spanish & Portuguese Studies, University of Washington
Paper 1725-c: ***Sane memoria*, Law, and the Custom of Memory in Medieval England** (Language: English)
Wendy J. Turner, Department of History, Anthropology & Philosophy, Augusta University, Georgia

Session: **1726** **Social Sciences Building: Room 10.07**
Title: **GEARS OF MEMORY: READING, LEARNING, AND WRITING IN THE NUNNERY**
Organiser: Sergi Sancho Fibla, Temps, Espaces, Langages, Europe Méridionale - Méditerranée, Aix-Marseille Université
Moderator: Sergi Sancho Fibla
Paper 1726-a: **Devotion and Learning: Presence of Liturgical Books in Barcelona during the 15th Century** (Language: English)
Oriol Murall Debasa, Departament d'Història i Arqueologia, Universitat de Barcelona
Paper 1726-b: **Female Scribes at the Royal Convent of Las Huelgas of Burgos** (Language: English)
David Catalunya, Lehrstuhl für Musikwissenschaften, Julius-Maximilians-Universität Würzburg
Paper 1726-c: **'Ego, Flora, abbatissa': The Making of Female Memory in 10th-Century León** (Language: English)
Laura Cayrol Bernardo, Centre de Recherches Historiques, École des Hautes Études en Sciences Sociales (EHESS), Université de recherche Paris Sciences et Lettres

---

Session: **1727** **Maurice Keyworth Building: Room 1.32**
Title: **EARLY MODERN MEDIEVALISMS**
Organiser: IMC Programming Committee
Moderator: Kirsty Day, School of History, Classics & Archaeology, University of Edinburgh
Paper 1727-a: **A House of Holiness at the Ends of the Earth: Medieval Memories in the Convents of New France** (Language: English)
Karen Blough, Department of Art, State University of New York, Plattsburgh
Paper 1727-b: **Remembering the Virgins: Women and the Medieval Past in *The Lives of Women Saints of Our Country of England*** (Language: English)
Hwanhee Park, Department of English Language & Literature, Incheon National University, South Korea
Paper 1727-c: **'Atlante que fuerte acaudilla': Reception, Construction, and Reconstruction of Castilian Epics in Modern Spanish Theatre** (Language: English)
Alberto Escalante-Varona, Facultad de Filosofía y Letras, Universidad de Extremadura, Cáceres
Paper 1727-d: **Echoes of St Bernard in a 16th-Century *Libellus* to Pope Leo X** (Language: English)
James Kroemer, Department of Theology, Concordia University, Wisconsin

Session:	**1728** **Maurice Keyworth Building: Room G.02**
Title:	**MEMORIES OF HERESY AND COUNTER-HERESY, III: TEXTUAL FORMATION**
Sponsor:	Department for the Study of Religions, Masarykova univerzita, Brno / Medieval Heresy & Dissent Research Network, University of Nottingham
Organiser:	David Zbíral, Department for the Study of Religions, Masarykova univerzita, Brno
Moderator:	Louisa A. Burnham, Department of History, Middlebury College, Vermont
Paper 1728-a:	**Looking through Someone Else's Eyes: Heretics, Inquisitors, Scholars, and the Sources** (Language: English) Luca Fois, Independent Scholar, Robbiate
Paper 1728-b:	**Waldensian Textual Memory of Durand of Huesca's *Liber Antiheresis*** (Language: English) Jack Baigent, Department of History, University of Nottingham
Paper 1728-c:	**Holy Simplicity and the Simple Souls: Forgotten Heresy in a 15th-Century Camaldolese Manuscript** (Language: English) Justine Trombley, Pontifical Institute of Mediaeval Studies, University of Toronto, Downtown

Session:	**1729** **Maurice Keyworth Building: Room 1.06**
Title:	**RELIGIOUS ART AS A REFLECTION OF CONTEMPORARY CONCERNS**
Organiser:	IMC Programming Committee
Moderator:	Maria Portmann, Kunsthistorisches Institut, Universität Zürich
Paper 1729-a:	**Between Word and Image: The Frescoes of San Vittore in Bologna, 12th Century** (Language: English) Fabio Massaccesi, Dipartimento delle Arti visive, performative e mediali, Università di Bologna
Paper 1729-b:	**The Remembrance of Death: Ascetic Example in 13th-Century Italy** (Language: English) Amelia Hope-Jones, Department of History of Art, University of Edinburgh
Paper 1729-c:	**Remembering the Middle Ages in Post-Colonial Religious Paintings in Santiago de Chile** (Language: English) Maisa Candela Cardemil Barros, Departamento de Teoría e Historia de las Artes, Universidad de Chile, Santiago

Session:	**1730** **Charles Thackrah Building: 1.03**
Title:	**MEMORY AND CONFLICT**
Sponsor:	University of Kent
Organiser:	Noah Smith, Centre for Medieval & Early Modern Studies (MEMS), University of Kent
Moderator:	Emily Davenport Guerry, School of History, University of Kent
Paper 1730-a:	**The Chest of Courtrai: Remembering the Battle of the Golden Spurs** (Language: English) Noah Smith
Paper 1730-b:	**Robert Dod, Edward the Confessor, and the Memorialisation of a Century of Conflict Within the Parish Church of Faversham, Kent** (Language: English) Angela Websdale, Centre for Medieval & Early Modern Studies (MEMS), University of Kent
Paper 1730-c:	**The Memory of an Heir: The Commemoration of the Black Prince in Word and Image** (Language: English) Sophie Kelly, Centre for Medieval & Early Modern Studies (MEMS), University of Kent

Session:	**1731** **Maurice Keyworth Building: Room 1.05**
Title:	**MEMORY, THE MATERIAL, AND THE MIDDLE AGES, III**
Sponsor:	National Museums Scotland
Organiser:	Katie Stevenson, St Andrews Institute of Mediaeval Studies, University of St Andrews
Moderator:	Katie Stevenson
Paper 1731-a:	**A Sign of Victory?: 'Scottish Swords' and Other Weapons in the Possession of 'Our Enemies' in the Late Middle Ages** (Language: English) Ralph Moffat, Glasgow Museums, Glasgow
Paper 1731-b:	**The Eglinton Tournament and Medieval Romanticism in Scottish National Identity** (Language: English) Sonny Angus, Department of Scottish History & Archaeology, National Museums Scotland, Edinburgh / University of Edinburgh
Paper 1731-c:	**Knights of the Gael: The Tartan-Medieval Hybrid in 19th-Century Scotland** (Language: English) Stuart Allan, Department of Scottish History & Archaeology, National Museums Scotland, Edinburgh

Session:	**1732** **Social Sciences Building: Room 10.09**
Title:	**AT THE CROSSROADS OF EMPIRES: SANT'AMBROGIO AT MONTECORVINO ROVELLA - A *LOCUS MEMORIAE* IN SOUTHERN LOMBARDY, III**
Organiser:	Francesca Dell'Acqua, Centre for Byzantine, Ottoman & Modern Greek Studies, University of Birmingham
Moderator:	Leslie Brubaker, Centre for Byzantine, Ottoman & Modern Greek Studies / Institute of Archaeology & Antiquity, University of Birmingham
Paper 1732-a:	**The Mother of God Takes Centre Stage: In Memory of Rome and Byzantium?** (Language: English) Francesca Dell'Acqua
Paper 1732-b:	**Tracing Radiation: Physical and Rendered Light in Sant'Ambrogio at Montecorvino Rovella** (Language: English) Andrea Mattiello, Centre for Byzantine, Ottoman & Modern Greek Studies, University of Birmingham
Respondent:	Daniel K. Reynolds, Centre for Byzantine, Ottoman & Modern Greek Studies, University of Birmingham

Session:	**1733** **Baines Wing: Room G.36**
Title:	**IN HONOUR OF RICHARD HOLT, III: OF MILLS AND MEDIEVAL TECHNOLOGY**
Sponsor:	'Creating the New North' Research Programme, Universitetet i Tromsø - Norges Arktiske Universitetet
Organiser:	Stefan Figenschow, Institutt for historie og religionsvitenskap, Universitetet i Tromsø - Norges Arktiske Universitetet
Moderator:	Eleanor Rosamund Barraclough, Department of History, Durham University
Paper 1733-a:	**Resistance and Recidivism in Scholarly Attitudes toward Technological Change in the Middle Ages** (Language: English) Adam Lucas, School of Humanities & Social Inquiry, University of Wollongong, New South Wales
Paper 1733-b:	**Scholastics and Humanists on the Medieval Technological Revolution** (Language: English) Steven A. Walton, Department of Social Sciences, Michigan Technological University
Paper 1733-c:	**Discovering the Plough in John Whethamstede's *Invenire*** (Language: English) Shana Worthen, Department of History, University of Arkansas at Little Rock
Paper 1733-d:	**Vitruvius and Mills in the Low Countries** (Language: English) Karel Davids, Faculteit der Geesteswetenschappen / De Faculteit der Economische Wetenschappen en Bedrijfskunde, Vrije Universiteit Amsterdam

Session:	**1734** **Leeds University Union: Room 2 - Elland Road**
Title:	**MEMORY AND IDENTITY IN HIGH MEDIEVAL CANTERBURY**
Sponsor:	Marco Institute for Medieval & Renaissance Studies, University of Tennessee, Knoxville
Organiser:	Katie Hodges-Kluck, Marco Institute for Medieval & Renaissance Studies, University of Tennessee, Knoxville and Alexandra Reider, Department of English, Yale University
Moderator:	Katie Hodges-Kluck
Paper 1734-a:	**Re-Writing the Defeat: Eadmer of Canterbury and the Norman Conquest** (Language: English) Pia Zachary, Historisches Seminar, Ludwig-Maximilians-Universität München
Paper 1734-b:	**Anselmiad?: The Wanderings of Aeneas and Anselm and the Memory of the Council of Bari in William of Malmesbury's *Gesta pontificum*** (Language: English) Jesse Harrington, Faculty of History, University of Cambridge
Paper 1734-c:	**The Eadwine Psalter and Its Inherited Innovations** (Language: English) Alexandra Reider

Session:	**1735** **Maurice Keyworth Building: Room 1.09**
Title:	**PARTNERSHIPS OF POWER IN THE HIGH MIDDLE AGES**
Sponsor:	Centre for Medieval Studies, University of York
Organiser:	Jessika Nowak, Departement Geschichte, Universität Basel and Danielle Park, Department of History, University of York
Moderator:	Jessika Nowak
Paper 1735-a:	**Fulk and Melisende: Co-Rulers of the Latin East** (Language: English) Danielle Park
Paper 1735-b:	**How Wives and Sisters Further Allegiances and Relationships: The Case of Donations to High Medieval Monasteries in South-West Germany** (Language: English) Johannes Waldschütz, Stadtmuseum und Archiv, Stockach
Paper 1735-c:	**A Partnership in Power: The Coordination of the Government in the Crown of Aragon between Eleanor of Sicily and Peter IV of Aragon** (Language: English) Sebastian Roebert, Historisches Seminar, Universität Leipzig
Respondent:	Anne Foerster, Historisches Institut, Universität Paderborn

Session:	**1736** **Leeds University Union: Room 4 - Hyde Park**
Title:	**LAW AND MEMORY IN WESTERN FRANCE, 1000-1300**
Organiser:	Tracey L. Billado, Department of History, Queens College, City University of New York
Moderator:	Justine Firnhaber-Baker, St Andrews Institute of Mediaeval Studies, University of St Andrews
Paper 1736-a:	**Custom and Memory in Some Disputes in 11th-Century Greater Anjou** (Language: English) Tracey L. Billado
Paper 1736-b:	**Remembering Order and Disorder in Angevin France: The Strange Case of Count David of Maine** (Language: English) Richard E. Barton, Department of History, University of North Carolina, Greensboro
Paper 1736-c:	**Remembering Justice and Constructing Law in Medieval Brittany** (Language: English) Jehangir Yezdi Malegam, Department of History, Duke University

Session: **1737** **Leeds University Union: Room 5 - Kirkstall Abbey**
Title: **THE MEANING OF MEMORIES AND IDENTITIES IN RENAISSANCE FLORENCE**
Sponsor: Prato Consortium for Medieval & Renaissance Studies, Monash University, Victoria
Organiser: Peter Francis Howard, Centre for Medieval & Renaissance Studies, Monash University, Victoria
Moderator: John Henderson, Department of History, Classics & Archaeology, Birkbeck, University of London / School of Philosophy, History & International Studies, Monash University
Paper 1737-a: **'I am very much indebted to this city': The Papal Residencies and Florentine Memory in Leonardo Bruni's *Memoirs*** (Language: English)
Luke Bancroft, Centre for Medieval & Renaissance Studies, Monash University, Victoria
Paper 1737-b: **Remembering Nuns: Miraculous Visions and the Narration of Spiritual Identity in Post-Tridentine Italy** (Language: English)
Rosa Martorana, School of Philosophical, Historical & International Studies, Monash University, Victoria
Paper 1737-c: **The Prudence of Memory: Remembering the Past in 15th-Century Florence** (Language: English)
Matthew Topp, Centre for Medieval & Renaissance Studies, Monash University, Victoria / Centre for the Study of the Renaissance, University of Warwick, Coventry

Session: **1738** **Michael Sadler Building: Room LG.15**
Title: **MAPPINGS, III: (RE)CONTEXTUALISING MAPS**
Organiser: Felicitas Schmieder, Historisches Institut, FernUniversität Hagen and Dan Terkla, Department of English, Illinois Wesleyan University
Moderator: Arnold Otto, Erzbischöfliches Generalvikariat Erzbistumsarchiv, Paderborn
Paper 1738-a: **Explanations of Grid-Maps: Johannes Poloner, Maurice Paris, and Marino Sanudo** (Language: English)
Susanna E. Fischer, Abteilung für Griechische und Lateinische Philologie, Ludwig-Maximilians-Universität München
Paper 1738-b: **Expert Culture in Regional Cartography, 1500-1650** (Language: English)
Sabine Hynek, Historisches Institut, FernUniversität Hagen
Paper 1738-c: **Using GIS to Illustrate and Understand the Influence of St Æthelthryth of Ely** (Language: English)
Ian Styler, Department of History, University of Birmingham

Session: **1739** **Maurice Keyworth Building: Room 1.03**
Title: **SELECTIVE RECALL: MEMORY AS DECISION-MAKING RESOURCE**
Sponsor: Mediävistenverband
Organiser: Maximiliane Berger, Sonderforschungsbereich 1150 'Kulturen des Entscheidens', Westfälische Wilhelms-Universität Münster
Moderator: Wolfram Drews, Sonderforschungsbereich 1150 'Kulturen des Entscheidens', Westfälische Wilhelms-Universität Münster
Paper 1739-a: **Legislation through Negligence?: On the Importance of Forgetting for the Roncaglia Assembly, 1158** (Language: English)
Konstantin Maier, Sonderforschungsbereich 1150 'Kulturen des Entscheidens', Westfälische Wilhelms-Universität Münster
Paper 1739-b: **The Hero's Decision and the Judgement of Others: Decision-Making in the Perspective of Future Memory** (Language: English)
Susanne Spreckelmeier, Sonderforschungsbereich 1150 'Kulturen des Entscheidens', Westfälische Wilhelms-Universität Münster
Paper 1739-c: **The Spanish Inquisition Remembers: Orality and Literacy in Inquisitorial Decision-Making** (Language: English)
Sebastian Rothe, Sonderforschungsbereich 1150 'Kulturen des Entscheidens', Westfälische Wilhelms-Universität Münster

---

Session: **1740** **Stage@leeds: Stage 3**
Title: **ANCESTRAL ROOTS: MEMORY AND ARBOREAL IMAGERY ACROSS CULTURES, III - ORIGIN AND APPROPRIATION**
Sponsor: Trames Arborescentes Project
Organiser: Pippa Salonius, School of Philosophical, Historical & International Studies, Monash University, Victoria and Naïs Virenque, Centre d'Études Supérieures de la Renaissance, Université François Rabelais, Tours
Moderator: Pippa Salonius
Paper 1740-a: **Christian Trees and German Roots: Otto Huth's *Völkisch* Christmas Tree** (Language: English)
Lays Farra, Faculté de théologie et de sciences des religions, Université de Lausanne
Paper 1740-b: **Tree Symbolism in Medieval Islamic Art and Culture: A Qur'anic Perspective** (Language: English)
Valerie Behiery, Independent Scholar, Ontario
Paper 1740-c: **Adorned and Adored: India's Sacred Trees** (Language: English)
Louise Fowler-Smith, Faculty of Art & Design, University of New South Wales

Session: **1741** **Stage@leeds: Stage 2**
Title: **MEMORY AND METHODOLOGY: ANCHORITIC LEGACIES AND HISTORICAL RECONSTRUCTION**
Sponsor: International Anchoritic Society
Organiser: Alicia Smith, Queen's College, University of Oxford and Victoria Yuskaitis, Institute for Medieval Studies, University of Leeds
Moderator: Laura Kalas Williams, Centre for Medieval & Early Modern Research (MEMO), Swansea University
Paper 1741-a: **Archaeology and Anchoritism: A New Methodology** (Language: English)
Victoria Yuskaitis
Paper 1741-b: **Anchoritic Legacies in the Vernon and Simeon Manuscripts** (Language: English)
Catherine Innes-Parker, Department of English, University of Prince Edward Island
Paper 1741-c: **'Each way means loneliness - and communion': Anchoritic Practice Refracted and Remembered in T. S. Eliot** (Language: English)
Alicia Smith
Paper 1741-d: ***Ubi cor, ibi oculus*: Reading *Ancrene Wisse* with the Eyes of the Heart** (Language: English)
Samira Lindstedt, Pembroke College, University of Oxford

Session: **1743** **Leeds University Union: Room 6 - Roundhay**
Title: **SHARP THINKING, II: EARLY MEDIEVAL SWORDS PUT TO THE TEST**
Sponsor: Rijksmuseum van Oudheden, Leiden
Organiser: Annemarieke Willemsen, Rijksmuseum van Oudheden, Leiden
Moderator: Nelleke IJssennagger, Faculteit der Letteren, Rijksuniversiteit Groningen / Archaeological & Medieval Collections, Frisian Museum, Leeuwarden
Paper 1743-a: **A Reassessment of Irish Sub-Roman Swords: Iron Age Introduction and Medieval Legacy** (Language: English)
Sam Hughes, Independent Scholar, Terenure
Paper 1743-b: **Ulfberht Swords: Material, Development, and Use** (Language: English)
Ingo Petri, Museum und Park Kalkriese, Bramsche
Paper 1743-c: **The Viking Sword: Development, Use, and Myth of a Glorified Weapon** (Language: English)
Florian Messner, Institut für Archäologien, Universität Innsbruck

---

Session: **1744** **Fine Art Building: SR 1.10**
Title: **MEMORIES OF THE ROMAN PAST IN 5TH- AND 6TH-CENTURY NORTH AFRICA**
Organiser: Marguerite Ronin, Ioannou Centre for Classical & Byzantine Studies, University of Oxford
Moderator: Nicolas Lamare, Antiquité classique et tardive, Orient et Méditerranée (UMR 8167), Université Paris IV - Sorbonne
Paper 1744-a: **Historical Memory in Justinian's African Legislation (*Codex Justinianus* 1.27.1-2)** (Language: English)
Miranda Williams, Ioannou Centre for Classical & Byzantine Studies, University of Oxford
Paper 1744-b: **Recalling the Romans?: Fortified Architecture and Settlement in the Late Antique Tripolitanian Countryside** (Language: English)
Nichole Sheldrick, School of Archaeology, University of Oxford
Paper 1744-c: **Memory of the Roman Past in Vandal North Africa** (Language: English)
Philipp von Rummel, Deutsches Archäologisches Institut, Berlin

Session: **1745** **Michael Sadler Building: Room LG.19**
Title: **TRUE STORIES AND OTHER LIES: ORALLY-DERIVED HISTORICAL TRADITIONS IN THE EARLY MEDIEVAL BRITISH ISLES**
Organiser: Paul Gorton, Institute for Medieval Studies, University of Leeds and Catalin Taranu, Institute for Research in the Humanities (IRH-ICUB), Universitatea din Bucureşti
Moderator: Alaric Hall, School of English, University of Leeds
Paper 1745-a: **'Vera lex historiae' from Bede to Beowulf: Constructing Truthfulness in Early Medieval History-Writing** (Language: English)
Catalin Taranu

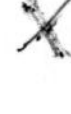

Paper 1745-b: **Remembering the North: Oral History or Historic Inspiration?** (Language: English)
Paul Gorton
Paper 1745-c: **Authority Strategies: A Brief Analysis of Gildas's *De Excidio Britanniae*** (Language: English)
Helena Schütz Leite, Departamento de História, Universidade Federal do Paraná, Brazil

Session: **1746** **Stage@leeds: Stage 1**
Title: **CLERGY AND WAR IN 'YOUNGER EUROPE' IN THE MIDDLE AGES**
Sponsor: Uniwersytet Kazimierza Wielkiego, Bydgoszcz / EPISCOPUS: Society for the Study of Bishops & the Secular Clergy in the Middle Ages
Organiser: Jacek Adam Maciejewski, Instytut Historii i Stosunków Międzynarodowych, Uniwersytet Kazimierza Wielkiego, Bydgoszcz
Moderator: Jacek Adam Maciejewski
Paper 1746-a: **Violent Christianisation and the Orthodox Clergy of the Rus'** (Language: English)
Anti Selart, Institute of History & Archaeology, University of Tartu
Paper 1746-b: **Polish Medieval Bishops at War: Conclusions Drawn from the Historiographical Sources** (Language: English)
Radosław Kotecki, Instytut Historii i Stosunków Międzynarodowych, Uniwersytet Kazimierza Wielkiego, Bydgoszcz
Paper 1746-c: **The Church at War: The Military Role of the Bishop of Zagreb in the Later Middle Ages** (Language: English)
Mišo Petrović, Department of Medieval Studies, Central European University, Budapest

Session: **1747** **Baines Wing: Room 2.14**
Title: **MEMORY OF DEATH, MEMORY AFTER DEATH: SALVATION, CHURCH, AND MONEY IN THE HANSEATIC ZONE**
Sponsor: Towarzystwo Naukowe, Toruń
Organiser: Piotr Oliński, Instytut Historii i Archiwistyki, Uniwersytet Mikołaja Kopernika, Toruń
Moderator: Emilia Jamroziak, Institute for Medieval Studies / School of History, University of Leeds
Paper 1747-a: ***Pfarrers sele nicht vorgessen*: The Parish Clergy's Concern to Obtain Salvation** (Language: English)
Marcin Sumowski, Instytut Historii i Archiwistyki, Uniwersytet Mikołaja Kopernika, Toruń
Paper 1747-b: **Sword and Redemption: Efforts of the Knights to Obtain Salvation** (Language: English)
Alicja Sumowska, Towarzystwo Naukowe, Toruń
Paper 1747-c: **Memory in a Mobile World: Strategies of the Economy of Salvation of the Hanseatic Burghers** (Language: English)
Piotr Oliński

Session: **1748** **University House: St George Room**
Title: **ENGAGING THE CRUSADES, III: WEAPONIZING THE CRUSADES**
Sponsor: Routledge
Organiser: Kristin Skottki, Lehrstuhl für Mittelalterliche Geschichte, Universität Bayreuth
Moderator: Susanna A. Throop, Department of History, Ursinus College, Pennsylvania
Paper 1748-a: **Academic Histories of the Crusades and the 21st-Century Debate about Religious Violence** (Language: English)
John D. Cotts, Department of History, Whitman College, Washington
Paper 1748-b: **Islamic State and the Appropriation of the Crusades** (Language: English)
Jason T. Roche, Department of History, Politics & Philosophy, Manchester Metropolitan University
Paper 1748-c: **The *Reconquista* Revisited: Contemporary Political Uses of Iberian Medieval History** (Language: English)
Tiago Queimada e Silva, Department of European & World History, University of Turku

Session: **1749** **Parkinson Building: Nathan Bodington Chamber**
Title: **MEDIEVAL ECOCRITICISMS, II: COMPLICATING DEFINITIONS OF HUMANS AND NATURE**
Sponsor: Medieval Ecocriticisms
Organiser: Heide Estes, Department of English, Monmouth University, New Jersey
Moderator: Michael J. Warren, Department of English, Royal Holloway, University of London
Paper 1749-a: **Domesticating the Devil: The Ambiguities of Aldhelm's Cat Riddle** (Language: English)
Megan Cavell, Department of English Literature, University of Birmingham
Paper 1749-b: **Trial by Fire: Re-Examining the Furnace Episode in Daniel** (Language: English)
Emma Knowles, Department of Anglo-Saxon, Norse & Celtic, University of Cambridge
Paper 1749-c: **Ecocriticism, Intersectionality, and Early Medieval England** (Language: English)
Heide Estes

Session: **1750** **Maurice Keyworth Building: Room 1.31**
Title: **RECONSTRUCTING AND CONSERVING THE MEDIEVAL PAST**
Organiser: IMC Programming Committee
Moderator: Siegrid Schmidt, Interdisziplinäres Zentrum für Mittelalter und Frühneuzeit (IZMF), Universität Salzburg
Paper 1750-a: **More Medieval than Ever: Rebuilt Castles in East Central Europe** (Language: English)
Béla Zsolt Szakács, Department of Medieval Studies, Central European University, Budapest
Paper 1750-b: **Bastaxii, Bavastelz, and Kobolte: Remembering Medieval Puppet Theatre** (Language: English)
Yanna Kor, Représenter, Inventer la Réalité du Romantisme à l'Aube du XXIe siècle (RIRRA 21), Université Paul-Valéry Montpellier 3
Paper 1750-c: **Ethiopian Medieval Heritage Action Research, Notable Failures, and Limited Success after the Discovery of Massive Unexpected Ruins** (Language: English)
Marco Viganò, Center for Environmental & Developmental Studies, Addis Ababa University, Ethiopia

Session:	**1751** **Baines Wing: Room 2.15**
Title:	**SETTLEMENTS, NATURAL RESOURCES, AND ECONOMY: NEW STUDIES ABOUT MEDIEVAL CENTRAL EUROPE**
Sponsor:	Department of Medieval Studies, Central European University, Budapest
Organiser:	Balázs Nagy, Department of Medieval Studies, Central European University, Budapest
Moderator:	József Laszlovszky, Department of Medieval Studies, Central European University, Budapest
Paper 1751-a:	**Towns and Their Environment: Urban Law Books in the Magdeburg-Saxon Tradition from the 14th Century** (Language: English) Sébastien Rossignol, Department of History, Memorial University of Newfoundland
Paper 1751-b:	**Transformation of the Settlement Network in the Carpathian Basin between 1200 and 1500** (Language: English) Beatrix F. Romhányi, 'Hungary in Medieval Europe', Lendület Research Group (MTA-DE), University of Debrecen / Hungarian Academy of Sciences, Budapest
Paper 1751-c:	**Nature Conservation: A Revival of Medieval Resource Management?** (Language: English) Peter Szabó, Department of Vegetation Ecology, Botanical Institute, Czech Academy of Sciences, Brno
Paper 1751-d:	**Towards a New Synthesis of Medieval Economic History of Hungary: Questions and Lessons** (Language: English) Balázs Nagy

Session:	**1753** **Baines Wing: Room G.37**
Title:	**CONSTRUCTION AND RECONSTRUCTION OF THE MIDDLE AGES: MEMORY OF DELIGHTS**
Sponsor:	Taiwan Association of Classical, Medieval & Renaissance Studies (TACMRS)
Organiser:	Hui-zung Perng, Department of English, National Changhua University of Education, Taiwan
Moderator:	Matthew Treherne, School of Languages, Cultures & Societies - Italian / Leeds Centre for Dante Studies, University of Leeds
Paper 1753-a:	**The Spiritual Joy in Johannes Witte de Hesse's *Itinerarius*** (Language: English) Francis K. H. So, Center for Languages & Culture, Kaohsiung Medical University / Department of Foreign Languages & Literature, National Sun Yat-Sen University, China
Paper 1753-b:	**Forgetting to Remember, Remembering to Forget: Incarnational Recapitulation in Dante's Earthly Paradise** (Language: English) Brian Reynolds, Department of Italian, Fu Jen Catholic University, Taiwan
Paper 1753-c:	**Christian Ideals Challenged in *Sir Gawain and the Green Knight*: Generic Hybridization in the Pastoral Movement** (Language: English) Chin-ching Lee, Department of English, Da Yeh University, Taiwan

Session: **1801** **Baines Wing: Room G.36**
Title: Public Medievalism for Social Change: A Workshop
Sponsor PublicMedievalist.com
Tutors: Victoria Cooper, School of English, University of Leeds, Robert Houghton, Department of History, University of Winchester, Amy S. Kaufman, PublicMedievalist.com, Paul B. Sturtevant, PublicMedievalist.com, and Richard J. Utz, School of Literature, Media & Communication, Georgia Institute of Technology, Atlanta
Purpose: *Many medievalists have watched the news in horror as people have used the Middle Ages to promote and justify hate. The difficult question can be: as medievalists, what can we do? Is there a way for us to responsibly connect the present and past with rigor and nuance? How could we use our knowledge of the Middle Ages to educate the public against these warped ideas of the period we love?*

The staff and contributors of The Public Medievalist *will lead this workshop, teaching public history principles developed in tandem with the* History Communicators *group. We will discuss the incredible potential, and possible pitfalls, of writing for a wider public with an eye toward effecting social change. We will then work with participants to build the skills necessary to turn their research into an article that could thoughtfully engage a wider audience.*

The Public Medievalist *is a popular, volunteer scholar-run web-zine. It regularly publishes articles at the intersection of the medieval past and contemporary culture and politics. The Public Medievalist has featured articles on a wide range of topics, in all disciplines in Medieval Studies, by over 50 scholars at all stages in their careers, and has been used in teaching at more than 60 universities worldwide. In 2017, it inaugurated its first special series,* Race, Racism, and the Middle Ages, *which ran for 10 months and was viewed over 250,000 times. At the beginning of this year it launched a complementary series on* Gender, Sexism, and the Middle Ages.

Although this workshop is open to all IMC participants, the workshop leaders request that those interested in participating contact the IMC in advance so that they will have an idea of the numbers attending.

Session: **1802** **Baines Wing: Room G.37**

Title: **A DATABASE OF CRUSADERS TO THE HOLY LAND, 1095-1291: A WORKSHOP**

Tutors: Alan V. Murray, Institute for Medieval Studies, University of Leeds and Guy Perry, Institute for Medieval Studies / School of History, University of Leeds

Purpose: *The Crusaders to Holy Land, 1095-1291 database will bring together information on men and women who took part in the crusades to the Holy Land in the period between the Council of Clermont (1095) and the end of the 12th century. Its purpose is to enhance understanding of the motives and dynamics of the crusading movement by collating data on issues such as the identity and social status of crusaders and their relationships, family traditions and regional patterns of crusading, finance, mortality rates, and gender issues. It can thus be used to gain information on the lives of individual crusaders, as well as on the composition of individual crusades and their contingents and the contribution made to crusading by different families, countries, and regions of Europe.*

Currently a pilot study for the creation of a searchable database of crusaders to the Holy Land from 1095 to 1291 is available online. It includes data on individuals who were involved in crusading in the period from the First (1096-1099) to the Second (1145-1149) Crusades. The original material was put together in 2007-2008 from basic databases compiled by Jonathan Riley-Smith (mainly for the First Crusade) and Jonathan Phillips (mainly for the Second Crusade). This data was entered into an Access database constructed by Nicholas Morton. Subsequently, Alan Murray and Guy Perry (both of the University of Leeds), who had both independently worked on crusade participation in the 12th century, offered their assistance to the project, and during 2014-2015 they checked and harmonised the complete database and added further biographical and geographical information and additional references. In 2015-2016 a more user-friendly interface was developed by the Digital Humanities Institute at the University of Sheffield. The database now comprises some 1100 records.

For further information, please see: www.dhi.ac.uk/crusaders/

DINNER

Meal Times

Refectory 18.00-20.00

See Map 9, p. 51.

---

*   *   *   *   *

IMC CEILIDH

REFECTORY
20.30-22.30

This event is free of charge

Pronunciation: 'kay-lee'
Forms: Also **ceilidhe**.
Etymology: < Irish *céilidhe*, Scottish Gaelic *cēilidh*, < Old Irish *céile* companion
In Scotland and Ireland:
a. An evening visit, a friendly social call
b. A session of traditional music, storytelling, or dancing

To bring IMC 2018 to a festive close, the Assumption Ceilidh Band will be performing in the Refectory. No prior experience is required as all dances will be taught beforehand, so please come to kick up your heels.

The Assumption Ceilidh Band primarily play for local charities and schools, but they also perform for special occasions such as weddings and birthdays. They play a mixture of traditional instrumental Irish music, folk songs, old tyme waltzes, and Irish set dances such as the 'Bridge of Athlone' and the 'Walls of Limerick'. The band ranges from seven to nine people (including a caller). Members of the band (who are very good friends and thoroughly enjoy each other's company) are a mixture of some mid-twenties members and some mature members (i.e. retired, albeit only recently!).

*   *   *   *   *

Session:	**1901** **Social Sciences Building: Room 10.06**
Title:	**7 WAYS A MEDIEVALIST CAN EARN INCOME OUTSIDE ACADEMIA**
Sponsor:	Medievalists.net
Tutors:	Danièle Cybulskie and Peter Konieczny, Medievalists.net
Fee:	£7.50
Purpose:	*The scholars coming to the International Medieval Congress know that it is challenging to find career opportunities once they have finished a PhD. There is much competition for work at universities, and not all graduates will be able to find work as an academic. But there are other options.*

This three-hour seminar will take a look at how a medievalist can earn money, and perhaps find a career, using their knowledge of the Middle Ages. Specifically, we take a look at the following possible paths:

1) Books - writing for publishers and self-publishing
2) Magazines - writing for history and non-history magazines
3) The Internet - creating your own website or digital content
4) YouTube and Podcasts - finding ways to create your own media brand
5) Publishing - working in publishing or creating your own business
6) Travel and Tourism - using your knowledge of local history
7) Public History - working for museums, historical sites, fairs, and festivals

Leading the discussion is Peter Konieczny, the founder of Medievalists.net, the largest website devoted to the Middle Ages. He is also the editor of Medieval Warfare *magazine. Joining him will be Danièle Cybulskie, author of* The Five-Minute Medievalist.

Peter Konieczny was a librarian at the University of Toronto before becoming part-owner of Medievalists.net. He has been developing websites for 15 years and is based in Toronto. Peter has extensive experience in web design, blogging, social media, and the use of digital media to support the dissemination of scholarship to wide-ranging audiences.

Danièle Cybulskie studied Cultural Studies and English Literature at Trent University, earning her MA in English Literature at the University of Toronto. A featured writer at Medievalists.net, she has been published in three international magazines, and her book, The Five-Minute Medievalist, *debuted at No.1 on Amazon's Canadian charts. She also worked as the subject matter expert for OntarioLearn's 'The Middle Ages and the Modern World: Facts and Fiction', currently offered at nine colleges. Having left college teaching behind, she now divides her time between giving workshops, writing articles, and working on her second book.*

Since 2008, Medievalists.net has billed itself as the media site for the Middle Ages, offering news, articles, and videos about medieval studies. It is one of the largest online resources about the Middle Ages, and has amassed over 35 million page views.

Session: **1902** **Social Sciences Building: Room 10.07**

Title: **MEDIEVAL RECORDS AND THE NATIONAL ARCHIVES: A WORKSHOP**

Sponsor: The National Archives

Tutors: Sean Cunningham, Paul Dryburgh, and Euan Roger, The National Archives, Kew

Fee: £7.50

Purpose: *For all medievalists the ability to locate, read, and understand archival sources is fundamental to their research whatever their discipline and stage in their career. The National Archives of the United Kingdom (TNA) holds one of the world's largest and most important collections of medieval records. The vast archive of English royal government informs almost every aspect of medieval life from the royal court to the peasantry, land ownership and tenure, the law, warfare and diplomacy, trade and manufacture, transport, credit and debt, death and memory, material culture, literature, art and music. However, finding, using, and interpreting the rich diversity of material is not always entirely straightforward, and its potential for a wide range of research uses is often unclear. This workshop will offer an introduction to TNA, show you how to begin your research into its collections, and access research support. A course-pack with facsimiles of original documents will be used to illustrate the range of disciplines and topics TNA records can inform and illuminate. Short, themed sessions will also introduce attendees to the Mechanics of Medieval Government, Law and Justice, and Material and Literary Culture.*

This workshop is aimed at all medievalists, from masters students through to experienced academics in any discipline, who wish to discover more about the rich archive collections at TNA and how they might use them in their research. There are no pre-requisites for attending the workshop, although a basic knowledge of Latin is recommended.

Sean Cunningham is Head of Medieval & Early Modern and specialises in 15th- and 16th-century records of English royal government. Euan Roger is a Medieval Records Specialist whose research has focussed on church, government, and law in the late Middle Ages. Paul Dryburgh is a Principal Medieval Records Specialist with interests in government, politics, and warfare in the British Isles in the 13th and 14th centuries.

Session: **1903**

Title: **'OF ARMED ALABASTER': MEDIEVAL MILITARY EFFIGIES OF WEST YORKSHIRE - A WORKSHOP**

Sponsor: Royal Armouries

Tutors: Keith Dowen, Royal Armouries, Leeds

Fee: £39.50

Purpose: *Found in their hundreds in Britain's churches, the knightly effigy is one of the most impressive memorials of the Middle Ages. Emerging in the second or third decade of the 13th century, the secular military effigy was designed not only to act as an impressive reminder of the identity and status of the individual, but as a focal point for intercessory prayers designed to speed the deceased's soul through the torments of Purgatory. As works of sculpture, the finest are so lifelike that the figures seem poised, ready to leap into action on the Day of Judgement.*

For the scholar of medieval arms and armour, military effigies are an invaluable resource, tracing the development of knightly equipment from the age of mail to that of full plate. With comparatively little armour surviving from the Middle Ages, military effigies provide details of materials, styles, and construction which have otherwise been lost or are difficult to interpret from other sources.

This workshop will explore the development of armour in England from the early 14th century to the second half of the 15th and the Wars of the Roses. The day will begin at the Royal Armouries where there will be a short session tracing the development of medieval armour. We will then visit three churches in West Yorkshire, starting with All Saints at Harewood, which is home to some of the finest alabaster effigies in England, before moving on to St Michael and All Angels at Thornhill with its collection of tombs belonging to the Savile family. Finally we will conclude by visiting St Oswald's in Methley and the tomb of Lionel, Lord Welles, who was killed fighting for the House of Lancaster at Towton in 1461.

Keith Dowen is the Assistant Curator of Armour at the Royal Armouries in Leeds. He has lectured widely, both in the UK and abroad, on arms and armours and British military history. In 2012 he was appointed Honorary Deputy Editor of the Journal of the Arms and Armour Society *and in 2016 he joined the editorial board of* Acta Militaria Mediaevalia. *Since joining the Royal Armouries in 2014, he has been heavily involved in a number of on-going museum projects across the UK concerning the display and interpretation of 17th century arms and armour and has organised a number of specialist seminars. Keith is also involved with the identification and cataloguing of finds of medieval arms and armour from archaeological sites in Poland.*

Participants in this workshop should assemble at the Parkinson Steps at 09.20. Packed lunches will be included.

Notes

Notes

Guide to Excursions

Places on our excursions are allocated on a first-come, first-served basis, so early booking is recommended to avoid disappointment. Please make a note of how participation in excursions will affect your meal requirements, and note also the time of departure from and return to the Parkinson Building in relation to other commitments, and book accordingly. Sensible footwear and raincoats are recommended. The wearing of high-heeled shoes is impractical at most sites and prohibited at some. Most excursions will involve a significant amount of walking and/or standing. Please contact the IMC if you have any questions or concerns about a particular excursion. Children under the age of 18 must be accompanied by a responsible adult.

We ask that those participating in excursions arrive at the steps outside the Parkinson Building 15 minutes before the excursion is due to leave. A member of staff will be present in this area to provide information.

The IMC administration reserves the right to cancel excursions due to unforeseen circumstances and to alter the schedule at short notice if necessary. Please note that all times are approximate. Prices for the excursions include coach transport, entrance fees, and donations to the sites, fees for the guides, staffing, and administration costs. Meals are not included in the price unless otherwise indicated.

Sunday 01 July

Mount Grace Priory and Jervaulx Abbey

Price: £38.50

Depart Parkinson Steps: 09.00 — Arrive Parkinson Steps: 19.00

Even in Yorkshire, with its many surviving monastic sites, Mount Grace Priory and Jervaulx Abbey are both very special: significant for their setting, as well as for their physical remains.

Mount Grace Priory is the best preserved and most accessible of the nine English medieval Carthusian charterhouses, and one of the most intensively researched in Europe. 2018 will see the publication of that research. The last monastery to be established in Yorkshire before the suppression, it retains the well-preserved ruins of its church, the individual cells of its choir-monks and lay-brothers, and the guest houses and service ranges of the inner court. The site was substantially excavated between 1968 and 1992, providing exceptional evidence for the reconstruction of a single monk's cell and its garden to demonstrate the setting of late medieval Carthusian life.

Jervaulx Abbey, in comparison, was a Cistercian monastery primarily of the late 12th-15th centuries, maintained as a semi-natural ruin in a post-medieval parkland landscape that still contains extensive evidence of the monastic precinct on which it is based. Its ruins are conserved as they were left by its early 19th-century excavators with fallen stones placed on the wall-tops close to where they were found. Because of this, the ruins are remarkably informative, showing the building of a revolutionary new church in the 1190s, the development of the cloister buildings throughout the second half of the 12th century, and their late medieval modification for the developing monastic life that is usually better documented than found in surviving buildings.

Though heavily ruined, sufficient evidence survives in the church to show it was the model for the eastern arms of both Fountains Abbey and Beverley Minster, and an increasing number of early 13th century churches in eastern England.

This excursion will be led by Glyn Coppack (Archaeological and Historical Research), who was responsible for the development of conservation and research on both sites for English Heritage, and Stuart Harrison (Ryedale Archaeology Services). A packed lunch will be included.

For more information on the sites, please visit

www.english-heritage.org.uk/visit/places/mount-grace-priory/

www.jervaulxabbey.com/

Sunday 01 July

Middleham Castles: The Wensleydale Domain Lord, Rebel Earl, and Plantagenet Prince

Price: £26.50

Depart Parkinson Steps: 13.00 Arrive Parkinson Steps: 19.00

This tour visits two castles on one site that at different times dominated this area of the Yorkshire landscape, overlooking the roads between the important towns of Richmond and Skipton. The earlier castle, 'William's Hill', is the remnant of a Norman ringwork-and-bailey castle, built about 1086, and the later stone castle has connections with Richard III (r. 1483-1485), the last Plantagenet king of England. Both castles had their origins in land granted to the Norman lord, Alan Rufus ('the Red') of Brittany (a second cousin of William the Conqueror) who fought at Hastings in 1066. He helped stamp Norman authority on the area by leading the infamous 'Harrying of the North' during 1069-70, the savage suppression of a rebellion against the new Norman masters that led to the loss of over 150,000 lives. Alan was well rewarded for his efforts: it has been estimated that when he died in 1093 his fortune was worth over £107.5 billion (at 2017 prices).

During the 15th century, however, the stone castle became the property of the Neville family and, for a while, the property of Richard III. In 1462, Richard, the young Duke of Gloucester, was placed in the household of his cousin Richard Neville, Earl of Warwick ('the Kingmaker') and was brought up at Middleham Castle for a short period of three years (1465-8), as well as at other Neville houses. Both Edward IV (1469) and Henry VI were held captive at the castle and, following Warwick's death at the battle of Barnet in 1471, Edward IV gave Middleham to his brother, Richard, who had married Warwick's daughter Anne Neville. Despite the short time he would have stayed here, it later became Richard's principal seat in the North, and it was here, in about 1476, that his one legitimate son, Prince Edward of Middleham, was born, allegedly in the castle's 'Prince's Tower'. Prince Edward's wet-nurse was one Isabel Burgh (who was later rewarded by Richard with a generous annuity from the revenues of Middleham) and an Anne Idley was appointed 'Mistress of the Nursery'. Her late husband, Peter Idley, had written a book entitled *Instructions to His Son*. In 1484 Edward died at the castle and possibly lies, buried still, in the local parish and collegiate church of St Mary and St Alkelda. The size and scale of Middleham castle shows that it was well able to cater for noble and royal households of upwards of 200.

This excursion will be led by Kelly DeVries (Professor of the Department of History, Loyola University, Maryland and Historical Consultant to the Royal Armouries) and Robert C. Woosnam-Savage (Curator of Armour and Edged Weapons, Royal Armouries, Leeds).

Although this excursion is self-contained, it will act as the perfect complement to this year's IMC Post-Congress Tour, with its Ricardian connections. Sensible footwear is recommended, as there will be a significant amount of walking on uneven surfaces and climbing steep stone steps. It would also be advisable to bring raincoats and sunblock.

For further information about Middleham Castle, please visit www.english-heritage.org.uk/visit/places/middleham-castle/

Sunday 01 July

Stank Old Hall, New Hall, and Barn

Price: £15.00

Depart Parkinson Steps: 14.00 Arrive Parkinson Steps: 18.00

The Stank Old Hall, New Hall, and Barn site in South Leeds had constant occupation from prehistoric times, as witnessed by the Iron Age defensive earthworks visible on the hillside immediately behind the site, which were excavated just before the Second World War. Stank Old Hall (with prominent garderobe) was rebuilt in 1280 from an earlier hall to provide a royal hunting lodge attached to Rothwell Castle. It was originally surrounded by a quadrangle of guest halls, domestic buildings, and offices such as hawking mews, kennels, stables, as well as butchery and smoking lodges. After the sudden cessation of the royal use of the site after the Wars of the Roses, when Rothwell Castle itself had fallen, these offices were demolished so quickly that the flagged floor of one long hall - probably guest quarters - still exists crosswise under the floor of the large timbered barn that was built on the site. At this time the Old Hall was re-purposed into a more domestic building by adding another hall cornerwise onto one end to form a larger L-shaped hall, although the garderobe was retained. A local family, the De Beestons, held the site for several centuries, although it seems likely that a form of hunting park surrounding the site was revived briefly in the 16th century, utilising the long redundant earthworks and chases.

In the 17th century, when the site was owned by the Puritan Major Greathead, one bay of the barn was rebuilt to form a courthouse presided over by the Major himself. This became known locally - probably not without humour - as Major Greathead's Chapel. Looking at the interior stonework, especially of the doorways and the external carvings, it appears to be repurposed stonework of a medieval chapel.

In 1847 disaster struck the site: an underground explosion known as the Beeston Mining Disaster demolished the end of New Hall and flattened a wattle and daub timber-framed wing that had been added in the 17th century. The owner of the site took out an advertisement in the *Leeds Mercury* stating that the disaster had revealed many pieces of carving and antiquity from the structure of the halls and invited local historians to come and barter for it. The cost to bring a horse and cart or carriage was two shillings, and thereafter the price of each item would be negotiated individually. Once the site had been rifled, Old Hall and New Hall were shored up, and the timber-frame structure of the barn, which had listed to one side, was straightened with the aid of a team of oxen.

Now owned by Leeds City Council, the site is sadly falling into dereliction, but it is supported by volunteers from the local community who have formed the Friends of Stank Hall and who are working to acquire the site for community housing, a community centre, and a small museum, together with a garden providing free vegetables for members of the local community. A programme of heritage activities and events is run each spring, summer, and autumn by the Friends, together with open days to let visitors access the inside of the barn and archaeological activities to clear finds from spoil heaps left from Leeds City Council's work on the site. The Old and New Halls can only be viewed from the outside, but the barn, which is one of the oldest secular buildings in Leeds and Grade II* listed, will be open.

This excursion will be guided by members of the Friends of Stank Hall. This tour will involve a significant amount of walking over rough ground. Participants are advised to wear study walking shoes and comfortable clothing that they don't mind getting dirty.

For more information, please visit https://friendsofstankhallbarn.wordpress.com/

MONDAY 02 JULY

JOHN RYLANDS LIBRARY, UNIVERSITY OF MANCHESTER

Price: £23.50

Depart Parkinson Steps: 13.00 Arrive Parkinson Steps: 19.00

The John Rylands Library was founded by Enriqueta Rylands in memory of her husband John Rylands, Manchester's first multi-millionaire. She commissioned architect Basil Champneys to design the striking neo-gothic building, which took ten years to build and was opened to the public on 01 January 1900.

The library became part of the University of Manchester in 1972 and currently houses the majority of the Special Collections of the University of Manchester Library. Mrs Rylands's memorial to her husband is now part of the third largest academic library in the United Kingdom, and the Deansgate building houses over 400,000 printed volumes, and well over a million manuscripts and archival items.

Participants in the excursion will have the opportunity to tour the building, learning about its history and architecture, including the historic entrance and main staircase, where readers would have originally entered the building, and the Reading Room, the layout of which resembles a church, but with alcoves designed for private study. The tour will be followed by a private collections encounter with a range of medieval manuscripts, charters, and early printed books from the library's collections.

This excursion will be led by John Hodgson, Manuscripts and Archives Manager, and Julianne Simpson, Rare Books and Maps Manager at the John Rylands Library.

For further information, please visit www.library.manchester.ac.uk/rylands/

Tuesday 03 July

Kirkstall Abbey

Ticket: £17.50

Depart Parkinson Steps: 13.30 Arrive Parkinson Steps: 17.00

One of the best-preserved examples of a medieval Cistercian monastery in England can be seen within two miles of the International Medieval Congress. A daughter-house of Fountains, Kirkstall Abbey is remarkable for both the quality and extent of its preservation. Large parts of the church, chapter house, cloister, south range, and abbot's lodging survive up to roof height. Complementing these impressive standing remains is the guest house, a rare survival in monastic precincts, which has been excavated extensively so that its structural developments are understood in great depth.

Despite its extensive architectural and archaeological remains, Kirkstall has received little scholarly attention, and the importance its material culture holds for understanding medieval religious life has consequently been neglected. However, the guesthouse has recently been the focus of extensive archaeological and historical enquiry and a subsequent AHRC-funded cultural engagement project has ensured that the findings of this research will be made freely available. This work has highlighted the importance of the guesthouse for the social life of the abbey, revealing how the monastic community provided hospitality to guests and entertained them within the precinct. New information concerning finds from the guesthouse, such as dress accessories, provides greater clarity regarding the identity of guests and what they did while at the abbey; the animal bones, meanwhile, provide an indication of the food eaten by guests and enable comparison with monastic fare. As a result, the guesthouse can now be set in the wider context of Kirkstall's structures, which have been the subject of a number of modern restorations, permitting a more holistic appreciation of the life in the abbey during the Middle Ages.

The tour provides an overview of the history of the abbey from its establishment in 1152 and gives particular attention to the guesthouse and its importance in monastic life.

This excursion will be led by Katherine Baxter (Curator of Archaeology, Leeds Museums & Galleries) and Richard Thomason (Department of Classical & Archaeological Studies / Centre for Medieval & Early Modern Studies, University of Kent).

For further information about Kirkstall Abbey, please visit: www.leeds.gov.uk/museumsandgalleries/Pages/Kirkstall-Abbey.aspx

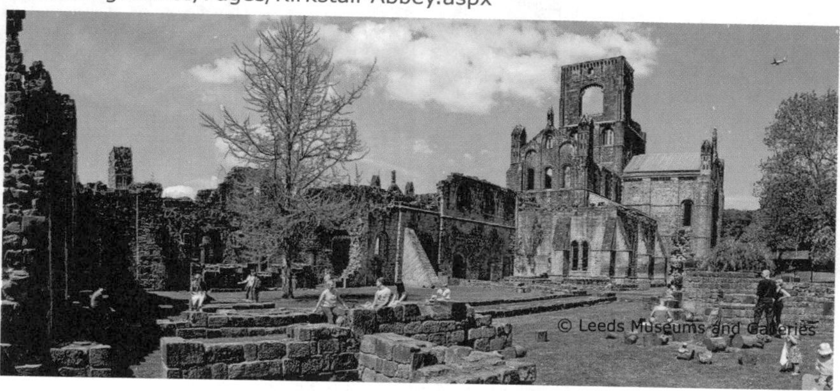

WEDNESDAY 04 JULY

YORK MINSTER

Ticket: £28.00

Depart Parkinson Steps: 13.30 Arrive Parkinson Steps: 19.00

York Minister is the second largest Gothic cathedral in Northern Europe. At 70 m (230 ft), the top of York Minster's central tower offers the best vantage point for viewing the city. Though the first church was erected on the site in 627, the present building was begun c. 1230 and completed over two centuries later. York Minster is also known for its remarkable collection of stained glass including the Great East Window, which is the largest expanse of medieval stained glass in Britain.

Yet the Minster is also important for what lies beneath ground level. Emergency excavations during the 1970s revealed not only the remains of the former Norman Minster, but also an Anglo-Saxon cemetery and Roman barracks. More recently, the Undercroft has been developed into 'Revealing York Minster', an interactive exhibition detailing the history of the site over the last 2,000 years, incorporating recent archaeological finds and artefacts never seen before on public display, such as the 1,000-year-old York Gospels.

This tour will involve a guided tour of York Minster as well as the opportunity to explore the new 'Revealing York Minster' Galleries in the Undercroft. Afterwards, there will be time for independent exploration of the Minster and the surrounding area.

This excursion will be led by Stuart Harrison (Ryedale Archaeology Services), who is the Cathedral Archaeologist at York Minster.

For further information about York Minster, visit: www.yorkminster.org/

Thursday 05 July

Southwell Minster and Town

Price: £38.50

Depart Parkinson Steps: 09.00 Arrive Parkinson Steps: 19.00

Southwell is a well-concealed secret in the centre of Nottinghamshire. It is a very small town, with a grid of Georgian and Victorian houses and shops, surrounding the ruined former palace of the Archbishops of York, the remains of a square of medieval canons houses, rebuilt at the end of the 18th century, and one of the finest English small cathedrals, Southwell Minster.

The earliest occupation at Southwell has recently been found to be a 1st-century Roman site, perhaps originally built as a temple to the north of the main Roman road, the Fosse Way from Lincoln to Exeter. This was rebuilt several times, and seems to have ended as a large courtyard villa, perhaps connected with the nearby Lindum Colonia, the capital of Britannia Secunda. The villa was abandoned, and part of the site was used for a small pagan cemetery. During the 8th century a small church with a Christian cemetery was built on the villa site.

In the middle of the 10th century the villa and its associated territory were given to Oscetyl, the first West Saxon archbishop of York, to strengthen his authority at the start of the reconquest of Viking Yorkshire. He set up a community of canons beside his manor house, together with a small church. This was enlarged on a grand scale during the 12th century, expanded with a new east arm after 1234, and was finally adorned with an exquisite chapter house at the end of the 13th century, famous for its carvings of leaves and flowers, called by Pevsner the 'Leaves of Southwell'. At the Reformation the college of canons and archbishop's chapel were converted to a parish church, with a couple of priests who served the needs of the small town. The palace was abandoned. The 18th century saw steady decay, with a major fire which destroyed the medieval roofs. All of this was remedied during the middle and later 19th century, when the Church Commissioners funded a thorough restoration under their architect, Ewan Christian. At the end of the process the church was adopted as the cathedral of the new diocese of Nottingham and Derby, one of the several new dioceses created for the industrial towns of the Midlands and North, and part of the palace ruins was rebuilt to provide a house for the new bishop. The cathedral also has a fine series of stained glass windows by the notable 20th-century artists Christopher Whall and Patrick Reyntiens, as well as four 16th-century panels rescued from destruction in Paris at the Revolution and now housed in the choir. This excursion will trace the history of this important site, from the Romans to the 19th century, and will visit both the cathedral and the former archbishop's palace.

Philip Dixon (Archaeological Consultant for Southwell Minster) and Jenny Alexander (Department of the History of Art, University of Warwick) will lead this excursion. Packed lunches will be provided.

For further information, please visit www.southwellminster.org/

Thursday 05 July

Conisbrough Castle

Price: £24.50

Depart Parkinson Steps: 13.30 Arrive Parkinson Steps: 19.00

Although famously depicted in Sir Walter Scott's novel *Ivanhoe*, the little-visited Conisbrough Castle remains one of Yorkshire's best-kept secrets. The cylindrical keep, which is supported by six semi-hexagonal buttresses, remains largely intact. The late 12th-century round keep is described as 'one of the finest examples of late Norman defensive architecture'. The four-storey Norman keep is exceptionally well-preserved, both internally and externally, and reaches a height of 27 m (90 ft). The keep speaks of authority, security, and strength.

At the time of the Norman Conquest the manor of Conisbrough was held by King Harold. After Harold's defeat at Hastings, the property was given to William, the first Earl Warenne and the son-in-law of William I. Little remains, however, of the original castle that he built on the site. The surviving keep dates from the time of the fifth earl, Hamelin Plantagenet, the illegitimate son of Geoffrey of Anjou; its cylindrical shape is unique amongst English castles, the nearest parallel being the keep at Mortemer, near Dieppe in France, a castle also held by the Warenne family.

It is not just defensive in nature; the surviving remains are a great reminder that it was a residence. Within its walls sits the largest hooded fireplace of its date, an impressive private chapel, and a fine processional staircase. There are, moreover, private latrines and fresh running water supplied by the two large water-storage tanks on the roof, which are fully accessible since the keep has been re-roofed and re-floored, making it possible for visitors to climb to the top of the tower.

As well as being a royal castle at various periods in its history, Conisbrough also bears an aura of romance and legend, having partly inspired, and appeared in, Scott's *Ivanhoe,* published in 1819. Set in 1194, Scott described the castle as a 'Saxon fortress' and one that was used by the thane Athelstane, the last of the Saxon royal line. This is, of course, incorrect as the entire work is fictitious. However, it has not prevented Conisbrough becoming a centre for Scott aficionados.

This excursion will be led by Audrey Thorstad (School of History, Welsh History & Archaeology, Bangor University).

For further information about Conisbrough Castle, please visit www.english-heritage.org.uk/visit/places/conisbrough-castle/

Guide to Events

The IMC administration retains the right to cancel events due to unforeseen circumstances, and to alter the schedule at short notice if necessary. Please note that all times are approximate. Children under the age of 18 must be accompanied by a responsible adult.

Sunday 01 July

'No gold glitters like that which is our own': Medieval Goldwork Embroidery Workshop

Directed by

Tanya Bentham

University House: De Grey Room

11.00-17.00

Price: £32.50

From the earliest times, embroidering with gold thread has been a popular way to decorate items and display wealth and prestige across Asia, Europe, and the Middle East. Among the oldest surviving examples of English goldwork are the fragments of the stole and maniple of St Cuthbert, which were found in his coffin and are now on display in Durham Cathedral. Many of the later surviving examples of goldwork are various forms of ecclesiastical embroidery. In the 13th and 14th centuries, English luxury embroidery, sometimes called 'Opus Anglicanum' (English work), enjoyed an international reputation and was imported across Europe. Recently, Opus Anglicanum was the subject of an exhibition at the Victoria and Albert Museum.

This workshop provides a rare opportunity to learn the goldwork embroidery techniques used throughout the medieval period. Participants will learn the basic stitches of goldwork embroidery – surface and underside couching - as well as how to incorporate pearls into their designs. The workshop fee includes all materials. Each participant will produce a compact lozenge-shaped piece that can be converted into a pendant or a key fob.

Tanya Bentham has been a re-enactor for more than 30 years, working for the last 20 as a professional living historian. Her main focus has always been on textiles, especially embroidery, but also making detours into costume, natural dyeing, weaving, millinery, and silversmithing. She has delivered workshops for numerous museums, schools, and community organisations throughout Yorkshire.

The workshop can only accommodate a limited number of participants. Early booking is recommended. Lunch is not included.

Sunday 01 July

'Draw thy sword in right': Combat Workshop

Directed by

Dean Davidson and Stuart Ivinson, *Kunst des Fechtens* (KDF) International

Leeds University Union: Riley Smith Hall

14.00-16.30

Price: £15.00

Have you ever had a desire to learn how to fight like our historical forbears or study the highly effective fighting style that was taught throughout the medieval period? This year Kunst des Fechtens (KDF) International brings a workshop on the use of medieval longswords to the Congress participants.

KDF workshops bring a dynamic approach to training, with a martial application of this historical art through practical drills combined with interpretations from historical treatises. Our professional and experienced instructors will be on hand to provide tuition in this noble fighting style.

KDF International is an association of like-minded clubs from across Europe, whose aim is to promote the study, development, and practice of the martial arts tradition of medieval and renaissance Germany, in particular the work of the Master Johannes Liechtenauer. These martial arts have been preserved in numerous treatises and have been unearthed, transcribed, translated, and interpreted into a modern understanding of a subtle, dynamic, and effective martial arts system that looks at the use of a number of weapons and unarmed combat of the time. Founded in 2006, KDF was born from a desire to focus attention on Liechtenauer's works as well as bringing a dynamic approach to training, adding the use of protection as well as free play exercises and bouts to drill and practice as a part of trying to triangulate a truth within their interpretations.

Dean has over 20 years' experience in martial arts and training in historical weapons. He is the KDF International Senior Instructor and European Historical Combat Guild Chapter Master at the Royal Armouries, Leeds. He is an active member of the Society for Combat Archaeology, an international organisation committed to the promulgation of systematic knowledge related to combat and warfare in the past. Dean is passionate about sharing knowledge on this subject and regularly presents at renowned international conferences and seminars, providing a unique insight in to the arms and armour used throughout medieval warfare. He is also a founding member of the Towton Battlefield Frei Compagnie and 3 Swords, a prestigious medieval historical and armed combat interpretation group. Dean holds a Masters in Health Informatics from the Faculty of Medicine at the University of Leeds and is a member of the Leeds University Medieval Society.

Stuart Ivinson has been involved with historical combat for 16 years, joining the European Historical Combat Guild in 2000 and KDF upon

Instructor at the Leeds Chapter of both organisations. Stuart is also a member of the Society for Combat Archaeology and a founder member of both the Towton Battlefield Society Frei Compagnie and 3 Swords. He has made presentations regarding the display arms and armour for organisations such as the National Archives at Kew, English Heritage, and numerous British museums. Stuart has an MA in Librarianship, an MA in Medieval History, and a P.Dip in Heritage Management. When he is not being Dean's sidekick, he is the Librarian at the Royal Armouries Museum in Leeds.

All weapons are provided by KDF and attendees are asked to arrive wearing indoor training shoes and appropriate and comfortable gym training gear that will allow freedom of movement (i.e. t-shirt and tracksuit bottoms). Please make the instructors aware of any prior medical conditions.

This workshop can only accommodate a limited number of participants. Early booking is recommended.

Sunday 01 July

Strange Adventures and Otherworldly Journeys

Performed by

Matthew Bellwood

Leeds University Union: Room 6 - Roundhay

19.30-21.00

This event is free of charge.

Master storyteller Matthew Bellwood brings to life Norse sagas, Celtic legends, and European folk stories in this collection of long-remembered tales from the Middle Ages. Enter into realms where gods battle frost giants, kings hide unexpected secrets, little girls fight wicked witches, and husbands reach out from other worlds to reclaim lost brides.

Matthew Bellwood is a Leeds-based writer and storyteller. His background is in devised theatre, and he has performed at drama festivals in Canada, Germany, and New Zealand, as well as throughout the UK. He currently runs Moveable Feast Productions, a touring Theatre in Education company, for which he has written and produced a wide range of shows and workshops for young people. He also works regularly with A Quiet Word, who create site-specific theatre work in unusual places.

Monday 02 July

'To lerne the tretis of the astrelabie': Astrolabe Workshop

Directed by

Kristine Larsen

Maurice Keyworth Building: Room 1.31

19.00-20.30

This event is free of charge.

Most medieval scholars have heard of the astrolabe, part work of art and part personal computer. For centuries the instrument was used across both the Christian and Islamic worlds in order to calculate times of prayer, measure the height of the sun and stars above the horizon for navigation, and aid in surveying. It is a two-dimensional model of the three-dimensional heavens that you can hold in your hands.

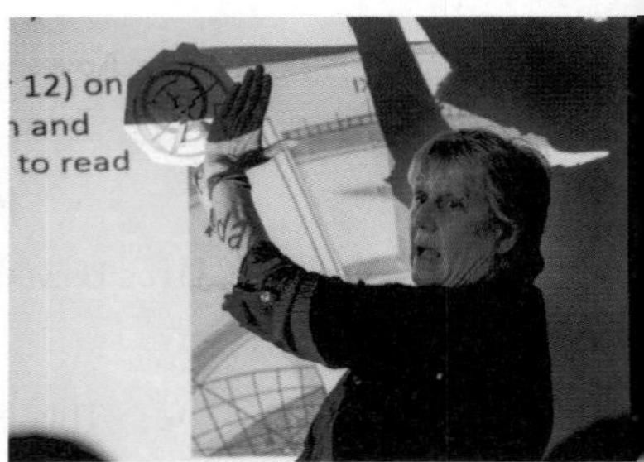

Anyone who has ever tried to work their way through Chaucer's *Treatise on the Astrolabe* without a basic astronomical knowledge might have (understandably) given up after the first few steps, but the astrolabe is actually not a daunting device if you just have some basic background. This hands-on workshop is a step-by-step walk-through of selected computations from Chaucer's work, including computing the current local time from the apparent position of the sun and stars and finding one's latitude.

The workshop is presented by Kristine Larsen (Professor of Astronomy at Central Connecticut State University), who has made similar presentations at the International Medieval Congress at Western Michigan University for several years, as well as numerous other universities and educational centres. The first 50 attendees will receive a free cardboard astrolabe as well as an instruction sheet (both theirs to keep).

Monday 02 July

'All thy best parts bound together': Coptic Bookbinding Workshop

Directed by

Linette Withers

Clothworkers Building South: Room G.11B

19.00-21.00

Price: £28.50

In 1945, a collection of early Christian and Gnostic texts was discovered near the Egyptian town of Nag Hammadi. These leather-bound vellum codices, dating from the 3rd and 4th centuries, were sealed within a jar which was found by a local farmer. These volumes were written in the Coptic language and bound in a single-section Coptic style, with covers of soft leather that were stiffened by sheets of waste papyrus. The first true form of the codex, the Coptic style of binding continued to be used until the 11th century.

Participants in the workshop will recreate one of the types of Coptic bindings used in the Nag Hammadi finds with goat leather and papyrus covers and linen thread. The internal pages of the book will be blank sketch paper. All materials will be provided.

Linette Withers completed an MA in Medieval Studies at the University of Leeds before joining the IMC team as Senior Congress Officer. She has been binding books since 2005 and since 2012 has worked as a professional book binder, producing codices that are inspired by historical books.

Recently one of her works was shortlisted for display at the Bodleian Library at the University of Oxford as part of their 'Redesigning the Medieval Book' competition and exhibition. She also regularly volunteers for library conservation projects and teachesbinding techniques in her studio in Leeds.

This workshop can only accommodate a limited number of participants. Early booking is recommended.

Monday 02 July

Music from the Ritson Manuscript

Performed by

The Clothworkers Consort of Leeds

Directed by

Bryan White

School of Music: Clothworkers Concert Hall

20.30-21.30

Price: £12.50

The Clothworkers Consort of Leeds performs music from the Ritson Manuscript. This manuscript contains a diverse collection of carols, masses, Latin liturgical and devotional texts, sacred chant, and secular and religious songs in English, representing a compendium of vocal music from the mid-15th to early 16th centuries. This programme will explore the diversity of collection including two large-scale works by Thomas Pack ('Lumen ad revelacionem gencium' and an English Te Deum), a setting of the prayer to the Blessed Virgin Mary against the plague, 'Stella celi extirpavit', the Marian antiphon 'Salve regina', and a range of carols and songs for small ensemble.

The Clothworkers Consort of Leeds (CCL) was formed in 2001 as a chamber choir which included the performance of sacred choral music in liturgical settings as one of its important aims. Since that time, it has developed into one of the finest choral ensembles in the north of England. The choir performs at services and gives concerts; it has collaborated with professional ensembles including Fretwork, QuintEssential Sackbut and Cornett Ensemble, Skipton Building Society Camerata, and Leeds Baroque Orchestra. The choir has performed in prestigious venues throughout the UK, including the Howard Assembly Room, St. Paul's London, York Minster, and 15 English cathedrals. It has toured to the Czech Republic, Germany, Italy, Poland, and Hungary, and recorded three CDs: *Songs of Praise: Music from the West Riding* (2004), *Vox Dei* (2006), and

No Man is an Island (2008). The choir has staged performances of *Dido and Aeneas* at Temple Newsam House and joined with Rambert Dance Company and London Musici for performances of Howard Goodall's *Eternal Light* at the Grand Theatre in Leeds.

The choir appeared on Corinne Bailey Rae's second album, *The Sea* (2010), and recorded Stephen Kilpatrick's title music for Michelle Lipton's play, *Amazing Grace*, broadcast on BBC Radio 4. CCL has been involved in modern premieres of Philip Hayes's *The Judgment of Hermes* (1783), with Skipton Camerata, and E. J. Loder's music for Lord Byron's *Manfred* at the Ilkley Literature Festival. In 2017 the choir made its Wigmore Hall debut in *Music on the Verge of Destruction*, subsequently broadcast on BBC Radio 3. This is the choir's third appearance at the IMC.

Tuesday 03 July

Art of the Sofer: Jewish Calligraphy Workshop

Directed by

Joseph Isaac Lifshitz

Clothworkers Building South: Room G.11B

19.00-20.30

Price: £7.50

Were all the skies parchment,
And all the reeds pens,
And all the oceans ink,
And all who dwell on earth scribes,
God's grandeur could not be told.

Akdamut Millan, Rabbi Meir Ben Isaac Nehorai (died c. 1095)

'Sofer' is the Hebrew word for a scribe who can copy out the Torah, tefillin, and mezuzot, as well as other religious writings according to the laws of 'sofrut'. If these laws are not followed, the text is not deemed to be valid. A sofer would be also responsible for preparing the *kulmus* (quill), *klaf* (parchment), and *d'yo* (ink) according to traditional methods.

In this workshop, Joseph Isaac Lifshitz will demonstrate the techniques of the medieval sofer. Participants will also learn to write medieval Hebrew characters with a quill on parchment. All materials will be provided.

Joseph Isaac Lifshitz is an expert on Jewish philosophy and history, with an emphasis on the philosophy of Ashkenaz in the high Middle Ages. He received his rabbinical ordination from Rabbis Yitzhak Kulitz and David Nesher. He earned his PhD in Jewish Thought from Tel Aviv University, and holds an MA in Jewish history from Touro College.

Author of numerous books, most recently *Judaism, Law & The Free Market* (Acton, 2012), he has written both scholarly and popular articles on subjects related to Judaism and economics. He is also a qualified Hebrew scribe.

This workshop can only accommodate a limited number of participants. Early booking is recommended.

Tuesday 03 July

Detour to Paradise:

Oswald von Wolkenstein and the Council of Constance (1414-1418)

Performed and Staged by

Silvan Wagner

Stage@Leeds: Stage 2

20.30-21.30

Price: £12.00

Oswald von Wolkenstein (1376/77-1445), the travelling knight and courtly singer, paid several visits to Constance, the city of the famous Council. In his poetry, he praised the city as 'wünnikliches paradis'. Indeed, one area of the city, the site of a former monastery for Poor Clares, was called Paradies (literally 'paradise').

©Sieglinde Hartmann Innsbruck, Universitäts- und Landesbibl., Cod. ohne Sign. (Wolkenstein-Handschrift B)

In 1415, he visited before joining the crusading army gathered by King John I in Portugal for the 'Reconquista' of Ceuta in North Africa. In contrast to the glories of Constance, this expedition, like so many of the other journeys that he had undertaken since his early years, greeted him with hardship and pain rather than paradisiacal pleasure. Recalling his many travels in his poetry, Oswald frequently invokes the sufferings he had to endure in other parts of the world from Europe to Africa and further east to Asia. From this perspective, the city of Constance in Germany, not far from Oswald's home county Tyrol, offers a brief detour to Paradise.

Silvan Wagner, who has a PhD in medieval German literature from the University of Bayreuth, has gained a rich experience as a professional musician directing and producing multimedia dramas featuring the texts and illustrations of medieval love poetry and courtly epics. His productions bring together the musical principles of historically informed performance with acting medieval narrative literature, making him the ideal person to perform the music and poetry of Oswald von Wolkenstein. Accompanying himself with gittern and drum, he will bring the cosmopolitan knight to life in a programme that features the Council of Constance, its city, and its world in songs full of realistic detail, sparkling with wit, irony, and humour.

The International Medieval Congress and the Oswald von Wolkenstein-Gesellschaft are proud to sponsor this unique musical event, creating new aesthetic means of bringing medieval poetry to life.

WEDNESDAY 04 JULY

DEAD SISTERS DO TELL TALES: A THEATRICAL READING OF MODERN DEVOUT SISTER-BOOKS

WRITTEN AND PRODUCED BY

MARLY TERWISSCHA VAN SCHELTINGA, UNIVERSITEIT ANTWERPEN
LIEKE SMITS, UNIVERSITEIT LEIDEN
GODELINDE GERTRUDE PERK, MITTUNIVERSITETS, SUNDSVALL

CLOTHWORKERS BUILDING SOUTH: ROOM G.11B

19.00-20.00

This event is free of charge.

On a winter's day, in the Dutch city of Deventer, a group of semi-religious women, all Sisters of the Common Life, start telling each other devotional tales, but their storytelling soon reveals that being a Sister does not make you a saint...

Retelling biographies from two collections from Modern Devout Sisters' Houses, this theatrical reading in English reconstructs a medieval reading experience, including the modern audience in the community of holy women. We would like to welcome you to Master Geert's House: join the Sisters as they wish to hear 'edifying points of our elder Sisters', but cannot agree on the most spiritually exemplary and enjoyable tale. At the same time, each Sister strives to tell the story of her own life, trying to fit into the community by adapting and adopting Modern Devout narrative conventions. Whose story will be heard and whose forgotten?

This performance brings to life the Sister-Books of Deventer and Diepenveen, two female-authored Middle Dutch texts. Originating from the bookish *Devotio Moderna*, a late-medieval religious movement encompassing both monastic and semi-monastic communities, these *vitae* are brimming with unforgettable scenes and local colour. Written and read in the very same Sisters' House in which the narratives are set, these 15th-century texts not only recount Sisters' lives; they also prompt the Sisters to overlay their lives with those of their predecessors and stage the departed Sisters' devotional feats in the spaces inhabited by the living Sisters.

This theatrical reading explores how the Sister-Books construct the very community they describe, investigating how the Sister-Books surround the living Sisters with the presence of those gone before them. According to the Deventer Sister-Book, hearing these lives makes the departed Sisters 'seem alive after death'; this research-by-performance event therefore also examines how the text includes and engages its audience. Ultimately, this performance illuminates medieval reading practices, the effect of aurality on text and reception, and medieval women's literary activity. After the 45-minute performance, there will be time for discussion.

Wednesday 04 July

Remember Death: Johannes Kolross's *Spil von Fünfferley betrachtnussen zur Buss* (*Play of Five Tableaux about Repentance*), 1532

Performed by

Theatergruppe des Instituts für Germanistik, Justus-Liebig-Universität, Giessen

Directed by

Cora Dietl

Live Music provided by

Peter Bull

Beech Grove plaza

19.00-20.30

This event is free of charge.

'Always be awake, and pray, / That I will not find you asleep in sin', says Death, warning a young man, whom he had just struck down in the midst of a sinful dance. The youth begs for pardon, and Death allows him some extra time to repent before he finally has to die. 'Memento mori' is the central message of the play that the Reformed School teacher Johannes Kolross performed with his pupils in Bâle. The youth is quickly converted to a holy life, but will he succeed? The 'Friends of World' and Devil try to lead him into temptation, but he firmly holds onto his new way. Devil and his Seven Deadly Sins, though, are successful in convincing others, and thus the epilogue can only repeat the call to remember death.

The aesthetics of the play are very different from those of 16th-century comedies that are often influenced by Terence. It can sometimes resemble an extended sermon, which can be unfamiliar to a 21st-century audience. The theatre group of the University of Giessen's German Department stages the play as part of the international research project 'Theatres of Persuasion', which focusses upon European morality plays of the 16th century and uses experimental performances of these plays (preferably full length) in order to examine the theatrical potential of the seemingly merely rhetorical texts, once visual and acoustic effects are added, which are not recorded in the texts.

The Theatregruppe was founded by Cora Dietl in 2007, and has since been staging two medieval or early modern plays per year. The performances are always part of seminar courses in German literature, running from April until June/July or from October until December, with 50 per cent new students each term, but with constant success, see: www.staff.uni-giessen.de/~g91159/archiv.htm.

This production will be performed in German.

Wednesday 04 July

Open Mic Night

Emmanuel Centre: Claire Chapel

20.30-22.00

This event is free of charge.

Not with an actual microphone (that would be silly!), the IMC Open Mic Night offers a variety of fare from poetry readings to music, song, even dance sometimes. We have had music from the troubadours, Viking sagas, medieval poetry, and a variety of musical instruments. Medieval contributions are particularly welcome but it is an opportunity to share anything you always wanted to perform with the international audience the IMC provides. Whether you come to perform or listen you will find the ambience of the Emmanuel Centre Claire Chapel and emcee Robin Fishwick's famous spiced fruit punch unforgettable.

Robin Fishwick, the host, is the Co-ordinating Chaplain at Leeds Universities and a local musician and singer-songwriter.

Wednesday 04 July
IMC Dance

Leeds University Union: Stylus

21.30-02.00

This event is free of charge

This year a local DJ will provide the entertainment.

Thursday 05 July
Making Leeds Medieval

Leeds University Union, University Square, and the Marquee

10.30-18.00

This event is free of charge

As the IMC 2018 draws to a close, join us in and around University Square for a range of activities, including a market featuring local produce and historical craft demonstrations. The Medieval Craft Fair will once again be extended to include a second day of trading during 'Making Leeds Medieval'. Come and browse a range of hand-crafted items including hand-bound books, historically-inspired woodwork, haberdashery, historic beads, and jewellery.

The Historical and Archaeological Societies Fair will be scheduled to coincide with 'Making Leeds Medieval', providing a unique opportunity to find out more about some of the many independent groups within the UK actively involved in preserving local and national history.

As last year, 'Making Leeds Medieval' will also feature live entertainment including music, combat displays, falcons, and hawks. The King Edward's Living History Group will also join us with a mixture of hands-on activities, demonstrations, and displays.

Thursday 05 July

IMC Ceilidh

Refectory

20.30-22.30

This event is free of charge

Pronunciation: 'kay-lee'

Forms: Also **ceilidhe**.

Etymology: < Irish *céilidhe*, Scottish Gaelic *cēilidh*, < Old Irish *céile* companion

In Scotland and Ireland:

a. An evening visit, a friendly social call
b. A session of traditional music, storytelling, or dancing

To bring IMC 2018 to a festive close, the Assumption Ceilidh Band will be performing in the Refectory. No prior experience is required as all dances will be taught beforehand, so please come to kick up your heels.

The Assumption Ceilidh Band primarily play for local charities and schools, but they also perform for special occasions such as weddings and birthdays. They play a mixture of traditional instrumental Irish music, folk songs, old tyme waltzes, and Irish set dances such as the 'Bridge of Athlone' and the 'Walls of Limerick'. The band ranges from seven to nine people (including a caller). Members of the band (who are very good friends and thoroughly enjoy each other's company) are a mixture of some mid-twenties members and some mature members (i.e. retired, albeit only recently!).

LUU Medieval Society

The Leeds University Union Medieval Society was formed in 2013 in order to promo a thriving community of medievalists in the University and City of Leeds. As such, w warmly encourage anyone with an interest in the Middle Ages to join. We are dedicate to building a strong interdisciplinary community; so whether you study, teach, or are ju really interested in the Middle Ages, this is the Society for you.

Medieval Society Pub Quiz

MONDAY 02 JULY: 19.15-20.30

LEEDS UNIVERSITY UNION: OLD BAR

This event is free of charge

Come wind down after your first day of sessions with the annual Medieval Society P Quiz! The LUU Medieval Society will re-imagine the traditional British Pub Quiz by aski IMC delegates to form teams and answer questions posed by the Medieval Soci quizmaster. Pool your knowledge with your colleagues for quiz topics such as: Na the Century, Latin Translation, and Match the Illuminations. Teams will be competing everlasting glory and a small prize.

The International Medieval Film Festival

The Leeds University Union Medieval Society would like to invite delegates to a f screening at The Hyde Park Picture House, a short 13-minute walk from the Univer Union. A walking party will be leaving from in front of the Union building 20 minutes bef the start of the film. Alternatively, the 56 bus stops directly outside the Hyde Park Pict House.

The Little Hours (2017)

TUESDAY 03 JULY: 18.00

HYDE PARK PICTURE HOUSE

This event is free of charge

Presented by LUU Medieval Society as part of the fourth International Medieval F Festival, *The Little Hours* (2017) has been described as 'one of the most faithful adaptati of a piece of medieval literature yet put to screen'. When a handsome fugitive preter to be deaf and without speech and takes up refuge in a convent, the bored you nuns are delighted to have such an attractive man in their midst. Jeff Baena's (*Life A Beth*) latest comedy adapts a tale from *The Decameron* into an alternatively hilari and heartbreaking film.

After the film the panel will discuss the film and take questions from the audience.

Want to know more?

If you are interested in learning more about LUU Medieval Society, there are many ways to get in touch with us:

Visit our webpage: www.leedsuniversityunion.org.uk/groups/18129/

Facebook: www.facebook.com/LUUMedievalSociety

Twitter: @luumedievalsoc

Email: luumedievalsociety@gmail.com

Notes

Exhibitions and Bookfairs

IMC Bookfair

Opening times:

	Parkinson Court, Parkinson Building
Monday 02 July	10.00-19.30
Tuesday 03 July	08.30-18.30
Wednesday 04 July	08.30-18.30
Thursday 05 July	08.30-13.00

All the exhibitors confirmed so far are listed below. To find a specific exhibitor at the IMC Bookfair, please refer to the floor plan you will receive in your registration pack when you arrive.

- Amsterdam University Press with Arc Humanities Press
- Austrian Academy of Sciences Press
- Boydell & Brewer
- Brepols Publishers
- Brill
- Cambridge University Press
- Chaucer Studio / Chaucer Studio Press
- Combined Academic Publishers Ltd
- De Gruyter
- Edinburgh University Press
- Gazelle Book Services
- Harvard University Press
- Ian Stevens Distribution
- Liverpool University Press
- Macmillan Publishers Ltd
- Manchester University Press
- Medieval Institute Publications
- Oxbow Books
- Princeton University Press
- Royal Armouries Museum
- Shaun Tyas Publishing
- SISMEL - Edizioni del Galluzzo
- University of Chicago Press
- University of Wales Press
- Yale University Press

Second-Hand and Antiquarian Bookfair

Opening times:

	Leeds University Union Foyer
Sunday 01 July	16.00-21.00
Monday 02 July	08.00-19.00
Tuesday 03 July	08.00-17.00

Confirmed exhibitors:

- Bennett & Kerr Books
- Chevin Books
- Northern Herald Books
- Pinwell Books
- Salsus Books
- Unsworth's Antiquarian Booksellers

Medieval Craft Fair

Opening times:

	Leeds University Union Foyer
Wednesday 04 July	10.30-19.30
Thursday 05 July	10.30-18.00

Confirmed exhibitors:

- Anachronalia
- Ana Period Shoes
- Corium Artificium
- D-Art Francisca
- Early Music Shop
- FiftyEleven
- Gemmeus
- Hare and Tabor
- John Hudson Claypotter
- The Mulberry Dyer
- Pen to Press
- Pretender to the Throne
- Runesmith
- Tanya Bentham
- Tillerman Beads handmade by Mike Poole
- Trinity Court Potteries

Historical and Archaeological Societies Fair

Opening times:

	The Marquee
Thursday 05 July	10.30-18.00

Confirmed exhibitors:

- British Brick Society
- Church Monuments Society
- The Corpus of Romanesque Sculpture in Britain and Ireland
- Friends of Stank Hall
- Leeds Symposium on Food History
- The Thoresby Society, The Historical Society for Leeds and District
- Yorkshire Archaeological and Historical Society
- Yorkshire Vernacular Buildings Study Group

Receptions

The IMC 2018 Bookfair will be launched with a wine reception on Monday 02 July, 18.00-19.00. This reception will be accompanied by later opening hours, offering a longer opportunity to talk to publishers' representatives.

On Wednesday 04 July, 18.00-19.00, we will also be hosting a very special reception to celebrate the 25th annual Congress.

As usual, individual publishers and other organisations will also host wine receptions to promote their new titles, talk to existing and potential authors, and maintain close relations with their market. See the following pages for more information on their events:

- Brill (p. 164)
- British Archaeological Association (p. 262)
- Centre for Medieval Studies, University of Bristol (p. 154)
- Centre for Medieval & Early Modern Studies, University of Kent (p. 367)
- Centre for the Study of the Middle Ages, University of Birmingham (p. 262)
- Charlemagne: A European Icon, University of Bristol (p. 367)
- De Gruyter (p. 261)
- *Early Medieval Europe* (p. 164)
- Graduate Student Committee, Medieval Academy of America (p. 154)
- International Center of Medieval Art (p. 375)
- *International Medieval Bibliography* (p. 154)
- Mediävistenverband (p. 273)
- Medieval Academy of America (p. 375)
- National Museums Scotland & The Glenmorangie Company (p. 262)
- Prato Consortium for Medieval and Renaissance Studies (p. 273)
- St Andrews Institute of Mediaeval Studies (p. 273)
- University of Wales Press (p. 261)

Programme Advertisers

- Amsterdam University Press, with ARC Humanities Press
- Brepols Publishers
- Brill
- Centre for Medieval & Early Modern Studies, University of Kent
- De Gruyter
- Department of Anglo-Saxon, Norse & Celtic (ASNC), University of Cambridge
- Duke University Press
- Early English Text Society
- Erich Schmidt Verlag, Berlin
- Faculty of History, University of Cambridge
- *International Medieval Bibliography*
- Medieval Institute Publications
- Saint Louis University
- SISMEL – Edizioni del Galluzzo
- St Andrews Institute of Mediaeval Studies
- University of California Press
- University of Chicago Press
- University of Pennsylvania Press
- Yale University Press

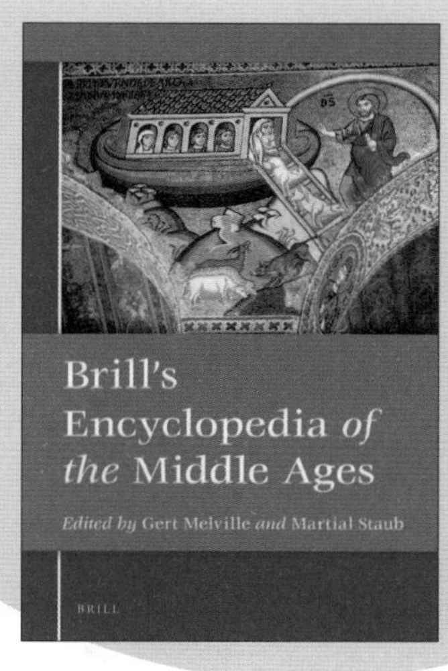

BRILL

December 2016
Hardback (xxxvi, 1332 pp.)
ISBN 9789004293151
Price € 350 / US$ 420

Brill's Encyclopedia of the Middle Ages (2 vols.)

Edited by **Gert Melville**, Technische Universität Dresden, **Martial Staub**, University of Sheffield. English edition supervised by **Francis G. Gentry** and **Tim Barnwell**

Brill's Encyclopedia of the Middle Ages offers an accessible yet engaging coverage of medieval European history and culture, c. 500-c. 1500, in a series of themed articles, taking an interdisciplinary and comparative approach. Presenting a broad range of topics current in research, the encyclopedia is dedicated to all aspects of medieval life, organized in eight sections: Society; Faith and Knowledge; Literature; Fine Arts and Music; Economy; Technology; Living Environments and Conditions; and Constitutive Historical Events and Regions. This thematic structure makes the encyclopedia a true reference work for Medieval Studies as a whole. The encyclopedia is supported by an extensive bibliography, updated with the most recent works and adapted to suit the needs of an Anglophone audience.

January 2018
Hardback (approx. 416 pp.)
ISBN 9789004288706
Price € 215 / US$ 247
E-ISBN 9789004352162
E-Price € 195 / US$ 224

Clothing the Past: Surviving Garments from Early Medieval to Early Modern Western Europe

Elizabeth Coatsworth and **Gale R. Owen-Crocker**

October 2017
Hardback (xvi, 408 pp.)
ISBN 9789004349933
Price € 171 / US$ 197
E-ISBN 9789004351905
E-Price € 155 / US$ 179
Brill's Companions to European History, 13

A Companion to the Abbey of Le Bec in the Central Middle Ages (11th–13th Centuries)

Edited by **Benjamin Pohl**, University of Bristol, and **Laura L. Gathagan**, SUNY Cortland

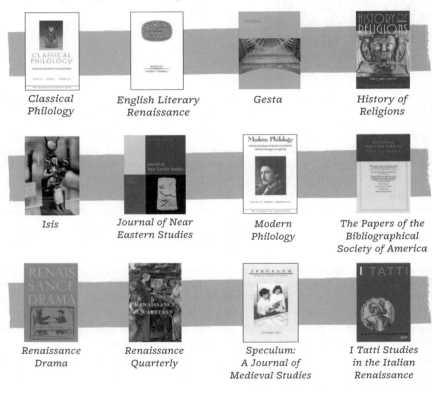

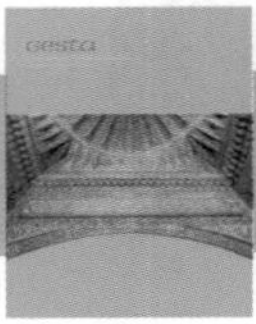

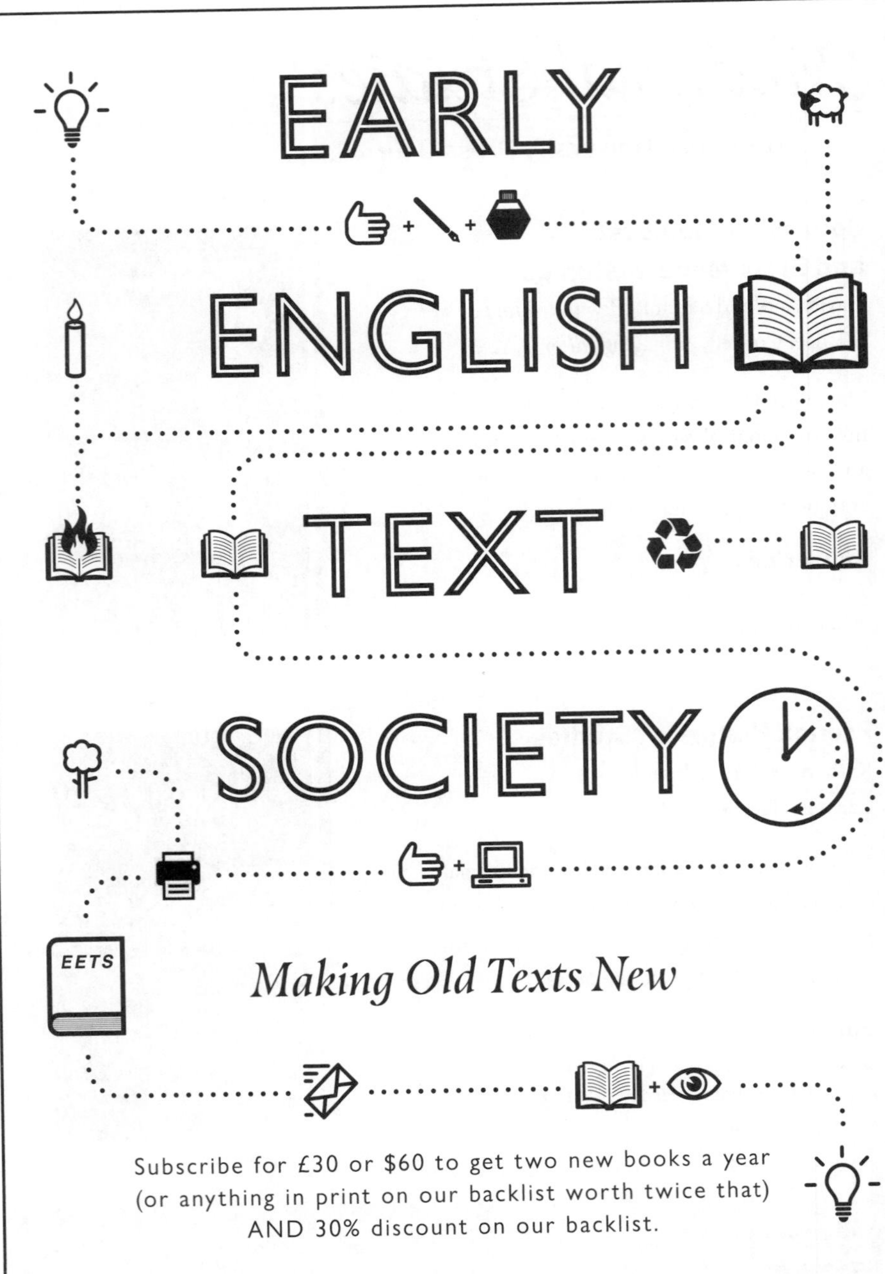
EARLY
ENGLISH
TEXT
SOCIETY
EETS
Making Old Texts New
Subscribe for £30 or $60 to get two new books a year
(or anything in print on our backlist worth twice that)
AND 30% discount on our backlist.
www.eets.org.uk
eets@ell.ox.ac.uk
@EEngTextSoc

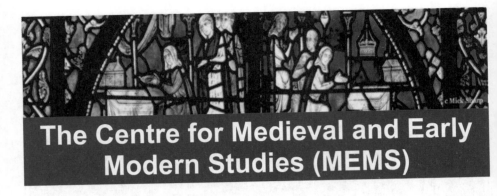

Exhibitions

NOTES

B. Guy. Welsh conquest of NW Mercia

NOTES

Notes

Notes

Index of Papers

Index of Papers

Index of Papers

Index of Papers

Index of Participants

Index of Participants

Index of Participants

Index of Participants

Index of Participants

Index of Participants

INDEX OF PARTICIPANTS

Index of Participants

Index of Participants

Index of Participants

Index of Participants

Index of Participants

Index of Participants

Index of Participants

Index of Participants

Notes

Kiri Kelt, 12th C origin stories

Gesta Hungarorum: 'write truthfully + plainly so readers can know exactly what happened.

Alluded to authoritative sources. Concepts + models.

How did they use Scythians re Hungarians. Regino of Prüm c. 908

Saxo Grammaticus influenced by Aeneid. Audience would have been familiar with Virgil.

Could take a classical concept + incorporate it. Or could model it more covertly on a classical model.

Tom Foster, Gesta Stephani

One of only 4 narratives spanning Anarchy: J. of Hexham + Torigni more locally focus, Huntingdon broader.

Henry of Blois the link to likely author bp of Bath?

Duchesne 17th C from now lost MS, 20th C discovered Valenciennes MS with later narrative. Literal analysis well overdue.

Typological + rhetorical readership. Davis gave brief linguistic overview.

Didn't identify many allusions.

Always seemed strained style. Author's intentions front-loaded. Could only discern 15.

'Omne nefas'; quote from Terence's Eunuch; Lucan's Pharsalia.

Judges 9:42: Abimelek. Woman throws down stone.

Polina Ignatova: Walking dead

About 19 stories in Britain 11th – early 15th C.

Icelandic sagas: Grettir, Eyrbyggja

Iliad: ghost of Patroclus begged Achilles to burn body; similarly in Lucan's Pharsalia, Erictho the witch burns revived corpse. Also Lucian, Herodotus.

WN uses classical word 'rogus' for funeral pyre.

[allusions accidental?]

Abbey Monk: OV

Isidore defines exile (exul): outside native soil

In Epilogue OV defines himself as an exile. Talks about departure of Abraham. 'Like Joseph in Egypt'. Parallels with rejection by family.

Being a stranger in a foreign land (Exod.). Biblical concept of wanderer.

St Evroult a hermit in Normandy.

Richard of Dover to TB on mendicancy.

J. Burah: Bede in 12th C

Rhetorical function of refs + allusions. Connection of memory + composition. Role of audience in refs.

intertextuality; reference must be explicit; allusion unmarked.

Use them to exert power over lit. trad, shape reader's understanding of that trad. Those in the know v those not

Driven by desire of historians to give authority to readers ~~that~~ to use older ~~texts~~. Encourages them to compose own works.

Storing + recalling texts are acts of composition.

Ref to 'true laws of history' (WM) stimulates discussion

Geared towards actively engaging readers.

A. Grabowski. Helinand of Froidmont (Antoni)

1211x1223. Gives full refs eg to book, section.

Hubert of Bosham. PL's Sentences. Seek + find info. Alberic of St Fontaines

Notes

A. Marx:
Imad ad-Din on taking of Cross 1187
Cross's theological/symbolic/salvific meaning
Ezek. 9 used to interpret loss: Draw through midst of J, put mark on foreheads!
Unique character of relic: Helena, tied to Jerusalem, proven as battle standard
Helinand of Froidmont, In vanitis psalmorum, sermon post-1187
Sign of the Tau on foreheads of men: 6 types of linear movement in cross
P. of Blois, Conquestio: Tau not a mere sign, means an attitude
Patrio Reginaldi: allowed cross to be captured on purpose so our redemption induced
Ralph Ardens, In festo omnium sanctorum, sermon 1187-90: Tau symbolises inner state.
Associated with Christ as eschatological warlord (Rev. 19); external + internal sign; comparison to Ark as danger.

K. F. Hojgaard
Reaction at David's camb
Cultural memory study. Loss cannot be seen as isolated event, rather as lieu de memoire. Assmann: Communicative v cultural memory.
Ann Rigney (2005): convergence – sites of memory continually imbued with new meaning.
Bolter + Grusin: Remediation + premediation
Astrid Erll on premediation: existing schemata for new experience + its representation
Letters + Howden refer to Babylonia Safeguard at top of
Historia de Expeditione p. I: much more serious than previous lamentation; gender holy city like Lamentations. 'Jerusalem as mother' article.
Arnold of Lubeck, P. 169
R of Diceto: attacks on Jerusalem
Howden: names of popes etc the same

J. Kane:
Libellus de Exp. Terrae Sanctae: argued written by knight or member of military order. Personal memory. Heartfelt lament for loss.
Survives in 3 13th C copies, one later MS + transcripts
Willoughby: Cott. Cleop. MS hand changes. Argues all 3 MS originate at Coggeshall. Cleop. has same hand as Coggeshall.
Part I existed in some form by start of 13th C. Period maps onto Ralph's abbacy.
March to Hattin as inversion of Exodus. Links relic of cross to bronze serpent of Moses. Exegetical reflections on places captured.
Ends with Christ on the cross.
Cresson: support for martyrdom.
Siege ~~[illegible]~~ were Christians drawn so much they yearned for death
Memory of not being martyred haunts him.
ligno / ferrum
Linda Paterson on crusader songs

Notes

wed after 3-45

Notes

Call for Papers IMC 2019: Materialities

The IMC provides an interdisciplinary forum for the discussion of all aspects of Medieval Studies. Proposals on any topic related to the Middle Ages are welcome, while every year the IMC also chooses a special thematic focus. In 2019 this is 'Materialities'.

Recent attention to objects, artefacts, matter, and material culture has reshaped scholarship in many fields. This strand seeks to address the impact of this new interest in things, theories, and methods as they relate to an expansive understanding of 'materiality'. The study of materiality brings together a host of scholarly and theoretical concerns and puts them into dialogue to understand how conceptions of matter, and matter itself, shaped the creation of the material world, regimes of labour and supply, connectivity, entanglements, trade networks, movements of things and people, concepts of agency and network theory, and constructed notions of the sublime, of replication, and of 'reality', as an abstract concept and category during the Middle Ages.

This strand seeks to bring into conversation recent work on materialities by art historians, archaeologists, paleographers, historians, economists, musicologists, liturgists, philosophers, philologists, and scholars of literature, critical theory, and religious studies, among other fields. Material objects and practices served as markers of cultural difference, but could also - simultaneously - become part of a shared culture of consumption, proximity suggesting gender and class affinities. Material dynamics were embedded in the making of objects, the trade in raw materials, and the roles of men and women in the fabrication of things spanning the luxurious to the mundane. Materialities shaped cultures of consumption, created regimes of circulation, and informed networks that defined both subjects and objects. Materialities encompass interactions between peoples both near and far and offer an analytical framework that suggests the unity of the medieval world across religious, ethnic, and spatial distances and differences.

Themes to be addressed may include, but are not limited to:

- Material culture and consumption
- Materiality and the archaeological record
- Agency of people and things
- Medieval 'thing' theory
- Material connections: regimes of circulation
- Materialism and the Middle Ages
- Labour and production of things
- The social life of things
- Fabrication: production of specific objects
- Replication and reproduction
- Materiality of coins, money, and circulation
- Manuscripts: material and making
- Material textual and writing cultures
- Soundscape: material and musical culture
- Light and form
- Representing the material
- Body and spirit: spirituality and the material
- Space and materialities
- Materials: mundane (e.g. wood, water, dust) and luxurious (e.g. gold, silver, gems)
- Intimacies of things
- Abundance and/or scarcity
- Imagined materials
- Material landscapes: urban, suburban, rural
- Loans, debts, credit
- Materialities of power/empire
- Race and subjectivity
- Transformations: recycling, reuse, destruction
- Material religions: beliefs and practices
- Materials and memory
- Materialities and/of conflict
- Gendered materialities
- Digital/virtual/material archives
- Conservation and preservation
- Text and/as object

Proposals should be submitted online at www.leeds.ac.uk/ims/imc/imc2019_call.html.

Paper proposal deadline: 31 August 2018

Session proposal deadline: 30 September 2018

The IMC welcomes session and paper proposals in all major European languages.